Un introducción
      de American
  gobierno o régimen

An Introduction
to American
Government

An Introduction to American Government

Kenneth Prewitt

University of Chicago

Sidney Verba

Harvard University

Harper & Row, Publishers

New York   Evanston   San Francisco   London

To Walter, Luther, and Firth,
who helped us get started.

Credits for photographs appearing on chapter opening pages:

Chapter 1: Mickey Palmer, DPI; Chapter 2: Culver; Chapter 3: Bonnie Freer, Rapho Guillumette; Chapter 4: Wide World; Chapter 5: Bob West; Chapter 6: Wide World; Chapter 7: Virginia Hamilton; Chapter 8: George Butler, Rapho Guillumette; Chapter 9: New York Public Library Picture Collection; Chapter 10: Sybil Shackman, Monkmeyer; Chapter 11: Philip Jones Griffiths, Magnum; Chapter 12: Robert Smallman, DPI; Chapter 13: Wide World; Chapter 14: T. Russell, DPI; Chapter 15: Wide World; Chapter 16: UPI; Chapter 17: Jan Lukas, Rapho Guillumette.

Sponsoring Editor: Ron Taylor
Project Editor: Elizabeth Dilernia
Designer: Howard Leiderman
Production Supervisor: George Buckman

An Introduction to American Government

Library of Congress Cataloging in Publication Data
Prewitt, Kenneth.
  An introduction to American government.

  1. United States—Politics and government—Hand-
books, manuals, etc. I. Verba, Sidney, joint author.
II. Title.
JK274.P76   320.4'73   73-15251
ISBN 0-06-045284-6

CONTENTS

Introduction

Why Government?

The question "Why Government?" is deceptively simple. It has puzzled astute thinkers for several thousand years. Part of the puzzle comes from the fact that there is a good argument *against* government: Government makes us do things, and thus it takes away individual choice and freedom. If we agree that individual choice and freedom are good, then the case against government is a very strong one. What's more, we cannot choose to obey government directives; we are forced to obey them. The punishment for not obeying is often severe—the government may take away your property (by fining you), your freedom (by imprisoning you), and, until recent Supreme Court decisions, even your life (by executing you). Not only can governments restrict you and punish you, they can also tax you, and they always do. All governments depend on involuntary payments to support their personnel and programs.

What is the justification for allowing such distasteful activities as coercion, regulation, restriction, taxation, and imprisonment? Why do people put up with government?

Maintaining Social Order

The usual answer stresses the importance of social order. Without government there could be no civilized life. If each individual were allowed to do his own thing, society would degenerate into a war of all against all. We support government because government in turn provides law and order. It provides the social context within which families can be raised, jobs can be performed, educations can be pursued, leisure can be enjoyed, and the future can be planned.

Take, for instance, economic activities. To work for a salary, to invest savings, to buy a product, or to produce one depends on contracts, perhaps between worker and manager, or between lender and borrower, or between seller and buyer. Some guarantee is needed to ensure that people don't unfairly back out on contracts—that the car buyer doesn't just drive off and quit making his payments; that the employer doesn't decide at the end of the month not to pay his workers; that the bank doesn't close its doors and keep the savings deposits. Contracts that sustain economic exchanges are usually honored, and at least one compelling reason is that they are backed up by the authority of the government. Or take the more simple issue of

A parent will not want his five-year-old to start school unless street crossings are safe.   (Photo: Robert Benson, Black Star)

social life and leisure activities. A man will be reluctant to buy a hi-fi set if he thinks it will soon be stolen; a parent will not want his five-year-old to start school if there are no traffic laws to make street crossings safe; a woman will refuse an invitation to a party if going across town at night is to risk attack. We depend on government to provide security and safety from theft, reckless driving, and street attacks. More than this, government is expected to protect national borders from foreign invasions or international outlaws. In the absence of national defense there would be little reason to make the sacrifices in time and effort to build homes, schools, factories, and parks.

Here, then, is the classic justification for government. The legal processes, the police powers, and the national security policies establish the social order crucial to civilized life. The justification seems reasonable enough, or at least it does until one starts asking additional questions. For instance, what is the connection between providing basic law and order and such government activities as repaving seven miles of Interstate 80 in the middle of Nevada; supporting a graduate student writing a dissertation on the stone tools used by prehistoric man in Central Africa; giving cash to a Montana farmer if he does not grow wheat on the back forty; publishing a brochure naming the trees and plants along a hiker's trail in the Smoky Mountains; sending a monthly check to a blind pensioner in New York?

Obviously we must look beyond the maintenance of social order to answer the question "Why Government?"

Providing Collective Goods

Governments make decisions (or laws) when individuals have goals that cannot be achieved without them. Automobile drivers have a mutual interest in seeing that all cars drive on one side of the road or the other. It matters little which side is chosen, right or left, as long as all drivers choose the same side. In such circumstances, all benefit if they can turn over to the government the power to make a rule *obliging* each driver to drive on a particular side.

To understand why social goals may require binding decisions by government, we must understand the concept of "collective goods." Governments often provide collective goods—benefits that are available to all

Government provides benefits that are available to all.   (Photo: Dennis Stock, Magnum)

individuals whether or not any particular individual worked toward the attainment of that benefit. If the government opens a new park, say, this park becomes available for my use whether or not I actively worked to create it. This helps explain why *binding* decisions are needed to create such public facilities. If I benefit in any case, why should I voluntarily help to create the park? I will benefit from it if *others* work to create it; so I will be wise to sit back and take advantage of their effort. Conversely, even if I were to try to work for a public park, it would probably do no good, because my effort—the money or labor I could contribute—would be relatively small (unless I were a millionaire who could personally buy a large public park).

The situation with a park is quite different from that with a noncollective good such as a camper. I can get access to a camper only if I use my private resources. Therefore, my efforts to buy a camper can be quite effective. If I put my resources into it and if I have enough resources, I can have the camper.

In short, for any *single* individual it makes a lot of sense to wait until others have created the collective good and then to take advantage of it at that time. Under such circumstances, however, collective goods would never be created. Only a binding governmental decision that *makes* all people contribute to the park through tax revenues can lead to a beneficial collective gain for all citizens that could not be obtained by the voluntary activity of individuals. No government has ever been supported through voluntary payments by its citizens.

Consider another example. Air pollution caused by automobiles is, as we all know, a serious problem facing many American communities. Reduction of air pollution would be a collective good in that all would benefit whether or not they did anything to help reduce it. Suppose that a highly efficient pollution control device for automobiles is invented that costs $300. All Americans would benefit from the elimination of pollution that would come from the installation of such a device on all cars. But can the installation and the beneficial social goal of pure air come from the voluntary activities of the citizens? It is unlikely.

The situation from the point of view of the individual citizen considering whether to spend his $300 is as follows: No citizen acting as an individual can have much impact on the overall pollution rate in his community. Even if Citizen A buys an antipollution device, the quality of the air in the city will not change very much if others do not do likewise. Conversely, if Citizen A does not buy a pollution device but all the other citizens in the community were to do so, he would benefit from the pure air (or almost pure air except for his small amount of pollution) and save himself $300.

Under such circumstances, it is rational for the individual citizen not to purchase such a device. He does not get clean air if he purchases one and others do not; and he gets fairly pure air even if he does not purchase one if others were to do so. Thus if every individual acts in a way that is most rational, a social situation is created in which all lose. This is why all citizens gain if there is some way of *coercing one another* to purchase such a device. And the most likely means of coercion is a law requiring all cars to be equipped with the pollution control device. Only when individual choice is taken away can the overall social goal be achieved.

Summary Thus Far

You should now have in mind two answers to the question "Why Government?" First, a government provides domestic law and order and national security from external threats so that citizens can go about such normal activities as raising a family, going to school, earning a living, or enjoying leisure hours. Second, a government decision can provide the coordinating mechanism that makes it possible for individual goals to be converted to a social benefit, and thereby satisfy the desires of the members of society.

Why Politics?

Government would be a very simple matter if it involved using state authority to obtain goals all citizens favored and from which all benefited equally. Thus the policy that all cars drive on the right presents few difficulties. For one thing, most drivers are indifferent as to whether they drive on the right or the left side, as long as there is uniformity. Besides, this is the type of policy that is costless. No one loses money because traffic laws in this country require right-hand driving.

Differential Preferences

Government, however, is not always a simple matter of achieving goals all citizens favor and that benefit all citizens equally. In fact, making government decisions is nearly always conflict ridden. The reasons are apparent. It is not easy to get agreement on *what* collective goods government should provide or on *who* should pay how much for them. Not every group benefits equally from every collective good, and not every group pays equally, or even pays in proportion to its use of the collective good. Thus there is always a political struggle to maximize the benefits of government decisions while minimizing the costs.

Consider public highways. Certainly public highways are a collective good in the sense that no single individual could afford to build one, no matter how much he wanted to drive between two points. They are a collective good also in the sense that they are not reserved for particular groups but are open to any who obey uniform traffic laws. Yet the politics

Most drivers are indifferent as to whether they drive on the right or the left side, as long as there is uniformity.   *(Photo: The Port of New York Authority)*

of highway construction and location can become very intense indeed. Downtown merchants may want an expressway coming directly into the central city; apartment dwellers about to lose their homes to the bulldozers will fiercely oppose such a plan. Truckers and automobile manufacturers line up on the side of more and faster expressways; conservationists insist that cities would be more livable if resources went to mass transit and public parks instead. Another group, favoring lower taxes, doesn't want the expressway no matter where it is located and opposes public transit and public parks as well. And in all likelihood another group, perhaps the largest one, is indifferent to the whole issue.

Thus we establish the first important point about politics and government. *Groups in America have different preferences.* A large, diverse nation such as ours inevitably includes groups with different goals: labor and management, doctors and patients, Whites and Blacks, Catholics and Protestants, producers and consumers, and on and on.

Doctors may want a limitation on governmental involvement in medical care; elderly citizens may want more comprehensive care programs. Blacks may want governmental intervention to promote integrated housing in suburbs; White suburbanites may want the government to stay out of it. Catholics may prefer governmental aid for parochial schools; Protestants oppose it.

The number of alternative preferences to be found in America is vast indeed. There are many issues. And on any issue we are likely to find some citizens on one side, some on the other side, and many other citizens indifferent.

Different preferences by different groups lead of course to arguments over what collective goods the government should provide, and who should pay the costs of these goods. It is these arguments that set in motion the political struggle to control government offices and government resources.

Differential Impact on Citizens
Leads to Differential Involvement

If the political struggle begins with differential preferences, it is intensified because of a second fundamental point about government and society: *Government decisions have differential impact on citizens.* Any given governmental policy is likely to benefit one group a great deal, benefit another group a little, and leave another group unaffected. Conversely it may hurt some people a lot, others a little, and again a third group not at all. The decision to build a highway next to my house benefits the highway builders a lot, benefits certain commuters somewhat, leaves most citizens unaffected, but may hurt me and a few of my neighbors substantially. The fact of *differential impact* means that on any particular issue there will usually be only a few citizens who are concerned and active. These are the ones who are most severely affected. Thus, *differential impact* leads to *differential involvement.* Differential involvement means that in relation to any particular governmental policy, some individuals and groups will be more active and will try harder to affect the outcome. Differential involvement means that the struggle over governmental policy is likely to be unequal.

Differential Resources

Citizens differ in the resources they bring to bear on influencing the government. In one sense that is not the case: All citizens are roughly equal in relation to a basic political resource—the vote. Each man and woman gets one vote. But beyond that equality, there are many inequalities. Citizens differ in their economic resources, and this makes some more politically powerful than others. Each citizen may have one vote, but heavy campaign contributors can influence a lot more votes than can those who have no money to contribute to a campaign. And citizens are unequal in more than economic resources—they are unequal in the skills they bring to bear on political matters, in how well they are organized, and in the connections they have with the government.

Government and Politics

Our introductory comments have come to an interesting conclusion. We started by asking why governments are tolerated, given their many distasteful activities and their coercive limitations on individual freedom, and we answered that they are tolerated because they provide collective goods such as national security, internal order, and state services. But then we learned that such collective goods can have very specialized benefits, aiding some groups in society but perhaps harming the interests of other groups. Even such collective goods as transportation systems, educational facilities, defense policies, and social security programs are not provided at equal cost to all citizens and are not equally beneficial to all citizens.

Thus there is in society a continuous, often intense, political struggle to influence what collective goods will be provided, who will mostly pay for them, and who will mostly benefit from them.

Who wins in this struggle? One easy answer comes to mind. In a democracy, when there is disagreement, the majority *should* win. But that answer is too easy, and not often correct. For one thing, there may not be a majority on one side or the other. Any given issue can have as many as half a dozen major groups all wanting something very different. Take the road-building example. Downtown merchants want the expressway to come to the center of the city; suburban residents and merchants want the expressway to circle the city; commuters want the expressway only if ample parking space is provided; construction firms don't much care where the expressway is built, as long as it *is* built; supporters of mass public transit want to stop all expressway building in and around cities; and conservationists prefer that public monies be spent on collective goods for cities other than transportation systems, which can only result in greater congestion and urban problems.

Differences in Intensity of Preferences

Furthermore, not all groups feel equally intensely about the issues. Should the voice of someone whose home will be bulldozed and whose neighborhood will be destroyed by the expressway count equally with the voice of another citizen who simply wants to reduce by five minutes how long it takes to get from his suburban home to a movie in the central city? Simple majoritarian democracy would ignore differences in intensity of preferences. But the actual political process makes room for them (as we shall see when we study political participation and pressure group activity).

Even if we were to conclude that the majority *should* win, we would have to recognize at once that it seldom does. Groups bring different resources, economic and otherwise, to the political struggle; hence very often the resources of a small group outweigh those of a majority. Many collective goods are highly specialized responses of government to an intense and well-organized minority—for example, subsidies to farmers, tax allowances to oil interests, research grants to university professors, training programs for Blacks, and loans to home builders.

The political struggle in America over what collective goods the government will provide for whom involves a complex, many-sided conflict. The contestants in the struggle differ in the policies they prefer and in the resources they have for political activity. What determines the outcome of this struggle over government policy? Which groups succeed and which groups fail? And why do some succeed and others fail?

The answers to these questions are not easy. We will try to answer them in this book.

A Note to the Student
On Understanding Politics

Few of us would argue with the assertion that politics is important. The outcome of the political struggle to control government affects us in many, many specific ways — the cleanness of the air we breathe and the water we drink, the standards (and costs) of the health care and education we receive, the security of the contracts we sign, the safety of the planes and trains we travel in, the honesty of advertisements we hear and the quality of merchandise we purchase. The ongoing and seemingly mundane activities of government add up to public policies that go far toward determining whether our own lives are healthy and happy, or perhaps mediocre and disappointing.

Yes, politics counts. And it does so whether we like it or not, whether we pay attention or are indifferent, whether we understand or are puzzled. Politics counts because, finally, some of the largest issues of life are at stake: security and safety, justice and liberty, equality and happiness. The unceasing, frequently intense struggle to control the offices and activities of government matters — very much indeed.

For this reason, if for no other, some effort to understand politics is worth our while.

But understanding is not easy. Politics is puzzling. Issues are complicated, changeable, and often seem to be affected by distant history. The legalistic language that surrounds political debate is obscure at best, as if an effort were being made to disguise the "real" facts deliberately. Besides, political personalities come and go. Yes, the effort to "keep up with politics" can indeed be very great. A busy undergraduate hardly has time to read a daily newspaper, let alone listen to and digest the extended commentary necessary for even a minimal grasp of current events. And even when you might know what is going on, you may continue to be puzzled as to why it is happening.

In this book we wish to help the student understand why things happen as they do in American political life. We will concentrate on the political struggle over governmental policies. Although we take for granted that the government provides collective goods, we know also that these goods are not equally valuable or equally costly to all citizens. Our focus will be the issue of who reaps the benefits and who pays the costs.

We will first investigate several aspects of American society that affect the way in which political struggle takes place. For one thing, the beliefs of American citizens about politics affect how policies are selected and implemented. Also important are the many conflicts and cleavages among political groups in America. We will study the economic system as well, because economics and politics are very closely intertwined in our society.

Our attention then will turn to the various actors in the political struggle. Chief among these are the pressure groups, the political parties, the voting public, and the political leaders. These actors play out the political game within a definite framework—a framework which in the first instance is provided by the basic features of American government: constitutionalism, federalism, separation of powers, due process of law, majoritarian democracy. We will examine these principles and will examine the institutions that give them substance: the Supreme Court, the Congress, the Presidency. Of constant concern will be the question, How do these principles and institutions affect the democratic struggle over governmental policies? In the final chapters the policy-making process itself will interest us, as will some specific policies.

This is a lot to cover, considering there are literally millions of facts we could recite about the politics, the principles, the institutions, and the policies of American government. We will be very selective in the facts we recite, and you as a student deserve from us an account of our criteria for selectivity: Why this set of facts and not that one?

An understanding of politics rests on two kinds of knowledge: knowledge of facts and explanations of facts. We cannot study politics without some knowledge of the two parties, the role of pressure groups, the meaning of judicial review, the significance of federalism. It is useful also to have some detailed information about public policies and the way in which they have come to be.

But all facts are not equally important to an understanding of politics. The child who has memorized every state capital knows some political facts, but does not understand much about politics. Even the adult citizen who can name his congressman and all the members of the President's cabinet does not necessarily have very useful knowledge.

Such facts are of relatively little use for a variety of reasons. For one thing they constitute temporary knowledge: Congress and the cabinet change with each election. Moreover, names by themselves do not answer the more important questions one might have about the operation of the government. Why does the President and his cabinet often favor one kind of legislation, while the Congress favors another? Why does the Congress more often than the cabinet consider the particular need of local areas? Why can there be wide shifts in the proportion of the vote going to the Democratic and Republican candidates for President (Johnson, a Democrat, won in a landslide in 1964; Nixon, a Republican, barely won office in 1968, but then won by a landslide in 1972) with the Congress remaining steadily in the hands of the Democrats? And why do the Democratic Congresses sometimes give as much support to Republican presidents as to Democratic ones?

To answer questions like these, we need more relevant facts than the names of the members of Congress. We need to know about the social backgrounds and professional careers of cabinet members and congressmen, for these facts help explain different views about policy. We need to know about party loyalties among voters and how these sometimes lead voters to support a candidate from one party for President and from the other for Congress, for this will help explain why a Republican can win the White House but then face a Congress controlled by the Democrats. And we need to know about the organization of the Congress and the nature of the party ties of congressmen, because this will help explain why Congress may support a President whose party affiliation is opposite to that of the majority of its members.

Why are facts about the backgrounds and professional careers of congressmen useful? The answer is that some facts can be used as parts of explanations in that they can be linked to other facts. The social background and careers of members of Congress help us understand how they act in office. Most important, the information is generalizable. It is useful in understanding congressional action on such topics as why Congress takes the stand it does on tax bills, or why it usually leaves control over foreign policy to the President.

This discussion gives some clues as to the principles of selectivity we use in this book. We cannot describe all the facts of American politics and even less draw connections among all of them. Nor can we keep up with the latest events as reported in the daily press. Rather, we must select what to discuss. Our principle is to select our material in terms of what will give us the most generalizable knowledge.

Politics and Controversy: "Let's not talk about politics. It will ruin the evening." Why does political discussion often lead to argument, and sometimes very bitter argument? Because of values and passion. People have different political values, and they often hold those values with passionate conviction. Objectivity about politics is difficult.

Those who write about politics — in the press, in magazines, in books — also usually have commitments to one political position or another. And the temptation is to describe and explain politics from that viewpoint. Thus on any political issue we can usually find many interpretations, often completely opposed to one another. Nor is the study of politics an exact science such that the objective observer can always find one side clearly right and the other clearly wrong.

In this book, we have tried to pay attention to the varying interpretations of American politics. We do not present one interpretation as gospel truth to be noted down and remembered by the student, for this would be misleading. Indeed, we have tried in every chapter to focus on some of the leading controversies in the interpretation of American politics. The result may be to leave an uncertainty in your mind: Which is right, position A or position B? But that uncertainty may represent a deeper understanding of American politics than would your belief that you knew all the answers, for the authors of this book do not know all the answers, nor does anyone else writing or thinking about American politics. To understand political controversies may well be the first step toward understanding politics.

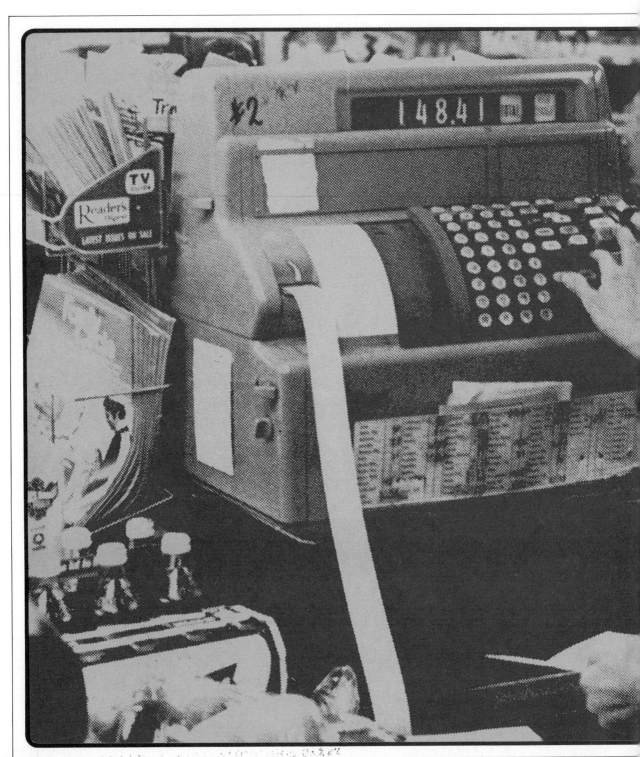

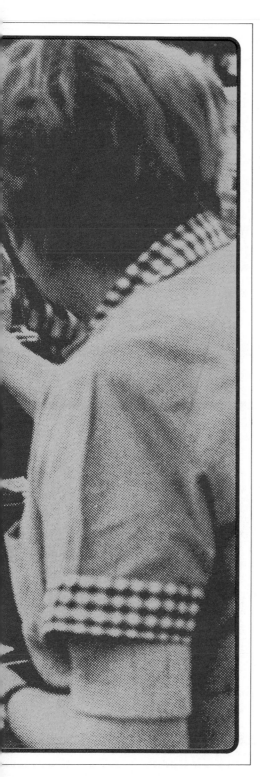

Political Capitalism: The U.S. Economy

The U.S. economy is almost entirely privately owned and is largely run for private profit, but it is managed in active cooperation and close consultation with the government. The relationship between an economy that is privately owned and a government of elected officials has led observers to describe the U.S. economy as *political capitalism*, a term whose significance will become clearer as we proceed.

We begin this textbook on American government with a chapter on political capitalism because we believe that the partnership between a private economy and an elected government provides the context within which economic *and* political life is carried on in America today. Think of the following topics: taxation, wage and price guidelines, welfare benefits, space exploration, public utilities, international trade, interest rates, farm subsidies, social security, inflation, and gross national product. These are neither solely economic matters nor solely political matters. Rather, they are both.

Think next of what are sometimes called an individual's economic roles: worker, owner, investor, consumer, entrepreneur, welfare recipient. Would anyone believe that these roles are unrelated to how the citizen thinks and acts politically? Not likely. From the citizen's point of view, who he is economically and who he is politically are inextricable.

Our premise, then, is the interrelatedness of political and economic life. Our thesis is that in American society this interrelatedness spells political capitalism. The thesis does not pronounce one economic philosophy to be superior to another. It does not lead to a celebration of the U.S. economy or to a censure of it. Some readers will find much to celebrate, others much to censure. Our thesis does not hold that "economics explains all" any more than it holds that "politics explains all." We have no hidden agenda saying that one set of activities is "basic" and all other activities are peripheral. A democratically elected government throws its weight around in the economy, but a privately owned economy throws its weight around in politics.

What we are saying is that the growth of political capitalism has resulted from a fascinating partnership—a partnership between an economy largely privately owned and organized according to the capitalistic creed on the one hand, and a government of elected officials that is organized according to democratic principles on the other. We are ill equipped to understand American politics without a few basic facts about this partnership. Before we proceed to the question of how this partnership came to be, let us get firmly in mind three such facts about the American economy: (1) It is privately owned. (2) It is dominated by a relatively few giant corporations. (3) It encourages substantial inequalities in income and wealth.

The Privately Owned Economy

You might have been told that the United States has a "mixed" economy, which usually means that there is a mixture of private and public ownership. This is a half-truth at best, because it confuses government regulation of the economy—of which there is a great deal in the United States—with government ownership—of which there is very little. Although many substantial changes have taken place in the American economy since its impressive growth in the late nineteenth century, these changes have not included public ownership.

We know of course that in such socialist nations as the Soviet Union or East Germany much of the economy is state owned and state managed. But we sometimes overlook that public ownership of economic enterprises is extensive even in Western democracies such as France or Britain. The United States is an exception to the worldwide trend, for in the United States important natural resources, transportation and communication systems, and other services are not owned and operated by the government. Table 1.1 makes this very clear. Public ownership of various industries and facilities in the United States is compared with public ownership in three leading capitalist countries in the world. Three stars in the table indicate that a particular industry is predominantly government owned; two stars indicate a heavy element of government ownership; one star indicates a balance between government and private ownership; no stars indicate predominant private ownership.

The contrast between the United States and three other major Western democracies is evident. It should be stressed that this table presents data on *ownership*, not on government regulation or government support. The airline industry is as closely regulated in the United States as it is in the

Table 1.1 Comparison of Public Ownership of Industries
and Services in France, Britain, West Germany, and the United States

	ROADS	POSTAL SERVICES	ELEC-TRICITY	RAIL-WAYS	TELE-PHONES	AIR-LINES	RADIO, TV	GAS	COAL	OIL	STEEL	BANKS
FRANCE	***	***	***	***	***	**	***	***	***	***		**
BRITAIN	***	***	***	***	***	**	**	***	***	**	***	
WEST GERMANY	***	***	***	***	***	***	***	***	**			
UNITED STATES	***		**									

Three stars = predominant public ownership
Two stars = heavy element of public ownership
One star = mixture between private and public ownership
No stars = privately owned
Source: Data based on Anthony King, "Ideologies as Predictors of Public Policy Patterns: A Comparative Analysis," as presented to the 67th Annual Meeting of the American Political Science Association, 1971.

other three nations. But each of the other nations has a major government-owned airline: Lufthansa in Germany, Air France in France, and BOAC in Britain. There is no publicly owned airline in the United States. Gas and electricity are wholly state owned in the three European democracies. In the United States, the manufacture and distribution of gas are overwhelmingly in private hands. The ownership of electricity is mixed; some firms are privately owned (Pacific Gas and Electric) and some are publicly owned (Tennessee Valley Authority).

This evidence is a useful corrective to those who believe the government to be increasing its ownership of industry and business. Government is big in the United States, but it is big because of an expansion of such services as education, roads, research, space exploration, and mostly, national defense. It is big also because it regulates a complex economy. It is not big because of public ownership.

The Domination of Giant Corporations

The romanticized version of early American capitalism maintained that the driving force behind economic expansion was the individual small businessman. This was not the case. Starting in the nineteenth century and continuing until today it has been the industrial corporations, not the small businessmen, that have amassed the capital and technological know-how necessary for opening canals and harbors, cutting the timber, mining the oil and coal, building railroads, innovating in production techniques, and experimenting with new products. The early "captains of industry" are remembered for the industrial empires they established: Rockefeller (oil), Carnegie (steel), Armour and Swift (meat-packing), Pillsbury (milling), Vanderbilt and Stanford (railroads), and Morgan (banking). John D. Rockfeller, founder of Standard Oil, recognized many years ago that the giant corporation would revolutionize "the way of doing business all over the world . . . . The day of combination is here to stay. Individualism has gone, never to return."[1]

Rockefeller was as much a prophet as businessman. The economy of America is today dominated by a very small number of corporations and banks. Consider the following facts:

1. In 1970 the Securities and Exchange Commission listed 202,710 manufacturing corporations. But only 100 of these corporations (.05 percent) controlled more than half of all manufacturing assets in the nation. This concentration has been steadily increasing for the last two decades. Here is the proportion of all manufacturing assets controlled by only 100 corporations:

1950	1955	1960	1965	1970
39.8%	44.3%	46.4%	46.5%	52.3%

[1] Quoted in William Miller, *A New History of the United States*, rev. ed. (New York: Dell, 1962), p. 300.

2. Fewer than 1600 persons, the corporation presidents and directors, have legal authority over the 100 largest corporations.
3. The largest single corporation, General Motors, has annual worldwide sales of approximately $25 billion, a figure that is greater than the gross national product of all but about 15 nations of the world.
4. There are 67,000 corporations actively involved in utilities and communications. But only 33 of these control half of all assets in electricity, gas, transportation, and communication.
5. Similar concentration is true in banking, where less than one-tenth of one percent of all banks control nearly half of all banking assets. (These are the 50 largest commercial banks out of a total of 13,511.)
6. Although there are nearly 2000 insurance companies in the United States only 18 of them control two-thirds of all insurance assets. Such concentration is also true in the trust business, with approximately three-fifths of all trust assets being held by less than 2 percent of the national banks.

Not all U.S. industries display an equal amount of concentration. It is in the key sectors of the economy—transportation, iron and steel, oil, banking and finance, communication, industrial chemicals—that concentration is most advanced. In less critical industries and services—retail clothing, for instance—the assets are more evenly distributed. But of course these less critical industries play a comparatively lesser role in political capitalism. The important features of political capitalism emerge in the close relationship between the U.S. government and the leading corporations in transportation (General Motors, Ford), in communication (American Telephone and Telegraph), in aeronautics (Lockheed, Douglas, Boeing), in iron and steel (U.S. Steel), and so forth.

These two important facts—first, that the economy is owned and operated privately and for the purpose of private profit and, second, that the economy is largely controlled by a comparatively few huge corporations and thus by a tiny, tiny group of men—have led to the emergence of the economic system best described as *political capitalism*. How this has happened and what it means will interest us in the remainder of this chapter. But first we must quickly review one more fact, which is of less immediate importance but which will loom large in the next chapter when we turn our attention to the issue of how political capitalism encourages social inequalities.

The Encouragement of Inequalities in Income and Wealth

Capitalism encourages substantial economic inequality in two ways. First, the ideology of capitalism asserts that economic growth is related to material reward. It is taken for granted that there are inequalities among men, some being more intelligent, ambitious, and talented than others. Economic expansion and innovation depend on attracting the superior people into positions of leadership and responsibility. This is simple to accomplish, because it is also taken for granted that men will work for money. Thus, by attaching the highest salaries to the most important positions, the flow of the most talented people to the most important positions can be guaranteed. Persons in the less important positions, presumably the persons with fewer skills or less ambition, should be rewarded at a lower rate of pay. In 1971 the president of International Telephone and Telegraph earned $812,494, or more than $15,000 per week. A clerk in ITT earned $8,000 a year, or less than 1 percent of what the top executive received.

Capitalism encourages economic inequality in a second and even more significant way. The capitalist creed emphasizes the sacredness of private property. There are two forms of private property: what we commonly call private possessions (a car, a home, a television set) and what we call income-producing property (stocks, bonds, real estate, patents). Those in society fortunate enough to own income-producing property will in almost every case be far wealthier than those not so favored. This is because of the simple principle that money makes money. For instance, if you are a millionaire (and more than 100,000 persons in the United States are) and you invest your wealth in income-producing property, at a conservative 6 percent, your yearly income would be $60,000. If you are a multimillionaire, your income from investments would of course be even greater. Indeed, *Fortune Magazine* recently named 66 Americans, each of whose net worth exceeded $150 million. This tidy sum invested at 6 percent would guarantee each of them a yearly income of $9 million. (In Chapter 2 we will see just what effect income taxes have on this type of wealth.)

By this time, it may have occurred to the reader to wonder if there is an inconsistency between a capitalist economy and a democratic polity. Many astute political scientists have wondered the same thing; in fact, there is a long-standing debate in political thought on the subject. We review this argument as background to our analysis of how *democratic* political processes have shaped what today is called political capitalism.

Democracy and Capitalism: A Paradox?

The Argument on the Left

Capitalism is such a strong and domineering economic system that it undermines true democracy. Great wealth in the hands of the capitalist class is used, the argument goes, to purchase political control, for if there are great inequalities of wealth it is difficult to see how there can be any equality in political influence. This argument owes much to the Marxist proposition that industrial capitalism is a coercive economy that submits the masses to the direction of a wealthy minority who own the institutions of economic production.

Baran and Sweezy, noted Marxist economists, claim that "the incessant repetition that the political regime in the United States today is a democracy" is a falsehood "devoid of all descriptive or explanatory validity." In the United States, they continue, "the propertyless masses have never been in a position to determine the conditions of their lives or the policies of the nation's government." A tiny group "resting on vast economic power and in full control of society's political and cultural apparatus makes all the important political decisions. Clearly to claim that such a society is democratic serves to conceal, not to reveal, the truth."[2]

The Argument on the Right

In conservative political thought one can also find the idea that private property and democracy are incompatible. But here the argument is reversed. Democracy, say some conservatives, puts property in peril rather than private ownership putting democracy in peril. The property and wealth of intelligent and hardworking citizens will be snatched away by less able and less industrious citizens, who will use the ballot box to radically redistribute wealth. Once the wealth has been redistributed, the incentive to invent or to work will fade away, and economic stagnation will set in. Even as long ago as 1821 a constitutional convention in New York State debated the merits of democracy. Speaking in vigorous opposition to universal suffrage was the highest political official of New York, Chancellor James Kent:

> That extreme democratic principle, universal suffrage, has been productive of corruption, injustice, violence, and tyranny. . . . The apprehended danger from the experiment of universal suffrage applied to the whole legislative department, is no dream of the imagination. It is too mighty an excitement for the moral constitution of men to endure. The tendency of universal suffrage is to jeopardize the rights of property and the principles of liberty. There is a constant tendency in human society, and the history of every age proves it; there is a tendency in the poor to covet and to share the plunder of the rich — in the debtor to relax or avoid the obligation of contracts — in the indolent and the profligate to cast the whole burthens of society upon the industrious and the virtuous. . . .[3]

Echoes of this sentiment can be heard today in debates over public welfare programs. Some citizens view public welfare programs as government-sponsored theft and characterize welfare recipients as lazy citizens using political pressure to grab an unfair share of the profits earned by the hardworking citizens.

[2] Paul A. Baran and Paul M. Sweezy, *Monopoly Capital: An Essay on the American Economic and Social Order* (London: Pelican, 1968), p. 327.

[3] Quoted in Alpheus T. Mason, ed., *Free Government in the Making*, 2nd ed. (New York: Oxford University Press, 1956), p. 399.

The Facts of the Matter

The facts of American history lend partial support to both arguments, but total support to neither. It is true that the elites who largely control the economy have political power far in excess of that available to the average citizen, but to conclude that democratic processes have no significance for political decisions ignores much that is central to American politics. It is true also that voting and other democratic processes have redistributed some of the wealth from the owners of private property to the working classes, but this redistribution has stopped very far short of the radical egalitarianism feared by some conservatives. The connection between democracy and capitalism will be reviewed at many points in this text, but let us first get in mind the larger political-economic context.

The Origin and Significance of Political Capitalism

The term *political capitalism* suggests a close partnership between a privately owned economy and a publicly elected government. The powers of the state are used to sustain the private sector, and the private sector contributes resources and personnel to the state. The private sector is dominated, as we have seen, by the giant corporations. The public sector is dominated by the federal government. Political capitalism, then, is largely an outgrowth of the partnership between the corporations and the federal government. The mutual goals that bind this partnership together are (1) economic and social stability, (2) continuous economic expansion, and (3) national defense.

Political capitalism has evolved out of the politics and policies of many generations—and it is still evolving. To understand political capitalism fully, we must go back into American history and inquire into the major stages that have shaped our political economy.

The First Component: Establishing the Legal Framework for a Free Enterprise Economy

When James Madison, chief draftsman of the American Constitution, wrote in 1787 that the first object of government is to protect the different and unequal faculties of men for acquiring property, he was echoing themes from Europe and England. In its European origins democracy was a reform movement led by a commercial middle class against the oppressive practices of absolute monarchs and hereditary aristocracies. The privileges and special statuses enjoyed by the monarch and his noblemen blocked the commercial activities of a small but growing group of merchants, traders, and craftsmen.

These early "capitalists" knew that a free enterprise economy depends on the right of individuals to enter into valid contracts and to have those contracts upheld in a court of law; it depends on the right of individuals to sell their products and labor in the free marketplace; and it depends on one's right to strive for such material goods as individual talent can achieve. Free enterprise cannot flourish when legal restrictions block the exchange of goods and labor; and it cannot flourish where social position is fixed at birth, and the entrepreneurial spirit is denied an outlet.

The assault on class privilege was in the first instance a reform movement that freed commerce and trade. But in doing so the reform movement introduced such critical democratic principles as due process of law, equal status as citizens, protection from arbitrary arrests and unfair seizure of property, parliamentary representation, and at least limited voting. Stated differently, the U.S. Constitution reflects the victory of individual rights and limited government over class privileges and royal absolutism. And just as the European middle-class reformers expected, such a Constitution would also establish a free enterprise economy.

Although capitalism as we know it today did not take hold until after the Civil War, the legal framework and constitutional system necessary to a free enterprise economy was fairly well established as early as 1800. Even then as today, a police force protected the private property of citizens, a government court system settled disputes arising from violations of economic contracts, a government monetary system provided the bills and coins necessary to economic transactions, a government postal system circulated the mail indispensable to commercial activities, and a government system of common weights and measures, patents, and copyrights provided the necessary uniformity and protection for exchanges of goods and titles. These have been accepted governmental functions since 1789, and they continue today—in a very much enlarged sense—to establish the legal framework that allows a capitalistic system of production and exchanges to operate.

The Second Component:
Establishing the Practice of Government
Subsidies to Private Enterprise

The direct support of private enterprise through state powers and with public monies is as old as the nation itself. Alexander Hamilton, first Secretary of the Treasury, was insistent that the new federal government establish a national bank. Credit would be increased in this manner and, according to Hamilton, this would help "the operations of commerce among individuals. Industry is increased, commodities are multiplied, agriculture and manufacturers flourish; and herein consists the true wealth and prosperity of a state." As the most decisive member of President George Washington's cabinet, Hamilton got his way, and the federal government has been in the business of supporting private business ever since.

Support for Means of Transportation: The first really massive government support began in the post-Civil War period. These were the years in which the economy of the United States was transformed. The nation was being crisscrossed with railroads, and canals and harbors were opened up to shipping. Natural resources—especially coal, lumber, and oil—were everywhere being put to industrial use. Factories were making everything from shoes to stoves. Telegraph and then telephones were spreading. Electricity was being introduced into the American home. American exports were being shipped around the world.

The tremendous economic expansion between the 1860s and the end of the century was accomplished by a vigorous and innovative private sector. But direct government support was not lacking. The most notable subsidy was for the railroads. By 1870 some 183 million acres of land had been granted to private railroad builders, in return for which the railroads agreed to transport the U.S. mail at very low costs. The "Indian removal" project of the U.S. cavalry cleared the way for the railroads and the settlements that accompanied the westward expansion. Other such internal improvements as canals, harbors, and roads necessary for commercial expansion were built and maintained at public expense.

By 1870 some 183 million acres of land had been granted by government to private railroad builders.   *(Union Pacific Railroad Photo)*

One hundred years later the practice of direct public support for the private sector has been greatly enlarged, and for reasons similar to those given in defense of the earliest programs, the main reason being that certain industries and social services are "collective goods" (as defined in the Introduction), and yet no single corporation has sufficient capital to provide them. Thus a contemporary version of the nineteenth-century railroad subsidy is the federal highway program, which is of great benefit to the trucking, automobile, and oil industries, but also, of course, to millions of daily users. Equally important are various forms of direct assistance to the airline companies. Airports are built with public money, and weather information and navigational aids are provided at public expense.

Protection of American Industry—the Protective Tariff: Another venerable institution is the protective tariff. By placing high import taxes on foreign products the government protects American industry from foreign competition. When President Nixon in 1971 imposed a surtax on foreign cars he was following a familiar Republican tradition, for the Republican party platform of 1896 stated: "We renew and emphasize our allegiance to the policy of protection as the bulwark of American industrial independence and the foundation of American development and prosperity. This true American policy taxes foreign products and encourages home industry. . . . It secures the American market for the American producer."

Federal Aid in the Form of Loans: The government subsidizes and protects; it also lends money. The Small Business Administration regularly provides loans to small businessmen, and the Federal Home Loan Bank system makes loans to private lending agencies in order to encourage the flow of private capital into housing construction. Federal-guaranteed loans to help a particular corporation out of economic difficulty have been made from time to time, a recent example being the Lockheed Aircraft Corporation.

Agriculture Subsidy Programs: One of the largest government subsidy programs is in agriculture. Farm prices are subject to many uncertainties; they fluctuate more widely than does farm production itself. Supply and demand are more difficult to keep in balance in agriculture than in industry. As a result the individual farmer can easily suffer from considerable income instability, often due to causes over which he has no control. That is, he would suffer from such instability were it not for a massive government program which ensures the farmer a fair price for his products. The various parts of this program amount to a $5 billion item in the national budget each year.

Government subsidies constitute, then, the second major component of political capitalism. As was true of the first component—the legal framework necessary for a free enterprise system—government subsidies have their origins in an earlier period but are today greatly amplified. Support of the private sector with public money is not an occasional practice but is, rather, part of the continuous pattern of interaction between government and the corporate economy.

The Third Component: Establishing Precedents for Government Regulation of the Economy

The next major modification of the capitalist economy took place through the regulatory activities of the government, a major step in the progression toward political capitalism. Although some regulations have been present since 1789 (for instance, licensing of certain occupations), major attention to regulatory legislation did not occur until the end of the nineteenth century. There were two main reasons.

First, the capitalist economy, and especially the capitalist class, was by no means universally admired. Ruthless business practices by monopolies such as Standard Oil forced the small businessman out of the market; farmers resented the high prices charged by railroads for transporting produce to market; workers suffered heavily from long hours at low pay in unsafe and unsanitary working conditions; consumers resented price-fixing practices of trusts and monopolistic corporations. The government provided little help to those groups most penalized by unregulated capitalism. Indeed, judges, legislators, party leaders, and even Presidents depended for their power base on the industrial interests: "Capitalists, seeking land grants, tariffs, bounties, favorable currency policies, freedom from regulatory legislation and economic reform, supplied campaign funds, fees, and bribes and plied politicians with investment opportunities."[4] It was the rare politican who resisted the temptations: "One might search the whole list of Congress, Judiciary, and Executive during the twenty-five years 1870 to 1895," concluded Henry Adams, "and find little but damaged reputation."

By the 1890s discontented farmers, middle-class reform groups working with small business interests, protesting consumers, and labor agitators began to call for government regulation of the economy. They enjoyed only limited success, but they established a political climate that eventually led to a critical modification of capitalism. The rhetoric of the day made popular the idea that even a capitalist economy had flaws. These flaws—child labor, economic insecurity, deceptive advertising, price fixing, shoddy merchandise, unsafe working conditions—could be corrected through regulatory legislation enforced by the government.

[4] Richard Hofstadter, *The American Political Tradition* (New York: Vintage, 1954), p. 170. The quotation from Henry Adams appears in this work as well, p. 107.

Antitrust Legislation: The most important goal was to break up the enormous concentrations of economic power. "Trust-busting" became a popular political slogan; Supreme Court Justice Louis D. Brandeis, speaking of "industrial absolutism," warned of the danger to democracy when "there develops within the State a state so powerful that the ordinary social and industrial forces existing are insufficient to cope with it." Regulatory legislation was passed, such as the Sherman Antitrust Act of 1890, which prohibits monopolistic practices in restraint of trade, and the Federal Trade Commission Act of 1914, which prohibits unfair competition. Laws were also passed regulating working conditions and hours of work, especially for children and women.

Regulatory Legislation for the Business Community: The second and perhaps more significant impulse for regulatory legislation came from the business community itself. A totally unregulated economy was proving difficult to manage. It was necessary to standardize products, accounting procedures, prices, professional qualifications, and so forth, and the more enlightened corporation chiefs recognized that the federal government could be immensely helpful in bringing order to the sometimes chaotic economic situation. It was only necessary that the business community define the limits of political intervention in the economy—and this it was largely successful in doing. The early regulatory legislation did not signal the "triumph of small business over the trusts, as has often been suggested, but the victory of big business in achieving the rationalization of the economy that only the federal government could provide."[5]

The Scope and Amount of Governmental Regulatory Activities: Taken together, the demand for reforms from outside business circles and the desire for uniformity and economic stability within business circles led to an increasingly active role by the federal, state, and even local governments in the economy. It is often difficult for the student to imagine the amount of regulations enforced by the government. But consider just the following: There are government regulations that establish the training necessary to become a licensed barber (let alone a licensed doctor or lawyer or teacher); that fix the number of exits from an airplane or a movie theater or a day nursery; that determine the wording appropriate for wills and contracts; that restrict the advertising claims made by a medicine or food or automobile manufacturer; that limit the price of electricity and gas and of air, railroad, and water transportation; that set interest rates charged by banks and fees collected by stockbrokers. Government regulations affect how a corporation sells stocks, whether it will be allowed to expand operations, the way in which it advertises its products, how often and in what

---

[5] Gabriel Kolko, *The Triumph of Conservatism* (New York: Quadrangle, 1967), p. 284.

manner it must make a public accounting of its transactions, and how it acquires its raw materials and ships its finished goods.

It is evident that such an enormous range of regulatory activities brings the government and the corporate world very close together. Regulation, then, fosters the partnership that results in political capitalism. As we shall see later (in Chapters 15 and 16), the regulatory agencies themselves almost become part of the economic sector they are supposed to regulate. Thus the Civil Aeronautics Board works in close harmony with the commercial airlines, the mutual goal being the economic health and stability of the air industry. The aim of government regulations is as often to promote as to restrict particular industries.

The Fourth Component: Establishing Government Fiscal Policy and Public Welfare Programs

Regulatory legislation was and continues to be largely specific in application; it sets standards for licensing a particular profession or for marketing a particular product. This type of piecemeal legislation was never intended to manage the entire economy. Indeed, the dominant economic philosophy had long held that a capitalist economy was self-adjusting. Full employment and price stability could be attained if workers freely exchanged their labor for earnings, if supply and demand regulated production and prices, and if profits guided the rate of expansion and investment. This orthodox economic view dominated American public policy during the period of industrial growth from approximately 1860 to 1930.

Only a few "radical" economists and political leaders challenged the orthodox view. They held that an unmanaged capitalism is inherently unstable, because it operates in a "boom-bust" cycle, with first a period of economic expansion that brings about inflation and runaway prices and then a period of economic recession that creates unemployment and underused productive facilities. Very few leaders paid much attention to this criticism of capitalism, until the enormous worldwide depression of the 1930s.

Fiscal Policy in the 1930s: As unemployment in the United States climbed to a high of 25 percent, as banks failed and factories closed, and as bread lines grew longer and longer, voices insisting that somehow the economy would straighten itself out became less prominent. Government leaders began to listen to a different viewpoint. Sir John Maynard Keynes, in his book *The General Theory of Employment, Interest, and Money*, stated the argument for government intervention in the economy. The boom-bust cycle could be arrested, according to the new economics, if government used its tremendous fiscal power to stabilize the economy. Ad-

As banks failed and unemployment grew in the 1930s, the cry came for new economic policies. (Photo: Wide World)

justing taxes, increasing or decreasing government spending on public projects, and altering the supply of money and credit through control of bank reserves and interest rates are major economic tools available to the government.

These economic tools began to be used in the 1930s, during what is generally called the New Deal of Franklin D. Roosevelt. Government fiscal policy is today a major force in the free enterprise system. In accepting such policies the business and political leaders were in effect admitting that no citizen—whether worker, pensioner, investor, or owner—was immune to the ravages of an economic depression. Government assumed responsibility for monitoring the business cycles, and for attempting to maintain a relatively low level of unemployment while at the same time preventing prices from creeping up to destroy the value of the dollar.

Fiscal policy has not, of course, been entirely successful in this regard. American capitalism is still a free enterprise economy; and government has stopped short of imposing rigid controls on prices, wages, investments, and spending. We still suffer through business cycles, though none to date so severe as that of the 1930s. It is for this reason that the New Deal is sometimes said to have "humanized" or tamed capitalism. Excessively severe depressions, massive unemployment, and rampant inflation have presumably been modified by Keynesian economics.

Public Welfare Programs: But the New Deal did more than this to humanize capitalism. The right of labor to organize and to bargain collectively with management received major support in the legislation of the 1930s. This in turn has led to numerous economic reforms: minimum wage laws, unemployment insurance, social security, improved health standards for factory workers, paid vacations, and so forth. Some of these reforms (paid vacations, for instance) are the result of bargains struck between worker and management, and are presumably paid for out of corporate profits (though the evidence is that the costs are mostly transferred to the consumer). Other reforms (social security, for instance) have become citizenship rights, and are under the direct control of government agencies. We will discuss these more fully in the next chapter.

The responsibility of the federal government for the health of the privately owned economic sector was firmly established by legislation in the Employment Act of 1946, which declared that "it is the continuing policy and responsibility of the federal government . . . to promote maximum employment, production, and purchasing power." The economy remains privately owned but is increasingly subject to public management. This legislation and the philosophy it embodied has of course become one of the major components of political capitalism.

The Fifth Component: The Government as Customer for Private Enterprise

The U.S. government has become since World War II the single largest customer for American industrial products and services. Approximately 30 percent of the gross national product is due to government expenditures. Were government purchases to cease, huge gaps would be left in the private enterprise system. This is especially true of the industries that supply the defense establishment. Billions of dollars—if such sums can even be imagined—have been spent on military hardware and personnel over the past two decades. This simple if enormous fact has transformed the economy once again, moving to a new level the partnership between private corporations and the federal government.

The Contract Economy: Sizable sections of the free enterprise economy are under direct contract to the federal government, especially to the Pentagon, the Atomic Energy Commission, and the National Aeronautic and Space Administration (NASA). A list of the leading military contractors

Table 1.2 The Military-Industrial Alliance: Contracts and Colonels

SELECTED CONTRACTORS	PRIME MILITARY CONTRACTS, 1968 (IN BILLIONS OF DOLLARS)	MILITARY CONTRACTS AS PERCENTAGE OF 1968 TOTAL SALES	NUMBER OF RETIRED COLONELS OR NAVY CAPTAINS EMPLOYED, FEBRUARY 1968
General Dynamics Corporation	$2.24	84%	113
Lockheed Aircraft Corporation	1.87	84%	210
General Electric Company	1.49	18%	80
United Aircraft Corporation	1.32	55%	48
McDonnell-Douglas Corporation	1.10	34%	141
Boeing Corporation	.76	23%	169
North American Rockwell Corporation	.67	26%	104
Grumman Aircraft Engineering Corporation	.63	55%	31
Martin Marietta Corporation	.39	57%	40
Northrop Corporation	.31	64%	48

Source: Based on data from *Congressional Record*, March 24, 1969, p. S3074; "500 Biggest Industrial List," *Fortune*, May 15, 1969; and "Where the Military Contracts Go," *Fortune*, August 1, 1969.

overlaps to a considerable degree a list of the most powerful industrial corporations in America. (See Table 1.2.) The largest defense contractors include General Electric, General Motors, Lockheed, IBM, DuPont, Union Carbide, Dow Chemical, and nearly all of the major aeronautics corporations. It is estimated that 65 of the 100 leading firms in the economy are significantly involved in the military market. However, as one report states, focusing on the prime contractors "is like looking at only the visible part of an iceberg. This is only the direct impact of the military budget; the indirect impact on subcontractors, on producers of intermediate goods and parts, and on suppliers of raw materials ties military spending into the heart of the economy."[6] The major components of the contract economy are weapons development, space exploration, atomic energy, technical training, and research development.

Economist John Kenneth Galbraith, in his aptly titled *The New Industrial State*, spells out the chief goals of the state: "The state is strongly concerned with the stability of the economy. And with its expansion or growth. And with education. And with technical and scientific advance.

[6] From Michael Reich and David Finkelhor, "The Military Industrial Complex: No Way Out," in Richard C. Edwards, Michael Reich, and Thomas E. Weisskopf, eds., *The Capitalist System* (Englewood Cliffs, N.J.: Prentice-Hall, 1972), p. 394.

And, most notably, with the national defense."[7] These national goals all have their counterpart in the corporate sector of the economy; stability is necessary to long-term planning desired by the large corporation; economic growth brings profits, promotions, and prestige; trained manpower, scientific research, and technical development are necessary components to a modern industrial system; defense spending directly supports, through government contracts, a large part of the economy. There are, then, shared goals between the public and the private sectors, between government leaders and corporation leaders.

The similarity of interests between government officials and corporate leaders makes for a free exchange of viewpoints. It also facilitates movement from the private sector to the government. Nearly all top political executives come from careers in the corporate economy. Many have been corporation lawyers, and a sizable number have been corporation presidents or directors. The career pattern works in the opposite direction as well. Persons leaving government service frequently turn to the huge corporations for a new position. This is especially true of ex-generals and Pentagon officials, who find it comparatively easy to find a top position in one of the firms that do major contract service for the Department of Defense. Illustrative evidence appears in Table 1.2. This table also shows the extent to which leading corporations depend upon military contracts to maintain high sales.

And even when direct exchange of positions does not take place, the many committees and advisory agencies that work closely with the federal government are filled with recruits from the corporate world. For example, the Council on Foreign Relations (CFR) is a small but prestigious, tax-exempt, nonpartisan organization which serves as a training ground for recruits into the State and Defense Departments and which provides research and advice—at very high levels—on foreign policy. Important names associated with the CFR in recent years include Henry Kissinger (national security advisor to Nixon), former Secretary of State Dean Rusk, John Foster Dulles, and many others. The chief occupations of Council members—in order of numerical strength—are corporation directors, corporation lawyers, bankers (especially from banks with large international services), educators (especially college presidents and deans), and publishers. The Committee for Economic Development (CED) is a counterpart organization whose major involvement is with monetary and economic problems.

Political Capitalism: Strengthening the Free Enterprise System

It is generally accepted that political capitalism has strengthened rather than weakened the free enterprise system based on private ownership. Cer-

---

[7] John Kenneth Galbraith, *The New Industrial State* (Boston: Houghton Mifflin, 1967), p. 304.

The framework provided by government for commercial activities and economic transactions has been indispensable to capitalism. *(Photo: U.S. Postal Service)*

tainly the legal framework provided by government for commercial activities and economic transactions has been indispensable to capitalism. The various government subsidy programs have bolstered faltering parts of the economy (such as the railroads today) and have greatly strengthened other parts (such as agriculture). Regulatory activities have helped rationalize the economy. Collective bargaining between labor and management, for instance, has stabilized industrial relations, and yet not seriously challenged private ownership. Government fiscal policies and general management of the economy have lessened the likelihood of severe business cycles, and have helped maintain a steady flow of investment capital into the private sector. Public education has furnished trained manpower for private enterprise; and government-sponsored research has produced technologies of direct and considerable profit to private corporations (atomic energy, for example).

Political Capitalism: Strengthening the Political System

A further point often made about political capitalism is that it strengthens the political system. It does so by creating a large, satisfied majority in the population. A steadily increasing gross national product (now approximately $1,000 billion) has meant a steadily increasing per capita income. Although pockets of poverty persist and inflation threatens savings, more persons in the United States have more material goods than is true of any other nation in the world. Median income levels continue to increase as do the number of things one can purchase with one's income. Private cars are nearly universally owned in the United States, and the same is true of such labor-saving devices as washers and dryers. Only a small number of families are unable to afford such entertainment facilities as television and radio. Newspapers, books, magazines, and journals are published in the millions—and available to suit every taste and hobby. Life is good for many, many Americans. There are flaws—unemployment, poverty, disease, poor housing. These can be readily admitted and strongly disapproved. But the fact remains that the prosperous middle class of America is the majority class, and that it continues to grow.

In this argument, political capitalism has effectively neutralized radical political movements that question private ownership, concentrations of economic power, or great inequalities in wealth. Such challenges have been diverted by the reforms and regulations that have modified and "humanized" capitalism while stopping short of public ownership, breaking up the corporate giants, or redistributing wealth. Thus the attack on private property by the Black Power movement in the early 1960s is now partly channeled into "Black capitalism" and a radical critique thereby moderated. Or, at an earlier time, the American Socialist party was a thriving organization from the 1900s to the 1930s, but the New Deal policies of the Democratic party, which have been retained and expanded by subsequent Republican and Democratic administrations, seriously undermined the attractiveness to voters of the socialist alternative.

Conclusion

The close cooperation and shared goals between the government leaders and the corporate leaders affect much of our analysis in the remainder of this book. In the next chapter we will see how the interplay between democratic principles and economic practices influences basic citizenship rights. Later, we investigate how mass political participation and the recruitment of leaders are affected by the distribution of wealth in the society. Political capitalism also sets the context within which many conflicts in this society take place, and thus it influences the activities of pressure groups, electorates, and political parties. And the process of formulating public policies in the legislative, executive, and judicial branches of government — as well as the substance of the policies themselves — reflects the partnership between government and economy.

Controversy

Is our political-economic system serving the needs of citizens. Or is it frustrating their basic wishes and goals?

One Side

The fundamental problems of reconciling capitalism and democracy in the United States have been solved. A powerful government and an equally powerful economy are committed to similar goals, which include: a steady expansion of production, always benefiting from improved efficiency; an equally steady expansion of consumption, thereby raising the standard of living for more and more Americans; international stability and larger world markets for American goods; unabated technological advance based on increasingly sophisticated research; constant improvement and enlargement of public education; and an unending supply of trained manpower. Many, indeed most, Americans are happy with the steady growth of the economy, for this translates into higher standards of living for themselves and their children. In no other nation of the world is so much within reach of so many: higher education, white-collar occupations, labor-saving devices, leisure time and an abundance of entertainment facilities, and decent housing and decent health care.

The authority of the government has been joined with the economic goals of a free enterprise system. The result is a society in which the basic needs and the hopes of a large part of the population are being cared for. There are, to be sure, still groups left out of the affluent American society. But the number of persons left out grows smaller and smaller as the political economy becomes stronger, and as the gross national product continues to grow. The ideals of democracy combined with the technology of capitalism will someday produce a society in which even poverty is eliminated.

All in all, there are good reasons to celebrate the establishment of political capitalism in the United States. This is clear if you compare today's living conditions with those of the nineteenth century, and if you compare the living conditions in the United States with those in most other parts of the world.

The Other Side

Living conditions in the United States are indeed very high for many citizens, but the social costs imposed by political capitalism have been enormous. First, there is the question of *priorities*. In worshipping economic growth we have endangered other, more fundamental values. At the same time that we have several dozen varieties of hairspray, we have understaffed and inadequate health clinics. A social service that is not sponsored by the industrial system becomes neglected. We have also allowed economic criteria to prevail over cultural and aesthetic criteria. This can be seen when a factory is located where it is economically efficient to do so, rather than locating it where it least fouls the air or pollutes the water or snarls the traffic.

Second, there is the question of *social justice*. A truly democratic society would not tolerate an economic system that allowed for a permanent group of unemployed poor persons. But our economic system does just that. Perhaps living conditions have been rising for the majority of Americans. However, the very poor class is still with us, and it shows no signs of disappearing despite national affluence. The poor can be found in urban ghettos, in nursing homes, in Appalachia, in migrant worker camps, and elsewhere. Political capitalism has not solved the question of poverty, and it is wrong to think that it can.

Third, there is the question of *foreign interventionism*. Our foreign policy over the past few decades has rested on protection of American commercial interests and intervention in the political life of other nations. This policy may be necessary to sustain the economic expansion of American business, but there have been social costs to pay. One such cost is the damaged reputation of America abroad. Another is the destruction that has sometimes accompanied our efforts abroad—especially, but not only, in Vietnam. Still another cost is the amount of our national resources that go to the military budget.

Finally, there is the question of *bigness*. Political capitalism has led to an enormous concentration of wealth and power in giant corporations and a huge federal government. There has been a corresponding sense of loss of control over one's own life.

These social costs are considerable ones. They are leading some persons to take a second look at the goals and workings of our political economy. These persons are asking whether a steadily increasing gross national product is not the wrong goal. Perhaps it is time to transform our economy once again. Perhaps the quality of the environment is more important than the economic efficiency of a manufacturer. Perhaps social services for the poor are more important than high salaries for the doctor or lawyer. Perhaps the role of "world policeman" should be dropped. Perhaps local control in small political and economic units is preferable to the economies of scale of the giant corporations.

Suggested Readings

A classic work on capitalism and democracy is Joseph A. Schumpeter's *Capitalism, Socialism, and Democracy*, 3rd. ed. (New York: Harper & Row, 1950). For a less favorable view of similar issues, written from a Marxist point of view, see Paul A. Baran and Paul M. Sweezy, *Monopoly Capital: An Essay on the American Economic and Social Order* (London: Pelican, 1968); and Ralph Miliband, *The State in Capitalist Society* (New York: Basic Books, 1969).

Two works by John Kenneth Galbraith provide useful perspectives on American economic society. These are *The Affluent Society* (Boston: Houghton Mifflin, 1958) and *The New Industrial State* (Boston: Houghton Mifflin, 1967).

A textbook by Paul A. Samuelson provides not only basic facts about the American economy but also lucid interpretation; see his *Economics*, 7th ed. (New York: McGraw-Hill, 1967).

Current statistics on government programs and expenditures can be found in various publications by the Office of Management and Budget and in publications of the Congressional Quarterly Service. See, for instance, the latter's *Federal Income Policy*, a background report on economic developments and legislation.

Political Equalities and Social Inequalities

2

Political capitalism encourages social inequalities, whereas political democracy promises equality. That is, the democratic principle of "one man, one vote" is a way of saying that all citizens share equally in the exercise of political power. Capitalism, however, does *not* rest on the principle of "one man, one dollar," and thus does not presume that all citizens will share equally in the wealth of the society.

We are left with the coexistence of seemingly inconsistent principles. This paradox is nicely summarized in a passage from Charles A. Beard's famous book, *The Economic Basis of Politics*:

> *Modern equalitarian democracy, which reckons all heads as equal and alike, cuts sharply athwart the philosophy and practice of the past centuries. Nevertheless, the democratic device of universal suffrage does not destroy economic classes or economic inequalities. It ignores them. Herein lies the paradox, the most astounding political contradiction that the world has ever witnessed.*[1]

The paradox identified by Beard is truly an interesting one, and one that is basic to our understanding of American politics. In this chapter we will review first the various types of equality promised by and somewhat created through democratic politics. We will then consider the inequalities in wealth that persist in this society. And then we will go on to ask why political capitalism can simultaneously encourage many forms of inequality and yet presume to rest on the principle of democratic equality.

Democracy and Equality

"We hold these truths to be self-evident," asserted the Declaration of Independence, "that all men are created equal." The men who signed this document knew, of course, that indeed all men were not created equal; differences in ability, intelligence, ambition, and talent could hardly be denied. Yet the Declaration was not just empty political sloganeering. The signers wanted to be on record against a political order in which members of society were *legally* unequal.

In medieval political life, citizenship was classified, and privileges and rights were allowed to one class of citizens but denied to other classes. The nobility, for instance, was allowed to participate in the exercise of public authority, but commoners or serfs were by law politically subordinate. The

[1] Charles A. Beard, *The Economic Basis of Politics* (New York: Vintage, 1960), p. 69.

aristocratic ideology which justifies first- and second-class citizenship is well summarized in the following passage:

> *The lot of the poor, in all things which affect them collectively, should be regulated for them, not by them. They should not be required or encouraged to think for themselves, or give to their own reflection or forecast an influential voice in the determination of the destiny. It is the duty of the higher classes to think for them, and to take responsibility for their lot. . . . The rich should be in* loco parentis *to the poor, guiding and restraining them like children.*[2]

Democratic ideology contrasts sharply with this aristocratic way of looking at things. The notion of citizenship embraced by democratic thinkers rejects the idea that the richer, the more accomplished, the more intelligent, or the higher born are somehow "better" people. The principle of citizenship elbows aside those ancient beliefs that had long been the bulwark of monarchies, aristocracies, hereditary privileges, class prejudices, and racial distinctions. It is no accident that the democratic principle of equal worth emerged nearly simultaneously with radical religious movements. The idea that all men are equal in the eyes of God became extended to the principle that all men are equal in the eyes of the state.

It is of course true that the principle of equal worth is not yet completely accepted, and probably never will be. But nevertheless it is deeply rooted now in Western political systems and has discredited, probably forever, certain ways of thinking about political relationships. Justifications for special and privileged statuses or for hereditary rights have been undermined, and this in itself is a major accomplishment. This does not mean that privileges and special rights no longer exist, but it does mean that they no longer have the overt protection of the state.

Equal Status Before the Law

We observed in Chapter 1 that the first century of our political history was preoccupied with legal-constitutional issues. Predominant among these issues was the proper definition of citizens' rights and the gradual extension of those rights to various elements of the population. The earliest decades concentrated on legal citizenship, or what we today might call civil rights.

Civil rights are the individualistic rights of free speech and thought and faith, the basic economic rights to acquire and dispose of property, the right to choose one's place and type of work, and the right to enter valid contracts in confidence that they will be upheld by courts of law.

---

[2] John Stuart Mill, *Principles of Political Economy*, II (Boston: Little, Brown, 1848), pp. 319–320. Here Mill is summarizing the aristocratic viewpoint, not endorsing it.

The Due Process of Law: Undergirding these legal rights is the fundamental principle of *due process of law*. Neither the state nor a fellow citizen may deny any man his right to speech, religion, property, or contract without first having the case tried in an impartial court of law according to prescribed rules and principles. The most important institutions connected with legal citizenship are, of course, the courts.

Fundamental Rights of Citizens: The principles of legal citizenship were accepted by the latter part of the eighteenth century. The Constitution and the Bill of Rights made it illegal to interfere with a citizen's expression, beliefs, or his right to act in the free marketplace. Furthermore, a citizen was innocent until proved guilty, was to be tried by a jury of peers, could not be detained without evidence, had the right to legal counsel, was protected against self-incrimination, could confront and cross-examine witnesses, and was not subject to unreasonable searches and seizures.

These citizenship rights were generally accepted, but in the eighteenth century they were *not* universally applied. Only certain groups of people living within the boundaries of the United States initially were given the status of citizenship—namely, White male property owners. Women, it must be remembered, were not allowed to vote until 1920. And the American Black, in some areas of the country, was effectively disenfranchised until the Civil Rights Act of 1964 was passed.

Dual Citizenship: The denial of citizenship is the essence of slavery, and in the eighteenth century most American Blacks were slaves. Slaves were not to speak out as they wished, were not to associate with whom they wanted, were not to do with their labor as they pleased, and were not to conclude binding contracts. American citizenship gave a man title to the product of his labor; American slavery forbade this title. The egalitarian promises of the Declaration of Independence notwithstanding, the American Constitution allowed a double standard. One class of people had rights and privileges denied to another class.

At first this double standard was not solely a racist doctrine. It separated free men and slaves, but it did not separate Whites and Blacks. And there were free Blacks. Nearly 100,000 of them had escaped slavery; they had purchased their freedom or had been given it by their owners (manumission), and lived in the North and West much as other citizens. They paid taxes, voted, and in a few cases held political office. But in 1857 this was changed by the infamous *Dred Scott* case, which held that Blacks, free or slave, "had no rights which the white man was bound to respect."

Dual citizenship based on race persisted long after the Civil War had officially ended slavery. The clear language of the Fourteenth Amendment, "all persons born or naturalized in the United States, and subject to the jurisdiction thereof, are citizens of the United States. . . . No state shall make or enforce any law which shall abridge the privileges or immunities

Dual citizenship based on race persisted long after the Civil War had officially ended slavery. *(Photo: Wide World)*

of citizens," was modified by subsequent court decisions and thwarted by the "Jim Crow" society.

Jim Crow laws allowed nearly total segregation of the Blacks into separate and inferior institutions. As described by the Commission on Civil Rights (1963), Jim Crow was applied to "waiting rooms, theaters, boardinghouses, water fountains, ticket windows, streetcars, penitentiaries, county jails, convict camps, institutions for the blind and deaf, and hospitals for the insane." This is of course but a partial list. Jim Crow laws affected schools, businesses, clubs, and churches, and the U.S. Armed Services. Facilities reserved for Blacks were always inferior, though equal prices had to be paid for the unequal services.

Racist ideologies received the backing of the Supreme Court. As Justice Brown ingenuously remarked in *Plessy v. Ferguson* (1896), the case that established the "separate but equal doctrine," which remained in force until 1954: "If one race be inferior to another socially, the Constitution of the United States cannot put them upon the same plane. . . ." So much for the Fourteenth Amendment, and so much for the idea that citizenship placed everyone on an equal footing before the law (see Chapter 11).

Other classes of citizens also have been denied equal protection of the laws. Religious minorities such as the Mormons migrated west to escape persecution and discrimination. Jews have long been subjected to quota systems in universities and associations and businesses. Racial groups other than Blacks have suffered legal discriminations, as in the detention of citizens of Japanese ancestry during World War II and the continued mistreatment of the American Indian. And of course today the entire issue of "second-class citizenship" is central to the Women's Liberation movement, as the women strike out at laws and regulations that relegate them to secondary positions in the society.

These flaws notwithstanding, the principle of equal status before the law remains politically significant in the ongoing attack on unfair status distinctions. The principle is, after all, the chief weapon in reform movements. In the absence of such a principle, the entire history of status privileges and rights would have taken a very different route. And it is likely that the legally protected privileged classes of earlier centuries would still be with us. That they are not is in no small way due to the concept of legal citizenship and its egalitarian implications.

Equality of Political Participation

Closely associated with the principle of equal rights under the law is the right of citizens to participate in the exercise of public authority. That government "should rest on the consent of the governed" is a major claim in democratic ideology.

The central promise of democracy that all citizens have equal influence in setting the goals for society and in choosing the means for reaching those goals was set forth in *The Federalist Papers* (No. 57):

Who are to be the electors of the federal representatives?

Not the rich, more than the poor; not the learned, more than the ignorant; not the haughty heirs of distinguished names, more than the humble sons of obscurity and unpropitious fortune. The electors are to be the great body of the people of the United States.

Who are to be the objects of popular choice?

Every citizen whose merit may recommend him to the esteem and confidence of his country. No qualification of wealth, of birth, religious faith, or of civil profession is permitted to fetter the judgement or disappoint the inclinations of the people.[3]

The authors of *The Federalist Papers* clearly believed that the Constitution they had helped write did indeed guarantee these equalities of suffrage and of access to political office, but they ignored the very many barriers that

---

[3] A series of brilliant essays written by Alexander Hamilton, James Madison, and John Jay in defense of the Constitution that will be discussed in greater detail in Chapter 9. The essays are known both as *The Federalist* and as *The Federalist Papers*.

were placed between the voter and his participation in choosing a government. In the eighteenth century, members of the House of Representatives were directly elected. Until the ratification of the Seventeenth Amendment in 1913, senators were chosen by the various state legislatures, whose members were presumably more mature and reliable than the mass electorate. The selection of the President was even further removed from the mass electorate, the holder of this office being chosen by an electoral college which in turn was chosen by state legislators. The most significant members of the judicial branch, especially Supreme Court justices, were completely protected from electorate choices—they were and still are appointed and for lifetime tenures.

The Constitution did not impose suffrage restrictions, but it did allow the individual states to do so, and it did stipulate that unless you could vote in state elections you could not vote in federal elections, in itself a restriction of the first magnitude. The electorate during the colonial and revolutionary period was largely restricted to White male property owners, though the last of these three restrictions was nearly eliminated during the administration of Andrew Jackson (1829–1837).

Universal suffrage was much longer in coming. Blacks of course were legally barred from voting until the passage of the Fifteenth Amendment after the Civil War, which read, "The right of citizens of the United States to vote shall not be denied or abridged by the United States or by any State on account of race, color, or previous condition of servitude." But if Black citizens were granted the vote by this constitutional amendment, they had it taken away almost immediately, especially in the South, by literacy tests, poll taxes, and closed primaries. Blacks have slowly been getting the vote back through court action and civil rights legislation.

The electorate was restricted not only by skin color but also by sex. Allowing the women into the electorate began in a piecemeal fashion, mostly in the thinly settled territories and states of the West in the late 1800s. It was in 1920 that the federal Constitution was amended (Nineteenth Amendment) to provide that the right to vote cannot be denied on account of sex. The most recent extension of the suffrage has been to lower the voting age to 18.

Usually when we think of citizenship we think only of the two ideas just reviewed—legal rights and political rights. It is thought that if these rights can truly be equally available to all members of society, then the egalitarian promise of democracy will have been realized. But there is a third form of citizenship, one that occupies much more political attention today than either of the other two.

Social Citizenship:
A New View of Equality

Speaking in 1944, President Franklin D. Roosevelt made a remarkable statement. He began his twelfth State of the Union Address with a familiar litany: "The Republic," he said, "had its beginning, and grew to its present strength, under the protection of certain inalienable political rights—among them the right of free speech, free press, free worship, trial by jury, freedom from unreasonable searches and seizures. They were our rights of life and liberty."

Had the President stopped at this point, nothing notable would have distinguished his speech from many others. He did not stop, however; he continued with what surely must be one of the most amazing confessions ever voiced by a U.S. President: "As our Nation has grown strong in size and stature, however—as our industrial economy has expanded—*these political rights proved inadequate to assure us equality in the pursuit of happiness.*" The often celebrated legal and political rights, enshrined in the Constitution and expanded over the course of American history, had been found wanting when confronted with the economic dislocations and discrepancies of a powerful if erratic industrial economy.

Looking back on his twelve years in office the President claimed, with some justification, that "we have come to a clear realization of the fact that true individual freedom cannot exist without economic security and independence." The concept of citizenship, he suggested, must be extended to include social well-being and security against economic injustices. The President did not even stop at this point, with the proclamation of a principle. The next section of his speech is worth quoting in full:

> We have accepted, so to speak, a second Bill of Rights under which a
> new basis of security and prosperity can be established for
> all—regardless of station, race, or creed.

Among these rights are:

- The right to a useful and remunerative job in the industries, or shops or farms or mines of the Nation.
- The right of every farmer to raise and sell his products at a return which will give him and his family a decent living.
- The right to earn enough to provide adequate food and clothing and recreation.
- The right of every businessman, large and small, to trade in an atmosphere of freedom from unfair competition and domination by monopolies at home or abroad.
- The right of every family to a decent home.
- The right to adequate medical care and the opportunity to achieve and enjoy good health.
- The right to adequate protection from the economic fears of old age, sickness, accident, and unemployment.
- The right to a good education.

Note Roosevelt's stress on the term "right," and, consequently, what a different conception of citizenship is here being described—a citizenship enlarged far beyond what was intended when due process of law was written into the Constitution or when suffrage was extended.

This new conception of citizenship takes on even greater significance when one realizes that beginning with Roosevelt's first term (1932) successive administrations, whether Democratic or Republican, have all passed legislation elaborating social citizenship in law.

The first great social legislation was the Social Security Act of 1935. Until the 1930s the prevailing economic viewpoint insisted that each individual was responsible for planning and saving against emergencies, such as unemployment or sickness. But when the depression came, and one of every four workers was without work and about one of every three families was receiving some sort of relief, this ethic of individualistic responsibility was no longer tenable. Three major components of the Social Security Act resulted from the economic realities of that era: (1) a worker's insurance program designed as a protection against unemployment; (2) a retirement and a survivors insurance program designed as a protection against old age, and a disability insurance program (commonly thought of as the Social Security program); and (3) a public assistance program to provide aid to the blind, the permanently disabled, dependent children without support, and similar persons not covered by other programs. The Social Security Act has been elaborated and extended over the past three and a half decades.

At the same time an enormous range of new programs has been initiated—some under Democratic administrations and some under Republican administrations—urban renewal and housing, job training and man-power-development programs among them. In 1965 Medicare was added to the basic social security program; thus, in the perhaps overly optimistic words of Lyndon Johnson, under whose leadership Medicare was passed, "No longer will older Americans be denied the healing miracle of modern medicine. No longer will illness crush and destroy the savings that they have so carefully put away over a lifetime so that they might enjoy dignity in their later years. No longer will young families see their own incomes, and their own hopes, eaten away simply because they are carrying out their deep moral obligations to their parents, and to their uncles and their aunts." Today the debate continues over how far to extend public health services.

During all this time, of course, the earliest "welfare program," public education, has continued to expand. At local, state, and federal levels, expenditures on education have risen enormously, both absolutely and relative to other government expenditures. More than $60 billion a year is spent on education, and education is said to be the largest and fastest growing "industry" in the United States.

Social-Rights Citizenship:
A Break with Tradition

With the exception of public education, social-rights citizenship did not become a matter for public concern until the twentieth century. Today it is one of the most important political battlegrounds in American society.

The establishment and extension of social-rights citizenship breaks with tradition in two significant ways. First, it transforms what has traditionally been a responsibility of private charity into an obligation of the state. To say that a decent standard of living is a citizenship right is to deny that it is any longer dependent on the charitable impulses of the wealthier classes. Critics claim, not without cause, that replacing the Christmas basket from the local church with a welfare check destroys one of the most important traditions in American society, the act of charity. But these critics may overlook the implicit snobbishness in the act of charity and the explicit self-degradation in the acceptance of charity. They may also overlook the fact that hunger does not occur only at those times when the wealthy are moved to charity. Charity is whimsical; social welfare is regular and consistent.

The second break with tradition implied by social-rights citizenship is a more substantial one. Social-rights citizenship severs social services from the price system. This is a situation not welcomed by persons most committed to the free enterprise system. Medical care, housing, food, security in the form of insurance, and even education have traditionally been priced in terms of what the market will bear. Who gets what quantity of these various social benefits depends on the purchasing power of the claimant. Those members of society who are "worth more" pay the price and receive better medical treatment, better housing, more nourishing food, more security against illness and old age, and superior education. Those members of society who are "worth less" get proportionately fewer of these benefits of society, or get a poorer quality of them.

Social-rights citizenship separates social services from the price system by shifting the services from the private to the public domain, in the name of citizenship. A decent standard of living is said to be a right rather than a privilege to be paid for or a gift to be bestowed.

The process of shifting social services from the private domain to the public domain, from the price system to the citizenship system, received a major impetus in the depression legislation of the 1930s. The Social Security Act and unemployment compensation laid the groundwork for what today we call the welfare state, a society in which government responsibility for the minimal well-being of every citizen is assumed. Many of the most hotly debated issues today are in the area of social-rights citizenship: federal support for education, the negative income tax, a minimum wage, a national health insurance program, public housing, and, increasingly, consumer protection. Consumer protection is particularly interesting because it represents yet a new area in which the "rights of equal citizenship" are being proclaimed—the right to get your money's worth.

What is striking about these political debates is not so much that they are taking place, but that they concern the means, not the end. Today even conservatives accept some form of the welfare state. The "voucher system" of welfare—a program appealing to some conservative elements—ingeniously combines welfare with the virtues of the free enterprise system while not denying basic social services to the sick or the poor or the unemployed. For example, every family would receive "educational vouchers" with which to pay for educational services at the schools of their choice. Schools would compete to provide the best education. An ineffective school would attract few customers and would, literally, go out of business. Such a system would reunite the competitive market with social services, but would still attempt to guarantee equal social citizenship.

Is There Equal Citizenship?

The rights, privileges, and obligations embraced by citizenship theoretically place members of society on an equal footing. Many early commentators felt that citizenship egalitarianism would lead to a gradual but total leveling of society. Less well-off groups, they believed, would use legal and political powers to redistribute wealth radically. Some argued that the advent of social citizenship was a major step in this direction.

But a radical equality of condition has not occurred in the United States, nor has it occurred elsewhere in the world as a result of political and legal citizenship. Members of our society are not equal in wealth, and even the newest form of citizenship—social welfare—is not likely to bring about such equalities.

Why this is so will interest us in the remainder of this chapter. We will see in later chapters that the persistence of inequalities of wealth is related also to inequalities in legal and political citizenship.

Social and Economic Inequalities

Demonstrating the realities of social and economic inequality in the United States is not a difficult task. The income gap between the wealthiest citizens and the poorest citizens is enormous. In 1971, according to government estimates, the absolute minimum that a family of four persons needed for a decent, subsistence life was $3968. This of course is a very low "poverty line"; nevertheless, more than 25 million people, about 12.6 percent of the nation's families, had incomes under this amount. In Table 2.1, in contrast, are salaries and bonuses paid in 1971 to top executives of leading U.S. corporations. The combined salaries of these fourteen men are equiv-

Table 2.1   Salaries and Bonuses of Leading Executives

COMPANY	NAME AND TITLE	REMUNERATION
A.T. & T.	H. L. Romnes, Chairman–President	$350,000
City Investg.	G. Scharffenberger, President–CEO*	443.300
Eastman Kodak	L. K. Ellers, Chairman	385,000
General Motors	J. M. Roche, Chairman–CEO	822,000
Goodyear	Russell DeYoung, Chairman–CEO	374,112
Gulf Oil	E. D. Brockett, Chairman–CEO	385,000
IBM	T. V. Learson, Chairman	394,331
I.T. & T.	H. S. Geneen, Chairman-President	812,494
Johnson & Johnson	Philip B. Hoffman, Chairman–CEO	462,203
Mobiloil	Rawleigh Warner, Jr., Chairman	410,000
Proctor & Gamble	H. J. Morgens, Chairman–CEO	486,495
Sears, Roebuck	G. M. Metcalf, Chairman–CEO	385,000
Standard Oil (Ind.)	J. E. Searingen, Chairman	395,000
Standard Oil (N.J.)	J. K. Jamieson, Chairman	485,000

* CEO means Chief Executive Officer.
Source: *The New York Times*, April 30, 1972. © 1972 by The New York Times Company. Reprinted by permission.

alent to the income of 1662 persons living at the official poverty line. Indeed, in one single corporation, the Ford Motor Company, salaries and supplementary payments to the top 8 executives totaled $4 million. These 8 men, among them, earned approximately what 500 men on the Ford assembly line might have earned.

Persons who earn huge executive salaries are not, however, the "very wealthy." The very wealthy are, as we pointed out in Chapter 1, those who own many shares of corporate stock or who control valuable income-producing land. At the top of this small elite are the estimated six billionaires in the United States. The annual income of a billionaire is difficult to imagine; estimates for oilman J. Paul Getty go as high as $300,000 a day. (Nevertheless, he is reported to have paid less than $5,000 in federal income taxes in 1970.) Just below the billionaires in the wealth hierarchy are the fifty or so American families whose assets approach or exceed $100 million. Below this group are several hundred families whose wealth is approximately $10 million; and below them there are nearly 100,000 millionaires.

The income from such assets can be enormous indeed. Wealth of the sort that allows persons to live off the interest it earns is mostly inherited wealth. It is estimated that more than 90 percent of the very rich families in America today have inherited much or most of their wealth. Inheritance

The gap in living conditions between the wealthy and the poor is enormous.

(Photos: Lizabeth Corlett, DPI; Ted Spiegel, Black Star)

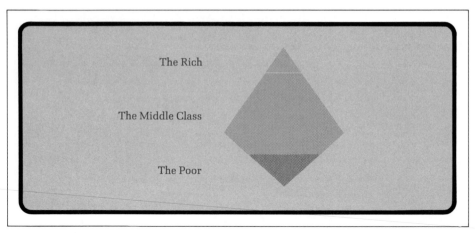

Figure 2.1 The Income Hierarchy, U.S.

taxes are less of a barrier than is commonly thought; marital deductions, transferring assets to children, trust funds and gifts, and family-owned "charitable" foundations are important loopholes that allow the rich to retain and pass along their wealth.

If the top of the wealth hierarchy is reserved for billionaires and millionaires, the bottom of course belongs to Americans below the poverty line. The 25 million such persons in this category live as best they can on unemployment insurance, charity, or welfare payments.

Somewhere between the poverty line and the wealthiest classes are scattered the rest of the citizens. Median family income in America today is approximately $11,000, which is to say that half of the families in America earn this amount or more and half earn less. The income hierarchy is bulged in the middle, shaped more like a diamond than a pyramid, as it is sometimes depicted. This is shown in Figure 2.1.

The Persistence of Wealth Inequalities in America

Inequalities of income and wealth persist in the United States despite citizenship egalitarianism. Although many factors contribute to this fact, of particular importance are two doctrines well established in the American tradition: (1) the rights of private property, and (2) the value of material incentives.

Private Property Rights: One of the tenets on which the nation was founded was the Lockian principle that governments are instituted among men to secure life, liberty, and *property*. The constitutional framers protected property rights in many ways, though what they had in mind by property was not what we today accept it as. They were concerned that the pioneer's homestead or the trader's merchandise should not be jeopardized, either by state action or by fellow citizen.

What constitutes private property has changed enormously since the 1780s, though the constitutional principle of property rights is as important now as it was then. Today much of the most important property in the United States is neither land nor tangible possessions. Stockholdings in General Motors are a form of property; so also are a franchise to drill an oil well, a license to use a particular air frequency, a patent for a chemical process, and a royalty on a book. It is these forms of property that are income producing, and it is these forms of property that are very unequally distributed in American society.

Although large numbers of Americans own their own homes (65 percent), their own car (80 percent), and such consumer goods as television sets, refrigerators, washing machines (over 90 percent), ownership of stocks and bonds, rental property, royalty rights, and patents is much more concentrated. The most detailed study is now somewhat dated, having been carried out in 1954.[4] At that time, however, the wealthiest 1.5 percent of the adult population owned approximately a third of all privately owned wealth, consisting of 82 percent of all stock, 100 percent of state and local bonds, 38 percent of federal bonds, 88 percent of other bonds, 29 percent of the cash, 36 percent of mortgage notes, and so on. A survey carried out at the beginning of 1960 by the University of Michigan found the basic pattern little changed, and many economists feel that the concentration of income-producing property is as great now as it was twenty years ago.[5]

All told nearly one-third of the total income paid to the United States population comes not in the form of wages or salaries for services performed, but rather as dividends, interest payments, rents, royalties, and similar returns on inherited or acquired wealth. This income from "working money" rather than actual work goes primarily to a very small group. It is in this sense that the Lockian principle of private property contributes to income inequalities in the United States today.

A Material Incentive System: Democratic ideology rejects inequalities based on assumptions about "natural" superiority or inferiority. In the words of the French Declaration of the Rights of Man and Citizens in 1789, "Men are born and remain free and equal in rights." But democratic ideology does not reject the idea of inequality itself, as that radical document makes clear: "Social differences," the French Declaration continues, "can only be based on general utility."

[4] Robert J. Lampman, *The Share of Top Wealth-holders in National Wealth, 1922–1956* (Princeton, N.J.: Princeton University Press, 1962), as reproduced in Maurice Zeitlin, ed., *American Society, Inc.* (Chicago: Markham, 1970), chap. 9.

[5] University of Michigan, "Survey of Consumer Finances," as summarized in Ferdinand Lundberg, *The Rich and the Super-Rich* (New York: Bantam, 1968), pp. 12–14.

"Social differences based on general utility" can be translated into three propositions:[6]

1. Certain tasks are more important to society than other tasks; some are so critical that if poorly performed society itself is jeopardized.
2. Certain tasks, often the same as the socially important ones, require long and difficult training periods and are, once undertaken, not easy to carry out.
3. Men will work only if given suitable material rewards.

It follows from these three propositions that the most critical and difficult positions in the society are unlikely to be filled unless they carry special rewards. In a money economy, the incentive is money. The more intense the competition for the critical jobs—that is, for the best-paying jobs—the better for the entire society. Society—which is to say you and me—prospers to the extent that critical tasks are well performed by able persons. It suffers to the extent that critical tasks remain unfilled or are poorly performed by the less able. The soldier being sent to the front lines doesn't want an inexperienced dullard planning military strategy; he wants someone in charge of staff headquarters who is experienced at planning troop movements with a minimum of casualties. The victim of a car accident doesn't expect to be wheeled into an operating room only to be met by a medical quack; he expects a professional expert to attend him.

Fields that require costly or arduous training—such as medicine and nuclear physics—professions that require skills not widely available—such as a professional football quarterback and astronaut—and positions that are deemed socially important—such as corporation executive and political leader—all these must compete for personnel, and thus it is advisable that these positions provide high rewards. These rewards are usually monetary, but they can be supplemented with other kinds of rewards such as leisure time, travel, prestige, or power.

Thus, even radical democrats realize that there are many different social tasks. These tasks are not equally easy or equally important. An incentive system is society's insurance program that the difficult and unpleasant ones will be carried out; it is a program that makes no naive assumptions about human nature, and especially no assumptions about how hard men will work. Different wages for different tasks is not just a capitalist invention. It is also the practice in such Communist economies as China and the Soviet Union, and such socialist nations as Cuba and Tanzania.

In the United States, as elsewhere, the incentive system contributes to inequality. Wage differentials are deliberately spread out so that society has one huge carrot and stick at its disposal to motivate competition and per-

[6] What is often called "the functional theory of social stratification" is an elaboration on these propositions. The argument is developed in Kingsley Davis and Wilbert E. Moore, "Some Principles of Stratification," *American Sociological Review*, 10 (April 1945), 242–249.

formance. If the shop foreman earns twice what the assembly-line worker does, this is because the foreman's job requires more experience, skill, and responsibilities. If the owner of the factory in turn earns several times what the foreman does, this is because the owner, after all, took the initial risk and established the enterprise which now provides employment and income in the community. If a line worker excels at production, his reward is reflected in his paycheck, and perhaps even in a promotion. If the foreman fails to manage his workers, his punishment is a pink slip suggesting that he seek a position elsewhere. If the owner makes an error in judgment, perhaps bankruptcy follows. If he is innovative, perhaps a fortune follows.

The Political Challenge to Wealth Inequalities

These two economic principles—private property and material incentives—go far toward explaining the persistence of social inequalities in America, despite, at the same time, the spread of such democratic ideals as extending the franchise to wider and wider segments of the population. Americans, however, have not had a difficult time adjusting the legal-political equalities associated with citizenship and the social status inequalities associated with capitalism. Indeed, it is no exaggeration to claim that the economic values that lead to inequalities are every bit as central to our culture and our traditions as are the political values that seem to promise equality.

This is not to say that political action has not affected the distribution of wealth in the nation. We have already seen the considerable reforms announced in the name of the "welfare state," and there is some evidence that wealth in the United States is more equitably distributed than it was 30 or 40 years ago. The Nobel Prize-winning economist Simon Kuznets has estimated that the wealthiest 5 percent of the population held about one-third of total income in 1929, but only one-fifth in 1948.[7]

Kuznets' figures are, however, disputed by other economists, who compute income figures somewhat differently and conclude that the drop has been nowhere near this sharp, if indeed it has taken place at all.[8] Using after-tax figures, and reporting the share of family personal income received by the highest 20 percent of the population, another economist reports the data shown in Table 2.2. And, according to a report of the Joint Economic Committee of Congress, the income gap between America's poorest and richest has nearly doubled in the last two decades. The gap between the poorest one-fifth and the richest one-fifth was $10,565 in 1949, but in 1969 it was $19,071. Thus substantial inequalities remain even after a half-cen-

[7] Simon Kuznets, *Shares of Upper Income Groups in Income and Savings* (Washington, D.C.: National Bureau of Economic Research, 1953).

[8] For important criticisms of Kuznets' conclusions, see articles by Selma F. Goldsmith and Victor Perlo, reprinted as chaps. 11 and 12 in Zeitlin.

Table 2.2   Percent of Total Income Received by
Highest 20 Percent of the Population, After Taxes

1929	1941	1959	1954	1956	1959	1962[a]
54%	47%	44%	43%	43%	43%	44%

[a] Recent figures do not report any marked change between 1962 and the present.
Source: "Inequality in Income and Taxes," by Edward C. Budd. Reprinted in Maurice Zeitlin, ed., *American Society, Inc.* (Chicago: Markham, 1970), p. 148. Originally published by W. W. Norton & Company, Inc., © 1967. Reprinted by permission.

tury of social welfare policies and progressive income taxes. There are many reasons for this, some political and some economic, but we can concentrate on three programs: the war on poverty, the progressive income tax, and social welfare.

The War on Poverty: Conventional approaches to social services and public welfare were significantly extended in the mid-1960s. The much-heralded antipoverty programs, with an annual budget of around $2 billion, introduced Head Start, Job Corps, VISTA, and various other community action programs. We will not here review the failures and successes of President Johnson's War on Poverty (substantially modified by President Nixon), but will simply ask how antipoverty programs affect inequality.

The purpose of antipoverty policy is to raise the floor level of society. The poor are those living below some socially acceptable standard. An affluent society should not have poor in its midst. No one should be so poor that he cannot effectively exercise his political and economic rights. A successful antipoverty program moves every citizen above the tolerable level, which, in the words of the War on Poverty, eliminates poverty "by opening to everyone the opportunity for education and training, the opportunity to work, and the opportunity to live in decency and dignity."

A program such as envisioned in the War on Poverty, however, even if completely successful, has little bearing on inequality. The goal is to increase the proportion of the population, hopefully to near 100 percent of the physically able, who compete in an economic system based on wage differentials and wealth earned from private property. This is no insignificant accomplishment, but it should not be confused with egalitarianism. The only way in which the elimination of poverty can affect inequality is by reducing slightly the distance between the rich and the poor, not by making the rich less wealthy, but by making the poor less impoverished. But if the high-income class makes only 10 instead of 15 times what the lowest income class makes, we can hardly call this an egalitarian system.

Thus in our quest to understand how citizenship equality alters economic inequality we can dispose of antipoverty programs easily. They introduce very little equality (though this is hardly a reason to treat them lightly, especially if you are below the poverty line or have humanitarian concern for those who are).

The Progressive Income Tax: The principle behind the progressive income tax is simple enough: The more money you earn the higher the proportion you pay in taxes. The present official range is 14 to 70 percent, fourteen cents out of every dollar of the lowest income earner, and seventy cents out of every dollar of the highest earners. (The 70 percent refers to all income sources; for salary income the top is 48 percent.) While such a taxation policy, if enforced, would indeed be redistributive and egalitarian, the actual rates paid by the higher income groups are a great deal less than what the law says they should be.

The Sixteenth Amendment, which first authorized the progressive income tax, empowers Congress to tax income "from whatever sources derived," but subsequent tax legislation has played havoc with this principle. Dollars earned from some sources, though they are worth just as much when translated into consumer goods or leisure time or what have you, are *not* taxed at the same rate as dollars earned from other sources. The dollars most heavily taxed are those earned in wages and salaries; the dollars least heavily taxed are those earned on various types of investments: long-term capital gains, real estate, stock options, oil, and state and local bonds. For example, a family of four earning an income of $10,000 would, under existing laws, pay the following federal income taxes:

- $905 if the income is all from wages and salaries.
- $98 if the income is all profits from selling stocks or land.
- $0 if the income is all from interest on state and local bonds.

Since the income of the wealthy derives primarily from nonwage sources, it is the wealthy, not the low- and middle-income wage earner, who benefit from tax deductions.

Dramatic demonstration of this comes from a 1972 study by The Brookings Institution in Washington, D.C. In an analysis of actual tax returns the authors computed the average tax savings of families at different income levels. A tax saving is how much less is paid because of various loopholes and deductions than would be paid if income from every source were indeed taxed at the official rate. Table 2.3 shows what they report.[9] Thus the family that has an *annual income* of $1 million (and 3000 families did in 1971) has nearly three-quarters of $1 million more because of loopholes in the tax laws and other deductions. The family that earns between $5,000 and $10,000 benefits from the same deductions at a much lesser

---

[9] This study is reviewed by Philip M. Stern in "Uncle Sam's Welfare Program—For the Rich," which appeared in *The New York Times Magazine*, April 16, 1972.

Table 2.3　Average Tax Savings of Families at Different Income Levels

YEARLY INCOME	YEARLY TAX SAVINGS FROM LOOPHOLES AND DEDUCTIONS
Over $1,000,000	$720,000
$500–1,000,000	$202,000
$100–500,000	$41,000
$50–100,000	$12,000
$25–50,000	$4,000
$15–20,000	$1,200
$10–15,000	$650
$5–10,000	$340
$3–5,000	$48
Under $3,000	$16

Source: Philip M. Stern, "Uncle Sam's Welfare Program – For the Rich," *The New York Times Magazine*, April 6, 1972. © 1972 by The New York Times Company. Reprinted by permission. (Data based on a study by the Brookings Institution, Washington, D.C., 1972.)

rate. This study concludes that $77.3 billion is lost to the public treasury each year because of "handouts based on capital gains (which are taxed at one-half the normal rate), depletion allowances, bookkeeping farm losses, interest on local bonds, interest on mortgages, and so forth." This is of course an enormous loss; if these moneys could be collected, the official tax rates could be cut nearly in half, or perhaps needed social services such as urban transport or clean air and water could be provided. It is ironic that the annual budget of the antipoverty program is less than 3 percent of the loss from the "tax welfare" program, but what is even more ironic is the distribution of these tax handouts: The 6 million poorest families in the nation receive about $92 million; the wealthiest 3000 families in the nation receive $2.2 billion, or about 24 times as much.

The progressive income tax does flatten out the income distribution at the lower end of the scale. For example, the income tax brings the family with an income of $16,000 closer to the family with an income of $8,000. But its impact on the top of the income scale is much less. On a before-tax basis the average income of the richest 20 percent in the country is about ten times that of the poorest 20 percent; the effect of the income tax is to reduce this only to nine times as much. In general, under present laws, the progressive income tax is not nearly so progressive as it is often thought; it does not substantially reduce the distance between the wealthy and the poor.

Other types of taxes are even less progressive. The sales tax, for instance, takes a much larger share of the income of the poor than it does the rich. If a family earns $5,000 and spends, say, $4,000 on consumer goods and basic necessities on which it pays a 5 percent sales tax, the family is being taxed at a much greater rate than one earning $25,000 and spending, say, $8,000 on goods that have a sales tax. (You can easily figure this out for yourself. In fact, it is an understatement to say that a sales tax is "less progressive" than an income tax. It is actually regressive, taking a proportionately higher share from the less wealthy groups in the society.) The "Value Added Tax" suggested by the Nixon administration would be in effect a national sales tax, and thus its burden would fall more heavily on low- and middle-income groups than on the higher-income groups.

Social Welfare Programs: The connection between social welfare pro-grams and inequality is more complicated. A strong case can be made that such programs as unemployment compensation, Medicare, public edu-cation, and social security have made important contributions to equality of conditions in American society. But let us first distinguish between two forms of inequality: inequality of distance and inequality of scope.

Inequalities of distance refer to the size of the gap between the richest and the poorest, or between any two points along the wealth continuum. If the richest 5 percent of the population has only ten times the wealth of the poorest 5 percent, the inequality of distance is much less (there is more equality) than if the richest group has twenty times the wealth. We have already seen that American society tolerates enormous inequalities of dis-tance. We have seen as well that antipoverty programs or progressive in-come taxes make little dent on this type of inequality. We now observe that social welfare services are also inconsequential. Indeed, making social ser-vices such as education or health care available to the entire population can actually increase inequalities of distance. It has been pointed out that the main accomplishment of welfare policies has been to provide free social services to the middle class, thus releasing their income for expendi-ture on consumer goods and luxuries. However controversial this remark, it is true that simply providing social services or instituting compulsory insurance programs does not affect wage differentials or income earned from private property, the two major sources of inequality in America.

Inequalities of scope refer to the number of socially desirable values that are available to the rich more than to the poor citizens.

Assume the following extreme case: *Every* desirable social benefit is available only through the private sector and is priced such that its owners make the highest profit possible. Education, medicine, the attention of doctors, insurance, recreational facilities, transport, communication ser-vices, and even security against personal attack, are stratified. That is, they are available in unequal amounts and unequal quality. The wealthy person, therefore, has greater access to these services than the poor. He even hires his own security force to protect his possessions. The less wealth you have, the less of any of these services you can get, until we get to the bottom of the scale where none are available—there being no public education, no free medical care, no public parks, no social security, no transport or communication systems except those used by the wealthy, and not even a common police force. Under such conditions inequalities of scope would be enormous. Every social value would be more available, and in a superior form, to the wealthy than to the poor.

Now, assume the opposite extreme case: No social benefit is priced; all are equally available to every citizen. Public schools are excellent, and level of educational attainment is based on intelligence and merit; health and insurance programs protect all citizens equally against illness, accident, and disability; public parks are abundant and entertainment widely available; transportation is efficient, as are telephone and mail services; and the standing army and police force protect modest possessions, just as they protect huge investments abroad and expensive luxuries at home. Under such conditions, inequalities of scope are greatly narrowed. It is not that there are no rich and no poor; and it is not that the rich cannot afford luxuries and comforts denied the poor. But the rich cannot buy superior social services. The advantage of wealth is confined to limited areas of consumption.

Inequalities of distance, therefore, refer to *how much* better off the better-off are; inequalities of scope refer to *how many ways* the better-off are better off. *Welfare policies are egalitarian in the sense that they increase the number of services for which purchasing power is unnecessary.* The point is well made by Julius Nyerere, socialist President of Tanzania, when he urges that inequalities be reduced through "the provision of social services which are available to all, regardless of income; for a man who suddenly has new medical services available to him and his family, or a new house, or a new school or community center, has had an improvement in his standard of living, just as much as if he had more money in his pocket."

Insofar as citizenship reduces inequalities of scope it has made a substantial contribution to equality. This has happened, though to a lesser extent than either supporters or critics of the welfare state admit. For one thing, benefits of welfare programs are not always directed toward the less-well-off groups in society. Free higher education, for instance, has serviced the middle class, to a lesser extent the working class, and not much at all the really poor families. Benefits of even the programs specifically directed to the poor only partially end up in their pocketbooks or bank accounts. A sizable proportion of antipoverty money enriches the middle-class professionals who administer the programs and provide the services. Research grant money to university professors to evaluate antipoverty programs is money subtracted from what was to have reduced poverty. The impact of welfare programs and services on inequality has also been lessened by the method of paying for them. For the most part the relevant taxes are spread across the population, meaning that the poorer groups pay for services designed to equalize their income in exact proportion to what they pay in taxes anyway. Their payments would have to be subtracted from any exact calculations of benefits.

The consequences of social citizenship have been less egalitarian than some hoped and others feared; nevertheless, if decent social services are provided by the government, either free or at minimal cost, then the ways in which the rich are unequal become reduced. The rich can still support private universities, and send their children to them, but the availability of excellent public universities reduces the advantages this provides.

Controversy

Are substantial differences in wealth and social status justified in a democracy? This chapter has documented the considerable differences in income available to different social classes in the United States. Inequalities of wealth have been only moderately affected by such important government policies as progressive income tax, social welfare programs, and even the war on poverty. Should gross inequalities in living conditions be tolerated? Should not government be using its powers of taxation and redistribution in order to bring about more substantive equality in society?

One Side

Politically enforced egalitarianism is not practical and it is not fair. It is not practical because it would slow down economic growth and eventually bring stagnation to the economy. The American system of private ownership and material incentives has brought about a tremendous increase in the standard of living for all Americans. Certain income inequalities have ensured that the most talented and able persons are attracted to the critical leadership positions in society. All members of society benefit from this arrangement. To tamper with the system of differential rewards would be to invite laziness and underachievement. Eventually we all would suffer.

In addition, a politically enforced egalitarianism is unfair. Americans believe strongly in the value of equality of opportunity, but they have doubts about equality of condition. In our society social position is not fixed at birth. Anyone can improve his lot if he applies himself and takes advantage of opportunities. Listen to a janitor comment on his status:

> I can't complain. I had a chance to finish high school, but I dropped out. If a guy finishes school and gets a better job, he deserves it.

And to a lawyer:

> *Well, we all have the same opportunity. Some of us applied ourselves in school, some of us did not. Now I am a success, and you can't blame me for wanting the things my salary will buy.*

It would violate the American sense of "fair play" if government were to take away from the lawyer and give to the janitor. It would downgrade effort and achievement.

The Other Side

The idea that social inequalities are somehow beneficial to society is flawed in several major respects. For one thing, the magnitude of differences in economic rewards is not necessary to attracting talent and motivating effort. Top corporate executives are making 150 times more than their lowest paid employees. But isn't it likely that the president of General Motors would stay on the job even if his salary were $1000 a day instead of $3500 a day? The problem with our income-incentive system is that it allows the lower end of the salary scale to be fixed in the marketplace, thus depressing wages of the unskilled or semiskilled in a labor surplus situation. At the same time it allows the upper end of the salary scale to be fixed at the discretion of corporation managers and other powerful persons.

There is a second flaw in the argument that great inequalities of wealth are somehow beneficial to the society. Who is to decide which occupations are the critical ones? A heart transplant specialist is highly rewarded for his skill; a lab technician working on infectious diseases much less so for his skill. But ask the ghetto mother which skill is more socially beneficial. The designer of a new weapons system is better paid than the designer of a new curriculum for sixth graders. Who decides that weapons are more important than sixth graders? It is groups already powerful and wealthy that decide which occupations are to be rewarded, and the magnitude of the rewards.

If the practical defense of inequalities is flawed, so also is the "fair play" argument. In the first place, it simply is not true that there is equal opportunity in this society. People inherit wealth and educational opportunities. Children born into the upper classes begin life with a head start far more significant than the government Head Start programs designed to equalize opportunities. If we were to take equality of opportunity seriously, we would increase and enforce inheritance taxes.

Moreover, values other than "getting ahead" are — or should be — important to Americans. Humane treatment of the old, the sick, and the poor are also American values. But millions of Americans do not get a decent meal even once a day, do not have heat in their room on cold days, do not get medical attention when they need it, and do not begin to receive an education worth anything. Social justice demands a fairer distribution of the wealth of this society. Although no one would expect complete equality of conditions, certainly it would be better to reduce sharply the enormously inflated incomes of a tiny elite and at the same time improve the living conditions of the 25 million Americans living below the poverty line.

Suggested Readings

The classic treatment of American egalitarian values is Alexis de Tocqueville, *Democracy in America*, ed. Phillips Bradley (2 vols.; New York: Knopf, 1945), a report on this perceptive Frenchman's visit to the United States in the 1830s. Similar historical comments, though written from a contemporary perspective, can be found in Seymour Lipset, *The First New Nation* (London: Heineman, 1963). Perhaps the most cogent essay ever written on citizenship is that of T. H. Marshall, "Citizenship and Social Class," as reproduced in his *Class, Citizenship, and Social Development* (Garden City, N.Y.: Doubleday, 1964). The distinction between legal, political, and social-rights citizenship used in our chapter is drawn from this essay.

The literature on inequality in America is very large indeed. Useful data can be found in Christopher Jencks et al., *Inequality: A Reassessment of the Effect of Family and Schooling in America* (New York: Basic Books, 1972). A collection of critical essays is in Maurice Zeitlin, ed., *American Society, Inc.* (Chicago: Markham, 1970). Michael Harrington's *The Other America* (Baltimore: Penguin, 1963) is credited with helping to bring poverty forcefully to the attention of the government, and thus helping to prepare the way for the antipoverty programs. For facts and figures about the wealthier classes, see Ferdinand Lundberg, *The Rich and the Super-Rich* (New York: Bantam, 1968).

A Note to the Student
How to Study Political Behavior

Political scientists spend a lot of time worrying about the methods by which they study the political world. Do the methods they use produce accurate pictures of the political world or do they produce inaccurate ones? Are the methods objective or are they biased?

There is good reason to be concerned about the methods by which one learns about politics. The realities of politics are complex and sometimes hidden. It is easy to get distorted information. And there are two reasons for this: First, those active in politics are likely to give out somewhat distorted information because they want to "look good." And, second, those observing politics often observe it in such a way that they see what they want to see.

An example of the first phenomenon would be the political candidate eager to demonstrate that he has strong support behind him. The information he gives out about his public support often presents an overly optimistic picture. An example of the second phenomenon—where the observer distorts reality by seeing what he wants to see—would be the newspaper reporter with strong views about a particular administration in power. If he has negative views of the administration in power (or, perhaps, if his publisher has such views), he is likely to look for and probably find examples of scandal and mismanagement in that administration. If he or his publisher have positive views, he is likely to look for and probably find examples of successful policy. Both sets of findings may in fact be true—administrations have both failures and successes. The emphasis on one or the other may largely reflect the biases of the observer as he studies political reality.

The serious student of American politics will, when presented with some "information" about that subject, always keep in mind the questions: Where did that information come from? How was it gathered? What are the possible biases in that information?

Public Opinion:
How Do We Find Out About That?

In the following chapters of our book, we shall present information about attitudes and behavior of the American public. We review their political beliefs, the ways in which they act politically, how they vote, and how they decide to vote the way they do. How is it that we find out about the American public?

Everyone has an opinion about public opinion. We all think we know how the American public feels on this or that subject. And in some sense we have a right to feel that way. For one thing, each of us is a member of the American public and thus our own views are part of public opinion. Second, we talk to many other people who are also members of the public, we read the newspapers where we see reports of public attitudes or letters to the editor, and we watch television. But such information—based on our observations of the world around us—can often be wrong, sometimes seriously wrong.

Our views of public opinion may be distorted for any of the following reasons:

1. We often look at our own views and generalize them to others. We believe that other people believe what we do; we believe that other people react to events the way we do. But, of course, this is not the case. People are much more varied than that.

2. We often look beyond our own personal views to those views we find around us. We talk with friends and neighbors or with colleagues at work and thereby learn more about public opinion. But such views of public opinion are also likely to be distorted since most of us move in relatively narrow circles and meet only certain kinds of people. The more this is the case, the more likely we are to obtain images that differ from the reality of public opinion.

An obvious example of such a closed circle of acquaintanceships is the college campus. Students spend most of their time interacting with other students (and faculty members interact with faculty members). If they are incautious, they may generalize from these experiences to the public at large. In the late 1960s and early 1970s, for instance, many students talked of a "generation gap" between a radical younger generation opposed to war and racism and an older generation more tolerant of these evils. More precise studies showed, however, that radicalism among the young tended to be concentrated on the college campuses and, more particularly, on various prestige campuses. If one looked at all those in the young generation—at those who were in college and those who were not—one found a much wider range of opinions. Indeed, one found the noncollege youth were quite conservative on a large number of issues.

3. The mass media, of course, provide us a wider view of the public than our own personal experiences. We can read letters to the editor; we can see the expressions of public opinion as reported on television and as reported in the press. But such information

may also give us a distorted view of the public. Those who write letters to the editor are not representative of the general public — they are often people with axes to grind or just people with lots of time to write letters. One can be certain only that they speak for themselves, not that they speak for the public at large. Furthermore, the mass media have a well-known tendency to look for the spectacular and for the dramatic. Those expressions of public opinion that wind up on the evening news are likely to have that characteristic — a demonstration by a small minority, a speech by a well-known celebrity. This, too, is information about one part of the public, but one cannot easily generalize from that to the public as a whole.

The Sample Survey: Its Strengths and Weaknesses

The systematic sample survey — more commonly called the public opinion poll — was developed to get around the weaknesses of the commonsense approach to public opinion. Such systematic surveys — the Gallup or Harris polls, surveys by scholarly organizations, and surveys done for political candidates — can be very accurate in estimating public opinion. But they, too, can give us distorted views of the nature of the American public if they are not well understood and used with care.

To understand how sample surveys can give us more accurate information than can our commonsense observations of public opinion, let's consider two characteristics of such surveys: the sample used and the instrument, or questionnaire, applied to the sample. That is, we must consider who it is to whom the pollster talks and what questions he asks.

Sampling

The notion of sampling is basic to the systematic survey. To understand public opinion, the ideal, of course, would be to talk to all Americans. But obviously that is not feasible; it would be too costly and time consuming. One can talk to only some Americans. The important point is that one should try to select those Americans to whom he talks in such a way that they are representative of the public as a whole. That is, one takes a sample of the American population and tries to generalize to the population as a whole.

But what characteristics should a good sample have? What makes a good sample may be clearly understood if we turn to an entirely different subject from that of public opinion. Imagine a company that manufactures jars of jam and a government inspector who wants to find out whether this jam meets government standards of purity. To find out if the jam is pure, he must open a jar and test it. But he cannot open all the thousands of jars that are produced by this company, for that would be too costly for him and leave the company with no unopened jars to sell.

Thus the inspector decides to take a sample of the jars and check them—just as a public opinion pollster takes a sample of citizens. What kind of sample does he look for?

1. An adequate number: The government inspector will probably not be satisfied by looking at one or two jars of jam. Any particular jar may be unrepresentative of all the others. He will want a sufficient number so that he is likely to find contamination if it exists.

2. A wide geographical spread: If the company produces jam at a large number of factories in the country, the government inspector should not be satisfied to go to that factory nearest his own office, even though that saves him time and effort. The company may be doing very well in that particular plant but that factory may differ from factories elsewhere in the country.

3. A wide range of types: If the company makes all kinds of jam, the inspector would do well to sample the various kinds and not to limit his inspection to strawberry jam. Again, the reason is simple: what he finds out about the strawberry jam will not tell him about the raspberry jam.

4.   The inspector selects at random; he does not let anyone else select for him: The clever inspector will be careful to try to avoid systematic bias in the particular jars he looks at. He will not sit in his office and allow company officials to bring him a few examples of each of their kinds of product. Rather, he will go himself and select the jars to inspect. If he used the former procedure, there would be a great possibility of bias since the company officials would bring to him only those jars in which they have fairly high confidence.

Let us now turn to the sample survey to see how the public opinion pollster deals with this kind of issue.

1. An adequate number: A good survey researcher will not be satisfied to talk to one, two, or a few dozen citizens. Even if they are selected at random, their numbers will be too small to allow generalization to a much larger population. There is too much chance that one will accidentally find people who differ substantially from the rest of the public. Most good public opinion polls interview about 1500 respondents. The number is not accidental. Statisticians can show that with that number of interviews, properly selected from a cross-section of the population, they can estimate quite accurately the attitudes or voting behavior of the public at large — that is, to within about 3 percent of the public's actual position.

2. A wide geographical spread: It is important that those interviews come from a wide range of places, not simply from the pollster's hometown. For this purpose, survey organizations maintain staffs of interviewers throughout the country and, indeed, samples are drawn in such a way as to cover a wide range of geographical areas.

3. A wide range of types: The most important thing about a sample is that it be designed to allow all types of citizens an equal chance to be interviewed. Various biases can occur if the criteria of selection systematically eliminate one type of person or systematically lead to the overrepresentation of another. For many years surveys were taken of people who happened to pass by in public places, such as railroad stations. Such surveys were usually inaccurate, as only certain kinds of people use railroad stations. A classic example of such selection bias occurred in one of the earliest attempts to predict a Presidential election on the basis of the systematic sample. In the 1936 election, a magazine called the Literary Digest conducted a sample survey via telephone on the Presidential race between Alf M. Landon and Franklin Delano Roosevelt. The results predicted a landslide victory for Landon; in fact, the opposite happened. The cause of all this was a simple sampling error. People who had telephones — particularly in the 1930s — came disproportionately from the wealthiest segment of society; these people were more likely to vote for the Republican Landon. If the Literary Digest had sampled everybody equally — those with and those without telephones — it might have predicted the election accurately.

4. The pollster selects; he does not let the respondent self-select:
Another important aspect of a good sample is that a pollster chooses — on the basis of his statistical criteria — who it is that he wants to interview. He does not wait for people to come forward and volunteer to be interviewed. This point is crucial, and it is this point that most clearly distinguishes the sample survey from the means of tapping public opinion used in everyday politics. The

congressman who judges public opinion on the basis of letters written to him does the opposite from that done by the professional pollster. The congressman looks at the opinion of those who volunteered their views by writing to him. These people are likely to differ substantially from the rest of the public or from the rest of his constituents. Citizens are more likely to write letters to those congressmen with whose views they are in agreement. Conservative citizens write to conservative congressman; liberal citizens write to liberal congressmen. What the congressman sees then becomes a portrait of public opinion much more supportive of him than may in fact be the case.

The situation is similar to that of the ordinary citizen who gauges public opinion based on the views of those he finds around him. He is likely to find that many people agree with him among those friends and neighbors with whom he talks. The reason, again, is that we all move in homogeneous circles. Some people who are devoutly religious simply do not know persons who are agnostics or atheists. Some people who are political liberals on social welfare, civil rights, and international politics never spend much time with people who take conservative positions on these issues. To think that what we and our friends believe is believed more generally can easily be a mistake.

There may be quite a distinction, this suggests, between opinions volunteered by people, as when someone talks to a friend or writes a letter to a congressman, and opinions discovered by a pollster when he seeks out a sample to interview. This distinction, in turn, reflects the greatest strength as well as the greatest weakness of the public opinion poll. The great strength of the systematic poll is that it gets at the opinions of all citizens, whether or not they have chosen to volunteer their views. The pollster chooses them; it is not that they have chosen to speak. In this sense a good survey represents all citizens—the articulate few who volunteer their views as well as the "silent majority."

But this fact can be a source of weakness as well. This is so because the pollster records the opinions of many citizens who basically have no opinion. Often people have not thought about any particular problem until a public opinion pollster appears at their door to ask about it. Under such circumstances, they are likely to give offhand answers or answers that are highly changeable. If the pollster were to come back in an hour or a day, he might find a different opinion. Respondents will also give opinions even when they have relatively little information on the subject about which they are talking. Under certain circumstances, one might expect the respondent to say that, indeed, he had no opinion. But in fact this is not so and most will answer questions. The point is that one must be most careful in interpreting a meaning out of those answers.

The Instrument Used

Most survey organizations have solved the problems of sampling, and the samples used by the major commercial polls are accurate. At times, though, there will appear to be a sharp divergence in the results found by, say, the Gallup and the Harris polls. One poll will find the public more in favor of a particular measure or a particular candidate than will the other. When that happens, the most likely reason is that the two survey organizations were asking different questions. Which brings us to another general principle of sampling survey: The answers you get depend upon the questions you ask.

Those who have worked professionally with sample surveys are aware of the way in which even subtle changes in question wording can change the results that one gets. People respond to the symbols contained in questions. If you ask a question about "Russia," people will respond one way. If you ask a question about "Communist Russia," people will respond more negatively, simple because you have added the negative symbol of communism.

The careful observer of public opinion polling will always keep this in mind. The polls are quite accurate in telling you how Americans responded to a particular question. But the wording of the question always has an effect on the response. Public opinion polls provide very useful information about the American populace, but the information is useful only if used with caution.

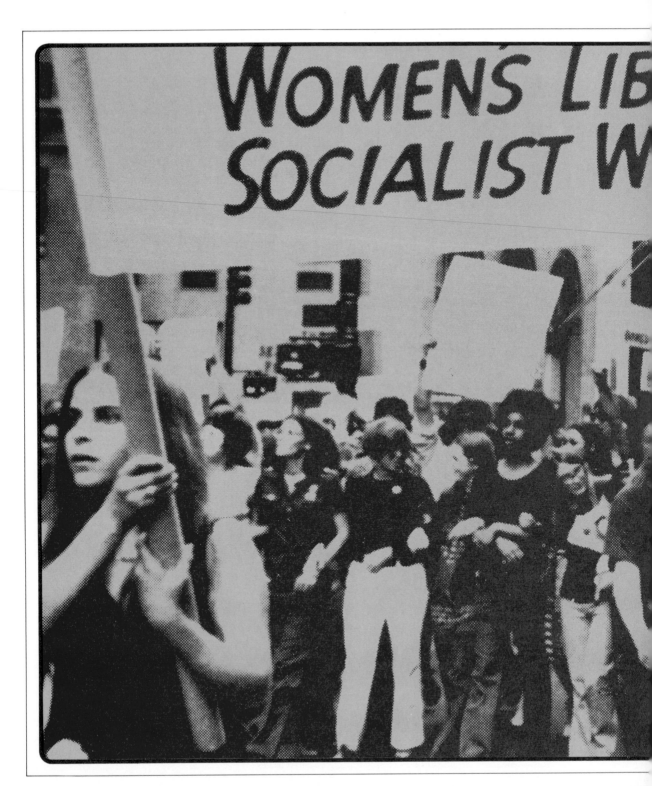

The Political Beliefs of Americans

3

To understand American politics, we must understand the American people—their beliefs and feelings about politics and government, and how they act in politics. The point seems obvious, but it is one that is often ignored. Some observers of politics have believed that politics is adequately understood by considering certain formal structures of government. If we were to ask them what the important features of the American political system are, they would reply: In the United States we have a Presidential rather than a parliamentary system; we have a federal system with power divided between the national and the state governments; we have a Constitution with formal guarantees of liberty. These features of the formal structure of government are, of course, important, and we shall look at them closely in later chapters. But we are starting in this chapter with something that may be more fundamental—the beliefs and feelings about the American political system that are held by the American people.

There is a simple reason why knowledge of the formal structure of government is inadequate unless one understands the beliefs of those who live under that structure: The beliefs affect how the political structure works. This lesson has been forcefully impressed on those who have seen the results of the attempt to transfer political forms from one society to another. A classic example is the Weimar Republic in Germany that was founded after World War I. This new republic replaced the relatively authoritarian empire of the Kaisers and had one of the most carefully worked-out democratic constitutions ever written. But the constitution never took root among the people—it was not respected; the democratic institutions it set up were constantly challenged from left and right. And after a short tumultuous existence, the new democracy succumbed to the totalitarian regime of the Nazis.

Similar results have been noted in many of the new nations in Africa and Asia. Constitutions have been borrowed from countries with long histories of functioning democracy—from Britain or the United States. These constitutions contain provisions for the basic institutions of democracy: periodic elections, guarantees of the right of political opposition, basic freedoms, and so forth. But in many cases the democratic governments have been replaced by military regimes or one-party authoritarian states. The explanation given is that the institutions were "motivationally hollow"; the democratic forms were there, but the democratic beliefs were not.

The experience of other nations has reinforced a widely held belief about American democracy: that it has its roots in the "hearts and minds" of the American people. In this chapter we will first spell out a speculative model of the role that political beliefs play in American democracy—a model expounded by many political philosophers. We can then compare this model to what we know about political reality.

Political Beliefs and Democracy: A Speculative Model

The speculative model goes as follows: If a democracy is to work, certain political features are needed. There must be opportunity for opposing groups to organize and express dissenting views; there must be provision for public control over officials through periodic elections; government leaders must be willing to step down when the voters choose other leaders. These features are found in the Constitution and in written laws. But—and here is where the political beliefs of the American public become important—these features survive and work only because the people of the United States are committed to them. Thus—according to this model—freedoms are guaranteed in the Bill of Rights, but these freedoms are maintained only because of the commitment of Americans to the maintenance of such freedoms. The Constitution provides that the winning Presidential candidate takes office and replaces the former President, but this happens not because it is written in the Constitution but because there is *consensus* among the American people that this is the way things ought to be—an agreement shared by those who supported the loser in the election. In other words, Democrats as well as Republicans believe it is *right* that a Republican President should replace a Democratic one if the Republican wins the election.

If American democracy depends on the consensus of the American people around some important political beliefs, what are these beliefs? Again, political philosophers, considering the problems of democracy, have suggested an answer. It is not necessary, they argue, that Americans agree on everything, as long as they agree on certain fundamentals. These fundamentals include *the nature of the political community and procedural rules.*

The Nature of the Political Community

If American democracy is to work, Americans must be committed to the United States as a political community; that is, there must be that kind of deeply felt, implicit attachment to the nation that individuals also feel toward their family or church. One must identify with the national community. Unless those who live within American society identify with it, pressures from separatist groups will prevent the effective working of the democratic process.

Procedural Rules

Equally important is the need for agreement on the "rules of the game," on the way in which political decisions are made. In the United States this refers to agreement on the rules of political competition—those constitutional rules about elections and free speech mentioned above.

Agreement on fundamentals is important because it allows for disagreement on less basic matters. Americans may disagree on specific policies:

To have a game there must be "rules of the game."

(Photo: George Butler, Rapho Guillumette)

Should there be federal control of the railroads? Should bussing be employed to overcome *de facto* school segregation? But if they believe that this is a matter for an elected Congress and an elected President to decide (within a framework set by constitutional limitations and enforced by the Supreme Court) and if the dispute is decided in that way, they will go along with the result even if that result is not what they want. Similarly, though some Americans prefer one Presidential candidate and others prefer the other, both sides accept the electoral outcome if that outcome derives from an election in accord with the rules.

Habitual Commitment and Rational Calculation: This model of politics has two components. The one we have been discussing we can call the *habitual-value-commitment* component. The other is a *rational-interest-calculation* component. On the one hand, citizens have deeply ingrained habitual commitments to the fundamental values of democracy and accept these under all circumstances. This is the consensus on fundamentals we have discussed. On the other hand, they have specific interests, and they want the government to carry out policies that will further these interests. They try to achieve this by rational calculation—they see which party or candidate offers policies that further their interests and they vote accordingly. Thus an individual prefers greater farm subsidies. He sees which party or candidate offers to increase such subsidies, and he votes—or engages in campaign activity—accordingly. In this model of politics, individuals pursue their varied and often conflicting interests by taking part in politics—voting, trying to influence others—while at the same time maintaining a general agreement on how these interests ought to be pursued.

This model (and we remind the reader that it is a "model" of how American politics operates; we will compare it to reality shortly) offers a most powerful answer to one of the basic questions we raised at the beginning of this book (and that political philosophers have raised many times before). How is democratic government possible? If all societies (the United States, of course, included) contain people with varied needs and interests, and if some of these needs and interests are held quite intensely and are in conflict with the needs and interests of others (some want bussing, others bitterly oppose it), and if democracy allows the free expression and competition of these alternative positions, what keeps the society from flying apart? Why is there not constant warfare and conflict? And how can disputes be settled peacefully? The answer, according to this model, is that though some are committed to bussing and others opposed, both sides are more committed to the procedural rules for settling that dispute. If the matter is settled in accord with these rules, the decision on what to do will be considered legitimate, and citizens will accept the decision even if they preferred an alternative outcome. In the same way the supporter of the Democratic candidate accepts the Republican President even though he preferred the opponent.

By this time the discerning reader should be getting a bit impatient. The model we have been describing sounds like a simple and smooth-working one, but things do not always seem to work so smoothly in the United States. But the even more discerning reader will remember that we are talking of a "model" of the way in which the political beliefs of Americans support the functioning of democracy in this country, not necessarily of the way in which things actually work. The model has been expounded by many political philosophers, and it is a compelling explanation of the workings of a complex phenomenon—American democracy. But, fortunately, in recent years social scientists have developed techniques that allow one to go beyond conjecture about the beliefs of Americans and beyond speculation about the consequences of such beliefs. Using such techniques as the in-depth sample survey of public attitudes, we have learned much about the structure of political beliefs among the American people. These studies indicate that the political beliefs of Americans are something like what we have assumed, but not exactly. And these studies show that the model we have been describing "works"—in that it accurately describes what goes on in America—but only in part. Let us first consider the information we have on the belief systems of Americans, and then we can reconsider the model.

The Political Values of Americans

Attitudes Toward the Political Community

Over the years, studies have found that Americans are, in general, deeply committed to the political community. Reverence for the general symbols of that community—the flag, the Constitution—is taught in the schools and reinforced by ceremonies and observances throughout the life of the average American. And there is evidence that the commitment to these symbols is deep. A major study of democratic attitudes in 1959 compared the political beliefs of Americans with those of citizens in four other countries. (See Table 3.1.) The researchers asked representative samples in each of these countries what it was that they were proud of about their countries. Two results are important. For one thing, few Americans—only 4 percent—replied that there was nothing of which they were proud, a response indicating general hostility to the overall political community. (In the other four countries, the proportions who were proud of "nothing" ranged from 10 to 27 percent.) More interesting is what they were proud of. Compared with the citizens in other nations, Americans expressed pride in political aspects of their society—in the Constitution, in political freedom, in democracy. Eighty-five percent of those interviewed in the United States—twice the proportion of the next highest country—spontaneously

Table 3.1   What Citizens Are Proud of About Their Country

	UNITED STATES	GREAT BRITAIN	GERMANY	ITALY	MEXICO
Proud of "nothing"	4%	10%	15%	27%	16%
Proud of the political institutions	85%	46%	7%	3%	30%

Source: Based on data from Gabriel Almond and Sidney Verba, *The Civic Culture: Political Attitudes and Democracy in Five Nations* (Princeton, N.J.: Princeton University Press, 1963).

mentioned such political aspects. Other evidence shows that Americans have a high level of faith in the "system." Studies show that Americans think most government officials can be trusted (compared with much higher levels of distrust elsewhere); the prestige of such positions as Supreme Court justice is high; public opinion studies show that people will rally around the President whenever he makes an appeal to the country. This general commitment has been the dominant pattern of American beliefs.

But the pride of Americans in their system has been undergoing serious strain. Events of the late 1960s and early 1970s seem to have shocked their political optimism. One group of scholars has been studying the hopes and fears of Americans for a number of years. They measure the evaluation of citizens as to the progress of the nation by using a "self-anchoring scale." (See Figure 3.1.) People are shown a ladder on which the topmost rung represents their ideal for America, the best possible circumstances for the nation that they can imagine. The bottom rung represents the worst circumstances. They then are asked to place the current United States on that ladder, and also where it fell five years earlier and where it will be five years in the future. In 1959 and 1964 the scholars found that Americans had a clear view of steady progress. The present was better than the past; the future would be better yet. But in 1971 they found a striking change. The citizens viewed the last half of the 1960s as an era of decay, not of progress. Things had gotten worse. In fact, as can be seen from the figure, in 1971 they rated the future and the past about equally. American optimism was reflected in a belief that we would recover lost ground. They still retained their hope for future progress, but the view of steady, undeviating progress had been shattered.

Table 3.2 shows clearly why the optimism had declined. Americans were asked what their greatest fears were for America. The table shows what they replied in 1959, in 1964, and in 1971. The fear of nuclear war

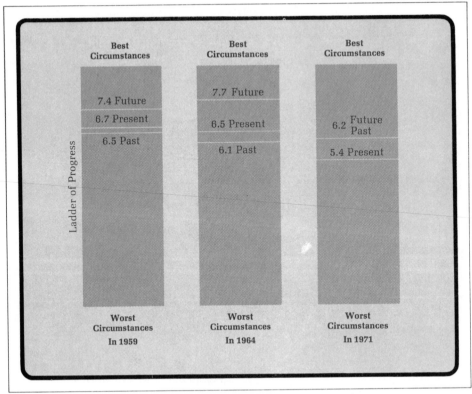

Figure 3.1 Where Citizens Put the Past, Present, and Future of America

SOURCE: Albert H. Cantril and Charles W. Roll, Jr., *The Hopes and Fears of the American People* (New York: Universe Books, 1971). Reprinted by permission of Universe Books and Potomac Associates.

that had dominated in 1959 declined, but it was replaced by a catalog of new fears that sum up the turbulence of the late 1960s: national unity and political instability, lack of law and order, pollution, drugs, and racial tension. None of these had been on people's minds before 1960, but they were on their minds a decade later.

Just as the optimism of the average American about the future was declining, so was another indicator of the citizen's faith in the political system. During the late 1960s and early 1970s there was a steady decline in the number of citizens saying that they "trusted" government officials in Washington. Most commentators believe that excessive secrecy in government, especially over the conduct of the Vietnam War, helped bring about this decline in trust. In 1973, when the Watergate scandal hit the front pages of the newspapers, the level of citizen trust in government leaders dropped much further. The revelation that highly placed government leaders were involved in illegal campaign activities and immoral use of campaign funds convinced many citizens that "you can't trust politicians."

Table 3.2. National Fears of Americans

NATIONAL FEARS	Percentage Mentioning a Fear		
	1959	1964	1971
War (especially nuclear war)	64	50	30
National disunity, political instability	3	8	26
Economic instability, inflation	18	13	17
Communism	12	29	12
Lack of law and order	3	5	11
Pollution	—	—	9
Drugs	—	—	7
Racial tension	—	9	7
Unemployment	7	6	7
Lack of public morality	4	5	6
Loss of personal freedom	4	5	5

Source: Albert H. Cantril and Charles W. Roll, Jr., *The Hopes and Fears of the American People* (New York: Universe Books, 1971). Reprinted by permission of Universe Books and Potomac Associates.

The long-term implications of this decline in optimism about America's future and in trust in government are unclear. But the decline does introduce tension between leadership and citizens. Such tension can create serious problems if, as the speculative model outlined above indicates, it is the case that successful democracy ultimately rests on public confidence and political loyalty.

The data presented show that Americans have a general commitment to the symbols of nationhood—even if doubts have begun to appear. But pride in nation and commitment to the symbols of nationhood do not necessarily represent commitment to democratic government. Indeed, intense commitment to the symbols of the nation may be the kind of nationalistic commitment that can undermine democracy. What may be more important for democracy is the content that is given to those commitments. Is the commitment to the symbols themselves, or is it to some democratic content that lies behind the symbols? This brings us to the next fundamental set of beliefs of Americans—beliefs about "rules of the political game."

Procedural Consensus

Do Americans generally agree with the rules of the democratic game? In part the answer is implied in the fact that the symbols to which they are committed include the Constitution and the Bill of Rights. When they talk about the specific political institutions of which they are proud, it is the symbols of democracy that are mentioned. Furthermore, several studies have shown that the American people generally will agree with the principles of democratic government. (By "generally" we mean that usually more than nine out of ten will agree.) They will agree, when asked, that the rights of minorities to free speech ought to be protected, that all people should have the right to vote, that political leaders should be responsive to the demands of the people, and that democracy works best where there is strong competition between political parties.[1] In short, one can ask Americans about many of the fundamental rules of the democratic political game, and they will overwhelmingly support them.

Commitment to Democratic Procedure—How Intense Is It? But there is other research on the political beliefs of Americans that offers a major qualification to the rosy picture of democratic consensus that emerges from the data just mentioned. Commitment to the rules of democratic procedure seems to be greatest in the abstract; it seems less firm when applied to particular cases. The same American population that overwhelmingly agrees that free speech in general is a good thing is less convinced that particular deviant groups ought to be allowed that freedom. When one asks whether opportunities to make speeches should be allowed to groups with unpopular views (Communists, socialists), the American people are by no means so sure that speech should be that free. Indeed, one finds a large proportion of Americans opposed to letting groups of this sort give a speech in their community, and large numbers would remove their books from the local library. For Communitsts or atheists, about two-thirds would oppose such freedom. One study in Tallahassee, Florida, found that there was overwhelming agreement that minority groups should have full right to participate in politics. But among the same people, 42 percent thought that a Black should not be allowed to run for mayor of their city.[2]

Much of the research on which this generalization about the difference between the abstract values of Americans and their views about the application of these values was done in the 1950s and early 1960s. But things have not changed much since then. In 1971 the National Opinion Research Center did a study of American attitudes toward free speech. In abstract democratic theory, one should favor free speech no matter how he feels about the speaker or the content of his speech—at least until the speaker reaches the point of directly advocating violence or breaking the

---

[1] James W. Prothro and Charles M. Grigg, "Fundamental Principles of Democracy: Bases of Agreement and Disagreement," *Journal of Politics*, 22 (Spring 1960), 276–294; and Herbert McClosky, "Consensus and Ideology in American Politics," *American Political Science Review*, 58 (June 1964), 361–382.

[2] Prothro and Grigg, 294.

law. But it is clear from the results of this 1971 study that citizens differentiate between free speech for things they favor and free speech for things they oppose. "Should a group of people be allowed to circulate an anti-pollution petition?" Ninety-three percent of the people said Yes. "Should a group be allowed to circulate a petition calling for the legalization of marijuana?" Only a bare majority, 52 percent, said Yes.

Similarly, people differentiated between freedom for those they like and freedom for those they like less. Ninety-five percent of the population approved when asked whether "a group of your neighbors" should be allowed to circulate petitions to ask the government to act on some issue—a clear commitment to democratic procedures. But only about 70 percent thought that "Black militants" or "radical students" should be allowed to circulate a petition. (See Tables 3.3 and 3.4.)

That citizens like free speech in the abstract does not mean that they support it where it really counts—when the speakers come from unpopular groups with unpopular views. Nor does this mean that all Americans are hypocrites about democratic values. General values often require modification in the light of particular values. Yet the commitment to democratic rules is hardly meaningful if whenever they are applied they are applied narrowly.

So the data present a puzzle. If democracy depends on commitment to the values of democracy, such a foundation would be weak indeed if those values are supported only in their most abstract formulation. But fortunately we can go one step further. We have seen that the citizenry takes a strong position in favor of democratic freedom when asked abstract questions and a more restrictive one when asked more concrete questions. But how in fact do they act? They act differently from what one might expect from some of their answers. In Tallahassee, Florida—where 42 percent of a sample had said that a Black ought not to be allowed to run for

Table 3.3 Citizens Approve Free Speech More When They Like the Group

	PERCENTAGE SAYING YES
Should a group *of your neighbors* be allowed to circulate a petition?	95%
Should a group *of Black militants* be allowed to circulate a petition?	69%
Should a group *of radical students* be allowed to circulate a petition?	71%

Source: Study by the National Opinion Research Center, University of Chicago, 1971.

Table 3.4 Citizens Also Favor Free Speech
More When They Approve the Views of the Speakers

	PERCENTAGE SAYING YES
Should a group be allowed to petition to *stop·a factory from polluting the air?*	93%
Should a group be allowed to circulate a petition expressing *concern with crime* in their community?	95%
Should a group be allowed to circulate a petition calling for the *legalization of marijuana?*	52%
Should a group be allowed to circulate a petition calling on the government to make sure that *Blacks can buy and rent homes in White neighborhoods?* (asked of Whites only)	70%
Should a group be allowed to circulate a petition calling on the government to *prevent Blacks from buying or renting in White neighborhoods?* (asked of Blacks only)	51%

Source: Study by the National Opinion Research Center, University of Chicago, 1971.

mayor—there had been a contest for mayor a few months earlier in which a Black *had* campaigned with vigor. No one had tried to stop him. And in the communities in which citizens said that various unpopular speakers ought not to be allowed to speak and their books ought to be removed from the library, such restrictions were not put into effect.

Thus the position of the American people on the "rules of the democratic game" is by no means as clear as those political philosophers who speculated about it thought. Americans support the rules in the abstract; when you get closer to reality and ask about specific cases, they are less supportive of democracy; but when you get even closer to reality and ask about what they do, you find that they do not act on their restrictive political views. One thing this tells us is that people are by no means consistent—the general values may not be totally consistent with the specific ways they apply these values; and their values and attitudes may not be consistent with their behavior.

One possible explanation of why the citizens of Tallahassee would report in large numbers that they thought a Black should not be allowed to run for mayor and yet do nothing to stop him is that these citizens were expressing negative feelings toward Blacks when the question about a Black running for mayor was asked, but were guided in their behavior by the more general value of equal access for all to political office. And this may in part be true. But there is another explanation. Individuals express political views to survey researchers, but often these views are lightly held and are not the kinds of attitudes on which people act. Studies suggest that most of the positions that individuals take on public issues during a survey interview are of this sort. They represent positions in which they believe, but not very strongly, or at least not strongly enough to motivate them into action.

This is not true of all Americans. For some, politics is a very important activity. The stratum of the American people that is politically concerned and active is an important group about which we shall have more to say later. They are also a minority of the population. But what is relevant for our understanding of how American democracy survives in the face of what seem to be some fairly uncongenial attitudes is that, like the rest of the public, political activists agree with the abstract principles of democracy, but they are more likely than the general public to support these general principles when they are applied to specific cases.

Thus the study that found Americans—up to two-thirds—opposing free speech for various unpopular groups also found that most Americans who were the *leaders* of local organizations or were local governmental officials were in favor of allowing such unpopular speech. (See Table 3.5.) Two-thirds of a cross-section of the American people would bar a Communist from speaking in their community, but a majority of the leaders (though a bare majority) would allow it. Or, as another study found, almost one-third of Americans thought that the majority has the right to abolish minorities; a much smaller percentage—7 percent—of the political leaders (in this case, delegates to the national conventions) took this undemocratic position.[3]

These data suggest that democratic values may be less well established

Table 3.5   Community Leaders Were Found More
Tolerant of Unpopular Views Than Were Ordinary Citizens

PERCENTAGE WHO WOULD ALLOW THE FOLLOWING:	AMONG A CROSS-SECTION OF CITIZENS	AMONG COMMUNITY LEADERS
An admitted Communist to speak in public	27%	51%
A socialist to speak in public	58%	84%
Percentage categorized as "more tolerant" of minorities	31%	66%

Source: Samuel Stouffer, *Communism, Conformity and Civil Liberties.* Copyright © 1955 by Samuel A. Stouffer. Reprinted by permission of John Wiley & Sons, Inc.

[3] McClosky, 365.

among the bulk of the American people than one imagined, but better established among those who are likely to have a greater voice in how things in fact are run—those who are active in politics and active in organizations. Democracy may rest on a foundation of democratic political commitments, but the foundation may be narrow.

Several additional points can be made—some discouraging, some encouraging for democracy. A discouraging point is that a large group in the population is not in favor of political freedoms for deviant groups and hence is a potential public for antidemocratic politics. This discouraging thought must be tempered by two others. For one thing, the general commitment to the values of democracy—vague though that commitment may be—provides a counterforce to the more restrictive views. At least it provides a set of values to which one can appeal. And further, all evidence shows that commitment to democratic values—in both the abstract and the applied sense—is strongest among those with higher education. As the population becomes more and more educated—as will happen over time with the increase in the college population—one can expect a large proportion of the population to have political views that are consistently democratic.

A Few Other "Fundamental" Beliefs

There are a few other fundamental political beliefs of Americans that ought to be mentioned, for they are important in understanding how Americans act in politics. Two characteristics of Americans are their belief in their *efficacy* as citizens and their belief in *rugged individualism*.

Citizens' Belief in Their Political Efficacy: Americans consider themselves to be politically efficacious; that is, they believe that they can influence the affairs of government by their actions. Most believe that the vote is an effective instrument for controlling government officials and they believe that government officials are basically responsive to the people. In short, they feel that they can have some political influence. Again this can best be seen in comparative perspective. (See Table 3.6.) If we compare Americans to the citizens of other nations, we find that they are more likely than most others to think that they can have some effect on a local government regulation or a law of Congress they consider unfair or unjust. About three out of four Americans say they could do something about such a regulation. The percentages are generally smaller elsewhere.

American citizens, this suggests, do not consider themselves helpless before the government. And, to some extent at least, believing that they are not helpless makes them in fact less helpless. This same study shows that just those Americans who consider themselves able to influence the government are, in fact, likely to try. In addition to the sense that one can influence the government, Americans believe that one has an obligation as

Table 3.6 Can You Do Something About a Regulation You Consider Unfair?

	Percentage Saying Yes				
	UNITED STATES	BRITAIN	GERMANY	ITALY	MEXICO
In relation to local government	77%	78%	62%	51%	52%
In relation to national government	75%	62%	38%	28%	38%

Source: Based on data from Gabriel Almond and Sidney Verba, *The Civic Culture: Political Attitudes and Democracy in Five Nations* (Princeton, N.J.: Princeton University Press, 1963).

a citizen to do so. When asked what role the individual should play in his local community, a majority of Americans replied that they should take some *active* part—a proportion higher than that found in the other countries studied.

The data reported in the preceding two paragraphs come from a study in 1959. How have things changed since this study? We have no information from other nations—to see if the relative position of the United States has changed. But we do have periodic measures of "citizen efficacy" during the fifties and sixties. And the best evidence shows that feelings of efficacy rose in the fifties, to fall somewhat in the sixties. In 1952, 69 percent of a sample agreed that "people have some say about what the government does"; by 1960 the figure had risen to 72 percent. But by 1968 the proportion agreeing with that statement had fallen to 60 percent. The figure is still high—higher probably than that in other nations—but the decline is significant.[4]

Belief in Rugged Individualism: In addition to their beliefs in their political efficacy, many Americans can be characterized by a belief in "rugged individualism"—a belief that the individual is responsible for his own fate, that his success or failure depends on his own effort. This general attitude colors the political thinking of many Americans.

But this is another case where the difference between general principles and specific positions appears. Americans seem to be more ruggedly individualistic in general principle than in relation to specific situations. Thus one political inquiry found that fully half of those studied could be classified as "conservatives" when it came to agreeing with such general principles as that "the government ought not to interfere in the lives of people

[4] Philip E. Converse, "Change in the American Electorate," in Angus Campbell and Philip E. Converse, eds., *The Human Meaning of Social Change* (New York: Russell Sage, 1972), pp. 327–328.

too much," or that "we ought to rely more on individual initiative and less on governmental help"; but only 14 percent could be classified as "conservatives" when it came to their positions on such specific government programs as medical aid, unemployment insurance, and the like.[5] The general principle of rugged individualism may be believed by the average American. But he does not let it stand in the way of government programs he finds of benefit to himself.

Summary Thus Far

We started with a speculative model of how democracies function whereby all Americans were committed to the rules of democratic procedures and, under the cover of those rules, could debate and dispute about more specific issues. The cohesive glue of common value commitment prevented issue debate from tearing the society apart.

The model fits the data in part. On the most abstract level there is commitment to democratic values. But on the more specific level of the application of these rules, the commitment of the populace to democracy is more ambiguous. However, this lack of clear commitment to applied democratic values is tempered by another fact: Those who are the least consistently committed are also the least active.

Thus the system works, but not exactly as the model describes. For the data also suggest that there may be a lot of built-in fragility—particularly when intense issues such as race or Vietnam come to the fore. The commitment to fundamental democratic values may not be as strong a support for American democracy as observers once thought.

Political Interests and Political Calculation

We have thus far concentrated on certain fundamental beliefs that individuals hold about government and politics. These we said were likely to be habitual beliefs—held from early years as part of the implicit understanding of the world. But beneath this high level of principle is a politics of interest conflict. Politics is, after all, about the allocation of benefits to the members of the society and the clash among citizens for a larger share of those benefits.

In the model of democratic functioning that we described at the beginning of the chapter, this clash of interests can take place without tearing the society apart because it takes place under the protective cover of commitment to fundamentals of democratic rule. Within a framework of habitual

---

[5] Lloyd A. Free and Hadley Cantril, *The Political Beliefs of Americans* (New Brunswick, N.J.: Rutgers University Press, 1967).

commitment to these rules, the individual citizen—so this model says—acts as a rational calculator of his interests. This means that he knows his own interests, he looks around to see which candidate or party offers to further those interests the most, and he votes accordingly or is politically active in other ways to further those interests. Our data suggest that the first part of the model, commitment to fundamentals, is only in part confirmed by the facts. And the data suggest the same about the second part of the model.

Opinions on Policy

Americans are opinionated; they have opinions on all sorts of subjects. And these opinions have been studied and analyzed more than those of any other people. Read the public opinion poll results in the newspapers—Americans have opinions on farm subsidies, on wage control, on the miniskirt versus the maxiskirt, on drug control, on antiballistic missiles, and on whether there is life on Mars. The holding of such opinions—at least on social and economic issues, if not on skirt length or life on Mars—is a crucial component of the model of democracy whereby citizens take part in a game of rational calculation to see how they can benefit most from the government. The informed citizen who knows what he wants can then act politically in a rational manner to achieve what he wants.

But if modern techniques of survey research can inform us about these policy positions of Americans, they can also tell us a little about what these policy positions mean. Scholars who have probed deeply into the content and structure of these policy positions have found that, for most Americans, such positions on specific policies may hardly be opinions at all. When individuals are questioned at their doorstep by the pollster they will express opinions on all sorts of matters. (Indeed, in one study a researcher asked a sample of Americans for their opinion on the "Metallic Metals Act." The act was fictitious, but 70 percent had an opinion for or against it.[6])

Other evidence shows that these opinions are often based on very limited information; citizens are often unaware of the issue at stake. Furthermore, they are usually uninformed of the position that parties or candidates take on the matter and, in that sense, they are unable to perform as the model of democratic citizenship says they should—by choosing that party or candidate who best suits their position. Sometimes the examples of this are quite dramatic. In 1968 Senator Eugene McCarthy's well-publicized opposition to President Johnson's Vietnam policy was major news, particularly when he entered the New Hampshire primary to challenge LBJ. But

---

[6] Stanley J. Payne, *The Art of Asking Questions* (Princeton, N.J.: Princeton University Press, 1951), p. 18.

though McCarthy's antiwar stand had been stressed by the media, 54 percent of a sample in a study conducted in New Hampshire shortly before the Presidential primary in 1968 said they did not know his position on the war in Vietnam, 17 percent identified him as a "hawk," and only 29 percent correctly identified him as opposed to the war and in favor of de-escalation.

That the public lacks detailed information about political matters is documented most thoroughly in a series of studies of the American electorate that started in the 1950s. These studies found that the average American was not a very political animal. For most citizens, politics was of only marginal concern; the average citizen was more occupied with things closer to him such as family, job, or friends.

Furthermore, these studies showed that most Americans did not think about politics in ways that were familiar to more sophisticated citizens. Journalists, scholars, and politicians themselves are likely to have consistent positions across a large series of issues. One can assign them to "liberal" or "conservative" or "radical" categories, because on a variety of political matters they will be the same place on the political spectrum. Thus a "liberal" in this standard meaning of the term would be someone who took the following position on policy issues: He would favor faster school desegregation and support programs to reduce residential segregation; on matters of social welfare he would be in favor of increased federal spending; on foreign affairs he would be in favor of a more conciliatory relationship to the Communist world. And the "conservative" would hold the opposite position: He would want to go slow on integration, reduce welfare spending, and take a hard line in foreign affairs. In each case, the positions on specific issues would be the subparts of a more general world-view.

The studies of the American public in the 1950s and the early 1960s found that the average American rarely held such clear political world-views. People seldom thought in broad terms such as liberal or conservative when they evaluated candidates. Most striking was the fact that there was almost no relationship between the position that a citizen took on one issue and the position he took on other issues. If he was conservative on matters of race, the average citizen was as likely to be liberal as conservative on matters of welfare policy or foreign policy. Any one issue position could not be predicted from other issue positions.

These characteristics of the American "mass public" had important implications for American politics. They meant that elections were unlikely to be determined by the issues, since the public was uninformed about where the candidates stood on the issues and, in any case, did not itself hold consistent positions on the issues. The lack of clearly crystallized positions on issues also meant that there was less chance of a sharp polarization of the American people into opposing conservative and liberal camps. The citizen who was conservative on one matter was likely to be liberal on another matter—and therefore would not easily fit into one camp or the other.

This portrait of the apolitical American was painted in the 1950s and early 1960s. The portrait was quite accurate for that era, as many careful studies showed. More recent research, however, has indicated that the American public has become more politically involved. The 1950s—when Dwight D. Eisenhower was President—was a bland political period: There were few burning political issues. But the 1960s ushered in a new set of issues—race, Vietnam, the urban crisis. And with these new concerns emerged an intensified political awareness among Americans. Surveys found fewer Americans saying that they were uninterested in politics. More important, the political attitudes of citizens began to fall into more distinct patterns. Whereas in the 1950s one could not predict a citizen's attitude on one issue by his attitude on another, attitudes in the 1960s and early 1970s became more and more consistent. Figure 3.2 is based on periodic surveys of the American people. It shows an "index of consistency" on political issues; the higher the index, the more was the average American consistently a liberal or conservative across a variety of issues—race, welfare, big government, foreign policy. As we can clearly see, that index rose substantially in the 1960s.

What effect this heightened political awareness and increased political consistency will have on American politics is uncertain. We will consider how it may affect elections in a later chapter. But the change in the American public is clear and rather dramatic: Politics has become salient for more people who have in turn developed more consistent and better-defined political positions.

Figure 3.2 Index of Consistency on Political Issues

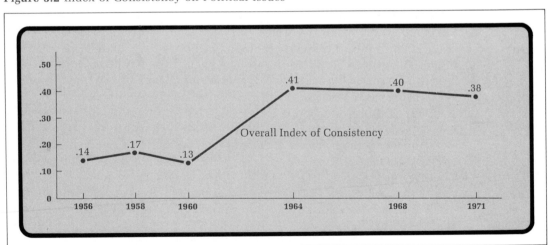

SOURCE: Norman H. Nie, "Mass Belief Systems Revisited: Political Change and Attitude," University of Chicago, August 1972 (mimeographed).

Where Do Political Attitudes Come From?

When individuals are acting—either by expressing an opinion or casting a ballot—they are likely to seek guidance. How do they know that their opinions or choices are right? Citizens usually have no direct information about an issue: "What really is going on in China?" "Who is to blame for inflation?" Under such circumstances, where one cannot test his opinions against reality, he tests them against the opinions of others. If a citizen does not have a view on the subject, he may be guided by the views of others. Or, if he has an opinion on a subject but finds that others have some alternative view, he is likely to modify his opinion to fit that of others. And this is especially the case if those "others" are individuals or groups whose views he respects or from whom he wants acceptance.

Who are these "others" against whom one can test his opinions and who are likely to influence the opinions a citizen has? We can mention three such "others": peers, political authorities such as the President or Supreme Court, and one's political party.

Peers

Studies have shown that groups of individuals in contact with one another are likely to have similar opinions. This is particularly true of what are called primary groups—groups of friends, families, neighbors, and others who come into face-to-face contact. In part the opinions of members of such groups are similar because they are in similar real circumstances—members of primary groups tend to come from the same occupational strata, to live near one another, and so forth. Thus they may be faced with similar political and social problems.

But beyond these reasons for similarity of opinion is the well-documented fact that individuals will change their opinions to fit those that are dominant within the groups to which they belong. This becomes a way of increasing one's acceptance within such groups, it reduces tensions with friends and relatives, and it gives the individual some sense that his view is right—because others agree with him when he presents his views.

Is such conformity to one's peers sheepish and irrational? Yes and no. It may be irrational in the sense that positions—how to vote, what to do about inflation—held by the individual do not derive from a confrontation with the "real" political situation. In other words, they are not based on a consideration of the issues or on the relative merits of a candidate. Rather the positions taken derive from social forces within the group— the desire to be socially accepted, for instance. On the other hand, such comformity may under certain circumstances be a perfectly reasonable way to come to a political position (given that one cannot afford the time and full effort to find out all the information on an issue). The opinions of one's associates are perhaps as good a guide as any to political beliefs.

Political Authorities

Another place where one can turn for guidance in moments of political uncertainty are leading political authority figures. The Supreme Court holds such a position for many Americans. If it has taken a position, it is one that many Americans feel must be the right one. Another such figure is the President. In one sense, he may be less potent than the Supreme Court as a guide for public opinion since he represents only one opinion and one political party, while the Supreme Court is a nonpartisan institution comprising nine opinions. But the President has great access to the news media and to popular prestige, and so his views are widely known and usually respected. This is particularly so on those issues that are "distant" from the average American, such as foreign policy.

Those who have followed the vagaries of public opinion on the war in Vietnam, for instance, noticed an interesting phenomenon. Over time, the general popular support for the war declined—as evidenced by the proportion of the people who thought that the President was not doing a good job handling the Vietnam situation. But whenever the President did something dramatic—increasing bombing or stopping bombing, taking a new hard line or a softer line—the proportion approving his activities went up (only to fall again shortly). In part this might be due to a desire on the part of the American people to see the war end, and their belief that some new initiative—in either a hawkish or dovish direction—might accomplish this. But in large part, the increase in Presidential support when he made a dramatic announcement is a reflection of his powerful prestige and the willingness of the American people to be guided by him in matters they do not understand. This is especially true in foreign policy. In fact, studies have shown that Presidential popularity goes up substantially even when the President does something that most (including the President) consider a mistake. After the disastrous U-2 incident (where President Eisenhower admitted that the United States had been caught red-handed in a spy plane incident we had tried to deny) and after the abortive Bay of Pigs invasion (which was the darkest hour of the Kennedy administration) the proportion of the American people who thought that the President was doing a good job *went up.*

One's Political Party

Perhaps the most important guiding force for political opinions is one's party affiliation. Over the years, scholars have found the party identification of American citizens to be one of the most important political beliefs they carry around in their minds.

1. Most people adopt a party affiliation—they come to think of themselves as Democrats or Republicans—early in their lives. And once they take that position they stick to it. Their opinions on specific issues may change, but

The most important guide to political opinions is one's political party.

(Photo: Lawrence Frank, Rapho Guillumette)

they are unlikely to change their partisan positions. We mentioned earlier a study that found that attitudes on racial matters were much more stable (when studied over time) than attitudes on other social issues. The same study also shows that one's party affiliation is about twice as stable as one's attitudes in racial matters. In some sense party identification becomes a part of one's social self-identification—something like religion.

2. Indeed, the origins of party affiliation go further back than one's early adult political experience. It is likely to be inherited as well. If you want to guess what party an individual supports, one bit of information that would enable you to guess correctly would be the party affiliation of his parents. If you know that both parents of an individual supported one or the other of the political parties, you will be right in about 70 percent of the cases if you guess that he supports the same party. And just as party affiliation is more stable over time than are attitudes on other issues, so is it more stable from generation to generation. An individual is more likely to differ from his parents on his political views than he is to differ from them on the party with which he identifies.

3. Party affiliation remains stable in many cases even though individuals may abandon their party to vote for the opposition candidate. Millions of Democrats supported President Nixon in 1972 just as millions of Democrats had supported President Eisenhower in two elections, but still considered themselves Democrats. And the same is true of the millions of Republicans who abandoned their party's candidate in 1964 to vote against Barry Goldwater. They continued to consider themselves Republicans.

These facts about the potency of party affiliation as a political belief tell us much about the way in which the American citizen organizes the political world in his mind. Party affiliation becomes a part of an individual's political self-identification; he carries it with him as an implicit and deeply held political belief. One reason why it survives from generation to generation while the specific political views of one's parents are less likely to be transmitted is that party affiliation is a general-purpose guide to political matters. The particular issue positions held by one's parents may be useless because the issues have changed. But parties persist over time and react to new issues. Thus one's party affiliation becomes a most useful simplifying mechanism for the individual citizen—issues come and go and are complicated. But one's party identification can give him some clue to the position to take on an issue. Or, even more likely, it can guide him on how to vote without getting concerned with specific issues.

Note how this reverses the model of rational calculation spelled out earlier. In that model, the citizen takes a position on an issue and then chooses the party to support on the basis of its conformance with the position he prefers. In actuality, the situation may be reversed. The individual is guided by his party affiliation to take a position or support a candidate.

We ought to end this section on a note of caution. The reader ought always to remember that we are talking of tendencies, not absolutes. There are many Americans who change their parties; there are many who choose a party based on its position rather than choosing a position based on what their party seems to believe. Indeed, we shall later look at the phenomenon of massive shifts in the party affiliations of Americans—when those rare but crucial realignments of support for the political parties occur. But, still, the tendencies reported here are the dominant ones. For most Americans most of the time, party affiliation is a "given" thing, and not something that changes.

Currents and Crosscurrents

One danger of a chapter such as this is that one may get the wrong impression. We have been trying to characterize the American public in rather broad and sweeping terms, and one may get the impression that all is homogeneous in America. The perceptive reader will see that this is not the message of the previous part of the chapter. Indeed, one thing found when we looked more closely at American opinion was that what seems at first glance like consensus—say, on democratic values—appears on closer scrutiny to represent much more diversity of opinion. All Americans (or at least most) agree with the abstract principles of democracy, but when it comes to their application the proportion supporting these principles falls to one-third, one-half, or two-thirds, depending on the groups about whose freedom we are inquiring. And figures such as one-third or one-half taking a particular position indicate just the opposite of consensus. They indicate quite a bit of disagreement.

Social Bases of Political Conflicts

We have not thus far raised the important question of which groups disagree with which groups in American society. This is, of course, one of the crucial questions one would want to raise in understanding politics in any society: What are the groupings of the population that are opposed to one another, or, in other words, what are the social bases of political conflicts? In the United States there are many such potential bases for political grouping—people in different regions, people with different occupations, people of different races, ages, religions, or ethnic origins may well have different political views. This theme is so important that we shall look at it more closely and intensively in later chapters. The struggle among contending groups—and the problem of which groups are important—go to the heart of American politics. Here we want to glance at some of the group variations in political viewpoint from the perspective of the main theme of this chapter: the underlying set of political values that exist in America.

There are, as just suggested, many ways to divide up the American population: into Northerners and Southerners, men and women, young and old, rich and poor, Black and White—that is, by region or sex or age or income or race—and by many other characteristics as well. Each such cutting of the population would reveal some interesting differences in political viewpoint. But when it comes to some of the basic political beliefs we have been discussing in this chapter—basic commitment to political freedoms, sense of ability to influence the government, basic trust in the government, and basic sense of obligation to participate in politics—many of these divisions of the population would reveal little difference in the overall pattern of attitudes. Although there are some differences, inhabitants of different regions, or young and old, or men and women do not radically differ on these fundamental political principles.

The division of the population that makes the most difference in attitude on these basic matters is that division which separates out the more affluent, more educated, more privileged on the one hand, and those less advantaged on the other. We have seen already that commitment to democratic values is most heavily ingrained among political activists and leaders of organizations. This is probably a reflection of the fact that such value commitment is most often found among those who have some higher education, and that such people are also likely to be the political activists and the organizational leaders.

The model of the democratic citizen—a man deeply committed to the values of democracy, with a strong sense of competence and an obligation to participate, and with well-thought-out and consistent political views—does not fit the American population very well, but it fits the educated part best of all. Americans, the reader will remember, were much more likely than citizens in other countries to report that the citizen had an obligation to be active in his local community—a major proposition in the democratic model. But there is quite a variation in the proportion who feel this obligation at different levels of education. Only a third of those citizens who have a primary education feel such an obligation in contrast with two-thirds among the college-educated. Or consider the sense of competence to influence the government. Most Americans (77 percent) felt that they could do something about an unjust local regulation. And even among those with primary education more than a majority (60 percent) have this belief. But when one comes to the college-educated, one finds almost unanimous (95 percent) agreement that one could have some influence in such a situation.[7] Also, when we turn to the issue positions of Americans, we find that those with higher education are more likely to have well-thought-out and consistent political beliefs.

---

[7] These figures come from the 1959 Almond and Verba *Civic Culture* study. But evidence from later studies makes it clear that things have not changed. In 1966, a sample were asked whether they agreed with the statement: "I don't think public officials care much about what people like me think." Over 70 percent of those who had not completed grade school agreed. Only 10 percent of the college graduates agreed. See Converse, 326.

Black Americans and White Americans

But suppose we turn from the "average" White, middle-class American to those Americans who have generally been deprived of the full benefits of their country and of the full opportunity to participate in its political life—the Blacks, the Chicanos, the Appalachian poor. What does one find about their political attitudes? One might expect less general acceptance of the "system," more demand for rapid change. Detailed data are hard to come by for all deprived minority groups, but we do know quite a bit about the political attitudes of Black Americans. And what we know confirms that they only partly share the perspectives of the average White American.

In some respects Black and White Americans have quite similar political attitudes. When it comes to some general views about the workings of the American political system, we do not find the amount of disparity that we might expect. Yet when asked more specifically about the workings of the government as it affects them, Blacks respond much more negatively than Whites.

Consider the question of the kind of treatment that citizens expect from officials of the government. A study of political attitudes found that Americans were much more likely to expect equal treatment in a governmental office than were citizens in most other nations. Table 3.7 shows how different the perspective of the average American is from that of the citizen in, say, Italy or Mexico. The American has much more confidence in governmental agencies. Indeed the percentages expecting equal treatment are so different that the authors of this study suggest that citizens in the United States and in Mexico live in "different political worlds." The former in overwhelming majority expect fair treatment; the latter are much less likely to.

But if the average citizen of the United States and of Mexico live in different political worlds, it can also be said that the average Black American lives in a different world from the average White American. Consider the

Table 3.7   Equal Treatment in Governmental Offices in Five Nations

	UNITED STATES	GREAT BRITAIN	GERMANY	ITALY	MEXICO
Percentage saying that they expect equal treatment in a governmental office	83%	83%	65%	53%	42%

Source: Based on data from Gabriel Almond and Sidney Verba, *The Civic Culture: Political Attitudes and Democracy in Five Nations* (Princeton, N.J.: Princeton University Press, 1963).

Table 3.8   Equal Treatment in Governmental Offices: Blacks and Whites

	WHITE AMERICANS	BLACK AMERICANS
Percentage saying that they expect equal treatment in a governmental office	87%	49%

Source: Based on data from Gabriel Almond and Sidney Verba, *The Civic Culture: Political Attitudes and Democracy in Five Nations* (Princeton, N.J.: Princeton University Press, 1963).

difference between the races on expectations of equality of treatment, as shown in Table 3.8. Almost 90 percent of White Americans expect equal treatment from the government; a little less than half of the Blacks have such expectations.

These differences between Blacks and Whites first uncovered in 1959 have appeared again and again in more recent studies. Most dramatic have been differences between the races in attitudes toward the police. Urban Blacks, when contrasted with their White counterparts, are found to have less confidence in the honesty of the police, less favorable expectations of fair treatment by them, and less favorable experiences in dealing with them. Furthermore, Blacks are less satisfied with public services in their neighborhoods; they complain more about high prices and the quality of goods in neighborhood stores.

In sum, when it comes down to their actual lives and their specific relations with the government, Blacks differ sharply from Whites in their attitudes.

Do the different perspectives of Black and White Americans mean that the overall consensus one seems to see when one considers the "average" American really masks fundamental differences when one looks more closely at a minority group like the Blacks? Since the issue of the relations between the races cuts to the heart of contemporary American politics, it is useful to look fairly closely at some evidence before answering the question.

Racial Hostility

Have Blacks and Whites become more hostile to each other in America over the years? Certainly someone comparing the newspapers in the early 1950s with those in the early 1970s would have to conclude that hostility had indeed grown. Twenty years ago, one read little about racial issues and conflict in the papers; today hardly a day goes by without some news of racial conflict. But this is merely to say that racial differences have come into the open. It does not imply that bitter race hatred has developed.

In 1971 the National Opinion Research Center asked people how they felt about various groups in America. The respondents were given a scale on which they could rate various groups in terms of how much they liked them. Consider Figure 3.3, which shows how White and Black Americans differ in the ratings they give each other: Note first that Whites have a more favorable view of Whites than they have of Blacks; Blacks favor Blacks more than Whites. That is not unexpected. More important, both racial groups place the opposite group on the favorable side of the neutral point. On the average, Blacks do not say they dislike Whites; Whites do not say they dislike Blacks.

The racial groups differ in their views toward Black militants. Whites, on the average, say that they dislike such militants and place them far down the scale. Blacks are not hostile to Black militants. But even if Blacks are more favorably disposed toward Black militants than Whites, they still rate them only neutrally. Indeed, the average Black reports more favorable views of Whites than he does of Black militants. The data suggest a significant difference of views, but not racial hatred.

In the years since the racial issue "exploded" in America, White attitudes toward Blacks have undergone striking, but somewhat ambivalent, changes. In general, Whites have become more favorable to Blacks, more responsive to their demands. In 1949 the National Opinion Research Center asked if "Negroes were as intelligent as whites." At that time, only 42 percent of Whites thought so. By 1956 the percentage had risen to 78 (where it has stabilized). In 1942 only 30 percent of White Americans said that White

Figure 3.3 How Whites and Blacks Feel About Each Other and About Black Militants

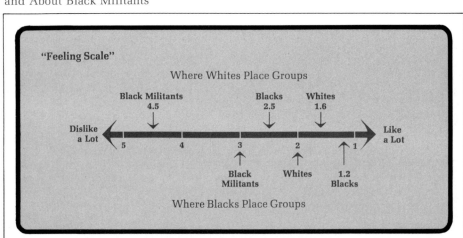

SOURCE: National Opinion Research Center, University of Chicago, 1971.

and Black children should go to the same schools. By 1956 (shortly after the Supreme Court decision), the percentage had risen to 48, and by 1968 to 60 percent. And the same has been true for attitudes toward residential integration. From 1942 to 1968 the percentage of Whites who would not object to residential integration had risen from 35 to 65 percent. The data make clear that the era of increasing salience of racial conflict was also one in which White attitudes toward Blacks improved considerably.

But there are several qualifications to that generalization. For one thing, as the data cited above indicate, a substantial proportion of Whites still oppose integration. Furthermore, White support for the goals of Blacks has been accompanied by a general and growing rejection of Black tactics — at least insofar as these take a militant form. We have seen the negative attitudes of Whites toward Black militants. And Whites have generally rejected direct action by Black groups, even when such action is peaceful and fully within the law. Thus the Harris poll found, in 1968, that 80 percent of Black Americans favored Martin Luther King's Poor People's March on Washington — a massive, peaceful rally at the Lincoln Memorial — whereas only 29 percent of the Whites did. Or consider the data in Table 3.9 on the proper speed of integration: There are some fluctuations, but Whites seem to think things are beginning to go too fast. Thus, just as Whites are coming to accept some of the goals of Blacks, they have come to feel that things are moving too quickly, that Blacks are pushing too hard with inappropriate tactics.

The picture is quite mixed: more favorable attitudes of Whites toward Blacks coupled with less favorable attitudes. One explanation of the ambivalence of Whites may lie in a fundamental characteristic of public attitudes in America — the "rugged individualist" beliefs of the Americans

Table 3.9   Percentage of People Saying That Integration Is Going Too Fast

February 1964	30%
April 1965	34%
July 1966	46%
September 1966	52%
August 1967	44%
April 1968	39%
October 1968	54%
July 1969	44%
March 1970	48%

Source: Gallup poll data, cited in Jerome H. Skolnick, *The Politics of Protest*, Staff Report to the National Commission on the Causes and Prevention of Violence (New York: Ballantine, 1969).

which we mentioned above. Whites have come less and less to believe in the inherent racial inferiority of Blacks, but they remain firm in a belief that people ought to get ahead on their own steam and that, in America, anyone who wants to get ahead can, if only he will try. Thus they come to interpret lower levels of Black education or income as a result of their lack of effort and motivation. If they do not succeed it is because they do not try hard enough. Such a view of the world leads to reluctance to favor massive social programs aimed at improving the conditions of Blacks.

The ambivalent nature of the White attitudes toward Blacks can be seen in Figure 3.4, which compares the attitudes of Whites and Blacks on racial issues in America. People were asked to choose between two polar positions on what to do about urban unrest and on the speed of progress for Blacks. The alternative positions can be seen at either end of the scales: On the question about what to do about urban unrest, people could choose between using all necessary force to suppress such unrest and solving the underlying problems of poverty. Blacks clearly favor the latter course. The position of Whites falls right in between the two alternatives. A similar pattern is seen in relation to the proper speed for further progress for Blacks. Blacks, as one might expect, want faster rather than slower progress. Whites would somewhat prefer a slower pace. On these two general issues, one finds Blacks firmly in favor of faster change in the underlying issues of

Figure 3.4 How Whites and Blacks Differ on What Should Be Done About Problems

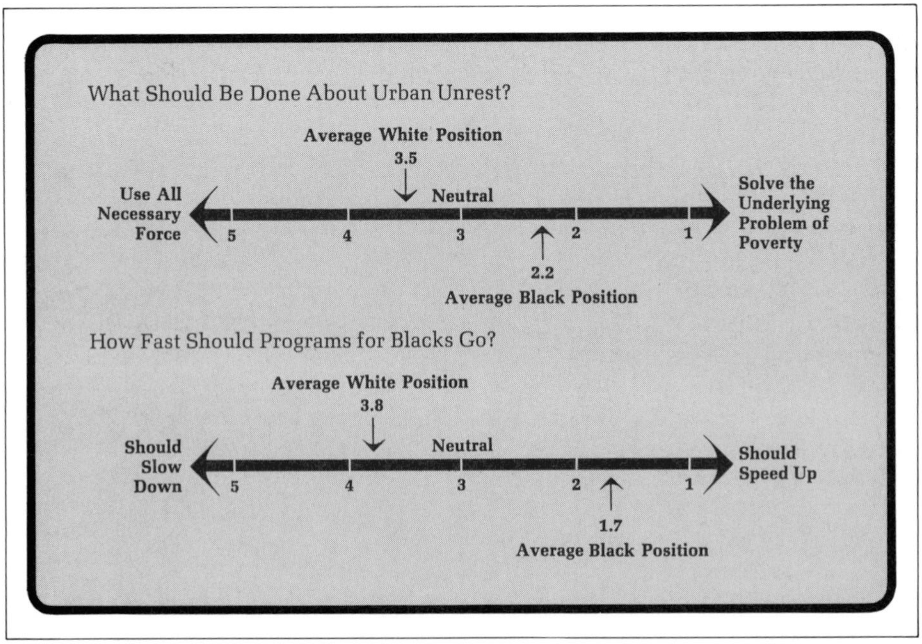

SOURCE: National Opinion Research Center, University of Chicago, 1971.

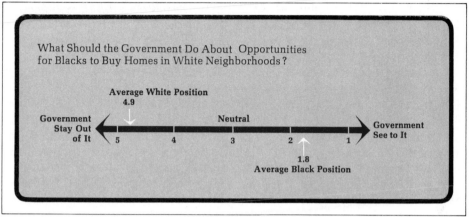

Figure 3.5 How Whites and Blacks Differ on What the Government Should Do About Residential Segregation

SOURCE: National Opinion Research Center, University of Chicago, 1971.

poverty; Whites are not completely opposed but they are certainly holding back compared with the Blacks.

Some issues, however, lead to more intense polarization. Consider Figure 3.5, which shows how Whites and Blacks differ in terms of what the government should do about residential segregation. Here is an issue that more sharply polarizes the population: Whites want the government to stay out of it; Blacks want the government to see to it.

The data on Black and White differences in political perspective suggest both the basis for sustained conflict and some hopes for cooperative progress. The progress could be based on the general shared commitment of the two groups to the democratic system, at least in a general sense. It also could be based on the absence of racial antagonism between Blacks and Whites, and on the greater acceptance by Whites of Black goals.

But the danger of protracted conflict lies in the greater differences between the races when one gets down to specifics. Blacks may trust the system in the abstract; they have less confidence in actual governmental officials. Whites may accept Black goals in the abstract; they are more hesitant about certain specific aspects of those goals, are opposed to pressure from Blacks to achieve those goals, and have come to feel that things are moving too fast.

Radical Politics in America

Traditionally, the United States has been described as an uncongenial society for radical politics. This, so the argument went, was not the case because radicals were suppressed. Rather, there were general tendencies in

American politics that took away many of the issues around which radical politics might be organized. And the two major political parties were very adept at "stealing the thunder" of such groups by taking up some of their positions.

The 1960s and early 1970s have rudely called into question the assumption about the absence of radicalism in America. The issue is crucial for understanding American politics, and we shall come back to it in a later chapter. But we cannot discuss the degree of consensus on basic political values in America without considering why some Black and Chicano and student radical groups came to challenge the fundamental workings of the political system in recent years.

We are not interested here in groups that are radical on some issue — who want basic changes in our foreign policy or in the economic structure of our country. Rather, we are interested in those who are radical from the point of view of the basic rules of the democratic process, who would prefer that decisions be made using some other rules. Such radicalism can come from either end of the political spectrum. Democratic procedures may be rejected by those who see them as blocking rapid social change — "Problems such as war, pollution, the cities, poverty, racism are too great to be dealt with through the 'system,'" so the argument might go. Or the rules of democracy might be rejected by those who see such rules as the cause of violence and decay in our society — "We have too much free speech. We cannot tolerate the political views of those who would destroy the 'system.'"

In fact, remarkably few groups — even in the context of the 1960s and 1970s — take such an explicit position. As we have seen, the commitment to the overall rules of democratic procedures (at least on the abstract level) is extremely widespread — even among those who would be expected to have deep grievances about the operation of that system. Blacks and college students have been found to be much more critical of political institutions in America than is the population as a whole. But when the Harris poll asked these two groups about the effectiveness of violence as a means of changing the system, only about one in ten in either group considered violence effective.[8] That is a much higher proportion than one would have found among other segments of the population, but still a small minority of even these somewhat more alienated groups.

And, indeed, many of the more radical critiques of the workings of American politics come not from those who would prefer other rules, but from those who see the rules working imperfectly and who would prefer to see more effective democracy in the United States. These would include those who want more real participation in the political process or who want a resurgence of local governmental power.

Where one sees direct radical critiques of the rules — rejection of elections or rejection of free speech — these seem to derive less from beliefs that

[8] Harris Survey of College Students, June 1970; Harris Survey of Blacks, September 1971.

such rules of democratic procedure are bad *per se* than from beliefs that these rules have impeded adequate performance on some issue.

As pointed out earlier, the model of democracy suggests that conflicts over issues can take place under the "protective covering" of general consensus on how those issues are to be resolved. The model fits reality imperfectly, but it still gives a good approximation. But what if some citizens have a position on an issue that they hold very intensely—as intensely or more intensely than they hold their commitment to the procedural rules? And what if they perceive that there is little or no chance that the issue will come out as they want under those rules? We have in recent years seen such issues—race and the war in Vietnam—for the sake of which some individuals will prefer to reject the procedures if the procedures do not produce the outcome they want.

Paradoxically the rejection of the procedures may have its roots in the basic acceptance of the procedures by most Americans. Most American schoolchildren are taught a generalized faith that the system "works" because of the procedures of democracy. When they then see that it does not "work"—in that humane decisions are not taken—or they see that the procedures are often violated in fact though supported in words, the disappointment is likely to create an even greater turning away from the system. In short, things are more fragile than one imagined.

Summary Thus Far

It may be useful to summarize what we have learned about the basic beliefs of Americans and how these beliefs affect politics.

Philosophers had long argued that democracy depended on consensus among a people on certain democratic values such as free speech. In the United States we find such consensus in the abstract, coupled with some tendency to limit these values in practice. The latter tendency is, however, balanced out in part by the fact that those citizens who are likely to be most politically involved and active—the better-educated, the leaders of organizations—have a somewhat more consistent commitment to democratic values.

Perhaps the most striking thing about the basic political beliefs of Americans is the fact that there have been important changes in the past decade. For one thing, Americans are no longer as optimistic about their nation as they once were. And this has happened at a time when politics has become more salient to the average citizen and when citizens seem to be developing more consistent sets of political attitudes.

These changes in political attitudes, coming at a time when powerful and possibly divisive issues emerged in America—race, the urban crisis, Vietnam—create the possibility of severe polarization in America, a situation in which hostile groups of citizens confront one another across a wide range of issues. The data on the political beliefs of Blacks and Whites suggest that this may be happening, but not to as great an extent as would be the case if one considered only the views of the most militant representatives of each group.

This last theme—the possibility of polarization—is so crucial to contemporary America that we will devote a good deal of the next chapter to it.

Does Public Opinion Make a Difference?

We have thus far looked carefully at the shape of American attitudes on general governmental matters and on some specific issues such as that of race. But there is a major question as yet unanswered: What difference, if any, does public opinion make? Does it shape government programs? Or do officials pay it some lip service and largely ignore it?

When the systematic public opinion poll was started in the 1930s, some enthusiasts hailed it as a new era for democracy. Now the officials in Washington could be guided by an accurate periodic referendum of the American people on the important issues of the day. Policy could really follow the views of the citizens: An accurate poll could tell one what the American people thought of unemployment insurance, of expenditures for defense, of farm supports. At the same time, other commentators expressed deep concern. Such a "permanent referendum" would be disastrous, for the public was too ill informed, too fickle, too "irrational" to guide public policy. Adequate policy requires careful study and deliberation, something possible only if officials are protected from the day-to-day opinions of the majority.

Actually, the pessimists and the optimists were both wrong. The public opinion poll never became a device for setting governmental policy as the optimists hoped and the pessimists feared. And it did not for the very reasons that had worried the pessimists. The governmental official could find relatively little specific guidance from public opinion for the important issues of the day.

The Impact of the Public on Government Policy

Two somewhat contradictory points can be made about the impact of public opinion on governmental leaders. One point is that most officials—especially elected ones—are avid readers of the public opinion polls, of the mail, of all sorts of indicators of public opinion. Not only do politicians follow the Gallup and Harris polls, they also have special polls taken for them to gauge the state of public opinion. Furthermore (and this is important), political leaders believe that public opinion is important and should be followed—at least up to a point. On the other hand, policy is rarely made directly on the basis of the expressions of public opinion.

How can one reconcile these two points? The answer lies in the fact that public opinion tends to be powerful as a *reactive* force, not as a guide to current policy. The public official trying to choose a policy does worry about the public, and usually tries to keep informed about its attitudes. But he finds little direct policy guidance there. On most issues the public is ill informed, and its policy preferences inchoate. We have seen evidence for this.

But the official also knows that the public may react negatively if he does badly. Thus much of the official's concern about public opinion is *in anticipation* of public reaction. He does not learn from the public opinion polls what policy specifically to pursue. But he often learns what troubles he is likely to face at the next election if he does not deal with certain problems. The public will not inform the political leader how to deal with inflation, but it will let him know if it is concerned with high prices.

The history of the involvement of the American public in relation to the war in Vietnam illustrates this point. No war has ever aroused so much public concern and so much public disapproval. From the time that the war first became a leading public issue—sometime around 1964 or 1965—the proportions of the American people satisfied with governmental policy went down and down. The low point was reached around the time of President Johnson's decision in 1968 not to run again. And public unhappiness with the war probably had something to do with that decision.

Yet public opinion was a far-from-adequate guide for specific policy. When pollsters asked citizens for their preferences on the war—should we escalate to win, de-escalate and get out, or keep up our present policy?—they typically found the public divided across all three positions. How can a President follow that lead? Furthermore, the public seemed to be pleased whenever the President did anything—increased our military commitment or decreased it—as long as something was done. The pleasure lasted only briefly when it became clear that the new move was not effectively ending the war. But the conclusion to be drawn was obvious: The public was unhappy and wanted some results to end the war. And public leaders had to pay attention to that unhappiness or they would suffer the consequences in the next election, as the Democratic party learned in 1968. But what specifically the public wanted to be done was less clear. The administrations involved—the Johnson administration and, later, the Nixon administration—were under pressure by public opinion to do something, but not under pressure to do something specific.

Limits to Public Tolerance of Policies: There is another interpretation of the role of public opinion in the policy process. This is that public opinion sets certain limits as to what is acceptable policy: some things the public will not stand for. There is probably some truth to this. Public tolerance sets some outer boundaries to acceptable policies. But even here the role of public opinion is by no means clear. One reason is that one never knows what these boundaries are simply by observing the answers to questions in public opinion polls. We do not know the limits to public tolerance in advance; we may have to probe those limits in order to find out.

An example will help make the point clear, and also teach us some important lessons about public opinion. For many years, observers claimed that the American public set definite limits to the foreign policy of the government. The public, we were told, would not stand for recognition of China or for support for a UN seat for that nation. Students of foreign policy often lamented that American political leaders were constrained in this way from regularizing U.S. relations with China. And, indeed, public opinion polls over the years indicated a large majority of the American public were hostile to recognition of China.

But when President Nixon made his historic trip to China in 1972, the Harris poll found that 73 percent of the people approved. The notion that public opinion had been impeding better relations with China had likely been a myth. This illustrates the importance of leadership in setting public

When President Nixon made his historic trip to China in 1972, the Harris poll found that 73 percent of the people approved.   *(Photo: Wide World)*

opinion. Rather than policy on China being a reflection of public attitudes, public attitudes were a reflection of government policy. Change the policy and the attitudes change.

The case of China may exaggerate the changeability of public opinion and the real flexibility this leaves to leaders. Such flexibility is probably greater in relation to foreign affairs, about which citizens do not have firmly fixed opinions. On issues closer to home, the constraints of public opinion may be more rigid. Attitudes on racial matters are less easily manipulated, and the threats of electoral punishment by an unhappy public on such an issue may be more real to an elected official than was the supposed threat of public disapproval for a new China policy. On such matters public attitudes may thus place great constraints on leadership. Yet even in these areas, where citizen opinion seems firmer, one can never be sure of the extent to which it is malleable. As we have seen, public support for integrated schools increased substantially after the Supreme Court declared segregated schools to be unconstitutional.

A Nation of Many Publics: Finally, we can end our discussion of the impact of the public on government policy by making one major point. In most cases, one cannot think of the *public* as a single entity. There are many *publics:* There are those citizens who are inactive in politics; there are those who are active. There are those uninterested in political matters, and a smaller attentive public. There are, above all, differences in what it is that interests citizens. Different citizens become interested and active in relation to different sets of problems. This set of facts is important in understanding how the attitudes of the public affect governmental policy. Governmental leaders are likely to be responsive to certain parts of the public, especially to those parts that are attentive to a particular issue and active in relation to it. Rather than asking about the impact of public opinion as a whole, we have to ask about the impact of the special publics. This subject is so important we will cover it more extensively in the next chapter.

Controversy

When public opinion polls first began, many argued that they represented a new and powerful mode of democratic control by the citizenry over the government. Elections came only periodically and could not reveal the details of the citizenry's preference for one policy or another. But the public opinion poll would allow the leaders of the government to learn much more quickly and precisely what the public thinks about all sorts of issues and so would allow them to be guided by that opinion. In recent years, technological innovations have led some to suggest schemes for electronic polling, something that could resemble an instantaneous national vote on major issues. Homes of the future may have small computer terminals on which citizens could receive and send messages, and this makes it possible to envision a time when the public can quickly express its views on some public issue.

One Side

Government by instantaneous public opinion polling would be a disaster. The public does not have the information necessary to make wise choices on most public issues. Only a small, select part of the population has the knowledge and skills needed to make complex policy decisions. Furthermore, such decisions require careful deliberation and debate, something that is not possible when one has an instantaneous national vote on what will be a necessarily simplified question. The mass of the citizenry is too easily influenced in one direction or another by leaders. And any scheme for mass voting on specific issues will degenerate into an undemocratic battle over who can manipulate public opinion most effectively.

The Other Side

No matter what criticisms one can make of the American people, it remains true that they must rule if there is to be democracy in the United States. It is not democratic when a few leaders in Washington make policies on which the public has never expressed its opinion and with which it may disagree. Thus a system for popular vote on major issues is a system that makes America more democratic. And while it is true that the average citizen is not fully informed on all issues, he is more informed than anyone else in one crucial way—he knows his own interests. A system of mass voting on important issues will ensure that those interests are adequately expressed.

Suggested Readings

Two classics about American political belief systems are Alexis De Tocqueville, *Democracy in America*, ed. Phillips Bradley (2 vols.; New York: Knopf, 1945); and James Bryce, *The American Commonwealth* (2 vols., 3rd ed.; New York: Macmillan, 1899). In these books one will also find a statement of the "model" of democratic beliefs.

Gabriel A. Almond and Sidney Verba, *The Civic Culture: Political Attitudes and Democracy in Five Countries* (Boston: Little, Brown, 1965), views the political beliefs in America in comparison to other democracies. It is the source for the comparative information in this chapter and for the data on education and attitudes.

A general discussion of the impact of public opinion on policy makers is found in Sidney Verba and Norman H. Nie, *Participation in America: Political Democracy and Social Equality* (New York: Harper & Row, 1972).

Two other major works on the American public are V. O. Key, *Public Opinion and American Democracy* (New York: Knopf, 1961); and Angus Campbell, Philip E. Converse, Warren E. Miller, and Donald E. Stokes, *The American Voter* (New York: Wiley, 1960). Both are sources for many specific items in this chapter.

For the best statement on the lack of structure of political opinion, see Philip Converse's essay "The Nature of Belief Systems in Mass Politics," in David E. Apter, ed., *Ideology and Discontent* (New York: Free Press, 1964), pp. 206–261. For the sources of political beliefs in the process of socialization, see Richard Dawson and Kenneth Prewitt, *Political Socialization* (Boston: Little, Brown, 1969).

Patterns
of Conflict

Politics in America—as everywhere—is about conflict and competition. The reason is obvious. The government allocates benefits to the citizens in the society. And the major decisions of the government involve the questions of who gets the benefits and who pays the costs. Conflict would arise in America even if there were no differences of opinion among citizens on what kinds of policy the government ought to pursue, simply because the pie that the government is dividing among the citizenry is not infinite. Suppose everyone thought that the most important thing for the government to do was to spend more on roads. Conflict over government policies would still arise since choices have to be made as to what kind of road to build and where. Citizens in one part of the country would try to pressure the government to favor their area and not some other. Citizens in one town would prefer to have the new superhighway close enough to be convenient, but not so close as to disrupt their community. They would prefer that it run through the neighboring town.

But of course not everyone wants roads. Some citizens think that more should be spent on mass transportation systems and less on roads. Some think that spending on transportation is not as important as spending on education or housing. And some think that what is most important is cutting spending to cut taxes.

Thus conflict arises not only about who should benefit from a particular policy but also about which policy to pursue. And, to take it one step further, conflict arises also because a policy to benefit one group is perceived by others as a policy that hurts them; a decision to place public housing projects in suburban communities may be favored by Blacks and others who want integrated housing, but opposed by some suburban residents. Higher tariffs on imports of textiles from Japan may be favored by American textile manufacturers, but opposed by some clothing manufacturers who like to use the cheaper Japanese textiles or by consumer groups who prefer the lower-priced imports.

This chapter is about the groups that take part in competition and conflict for benefits. What is the nature of the groups that compete in the United States? Note that we talk about "groups" that compete, not about individuals. Political competition is usually among groups, not among isolated individuals. Consider the following headlines on newspaper stories:

Auto Workers Question Wage Guidelines
Legislature Seat for Chicanos Demanded
Republicans Ask Court to Nullify Convention Seats
Pilots Call for Hijack Protection

Women's Group Challenges All-Male Court Nominations
Parents' Group Calls for Bussing Boycott
Fishermen Protest Shortened Season
Conservationists Sue to Block H-Blast

In each case, we see a group of citizens demanding something, challenging something, expressing some position. They become politically relevant because they are groups of citizens, not isolated individuals. Groups such as those in the preceding paragraph have sometimes been described as "interest groups," sometimes as "pressure groups." The members of these groups have *interests* in common. This forms the basis for their working together in politics. And they apply *pressure* on the government to further these interests. Both terms are crucial—for not all categories of individuals have interests in common, and not all of those that have such interests act to express those views through pressure brought on the government. Which brings us to the question: Which groups in America are politically important and why?

What Makes a Group Politically Relevant?

Anything that a set of individuals have in common can be the basis of a group—in the previous examples we see groups based on sex (women); on occupation (auto workers); on leisure time preference (fishermen); on political belief (Republicans); on ethnic background (Chicanos). But the number of characteristics we could name that might be the basis of a group is almost infinite: What about citizens of Japanese descent, tea drinkers, red-haired citizens, hot-rod racers, people who live in odd-numbered houses, people opposed to vivisection, sausage makers? Not all the groups are politically relevant. Chicanos and Blacks are relevant political groupings. A few years ago women were not; now they are. Suburbanites may or may not be, depending on the particular suburb. Hot rodders usually are not but might become such if they want a local town to set up a drag strip. But residents in odd-numbered houses are unlikely ever to be a politically relevant group.

Since politics is structured so centrally around groups making claims on the government, it is vital to ask why some social characteristics form the basis of politically relevant groups while others do not. Why are Chicanos politically relevant but tea drinkers not? Why women now, but not women fifteen years ago? Three attributes convert a set of people with some characteristics in common into a politically relevant group: common interest, self-conscious awareness of the interest, and organization.

Common Interests

A group is likely to be politically relevant if the characteristic that defines the group—sex or race or occupation or type of house—is some-

Not all groups are politically relevant.   (Photo: Wide World)

thing that creates a common interest, and, more particularly, a common interest for which governmental policy is relevant—that is, an interest that can best be furthered by some action on the part of the government. Blacks clearly have such common interests in housing policy, desegregation policy, voting rights, and so forth. Tea drinkers also have such interests in common, interests relating to government tariff policy on tea. But residents of odd-numbered houses do not, and it is hard to believe that they ever would.

However, we must add one other qualification, since not all common interests lead to the formation of politically relevant groups. Some interests are more important than others. Tea drinkers may have interests in common, but they are not vital enough to arouse them to action. The change in the price of tea that might come from a change in tariff has too little impact on them to make any difference. It is hard, on the other hand, for an American Black to be unaware of those policies that affect Blacks. They represent interests closely touching on their central problems.

But, though tea drinkers may not consider the price of tea to be important, tea importers do. The price of tea, as affected by tariff policy, has a large impact on the lives of those who earn their living from the import and sale of tea; it has a small impact on those for whom it is but one item in a shopping bag.

This illustrates a most important principle of politics, and one that structures much of American political life. Sets of citizens with different characteristics are interested in different areas of governmental policy. Tea importers and tea drinkers may be interested in tea tariffs. Coffee drinkers probably could not care less. Chicanos—citizens of Mexican-American descent—will be interested in Spanish-language instruction in the schools. Citizens in states with no Spanish-speaking minority will be uninterested. Furthermore, even when several sets of citizens have interests relevant to a particular area of governmental policy, the interests may be very intense for some, but relatively mild to others. Chicanos will be interested in Spanish-language instruction in the public schools, as will the non-Spanish-speaking residents of their communities. But for the former it represents a crucial issue relating to the integrity of their culture, to the latter perhaps a less crucial issue having to do with the cost of schools.

What this means is that in relation to any policy some citizens may be intensely concerned, others will be only mildly involved, and many others will be indifferent. This fact structures much of the political conflict in America. We will give some examples soon.

The word "interest" is a very general word and we have not defined it. Perhaps its meaning is clear enough so that it can be considered what logicians call a "primitive" term. What must be stressed though is the vast range of possible interests that citizens can have and that can form the basis of politically relevant groups.

Economic Interest: These are the ones that come to mind most easily when one thinks of the interests that citizens pursue in political activity. Workers seek higher wages. If the government tries to hold wages down by direct or indirect controls, this interest in wages is likely to form the basis of political activity on the part of workers and unions. Businessmen are concerned about price controls, about tariffs, and about government policies that affect the "economic climate"—all because such policies affect their incomes. And, of course, all citizens have interests in that inevitable governmental policy—taxes.

Power Interests: But economic interests are not the only ones that motivate citizens. We can also talk of power interests—citizens want, demand, and work for political control over their own lives and over the government of their community. Thus there are conflicts over what kind of person gets elected or appointed to office, who has access to the vote, how districts are zoned for elections. Such political control can, to be sure, be used to further economic interests. And it is often used for that purpose. But over and beyond the way in which political power is used, it is desired by citizens as an end in itself. Many of the most bitter conflicts in America are over the question: Who controls the government?

Way-of-Life Interests: It is hard to give a more precise term to this broad set of interests. They are not clearly economic or political, but represent desires to lead a particular kind of life. Citizens have interests in keeping a community the way it is—residential and not industrial; White and nonintegrated; small and not large. Or they may have interests in changing a community—to make it integrated, to improve its cultural life. These interests, as well, can form the basis of political groupings. They are interests that citizens can hold to be most salient.

Self-Awareness

It is not enough that a set of citizens have interests in common; they have to be aware of those interests. Interests become politically important when they are not merely objective, but subjective as well. American Blacks have such objective interests and, furthermore, are aware of them. Other groups may also have interests in common but have little self-awareness. American consumers come to mind as an example, as do women, though in both cases there has been a growing sense of self-consciousness among at least some members of each set of citizens.

Organization and Leadership

The last attribute that makes a set of citizens into a politically relevant group is organization and leadership. Groups that are organized can press their claims on the government more effectively; groups that have leadership have spokesmen who can represent them to the government. And such leadership can arouse the group members to greater efforts and commitment.

Self-awareness and leadership mutually reinforce each other. One of the prime tasks of a leader or potential leader is to arouse the self-awareness of his followers. When that happens social movements are born. If not, one has a spokesman, but no one for whom he speaks.

Common interests, self-awareness, organization—these make for relevant political groups. Blacks in America have all three. Many economic and professional groups such as unionized workers, farmers, and doctors have all three. In some cases one finds the first two components but not the last. Groups such as migratory farm workers have had till recently common interests and some self-awareness, but little organization. Groups with interests in common but little shared sense of group membership and little organization have been called potential groups. For a long time such a description might have fit consumers or city dwellers who suffered from polluted air. Potential groups are turned into more active groups as there begins to grow a consumer (or bad-air-sufferer) consciousness as well as organizations dedicated to furthering these interests.

Groups in America: Many and Varied

The United States is a vast and diverse country. There are many bases of politically relevant groups. Let us consider some of the more important bases of groups and cleavage in America.

Ethnicity and Race

If we wish to describe the various groups that make up the American political universe, it is best to start with something basic like ethnic identity. When we talk of ethnics or ethnic politics, we tend to think of Irish Americans, or Polish Americans, or Jewish Americans, or, perhaps, Black Americans. There is no generally agreed-upon definition of ethnicity, but the phenomenon to which we refer is fairly clear. Ethnicity refers to those basic ties or that fundamental sense of identity that comes with the assumption of common origin. This sense of identity has been called "primordial." It is transmitted through the family. It is associated with the place one lives or with the place one is from. It forms the core of the answer an individual might give if asked the vague but vital question "What are you?"

Such primordial ties that go to make up one's ethnic identity are often associated with more specific social characteristics. Language is one of these characteristics. If people speak a language in common, they have a fundamental bond—that of the ability to communicate. True, they may not communicate or they may communicate hostile messages. But the identification based on one's language—especially when there are others around speaking an alternative language—is crucial. Common place of residence is often associated with ethnicity—people who have lived together for a long time develop common characteristics and common bonds. Or—and this is relevant particularly to the United States—common place of origin may be vital. In addition common characteristics such as race or customs hold such primordial groups together.

The power of these primordial ties is apparent around the world. They divide nation from nation, and they divide within nations as well. And the divisions can create overt conflict. Nigeria, Belgium, Canada, Ireland, India, Ceylon—the list could be made quite long of nations where ethnic differences lead to divisions, disputes, and violence.

But, we are told, not in the United States; not where we are "one nation indivisible." America, so the cliché goes, is a melting pot. It is inhabited by people from Europe, Asia, and Africa who melted together, mixed, and formed a common American citizenry. Like all cliches, this one has some truth. For one thing, the immigrants from all these continents have by and large become American citizens. (In some countries, immigrants may live for generations without obtaining local citizenship—either because they prefer not to or because they are not allowed to. So this fact is not as obvious as it may sound.)

Furthermore, the stamp of "Americanization" was placed on all these immigrants in terms of language. The people who poured into the United States in the latter part of the nineteenth and early twentieth century wound up a generation later speaking a single language. The earlier language sometimes (but rarely) survived. But the dominant language became English. Again this is not an inevitable result of merging in a common country. In many lands, multiple languages remain side by side, and sooner or later form the basis of conflict. The linguistic homogeneity of America is in part the result of deliberate policy. Educators and government officials believed that to be an American meant to speak English, and the schools enforced this in their training of immigrant children. Former Justice Felix Frankfurter of the United States Supreme Court, who came to the United States from Austria as a youth, reports that he said something in German on one of his first days in school. The teacher slapped him and told the rest of the class not to speak to him unless he spoke English. It is important to note that the movement toward English was supported by the immigrants themselves, who largely accepted the argument that to be an American meant to speak English.

Thus, so the history goes, out of the multitudes from Europe and Asia and Africa, the melting pot made one nation. Not quite. Some groups did not easily melt. Those of other races did not fit the melting pot model. Blacks, of course, were in a separate category, denied citizenship and freedom until the Civil War. Even then they received only a token citizenship without its real benefits. Similarly—though not as drastically—immigrants from Asia were denied full citizenship. In the same way, the only Americans who were not immigrants—the American Indians—were denied full citizenship and assimilation through the melting pot. The melting pot never fully applied to non-Caucasians.

But to take the matter further, neither did it apply fully to White immigrants. Long after the melting pot was supposed to have created its homogeneous mix, ethnic identity remains, ethnic organizations flourish, and American politics is enlivened by the clash of ethnic interests.

The manifestations of this ethnicity are found throughout American politics. Ethnic voting patterns persist. Groups like Irish Catholics or Polish Catholics traditionally support the Democratic party, usually voting over 70 percent Democratic. Or ethnic voting patterns may take the form of support for candidates of the same ethnic group. Sometimes ethnic politics takes the form of particular concern for happenings in the "old country"—Americans from Eastern Europe have had a special concern with political problems in that area of the world, Jewish Americans with developments in Israel.

There are two reasons for the persistence of ethnic politics, both having to do with the interests of the various ethnic groups. One set of interests is directly associated with ethnicity, another indirectly. The direct interests involve the desire—despite the melting pot—to preserve and foster ethnic identity. At earlier times, these interests involved the desire to live near, depend on, marry with others who shared a similar background and language—for only in that way could one find security in an alien land. Nor have things changed that much. The hyphenated Americans who long ago should have been ex-ethnics have been rediscovering the language, the culture, the history, and the customs of the old country. The richness of American life that was almost lost through pressures for Americanization may still be preserved by self-conscious concern of ethnic groups for their heritage.

More important politically may be the fact that the various ethnic groups in America have had indirect interests associated with their ethnicity. The fact that many ethnic groups were immigrants is important here. The groups who today form the various ethnic communities tended to come as immigrant groups to the United States. And each successive group found itself to be the most deprived. The Irish when they came in the middle and late part of the nineteenth century found themselves to be in the poorest neighborhoods, to hold the most menial jobs, and to live in communities where the government was controlled by established residents. Their struggle was with the older Yankee residents for economic advance, residential mobility, and political power. A generation later, when the Italian immigrants came, history repeated itself—with the Irish now likely to be in a somewhat more stable economic position and in control of the local government.

The history of Black immigration from the South to northern cities resembles—at least in part—a recapitulation of this history. Like the older immigrants, the Blacks find themselves in the lowest positions in relation to housing, jobs, and income. And they often face a city government controlled by other ethnic groups. The struggle takes the same form—for better living conditions and for political control of the local government. But the analogy between Blacks and other ethnic groups is far from perfect, as we shall indicate shortly.

Let us consider some of these ethnic groups more closely.

The "White Ethnics": American politics—particulary in the large cities—was for many years an ethnic politics. The waves of immigrants who came to America in the late nineteenth and early twentieth centuries often settled in these cities. And because such immigrants came in groups, with one family member following another or groups of immigrants seeking places where they would find familiar faces or a familiar language, large numbers from the same place of origin would concentrate in particular cities. These groups—the Irish, the Poles and Slavs, the East European Jews, the Italians—usually occupied the lowest economic rungs in these cities. But their numbers, and the ease with which citizenship was available, gave them one basis of power—the vote.

The large urban political machines in New York, Boston, and Chicago grew on the basis of these ethnic voters. In return for the vote, the large urban machine offered the new immigrant help in getting a job, aid if there was trouble with the police, perhaps a Christmas basket—important comforts in a hostile new country. In precisely this way, support for the party machines was cemented.

These White ethnic groups have usually been overwhelmingly Democratic—and this is particulary true for Catholics and Jews. There are many reasons. The established groups—the White Protestant Yankees—tended to be Republican and to control the local government, and the Democratic party became the political channel available for their opponents. The Democratic party, furthermore, being somewhat less a party of the business elite, was more willing to provide the social services needed by these new groups—though such services more often took the form of specific informal benefits to the party faithful than the form of legislation to help those in need.

These immigrant groups must not of course be considered simply a single group. There were Jews and Italians and Irish and so forth. And the important point about them may be the order in which they came. Thus the Italian groups in many American cities started out supporting the Republican party because the Democratic was the province of the Irish who had come a generation earlier. New York provides an example of such a case. But the Italians switched allegiance to the Democratic party over time, often displacing the Irish in leadership positions.

The White ethnics illustrate the three characteristics that go to make a set of citizens into a politically relevant group. They had common interests because they were newcomers in an unfamiliar country; they were self-consciously aware of this commonality because they lived in ethnic neighborhoods; and they were organized by the political parties who courted their votes. This was in the early part of this century. For several decades now, observers have, for a number of reasons, been sounding the death knell of ethnic politics. As the generations pass, the common set of interests that hold the ethnic groups together fade. They are no longer new residents holding the most marginal jobs; their children move into the mainstream of the American economy. Many move out of the ethnic neighborhoods to the newer suburbs, into areas that are ethnically mixed. This reduces the level of common interest and the possibility of developing a strong self-awareness. Lastly the urban machine has lost much of its power and function; the welfare services it provided have been taken over by federal social security and other welfare programs. In short, the basis for ethnic politics seems to be fading.

But though ethnicity is not as powerful a political factor as it once was, it has remained remarkably resilient. After a generation of attempts to bury the customs and identities of the Old World, many third-generation immigrant children are returning to a sense of ethnic self-consciousness. Ethnic voting has persisted in many cities—the candidate with the right ethnic name can count on support from many of similar background. Ethnic associations and, in some cities like Chicago, ethnic neighborhoods remain intact.

Likewise, the Democratic party affiliation has remained generally intact. Many commentators expected such affiliation to weaken—as the White ethnics moved to the suburbs and improved their social and economic status it was assumed that they would switch to the Republican party. For a time in the 1950s it looked as if this was happening when the Republicans came close to capturing a plurality of Catholic votes in the Presidential elections of 1952 and 1956. (Even in those elections, the Jewish vote remained solidly Democratic.) But the defection of the Catholic ethnics to the Republican party may have been more a function of the appeal of Dwight Eisenhower than a permanent shift of allegiance. Today young, upwardly mobile Catholic college graduates, several generations removed from immigrant status, are still more likely than their Protestant counterparts to vote for Democratic candidates. Indeed, this situation may be considered an illustration of a general point made in the last chapter. Partisan affiliation tends to be a stable and long-term aspect of an individual's political makeup. Once it is formed, it is likely to be passed on from generation to generation. Thus the partisan affiliation of ethnic groups persists even after the historical circumstances that led to that affiliation fade. (See Table 4.1.)

In part this resurgence of ethnic politics represents a reaction to a

Table 4.1 Ethnic Support for the Democratic Party Persists

Percentage Identifying Themselves as Democrats Among the Following Groups:

White Protestants (Anglo-Saxon, Scandinavian, or German origin)	47%
Catholics (Irish origin)	70%
Catholics (Italian origin)	67%
Catholics (Polish origin)	77%
Jews	62%
Blacks	89%
Among all citizens	60%

Source: Based on data from Sidney Verba and Norman H. Nie, *Participation in America: Political Democracy and Social Equality* (New York: Harper & Row, 1972).

challenge from other groups—in particular from Black Americans. Many of the American ethnic groups have "made it"—skilled work, a reasonably good income, a house and car, children in a good school. Challenged by what they perceive as a threat from expanding Black neighborhoods, and challenged by a group with what seems to be a firmer sense of identity—the Black militants—White ethnics have begun to reaffirm their ethnic ties.

Blacks: The melting pot, as we have pointed out, never applied to Blacks. Other groups might come to participate fully in America but the racial barrier was harder to cross. Black Americans have been, from the beginning, important in American politics—but as the subjects of governmental policy, not as participants in politics. The history of America from the early nineteenth century through the Civil War was in large part a history of conflict about Blacks. And since the Civil War, a large part of our politics has revolved around the politics of race.

In the pre–Civil War United States, Blacks were excluded from participation in political life. Even in states where there was no slavery, free Blacks were usually denied the vote. As we have suggested above, there is some analogy between the current position of Black Americans as the newest immigrants to northern cities and the position of the earlier white immigrants. Such an analogy is useful, for it helps us to see some general patterns underlying the experiences of various groups. But one ought never to carry such analogies too far, and in relation to the position of Blacks in America it would be carrying it much too far not to notice as well the vast disparities in the position of the American Blacks and the Irish or the Italian or Eastern European White immigrants to America. The major differences are summarized in two words—slavery and race.

Consider the position of the White immigrants to the United States in the nineteenth century. They came impoverished and ill educated; large proportions were illiterate. They came into circumstances where they were looked down on and discriminated against. They were crowded into urban ghettos. But their situation was sharply different from that of Blacks. The White immigrants entered a nation where the dominant ideology—as numerous observers had noted—was one of equality; where the aristocratic tradition of Europe whereby one's position in life was fully determined at birth had been rejected. And they entered a society where the laws supported this egalitarianism. By the 1840s universal male suffrage was the general rule in the United States. But this ideology of equality and this openness of the electoral system were clearly limited to Whites—in the North as well as in the South.

The Civil War and the constitutional changes that followed it—the Thirteenth, Fourteenth, and Fifteenth Amendments—sought to change this situation. The American Black could not be denied citizenship, the vote, or the full protection of the laws.

Or at least so the Constitution said—it had still to be fully applied in practice. As part of the process of reconciliation of the North and South (of northern Whites and southern Whites, that is) the meaning of these amendments was watered down. Votes were effectively taken away from Blacks in the South. Segregated facilities were legally accepted. And in many ways the gains for Blacks at the end of the Civil War were seriously reduced.

Political conflict, as we have pointed out, arises when groups have conflicting goals but are mutually interdependent. If they have no conflicting goals, there is no conflict. If they are not mutually interdependent, they can each go their own way and there is no need for conflict over what policy the government ought to pursue. The conflict between American Blacks and American Whites arises because of a combination of mutual interdependence and the conflicting goals. Where the conflict between goals is severe and there appears to be little chance of agreement, one solution is to reduce the mutual interdependence—to separate. And throughout the history of the Blacks in America, this has been a theme. In the early days of the Republic many prominent White leaders thought that the solution to the issue of slavery would be a return of Blacks to Africa. And Black leaders have often supported that position—the most striking expression of it probably being the movement under Marcus Garvey in the 1920s for a return of Blacks to Africa. This movement—though it did receive support in a segment of the Black population—never received support among the bulk of American Blacks and never has been a fully realistic alternative. Its more recent forms—manifested in the various versions of Black nationalism and separatism—calls for separation within the United States: separate communities, separate schools and institutions, sometimes separate states or sections of the country.

The failure of the Garvey movement and the unreality of the movement for a fully separate state point up the fact that political conflict will continue, for mutual interdependence cannot be removed. The Black nationalist movements are nonetheless significant, not for the fact of their specific goal but for the increased consciousness of Black identity that they reflect and that they foster. As we have pointed out, one of the factors that makes a collectivity of citizens into a politically important and effective group is the sense of identity that binds them together. And this has been fostered to a large extent by the sense of identity that comes with the sense of deprivation of Blacks in America.

American Blacks have become a potent political force in recent years because they have developed two of the characteristics that make groups politically relevant—self-awareness and organization. The third characteristic—common interests—is something that has characterized American Blacks from the earliest time. But interests in common are not enough if the group is not self-consciously aware of these interests. This self-consciousness grew in the 1950s and 1960s.

The growth of Black self-consciousness has many sources. The role of the civil rights movement of the 1950s and 1960s is crucial. As important is the role of the mass media—especially television—in communicating the new movement across the entire Black community. In an earlier era, a civil rights demonstration in one part of the country might have little impact on others. But when a nation is linked together in a common communications network, the possibility increases of creating a community among people living in different regions, of people living in cities and in rural areas.

The increased importance of Blacks in American political life depends also upon organization. The history of the recent Black movement has been a history of organization as well: the NAACP, the Southern Christian Leadership Council, CORE, the Black Muslims, the Black Panthers, Operation Breadbasket. The list—and it could be made much longer—illustrates how many and diverse are the bases of Black political organization. They are by no means organized in one common group, nor are they all organized. But organizations, of all sorts, are the vital means of making Blacks a potent political force.

Other Minority Groups: Blacks are not the only racial or ethnic minority. We have seen how White ethnic politics has had a resurgence at least in part as a response to what is perceived as a Black challenge. Other minority groups—Chicanos, American Indians—have also moved into active politics. In each case their activity illustrates our principle of the three characteristics that make a group of individuals into a politically relevant group—interests or needs in common, self-awareness, organization.

Chicanos, for instance, long have had common interests and needs. Speaking a language that was foreign in the United States, often relegated to the lowest-paying agricultural jobs, discriminated against in housing and schools, these Americans of Mexican origin were largely politically quiescent until recent times. However—again perhaps in partial response to similar activities among Black Americans, but also in response to such leaders as Cesar Chavez—they have moved into the center of political conflict.

They form an interesting contrast to another group—Americans of Japanese origin—many of whom, like the Chicanos, live on the West Coast. Japanese Americans have also had a long history of common problems and common discriminations. For long they were barred from American citizenship and from owning land. And in World War II most Japanese Americans were shipped off to concentration camps—euphemistically called "relocation centers"—as dangerous aliens. In addition to this history of common problems and common discriminations, Japanese Americans have maintained a fairly strong sense of group identification.

But unlike Chicanos and Blacks, Japanese Americans are not an active political force. The reason for inactivity is that one of the three components is missing; in this case, though, there is a sense of identification and even some organization; there is little common political interest. Japanese Americans face almost no housing or schooling discriminations and have moved into high-status jobs in most places. With little common political interest—that is, no set of policies that they want the government to pursue or to stop pursuing—they do not become a potent political force.

Other Types of Groups

One could go on for many pages listing and describing the various politically relevant groups in America. And—there being so many ways in which citizens group together—we would never exhaust the description. Furthermore, as we began to exhaust the list of relevant groups at one point in time, new ones would be forming and old ones fading from political involvement. Let us, then, merely sketch some of the other *types* of groups one finds in America. We can then turn to the more interesting question of how they relate one to another.

Occupational Groups: Occupation represents a most important way in which Americans divide up into politically relevant groupings. For all individuals, the fate of one's occupational group—how well teachers, or farmers, or doctors, or plumbers are doing—is crucial. But occupational groups vary in the extent to which they are politically relevant—and they vary in this in relation to the three characteristics we have mentioned: common interests, self-awareness, and organization.

Not all occupational groups have common interests to the same extent. Small shopkeepers represent an important occupational grouping, but its members do not necessarily have a "common fate": One shopkeeper may flourish while another goes bankrupt. Of course, there are cases where they will have common problems. All shopkeepers may be hurt by inflation or a business downturn, but in these cases it will have an impact on them as members of the general economy, not specifically as shopkeepers. Or the shopkeepers in a particular town may be hurt by the development of a shopping center outside the town. But in this case, they will likely form a politically relevant group on a local basis.

Compared with shopkeepers or lawyers, such groups as teachers or automobile workers are much more likely to have a common fate and a set of common interests. Teachers have common interests because their salaries and working conditions are all set by the governments for which they work; automobile workers because they depend on a single industry.

In addition to having interests in common, there is the question of the extent to which these interests are affected by governmental policy. The more the government is active in relation to a particular occupation, the more the occupational group is likely to be politically involved. Doctors and lawyers offer a contrast here. Governmental policies that affect the practice of medicine—from the provision of community and state hospitals to Medicare to drug regulations—are much more extensive than those that affect the practice of law. And doctors as an organized occupational group have, through the American Medical Association (AMA), been most active in politics. Here is a good illustration of a point made earlier about the differential degree to which sets of citizens are concerned about particular interests. All citizens have an interest in health care. But the medical profession—because it earns its living through health care, because it is organized and has leadership—has had a more potent voice in such matters than has the much larger number of ordinary citizens.

Note that we are dealing here with the extent to which various occupational groups become politically active *in relation to the interests of that occupation.* Lawyers are generally more active in politics than are doctors; indeed, they are more active than most other professions. They are more likely than members of other professions to run for office or to take governmental appointments. But they do so not as representatives of the interests of the legal profession (though of course the legal profession's interests may get well represented that way).

This difference among occupational groups is related to a simple but important generalization about politics: Where the government is active, citizens are likely to be active as well. When new government programs begin that touch the lives of particular groups, they are likely to become more politically involved.

Occupational groups also differ in the degree of their self awareness and organization. These two characteristics are, of course, linked. The more a group is organized, the more it is likely that the members will be aware of their common problems and the common relevance of the government to them. Farmers have been a potent political force because they have been organized in a variety of farm organizations. Or, rather, those farmers who have been organized have been a potent force; those who have not (poorer farmers, tenant farmers, and so on) have not. A most important distinction is between organized and unorganized labor. Those workers who are not unionized are the ones from whom one hears the least—both because they have no organization to speak for them and because they have no organization to foster a sense of self-awareness. This was the case for many decades for such groups as teachers and migratory workers. Teachers remained unorganized because of a belief that unionization was not appropriate for such a professional group; migratory workers remained unorganized because the conditions of their work made it difficult for them to form groups. In recent years, as both groups have begun to develop organization, they have become more politically active and more potent.

We have not mentioned one way in which the American population might divide up occupationally. Rather than being divided into specific groups—auto workers, or high school teachers, or small shop owners, or doctors—politics could be structured around broad divisions between "workers" and "management." In other countries such has been the case, with workers organized into a Socialist or Communist party while another party or parties represents the more bourgeois segments of society. For a variety of reasons, some of which we shall discuss later when we consider the American parties, this type of alignment has not evolved in America. One can debate whether this is due to a lack of objective interests in common among workers, or a lack of self-awareness of their interests, or a failure of leadership and organization. Or perhaps, as some argue, the needs of workers are satisfied by a strong union movement. Whether this is good (because it lowers the intensity of conflict in America) or bad (because it prevents the adequate representation of the needs of workers) is also debatable.

Income Groups: Income is of course closely related to occupation, and the two go together to create what is often referred to as social class. Many have wondered why the poor in America do not form a more clear-cut and vital political movement. Why do not farmers and laborers join to form a political party that would redistribute the resources in America?

Attempts have been made to form such parties. And in recent years, one sees the formation of poor peoples' coalitions cutting across occupation and race. Such movements represent a potentially important force in America, and one cannot predict their future success or failure. But the fact that they are often described as "coalitions" indicates one of the problems with the formation of political groupings around income. It is true that the poor have interests in common, but they also have much that keeps them from coming together to work on those interests. For one thing, as we shall point out in the next chapter, political action depends on resources such as time and money. The poor have less money by definition, and time is often something that they can ill afford. And the poor are themselves divided by occupation—farmers and laborers have some interests in common but they have many that are not in common—and by race and ethnicity. As a political group, the poor remain potentially important, but income is not yet a strong basis for cohesive political action.

Regional Groups: The place where people live and work also forms the basis for common interests. Different regions, different states and cities, suburbs versus central cities—all these differences may have political impact. Regional politics has, of course, been historically important in the United States, the South being the most distinctive region in terms of culture, history, and political behavior. Its voters tended to vote in a distinctive way—traditionally for the Democratic party long after the ideological basis for that affiliation had faded. And its representatives in Congress formed a distinctive bloc—often voting with northern Republicans to form a strong conservative coalition. The solid South has become less solid since Republicans began to make inroads in the Eisenhower years. Industrialization and population migration, as well as the political awakening of the southern Black, have brought massive changes in the social and political life of that region. Yet it remains the most distinctive American region.

With the South one sees another example of the importance of common interests and common experiences with governmental policy. Southerners had the shared experience of the Civil War and Reconstruction. Even when long past, these experiences left traces that manifested themselves in heightened self-awareness of their distinctiveness as a region.

And note one other fact: Regional politics in the United States is important because it is always well organized. By that we simply mean that elections in America have a locational or regional structure. We elect representatives to Congress from particular geographically defined districts or particular states. The point is so obvious that we may miss its importance. Why not elect representatives from occupational groups—all plumbers elect a certain number, all lawyers, all farmers? Or representatives by race —the Blacks elect theirs, the Whites theirs, the Chicanos theirs? Why not indeed? Other countries have experimented with such alternative modes of representation and one can make an argument for such a scheme. The argument for geographic basis of representation is that citizens living in the same area have similar interests, but this is only partially true. In some respects we have interests in common with those who live in the same congressional district with us; but in some respects we may have more interests in common with citizens of similar occupation or religion or race living in other parts of the state or nation.

But whatever the basis of representation, and probably none is perfect, the fact is that the American system is organized on the basis of place of residence, and there is little likelihood that this will change. This automatically makes geography important as a basis of citizen interests. As we shall see in Chapter 13, where we discuss the representativeness of Congress, this territorial basis of representation has a major impact on how the government operates.

One major grouping concerned with location has recently emerged in America and has given rise to a conflict between those in central core cities of our metropolitan areas and their surrounding suburbs. The conflict is between the citizens who have moved to suburbs to avoid the noise, crowding, and social tensions of the cities and those who remain in the central cities for whom the noise, crowding, and social tensions are an unavoidable part of life. The latter claim that the problems of the central city could be solved if those in the suburbs would join in the solution—if their schools were open to central city children, if their communities would construct low-cost housing. The suburbanites often reply that these are the problems of the cities, and they are pleased to have left them behind. That the central city resident is often Black and the suburbanite White does not, as we shall see, make the problem easier to solve.

Religious Groups: In many nations, religious conflict is severe. In America religious divisions have been politically relevant but not the source of severe conflict. Catholics have had a more traditional allegiance with the Democratic party, Jewish groups have been active in relation to American policy in the Middle East, fundamentalist Protestant groups have lobbied for Blue Laws and the like. When the first Catholic candidate (Al Smith) ran for the Presidency in 1928, he was bitterly opposed by many Protestant groups who thought that his election would represent a take-over of the United States by the Catholic church. When the second Catholic candidate (John F. Kennedy) ran and won in 1960, he was also opposed by many for similar reasons. But his behavior in office in no way could be considered distinctively Catholic. It may be that the Kennedy experience will lead to a decline in the religious basis for political groupings.

Perhaps the major reason for the absence of severe religious conflict in American politics is the constitutional prohibition of laws affecting matters of religious belief. If our generalization is correct, groups become politically active when governmental policy is directed at them. The constitutional bar to legislation affecting religion may explain why religion has not been the explosive issue it might have been. On the other hand, constitutional prohibitions do not eliminate all religious-based issues. The exact meaning of the constitutional provision for the separation of church and state has given rise to conflict in the past and continues to do so. Is it a violation of the Constitution if a city pays for school buses for children going to Catholic schools? Is it a violation if there is prayer in the schools? On such issues one finds religious groupings active and concerned. Similarly, religion can affect a group's attitude on foreign policy—as is evidenced by the strong views of American Jews on relations with Israel.

Sex and Age Groups: Is either sex or age the basis for politically relevant grouping? Ten years ago one might have said "Maybe" for age (there having been politically relevant movements among old and retired people from time to time in American history)—but "No" for sex. Men and women, at least since the women's suffrage movement, did not seem to have differing political interests. In recent times, of course, age has become a potentially important political distinction with talk of a "generation gap," with the increasingly large numbers of elderly citizens, with the issue of the vote for 18-year-olds, with youth movements and the youth culture. Evidence suggests that the organized manifestations of youth represent a small proportion of that group and a rather distinct portion at that—those on college campuses. But youth may be a politically relevant group—at least for some youth. And the same is probably true of women. Although the proportion of American women active in women's liberation groups may be quite small, the potential group to be mobilized is, of course, large: 51 percent of the population, to be precise.

The case of women illustrates the importance of self-awareness as well as common interest in creating a politically relevant group. The leaders of women's groups complain of various forms of discrimination. But they do not refer to new grievances invented in the few years since that movement has burst on the scene. Rather the practices referred to—job discrimination,

Creating awareness and group identity is a prime task for the leadership of a new social movement.   *(Photo: Wide World)*

stereotyping, and so forth — are old ones. But the self-conscious awareness of such practices — fostered by a few active leaders and the mass media — is what creates the group.

Critics of social movements such as Women's Liberation or Black militant movements often accuse these groups of inventing the problems of which they complain. "Women never knew they were discriminated against until the Women's Lib types told them." But that is exactly what political leadership attempts to do and must do if it is to be successful in creating a movement. It must create awareness of problems within a group in order to mobilize that group for political action.

Special Concern Groups: We have been characterizing groups of American citizens in terms of certain of their enduring social characteristics — their ethnic background, occupation, sex, age, place of residence. These enduring characteristics are likely to be at the base of enduring political groupings, but they become politically relevant, we have argued, only if accompanied by an awareness of some interest related to that group characteristic — a Black political interest, a women's political interest.

But there are times when groupings are based more directly on shared interests, and less on basic social characteristics. As with basic social characteristics, the variety of specific interests is also vast. Groups form about common recreational interests (skiing, hunting, bird watching); around social concerns (mental health, pollution, governmental corruption); around intellectual or cultural interests (book clubs, literary groups, art groups).

As with the other groupings, these special concern groups become politically relevant when there is some way in which their interests are affected by governmental action or inaction. For instance, those recreational groups may begin as organizations with no particular interest in government policy; they may be simply groups of citizens with common interests in skiing or hiking or bird watching. But as the pursuit of these nonpolitical interests becomes dependent on governmental programs—on the preservation of a wilderness area, for instance—these groups can become important political actors.

The Effects of Multiple Groups: Crosscutting Affiliations

One could go on for a long time listing the groups that form the basis of American politics; there are many more candidates for the list presented above. And if one wished to speculate about the potential groups that might arise in the future, the list would go on indefinitely. New events, new issues, trigger off new political groupings. Recent commentators have talked of a potential "generation gap"—not between generations, but rather within generations. There is growing evidence of sharp difference in attitudes, expectations, and preferences between those young people who have gone to college and those who have not. The strongest opposition to "youth culture"—essentially a culture of the college generation and the middle class—often comes from the youth who have not gone beyond high school. One can think of other potential conflicts. The point is that these cannot be specifically predicted. And it is much more important to understand the general dynamics of group formation and the bases of conflict among groups.

Diversity of Groups

Let us consider several general conclusions that can be derived from the list of groups mentioned above. The conclusions will help us understand how the relations among groups work themselves out.

1. One point is clear: There is a wide diversity of groups and potential groups in America. There is no single set of dominant groupings.

2. More important is the fact that the groupings are not mutually exclusive. Each citizen belongs to many groups at once. Citizens have at the same time ethnic identities, occupational statuses, regional locations, religions.

Which of these affiliations will be important politically? The answer is that it varies. At some times and in relation to some issues, one affiliation will be important, at other times other affiliations will be important. The Catholic steelworker living in a suburb of Cleveland will sometimes act politically as a steelworker. He will support policies or candidates based on his views as to the interests of steelworkers or based on the advice of his union. At other times, he may act as a Catholic, perhaps voting for a candidate who is of the same faith or considering an issue such as abortion law or aid for parochial schools from that point of view. And at other times he may act as a suburbanite, perhaps opposing plans of the government of the central city to tax suburban dwellers who work in the cities.

In short, citizens have many potential political interests. At times they will act in relation to one, at times in relation to another.

Or, at least that is the case with most Americans. For some, one identification overrides all others—Black militants respond to all issues in terms of racial identity, militant members of women's liberation groups in terms of sexual identity, and so forth. The consequences for political life are important. If a citizen has a variety of identifications, he is likely to hold none as intensely as does the citizen who concentrates all his energies on one. The result for the citizen with multiple identifications is a greater willingness to compromise, less firmness in action. The "single-identity" citizen is likely to be more militant, firmer in position, less compromising.

Crosscutting vs. Reinforcing Affiliations

An important characteristic of group identifications in America is the extent to which they *crosscut* rather than *reinforce* one another.

Let us explain what we mean by these terms, since they help us to understand how political conflict in America works itself out. Imagine a society where people are divided by religion (into Catholics and Protestants), by occupation (into workers and managers), and by place of residence (into suburbanites and central city dwellers). If these three divisions of society were reinforcing rather than crosscutting, one would find that all citizens who were similar on one characteristic would be similar on the other two. The society might be divided into:

Catholic workers living   Protestant managers living
in the central city   in the suburbs

And insofar as there were interests associated with these identifications, the society would be divided into two groups having totally divergent interests. Catholics want aid to parochial schools; Protestants do not.

Workers want controls over profits; managers want controls over wages. City dwellers want suburbanites to share in the cost of urban services; suburbanites do not. Thus the society would be divided into groups with the following interests:

One group would be:	The other group would be:
a. In favor of aid to parochial schools.	a. Opposed to parochial school aid.
b. In favor of control over profits.	b. Opposed to controls over profits.
c. In favor of taxing the suburbs to pay for city services.	c. Opposed to taxing the suburbs to pay for city services.

Such a situation is likely to be one of high political tension. The two groups have nothing in common. They are divided on every issue. If governmental power were in the hands of the Protestant managers who live in the suburbs, the city-dwelling Catholic workers would have little reason to believe that their interests would be protected—for the group in power would differ from them in every respect. And the reverse would apply when the Protestant suburban managers contemplated a government led by their opponents.

But suppose the identifications were cross cutting, not reinforcing. In this case, some workers would be Protestant and others Catholic; some would live in the suburbs and some in the city. The important point about this circumstance is that citizens divided on one interest would be united on others. The Catholic worker would disagree with the Protestant worker on aid to parochial schools, but agree with him on controls over profits. If he lived in a suburb he would share interests with Protestants who lived there as well as with managers who did. And in his church, he would meet (maybe not socialize with, but at least see) people of different economic backgrounds.

In general, American politics has been characterized by cross cutting patterns of group cleavage. Catholic workers join with Protestant workers on some issues (economic ones), and with Catholic businessmen on others (parochial schools, perhaps). These patterns of crosscutting affiliations have an important impact on American politics, since they affect the nature of political coalitions that can be formed. People have often talked of forming a liberal (or radical) coalition in the United States, bringing together all those interested in major changes in the social and economic system. But such a coalition is very difficult to build, for any such grouping will contain people with very different views on some issues, much as they may agree on other issues.

Take a simple example: One of the major planks of a liberal or radical coalition is likely to be tax reforms that increase taxes on higher-income groups and eliminate many of the loopholes in tax laws that benefit such groups. Such a plank would find agreement among many of the groups that would form the core of a liberal or radical coalition—among Blacks, among White workers, among middle-class liberal intellectuals. But those three groups would differ when it came to other issues. The Blacks and the White workers might differ on matters of integration; both might differ from the middle-class intellectuals on matters of civil liberties. Such a coalition would, obviously, be hard to hold together.

Patterns of Cleavage and Competition

We have described the politically relevant groups in American society at some length because it is around such groups that the political struggle in America takes place. These groups have different interests and, therefore, press different claims on the government. Each seeks policies that benefit it and, in so doing, often comes into conflict with other groups.

The wide range of groups in America, the variation in the intensity of concern citizens have with one set of interests rather than another, and the fact that groups crisscross one another all suggest that no single pattern of cleavage and competition is found in America. From issue to issue, from group to group, the way in which segments of the society confront each other may differ. But the dominant pattern of cleavage may be changing as well. As we saw in Chapter 3, the political beliefs of Americans have been changing somewhat. More and more citizens are developing consistent political beliefs across a range of issues. How far this movement will go is uncertain. The following section will help one understand the implications for conflict in the United States of differing patterns of political belief.

Differing Patterns of Political Belief: Implications for Conflict

It will be useful to sketch, rather schematically, a variety of patterns of competition or conflict among groups, illustrating our analysis with some examples. The reader will understand a good deal about any particular issue or conflict in America if he can assign it to one of these patterns.

Scale of Political Positions: Political conflict begins with conflicting interests. One group of citizens prefers one policy (we can call it A); another prefers an alternative policy (call it B). In addition, some citizens feel strongly about the issue, others less strongly, and some are indifferent. Thus we can put various citizens and groups somewhere on the scale, as shown in Figure 4.1. "A" might stand for a hawkish position on Vietnam; "B" for a dovish one. Or perhaps they stand for being pro- or antiintegrated housing, or pro- or antigun control, or pro- or antivarious welfare measures. Some citizens will support A or B strongly, some more mildly, and some will have no position.

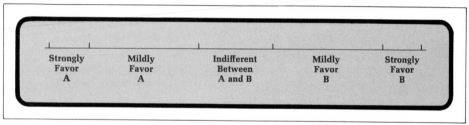

Figure 4.1 Scale of Political Positions

If we convert the Scale of Political Positions into a graph, with the amount of space under the curved line indicating how many people hold that position, we can see a variety of patterns of cleavage or competition. Consider Example 1. Here is an example where the largest group of Americans are indifferent as to A or B, and those Americans who do have a position hold that position rather mildly. Furthermore, the figure is quite symmetrical—about equal numbers of citizens appear on either side of the issue. Many issues take this form; and for obvious reasons they tend to be those on which there is little conflict, little excitement, and perhaps no governmental activity. Perhaps side A will have its preference adopted, perhaps B, or perhaps there will be a stalemate. It will make little difference because there is little intense concern on either side. With a distribution of political preferences of this sort, governmental leaders are fairly free to do anything they want about the issue—if they want to do anything at all.

Example 2 presents a different distribution of interests or preferences. Like Example 1, it is a situation where one would expect little conflict or

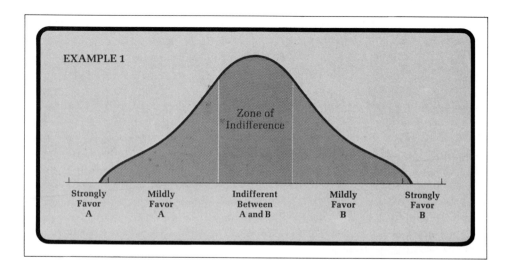

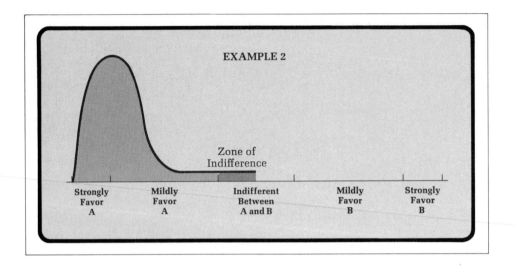

competition, simply because all citizens seem to agree in their strong support for position A. It is a circumstance of strong consensus, with almost no one indifferent or in support of position B.

Examples of such a situation might be the attitudes of Americans toward the enemy in most wars before Vietnam. Most Americans felt the same way and felt that way strongly. Such a distribution of attitudes does not lead to internal conflict. It can be a potent political force, a resource used by governmental leaders if they want to mobilize the public for an all-out war effort. Or it can greatly limit their freedom of action if, for instance, they want to pursue a more conciliatory policy toward the opposing foreign group.

A distribution of interests of this type, however, can have dangerous consequences for democracy—for woe be to the few citizens who are in favor of policy B! Even those who are indifferent may be in trouble. Free speech or rights of political association have been most severely limited when American opinion is shaped like that in Example 2. Thus, in wartime, we have often seen the suspension or diminution of constitutional guarantees contained in the First Amendment.

Example 3 differs substantially from those presented thus far. It is a pattern of preferences of intense cleavage—about half the citizens strongly prefer A and about half strongly prefer B. And very few are in between.

It is obvious that a population divided in this way—especially if the choice between A and B is an important one—is deeply divided indeed. This may describe the United States on the eve of the Civil War.

The point to be made, though, is that this pattern of cleavage in America has been relatively rare (though a variation on this pattern which we shall discuss below is becoming more common), simply because issues as sharply defined as in Example 3 that split the population down the middle

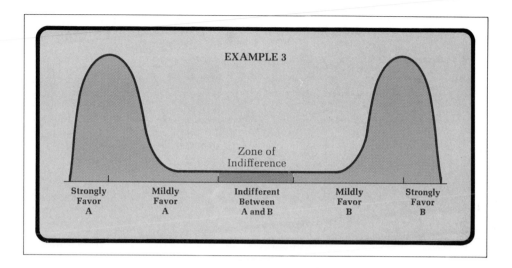

have been infrequent in America. Consider two of the most potent political controversies of recent years: Vietnam and the racial issue.

At the height of the controversy over what to do about Vietnam, citizens were asked to place themselves on a scale indicating their policy preference. They could place themselves at an "extreme dove" position indicating that they wanted to withdraw immediately from Vietnam no matter what; they could place themselves at an extreme hawk position indicating that they wanted to use all force to win. Figure 4.2 shows where they placed themselves. Some citizens took strong positions at either end of

Figure 4.2 Positions on Vietnam

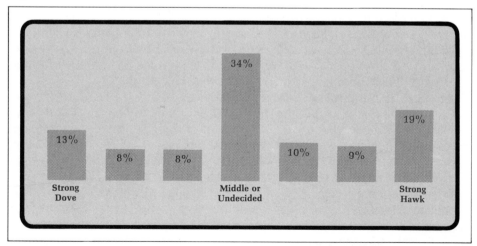

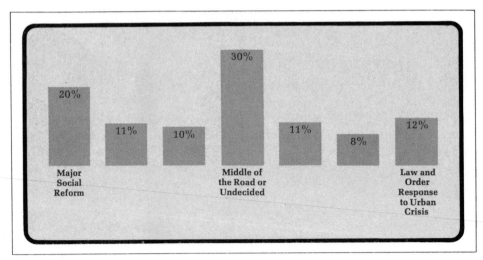

Figure 4.3 Positions on Urban Crisis

SOURCE: Based on data from an unpublished study on Vietnam and the urban crisis by Richard Brody, Benjamin Page, and Sidney Verba, 1968.

the scale. But the largest group is found in the middle, and many others took mild positions on one side or the other.

Or consider a similar scale of opinions on what to do about the "urban crisis" in America. Citizens were asked to place themselves on a scale that ran from favoring major reform to deal with the social and economic issues underlying urban unrest to favoring maximum enforcement of "law and order" to stop urban unrest. (See Figure 4.3.)

As with the Vietnam issue, one found many Americans in middle positions. On two of the most controversial issues of the day one did not find a clear polarization of positions.

Indeed, the general position of Americans on a broad political dimension such as liberalism and conservatism is probably well reflected in the results of a Gallup poll in 1970 when citizens were asked to describe themselves in these terms. Figure 4.4 shows what the Gallup poll found.

The results differ slightly from what the Gallup poll has found in previous years—largely in that the conservative group has become somewhat larger than the liberal. This may be due to a movement of the American people in that direction or, perhaps, to a redefinition of conservatism to stress such issues as sex, pornography, and drugs—rather than economic issues to which the term used to apply.

But the most important point is that opinions tend to lie near the center. In fact, the distribution of citizen preferences in America—when looked at across a number of issues—may often take such a form. It can be schematized in Example 4.

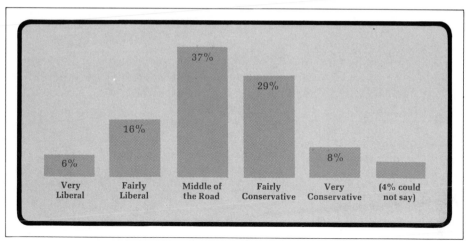

Figure 4.4 Positions on Liberalism and Conservatism

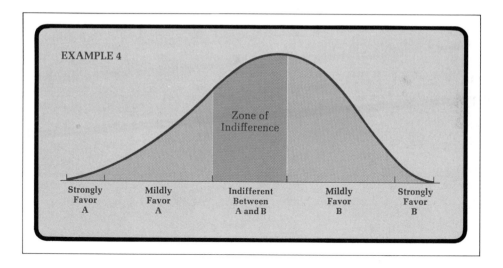

This situation represents a slight variation on Example 1. There is little intensity of political opinion, but somewhat of a balance of opinion in favor of B. Many ordinary political issues take this form — a fairly large proportion of the population mildly favors one alternative; another large, but not as large, group favors the other. And between is a large indifferent group. Policy B stands a good chance of being instituted, though it is by no means certain. Those holding position B may have no organization or leadership; the fact that they are so mildly in favor of position B means that such is likely to be the case. Or they may need to win over the support of some of the indifferents to carry the day, and because they feel mildly about the issue they may not try hard enough. In any case, if they succeed in instituting position B, it will cause little conflict because both those holding positions A and B do so mildly.

This pattern of cleavage is a fairly good representation of one major division of the American population—that into Democrats and Republicans. Most Americans have one identification or the other, whereas some lie in between in the independent camp. But few Americans hold their partisan identification so intensely that they would be fundamentally opposed to turning the reins of government over to the opposition (else elections would be potential civil-war situations). Over the years, more citizens have identified with the Democratic side than with the Republicans. But this does not mean a Democrat in the White House at each election. Since the identifications are relatively unintense, many citizens can be swayed from one side to the other. And as we shall see in Chapter 8 on parties and elections, election victory often depends on the pull of many forces over and above those that identify a citizen with a party.

In general, the pattern of cleavage in the United States has tended to resemble that in Example 4. This situation has often been applauded by students of American politics—because such a situation makes for stability. Granted, a society that resembles Example 3 with citizens far apart and hostile is more likely to fly apart. But such a circumstance as that depicted in Example 4 means stability in another sense of the word—nothing changes. And it is just this centrist tendency of American cleavage patterns—when one considers the nation as a whole—that may lead to stagnation in governmental policy.

The extent to which the pattern of cleavage found in Example 4 will remain the dominant one in America is uncertain. In the previous chapter we showed that the American public has changed over time in terms of the consistency of their political attitudes. More Americans now have consistently conservative or consistently liberal attitudes. And this implies that patterns of cleavage may be moving from the "consensual" pattern of Example 4 to the "polarized" pattern of Example 3. The extent to which that will happen is uncertain as we write this book; but the citizen who wants to understand the evolving pattern of American politics would be wise to follow this development closely.

Furthermore, there are two other patterns of cleavage that are relevant in America—one a traditional one that has applied to many issues, the other one that is becoming more apparent in recent years. Consider Example 5. Here is a small group of the population strongly in favor of a particular position, faced by the bulk of the population that is either indifferent or mildly on the other side. That such a distribution of preferences is common is suggested by the generalization presented earlier—different problems are of different intensity of concern to different groups of citizens. Drug manufacturers care intensely whether the government regulates the manufacture or sale of their product since such regulations may cut into their profits.

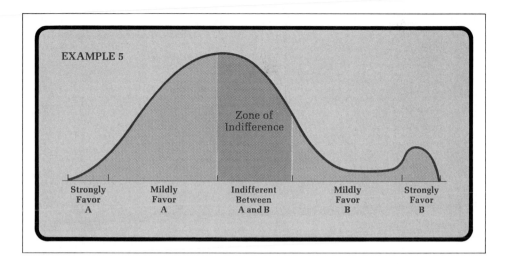

Citizens who do not consume many drug products will be indifferent. The citizens who consume a lot would prefer such regulations, but will care far less intensely than do the manufacturers.

The situation in Example 5 repeats itself in many areas. The special role of the medical profession vis-à-vis medical legislation is like this; so is the special importance of hunters and sportsmen vis-à-vis gun control; and so forth. Politics that takes place when there is a preference distribution of the form of Example 5 brings us to the realm of pressure group politics, a subject we shall discuss later. The main characteristic is that the intense minority is, under such circumstances, likely to win the day. They are more likely to be vocal and to be organized. What they lack in numbers they make up for in intensity.

Let us look at one last example (Example 6). Here we see an intense minority faced by an opposing but also intense majority. Such a situation would exist if there were groups in society that were severely deprived but that were cut off from the rest of the population by a set of reinforcing cleavages. Consider the situation that is emerging around many of America's metropolitan areas. In the decaying central city lives a population that is poor and Black; surrounding them are the suburbs, rich and White. They are divided by race, by economic condition, by place of residence. And, therefore, they have very few common interests. The central city dwellers want social services and want the costs shared by those outside the city; they want access to better schools; they want chances for housing outside of the cities. Those in the suburbs differ on all these issues. Further, they have few social ties with those in the cities; they differ in all respects. And they prefer to keep the problems of the city within the city. Here is a situation fraught with potentialities of conflict—and, of course, potentialities that have become real.

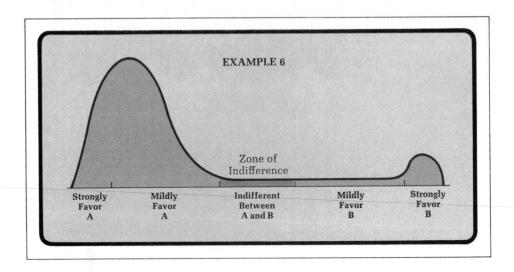

EXAMPLE 6

Zone of
Indifference

| Strongly
Favor
A | Mildly
Favor
A | Indifferent
Between
A and B | Mildly
Favor
B | Strongly
Favor
B |

Controversy

The majority of income in America is earned by a minority of families. For instance, the top 49 percent of Americans in terms of income earn about three-quarters of that income. Why does not the other 51 percent organize politically to change that situation? They are, after all, a majority of the citizens.

Yet American policy has rarely been organized into a struggle between the haves and the have-nots, as many radical Americans have hoped it would and as many conservative Americans have feared it would. Political conflict in America has never involved all the wealthy versus all the less wealthy. Most observers agree on this. But there is controversy over why this has not been the case and whether politics ought to be organized in this way.

One Side

What is needed in America is a poor people's coalition, a union of all those who do not receive the full fruits of American society. Such a union of poor people—the Blacks, Chicanos, and other minority groups; the factory workers; the low-paid clerks; the small farmers; the elderly living on pensions—could elect a government that would equalize the wealth in America. And such a coalition is "natural." Pocketbook issues are of greatest concern to Americans; such issues could overcome other differences among the poor. If this part of the population has not been aware of its common objective interests, it is because political leadership has been inadequate.

The Other Side

The reasons why America won't be divided into the haves and the have-nots in the future are the same that have prevented the growth of coalitions of the poor in the past. The only thing the poor have in common is low income. They do not think of themselves as members of the same group —the White unskilled laborer identifies with neither the White farmer nor the Black unskilled laborer. Nor do they have the same objective interests. They have a common interest in higher income. Who doesn't? But there is so much else that divides them; race, region, sex, and age are only a few of the characteristics that *divide* rather than unite the poor. They are unlikely ever to put a movement together. And it is a good thing too. If the nation were divided into the haves and the have-nots—if, that is, the other bases of political conflict were irrelevant—the possibility of severe domestic conflict would be very great.

Suggested Readings

Two of the best books of the group bases of American politics are: V. O. Key, Jr., *Public Opinion and American Democracy* (New York: Knopf, 1961); and Angus Campbell, Philip E. Converse, Warren E. Miller, and Donald C. Stokes, *The American Voter* (New York: Wiley, 1960).

For material on ethnicity in America, see Nathan Glazer and Daniel P. Moynihan, *Beyond the Melting Pot* (Cambridge, Mass: Harvard University Press, 1963); and Andrew M. Greeley, *Why Can't They Be Like Us?* (New York: Institute of Human Relations Press, 1969).

On American Blacks, see the classic by Gunnar Myrdal, *An American Dilemma: The Negro Problem and Modern Democracy* (20th Anniversary Edition; New York: Harper & Row, 1962); Donald R. Matthews and James W. Prothro, *Negroes and the New Southern Politics* (New York: Harcourt Brace Jovanovich, 1966); and Talcott Parsons and Kenneth B. Clark, eds., *The Negro American* (Boston: Beacon, 1967).

The American as Participant

5

How does the American citizen participate in the political life of his country: How active is he? In what way does he participate? And which citizens participate?

How American democracy works depends in large part on who participates and how. Participation is crucial because of its relationship to all other social and political goals. It is not committed to any social goal but is a technique for setting goals, choosing priorities, deciding what resources to commit to what purposes. Through participation citizens communicate their wishes in relation to the conduct of government: what goals they wish the government to pursue, and how they want the government to allocate resources. If the citizenry is passive and does not participate, governmental leaders are not likely to be responsive to its needs and desires. Or, if some citizens participate while others are quiescent, governmental leaders are much more likely to pay attention to the needs and desires of the activists and ignore the citizens who are inactive. Thus to understand what role participation plays in American politics we have to consider how active citizens in general are, as well as which citizens are active.

Participation is important for another reason. Not only does it communicate the citizen's needs and desires to the government, it has more direct benefits. The ability to participate in decisions that affect one's life is an important source of human dignity. Participation, thus, is an end in itself. In a democracy it is probably the best evidence of full membership in the society.

How Do Citizens Participate?

By participation we refer to all the ways in which citizens influence what the government does. And there are many ways available to the citizen.

Voting

This is the first activity that comes to mind when we think of the citizen as an activist. Through his vote, the citizen takes part in choosing his political leaders. The vote of any single individual is not a very powerful political tool. But elected officials are sensitive to the needs and desires of groups of voters.

Campaign Activity

Each citizen is limited to one vote in an election. That vote is but one of thousands or millions and can play only a small role in the outcome. But a citizen can increase his voting influence in one perfectly legal way—he can attempt to influence the vote of others. One of the most common forms of political activity takes place at the time of an election. Citizens ring door-bells, work at the polls, and talk to their friends and neighbors to try to af-fect their votes. And if political leaders pay attention to voters, they may pay even more attention to those citizens who supply the man-and-woman power for conducting a campaign.

Communal Activity

Elections are an important means by which citizens exercise control over government officials. But elections have a serious limitation—they are very blunt instruments of citizen control. Elections take place only at fixed intervals—every two, or four, or six years, depending on the office. And the choice facing the citizen is between two, or maybe three or four, candidates.

Citizens, on the other hand, as Chapter 4 made clear, have many and varied interests. In fact one can imagine each group of citizens as having an "agenda of priorities" on which they would like to see the government act. Sometimes these interests have to do with broad national policies — members of the American Jewish community are concerned with policy in the Middle East, conservationist groups are concerned with nuclear testing, Black groups are concerned with federal measures on segregation. Some-times the interests are localized to a particular community—a group of neighbors want to prevent the building of a road in their section of town, a group of parents want to improve school facilities, a group of highschoolers want the community to provide a recreation center.

Given the variety of citizens and groups in America, these interests are indeed varied. An election could not possibly offer a choice with regard to all of them. Citizens often find that their particular set of priorities is not an election issue, for both candidates take the same position or take no posi-tion. Furthermore, the problems and interests that citizens want the govern-ment to deal with do not arise neatly at election time; they often arise between elections. Thus the electoral mechanism is inadequate for com-municating citizen needs and desires to government officials.

Other means of participation are needed to fill in the gaps left by elec-tions—some modes of participation by which specific sets of citizens can communicate their more precise concerns to the government as those con-cerns arise. We have labeled much of the activity that serves this end "com-munal activity." We refer to all those activities whereby groups of citizens work together to try to influence the government. They may work through informal groups, as when a group of neighbors join together to protest to city hall about some issue. Or they may work through more long-lasting formal organizations such as unions, PTAs, or civic associations. This kind of activity—which, as we shall shortly show, is particularly characteristic of the United States—has two important features. First, citizens work together, a fact that is important because the government is sensitive to numbers; and a group of citizens is much more potent than a single individual. Second, the citizens are active on that set of problems that concern them most—parents will work in the PTA, welfare recipients in a welfare mothers' group, and so forth.

Citizen-Initiated Contacts

Thus far we have mentioned ways in which citizens participate in concert with others—either as part of the voting population, or in campaigns, or in cooperation with their fellow citizens. But some citizen activity is carried on alone—as when someone writes to his congressman or to a newspaper, or someone visits a government office to register a complaint. We do not often think of this as political participation, for citizens may be dealing with very narrow and specific problems that concern only them. They may ask their congressman to help a relative receive a discharge from the army or they may complain to an official about the condition of the sidewalk in front of their house. But such activity also represents a way in which citizens influence what the government does—and often on matters that are very crucial to them.

Protests, Marches, Demonstrations

Citizens sometimes use more dramatic and direct means of expressing their points of view. They may march to protest the war in Vietnam, to protest bussing, to protest the absence of school bussing. Such modes of participation have become more common in recent years. Some of these modes of activity represent ways in which political preferences can be expressed in a more dramatic way. Some represent ways in which citizens try directly to affect the workings of the government—by blocking the entrance to an induction center, by preventing the school buses from running. Such means of participation are used by citizens who consider the "ordinary" means to be ineffective or who think the problem so urgent that it cannot wait for the ordinary processes of politics.

How Active Are Americans?

One can hear quite contradictory things about participation in America. Some describe it as quite high and vigorous. Others will complain that it is very low and ineffectual. In part, the difference in evaluation may be due to one's preconception of what ought to be. If one expects all citizens to be fully active political men and women, the finding that only 10 to 20 percent of the population is active in political campaigns leads one to feel disappointment in the public. If one expects citizens to be essentially private creatures—concerned with matters of their household—he might express wonder that *as many as* two out of ten Americans bother to take part in election campaigns.

In part, the reader will have to judge for himself whether participation in America is high or low. But we will give some standards for comparison.

Table 5.1 reports the percentages of citizens who are active in various ways—in voting, in campaign activity, in communal activity, and in contacting the government.

A number of facts become clear by looking at the data on participation rates. Only when it comes to voting in Presidential elections do we find a

Table 5.1   What Activities Citizens Perform

MODE OF ACTIVITY	PERCENT ACTIVE
A. Voting	
Voted in 1964 Presidential election	72%
Voted in 1960 Presidential election	71%
Votes regularly in local elections	47%
B. Taking Part in Campaign Activities	
Persuade Others how to vote	28%
Ever worked for a party	26%
Attended political rallies	19%
Contributed money in a political campaign	13%
Member of a political club or organization	8%
C. Cooperative Activities	
Worked through local group	30%
Helped form local group	14%
Active member of organization engaged in community activities	32%
D. Contacting Officials	
Contacted local officials on some problem	20%
Contacted extralocal officials on some problem	18%
Written a letter to a public official	17%
Written a letter to an editor	3%

Source: All but the last two items in D are based on data from Sidney Verba and Norman H. Nie, *Participation in America: Political Democracy and Social Equality* (New York: Harper & Row, 1972). The last two items in D are based on data from the study of the 1964 Presidential election conducted by the Survey Research Center of the Institute for Social Research of The University of Michigan.

majority of the people active—about 70 percent say they vote in such elections. (In fact, voting turnout is slightly lower; people exaggerate their activity somewhat in questionnaires.) In local elections, a little less than half report that they vote regularly. Voting, it must be noted, is the easiest political act. It takes relatively little time and, more important, it takes relatively little initiative. Thus it is not surprising that one finds the highest activity rates in voting.

Campaign activity takes more time, more initiative, and more commitment to a particular candidate or party. And it is clear that this is not an activity for all the citizens. Less than a third of the citizens report that they try to persuade others how to vote; only about a quarter have done work for a political party; and other campaign activities are performed by even smaller proportions of the population.

Campaign activity takes time, initiative, and commitment to a candidate or party.
(*Photo: Cornell Capa, Magnum*)

Communal activity seems to engage about a third of the citizenry. This is the proportion that reports that it has worked with some local group to try to deal with some community problem. And a similar number has done so through a formal organization.

Finally, we can consider the citizen-initiated contacts. "I am going to write to my congressman!" is the stock phrase one hears in relation to all sorts of problems. But only about 1 American in 6 reports that he has ever written a letter expressing his opinion to any public official. And only about 1 in 5 has ever contacted a local official or an official outside of the community on a problem.

What about the frequency of more dramatic political activities — protest marches, demonstrations, and the like? It is hard to obtain accurate figures. But it is likely that relatively few citizens have taken part in such activities. One study conducted during the height of the Vietnam war protests in the late 1960s found only 8 citizens (out of 1500 interviewed) who had ever taken part in a demonstration about Vietnam — about one-half of 1 percent. And another study of a city in upstate New York found that only about 2 to 3 percent of the White citizens had ever attended a protest street demonstration, and only 4 percent said that they had attended a protest meeting.

But one point should be made about such activity. Only a small percentage of the citizenry as a whole may take part in demonstrations, but larger proportions of particular groups may be involved. Thus the same study that found only 2 to 3 percent of Whites had taken part in a street demonstration found that 11 percent of Blacks had. And we do not know the proportion of college students who have taken part in antiwar demonstrations, but it is certainly likely to be larger than the miniscule percentage of the population as a whole who have done so.

Is There Much or Little Participation?

As we suggested, the reader can look at the figures given above and judge for himself. But we can give some guidelines for such judgment. In the first place, we ought to be careful how we read the data on citizen participation. Remember that, aside from voting, we find that no other political act is engaged in by more than a third of the population — that's the proportion that is active in a local organization — and the most usual campaign activity is engaged in by only 28 percent of the citizenry. But this does not mean that only one-third of the American public engages in any activity beyond the vote. Remember that citizens who engage in nonpartisan activity within their local community are not always the same ones who work in campaigns. In fact, some citizens avoid political campaigning while taking an active part in more nonpartisan community activities. Thus the 28 percent who have tried to convince others how to vote and the 30 percent who have worked in an informal group on some community matter only partially overlap.

Types of Participants

We can, in fact, divide the American public into "types of participants" based on the degree to which they are active in politics and the kind of activity in which they engage. The political scientists who gathered the data on the amount of political activity in America did just that, and found six types of citizens.[1]

1. *The Inactives:* These are citizens who never take part in campaigns, who engage in no communal activity, and who never contact an official. They are by no means regular voters, though they may vote from time to time. They are 22 percent of the population. In other words, about one-fourth of all Americans take no part in political activity.

2. *Voting Specialists:* Some citizens are very dutiful about voting in elections; they rarely fail to register their vote. But that is all they do. And this group is similar in size to the inactives—about 21 percent.

3. *The Parochial Participants:* One interesting political group was discovered. These are citizens who do contact government officials. In this sense, they are active. But the reason for their contact is some problem affecting them or their family. And that is the full extent of their activity. They limit their involvement with the government to problems close to their personal lives and avoid all activity likely to affect more public issues. These "parochial" participants form 4 percent of the population.[2]

4. *The Communal Activists:* A fairly large segment of the population was found to be active in the life of its community, but only in nonpartisan activities—voluntary groups, school issues, and the like. These are the citizens who join civic groups, who work in charitable campaigns, and who keep all kinds of community activities going. These are about 20 percent of the population.

5. *The Campaign Activists:* A group of similar size takes part fairly regularly in political campaigns but is not involved as much in the less partisan community activities. They form 15 percent of the population.

[1] Sidney Verba and Norman H. Nie, *Participation in America: Political Democracy and Social Equality* (New York: Harper & Row, 1972), chap. 4.

[2] Note that this figure is lower than the number who contact the government, just as the figure for "voting specialists" is lower than the number of voters. We are dealing here with those who *limit* their activity to this one type.

6. *The Complete Activists:* This is a small—but important—segment of the population, numbering 11 percent. They are active in all respects. They rarely miss an election; they are active in nonpartisan community affairs; and they are found ringing doorbells and engaging in other partisan activities when election time comes around. There are only about half as many of them as there are inactive citizens.[3]

Does this profile of the American public represent a high activity rate or a low one? Should we say that a *full* quarter of the population is totally inactive, and another *full* quarter limits its activity to voting? Or should we say that *only* one-quarter is inactive and *only* another quarter never get beyond the vote, while *fully half* of the citizenry is active beyond the vote? The data are the same in either case.

Participation in the United States Compared to That in Other Nations: To help see whether American participation is high or low it may be useful to compare American citizens to citizens of other nations. One point should be made first: Americans are more "participation oriented" than citizens elsewhere. They are more likely to believe they can influence the government if they want to than do citizens in other countries, and this sense of efficacy or competence makes them more likely to act. And, perhaps more important, they are more likely to express the belief that the citizen has a *responsibility* to be active in the life of his community. In a study conducted in five democratic nations, people were asked what responsibility a citizen had to his community. In the United States, as Table 5.2 indicates, over half of those replying said that a citizen should take an active part in the life of his community—a figure much larger than that in any of the other countries. By an "active role" these people meant participation in local government (willingness to run for office, to serve on boards, and to attend meetings) as well as activity of a nongovernmental nature (to work for the local Red Cross, the PTA). If participation depends on a responsibility to be a participant, such responsibility is more widely distributed in America than elsewhere.

When it comes to actual participation, comparison shows a quite high level in the United States compared to that in other places. This is not the case with voting. Voting turnout in the United States has been traditionally lower than that in many of the democracies of Europe. Turnout in U.S. Presidential elections tends to be between 60 and 70 percent. In many European countries turnout is in the 80 or 90 percent category. This does not necessarily reflect a lower level of political interest and involvement in the United States than elsewhere. The best explanation of such low voting rates is that registration rules, residence requirements coupled with high mobility, and so forth, tend to make it difficult for many citizens to take part by voting.

[3] Seven percent of the sample studied was unclassifiable because of mixed patterns or missing information.

Table 5.2 How Active Should the Ordinary Man Be in His Local Community?

Percentage Who Say the Ordinary Man Should:	UNITED STATES	GREAT BRITAIN	GERMANY	ITALY	MEXICO
Be active in his community	51	39	22	10	26
Only participate in more passive ways (be interested, etc.)	27	31	38	22	33
Only participate in church affairs	5	2	1		
Total who mention some outgoing activity	83	72	61	32	59
Only be upright in personal life	1	1	11	15	2
Do nothing in local community	3	6	7	11	2
Don't know	11			35	30
Other	2			7	7
Total percent	100	100	100	100	100
Total number of cases	970	963	955	995	1007

Source: Gabriel Almond and Sidney Verba, *The Civic Culture: Political Attitudes and Democracy in Five Nations.* Copyright © 1963 by Princeton University Press. Reprinted by permission of Princeton University Press.

The frequency of those political activities that take more time and effort may be more important. Data on this subject are harder to come by, since they are not recorded officially as is voting turnout. But some are available. For instance, only a small minority of Americans report that they have ever tried to influence a decision of their local government (28 percent say they have) and an even smaller proportion say that they have tried to influence a decision of the national government (16 percent). But in both cases the proportions are substantially larger than those found in other nations, as Table 5.3 shows: Political activities may just not be the predominant activity of citizens in any country, either in the United States or elsewhere. But they are more likely to be an important activity in the United States than in other democracies.

In one particular way, participation in the United States seems particularly well developed compared with other nations. This is in the communal mode of participation, when citizens come together to work on some community problem or join in some group to pressure the government. Citizens in a variety of countries were asked how they would go about influencing

Table 5.3   Percentages Who Say They Have
Attempted to Influence a Government Decision

	UNITED STATES	GREAT BRITAIN	GERMANY	ITALY	MEXICO
Attempted to influence a decision of the local government	28%	15%	14%	8%	6%
Attempted to influence a decision of the national government	16%	6%	3%	2%	3%

Source: Based on data from Gabriel Almond and Sidney Verba, *The Civic Culture: Political Attitudes and Democracy in Five Nations* (Princeton, N.J.: Princeton University Press, 1963).

the government. In the United States over half of those who thought they could exert some influence felt that they could best do so by joining with others. In the other countries studied, citizens would more likely work alone or through some more formal organization like a political party. And the willingness to work with others—friends, neighbors, and others at work—found in the United States extends to all social groups.

Data on the actual behavior of citizens show that in the United States there is much more community-oriented activity involving the cooperation of citizens: more ad hoc groupings of citizens to deal with some local problem and more active associations connected with the schools, with recreational problems, with all the myriad problems that arise in a community. This characteristic mode of behavior is, in fact, not new in America. It was noted over one hundred years ago by the Frenchman Alexis de Tocqueville, who commented on the zest for cooperative activity he found in America compared with that in Europe.

And, as noted, such activity represents an important involvement of the citizenry in public affairs because it can deal with the most immediate problems of citizens. It is a means by which the individual citizen increases his own influence vis-à-vis the government—because the voices of many generally carry more weight with government officials than do the voices of a few.

The Equality of Political Access

Compared to other nations, the participation in the United States looks fairly rosy; citizens feel a fairly high level of responsibility to be active and are relatively active. But there is another standard we can use in judging the adequacy of participation in the United States—a standard that does not require us to look beyond our borders. How *equally* do citizens participate in America? Are all types of citizens equally active, or is participation concentrated in the hands of a few? The answer is, of course, very important in understanding how participation works in America. Citizens communicate their needs and desires to government leaders through participation, and also apply pressure on leaders to be responsive to these needs and desires. Thus the citizen who does not participate may be ignored. The government will respond to the participant.

But what may be most important is not that all citizens participate but that the citizens who do be *representative* of the rest of the citizenry. As we have seen, not everyone is active in politics; nor is it a realistic expectation that they should be. But if the activists have the same problems, the same needs, the same demands as the nonactivists, the former may effectively act as communicators for those who do not take part. On the other hand, if the activists are different from the rest of the population—come from different social groups, have different problems, want the government to engage in different policies—then the fact that only a subgroup of the population participates means that the government will respond only to some of the needs and desires of the population.

Who Are the Participants?

Do the participants come from all walks of life, or do they come from special segments of the population? The answer is: Citizens from all walks of life can be found among the participants in American politics—no group is totally barred. But certain kinds of citizens are overrepresented among the activists. These tend to be citizens of upper social status—the better-educated, the wealthy, those with higher-status occupations. Recall the six types of participants listed a few pages ago. Figure 5.1 indicates the extent to which those with a college background are over- or underrepresented in the various types of participants; we also indicate the over- and under-representation of citizens who have not finished high school. (A figure of "50" for overrepresentation, for instance, means that college graduates are 50 percent more likely to be in a certain category of participant than their proportion in the population as a whole would predict.)

The message of Figure 5.1 is quite simple and quite important. When we look at citizens with a college background, we find that they are underrepresented among those types of participants whose participation in politics is minimal—among those who are totally inactive, among those who limit their activity to the vote, and among those whose political activity is limited to the narrow personal problems facing their day-to-day lives. But among those citizens who are taking a fuller role in political life—among those who are active in nonpartisan communal work, among those who work in campaigns and, above all, among those who are active in all pos-

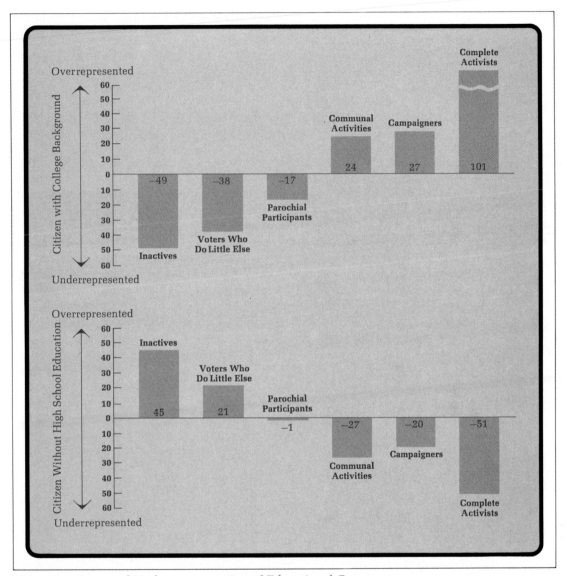

Figure 5.1 Over- and Underrepresentation of Educational Groups
Among Participant Types

SOURCE: Based on data from Sidney Verba and Norman H. Nie, *Participation in America:
Political Democracy and Social Equality* (New York: Harper & Row, 1972).

sible ways — we find the college-educated citizenry highly overrepresented.
They are, for instance, 101 percent more likely to be complete activists than
their proportion of the population would predict.

The exact opposite is the case among those who have never finished
high school. They are unlikely to be found in the highly active groups, and

very likely to be found among those citizens who are inactive or who never get beyond the vote. They are 45 percent more likely to be in the inactive group than their numbers would predict.

Let us look at a fuller profile of the citizens who take no part in political life. Figure 5.2 shows how various social groups are over- or under-represented among the inactive citizens. Again, a line on the side of over-representation indicates that a group is more likely to be inactive than we would expect, given their proportion of the population; a line indicating underrepresentation means that a group is less likely to be inactive than we would expect, given their proportion of the population.

The figure is worth a close look, for it gives a good profile of those citizens who take no part in American political life. It is quite clear that groups deprived in social and economic terms are also more likely to be inactive. If you do not have a high school degree, if you earn less than $4000 per year, if you are Black, you are more likely to be politically inactive. If you are in the groups that are advantaged in a social and economic sense—if you have a college education, an income over $10,000 a year, and are White—you are significantly less likely to be found in the inactive segment of the population. In addition, it is worth noting that women are a bit more likely to be inactive while men a bit less likely (though these differences are much less

Figure 5.2 Who Are the Inactive Citizens? (This diagram shows the types of citizens who are over- or underrepresented among the inactives.)

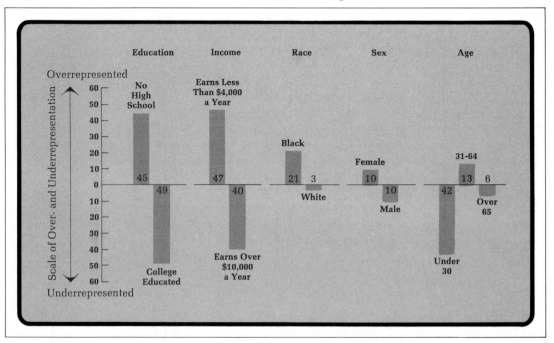

than one would find in almost any other country). Finally, we find that young citizens are more likely to be inactive and so are elderly ones. In the middle years of life, participation is the greatest.

Furthermore, the difference in participation rates among these various groups does make a difference in what messages are communicated to the government. Those who are inactive—the poor, the ill-educated, the Black—have different problems than those who are more active, and the inactive ones prefer that the government engage in different policies than do the more active citizens. Suppose we compare the problems that the most active citizens report they face in their day-to-day lives with those faced by the least active. (See Figure 5.3.) We find that the inactive citizens are nearly twice as likely to report that they have been faced recently with serious problems in the area of paying for medical care, or obtaining employment, or finding adequate housing than are the citizens who are the most active.

In other words, if participation is the mechanism by which government leaders learn of the problems facing the citizens, these leaders will be relatively unaware of some of the more serious economic problems that citizens face.

Similarly, the fact that those with the most severe problems are the least active will also have an effect on what government leaders see as the way the citizenry would like them to deal with social and economic problems. The activists are about twice as likely, for instance, to believe that the solution to the economic problems of the poor lies in the activities of the poor

Figure 5.3 What Problems Face the Inactive and Active Citizens?

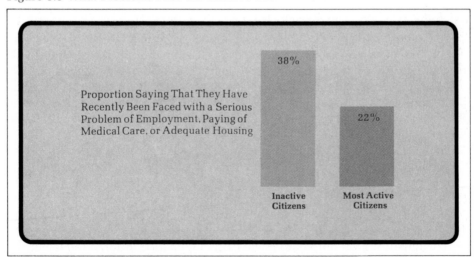

SOURCE: Based on data from Sidney Verba and Norman H. Nie, *Participation in America: Political Democracy and Social Equality* (New York: Harper & Row, 1972), chap. 15.

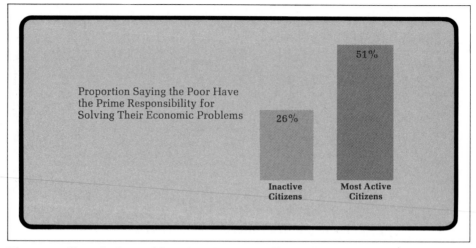

Figure 5.4 How Active and Inactive Citizens Differ in the Proportions Thinking the Poor Must Solve Their Own Problems

SOURCE: Based on data from Sidney Verba and Norman H. Nie, *Participation in America: Political Democracy and Social Equality* (New York: Harper & Row, 1972).

themselves. (See Figure 5.4.) Those who are inactive are more likely to think that the government has a prime obligation to deal with such problems.

Thus the government leader who learns what the public wants by considering the preferences of the active citizens will find a majority who feel that the economic problems of the poor are their own responsibility and not something to be dealt with by governmental intervention.

The Paradox of Participation: The data clearly illustrate a major *paradox of participation* in American politics: Those who need governmental help and intervention the most—the poor, the ill-educated, the victims of racial discrimination—are the ones who are least active. Those who need governmental help the least—in the sense that they are already the wealthier, the better-educated, the less discriminated against—are the most active. And through the inactivity of the former and the activity of the latter, the government may receive an impression of the state of the public that underestimates the extent to which citizens desire governmental intervention to deal with these problems.

What causes this paradoxical situation? Why do those who need help least participate the most? The answer is that just those characteristics that make them more advantaged in social and economic terms make them more participant as well. Education and wealth provide the resources needed for participation: the money to make campaign contributions, the leisure to allow involvement in political activity, the skills to be effectively active

In addition to the resources for participation, citizens with higher in-

Table 5.4   Which Citizens Think the Ordinary
Man Has a Responsibility to Be Active in His Community?

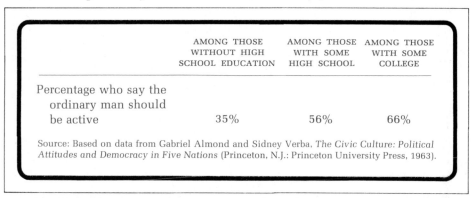

	AMONG THOSE WITHOUT HIGH SCHOOL EDUCATION	AMONG THOSE WITH SOME HIGH SCHOOL	AMONG THOSE WITH SOME COLLEGE
Percentage who say the ordinary man should be active	35%	56%	66%

Source: Based on data from Gabriel Almond and Sidney Verba, *The Civic Culture: Political Attitudes and Democracy in Five Nations* (Princeton, N.J.: Princeton University Press, 1963).

come or more education are likely to have greater motivation to participate. One of the most important characteristics of political participation is that it is *voluntary* — no one is forced to be a participant. Thus the law can provide for equal opportunity to participate. It cannot equalize participation. But with higher education comes a set of attitudes — a belief that one can be effective in politics, a belief that one has the responsibility to be active — that leads citizens to participate. We pointed out above that half the citizens in America think the ordinary man has a responsibility to be active in the affairs of his community — a figure much larger than that found in other countries. But in Table 5.4 notice the way in which educational groups differ in that sense of responsibility.

Among those with no high school education only a third report that the ordinary man has a responsibility to be active in his community; among those with some college training two-thirds think that the ordinary man has such a responsibility.

Table 5.5   Which Citizens Think They Could
Influence a Governmental Decision If They Wanted To?

PERCENTAGE WHO SAY THEY COULD	AMONG THOSE WITHOUT HIGH SCHOOL EDUCATION	AMONG THOSE WITH SOME HIGH SCHOOL	AMONG THOSE WITH SOME COLLEGE
Influence a decision of the local government	60%	82%	99%

Source: Based on data from Gabriel Almond and Sidney Verba, *The Civic Culture: Political Attitudes and Democracy in Five Nations* (Princeton, N.J.: Princeton University Press, 1963).

Similarly, citizens with more education are more likely to think that they can influence the government than are those who have more limited educational attainment, as Table 5.5 shows.

Thus in terms both of the resources available for participation and the psychological orientations that further that participation, those citizens who are already more advantaged in terms of education are found to be also advantaged vis-à-vis political participation.

Bypassing the Participation "Paradox"

How can groups with lower social status break through the reinforcing cycle whereby their social and economic status deprives them of the resources and motivation to be politically active? Our discussion of the basis of political groupings in America suggests the answer (see Chapter 4). There we argued that there are three characteristics that make a category of citizens into a politically potent group: common interests, self-conscious awareness of those interests, and organization. Obviously citizens with inadequate education, low income, and low-status jobs have interests in common. But do they have self-conscious awareness and organization? The answer — in large part — is No.

Self-Conscious Awareness: Observers of American politics — particularly those who compare it with politics as practiced in Europe — have frequently commented on the absence in the United States of any strong sense of class consciousness. And the absence is especially noticeable among American workers. This absence is particularly striking in the light of the existence of such a belief system in many other industrialized democracies. The American worker sometimes thinks politically as a worker, but sometimes in terms of other identifications that may separate him from other workers — he may think politically as a Catholic, a suburbanite, a White or a Black, and so forth. Thus a self-conscious ideology that might be most potent in motivating lower-status citizens to political activity is missing.

Organization: What about organization? Two kinds of organization might help lower-status citizens participate more in politics: political parties and voluntary associations. They might help by providing channels for activity and by increasing a sense of group identity. Again we can consider this in comparative perspective. In many countries, political parties are organized along class lines — they are parties of the working class, parties of the farmers, parties of the middle class. Parties that are limited to a particular class tend to do a better job of recruiting the members of that particular class to political activity. Thus socialist or workers' parties tend to mobilize working-class citizens to be politically active. But the parties in the United States are well known for the fact that they have no such clear class basis. Democrats are more likely to receive support from workers, and Repub-

Table 5.6 Which Citizens Belong to Organizations?

	AMONG THOSE WHO HAVE NOT FINISHED HIGH SCHOOL	AMONG HIGH SCHOOL GRADUATES	AMONG THOSE WITH SOME COLLEGE
Percentage who are members of an organization	49%	67%	78%
Percentage who are active in an organization	27%	43%	59%

Source: Based on data from Sidney Verba and Norman H. Nie, *Participation in America: Political Democracy and Social Equality* (New York: Harper & Row, 1972).

licans from business—true. But both parties reach across the social spectrum for their support. The result is that citizens of lower social status have no party organizations especially trying to bring them into politics.

The same can be said for voluntary associations. These organizations can help citizens become more participant. We shall discuss how this happens in Chapter 7. But here we can just note that members of these associations tend to be citizens of higher social status. As Table 5.6 shows, those citizens with higher education are more likely to be organizationally active: Only about one-half of those citizens who have not finished high school belong to any voluntary organization; over three-quarters of those with some college training do. And only about one-fourth of those without a high school degree are active in an organization, whereas over half of the college group is.

If organization is a means of making sets of citizens into politically meaningful groupings, then it is clear that this resource is also more available to upper-status citizens.

Black vs. White: An Example of the Political Mobilization of a Disadvantaged Group

Among Black Americans—at least in recent decades—one can observe the beginnings of a break in the reinforcing cycle of participation that leaves the disadvantaged even more disadvantaged. And the break comes, we believe, through the processes mentioned above—organization and self-consciousness. American Blacks have a history of relatively effective organization—at least, more effective organization than that of White Americans of similar social and economic status. There are many sources of this, perhaps the most important one being simply the fact of segregation and social separation. Forced to live apart from Whites, they are in a better position to organize as a separate group. In addition, numerous Black organizations — from the NAACP to more militant groups — have played an important role. Nor ought one to forget the role of the Black churches. Blacks, it is apparent, have developed an organizational base to aid their participation.

In addition they have developed — as their White counterparts have not — a clear sense of self-identity. The slogans "Black Power" and "Black Is Beautiful" are examples of this consciousness. And their separation from the mainstream of White society makes this possible. The point is that the segregation of American society — which finds Blacks living apart, going to school apart, holding particular kinds of jobs — produces less of the cross-cutting affiliation that impedes self-consciousness and organization among disadvantaged White citizens.

Studies show that Black consciousness represents a way in which citizens who might not otherwise participate can come to be active in politics. Black Americans, on the average, participate in politics somewhat less than do White Americans. This is what one would expect given the fact that Blacks are generally of lower income and education. But if we consider those Blacks who manifest a sense of group consciousness (who, for instance, mention problems of race when asked what are the most important problems for themselves or the nation), we find that they are as active in politics as Whites. In other words, the sense of Black consciousness appears to be a means by which the disadvantage — a result of not engaging in political activity — that faces Blacks because of their lower educational and income levels can be overcome.[4]

The situation can be seen even more dramatically if we look at the situation over a period of time. The long series of studies of American voting behavior conducted by the University of Michigan since 1952 allows us to trace the difference in Black and White participation rates over this long period — at least in relation to campaign activity. These data are presented in Figure 5.5.

In 1952 — two years before the Supreme Court's historic school desegregation decision and three years before the first bus boycott led by Martin Luther King in Montgomery, Alabama — it was found that Black Americans were much less active in political campaigns than the average White. According to the findings of the 1950s there was a rapid diminution of that difference, with Black Americans slightly outparticipating Whites in 1964. And though the average Black level of activity has remained a touch below that of Whites, the difference was much less than that at the beginning of the era of awakening of Black consciousness.

The data on Black-White differences ought not to be taken to mean that all political problems for Black citizens have vanished. Their participation

[4] Verba and Nie, chap. 10.

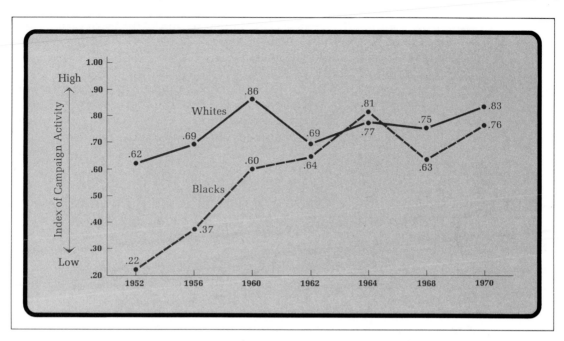

Figure 5.5 Level of Campaign Activity of Blacks and Whites

SOURCE: Based on data from Sidney Verba and Norman H. Nie, *Participation in America: Political Democracy and Social Equality* (New York: Harper & Row, 1972).

rate still remains below that of Whites. And, of course, we have presented information merely on how much activity they attempt, not on the all-important question of how effective is that activity. Thus they may have increased their political activity over recent years, but they remain a minority group and their political activity is not always — perhaps not often — decisive.

The weight of participation in the United States still comes from the White population — and among that population, from those who are more affluent and better educated, citizens who do not share the problems faced by Black Americans and other Americans of lower social and economic status nor the desire of the less-well-off citizens for governmental intervention on their behalf.

Two further conclusions can be drawn from these data. Both have to do with the relationship between the more ordinary modes of participation — through elections, through community work, and through letters to one's congressman — and the more dramatic, more direct, and sometimes illegal modes of activity through protest demonstrations, marches, and the like.

One conclusion is clear from the last figure on Black-White differences in campaign participation over the past two decades. Although much attention has been focused on direct political activity among Blacks and on the origin of that activity in an increased sense of Black consciousness, it is quite clear that this has been accompanied by a growth of activity of the more ordinary political kind. The last two decades have seen Blacks more and more active in political campaigns.

The second conclusion is that the increase in more direct political activities may in part be explained by some of the disparities in participation rate found among social groups in America. If indeed the ordinary modes of participation are so heavily weighted in favor of the "haves" rather than the "have-nots," citizens unhappy with the results of that weighted-influence process might seek other, more direct means of applying political pressure.

The Politics of Protest:
A Closer Look

We have thus far focused most of our attention on the "ordinary" means of political participation: through political campaigns and through commu-

New forms of political participation have grown in importance in recent years.
(Photo: UPI)

nity group activity. But a full account of participatory activities in America has to pay close attention to direct political activity: political demonstrations, political marches, and political violence. These are phenomena whose importance has grown in recent years—in particular in relation to protests on racial matters and to protests against the war in Vietnam. But they have spread to other issues as well. Although there are no clear data available on the subject, it does seem likely that the threshold of direct activity has changed in recent years. Groups are more willing to stop and disrupt (to seize a building, to march on an office) than in the past. Is this something new in America—a new political style that grew out of the tensions of the 1960s?

Violence, Protests, and the Historical Record

To begin with, we must make clear that protest and violence are not the same thing. A study done for the National Commission on the Causes and Prevention of Violence found that only about one-third of the protests recorded in the press involved violence; most were nonviolent. In fact, the figure of one-third may be somewhat large since the newspapers give disproportionate attention to violent incidents while nonviolent protests are less likely to be reported.

Furthermore, as the authors of that report make clear, what exactly is and is not violence is often hard to define. "Violent language"—rude and insulting—is often used in political confrontations, but is that violence? Also, as the studies of various direct confrontations between police and demonstrators have made clear, it is also ambiguous "who starts it" when confrontations turn violent. As the report to the National Violence Commission put it: "It is often difficult to determine who was 'responsible' for the violence. The reports of our study teams, however, clearly suggest that authorities bear a major responsibility. . . . Of the violent incidents [analyzed], in only half did the violence seem to be initiated by the demonstrators."[5]

Although it is common to consider the recent growth of political protest (and its sometimes accompanying violence) as a new phenomenon, such is clearly not the case. The history of America is filled with the uses of political violence and political confrontation. One need not remind the reader of the origins of the nation in violent protest against the British, but not as well known is the sustained history of violent protests against the government by poor Appalachian farmers throughout the last half of the seventeenth century. Violence was used by the southern states in trying to secede fron the Union and by the North in preventing it. It was used by WASPs (White–Anglo-Saxon–Protestants) against various immigrant groups in

[5] Jerome H. Skolnick, *The Politics of Protest*, Staff Report to the National Commission on the Causes and Prevention of Violence (New York: Ballantine Books, 1969), pp. 3–4.

American cities in the nineteenth century. It was used by worker groups to protest economic conditions; and it was used by the authorities to suppress these protests. If the 1960s saw demonstrations against the war in Vietnam, none of these demonstrations matched the violence of the antidraft riots in New York during the Civil War when draft offices were burned and many persons were killed.

Above all, one must mention the sustained pattern of violence in the South after the Civil War—violence against Blacks (with the tacit or open approval of the authorities) that quite successfully maintained the domination of White over Black in that area.

This is not to deny the increase of direct protests in recent years. But even that is uncertain because the media of communications are better and we now see more of what goes on than in the past. But it certainly suggests that demonstrations and violence have a long tradition in America.

What Are Protests About?

In recent years, protest activity has largely been linked with two issues: the war in Vietnam and minority rights. But, as the historical record makes clear, protests have arisen on many issues. One common interpretation is that such activities are "irrational" outbursts, involving no political goal. But such does not appear to be the case. Usually there is some political goal in mind. The goal may not be totally clear, but then neither is the goal of the act of voting totally clear in the mind of the voter.

Another common interpretation of political protest is the so-called riff-raff theory: Those who take part in such activities are those who are the least well integrated into society. Among Blacks these would be the jobless, the young, and the most poverty stricken. (Among students it would proba-bly refer to those closest to the margin of flunking out.) But studies of pro-test behaviors show that they do not have such a narrow base. Studies of participation in urban riots find that the rioters do indeed come disproportionately from the young and from the unemployed, but they are drawn from all segments of the community and have at least the pas-sive support of the majority. And student demonstrators are often those with quite respectable grades. Thus the composition of the protest groups also is consistent with a view that these are political activities.

The Motivation for Direct Action: Most protests have one thing in common: a belief that the ordinary channels of political activity are unre-sponsive or (what is perhaps the same thing) too slow for the urgency of the issue. As the Chicago Riot Study Committee put it, "There is a conviction on the part of a clear majority of our Black citizens that [political] repre-sentation is entirely unsatisfactory and must be improved."[6] As the data we

---

[6] *Chicago Riot Study Committee Report* (Chicago, 1968), p. 112.

presented on the belief systems of Americans showed, Black Americans do not share the belief of Whites in the responsiveness of government officials.

Direct action, furthermore, is likely to take place under particular circumstances: when a group lives in isolation from the rest of the society, when it has its own life-style, and when it has little (or believes it has little) in common with those around it. There are no overlapping affiliations to tie the group to the rest of the society or to lead it to believe that channels are open for it to influence policy. And such, of course, characterizes American Blacks living in racial ghettos. If the ordinary channels of political responsiveness are closed, the buildup of tensions and frustrations may result in the use of alternative, more direct means.

The Debate on the Propriety of Direct Action: Here, of course, lies the great dilemma of direct action, and is the point around which the debate on the propriety of such activity revolves. Some would argue that such activities are never appropriate in a democracy, where other more peaceful channels exist. Certainly the ordinary channels must be exhausted first. And, even then, the switch to direct action is inappropriate. If everyone who could not get his way in politics resorted to violence, society would decay into a war of all against all.

To this the counter-argument comes back: In many cases all channels have been exhausted; direct action is not premature. Furthermore, the democratic channels are not equally available to all: Some groups are systematically excluded from participation; they have no choice but direct activity. Finally, those favoring direct activity would argue that there are some issues of such an overriding importance—stopping a war or providing civil rights or preventing the bussing of one's children away from a neighborhood school (remember, protest is not always to foster change; it may be to block change)—that one must act firmly and directly.

It is not our task to decide who is right in such a debate. Part of the debate is a factual one: Are channels open to all and were all channels tried before the resort to direct action? But these are factual questions of such complexity that they allow of no easy answer. And the basic issues of the legitimacy of stepping outside of the ordinary political channels as well as the tougher question of the legitimacy of violence are not factual ones. Rather, it is a moral question of what circumstances warrant what kinds of action. One thing, though, is clear historically: At various times groups of all sorts have resorted to direct and even violent political activities.

Is Protest Effective?

Protests are political acts; they are engaged in by citizens who want some response from the government. In this sense we can judge them by asking how effective they are.

This again is an area where it is hard to find clear answers. It is difficult to measure the extent to which protest is more effective than the slower processes of ordinary participation. Many—particularly government leaders who would like to discourage such practices—claim that they pay no attention to them. President Nixon once made quite a point of watching a football game on TV while the White House was surrounded and much of Washington filled with protesters against the war in Vietnam. Others—particularly the leaders of demonstrations—claim that they are the only effective means of political activity.

Probably the truth lies in between. The most effective political activity often is the slowest and the most laborious—the doorbell ringing and the patient convincing that goes with attempts to elect a candidate. Protest activities sometimes flash quickly and then fade, leaving no results behind. But the opposite is often also the case. An urban demonstration bordering or crossing over into violence, a massive descent on Washington of outraged war protesters, attempts by citizens to block school integration forcibly—all such activities may cause government leaders to change their course sharply.

We can find examples indicating clearly that change was induced by direct action. As the Riot Commission Report summarized it:

> Northern violence ended Southern slavery, and Southern terrorism ended radical Reconstruction. The transformation of labor-management relations was achieved during a wave of bloody strikes, in the midst of a depression and widespread fear of revolution. And black people made their greatest political gains, both in Congress and in the cities, during the racial strife of the 1960s."[7]

Protests are likely to be particularly important as "signaling" devices. The very severity of the acts involved in the protest and the vast coverage they receive through the media make them a powerful tool for signaling discontent to political leaders. And they may often be signaling devices to potential participants as well. Such overt and powerful manifestations may help to mobilize others to become more active. It is not accidental that the growth of Black participation in the electoral process (on which we have reported data earlier in this chapter) came at a time of more direct protests.

Yet we cannot ignore the other side of the coin. Direct action is generally disapproved by the majority of the American people—even when they approve of the goals of those engaged in such action. An overwhelming majority (75 to 85 percent) of the American people have tended to reject student protests on the war in Vietnam. Indeed, one study showed that student protesters were viewed negatively by two-thirds of those citizens who thought the war in Vietnam was a mistake.[8]

[7] Skolnick, p. 16.
[8] Milton J. Rosenberg, Sidney Verba, and Philip E. Converse, *Vietnam and the Silent Majority* (New York: Harper & Row, 1970), pp. 44–45.

And much evidence from public opinion polls on racial matters makes clear that a "White backlash" may exist in relation to Black militant activities. In this respect it is interesting to note that the 1960s was an era of constantly increasing acceptance by Whites of the goals of Blacks—better housing, integration, and the like—coupled with a rising rejection of militancy.

How do these countervailing forces balance out? And does militant activity do more harm than good? These are not easy questions to answer. In part, this is the case because the factual results are mixed and hard to measure. In part, this is the case because one's judgment on these issues depends upon his values. Some may believe that violence (or the risk of violence) is unjustified in almost any case. Others may feel that social changes require any necessary means. Out of such differences come "ordinary" politics as well as violent politics.

Controversy

Upper-status Americans—those with higher education, those with higher incomes, and those with higher-status jobs—participate more in politics than do those citizens of lower status. The evidence is clear on this. And this probably means that the government pays more attention to the higher-status groups than to the lower-status citizens. But is the greater political activity of the rich simply the proper working of the democratic system in America, or does it reflect a fundamental flaw in American democracy?

One Side

That upper-status citizens participate more in American politics implies nothing bad about American democracy. They participate more because they *choose* to do so. Lower-status citizens *choose not to*. And if, because of that, the latter have less influence over the government than do their wealthier fellow citizens, it is they who are to blame, not the system. As long as citizens are *free to participate* democracy is ensured. If some do not take advantage of these opportunities, it does not mean that democracy is not working well.

The Other Side

Democracy flourishes only when all citizens have equal voice; the more the United States fails in this respect, the less effective a democracy it is. That the rich are more active is, therefore, a fundamental flaw in democracy in

America. Nor is it fair to say that poorer citizens do not participate because they choose not to. The opportunities to participate are not equal across social groups. If lower-status citizens participate less than others, it is not due to indifference on their part, but to lack of resources. If election campaigns cost millions, those who cannot contribute large sums are not "equally free" to participate effectively. And perhaps the nonparticipants have a realistic view that they may be wasting their time. Political leaders will pay less attention to them if they come from the wrong social background or the wrong side of the tracks.

Suggested Readings

For a comprehensive study of participation in America, see Sidney Verba and Norman H. Nie, *Participation in America: Political Democracy and Social Equality* (New York: Harper & Row, 1972). Robert A. Dahl's *Who Governs?* (New Haven, Conn.: Yale University Press, 1961) is a classic study of a small American city and contains important considerations of how citizens take part in the government of that city. The classic study of voting in America is Angus Campbell, Philip Converse, Warren Miller, and Donald Stokes, *The American Voter* (New York: Wiley, 1960).

For a study of the participation of American Blacks, see Donald R. Matthews and James W. Prothro, *Negroes and the New Southern Politics* (New York: Harcourt Brace Jovanovich, 1966).

For a consideration of participation in America in comparative perspective, see Gabriel A. Almond and Sidney Verba, *The Civic Culture: Political Attitudes and Democracy in Five Countries* (Boston: Little, Brown, 1965).

For a discussion of violence in American politics, see Jerome H. Skolnick, *The Politics of Protest*, Staff Report to the National Commission on the Causes and Prevention of Violence (New York: Ballantine, 1969).

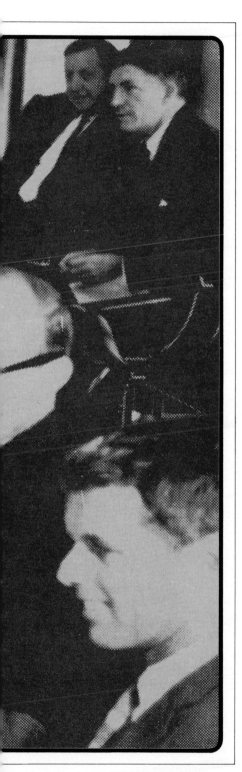

The
Recruitment
of Political
Leaders

6

Responsibility for running American society is of course not evenly distributed among all citizens. A particular group of citizens, which we can broadly call "the political leadership," has the task of managing the federal bureaucracy, passing the legislation, running the major parties, formulating action programs, interpreting the Constitution, and spending the public resources. The most striking fact about political leadership is how few persons are directly involved in it. As summarized by one scholar:

> In all assemblies and groups and organized bodies of men, from a nation down to a committee of a club, direction and decisions rest in the hands of a small percentage, less and less in proportion to the larger size of the body, till in a great population it becomes an infinitesimally small proportion of the whole number. This is and always has been true of all forms of government.[1]

This proposition is easily documented. There are 136 million adult citizens in the United States, yet how many of them are directly involved in planning and directing government programs? The answer is somewhere between 1500 and 2000 persons, which includes congressmen, higher officials in the executive branch, governors, top federal and state judges, big city mayors, national party committee members, and various other key state and local officials. From 136 million candidates, then, comes the tiny, tiny group of significant political leaders.

The ratio of leaders to nonleaders is similar in other sectors of American life. Approximately 1500 persons have authority over the 100 largest manufacturing corporations, and thus control more than 50 percent of all manufacturing assets in the nation. Indeed, one study reports that fewer than 4000 individuals

> control half of the nation's industrial assets, half of all assets in communications and utilities, half of all banking assets, half of the assets of diversified investment companies, two-thirds of all insurance assets. They control nearly forty per cent of all the assets of private foundations, half of all private university endowments; they control the most prestigious civic and cultural organizations; they occupy key federal government positions in the executive, legislative and judicial branches; they control the largest accumulations of personal wealth; and they make the largest contributions to political campaign finances.[2]

[1] J. Bryce, *Modern Democracies* (New York: Macmillan, 1924), p. 542.
[2] Thomas R. Dye, Eugene R. DeClerg, John W. Pickering, "Men in Authority," unpublished paper, Florida State University, August 1972.

In this chapter we will restrict our attention to political leadership, as conventionally defined, but the reader might keep in mind that much of what we describe of political recruitment is true of the recruitment process for top bankers, corporation executives, foundation directors, university presidents, and so forth, as well.

Political Recruitment and Democracy

The simple fact that the few govern the many is the starting point for the study of political recruitment. How do persons move into and out of the top circles? Are particular groups given special advantages, and other groups disadvantaged? What political viewpoints dominate within the governing group? What actions or errors of judgment typically result in the downfall of individual leaders or even in the collapse of entire ruling groups? These are the questions that the study of political recruitment sets out to answer. If, for instance, in Figure 6.1 the box on the left represents the entire adult population of the United States, and the speck on the right stands for the political leaders, which few citizens will succeed in reaching leadership positions?

For much of human history the answer to the question who would rule would have posed no problems. Persons were either born into the ruling class, or they were not. Genealogy determined recruitment into leadership positions, just as it determined who was wealthy and owned property, and who was poor and without property. Of course hereditary rulership did not prevent quarrels within the ruling group, and did not even prevent palace revolutions. But it did prevent the possibility of recruitment from the lower social orders. Political office and its privileges were matters of birthright.

The democratic revolution changed this. It separated birthright from

Figure 6.1 Which Few Citizens Will Achieve Leadership Roles?

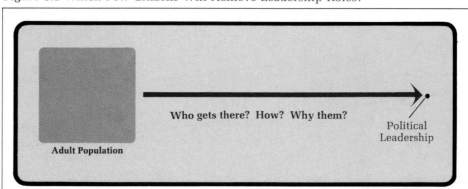

Who gets there? How? Why them?

Political Leadership

Adult Population

political officeholding. Authority over society could no longer be claimed because of family name. The powerful positions had somehow to be earned.

It is worth dwelling on this idea for a moment. Sometimes it is thought that the democratic revolution was a challenge to the idea of leadership itself. Although such might have been intended by a few radical egalitarians, this challenge was not a major part of the democratic revolution. What took place was the challenge to inherited leadership. Even our own Constitution acknowledged that a few would govern the many. But at the same time it was also acknowledged that power and position were to be achieved through merit, performance, and talent.

Criteria for Political Recruitment

We can begin our description of actual recruitment practices in American politics by expanding Figure 6.1. Think of the ancient Chinese Box Puzzle. In this puzzle different-sized boxes are designed so that the smallest box fits into the next largest one, which in turn fits into the next largest one, and so forth. The largest box contains all the boxes. To discover the very smallest box requires opening the whole series of boxes between it and the largest box.

Now imagine that the largest box represents the population of society and the smallest box represents the leadership group. The remaining boxes would represent smaller and smaller "recruitment pools" which supply persons from the larger to the smaller groups. Recruitment is the gradual but continuous process of selection and elimination which narrows the large population to the few who hold the highest positions. Figure 6.2 is a diagram of that process, showing four recruitment stages intervening between the many and the few.

Figure 6.2 Recruitment Criteria for Political Leadership

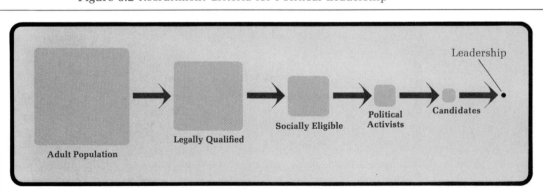

Legally Qualified: Within the adult population there is a subset who meet the legal qualifications for political officeholding. For instance, they meet the constitutionally set minimum ages. Other legal qualifications include residency requirements (you must live in the state from which you would like to be a senator, for instance) and, for certain positions, professional credentials (especially for judicial offices, which often are limited to persons with legal training). Legal qualifications, however, do not play a very significant part in political recruitment. With minor exceptions any adult citizen is legally qualified to hold public office. This has not always been the case. In the seventeenth century only property owners could stand for office; Blacks were barred from office as well as from voting until after the Civil War; and women were prohibited from holding certain positions until fairly recent times. One way to trace the evolution of democratic principles in any society is through the progressive elimination of legal restrictions that prevent particular groups from holding office.

"Socially Eligible": The next recruitment criteria in the diagram refers to those who are "socially eligible." Although there are no written rules concerning this criterion, there is evidence that a large percentage of our political leaders consistently come from particular social groups in the population. Far from being a representative sample of the population, the leaders are very atypical in their social origins, in their educational attainments, and in the occupations they hold before reaching political office.

To begin with, leaders are almost always recruited from middle- and upper-middle-income families, and from the business and professional classes. One technique for showing this is demonstrated in Figure 6.3. In

Figure 6.3 Social Eligibility: The Bias in Leadership

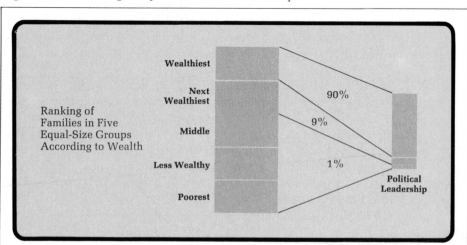

Ranking of Families in Five Equal-Size Groups According to Wealth

Wealthiest
Next Wealthiest
Middle
Less Wealthy
Poorest

90%
9%
1%

Political Leadership

this figure the adult population is ranked into five equal-size groups according to wealth. At the top is the wealthiest one-fifth of the population; at the bottom are persons near or below the official poverty line. Once we have this ranking it is a simple matter to calculate the proportion of leaders recruited from each income level.

The weathiest one-fifth of the population contributes approximately nine of every ten members to the leadership group. Stated differently, if you were to trace the social background of political leaders you would learn that 90 percent of them come from comparatively well-off and higher-status families. Most of the remaining come from the next social stratum. Only a sprinkling of leaders are drawn from the wage-earning working class. From this, one might conclude that the two or three hundred wealthiest families, the multimillionaires, thereby control American society. This is exaggerated propaganda. What is not exaggerated is that the wealthiest families oversupply those recruited into the elite political circles. Top positions in government tend to be held by men from prosperous professional or business families, or by men who themselves have become leading professionals or men of commerce.

Not only is the governing class composed almost entirely of men from better-off families, and has been so since the beginning of the nation, these men are atypical in terms of race, education, religion, nativity, and occupation. And they are men. If you aspire to the political elite it is advantageous to be male, White, well-educated, Protestant (and of Episcopalian or Presbyterian upbringing), native-born, and of British or northern European heritage, and, perhaps most important, successful in a prestigious occupation. A person lacking one or more of these traits might still reach the governing circles—Supreme Court Justice Thurgood Marshall is Black, Lyndon B. Johnson attended a teacher's college, John F. Kennedy was not a Protestant, and Harry S Truman began as a Kansas City haberdasher. But the fewer of the advantaging traits you have, the fewer your chances of reaching the governing class. However, the notable exceptions are important, and we return later in the chapter to the political conditions that explain the advancement of different types of persons into leadership circles.

Political Activists: Approximately one in twenty adult citizens are what we might call the political activists, and it is from this group that leadership eventually comes. As Chapter 5 made clear, the activists are persons who pay close attention to political matters, who serve on committees and work in campaigns, who know and are known by the persons actually holding office, and who are in positions that traditionally supply the recruits for public office. This group is largely, though not exclusively, made up of middle- and upper-middle-class citizens.

The boundaries that separate the politically active from the less active are neither firmly established nor easily recognized. Persons move back and forth across these boundaries as their interests shift, as their career experiences take them closer to or further away from the political sector, and as their own ambitions intersect with opportunities for a political career. In some important respects the actives are self-selected. There are no universally applied criteria for entry into the loose network which supplies the candidates for the highest position. Political activists do, though, often come from families with a tradition of political involvement; they are exposed to politics early in their life and simply carry on with these habits into their adult careers. Approximately one-third of the officeholders in the United States trace their earliest political involvement to the influence of the family. This is well illustrated in the careers of such families as the Roosevelts, Tafts, and Kennedys, and is a pattern that repeats itself at the less dramatic levels of political life as well.

Candidates: Within the politically active stratum is an even smaller number of persons who become the serious candidates for top leadership positions. This includes those who are actually nominated for elective positions as well as those whose names appear on lists when appointments are being made to the cabinet, the Supreme Court, executive agencies, and so forth. How some activists become serious contenders for the leadership positions, and others do not, is not well understood. One factor, however, is self-assertiveness. This is illustrated in President Lyndon Johnson's view of the world as "a vacuum of non-wills in which the strong man with a 'will to power' automatically takes charge. Most people drop off the political ladder at the bottom and middle rungs; private values intrude; conflicts arise. The restless few who remain become the political leaders of the day." It was no accident that Johnson himself belonged to the restless few: "As long as I can remember I've always been the kind of person who takes over in any group, who takes responsibility for calling the gathering together, getting the agenda for the meeting and carrying out the assignments."

Another factor influencing movement from the activist to the serious contender group is the attitude of those already in powerful positions. Persons in established leadership positions can nurture and sponsor careers in the way in which they make opportunities available and the way in which they fill key apprenticeship positions. It is said, for instance, that Lyndon Johnson, when he was majority leader in the Senate, greatly aided John F. Kennedy's career by assisting Kennedy as a freshman senator to his appointment on the prestigious Senate Foreign Relations Committee. This provided Kennedy with a platform from which he could launch his drive for the Presidential nomination of the Democratic party.

From the candidates of course come the officeholders. But what we see in this overview of the recruitment process is that the selection of leaders begins long before the attention of the voting public is engaged. It is not entirely correct to say that "electorates choose their leaders." Rather, it is more accurate to say that the electorate chooses between candidates who themselves have been "preselected" by a long process of sorting and picking and eliminating.

We cannot, therefore, understand important aspects of American politics until we see what kinds of persons successfully move through the recruitment processes. In your generation, which few will be chosen for the most powerful and prestigious position? Why them and not others? To answer these questions we consider three topics: (1) The Recruitment Plateau, (2) An Elite of Achievement, and (3) The Continuing Skill Revolution.

The Recruitment Plateau

Imagine that we were to study systematically the processes through which a tiny, tiny proportion of your own generation will eventually come to hold the highest offices of political authority and leadership in the society. We might make up a list of persons between the ages of 18 and 25, and then follow them through their careers until, say, 30 years from now, when a few of them will have risen to powerful and prestigious positions. Suppose that this list of younger citizens included the following:

> The son of an influential corporation lawyer who heads a law firm in Washington, D.C. He has just graduated from Princeton, where he was active in student politics and was chosen editor of the campus newspaper. Next year he will enter the Harvard Business School.
>
> A Black longshoreman in San Francisco who is keenly interested in trade union affairs. He has already been elected secretary of his multiracial local. His formal education is limited to community college, but he is an effective organizer and popular with fellow workers. He has campaigned actively for local candidates of the Democratic party.
>
> A student body president of a large state university in the Midwest. She is the daughter of a small-town mayor, and has served her father as an unofficial consultant on eliminating sex discrimination in the town's schools and hospitals. Although she is known to be very sharp politically, her academic record is mediocre. Still, she has been admitted to the university's graduate school of education.
>
> A farmer's son who graduated with honors from Jerseyville High School, but decided against further education. He was a football hero in the community and has recently joined the Elks, partly because some local businessmen have hinted that they would like him to serve on the town planning commission.

Now ask yourself, what are the chances that 30 years from now any one of these four will have reached the top governing circles? We probably would rank their chances in the order in which they are listed, and this despite each having political leadership skills. For every 100 persons with the traits of the Princeton graduate, perhaps one will end up in a top position, while for every 10,000 budding labor leaders, only one is likely to move that far. However, this particular labor leader is Black, which may be an advantage during a period when great attention is given to parity between races. The next person on the list is probably, on balance, disadvantaged by her sex, and by the fact that she is taking advanced work in education rather than law or business. Finally we come to our high school hero, whose chances of reaching elite status are practically nil. It is true that Richard Nixon comes from a small town, where his parents ran a grocery store, but Nixon went to college and then earned a law degree before getting into politics. Spiro Agnew, son of a hardworking immigrant, also started his political career with law degree in hand.

The Recruitment Pool
for Elite Positions

Predicting the probable success of different 20-year-old citizens illustrates an initial fact about political recruitment. Leaders are chosen from a distinct and comparatively small subset of the general population. This subset can be viewed as a plateau that it is necessary to reach before one is likely to gain an elite position (see Figure 6.4).

We can now make more sense out of the idea of social eligibility. To be well known, wealthy, highly educated, in a prestigious occupation, and the beneficiary of important family connections is to be on or very near the plateau which serves as the recruitment pool for the elite positions. Consider two persons from our list of young citizens. The Princeton graduate is launched on a career which has in the past placed persons such as himself in line for the highest governing circles. His family, his family's friends, his father's business associates, as well as his fellow students at Princeton and Harvard, would not consider it abnormal were he to an-

Figure 6.4 The Recruitment Plateau

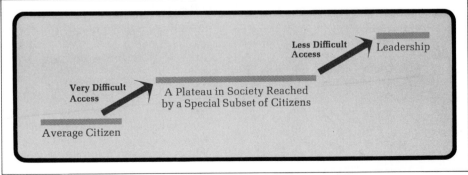

nounce that his ambition is to gain high political office. The social setting of the farm boy is in this regard far different. How unusual it would be were he seriously to consider himself as a future member of the highest political circles. There are few models for him to emulate, no contacts to put him into the right channels, and little reason for him to think of himself as hobnobbing with the very wealthy and the very powerful. His idea of success is to own his own farm and maybe become village mayor. Such a self-image is realistic, just as is the self-image of the Princeton graduate. The point is, however, that persons are constantly eliminating themselves from as well as selecting themselves for the competition for the few top positions. Patterns of self-elimination and self-assertion are not separable from the accidents of birth. Some are born with a foot on the ladder leading to power, but most are not. Those who are not have difficulty finding the ladder, let alone getting a foot on it.

Moreover, movement into leadership positions always to some extent is influenced by the judgments of persons already holding high office. This is true even if great stress is placed on "objective criteria," for the formulation and application of those criteria can never be separated from the prejudices and biases of men responsible for them. No matter how talent is defined, it must be discovered by those who have already proved themselves to have

Some are born with a foot on the ladder leading to power.   (Photo: Wide World)

the talent. It is natural that men who control the pathways into the governing class will perpetuate persons of similar status and background. Men look to familiar faces and well-known circles when choosing their associates or when promoting from among the many able young a few who thereby have the opportunity to reach yet higher positions. This selectivity from the top down contributes to a process wherein particular social groups continue to supply recruits for the top political positions.

Social eligibility, however, is only one among several factors that account for who reaches the plateau. All four of our illustrative cases listed earlier have a chance if for no other reason than that they have demonstrated some political leadership skill. In this regard their chances are higher than are the chances of schoolmates who have shown no inclination toward or competence in politics. Another Princetonian might come from an equally prestigious family, but his interests might have been concentrated on chemistry for the past six years. He is now in graduate school, and avoids activities that distract him from his academic work. Or the student body president might plan on getting married immediately after graduation, her chief goal to raise a healthy, happy family. Neither the chemist nor the future housewife is a realistic possibility for political leadership positions.

An Elite of Achievement

Because so many of our political leaders are White and male and from fairly well-to-do families, some observers of American politics reach the conclusion that *who you are* is the definitive criterion for recruitment into top positions. This, we believe, is a hasty and incorrect conclusion. It is true that the traits we have identified as making for "social eligibility" provide advantages, and the absence of these traits hampers a political career, but social background can neither guarantee a place among the political leaders nor completely block entry.

Achievement: A Determinant of Political Recruitment

The men who govern American society are all achievers. They have proved their ability to manage enterprises or to direct the efforts of others or to command the loyalty of large numbers of persons. Thus men do not become Presidents who yesterday were state legislators or small-town mayors. Since the end of World War II the men reaching the Presidency were either Vice-Presidents (three of them); or in the case of Eisenhower, a five-star general and popular war hero; or in the case of Kennedy, a forceful U.S. senator who happened also to come from an extremely wealthy family.

This emphasis on achievement in American politics is consistent with the democratic principle that political office should be open to any who are talented and ambitious. Of course not all achievements, not all talents, and not all ambitions are weighed equally in the calculus that determines recruitment into leadership circles.

The Display of Talent on a Grand Scale: The magnitude of talent and abilities is involved. It is necessary to display talent on a grand scale. It is better to be a success at running Ford Motor Company than to be a success at selling worn-out Fords on the used car lot, though the latter may involve greater skill and harder work than the former. It is better to be an innovative president of a prestigious university than an innovative grade school teacher where the president sends his children, though teaching a room full of 8-year-olds may demand more innovation than overseeing a university. It is better to be the popular vote-getting mayor of New York City than the popular vote-getting mayor of Brisbane, though it may take more magnetism to turn out the vote in Brisbane than New York.

It is therefore not achievement considered in the abstract but, rather, very specific achievements that move one into the governing circles. This suggests why the better-off contribute so regularly to the top leadership. They have initial advantages: They have the education and contacts necessary to reach positions through which ability can be demonstrated on a grand scale. The used car salesman may be as skilled, as personable, and as hardworking as the president of the company whose worn-out products he sells. But the salesman was born into the working class, not the upper class; he attended a local junior college, not Harvard Business School; his friends also sell used cars, not direct the corporations which manufacture them; he is sometimes active in precinct politics, not a contributor of thousand of dollars to Presidential campaigns. When the list is made of possible appointees to the cabinet or possible nominees for the governship or possible candidates for an ambassadorship, it seems never to include the skilled, personable, hardworking used car salesman, but often to include the head of the company whose cars he sells.

Top leaders are recruited from among men of considerable achievement. But the achievements that count are those easier to display if you start life as a White male from a Protestant and fairly well-off family. These are the traits that provide the education and the initial job opportunities that in turn launch the careers that take some people, but not many, to the plateau from which the jump into governing circles is made.

The Ability to Win Elections: This picture of an elite of achievement does not, however, tell the whole story. It is true that American politics often rewards with power those persons who have proved that they can direct the large institutions of commerce and business, of banking, and of law, education, and philanthropy. But also rewarded are persons who demon-

Eisenhower used his enormous popularity as a victorious wartime general in winning the Presidency. *(Photo: Wide World)*

strate a very different kind of talent and skill—the ability to win elections.

The electorate in a democracy necessarily controls entry into certain key leadership posts. Thus the achievement that matters is the simple achievement of winning elections. Nixon builds on a succession of election victories, starting with his campaign for the House of Representatives in 1946 and culminating in his landslide reelection to the Presidency in 1972. Lyndon Johnson before him also went from the House to the Senate to the Vice-Presidency to the Presidency. Of course not all major electoral victories represent the culmination of a series of lesser victories. Eisenhower transferred his enormous popularity as victorious wartime general into voter popularity, and won the Presidency without ever having been active in politics. The governor of California, Ronald Reagan, moved into that position directly from his career as a movie actor. Charles Percy was a corporation executive just prior to his election as Illinois senator.

Voter appeal is a resource that persons from any background can use to advantage. Indeed it is a resource that compensates in American politics for the lack of family wealth or a prestige education. Only one President out of the last five (Kennedy in contrast to Truman, Eisenhower, Johnson, and Nixon) started his career with the advantage of wealth.

We see, thus, that achievement is weighed in two different though not always unrelated ways. There is the achievement that is marked by becoming a corporation executive or a senior partner in a leading law firm or the president of a foundation or university. Persons whose talents are thus displayed are candidates for the highest political positions, as when Robert McNamara moves from head of Ford Motor Company to become the Secretary of Defense or Dean Rusk from president of Rockefeller Foundation to become the Secretary of State. There is also the achievement that is marked by election victories.

Although the first group of achievers come almost exclusively from the wealthier social classes, for the second group of achievers this is not necessarily so. It is this fact that gives to political recruitment in America one of its distinctive characteristics. Recruitment is comparatively closed to the lower classes insofar as the achievements leading to high *appointive* office are concerned. It is much less closed to those classes insofar as the achievements leading to *elective* office are concerned. Persons from higher-status groups will always be overrepresented in top leadership circles, but they are never the exclusive occupants.

The Continuing Skill Revolution

The central task of leadership can be simply stated: Anticipate and solve the problems of society. This task is always unevenly performed. Consider the agenda of today's social problems: the pollution of air and water; congested and poorly functioning cities; inflationary costs of social services; and racial, ethnic, and social class tensions. Would these problems be less severe today had the leadership of previous decades been more skilled at anticipating and correcting the drift toward pollution, urban decay, costly social services, and group tensions? Or, to put the question another way: Are there today signs of future problems that go unnoticed by the current leadership, but that will crowd the political agenda when today's college students are trying to raise their families?

Such questions as these are extremely difficult to answer, but they do illustrate an important issue for political recruitment. The skills necessary to give effective leadership to society change as the problems facing the society change. We ask, then, whether leadership skills have caught up to the social problems. The struggle to keep the leadership abreast with particular challenges is what sets in motion the continuing skill revolution.

The Link Between Skill Revolution
and the Political Agenda

One illustration of the link between skill revolution and the political agenda is demonstrated by the events of the 1930s. The nation was caught in the midst of a severe economic depression, and none of the traditional economic solutions seemed to be working. Then in 1932 the administration of Franklin D. Roosevelt took over the leadership of the country. In a spirit of pragmatism and experimentation dozens of new social reforms and programs were tried. The persons recruited to government positions had very different economic and social philosophies from those who had served in the preceding administrations. The new recruits, some elected and some appointed, displayed a new range of skills. Out of this "skill revolution" came the New Deal, a collection of government programs and social services and an attitude toward fiscal management which would have been alien to the leadership group of only a decade earlier.

This illustrates the link between a skill revolution and the political agenda as it conforms with social change. Pressing problems in a society define the agenda with which the leadership should deal. When suitable skills are lacking, the problems worsen. When the appropriate skills are provided, relevant programs are initiated. What are often called "national crises" occur during the lag time between the emergence of critical problems and the recruitment of persons with skills and outlooks capable of dealing with them.

To understand further the interaction between a nation's political agenda and the skills of its leadership, let us briefly compare the past three decades with the present decade. In the thirty years from 1940 to 1970, the political agenda of the United States was dominated by issues of national security and international politics: World War II, the containing of communism, the Korean War, the North Atlantic Treaty Organization (NATO) and other mutual security alliances, the Berlin crisis, the arms race and nuclear stockpiling, the missile gap between the United States and the USSR, the Cuban blockade, and of course the long-drawn-out Vietnam war.

This agenda of issues had a profound effect on the skills and outlooks recruited into top political leadership positions. Thus, for instance, the man elected to the Presidency in 1952, General Dwight D. Eisenhower, had no record and very few known positions on any domestic questions. Indeed, *both* of the major parties had approached him about running for the Presidency on their ticket. With national security and international politics at the forefront of public attention, leadership fell into the hands of persons skilled at diplomacy and military matters, persons such as John Foster Dulles, powerful Secretary of State to Eisenhower, or, more recently, Henry Kissinger, foreign policy advisor to Nixon. The 1950s and 1960s spawned the "military-industrial complex," but we should not be surprised that a nation with war, weapons, and security on its mind would turn for leadership to the Pentagon, the CIA, the weapons manufacturers.

Now, however, as we approach the mid-1970s the military-industrial complex is in disfavor. Americans have become disenchanted with the Cold War policies of the past decade, and they were even more disillusioned by the long-drawn-out Vietnam war. Domestic political questions are in the ascendancy: pollution, drugs, crime, social services, taxes, and inflation. This shifting of the social-political agenda is, according to some observers, setting in motion a skill revolution. We may be witnessing, they say, the transfer of political power from the military-industrial complex to the social services-industrial complex, with a demand for leaders able to solve the perplexing problems in health and education, transport, consumer protection, urban life, conservation, and environmental quality.

It is too early to see where this skill revolution will take American society, but two summary points suggest how it helps us understand the concept of political recruitment. First, we draw our political leaders from particular social groups and from persons of demonstrated achievement, but we draw them as well from particular skill groups; and, second, the challenge of any society is to recruit into leadership the skills appropriate to the problems it faces. The drift into one crisis or another is in some measure due to the failure to recruit leaders able to anticipate and solve social problems. Unattended to, the problems gather momentum until they become crises, as when the "problems" of city life become the "crisis" of urbanized America. Some feel that it is past time for a major skill revolution, arguing that those who have managed America over the past decades have been too preoccupied with anticommunism and national security and too unconcerned with the quality of life for American citizens.

Summary Thus Far

It may be useful to summarize the three things we have learned about political recruitment in the United States. First, some social groups are very overrepresented within leadership circles, whereas other social groups are underrepresented or not represented at all. Yet this simple fact should not disguise the equally important fact that the social composition of the governing group can and does change over time. The wealthy landowners who founded the nation did not expect that a century later the United States would be governed by aggressive industrialists. These same industrialists and capitalists so much in control by the latter part of the nineteenth century hardly anticipated that but a few decades later they would be sharing power with leaders of giant labor unions. But these changes have taken place, and even today it is obvious that new social groups are making their presence felt. The most dramatic contemporary instance are the Blacks. But the emergence of women as a social force is also having an effect. Each year there are a few more Blacks and women in public office; both groups are inching their way closer to the highest offices. Table 6.1 shows the increase of Blacks and women in Congress over the past quarter century.

Changes in the social composition of the leadership notwithstanding, it remains a fact that most leadership comes from the better-off social classes and from the more prestigious occupations. This observation led to our second comment on political recruitment. Despite a bias in political recruit-

Table 6.1 Number of Black Members and Women Members in Congress, 1947–1972

CONGRESS[a]	Black Members in the		Women Members in the	
	SENATE	HOUSE	SENATE	HOUSE
80th		2	1	7
81st		2	1	9
82nd		2	1	10
83rd		2	3	12
84th		3	1	16
85th		4	1	15
86th		4	1	16
87th		4	2	17
88th		5	2	11
89th		6	2	10
90th	1	5	1	11
91st	1	9	1	10
92nd	1	12	2	13
93rd[b]	1	15	0	14

[a] Each congressional session lasts two years. There are a total of 435 members of the House and a total of 100 members of the Senate.
[b] As of November 1972 election.
Source: Based on data from *Current American Government* (Washington D.C.: *Congressional Quarterly*, Spring 1973), pp. 25–26.

ment, it is not "who you are" but "what you accomplish" that guards entry into top positions. Political leaders are nearly always persons of impressive achievements. Often these achievements are in nonpolitical arenas, especially in business, law, education, or the military. It is achievements in these areas that can identify one as a good candidate for a high appointive position. The other main achievement is a string of electoral victories. In the final analysis, many powerful offices go to those with voter support; these same offices are denied those whom the voters reject.

This took us to our third comment: The talents and abilities of the leadership group do not always measure up to the challenges facing the society. It can easily happen that the problems on the political agenda change more quickly than the recruitment into leadership of new skills and new visions. Unless, and until, a "skill revolution" takes place, the nation will drift. Problems stack up, and solutions are elusive. This is a complaint heard often today. The agenda is crowded with unsolved problems: congested cities, racial justice, environmental pollution, unsafe neighborhoods, inflation, and unemployment.

New social groups are making their presence felt.   *(Photo: Wide World)*

Some critics of American society believe that the biases in our recruitment processes are blocking the type of skill revolution necessary if contemporary social ills are to be cured. This is a point of view to which we return at the conclusion of the chapter, when we raise a controversial question. First, however, another and related point should be made about recruitment and American politics.

A Debate About Political Leadership

The argument is sometimes heard that the political leaders in the United States all think and feel the same way about public policy. Differences of viewpoint within leadership circles are allowed only on trivial matters. The leaders are a cohesive group, and it is nearly impossible to introduce new ideas unless the "establishment" agrees to them.

Others counter that leaders are divided by arguments and differences of opinion. Leaders have conflicting career ambitions, and they speak for different groups in society. In this view, the important fact about leadership is internal competition, not internal cohesion.

Two considerations will put this debate into its proper context, one indicating leadership disagreements and the other indicating an important measure of leadership consensus.

Political Leadership in Disagreement

A great variety of policy viewpoints find their way into the governing circles. Sharply divergent views are held on such issues as tax reform, inflation controls, defense expenditures, and so forth. It could not be otherwise. *The political recruitment process carries into leadership circles some of the basic conflicts and divisions of society*. This happens in many ways. For instance, we see in Chapter 8 that Republicans and Democrats do differ. These differences become expressed within the leadership group whenever the two parties are pitted against each other. Factors in addition to two-party politics create sharp disagreements among leaders. Leaders become spokesmen for the many political and social cleavages in society: North versus South, Protestant versus Catholic, workers versus management. Then of course there are conflicting perspectives associated with different institutional roles: state leaders versus the federal bureaucracy, Congress versus the Presidency.

Two practical consequences follow from these conflicts. The first is that they put an enormous strain on government. It is not easy to settle on a policy when the policy makers cannot agree. The result is often policy through compromise and negotiation. The second consequence directs our attention to democratic theory. Disagreements within the leadership group allow the public to play off one set of leaders against another. The Democrats can be replaced by the Republicans; or leaders who favor an expanded military budget can be replaced by those who support military cuts. Thus it is that competing viewpoints and conflicting career ambitions within the leadership help establish some measure of popular control over public policy.

Conflict and competition among leaders are, however, only part of the story. The political recruitment process also ensures a measure of consensus and agreement.

Recruitment from the Political Mainstream

We mean two things by the "political mainstream." First, we mean those broad policies that most Americans actively support, or at least willingly tolerate. Take military policy as an example. Most Americans agree that the nation should maintain military preparedness, and that the United States should if necessary defend its national interests with military force. Most, but not all, citizens take this view. There are some who oppose the whole idea of military preparedness, and believe that the United States should totally and unilaterally disarm. Such a view is normally considered to be "outside the mainstream of American thinking." Equally outside the mainstream is the view that the United States should engage in preemptive nuclear strikes against its presumed enemies.

The political recruitment process tends over and over again to select leaders from the political mainstream. One reason is that the electorate is not likely to support candidates whose viewpoints are at sharp odds with its own. This does not mean that every political leader is equally acceptable to every voter. A congressman elected by White rural Mississippians probably has views on race relations that are obnoxious to northern Black voters. But if individual leaders are disliked by particular electorates, the leadership group as a whole has policy views that are not at odds with majoritarian, mainstream thinking.

Substantive Consensus: There is, then, a certain consensus among the leaders. It is a consensus established by the broad policy perspectives the American public is willing to tolerate. Our argument about consensus is not inconsistent with the previous point. Within the political mainstream, and thus within the leadership, are many divergent viewpoints. Take again the example of military policy. To say there is broad agreement that the United States should be prepared to defend its interests is not at all to agree about the size of the budget necessary to maintain "preparedness" or to agree about what poses a threat to "national interests." This is shown in Figure 6.5. Divergent viewpoints within the mainstream notwithstanding, the recruitment process does eliminate from the top leadership circles those views that strike most Americans as "extreme" or "going too far."

Figure 6.5 Inside and Outside the Political Mainstream

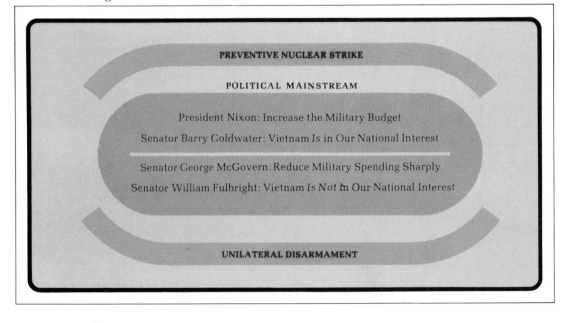

Procedural Consensus; Working Within the System: There is a second sense in which leaders are recruited from and reflect the political mainstream. Much that is important about American politics, or any politics, is captured in the oft-repeated phrase of the 1960s, "working within the system." Here the emphasis is not so much on substantive consensus as on procedural consensus. There is an acceptable way of doing things, and an unacceptable way. The political hostility shown toward peaceniks, eco-freaks, Black militants, and hippies should be understood in this context, because the hostility stemmed from a deep and pervasive belief that without "the system" there is no hope for the goals sought by dissident groups—no hope for lasting peace, clean air, racial justice, cultural tolerance. Political dissidents can vote the rascals out, but they will not be allowed to destroy the system which permits a later group of rascals to be evicted; they can petition and demonstrate, but they cannot abolish the system which allows petitions and demonstrations; they can renounce acquisitiveness, but they cannot be permitted to ruin the system which gives to others the right to acquire.

Leadership is agreed on the importance of "working within the system," and in this regard it reflects the political mainstream of American society. Consensus on *how* to bring about change cuts across sharp policy disagreements on *what* changes, if any, are necessary. The recruitment process nourishes this procedural consensus. The long climb to high office generally breeds in persons a commitment to the rules of the game, and these rules facilitate a common approach to governing despite differences of view within the elite.

Sometimes, however, certain members of the political elite fail to play by the "rules of the game." The discovery of this activity sends shock waves through the political system. Certainly such was the case with the exposure of the Watergate affair. Men in extremely powerful positions were caught in the act of distorting the workings of democracy to further narrow interests. Illegal raising of campaign funds, the dubious use of political spying techniques, and even attempts at undermining the election process were in wide practice during the months before the election of 1972.

Perhaps most disturbed by the revelations surrounding Watergate were certain key elite groups that fully understood the implications of the Watergate activities. These groups—an independent judiciary, influential newsmedia personalities, and congressmen—quickly saw the importance of ridding Washington of those persons whose ideas and ways of operating were alien to the "procedural consensus" on which the successful political guidance of the nation depends.

Watergate was not a dispute over this or that candidate, or this or that substantive policy. It was a challenge to an open, democratic politics. And this was an intolerable challenge to those whose careers, livelihoods, and principles are closely linked to such a politics. The uproar over Watergate is to be understood in this light. Disputes over who should govern and disputes over what policy goals they might seek can be accepted within leadership circles. Unacceptable are attacks on the very methods of choosing the leaders.

Controversy

The political agenda today is crowded with such unsolved problems as racial tension, costly and inadequate social services, and urban sprawl. Some critics of American society believe that these problems elude solution because of the skills recruited into leadership circles. They cite in particular the fact that leadership is generally recruited from very narrow social strata rather than from across a broad spectrum of groups.

One Side

The narrow base from which leadership is recruited hampers the "skill revolution" this society needs. The skills which might establish racial harmony, provide decent education and health care, and plan communities as places to enjoy life are not necessarily or even at all found in White upper-class males. Leaders should be drawn from those groups who have direct experiences with the problems of American life. Then we would have leaders with the skills and insights to find solutions.

Earlier we described four young citizens: the Princetonian headed for a career as a corporation executive, the Black longshoreman active in local politics, the politically astute feminist anticipating a career in education, the popular small-town boy who soon will have experience in community planning. The chances of the corporation executive's reaching high political office are much, much greater than the chances of any of the other three. But whose career is likely to develop the skill and insight necessary to ease racial tension within the American working class? And whose career will provide the experiences which could bring innovation and fresh approaches to the Department of Health, Education, and Welfare? And which of the four will develop sensitivity to the complexities of protecting community well-being against the encroachments of urban sprawl?

Is American society not penalizing itself by always turning leadership over to the successful business and professional classes?

The Other Side

Recruiting skilled and competent persons is difficult under the best of circumstances. Turning to the successful businessmen, lawyers, and civic leaders as candidates for high office helps minimize mistakes in recruitment. These persons have demonstrated that they can succeed where the competition is toughest. They have graduated from the most difficult schools. They have achieved in highly competitive situations. They have proved that they can run the largest institutions in American society, and governing requires the skill to run such superinstitutions as the Pentagon or the Department of Health, Education, and Welfare. We are well advised to recruit as top leaders those who have demonstrated their skills across a broad range of activities.

To reach the plateau from which leaders traditionally have come is already to have a grasp of the intricate *and* interacting problems in American society. Thirty years from now the Black trade union activist will know how to develop race relations programs which make sense for the docks of San Francisco. It is not clear, however, that he will have the national and international perspective necessary for a broadly based program on the same issue. A creative program will have to take into account the interracial conditions on Alabama farms, on army bases in Europe, in the sales forces of Boston insurance agencies. Moreover, it will have to coordinate with a program for police colleges in the Department of Justice or a student exchange program with Africa planned by the Department of State. Perhaps the Princeton graduate, now an IBM executive who spent two years as a consultant in Nairobi, who has served on the Civil Rights Commission, who is a member of the Board of Trustees of several colleges, and who recently advised the Ford Foundation on its program for grants to inner-city schools, is the best candidate for the directorship of a federal agency on race relations.

The argument we are making is for recruitment from the small group of citizens who have demonstrated their considerable talents and achievements. It is of course unfortunate that this small group is mostly White, mostly male, and mostly from wealthier and Protestant families. These facts should be changed, but they should be changed by eliminating race, sex, and class discrimination.

The color or sex or social background of leadership are not at issue. But the skills and visions are. American society will penalize itself if it attempts to recruit as top leaders persons whose careers have been limited and whose achievements do not command national recognition.

Suggested Readings

Material on the careers and social background of political leaders can be found in Donald Matthews, *The Social Background of Political Decision-Makers* (Garden

City, N.Y.: Doubleday, 1954); and in Suzanne Keller, *Beyond the Ruling Class* (New York: Random House, 1963). A report by W. Lloyd Warner and his associates, *The American Federal Executive* (New Haven: Yale University Press, 1963), has detailed information on the social and personal characteristics of civilian and military leaders in the federal government,

Important theoretical commentary on the process of political recruitment into top positions appears throughout C. Wright Mills, *The Power Elite* (New York: Oxford University Press, 1956). Elaboration of certain themes which appear in this chapter can be found in Kenneth Prewitt, *The Recruitment of Political Leaders* (Indianapolis: Bobbs-Merrill, 1970); and in Kenneth Prewitt and Alan Stone, *The Ruling Elites* (New York: Harper & Row, 1973). The idea of "skill revolutions" is developed by Harold Lasswell in *Politics: Who Gets What, When, and How* (New York: McGraw-Hill, 1936).

Pressure Groups in American Politics

7

O ur chapters thus far have dealt with a number of underlying characteristics of society and how they affect politics in America. We discussed the basic economic structure of America, the political beliefs of American citizens, ways in which Americans become active in politics, the kinds of group differences one finds in America, and the kinds of people who are recruited into political life. Together these characteristics form the framework for the struggle among citizens and groups of citizens over what policies the government ought to pursue.

Now we must turn to look at that struggle over governmental policy more directly. Who takes part in the struggle? How is it carried on? More important, what makes for success or failure in the struggle? Why is it that some groups and some interests are successful in obtaining from the government those policies that they want while other groups and interests are ignored?

The Role of Interest Groups

In this chapter we consider the role of organized groups or, as they are sometimes called, interest groups or pressure groups or lobbies. In Chapter 4 we discussed the factors that make groups of citizens into politically relevant forces. Two of the most important factors were that they have interests in common and that they become organized. This chapter will make clear why organization is important as we see the way in which organized interest groups operate to try to influence governmental policy.

Disputes over the Role of Interest Groups

There is some dispute over the power of interest groups. Some students of politics have argued that one can know all that one needs to know about American politics by understanding the role of such groups. The Congress and the President, these writers assert, do not initiate policy. Rather they merely respond passively to the demands of lobbies and organized interests. At best the government acts as a "broker" among such interests—seeing that each organized interest gets a little something in response to its demands. Thus it is the interplay of the conflicting pressures coming from organized groups that determines what policies the government pursues.

This view is considered by most writers on politics to be somewhat of an exaggeration. Governmental policy is not the mere mechanical sum of interest group pressures. Yet there is some truth to the view. Organized groups are not all-powerful. But interests represented by well-organized pressure groups are much more able to press their demands on the government than are unorganized interests. And this plays a major role in determining who will benefit from governmental policy.

There is a second dispute about the role of organized groups in American politics. This has to do with the extent to which the activities of such groups are detrimental to the welfare of the society as a whole. Pressure groups serve the "selfish" interests of particular groups of citizens. Organizations of clothing manufacturers lobby for the interests of clothing manufacturers, organizations of doctors for the interests of doctors, organizations of farmers for the interests of farmers. Nor are such "selfish" interests limited to the wealthier sections of society trying to get an even bigger share of the economic pie. Black organizations press the claims of Blacks, organizations of welfare mothers express their interests, labor unions press the claims of workers. The interests they express are "selfish," not because the demands they make on the government are necessarily unjustified but because they represent the specific interests of each group and do not take into account the needs and problems of other groups. Each group is out to take care of "its own."

The debate revolves around whether these group activities hurt or help the "public interest." And since the term "public interest" has itself no clear definition, the debate is often over how one defines that term.

For critics of the effects of pressure groups on governmental policy, the "selfish" interests of pressure groups are detrimental to the welfare of the society as a whole. Pressure groups vie for the attention of congressmen and administrators in order to obtain some benefit for their specific group. In this way, the broader public interest is ignored. No one plans for the problems of the society at large. Such a view of interest groups is reflected in the "muckraking" literature that became prominent through such writers as Lincoln Steffens at the beginning of the century. And this position has been an important one in political commentary ever since. Muckraking literature has revealed many instances of close association of specific interests with the government. Out of such close association comes a governmental policy that benefits particular interests to the possible detriment of the rest of society. This critique of the functioning of interest groups is, furthermore, not merely the province of journalists looking for sensational examples of corrupt relations between lobbies and policy makers. It is a position argued with vigor by a number of the most serious students of American politics.

These critiques make one further point. It is not only that the pressure group system leads to the ignoring of the interests of the nation as a whole in favor of particular "selfish" interests. It is also a fault of the pressure group system that only certain "selfish" interests are adequately communicated. In general, they agree, the interests of business and of the more affluent portions of society are communicated in this way.

A counter-position has also been taken by other analysts of American politics. The counter-argument is that there is no contradiction between the selfish interests pursued by particular interest groups and some more general public good. Indeed, the public good, so the argument goes, does not exist outside of and separate from the specific interests of groups of citizens. Rather, the public good represents the sum of the desires of these various subgroups, and *out of the clash among these groups* comes the most effective and responsive public policy.

And though defenders of the interest group system would admit that not all groups are equally represented, they would argue that the answer is more, and *more equal,* group representation. If some interests are well represented by interest groups and others are not, then the unrepresented should emulate the others and organize as well.

Which is the case? Does competition among organized interests subvert some more general public interest? Or is it the most effective way of seeing that the myriad of citizen interests are adequately represented before the government?

We will return to these questions later in this chapter after we have considered some of the facts about the role of organized groups in American politics.

How Much Organization?

America has often been called a society of joiners; foreign observers have been struck by the ease with which Americans form organizations and by the vast numbers and far-ranging concerns of such organizations. And when one compares the United States to other nations, he finds a somewhat higher percentage of organization members here than elsewhere. Current figures indicate that about 6 out of 10 adult Americans belong to some organization, a figure higher than in other comparable countries where a little less than half the adult population is likely to belong to some organized group.

Who Are the Members of Organizations?

Does the figure "6 out of 10" mean that most Americans have some organization that looks after their political interests? The answer is unclear. Although the data show that a majority of Americans belong to some organization, they also indicate a large minority—4 out of 10—with no affiliation. More important, perhaps, is that all social groups are not equally

Most organizations are not formed for political purposes.   *(Photo: Wide World)*

likely to be members of organizations. As we saw in the chapter on the participation of citizens (Chapter 5), it is the upper-status citizens who are more likely to be organizational members. If you are affluent, if you have advanced education, if you are White rather than Black, you are more likely to be an organizational member. Thus, not only is membership not universal in the United States, but what membership there is, is not spread equally across the society.[1]

[1] Sidney Verba and Norman H. Nie, *Participation in America: Political Democracy and Social Equality* (New York: Harper & Row, 1972), chap. 11.

Political and Nonpolitical Interest Groups

Furthermore, not all organizations to which citizens belong are explicitly organized to express political interests. Only 8 percent of the citizenry belongs to specifically political groups—political party clubs; nonpartisan political groups like the League of Women Voters; and groups like the NAACP, whose prime purpose is to exert pressure on the government. Rather, the bulk of memberships are in organizations that are formed for other purposes. They are related to recreational interests (fraternal groups, sports and hobby clubs); to economic interests (unions, professional associations, farm groups); to particular community concerns (parent groups, service clubs); or to specific citizen identifications (nationality groups, religious groups).[2]

But it would be a mistake to think that only explicitly political groups represent citizen interests before the government. All these types of groups may become politically active, and some are constantly so. Indeed, it is hard to draw the line between political and nonpolitical organizations. Since the interests of all groups may at times be impinged upon by governmental activity or require some governmental response, any group may become a political actor. A prime example on the national scene is the National Rifle Association. Essentially organized as a recreational group for hunters and sportsmen, it became a major political force when it considered its interests challenged by advocates of gun-control legislation. And the same can be said for every other type of group. Church-related groups do not have primarily political goals, but they become involved in controversies over issues they see impinging upon their interests—perhaps abortion laws, perhaps school prayer decisions, or any other issue they take seriously. And groups representing economic interests are constantly involved with the government.

Involvement in Trying to Influence Government

The range of organizations that are active in trying to influence the government is reflected in Table 7.1, taken from a congressional report on officially registered lobbying organizations. It lists those who report the largest expenditures to influence Congress—of the hundreds of such groups registered in Washington.

The data ought not be taken to reflect necessarily which groups are most active in Washington—the Lobbying Act is too vague in defining who has to register and too lax in enforcement to allow one to rely too heavily on these reports. But the list does give some indication of the range of types of organizations that are active.

[2] *Ibid.*

Table 7.1   The Major Lobbies in Terms of Spending in 1971

ORGANIZATION	AMOUNT
Common Cause	$817,856
Veterans of World War I of the U.S.A., Inc.	308,946
American Postal Workers Union (AFL–CIO)	257,093
AFL–CIO (national headquarters)	205,101
American Farm Bureau Federation	165,063
United States Savings & Loan League	158,727
National Association of Letter Carriers (AFL–CIO)	135,334
National Committee for an American SST	131,080
Disabled American Veterans	129,881
National Association of Home Builders of the United States	125,779
American Trucking Association Inc.	115,287
American Medical Association	114,800
National Association of Postal Supervisors	102,795
New York Committee of International Committee of Passenger Lines	100,342
National Housing Conference, Inc.	99,924
Farmers' Educational and Cooperative Union of America	97,438
United Mine Workers of America	93,352
Brotherhood of Railway, Airline & Steamship Clerks (AFL–CIO)	91,624
National Association of Real Estate Boards	74,952
Committee for Humane Legislation	74,241
National Federation of Federal Employees	67,856
American Insurance Association	65,812
International Brotherhood of Teamsters	63,716
American Hospital Association	62,496
National Citizens' Committee for Revenue Sharing	61,720

Source: *Congressional Quarterly Weekly Report*, Washington, D.C., August 19, 1972.

Some represent particular segments of the business community: the home building industry, truckers, insurance agents. Some represent professional groups with particular interests, as in the case of doctors via the American Medical Association. Particular groups of workers are represented by their unions — postal clerks, letter carriers, mine workers. And some organizations represent groups of citizens who want to further particular political principles — Common Cause, for example, a liberal group interested in such matters as environmental protection, social welfare legislation, and governmental reform.

The list illustrates the wide range of groups that become involved in trying to influence the government—and the list reveals only the tip of the iceberg. It also illustrates the main principle that explains why some groups are active while others are not: Groups become politically active when governmental policy impinges on them—that is, when they want the government to stop some activity they consider harmful to their interests or when they want it to take some action they consider beneficial. Thus it is no wonder that the labor groups found most active are the ones who are most dependent on government, either because they are direct employees of the government (postal clerks, letter carriers) or because their conditions of work depend on government decisions (as do the conditions of mine workers in the heavily regulated mining industry). Nor is one surprised to find such businesses as savings and loan associations or insurance associations on the list, heavily affected, as they are, by federal and state legislation. Where the activity of government is important, citizens and groups are likely to be active.

What Differences Do Organizations Make?

That there is much organized activity in America is clear. But how does this activity affect governmental policy? Does it have any impact? And, if so, who benefits from that impact?

Organizations as Pressure Groups

Exerting pressure on government to influence policy is of course the best-known role of organized interests; they act as lobbies in Washington, in state capitals, and in local governments. Observers of the activity of lobbyists have sometimes concluded that the government is dominated by lobbies. Analysts of American politics often describe governmental policy as if it were the mechanical result of a "parallelogram of forces," the forces being pressures placed on the government by organized groups. In such a situation the public as a whole plays no role. Nor does the government itself. The role of government is merely to react passively to group forces or, at most, to act as a broker among them.

Such a description of policy making—in Washington or in state capitals—probably greatly exaggerates the power of organized groups and underestimates the other forces acting on the government. One close study of the Washington lobbyists concludes that "there is relatively little influence or power in lobbying per se. There are many forces in addition to lobbying which influence public policy; in most cases these forces clearly outweigh the impact of lobbying."[3] These other forces include public opinion and

---

[3] Lester W. Milbrath, *The Washington Lobbyists* (Chicago: Rand McNally, 1963), p. 54.

the congressman's consideration about the next election. And, above all, one must add the dominant role of the executive branch of the government. Furthermore, as one congressman points out in the study, congressmen have their own opinions on subjects. They like to hear the views of lobbyists, but are not necessarily moved by them.

Organized interests are not all-powerful. But they are far from powerless. One has to be more precise, because groups vary in how effective they are. Thus it is useful to consider what kind of group is likely to be effective, on what issues it is likely to be effective, and where is it likely to be effective.

Which Groups Are Effective?

When we discussed what makes for a meaningful political group in America, we listed three characteristics—common objective interests, subjective awareness of those common interests, and organization (see Chapter 4). And we can use the same terms to help understand why some groups are more effective in Washington than others—the more the members of a group have common interests and the more they are self-aware, the more likely they are to have effective organization. Let's consider some examples.

The National Association of Retail Druggists (NARD): One of the more effective business groups in Washington for many years was the National Association of Retail Druggists (NARD). It was a potent force behind legislation allowing price fixing in retail trade—legislation that greatly benefited druggists. Such laws were passed despite the fact that they went against the general tendency of governmental policy to outlaw such price fixing.[4] On the other hand, other retail trades have been relatively ineffective politically; they either have no effective trade association or they have one that cannot produce beneficial outcomes vis-a-vis the government.

The success of druggists lies in their common interests. They tend to be a fairly homogeneous group of small independent businessmen—not divided into tiny marginal stores and supermarkets as is, for instance, the retail grocery trade. Furthermore, they have the advantage of self-awareness. To be a pharmacist is to be a professional—with special training and special commitment—and this is also a powerful resource behind NARD's ability to be effective.

With this base of effective political action, the National Association of Retail Druggists successfully pressured for passage of price laws favorable to them in Congress as well as in 44 state legislatures. A potent political record indeed!

But even this record of relative success for a lobbying group does not

[4] For a discussion of this group, see Joseph C. Palamountain, *The Politics of Distribution* (Cambridge, Mass.: Harvard University Press, 1955).

imply an all-powerful system of lobbies. For one thing, the druggists would not have succeeded if they had not had allies from other interests—in particular the drug manufacturers and the drug wholesalers, the other two involved business groups. Furthermore, the one group that could have opposed them—the consumers—was unorganized and only marginally concerned. In fact, we have here a prime example of that distribution of preferences that we called the pressure group syndrome in Chapter 4—whereby a small and intensely concerned minority (the druggists) face a large, mildly opposed but fundamentally unconcerned majority. Thus the success of the group depends very heavily on the right circumstances.

Indeed, the victory can be more apparent than real if the circumstances change. When price-fixing laws were first passed, the retail druggists had little strong opposition. In recent years, the rise of discount department stores has created a counter-constituency of retailers eager to bypass these restrictions, and who have been fairly successful in having the laws changed, or weakened, or ignored, so that the price-control gain of the druggists has largely vanished.

The American Medical Association (AMA):   Consider another example of interest group involvement in the policy-making process: the involvement of the American Medical Association (generally conceded to be one of the more powerful groups in Washington) in the making of the Medicare legislation.[5] Government medical insurance was an issue where there were both proponents and opponents, not simply proponents as in the case of the control of retail prices on drugs. During the 1960s a long series of hearings was held on medical-care legislation, with the same groups lining up opposed to one another. In favor of such legislation were the AFL-CIO, the American Nurses Association, the Council of Jewish Federations and Welfare Funds, the American Association of Retired Workers, the National Association of Social Workers, the Socialist party, and the American Geriatrics Association. Against such legislation were the American Medical Association, the American Hospital Association, the Life Insurance Society of America, The National Association of Manufacturers, the National Association of Blue Shield Plans, the American Farm Bureau Federation, the U.S. Chamber of Commerce, and the American Legion.

The variety of participants is quite wide. But this is merely a list of groups that testified at hearings. Not all were equally active; in fact, the main disputants were the AMA and the AFL–CIO, with the former putting in proportionately much greater effort. The reason for the AMA's effort should be quite familiar by now—the issue was of closer and more specialized concern to them than to the other groups.

What does a group like the AMA do? It uses the funds from its members

---

[5] For a full account, see Theodore R. Marmor, *The Politics of Medicare* (London: Routledge and Kegan Paul, 1970).

to support a variety of lobbying activities. It hires representatives in Washington to visit and convince congressmen, it provides speakers to testify at hearings, it supports friendly congressmen in election campaigns. At the height of the Medicare debate in 1965, the AMA spent almost $1 million dollars on a public persuasion campaign in newspapers and other media.

And in general the AMA was very successful. Although a Medicare bill was passed it was, to say the least, a long time in coming—many, many years longer than in any other society of comparable level of economic development. Furthermore the bill, when passed, bore the marks of having been shaped by the AMA. In its long delaying action on government medical care, in its successful opposition until now of any comprehensive medical-care plan—such as those in most industrial societies—the AMA is a model of a successful lobby. It has kept up firm pressure against change; it has set the agenda of the debate.

But as has been pointed out in a close study of the issue,[6] the AMA could not have done this alone. For instance, the role of Wilbur Mills, Chairman of the powerful House Ways and Means Committee (the committee of Congress that had to pass on such legislation), was all-important. The AMA applied pressure on this committee, but what was crucial was that the views of the AMA were quite congenial to Rep. Mills and his colleagues on the committee, of mainly conservative southern Democrats and conservative Republicans. Most of these congressmen came from quite safe districts where their reelection was almost automatic. Rep. Mills was, for instance, in little danger of losing his seat if he opposed the AMA position. If he supported the AMA, it was largely because he agreed with it. That Medicare legislation passed in 1964 was due in large part to a change in Rep. Mills' position on the subject.

In short, even a powerful lobby needs powerful allies.

On What Issues Are Pressure Groups Effective?

Perhaps the simplest and most exact generalization of the issues on which pressure groups are effective is: The narrower and more technical the issue, the greater the weight of organized groups is likely to be felt.

The Two Levels of the Policy-Making Process: The policy-making process—a subject we shall deal with more fully later—goes through many steps. On the one hand there is the making of general policy, a process fought out in Congress and resulting in the development of broad policy guidelines. But much of this policy making has symbolic meaning.[7] It sets a

---

[6] *Ibid.*, chap. 6.

[7] See Murray Edelman, *The Symbolic Uses of Politics* (Urbana: The University of Illinois Press, 1964).

general direction for policy. But the actual working out of the policy depends on quite specific features that are worked out in congressional committees and subcommittees, or worked out in the application of the legislation by government administrators, or worked out in the interpretation of the legislation in the courts.

The point is that while the broad guidelines of legislation seem to be the most important, it is often the courts' interpretation of legislation that really counts. The general rules set down by Congress are so general as to have little impact until the details of the law and its interpretations have been settled.

In the arena of struggle for major legislation, pressure groups are active, to be sure, but they are not at their greatest advantage. Congress, in such public activities, must keep its eye on the public and, in turn, the mass media are keeping their eye on Congress. But the specific details of a bill — worked out in committee or in some agency of the executive branch — offer a better arena for such interests.

In such cases they can use one of their greatest resources: the information they have on the particular subject at hand. Representatives of special groups are usually specialists; they have such facts as the number of yards of cloth imported from Hong Kong each month, the business failure rate among druggists, and so forth, depending on their area of specialty. And this information is of great use to government officials who cannot gather it on their own. Such specialization gives group representatives ready access to government officials.

The case of Medicare legislation is an example. Even after the AMA lost its fight over the Medicare bill and it was clear that the bill would pass, the AMA worked in close consultation with the congressional committee in shaping the law. And it has since had a major role in working out the details of the administration of Medicare.

Policy Making on Tax Legislation: A prime example of the "two levels" of policy making — the broad statement of principles and the detailed working out of practices — is found in relation to tax legislation. The broad principle of progressive tax legislation dates from the Sixteenth Amendment. It is one of graduated income tax, taxing those who can pay more at higher rates. Such a general plan could have major effects on redistributing income in America.

Aside from a few diehard opponents, no one argues with the general principle of a graduated tax. And there is no need to argue, because the principle is hardly ever applied.

Although broad attempts have been made to reform income-tax laws several times in the past few decades, the results are almost always the same. Congress sets some broad guidelines, and the tax bill is then riddled with a myriad of very specific exemptions approved by the House Ways and Means Committee or the Senate Finance Committee (the committees of

Congress in which tax legislation is shaped). These exemptions range from some to help a particular individual (the famous Louis B. Mayer amendment, which was designed to help the aging movie magnate protect his retirement benefits) to broader exemptions (such as the even more famous 22.5 percent depletion allowance for oil companies, which gives oil producers a substantial tax benefit). At the hearings on the major revenue bills, one will find hundreds of specific groups testifying on what seem to be relatively minute issues, but they are issues that affect them closely. On each specific issue, there is no one to oppose them since what is at stake is some narrow application.

The result, of course, is that though there is never any direct challenge to the overall principle of a graduated tax that falls most heavily on the wealthy, in fact, tax policy does not work out that way. As many have noted, the tax law allows for a maximum rate of 70 percent. Few pay as much as 50 percent.[8] This is not the result of a decision by some governmental body—say, Congress or the Treasury Department—that *as a general principle* a rate of 70 percent is too high. Rather, the principle of steeply graduated taxes holds, but the practice is to riddle it with so many exemptions—for tax-free municipal bonds, depletion allowances, capital gains, real-estate transactions—that the principle never takes effect. (See Chapter 2.)

Tariff Legislation and Business Regulation: This pattern of principle and practice in policy making can be found in many fields. Tariff legislation has long been an area where general tariff bills are watered down through a variety of specific decisions on specific goods. Another example is business regulation. Congress will enact a general statute for the regulation of some business practices, such as the quality of food products, the amount of pollutants allowed into waterways, and the flameproofing of fabrics. The general principle will be clear—sell pure food, don't pollute, manufacture only fireproof fabrics. But the details of the regulation—How pure? Is a little pollution all right? What about slow-burning fabrics?—are usually worked out in close collaboration with those who are to be regulated. This is not necessarily a venal arrangement. In some sense, it could not be otherwise, since only the businesses involved have the necessary information on which the detailed regulations have to be made. But it does give businesses a special role in setting the exact terms of their relationship with the government.

One of the reasons why such is the case is seen if we return to some of the patterns of cleavage described in Chapter 4. When it comes to broad issues in which a group with a specific interest wants something that many other citizens oppose in principle, the pattern of cleavage will look some-

[8] See William L. Cary, "Pressure Groups and the Revenue Code," *Harvard Law Review,* 68 (1955), 745–780.

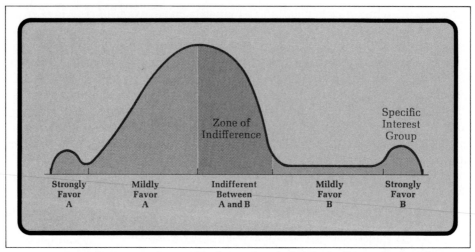

| | | Zone of Indifference | | Specific Interest Group |

| Strongly Favor A | Mildly Favor A | Indifferent Between A and B | Mildly Favor B | Strongly Favor B |

Figure 7.1 Specific Interest Group Confronted with the Opposition of Many Citizens

thing like that shown in Figure 7.1. On the right—favoring position B strongly—would be the specific interest group, small in number, but determined. On the left would be a populace generally opposed to the principle that the small interest group wants, and that populace will probably contain a number of citizens who feel strongly about the principle. In such a case, the specific group wanting B could only win after a public fight. And it would probably lose, since the bulk of the citizenry could be roused. In such a circumstance, congressmen might listen to the specific group but they listen more closely to election predictions.

If, for instance, representatives of top management in large corporations were to attempt—through the National Association of Manufacturers or the U.S. Chamber of Commerce—to have Congress enact a law severely reducing their rate of taxation, and were to base that attempt on a general denunciation of the principle of a graduated income tax, there is little doubt that strong opposition would be mounted and they would lose.

If, on the other hand, the House Ways and Means Committee can be induced to approve a stock option plan whereby profits from sales of stock received under such plans can be treated as capital gains if they are sold at least two years after the grant of the option and six months after the transfer of the stock, the public is unlikely to be aroused. As one commentator noted after looking at many examples of relief from taxes received by specific interest groups, "In each instance the character of the relief afforded is so technical as to make a simple explanation impossible. Being obscure or outright incomprehensible to the layman, it is not recognized as an outright favor to one individual or a highly selected group."[9]

[9] *Ibid.*

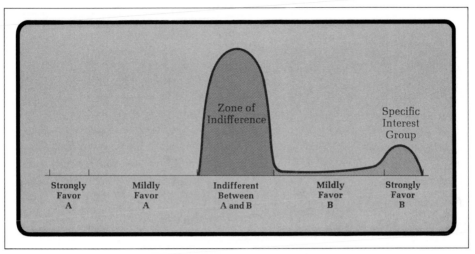

Figure 7.2 Specific Interest Group Not Confronted with Opposition Because of Ambiguity and Technicality of Issues

When it comes to an issue that is ambiguous and technical, the pattern of cleavage on the issue is likely to resemble that shown in Figure 7.2. A deeply interested, skilled, and technically competent group favors a position. The position, whatever its real consequences, appears as a technical issue on which the public has little knowledge or concern. Thus there is no opposition. In such circumstances, the specific interest group can be quite potent.

Interest Group vs. Interest Group: Balancing the Battle

Many of the activities of interest groups take place in the circumstances shown in Figure 7.2, where one group favors a policy, brings to bear technical skill on the issue, and has little opposition. But sometimes the battle is more evenly waged; such a situation is diagrammed in Figure 7.3. In this case, one interest group is directly opposed by another interest group equally involved with the issue. When that happens the outcome is by no means as clear.

Public-Interest Groups

In recent years, a number of *public-interest* groups have come to the fore to challenge those *economic-interest* groups that have, to a large extent, dominated American politics. Many of these public-interest groups have

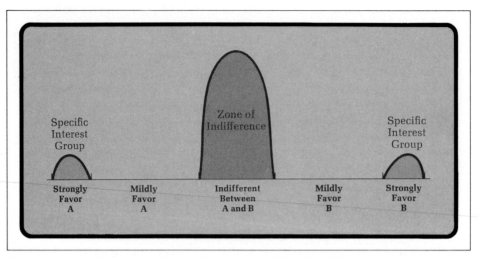

Figure 7.3 Specific Interest Group Confronted with Little Opposition Because It Has Access to Technical Skills

been involved in the fields of environmental or consumer protection. Such groups as the Sierra Club and those organized by Ralph Nader have begun to take an active role in many governmental policies that were formerly the subject of more one-sided lobbying. Through their highly professional investigations and through their willingness to pursue the battle in Congress and in the courts, these organizations have achieved some notable successes.

Prime examples of this activity are found in the area of public lands—national forests, the seashores, and so forth. Most citizens have some interest in the maintenance of natural beauty or open park lands or clean rivers. But for most citizens, such concerns are marginal; their major daily activities involve their own specific occupations and the narrower problems associated with their occupations. Thus when it came to decisions on the development of public lands, the groups that could devote concentrated energy to the issue would usually carry the day. And this was usually the business interests who favored a particular use for public lands—for mining, for private recreational development, for cattle grazing. The employees of these groups were professionally concerned with such matters; they had the skills to use administrative agencies of the government and the courts for their purposes and, because it was their *job* to do so, they devoted the time and the energy needed to be effective in these arenas. An unorganized public was an ineffective counterweight.

What organizations like the Sierra Club do is to place *professional* skills and energies on the other side. By having a full-time legal staff whose task it is to fight against private development of public lands, they redress the imbalance in the conflict over these matters before the government.

Public-interest groups active in environmental issues have achieved some notable successes. *(Photos: Los Angeles Air Pollution Control District)*

It is difficult to know how to categorize these new lobbying organizations devoted to consumer interests, to environmental concerns, and to other noneconomic interests. Are these organizations unlike other pressure groups in that they do not represent narrow "selfish" interests but rather care for the more general public welfare? Or are these groups different from other pressure groups only in that they lobby for a *different set* of "selfish" interests—consumer interests rather than producer interests, scenery-lover interests rather than mining interests?

The answer is not clear. But in either case these groups would seem to be a new and important addition to the system of organized pressures in the United States.

Where Are Pressure Groups Active?

The previous discussion of the kind of issue on which pressure groups can be most effective also tells us something about where they are most likely to be effective. One common impression is that they are most active in trying to arouse the public, through campaigns in the media (like the AMA's campaign against national medical insurance) or through support of candidates in elections. And interest groups do engage in such activities—they try to affect public opinion and they put their support behind particular candidates. In this way they try to influence public policy at the most general level—by affecting what the public wants and who is elected to office.

Congressional Committees

Interest groups are probably much more active and more effective in dealing with specific committees and subcommittees of the Congress. Here they can develop long and close relationships with specific congressmen—who often come from districts where that particular interest is well represented—and the staffs of the committees. They often provide the information and expertise needed to draft specific bills.

The Executive Branch

Interest groups are also active in relation to the executive branch. They may develop close ties with those agencies of the executive branch that regulate their affairs: farm interests with the Department of Agriculture, various businesses with the Department of Commerce, labor unions with the Department of Labor. In particular, quite close ties may emerge between independent regulatory agencies and the businesses they are created to regulate: trucking interests with the Interstate Commerce Commission, radio and television interests with the Federal Communications Commission,

Lobbyists develop long and close relationships with congressmen.   (Photo: Wide World)

airlines with the Civil Aeronautics Board. It is only natural that such relations should develop, since effective regulation depends on close ties with and much information about those regulated. But it also gives the businesses that are regulated considerable influence over these regulations.

The Court System

One arena of group activity — not often recognized as such — is the court system. The real impact of governmental policy is often felt through the interpretation of laws or the Constitution by the courts. And interest groups have been active in this area as well. Organizations provide the attorneys and expertise to prepare cases; they often carefully choose the test cases; and they appear in the cases through the filing of *amicus curiae* briefs. Perhaps the most dramatic example has been the long series of cases prepared and carried through by the NAACP, the school segregation cases being the best known. And this does not mean involvement only in the leading Supreme Court decision of *Brown v. Board of Education of Topeka* (see Chapter 11), but in the dozens of cases preceding that and following upon it — in lower courts as well as in the Supreme Court — that round out that decision.

Groups whose interest is in some right they believe guaranteed by the Constitution—civil liberties, or civil rights, or the separation of church and state—are particulary active vis-à-vis the federal courts. (See Chapter 12.) Thus one finds such groups as the American Civil Liberties Union, the Emergency Civil Liberties Committee, the NAACP, the Congress of Racial Equality (CORE), the Protestants and Other Americans United for the Separation of Church and State most active in this way.[10]

Economic organizations play a similar role in relation to their interests—sponsoring and supporting litigation on matters of concern to them. Again we see the way in which particular interests can be most effective. Litigation is a slow, costly, and technically difficult process. We hear of major court decisions, but the real impact of court action often comes through the slow accretion of decisions in a large number of narrower cases in the lower courts. And it is here that specific interest groups can be effective because they have the intense interest, the skill, and the staying power that make one effective under such circumstances.

Interest Groups as Quasi-Governments

There is one last, and important, way in which private interest groups play a political role in America. This is by taking on directly the functions of government. Government, the reader will remember from our Introduction, was abstractly defined as existing whenever binding decisions are made for a collectivity—that is, decisions that have the force of law and about which citizens have no choice but to comply. The abstract definition is useful because it allows us to locate and recognize instances where private organizations perform the governmental function of making such binding decisions.

It has long been an American tradition to delegate to private organizations the power to make such decisions vis-à-vis their area of concern. Let us consider some.

Controlling Access to a Profession

Many professions and craft groups control access to the particular type of work in which they are engaged. Medical associations have large control over the examination and accreditation process in that profession; bar associations control the nature of the bar examination; craft unions control access to apprentice programs that allow someone to become a practitioner of that craft; educational associations may control the accreditation process in teaching. Furthermore, these associations may control access to crucial

---

[10] See Clement E. Vose, "Interest Groups, Judicial Review and Local Government," *Western Political Quarterly,* 19 (March 1966), 85–100.

facilities without which one cannot effectively practice a profession—to hospitals, to labor exchanges, and so forth.

This activity represents control in the full governmental sense in that it is binding on citizens. One cannot practice law or medicine without accreditation; one cannot get employment as a plumber without union membership (and that in turn requires completion of an apprenticeship program). In this sense, the private associations that control the process of access to the profession act as governments.

Much of this activity, one can argue, is merely technical. Everyone wants a mechanism to accredit doctors or lawyers, some technique by which their adequacy as professionals can be judged so that laymen—who need medical care or legal advice but are not technically competent to tell a professional from a charlatan—can turn to them with confidence. And who, but the profession itself, has the competence to judge?

But such control over access to a profession can be used for other purposes as well. It can be used to keep members of a profession in line with policies favored by the leaders of that profession. The fact that the AMA controlled access to the medical profession and, often, doctors' access to such necessary facilities as hospitals, meant that it could control the behavior of doctors. It could, for instance, inhibit the formation of various types of group and cooperative practice it did not like. And the AMA wielded a power to keep doctors in line behind the policy on national medical care that the AMA favored.

Similarly, access to the practice of law depends on passing a bar examination in each state. The examination—particularly the rather general and vague examination of the "character" of the potential lawyer—has been used in various states to block applicants with radical records. And craft unions—plumbers, electricians, and the like—have used their control over accreditation to keep Blacks out of the profession.

Citizens who oppose these controls can, of course, challenge them in the courts or appeal to Congress or state legislatures for a change. But this does not in any way diminish the fact that the controls have the force of law—one can, after all, appeal any laws to the courts or appeal to a legislative body to change the law.

Controlling Standards and Making Regulations

In a variety of fields, the power to set industry-wide standards is delegated to a trade association or some other private group. Again the logic is that such regulations require the skill and knowledge of those most involved, and that such regulation brings with it the services and commitment of those to be regulated. Furthermore, those most involved and likely to be most affected are given a bigger voice. But, as with control of access to a profession, it turns over control to those who ought to be controlled.

Controlling the Allocation
of Public Funds

Many governmental programs are administered by essentially private groups. These groups receive government funds, which they then allocate. Of course, there are broad guidelines set by the government, but the control is essentially in the hands of the specific private group—and the guidelines are often so vague that the private group has a wide degree of latitude.

There are many examples from all fields of government activity. Urban renewal funds are often controlled by private developers; funds for hospitals and other welfare activities often are controlled by private charitable groups; and funds for much of the poverty program are channeled through local independent groups.

Such control over government funds by local groups does bring in the participation of many more citizens who are acquainted with local conditions. But it also delegates to essentially private groups—who are not as accountable to the public as are government officials and who may or may not be representative of those they are supposed to represent—an immense day-to-day power over governmental resources.

For Whom Do Interest Groups Speak?

Formally organized interest groups can be most effective—in certain circumstances—in pursuing specific interests. But it is not completely clear whose interests these are. Do such organizations pursue the interests of their members?

Interest Groups and Their Membership

When a representative of an interest group takes a position, he presents it as being that of the membership of the group—the AMA presents itself as speaking for doctors and the National Education Association (NEA), as speaking for teachers. Do they in fact do so?

The answer is that we do not often know. In the early part of this century, Swiss sociologist Roberto Michels wrote of the "iron law of oligarchy," by which he referred to an inevitable tendency for organizations to be run by a small group of leaders, unresponsive to the demands of the members. His argument was perhaps overstated; the law may not be an "iron" law. But much of what he noted applies to most organizations.

Most organizations are run by a relatively small number of members who give the time and effort to organizational activities. These members, furthermore, tend to become a special group—professional leaders. Trade union officials are professional officials—not workers who just happen to take a leadership role. Executives of the American Medical Association are similarly professional officials—not practicing physicians. Indeed, the AMA provides a classic case of an organization closely controlled by a leadership group.

Opponents of the AMA in the medical profession claimed it did not speak for that profession; the AMA claimed it did. In fact, it is unclear for whom the AMA spoke, since the profession as a whole was not active in Washington, nor was its opinion tapped. And this is true of most associations. The membership meets rarely, if ever, and the control over the activities of the association lies in the hands of a few elected officers—a board of directors—and, above all, a professional staff.

This potential disjunction between the views of the leaders of organizations and the views of the membership is reinforced by a tendency for members to join organizations, not because they want to support the political activities of that organization, but because of other benefits the organization provides. Doctors do not join the AMA because they are committed to the policies the AMA supports (though they may be), but because the AMA provides them with many services through its technical journals, through help in malpractice suits, and in many other ways. Similarly, businesses may join trade associations because those associations provide them with technical publications and other specific services, and not because of a support for the lobbying and other political activities of the organization. (One of the authors of this volume must admit that he joined the American Association of University Professors so that he could use their reduced-fare flights to Europe.) But their membership provides the base on which the organization can be politically powerful.

That organizations are generally controlled by a small professional elite makes the degree to which they represent the interests of their constituencies problematic. But there is another side to the coin. The centrality of control in a professional leadership makes is possible for organizations to be more effective in that they can mount careful campaigns with a distinct purpose. Thus when they do speak for their membership—and the discussion above does not imply that this happens rarely; rather, it just implies that it does not always happen—they can speak more effectively.

Controversy

If the extent to which interest groups represent the interests of their members is problematic, the extent to which they contribute to a more general public good is even more problematic. But let us stress that the word we use is *problematic*, meaning the issue is unsettled.

This returns us to a debate mentioned in the beginning of the chapter. Does the policy that emerges from a clash among interest groups further the common good?

One Side

Interest group politics represents a means by which specific citizen interests are communicated to the government. Without the activity of such groups, policy makers would not have the information about citizen and group needs to be adequately responsive to them. Such activity, particularly when it operates on the detailed level of the interpretation or the application of policy, allows governmental policy to be "fine-tuned" to the specific circumstances of groups. In a society with an infinite complexity of group circumstances, this is needed if the government is to avoid acting in a crude way that takes no account of variety.

Pressure groups do not discriminate against any particular group of citizens. It is true that all are not equally organized or equally active, but the right to organize and to petition the government is guaranteed to all. The fact that a group is organized and active indicates that it has interests it considers serious. If other groups do not organize to pressure the government it means that they do not really care enough.

The close relations of the government and interest groups represent a mobilization of the skills and energies of a broad segment of the society in the formation of government policy. In this sense the quality of policy improves.

Further, regulation through the cooperation of those regulated is essentially noncoercive. When citizens voluntarily work with the government in formulating such policies, it follows that they will voluntarily comply with the regulations they had a hand in framing. This is all to the good—the less coercion in a society, the better off everyone is.

Finally, the policy that emerges out of the clash of specific interests is not something that subverts the common good—for the common good is in fact the sum of the interests of specific groups.

In short, interest group politics produces the best overall governmental policy. It most adequately represents the views of specific groups; and it most adequately serves the needs of the country as a whole.

The Other Side

Interest group politics does a very uneven job of representing the most important interests of the citizenry. Many groups with serious needs are unorganized and have inadequate access. It is not necessarily a lack of interest that keeps particular segments of the society inactive; they may lack the resources to organize. Consequently, the interests that are most adequately represented are those of upper-status groups and, particularly, those of the well-organized business community. And in other sectors of society, the interests of groups vary in the extent to which they are represented—unionized workers do better than nonunionized ones, though the latter may need government protection more. The result is a general skewing of governmental policy in a conservative direction; policy tends to aid the privileged. This situation is compounded by the tendency for governmental power to be turned over to those whom the government should be regulating. Specific interest groups join in the making of regulations and thereby keep those regulations from affecting them adversely.

Interest group politics may be noncoercive, but progress and social change may require coercion—at least they may require that citizens be forced to accept changes they do not want. A more thorough change in American society—a change that many feel is needed—requires a more positive intervention by the government. And it is in this respect that interest group politics is weakest—there is no one to be concerned with a broader public interest, an interest that is not defined simply by the sum of contending forces. If the serious problems facing American society are to be dealt with, the government will have to become more than the mere sounding board for a multitude of narrow, selfish interests.

Which side is right? The debate will not easily be settled. It is fundamental to the way in which politics works in America. And whether one believes that interest group representation is salutary or not, such representation is a current fact of American politics.

Suggested Readings

The classic statement of the benefits of interest group representation is by David B. Truman, *The Governmental Process* (New York: Knopf, 1951). The counter-position is well expressed in Grant McConnell, *Private Power and American Democracy* (New York: Knopf, 1966), and in Theodore J. Lowi, *The End of Liberalism* (New York: Norton, 1969).

A subtle theoretical statement relevant to the dynamics of organization is found in Mancur Olson, Jr., *The Logic of Collective Action: Public Goods and the Theory of Groups* (Cambridge, Mass.: Harvard University Press, 1965). Murray Edelman's *The Symbolic Uses of Politics* (Urbana, Ill.: The University of Illinois Press, 1964) is relevant for the kinds of interests that can be served by group activity.

Political Parties in American Democracy

It is said that democracy is not possible without political parties, at least not in an industrial society with over 200 million citizens. The political party system solves the difficult task of organizing a popularly based government in a huge, complex society. In theory, it is through the party system that a mass public is able to gain access to the governing elite, to hold them accountable for their actions, to replace them when necessary, and to influence public policies.

American Political Parties: Organization and Program

If you have studied comparative politics you know that political parties in some societies regularly and effectively involve mass publics in the political life of their nation. For instance, some parties supplement the formal educational system to an amazing degree. They organize lectures and programs to inform the public about political issues; they print booklets and leaflets that review policy questions and invite the public to debate and take stands on these questions. Parties in many societies have youth groups and other auxiliary organizations. They have a chain of command that links local units with district headquarters and national officers.

None of these activities is much practiced in the United States. Indeed, in contrast to parties elsewhere, the Democrats and the Republicans do not even have formal members. It is the rare citizen in the United States who actually "joins" a political party, and an even rarer citizen who pays dues on any regular schedule.

It is difficult to imagine our political parties as truly mass based, if one means by that a series of activities that deliberately involve the citizenry in the policy-making process. Our parties hardly ever meet, and when they do, the meetings involve very tiny proportions of the possible party followers. Almost all party meetings—whether precinct, county, state, or national—take place around election time, and have as their primary purpose nominating candidates and planning campaign strategy. We would be surprised indeed to hear that the Santa Clara County Democratic party is meeting to debate and discuss tariff policy or school bussing, and that the party intends to express its considered judgment directly to representatives in Sacramento or Washington, D.C. And we do not expect the Republican party of Illinois to organize a series of public forums so that citizens can voice opinions about issues facing the Illinois legislature. Whether by intention or historical accident, political parties in America simply are not organized to involve the public in any continuous way.

Composition of the Political Party

Typically the political party in the United States is a small inner circle, composed of officeholders and those seeking office, along with a professional staff and a few loyal partisans. The staff and partisans come and go depending on the fortunes of their favorite candidates.

This small group and its activities are financed largely by wealthy individuals and contributions from interest groups. For instance, forty-six of the richest people in America gave a total of at least $1,494,502 for campaign costs in the 1968 Presidential election, an average of more than $32,000 per individual. Also in 1968, according to one study, at least half, and perhaps more, of Presidential candidate Hubert H. Humphrey's "general election campaign expenses were paid for through contributions and loans from about 50 individuals."[1] Neither of the two major parties has anything approaching a mass membership that provides funds for party operations.

Partisan Followers

In one sense only do American parties have a mass base: Both parties have millions of loyal followers who habitually cast their ballot for the candidates chosen by the small group of party professionals and activists. These loyal partisans are an important feature of American politics. They provide the electoral support that keeps each of the major parties contending for office. These loyal followers are the citizens described in Chapter 3 as partisan identifiers. Here is a Republican with a strong partisan identification: "I'm a born Republican, sister. We're Republicans from start to finish, clear back on the family tree. Hot Republicans all along. I'm not so much in favor of Eisenhower as the party he is in. I won't weaken my party by voting for a Democrat." And an equally fervent Democrat: "I was just raised to believe in the Democrats and they have been good for the working man—that's good enough for me. The Republicans are a cheap outfit all the way around. I just don't like the Republicans, my past experience with them has been all bad."[2]

All told, approximately three of every four voters in the United States identify themselves with one of the two major parties. The Democrats enjoy a sizable advantage: About half of all voters identify themselves with that party. The other half of the electorate includes a nearly even split between

[1] Herbert E. Alexander, *Financing the 1968 Election* (Lexington, Mass.: Heath, 1971), p. 152.

[2] These quotations are taken from Angus Campbell, Gerald Gurin, and Warren Miller, *The Voter Decides* (New York: Harper & Row, 1954), p. 92.

...can identifiers and those who claim to be Independents. Although ...san voters normally support the party they identify with, this does not always happen. If the opposition candidate is particularly attractive, the less committed partisans might shift their vote. This happened in the 1950s when the personal popularity of Eisenhower (a Republican) attracted many nominal Democrats. Similar shifts occur if the candidate of one's own party is disliked for some reason. Goldwater, the Republican candidate in 1964, was considered "too conservative" by many Republicans, a fact that contributed to Johnson's landslide victory. The election year of 1972 was a repeat of this, except that in this year many Democratic voters rejected their party's candidate, George McGovern, as too liberal, and shifted support to the Nixon-Agnew ticket.

Partisan loyalists provide what "mass base" there is to the American party system. This, as we shall see, is not an insignificant fact. The political parties are preeminently electoral organizations. And if millions and millions of voters use the party label as a guide to how they should vote, then political parties necessarily play a central role in the recruitment of political leaders. We shall turn to this issue shortly, but first let us get in mind two more facts about our political parties.

Decentralized Political Parties

Each of the major parties is much more a coalition of diverse and often disagreeing groups than it is a coordinated and single-minded organization. In the first place there are a variety of political viewpoints within each party. The Democrats and the Republicans each include a "conservative wing" and a "liberal wing." This is largely a result of historical development. Each party has attracted supporters in such a way as to create ideological diversity. The clearest example is the Democratic party. It is the party of the conservative South (conservative on civil rights and social welfare issues) because it was a northern Republican President, Lincoln, who brought on the Civil War and who signed the Emancipation Proclamation. The solid southern support enjoyed by the Democratic party is only now weakening, more than a century after the Civil War. But the Democratic party added new and very different social groups to its electoral coalition following the depression in the early 1930s. Franklin D. Roosevelt and his party chiefs cemented the loyalty of ethnic workers, Blacks, and the urban poor to the Democratic party by pushing such programs as unemployment insurance, public works jobs, and social security. The post-Civil War events and the Democratic coalition of the 1930s have resulted in the coexistence of a liberal, northern, urban group with a more conservative, southern, and rural group in the Democratic party. The Republican party has also been shaped by history. Partly because it was the party of the North immediately after the Civil War, it has become the political home of the commercial and industrial class in the Northeast. But the Republican party has also reflected the individualistic principles of Main Street America and the frontier spirit of the West, and thus today the Republicans include liberal northeastern business interests (e. g., Governor Nelson Rockefeller of New York) as well as more conservative midwestern and western interests (e. g., Senator Barry Goldwater of Arizona).

Ideological Diversity: The historical growth of each party and the resultant diversity of viewpoint within each pose formidable barriers in the way of cohesive, party-based programs. The issue that most unites Republicans is the desire to defeat Democrats, and the issue that most unites Democrats is the desire to defeat Republicans. Yet even in electoral politics there are defections. The nomination of McGovern in 1972 led many Democratic leaders to sit out the election, or even to support Nixon, the Republican candidate. And once we depart electoral issues, the possibility of party unity is much lessened. Each party tolerates many viewpoints, and little attempt is made to formulate a coordinated party policy perspective. Factional fights within the parties can be as sharp and divisive as struggles between the parties.

Organizational Fragmentation: Ideological diversity is compounded by organizational fragmentation. The federal structure of American politics has had a lasting effect on the parties. There are in fact fifty separate Republican parties and fifty separate Democratic parties, or even more if we include some of the strong and nearly autonomous organizations based at the county or city level. The state and local level parties are loosely linked together by a national committee, but the neat organizational charts that picture lines of communication from precinct to ward to county or district to state to national headquarters are misleading.

Decentralized Organization: National party headquarters has little control over what is done in its name at the state or local level. Party control is decentralized, localized. The active units of the party, insofar as there are active units, are based in constituencies much smaller than the national electorate. The decentralized nature of the parties contributes to diversity of viewpoint; the Democratic party of Biloxi, Mississippi, is a different political animal from the Democratic party of Palo Alto, California. Intraparty relationships are coalitional, a process of compromising and negotiation whenever a single party decision must be made, as is the case in the nomination of a Presidential candidate. On other types of party decisions, each unit goes its own way, comparatively indifferent to what another county or state party might be doing. For example, the nomination of congressional candidates is entirely under the control of the local activists, or perhaps the local voters if they participate in a primary. There is no effective command hierarchy, with instructions and policies formulated at the top and passed down through the constituent units. Even fund raising is mostly a local affair; national headquarters funds the Presidential campaign, but state organizations concentrate on statewide elections, and district and local organizations raise funds for their candidates.

The powers of state and local party units are related to federalism in the formal governmental structures. There is only one national elected office, but there are hundreds of state and local offices. This is where the action is, even more now that the mass media have taken over the Presidential campaign leaving less and less for the local organizations to do in national politics. And the decentralized aspects of party organization are bolstered by the doctrine of states' rights, a doctrine particularly persuasive to southern Democrats who resist any attempt to limit their considerable powers in Congress by including them in a centralized Democratic party under the control of northern liberals.

When the United States is described as a two-party system, it is not meant that there are two and only two major *party organizations*. Rather, it is meant that there are two and only two major *party symbols*. Elections take place between one diverse group of candidates and their personal organizations who invoke the symbols of the Republican party and another diverse group who invoke the symbols of the Democratic party; elections do not take place between two centrally directed, programmatic organizations. Ideologically and organizationally, each party is a loose coalition having in common the goal of gaining office under the party label, but not having in common a coherent program for the society.

Parties Without Programs

Neither the Republican party nor the Democratic party has a general program agreed to by all or even most of its officials. From time to time a party attempts to state a general program, but even these efforts usually come from a dissident group bothered by what another group is doing in the party name. For example, Republican governors might meet to formulate a program for revenue sharing between federal and state governments because they consider the Republican congressmen to be laggard on this issue. These are of course piecemeal attempts, touching only one of the many policy questions facing the government at any given time.

There are two documents proposed as party programs, but neither need be taken seriously. The first is the party platform put together at the Presidential nominating conventions. Platforms reflect their origins; they are campaign documents fashioned for the benefit of the particular Presidential nominee. They are not binding on party leaders, not even on the Presidential nominee himself. The second document is more serious, but it does not serve as a *party* program. This is the package of legislative proposals announced by the President in his State of the Union speech, his Budget Message to Congress, and related addresses. However important these proposals may be in other respects, it is stretching the language to call them a party program. The President's proposals are not formulated by his party; they are not even formulated in consultation with all the congressional members of his party, let alone in meetings with all governors, state legislators, local officials, or party professionals. It is easy to see why. Imagine the difficulties for the Democratic party of putting together a coherent program on, say, civil rights if the drafting committee included Representative Shirley Chisholm, a Black congresswoman from New York, and Governor George Wallace, a segregationalist governor of Alabama.

In summary, American political parties lack many things. They lack a mass membership and a regular dues-paying source of support. They lack central organization and any sense of uniformity across the many state and local units. They lack a coherent program and an ideology that can be clearly recognized and responded to. Despite these drawbacks, American parties are powerful actors on the political scene. They have been around for a long time, and they show few signs of disappearing. Their powerful position in American politics rests on one simple fact: They control the routes to political office.

Parties and the Selection of Political Leaders

In November 1972, the American electorate chose from among more than 1000 candidates 435 persons to serve in the House of Representatives in the 93rd Congress. Four hundred thirty-four of these persons were either Democrats (242) or Republicans (192); 1 gained a seat as an Independent. In that same election the voters in 33 states chose a U.S. senator, 16 of whom were Democrats and seventeen of whom were Republicans. All told, 99.8 percent of the current congressmen were elected under the label of one of the major parties. This is also true of every governor in the United States, as well as the vast majority of state legislators and other state officials.

Was the 1972 election unusual? Not at all. Recruitment to national and state office (and to many local offices as well) is "reserved" for those nominated by a political party. This is not a matter of law. The Constitution does not declare that political offices shall be held only by members of this or that political party. Indeed, the Constitution is entirely silent about political parties. But what is not a matter of law is very much a matter of tradition, custom, and practical politics. Ever since the Jeffersonians and Hamiltonians went their separate and partisan ways after the nonpartisan administration of President George Washington, the contest to control the government of the United States has been a party contest.

Nominating the Candidates

What we today recognize as political parties bear little resemblence to the political parties of two centuries ago. But then, just as now, the route to higher office in the United States detoured through some sort of party nomination process. The earliest political parties were nothing more than small groups of men gathered into party "caucuses," controlling who became candidates. Nominating caucuses for governorships and other state offices were generally made up of like-minded partisans in the state legislatures. Congressional caucuses nominated the Presidential tickets. The candidates then took their case to the general electorate, which itself was still a minority of male adult members of society (see Chapter 2).

"King Caucus," as this system was called, did not last long, but it was the first step in a historical process leading to party domination over access to public office. The second step in the development of political parties also has to do with nominating candidates. Jacksonian popular democracy, a social movement of the 1820s taking its name from Andrew Jackson (the seventh President), attempted to broaden the bases of participation in American politics. One of its notable successes was replacing the caucus system of party nominations with party conventions. Conventions were composed of delegates selected by state and local party organizations, and thus were supposed to be more broadly representative than caucuses.

Primary Elections: Throughout the nineteenth century, nomination for nearly all public offices was done by party conventions. Today nominating conventions retain their importance primarily for Presidential candidates. Candidates for most governorships, state and national legislatures, and many local offices are now nominated in direct primaries. Primaries — party elections that precede the general election — were introduced to reform "nondemocratic" politics. At the turn of the century various reform groups charged that party conventions had come under the control of political bosses, and that candidates were beholden to special interests. The reformers felt that a larger dose of democracy would cure this ill, and proposed primary elections.

Primary elections are a means of involving the party followers in the nomination process. From among numerous candidates of the same party the supporters of that party choose the person best qualified for the forthcoming general election. At least this is the theory. Some form of primary elections have now been adopted in every state, though the form and importance of primaries vary considerably from state to state. We cannot here review all the different kinds of primaries, and instead must satisfy ourselves with two very general conclusions.

On the negative side, the primary as a means of nominating candidates has many flaws. Voter turnout is always low. The choices presented are often not clear, resulting in considerable confusion among the electorate. At the same time the costs in campaign funds and effort can be very high, depleting the party of resources it needs for the general election. Certainly the primaries have not brought about mass political participation in the nomination process.

On the positive side, the primaries have lessened the control over nominations exerted by a small group of persons. They provide a channel by which an insurgent party group can proclaim its virtues and its candidate. Sometimes, as in the Democratic party of 1972, remarkable successes can be achieved by an insurgent group. In that year Presidential candidate George McGovern planned his strategy for nomination around key Presidential primaries. His primary victories helped immensely in gathering sufficient delegate strength to win the nomination at the Democratic National Convention.

The National Convention: If primary elections have replaced conventions in the nomination of most public offices, they have not replaced the Presidential nominating convention. The Democrats and the Republicans, as well as lesser parties, meet every four years for the express purpose of nominating a Presidential ticket. These are remarkable gatherings, as is well known to any readers who have stayed close to their television sets

The choice for President is predetermined; only the nominees of the two major parties have a realistic chance. *(Photo: Wide World)*

during a convention week. Several hundred party faithfuls convene in a city selected by the national party organization (in close consultation with the television networks) to debate and formulate a "party platform" and then to get down to the business of choosing a Presidential nominee. When the two party conventions have finished their business, two men from an adult population of more than one hundred million Americans are serious contenders for the White House. In this sense the choice for President is predetermined. Only the two nominees of the major parties have a realistic chance. Yet at the same time the choice is meaningful, for the party nominating process has provided the electorate with manageable alternatives.

How Delegates Are Selected: Delegates to the Presidential nominating convention are selected in a variety of ways. Some states have Presidential primaries which bind the delegates to the candidate winning the primary election; other states have primaries which allow the voters to register their preferences, but which still leave the delegates some autonomy. In yet other states the primary election chooses unpledged delegates. In some states the voters choose some delegates, but other delegates from that state are chosen by district or state party committees. All told, the use of some form of Presidential primary accounts for the selection of only a minority of delegates to either of the nominating conventions. The great majority of states rely on party committees or conventions to select convention delegates.

During the preconvention politicking, the states with primary elections receive the greatest news coverage and attract the greatest public attention. But the candidate who is seriously pursuing his party's nomination will use many of his organizational resources to influence delegate selection in the nonprimary states as well. John F. Kennedy in 1960 combined primary victories with careful delegate selection in nonprimary states, and received his party's nomination on the first ballot. Barry Goldwater in 1964 earned the Republican nomination by quietly influencing delegate selection in party conventions throughout the country. And George McGovern astounded observers in 1972 by his victories in several key Presidential primaries. Building on these victories, he was able to attract sufficient delegate strength from other states to ensure his first-ballot nomination at the Democratic convention in Miami.

Making sense out of the bewildering array of nomination procedures in the United States is not easy. Procedures vary from state to state and from office to office. But the seeming confusion should not lead us to overlook what is common in the nomination of candidates for public office. Primaries, conventions, committees, caucuses, and combinations among these forms all are under the control of the political parties. With the exception of some nonpartisan city and county offices (mostly in the western states), the route to a position of public authority is through a political party. This being so, we should explore one of the most perplexing questions in American politics: Just how different are the two major parties?

Just How Different Are the Two Major Parties?

Observers of American politics are unable to agree on whether the two major parties are essentially the same in political ideology, or whether they present contrasting personalities and policies. By asking the question, Does it make a difference who wins?—we can perhaps draw some conclusions of our own.

When the conservative senator from Arizona, Barry Goldwater, gained the Republican nomination in 1964, he argued that finally the voters would have "a choice, not an echo." Goldwater insisted that the two parties had become so alike in outlook that the American electorate was left with no choice between competing viewpoints. Many agree with this charge, claiming that a two-party system actually reduces choice, because each of the two mass parties must attract and hold the support of a wide variety of groups and individuals. The parties are coalitions, and coalitions cannot be held together unless they are ideologically flexible. Besides, so this reasoning goes, the big prize for each party is the White House. Because there can be only one winner it is natural that each party designs its overall strategy with that prize foremost in mind. This means that they must converge toward the middle, where the bulk of the electorate is supposed to be. The implicit image of the American electorate can thus be diagrammed as a normal bell curve, as shown in Figure 8.1.

Figure 8.1 The American Electorate

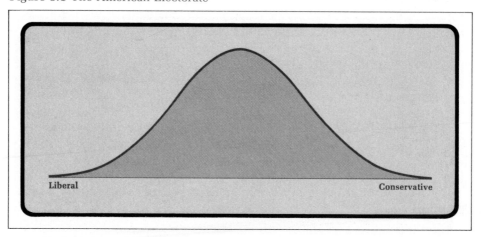

Other observers disagree. In a competitive political party system, they say, a very old dichotomy reflects itself in the parties. This dichotomy is the basic conflict between haves and have-nots, between rich and poor, property owners and propertyless, businessmen and workers, producers and consumers. The democratic class struggle plays itself out through electoral competition.

The "democratic class struggle" was foreshadowed in 1787 in the remarkable pamphlet *The Federalist* (No. 10):

> The most common and durable source of factions [political parties] has been the various and unequal distribution of property. Those who hold and those who are without property have ever formed distinct interests in society. Those who are creditors, and those who are debtors fall under a like discrimination. A landed interest, a manufacturing interest, a mercantile interest, a moneyed interest, with many lesser interests grow up of necessity in civilized nations, and divide them into different classes, actuated by different sentiments and views.

Early political history bore this out. The first political parties, or factions as Madison called them, were organized around conflicting economic interests. Under the leadership of Hamilton the Federalist party protected the interests of commerce, business, and hard money, while the Jeffersonians were more favorable to the small farmer and the debtor class. Class differences in the party system have been traced by scholars through nearly two centuries of party changes and adaptations, and, according to some observers, persist today in the form of the Republicans and Democrats.

The implicit image of the American electorate held by those who see party differences as reflections of class antagonisms suggests the diagram shown in Figure 8.2. In this figure the parties are seen to stand in opposi-

Figure 8.2 Party Differences as Reflections of Class Antagonisms

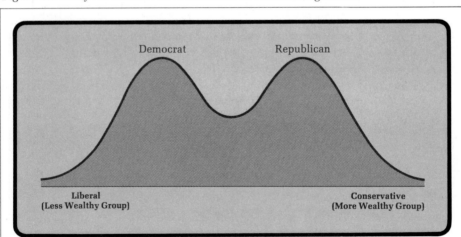

tion to each other, with the Democrats drawing their support from less wealthy social classes (liberals, presumably favoring a more egalitarian distribution of wealth) and the Republicans drawing their support from more wealthy social classes (presumably favoring a conservative, or status quo, viewpoint).

Which is correct—a picture of the parties as more or less the same in outlook, or a picture of them as reflecting conflicting social and public policies? For the answer, let us turn to five kinds of evidence:

1. Whether the parties draw electoral support from different social groups.
2. Whether the voters at large see any differences in the parties.
3. Whether the parties depend on different sources for campaign funds.
4. Whether the party leaders differ in their policy views.
5. Whether support for legislation differs between the parties.

Do Different Social Groups Support the Republicans and the Democrats?

The evidence is that the average income of Republican voters is several thousand dollars higher than the average income of Democratic voters. The Republican party traditionally draws its support from the wealthier business class, just as the Democratic party has traditionally enjoyed a voter advantage among the workers. These differences largely reflect the electoral coalition formed by the Democratic President Franklin D. Roosevelt in the midst of the depression of the 1930s. The Democratic party became the party of Blacks, of immigrant workers, and of the unemployed and marginally employed generally, because it was the Democratic party that aggressively introduced such public welfare measures as social security, unemployment insurance, and public aid. Meanwhile the Republican party was remaining close to its traditional principles of fiscal responsibility and individual effort. It continued to enjoy the support of business and commercial interests, and of White Anglo-Saxon Protestant voters (so-called WASPs). Although the electoral coalitions of the 1930s do persist in rough outline today, they are not nearly so cohesive as they were four decades ago. The reasons for this decline in cohesiveness are important in themselves, and will be discussed in a later section.

The tendencies for Democrats and Republicans to differ in social backgrounds and social statuses are just that, *tendencies*, not sharp polarizations. Both parties attract supporters from a variety of social groups. Part of the reason, of course, is that factors other than social class affect voter choice. Thus the businessman from the South is more likely to be a Democrat than a Republican, a fact that reflects regional differences in party support more than class differences. Regional, ethnic, and religious divisions cut across class lines.

Do Voters See Consistent Differences Between the Parties?

Many voters are able to describe significant differences between the Republicans and Democrats. Let us listen to some voters saying what they like or dislike about the two major parties:

Voters Stating What They Like About the Republican Party:
Retired Boston wholesaler *"The Democrats is all right but it's not a money party. I like to string along with big business and big money. Well, I'll also tell you under the Republicans the country has prospered.*
A Michigan janitor *"My dad and his dad were strong Republicans, and I guess it is in my blood too. Republican party is more of a party that promotes business and believes more in business principles."*

Voters Stating What They Dislike About the Republican Party:
A Texas janitor *"That party has always been for moneyed men. I don't like them. They are for the big man; people with money."*
A St. Louis policeman *"Republican leaders are controlled by moneyed men — that's what I don't like about the Republican party — it is run by large corporations."*

Voters Stating What They Like About the Democratic Party:
The wife of a Connecticut salesman *"I like what they do for the laboring class. They try to improve working conditions — work for shorter hours — a higher wage rate — and are more interested in benefits for the working man."*
Waiter in San Francisco *"I like the Democrats because they fulfill what they promise. With the Democrats I always had a job and with the Republicans I was in the breadlines. I feel the Democrats are for the small businessman and the poor people."*

Voters Stating What They Dislike About the Democratic Party:
North Carolina farm widow *"I like the high prices we get for our products and it's always been the Republican policy to do that. The Democrats have always been a low cost of living party. We always felt that the Republicans don't cheat over votes like the Democrats."*
Businessman in a small town in Illinois *"The Democrats are a giveaway party. Under their policies there would be no initiative left in the country. And they cannot keep the budget balanced, always spending more than the government has. Business suffers when the Democrats are in power."*[3]

These quotations are not systematic evidence, but they illustrate our hunch that voters see the Republican party as closer to business and com-

---

[3] With the exception of the last quotation, these are taken from V. O. Key, Jr., *Public Opinion and American Democracy* (New York: Knopf, 1964), pp. 436–438.

mercial interests and see the Democratic party as closer to working-class interests. National public poll data confirms this hunch. Different occupational groups in society report that Republicans and Democrats do not serve group interests uniformly; the Republican party is viewed as more favorable to business and professional groups, and the Democrats are viewed as more favorable to workers and farmer. Yet this too is a tendency, not a sharp polarization. Some businessmen see the Democratic party as serving business interests, just as some workers claim that the Republican party best serves workers' interests.[4] The attitudes of voters are not neatly dichotomous, just as the class support of the parties is not neatly dichotomous.

Does Big Money Support the Republicans?

Party activities and campaigns take a huge amount of money. Total campaign expenditures in 1968 were $300 million; in 1972 expenditures had increased to approximately $400 million. Costs have been steadily increasing; whereas in 1956 the expenditure per Presidential vote cast was 21 cents, this had nearly tripled by 1968 to 60 cents per vote. Much of this money is provided by a small group of wealthy individuals and pressure organizations. For example, fewer than one in ten citizens contributed to political parties in 1968. And of course a smaller proportion by far makes big contributions.

The money that comes from the wealthy class and from big businessmen greatly favors the Republican party. The money collected by trade unions and ad hoc reform groups greatly favors the Democratic party.

For example, the 46 very wealthy donors mentioned earlier in the chapter (who gave an average of more than $32,000 each in 1968) favored the Republican party by a ratio of 13 to 1. A similar pattern holds for contributions from members of the Business Council, a national group of corporate executives that advises the government. Members of this group gave at least $367,213 to campaigns in 1968; the Republicans received $280,913 compared to only $83,000 for the Democrats. Even more striking evidence comes from the breakdown in contributions by 12 prominent and very wealthy families in the United States. We see in Table 8.1 that of the nearly $3 million donated by these families, only 5 percent went to the Democratic party.

Contributions from executives of large corporations that are under contract with the Department of Defense, the Atomic Energy Commission, and National Aeronautics and Space Administration have also been tabulated. The Republican party was favored by a six-to-one ratio. For example, 24 of

---

[4] American Institute of Public Opinion, release of November 10, 1959. Reproduced in V. O. Key, Jr., p. 434.

Table 8.1   Political Party Contributions of Twelve Prominent Families, 1968

NAME	NUMBER OF MEMBERS CONTRIBUTING[a]	TOTAL CONTRIBUTIONS	Contribution Breakdown		
			REPUBLICAN	DEMOCRATIC	MISCEL-LANEOUS
DuPont	32	$ 107,000	$ 99,800	$ 1,700	$ 5,500
Field	4	39,000	2,000	17,000	20,000
Ford	8	109,750	57,750	52,000	—
Harriman	2	17,000	16,500	—	500
Lehman	7	51,000	2,500	48,500	—
Mellon	22	298,962	278,962	17,000+	3,000
Olin	7	70,000	70,000	—	—
Pew	11[b]	213,549	207,898	—	5,651
Reynolds	—	—	—	—	—
Rockefeller	21	1,714,375+[c]	1,700,875	13,500	—
Vanderbilt	2	12,000	11,000	—	1,000
Whitney	6	133,500	133,500	—	—
Totals	122	$2,766,136	$2,580,785	$149,700	$35,651

[a] In this analysis, husbands and wives were counted separately. Therefore, Mr. and Mrs. . . . would constitute two (2) contributing family members.
[b] The Estate of J. N. Pew Deceased was counted as one contributing member.
[c] This Rockefeller total does not include the $356,000 contribution made by Nelson Rockefeller for his own campaign.
Source: Herbert E. Alexander, *Financing the 1968 Election* (Lexington, Mass.: Lexington Books, D. C. Heath and Company, 1971), p. 180. Reprinted by permission of the publisher.

the 25 largest Department of Defense contractors had corporate executives who made political contributions in 1968. These military contractor executives gave only $110,000 to the Democrats but six times that, $671,252, to the Republicans. A leading contributor was Litton Industries; eleven of its officers and directors gave a total of $151,000 to Republican candidates, nothing to Democratic candidates.[5]

Of course there are a few leading businessmen who traditionally support the Democratic party. It is estimated that 10 to 20 percent of the total cost of a Democratic Presidential campaign comes from Wall Street sources. These sources quickly dry up, however, if a Democratic candidate does not show "sound fiscal sense." For example, George McGovern was not acceptable to many big contributors in 1972. Just before his nomination by the Democratic party one newspaper reported that Wall Street leaders who were "prominent backers of liberal candidates in the past express alarm at Senator McGovern's economic proposals and say that they will not support

[5] *Dollar Politics* (Washington, D.C.: Congressional Quarterly, Inc., 1971), p. 36.

him with funds. These proposals include income redistribution, welfare reform and changes in the nation's tax structure." John Loeb, senior partner of a major Wall Street law firm, said, "Frankly, his economic policies bother me. One of the important things in the United States that's made a lot of things possible is prosperous business. McGovern's policies as I see them would be a body blow to that."[6]

Much of the support available to the Democratic party comes from organized labor. National-level labor committees in 1968 spent $7.1 million in political campaigns, an average of 5 or 6 cents per union member, and nearly all of this went to Democratic candidates.

Do Democratic and Republican Party Leaders Differ in Political Philosophies?

Different studies confirm that Democratic party leaders take a more consistently liberal position than do Republican party leaders. Democratic leadership is more egalitarian in social philosophy and more willing to expand the social services of the government. Democratic leaders are more critical of big business and normally favor a more progressive income tax. In contrast, Republican leadership opposes many egalitarian programs, and believes that the government role in social services and welfare should expand slowly, or not at all. Republicans tend to fear the influence of trade unions, and to resist too much business regulation.

The political opinions of delegates to the Presidential nominating conventions in 1956 were studied, and here is what the authors concluded: The Democratic side of the two-party cleavage "is marked by a strong belief in the power of collective action to promote social justice, equality, humanitarianism, and economic planning, while preserving freedom." The Republican side "is distinguished by faith in the wisdom of the natural competitive process and in the supreme virtue of individuals, 'character,' self-reliance, frugality, and independence from government." Although the fit is not perfect, "the American parties do tend to embody these competiting points of view and to serve as reference groups for those who hold them."[7]

The strength of the differences between Democratic and Republican convention delegates can be seen in Table 8.2. A survey ten years later reports very similar differences. Evidence from two questions on social egalitarianism is presented in Figure 8.3, where we see that politically active Democrats are less willing than active Republicans to say that the poor

[6] Signed news story by Terry Robards, *The New York Times*, July 3, 1972.

[7] These findings on party leaders are taken from a study of the convention delegates to the 1956 Presidential nominating conventions of both parties. These delegates come from every part of the country and from every level of party and government. For a full report see Herbert McClosky, Paul J. Hoffmann, and Rosemary O'Hara, "Issue Conflict and Consensus Among Party Leaders and Followers," *American Political Science Review*, June 1960, 420.

Table 8.2 Comparison of Democratic and
Republican Party Leaders on Selected Policy Issues

		DEMOCRATS	REPUBLICANS
Public Ownership of Natural Resources	Increase:	57%	13%
	Decrease:	19	52
	Remain as is:	24	35
Government Regulation of Business	Increase:	20%	1%
	Decrease:	39	84
	Remain as is:	41	15
Tax on Large Incomes	Increase:	27%	5%
	Decrease:	23	57
	Remain as is:	50	38
Slum Clearance and Public Housing	Increase:	78%	40%
	Decrease:	6	22
	Remain as is:	16	38

Source: Based on data from Herbert McClosky, Paul J. Hoffmann, and Rosemary O'Hara, "Issue Conflict and Consensus Among Party Leaders and Followers," *American Political Science Review*, June 1960.

have the main responsibility for helping themselves; and the Democrats are more likely than Republicans to think that the income gap between rich and poor is too great in this country. These data reveal two additional points of interest. First, the more active partisans differ much more sharply than the less active partisans. Activists more than nonactivists spend their time with persons who share their political outlook, and thus reinforce them. The average voter spends his time in settings less partisan and less cohesive. Moreover the activists are attracted to politics by ideological considerations, whereas the average voter is often simply voting a family tradition or out of habit.

Second, Democratic Party activists are actually more conservative than rank-and-file Republicans. One important reason is that Democratic leaders are largely middle class in social origin and in current occupation. But the voters of a party are much more heterogeneous in background, and thus even the Republican party will include voters drawn from the working and lower classes. This has the result of sometimes pushing *both* sets of party leaders to the more conservative side of a question, and leaving *both* sets of party voters favoring more liberal policies. As Table 8.3 shows, one clear illustration is the proportion of different groups which favor an increase in taxes on large incomes.

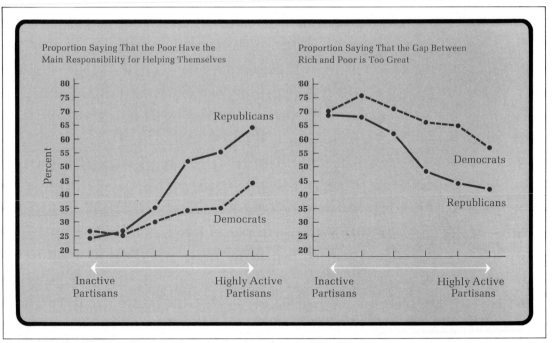

Figure 8.3 Welfare Attitudes of Democrats and Republicans
at Various Activity Levels

SOURCE: Based on data from Sidney Verba and Norman H. Nie, *Participation in America: Political Democracy and Social Equality* (New York: Harper & Row, 1972).

Summary Thus Far

Let us review what we have learned thus far. First, the parties draw electoral support from different social groups. Second, the average voter sees the parties aligned with different interests, the Republicans with the busi-

Table 8.3   Percentages Who Favor Increasing Taxes on Large Incomes

	DEMOCRATIC VOTERS	REPUBLICAN VOTERS	DEMOCRATIC LEADERS	REPUBLICAN LEADERS
Percentage who favor an increase in taxes on large incomes	47%	35%	27%	5%

Source: Based on data from Herbert McClosky, Paul J. Hoffmann, and Rosemary O'Hara, "Issue Conflict and Consensus Among Party Leaders and Followers," *American Political Science Review*, June 1960.

ness community and the Democrats with the working class. Third, the leaders themselves turn to different groups for campaign support and draw upon different groups for new recruits, and again the differences reflect the distinction between the business-oriented Republicans and the worker-oriented Democrats. And fourth, especially the leaders in the two parties and to a lesser extent the followers do indeed hold to different social philosophies.

Do Democratic and Republican Congressmen Support Different Legislation?

Shortly we will see that Democratic and Republican congressmen do not at all support the same legislative proposals, but first a word about political parties in Congress. Neither of the parties has the ability to enforce strict party loyalty or to impose a party program on its representatives in Congress. For reasons already outlined, the parties are loose coalitions of regionally based fiefdoms, not centrally organized or centrally directed programmatic parties. Although congressional leaders and the President have pressures they can exert on party members, these pressures go only so far. In the final analysis the Republican or the Democrat in Congress is more autonomous of his party than he is of his group supporters, his voting constituency back home, his financial backers, and his own judgment and philosophy. If, then, differences between the parties in congressional votes are found, these do not reflect organizational realities so much as substantive differences in philosophy between the parties.

Political scientists have studied how the parties vote in Congress, and have reached two conclusions: (1) There is significant internal cohesion within each party and significant policy differences between the parties, and (2) deviations from these patterns can almost entirely be attributed to constituency factors. Thus if a Democrat votes differently in Congress from his fellow Democrats it is usually because of particular pressures from the voters back home, or more likely from an important interest group in his home district.

Differences in voting records between the two parties are amply documented in roll-call votes in the House of Representatives. Table 8.4 lists votes on selected legislative proposals over the past quarter-century; the consistent contrast between Republicans and Democrats strikingly confirms party differences. On balance, the Republicans have been economic protectionists and the Democrats have been economic protestors. The Republican party has opposed government regulation of the economy, income equalization measures, social welfare programs, and has favored policies that create jobs and economic growth through free enterprise and private initiative. The Democrats introduced Keynesian economics with its emphasis on greater intervention by government in the economy; they have sought to

Table 8.4   Votes on Selected Legislative Proposals

YEAR	LEGISLATION	SELECTED PARTY VOTES IN HOUSE OF REPRESENTATIVES, 1945–1971			
1945	Full Employment Act	Favor:	D = 195 R = 58	Oppose:	D = 21 R = 105
1947	Reduce individual income tax rates	Favor:	D = 63 R = 236	Oppose:	D = 105 R = 2
1952	Invoke injunction provisions against the steel strike	Favor:	D = 82 R = 145	Oppose:	D = 117 R = 47
1954	Increase unemployment compensation	Favor:	D = 92 R = 17	Oppose:	D = 68 R = 173
1959	Curb on unions	Favor:	D = 95 R = 134	Oppose:	D = 184 R = 17
1961	Proposal to block an increase in minimum wages	Favor:	D = 74 R = 146	Oppose:	D = 142 R = 26
1961	Emergency Educational Act	Favor:	D = 164 R = 6	Oppose:	D = 82 R = 160
1964	Antipoverty program	Favor:	D = 204 R = 22	Oppose:	D = 40 R = 145
1969	Proposal to block tax reforms	Favor:	D = 56 R = 154	Oppose:	D = 179 R = 26
1971	Proposal to block loans to help low- and moderate-income families buy homes	Favor:	D = 78 R = 137	Oppose:	D = 111 R = 2
1971	Hospital construction	Favor:	D = 212 R = 67	Oppose:	D = 3 R = 95

Source: Based on data from Robert A. Dahl, "Key Votes, 1945–1964,"
Pluralist Democracy in the United States (Chicago: Rand McNally, 1967), pp. 238–242;
and *Labor Looks at the 91st Congress,* An AFL–CIO Legislative Report, 1971.

reduce income disparities through tax reform; and they have favored new and extended social welfare policies.

While this historical perspective is accurate, it is certainly not complete. There are many bumps and deviations. *Each* party can alternately be cast as protecting conservative principles *and* as pursuing a strategy of reform. The first major attempt to regulate commercial trusts and financial empires belongs to a Republican President, Theodore Roosevelt (1901–1909), who so disagreed with the conservative faction within his own party, a wholly probusiness and antilabor faction, that he eventually formed a third-party movement, the Progressive party, under whose banner he unsuccessfully sought the Presidency in 1912. (He split the Republican vote, and the election went to Democrat Woodrow Wilson.) The Democratic party has not been consistently reform-minded. Certainly the Democratic party within Congress, dominated by southern conservatives, must be credited with slowing down and blocking social welfare policies, especially when these policies are connected with civil rights. The liberal-labor coalition within the Democratic party is only one faction, and not always the one that controls legislation.

Qualifications notwithstanding, various types of evidence show meaningful differences between the two major parties, differences at least partially rooted in conflicting class interests. The argument that the Republicans and Democrats present "no choice" to the electorate cannot be sustained; and thus neither can the argument that it makes no difference which party controls Congress.

Political Parties
and Foreign Policy: A Footnote

There really are two types of foreign policy issues: those in which the political parties play a role and those in which they do not. Among the first type of issues are tariff policy and foreign aid. Even in listing them it is clear that they are as much domestic as foreign issues. Thus tariff policy reflects pressures and priorities of business and labor groups; on balance, the Republicans have been more protective of home industries and have favored high tariffs, whereas the Democrats have urged lower tariffs and free trade so that consumer products could be made available on as cheap a basis as possible. This distinction is breaking down, however, as the international business community (largely Republican) presses for less restrictive trade practices so that it can market abroad, and some labor unions (largely Democratic) now favor high tariffs in order to guard against unfair competition from "cheap labor" in other countries—a competition resulting in unemployment at home.

Foreign aid is more strictly a foreign policy issue, but it is never separated from domestic considerations. These include debates between balance-the-budget forces (mostly Republican) and humanitarian-spenders (mostly Democrats), and also debates sparked by strong ties between domestic pressure groups and one nation or another around the world. Aid to Israel has never been divorced from considerations of the Jewish vote in the United States. Black Americans are beginning to press for greater recognition and more favorable treatment of Black African nations, and for greater opposition to White-controlled African nations such as Rhodesia and South Africa.

In many other foreign policy issues, political parties play a minor role. These are the issues of war and peace, of national security and defense.

Here the prevailing position has been bipartisanship, with both parties accepting the leadership of the President and his executive advisors. *Bipartisanship* is perhaps the wrong term. More accurate is the term *nonpartisanship*, for major foreign policy since World War II has been made by a small group of experts isolated from party politics in any serious sense. This is evident in a long list of major foreign policy decisions, which would include most dramatically the Vietnam war but also involvement in military alliances such as NATO, participation in the arms race and nuclear stockpiling, the deployment of armed forces around the world, the use made of the United Nations for foreign policy concerns, and a host of other policies. These policies have not been made by political party leaders' getting together to formulate a bipartisan role for the United States in world affairs. Nothing of the sort. They have been made by the President, speaking as leader of the nation rather than as head of his party, in consultation with trusted advisors drawn from universities, major corporations, large law firms, and the career ranks of the State Department and the Pentagon.

Nothing so clearly documents the irrelevance of the parties to foreign policy than the divisive events of the 1960s and early 1970s, as the Vietnam venture began to sour. There was a split between hawks and doves within the government, but this split had little to do with party politics. Its institutional expression was a battle between Congress and the Presidency over who should control foreign policy. The principal antagonists, Senator Fulbright and President Johnson, were both Democrats.

Summary Thus Far

We have learned two important things about the American party system. First, the two major political parties control the selection of candidates for nearly all significant public offices, and thus effectively control the choice presented to the electorate. Second, there are sufficiently consistent differences between the two parties that this choice means something. Perhaps the choice is not as sharp as some would prefer, but the evidence shows that it does make a difference who wins. Keeping these two findings in mind, we turn to a third major topic—the political parties as electoral organizations.

Political Parties and Elections

American political parties come to life only at election times, with energies first going to the nomination process and then to the general campaign. The way in which parties become involved in the campaign, however, is different from what many of us might think. The one thing most expected of parties in active campaigning—"get-out-the-vote drives"—is not much practiced. Of course there are a few city and county party machines that deliver the vote, but these are exceptions. Certainly the image of the political party as a vast machinery of workers who blanket the country at election time is an exaggeration. Fewer than one of every twenty voters is actually visited by a party worker, and only about one-fourth receive any type of party literature. Most local elections, and even many campaigns for the U.S. Congress, are contested by two highly personalized campaign operations. A candidate depends more on his own loyal followers, on groups that traditionally support him, and on the campaign team he manages to put together than he does on the workings of a party organization. Of course the extent to which there is a party organization varies from area to area, and state to state. Yet even where parties are most organized, the candidate will supplement party effort with his own organization and his own fund-raising drives.

The role of the party in Presidential elections especially has been greatly modified by the mass media. For the most part the task of publicizing candidates and their views has been taken over by the pressmen who accompany a candidate (usually in a plane provided by the candidate), the television cameras which follow him around, and the paid spot advertisements on radio and TV. The chief task of the national party organization is to raise money—lots of it—to pay the campaign costs. The task of planning the campaign, writing the candidate's speeches, working out the strategy, and so forth, usually falls to the candidate's hand-picked staff. Sometimes this causes tension between the candidate and his party, as happened in the Democratic party in 1972. McGovern's campaign for the Presidency was often at cross-purposes with what the professional party workers wanted.

If local campaigns are largely controlled by the candidate's personal organization and if state and national campaigns are largely carried out in the news media and over the airwaves, what substance is left to the statement that parties are electoral organizations? This is a difficult yet fair question. Perhaps the single best answer is to stress again a point already made.

Were candidates not to have party labels attached to them (no matter who is running the campaign), the typical American voter would be left in confusion. Voters *expect* candidates to be supported by one of the major parties. Indeed the definition of a "major candidate" is one who has the Democratic or Republican nomination. The typical voter may know next to nothing about how the party is organized, how it goes about nominating its candidates, how it raises money, and how it campaigns. But he does know one thing. One candidate is a Democrat and the other is a Republican, and this fact more than any other helps the average citizen decide how to vote. This then is the significance of the party as an electoral organization. It legitimates the candidates. It stamps them approved. The typical American election is a process by which voter *party* preferences become translated into winning and losing candidates.

Elections and the Control of Government

A striking characteristic of American elections is that a voter can choose the candidate from one party for, say, the President, then choose the other party's candidate for state governor, and then switch back to the original party when he casts his ballot for congressman. In short, the voter can engage in "ticket-splitting." Not all or even a majority of voters do this, but enough do so that the party that controls the White House need not be the party that controls Congress. This was the case following the 1972 election. Although Republican Nixon gained 61 percent of the popular vote for President, the Democratic party sent 242 candidates to the House of Representatives compared to only 192 Republicans, and the Democrats gained a 57 to 43 majority in the Senate.

A few state election results dramatically illustrate ticket-splitting. In Arkansas, for example, 70 percent of the voters supported the 1972 Republican Presidential nominee, but only 39 percent supported the Republican senatorial nominee and even fewer (24 percent) supported the Republican candidate for governor. Nixon received 2 out of every 3 Presidential votes in Texas, but the voters of that state sent 20 Democrats to the House of Representatives, and only 4 Republicans.

Different branches of government—executive and legislative—and different levels of government—national, state, and local—will not often all be under the control of one party. Yet the different branches and the different levels must cooperate in order to govern the entire country. A Republican President cannot ignore congressional leaders just because they happen to be Democrats, and neither can the congressional leaders ignore the executive branch just because it happens to be filled with members of the opposition party. Cooperation across governing units is necessary, and this can often mean cooperation across party lines. A loosely organized, decentralized, and nonprogrammatic party system fits well, then, with the fragmentation of governing authority imposed by our constitutional system of separation of powers and federalism. Doctrinaire, programmatic parties unable to modify their programs would make governing very difficult when Congress and the White House were held by different parties, or when one level of government was primarily Republican and the other level primarily Democratic.

Elections and Social Change

No society stands still. Citizens become bothered by new social problems, and expect their leadership to do something about them. On the public agenda today are abortion, drug control, environmental pollution, amnesty, and street crime. None of these issues was very important twenty years ago. In the 1950s there was not much attention to space exploration;

in the 1960s "putting a man on the moon" dominated headlines and absorbed huge amounts of public resources; in the 1970s the space program is being quietly dismantled.

As the agenda changes (or perhaps causing it to change) changes occur in the kinds of social groups active in politics. No one thought of "youth" as a separate political group twenty years ago, but the readers of this book came of age in a period when the youth movement was something to be taken seriously in American politics. Today women's liberation has become a political issue, and very many active groups are concerned with the rights of women; this certainly was not the case even a few years ago. Civil rights has long been on America's political agenda, but Black protest groups of the type now active are a fairly recent phenomenon.

Is the political party system responsive to such social change? Do the major parties provide a channel for expressing new social concerns, an outlet for shifts in public sentiment, a home for new types of groups?

The evidence is sufficiently ambiguous that either *yes* or *no* can be argued. However, we intend to provide a less ambiguous answer. Our position is that the party system is responsive to social change, eventually. We can outline our position around two interrelated topics — protest movements and electoral coalitions.

Political Protest Movements

There have been four serious political protest movements in the last decade: first, the Black protest movement against accumulated grievances spanning centuries; second, the youth protest sparked by antiwar sentiment, and fueled by the insurgent political campaign in 1968 of Democratic challenger Eugene McCarthy; third, "Nader-populism," a middle-class movement embracing environmental issues and consumer protection, and hostile to big business, big labor, and big government; and, fourth, a protest led by Alabama Governor George Wallace, based in the South but receiving important support from northern working-class people and some White ethnic groups. The Wallace movement decries the national political elite that has "given in" to Black demands, but in addition to its "Negrophobia," it also expresses a "little-man" against the "power-bosses" mood and prizes traditional values against the cosmopolitanism and moral laxness of youth and other "modern" groups.

Although all of these protest movements shocked the two-party system, none of them, initially, depended on either of the two parties for its impetus. Take the antiwar movement. Citizens dismayed with our Vietnam policy did not turn to the political parties to express their discontent, for the parties provided very little leadership and certainly no institutional home for the antiwar movement during the 1960s. The institutions that mattered most were the national media and the universities, and in some cases the churches or local government. The same is true for the equally large number of citizens dismayed with the antiwar movement. The hawks among the citizens turned, just as the doves had turned, to more relevant institutions than the major parties. For the defenders of the Vietnam policy the relevant institutions were conservative business groups and in some cases trade unions, along with traditional groups such as the Veterans of Foreign Wars.

The other protest movements have been equally poorly serviced by the two major parties. The Wallace-led protestors used a third party in 1968. In that election year the American Independent party received a total of 10 million votes. In 1972 Wallace decided to run in the Democratic primaries, and though he received more than a fifth of the primary votes (only a few percentage points behind nominee McGovern), the nominating convention paid little attention to the causes he supported. An assassination attempt on Wallace crippled him prior to the convention, and he subsequently played little role in the 1972 election. So, too, have consumer protest and conservation movements been organized almost entirely outside of the political party system. Of the four major protest movements in the 1960s only the Black movement received some sort of attention and institutional home in the two-party system. Throughout the 1960s and early 1970s the Democratic party did attempt to respond to some of the pressing Black demands.

Many commentators conclude that the two-party system is not sufficiently flexible to accommodate such political protest movements as those that dominated the headlines and the politics of the 1960s. For this reason, they insist, the parties are not really responsive to what is going on in American society. This judgment, we believe, is premature.

Let us look more closely at the antiwar movement. Its leadership was totally frustrated at the 1968 Democratic Presidential nominating convention in Chicago, and much talk was heard about the inflexibility of the party system. After all, the antiwar movement had led to the decision of incumbent President Lyndon Johnson not to run for reelection, and yet here were the Democratic regulars nominating his Vice-President, Hubert Humphrey. But, only four years later, the Democratic party invited into the convention hall in Miami exactly the same protest groups that had demonstrated in the streets of Chicago in 1968. The convention nominated a strong antiwar candidate, Senator George McGovern. Thus in only four years the antiwar groups had a clear opportunity to take their case to the American electorate. That the results favored McGovern's Republican opponent, Richard Nixon, does not prove the inflexibility of the party system. It simply shows that a majority of Americans did not support George McGovern and his policies.

Indeed, all four of the major protest groups of the 1960s — Blacks, doves, Nader populists, and Wallacites — were in the 1970s receiving some sort of accommodation by the major parties. Blacks of course have been the most successful, but then they have been organizing for political action the

An important protest movement of the 1960s found expression through George Wallace's American Independent Party. (Photo: Wide World)

longest. They now have sixteen members of Congress, and they hold dozens of local and state offices. The successes of the Wallace movement are also evident. In 1972 the Nixon-Agnew ticket specifically addressed itself to the blue-collar suburbanites who feared bussing, to the southern businessmen who felt isolated, to the urban dwellers concerned about street crime, and to the lower-middle-class taxpayers outraged at the rising costs of welfare programs. The constituencies for whom George Wallace speaks were not ignored. Even Nader-populism, involving a much less clear-cut set of issues and groups, received attention in McGovern's campaign.

Minor Parties

The absorption of protest movements and minor parties into the dominant two-party system is an old theme in American politics. The two-party system has never for any length of time been pure in the United States. Numerous third parties have risen to challenge one or both of the dominant parties. And though these third parties disappear with time, their presence is seldom without influence. One variety of minor party has been the protest group, such as the Populist party in the late 1880s, which served as a channel for discontent with the monopolies and trusts. It also—with notable success—agitated for direct election of senators, the primary system as against the convention method of nominating candidates, the extension of suffrage to women, and other political reforms. With time these all became policies enacted into law by the major parties.

Another type of minor party is of the secessionist cast; it breaks away from one of the major parties when the politics of compromise fail to hold together the many factions that make up any large party. Theodore Roosevelt's Progressive party of 1912 is an example of a secessionist party resulting from a split in the national leadership of the Republican party. More recent examples are the largely regional parties of the South, which frequently have been led by "states' righters" within the Democratic party. Strom Thurmond (now Republican senator from South Carolina, having switched parties) led the Dixiecrats in 1948, a group of southern Democrats dismayed at the nomination of Harry Truman. The American Independent party of George Wallace in 1968 was a similar secessionist group, breaking away from the liberal northern wing of the Democratic party that nominated Humphrey to stand against Nixon.

Not all minor parties have resulted from splits within a major party. The Socialist party, for instance, deliberately supports an ideology that is generally outside the framework that guides the Republicans and the Democrats. Such a party will outlast secessionist parties, but will not usually have as much influence on public policy.

The chief function of minor parties has been to bring new issues, or new ways of looking at old issues, to the political agenda. As they succeed in forcing new policies on the older-established parties, they tend to disappear. What we witness in the 1970s, then, is a repeat of previous history. As the Democrats and Republicans absorb into their ranks the followers and goals of the protest groups of the 1960s, they simply are doing what major parties have always done. This is one of the ways in which the party system stays alive and remains responsive to changing conditions and issues.

Parties and Electoral Coalitions: Maintaining, Deviating, and Realigning Elections

Throughout this text we have stressed the strength of voting habits. The majority of American voters tend to identify with one or the other of the major parties, just as they identify with a particular religious creed. These party identifiers provide a great deal of stability to party politics. They become part of electoral coalitions that persist across a series of individual elections.[8] For example, the Democratic party was able to count on the urban working-class voters in every election from 1932 to 1968. And over the same electoral era the Republican party was able to count on the small-town, middle-class voters. Most elections, therefore, *maintain* the existing balance of forces.

From time to time, however, short-term electoral forces upset the existing balance. Voters *deviate* from their traditional loyalties, and sometimes in sufficient number that the outcome is not at all what we would expect if we predicted it solely on the basis of partisan identifications. Many different things can lead citizens to cross party lines and vote contrary to their long-standing partisan loyalties. Eisenhower was successful in 1952 and 1956 because many Democratic voters simply "liked Ike" and voted on the basis of their personal attractions rather than their economic interests. An important short-term electoral force in the 1960 election evolved around religious interests. Kennedy, a Roman Catholic, gained a few Catholic voters who normally would have supported the Republicans, but he lost many more traditionally Democratic Protestants to Nixon, the Republican candidate. This helps account for the extremely close election in 1960, less than a percentage point separating the winner Kennedy from the loser Nixon. The Republican candidate in 1964, Barry Goldwater, was much more soundly defeated than would have been expected on the basis of the normal strength of the two parties. In this case it was his strongly conservative stands that impelled Republican liberals into the Democratic camp. The important thing about such deviations is that they are temporary. The usual balance of forces reasserts itself in the following election.

In addition to such so-called maintaining and deviating elections, there is a third type—the *realigning* election. This type of election is a vehicle for substantial social change, for in this case the composition of one or both of the parties undergoes major transformation. Between 1932 and 1936 the Democrats constructed the electoral coalition that was to dominate American politics almost up to the present day. This was accomplished by their attracting entirely new kinds of voters into electoral participation—especially immigrant groups—but also by attracting many traditional Republican voters to associate themselves permanently with Democratic candidates. Black voters are an example. They had stayed with the party of emancipation, the Republicans, until it was crystal clear that the party which championed the needs and rights of the lower classes was the Democratic party. Then they switched.

Sometimes realigning elections are called "critical" elections, and this is an apt phrase. Very much that is critical to American politics happens

---

[8] The discussion of the next three paragraphs draws upon studies conducted by the Survey Research Center, University of Michigan. See especially Angus Campbell, Philip E. Converse, Warren E. Miller, Donald E. Stokes, *The American Voter* (New York: Wiley, 1960); and by the same authors, *Elections and the Political Order* (New York: Wiley, 1966).

jointly with a realigning election. The groups that had been ascendent drop into the political background; the groups that had been without political voice emerge into the foreground. The important shift in the political role of labor between 1932 and 1940 is a telling example. As the composition of the party support changes, so also does the political agenda. The range of issues which had been the focus of national debate changes, sometimes dramatically. Again the 1930s present a clear example. Social security, unemployment compensation, public welfare, and like measures were simply not on the political agenda throughout the 1920s, but the realignment which occurred in the 1930s put them very much on the agenda.

Throughout American history "critical elections" have helped transform the political agenda. The practice started as early as the 1800s, with the breakup of the Federalist party, as the strongly individualistic pioneer rejected the conservative, semiaristocratic outlook of the Easterner and trekked westward. This trek was to provide the popular support in the new territories for Jacksonian egalitarian democracy, and thus for a new party system in the 1830s. Another major realignment took place at the time of the Civil War, and yet another in the 1890s when the Populists challenged the dominance of conservative capitalism. The reoccurrence of critical elections suggests that the party system is at least partially responsive to changing popular preferences and social needs. Critical elections facilitate the emergence to power of new social groups, and such elections hasten the transformation of the political agenda.

The 1972 Election—Realignment?

Many observers believe that we are in the midst of an era of electoral realignment, the result of which will be a transformed Democratic and Republican party within a few years. They cite as evidence the following: (1) the variety of intra- and extraparty protests over the past decade, such protests indicating that "politics as usual" is under strain and that the parties will have to change to accommodate these strains; (2) the increasing numbers of voters now calling themselves Independents, indicating the presence of a large minority in the electorate now available to support either party; and (3) the upsurge in ticket-splitting, indicating a weakening of partisan loyalties even among those who continue to identify with one of the parties.

The most compelling evidence that realignment is taking place is the actual voting behavior of citizens in the 1972 Presidential race. There were dramatic switches of normally Democratic voters into the Republican camp. Large numbers of blue-collar Catholics and ethnics deserted the Democratic national ticket to give Nixon victories in the traditionally Democratic industrial states of the North; the Jewish vote remained Democratic, but only barely so, whereas it traditionally has supported the Democratic ticket by a 9 to 1 ratio; the southern support for the Democratic party continued to erode away; and the youth vote, which some had felt would strengthen the Democratic party, favored Nixon.

Yet not all the evidence points toward realignment. If groups are indeed changing party loyalties, this would be reflected in congressional, guberna- torial, and local elections, as well as in the Presidential election. But in all save the Presidential race the results of the 1972 election were fairly typi- cal. The Democratic party did not lose its majority in Congress, nor its edge in governorships, nor control of the state legislatures it traditionally domi- nates. Perhaps, then, the 1972 election was a deviating election, rather than one of realignment. If so, the Catholics, the workers, the ethnics, the Jews, the Southerners, and other traditionally Democratic voters will return to their habitual party abode at the next election, and the balance of electoral forces we have known since 1932 will reestablish itself.

Yet it is too early to draw this conclusion. And it is too early to predict with certainty an electoral realignment. The one firm conclusion that can be drawn is that the conditions that in past times led to electoral realign- ment are very much present in today's politics. The American public is showing restlessness with how the two parties have responded to the polit- ical problems of the past decade. Barely more than a majority of the eligible citizens even bothered to vote in 1972, a sign in itself of disaffection and dissatisfaction. As the major parties accommodate themselves to the protest groups of the past decade, and as they accommodate themselves to a politi- cal agenda now crowded with issues of pollution, consumer protection, drugs, tax reform, bussing, and street crime, they will not emerge unscathed. The inflexible party is a doomed party, and U.S. history gives ample evidence of the flexibility of both of our major parties.

Controversy

In selecting its Presidential ticket should a political party concern itself primarily with winning, or should it clarify the differences that divide the two parties? More often than not the two major parties nominate "centrist" Presidential candidates; that is, they nominate candidates who can appeal to the broad middle ground in American politics. In doing so they smooth over important differences in political outlook between the Republicans and the Democrats. Except occasionally the major parties deliberately pro- vide more echo than choice.

One Side

The American electorate responds favorably to Presidential candidates who stand midway between a broadly conservative and a broadly liberal orientation toward American society. Since it is the job of political parties to win elections, they should give the voters what they want. Recent examples of nominating "extreme" candidates have resulted in drastic election defeats. In 1964 the Republican Convention nominated Senator Barry Goldwater, an articulate spokesman for the conservative wing of the party. Goldwater led the Republican ticket to an overwhelming defeat, as the Democratic nominees Johnson and Humphrey won more than 60 percent of the Presidential votes. Election year 1972 was a repeat performance, except this time it was the Democratic party which, in Senator George McGovern, selected a candidate who spoke for its more liberal wing. McGovern's defeat at the hands of the Republican ticket of Nixon and Agnew was similar to Goldwater's defeat eight years earlier—and for many of the same reasons. To select a Presidential candidate well to the left or well to the right of center leads many voters to desert their traditional party. This shows that the electorate prefers candidates, at least presidential candidates, who are middle-of-the-roaders.

Besides, crushing defeats such as those suffered by Goldwater and McGovern can have unfortunate consequences. The winning party interprets the landslide victory as license to do whatever it wants. The checks imposed by a close victory are erased, tempting the party in power to take too many liberties with its authority.

The Other Side

While it is true that the electorate appears to prefer middle-of-the-road candidates, the major parties have a responsibility to values other than winning. They should provide the electorate with a clear choice, and should use the Presidential election as an opportunity for debating alternative goals and policies for the nation.

Such a choice is especially important in a Presidential campaign. Most American citizens pay attention to politics only at this time. If there is to be meaningful participation by the typical citizen in political life, it can best occur during a Presidential election year. If the typical citizen is going to think seriously about the alternatives facing his society, he will do so in response to debates between rival Presidential candidates. When the Presidential campaign smooths over substantive differences about how to handle the problems of the nation, the democratic process is subverted. The "me-too-ism" of most Presidential campaigns denies the one opportunity for a national debate about significant issues.

A candidate who clearly differs from his opponent plays an important educating role, even if he goes down to defeat. He reminds the nation that alternative policies are possible. This is part of the responsibility of leadership. In 1972, for instance, McGovern's strong antiwar stand might have contributed to his defeat, but perhaps it also contributed to the urgency with which the Nixon administration pursued peace negotiations that year. McGovern himself saw it this way, as reflected in his concession speech:

"There can be no question at all that we have pushed this country in the direction of peace, and I think each one of us loves the title of peacemaker more than any office in the land."

When the political parties fail to provide alternatives, they fail to provide leadership. Thus they fail the American public.

Suggested Readings

The standard reference work on American political parties is V. O. Key, Jr., *Politics, Parties, and Pressure Groups,* 5th ed. (New York: T. Y. Crowell, 1964). This work includes a detailed treatment of party organization, of the nominating process, of campaign techniques, of party finance, and related topics. It also includes some historical discussion. For additional historical treatment as well as analytic interpretation, see the collection of studies in William N. Chambers and Walter D. Burnham, eds., *The American Party Systems: Stages of Political Development* (New York: Oxford University Press, 1967).

For the argument that our political parties are not sufficiently programmatic and responsible, see the thesis developed in E. E. Schattschneider, *Party Government* (New York: Holt, Rinehart & Winston, 1942). For further analysis on the same topic the treatment of Austin Ranney, *The Doctrine of Responsible Party Government* (Urbana: University of Illinois Press, 1956), is very helpful.

The thesis that American political parties will converge toward a "centrist" position is ably developed in Anthony Downs, *An Economic Theory of Democracy* (New York: Harper & Row, 1957). Finally, the analysis of American voting behavior is best illustrated in two publications of the Survey Research Center at the University of Michigan: Angus Campbell, Philip E. Converse, Warren E. Miller, and Donald E. Stokes, *The American Voter* (New York: Wiley, 1960); and, by the same authors, *Elections and the Political Order* (New York: Wiley, 1966).

The
Constitutional
Framework

A farmer in the 1790s was free to grow whatever crops he wished, was free to pay his help any wages mutually agreed to, was free to prepare, transport, and market his commodities however he chose, and was free to set his own prices. Today, however, dozens of government regulations affect how foodstuffs are grown and processed and marketed. How much of which crops are planted is subject to government regulation; so also is the use of fertilizers and insecticides; so also are farm wages and crop prices.

If the farmer in 1790 was wealthy he sent his children to private schools or perhaps hired a tutor to educate them at home. If he fell ill he depended on his family or his neighbors to care for the farm until he could resume his work. As he grew old and could no longer run the farm, he lived off his accumulated savings and the goodwill of his children. Today the average farmer sends his children to public schools, and he can rely on public health services and a state social security system as a protection against sickness and old age.

It belabors a familiar point to say that the growth of government regulation and government services has transformed the relationship between citizen and state over the past two centuries. But no sooner do we recognize this than we come face to face with a fascinating issue: The same basic rule, by which we mean the Constitution, that governed American society in 1790 governs American society today. In other words, the growth of the "service" and "regulated" state has taken place within a legal framework and set of political principles hammered out one hot summer in Philadelphia nearly 200 years ago. What is this Constitution which could so long endure and accommodate itself to so totally transformed a society?

To answer this question we will need to do three things. First, we will need a quick review of American history. As we go back to the 1780s for an understanding of the politics that led to the Constitutional Convention and that influenced the Constitution itself, our purpose will be not to teach history, but to underline that our "basic rule," as a constitution is sometimes called, grew out of a period of political turmoil. We will point out that, although a constitution is supposed to "live for the ages," those who write it and those who argue for and against its adoption are living in their own present time, and they will likely have an eye on the immediate advantages and disadvantages of the new document, which are not always synonymous with its future effects.

Second, we will need to ask how our Constitution handles the fundamentals. To survive, a political community needs procedures for defending itself from external and internal enemies, it needs a means for settling disputes between its own members, it needs institutions for making and carrying out rules, it needs a basis for agreement on how to select the rule makers, and although it may not need them, it is wise that it have some provisions for limiting the uses to which political authority can be put. It often is said that the way the U.S. Constitution handled these fundamentals accounts for its staying power.

The third thing we will do is to examine how the Constitution has managed to adapt itself to political and economic and social conditions undreamed of back in the Philadelphia of 1787.

Writing the Constitution

Because some readers may have a hazy recollection of specific dates and events we include here an abbreviated chronology of major political happenings during the two decades that will concern us. While it is not necessary to memorize this chronology, it is necessary to keep in mind that a decade separates the Declaration of Independence (1776) and the framing of the Constitution (1787). What transpired during the intervening eleven years—when the states were governed under the Articles of Confederation—set the political context out of which the Constitution was born.

American Political History—1774 to 1791

1774 The First Continental Congress, formed extralegally. Fifty-six delegates from 12 colonies meet in Philadelphia to review problems common to all colonies.

1775 Military action between Britain and the colonies intensifies. The famous "ride of Paul Revere"; the British expedition against the Concord Minutemen; the Battle of Bunker Hill.

1776 Thomas Paine publishes *Common Sense*, a radical call to sever all ties with Great Britain.

1777 The Articles of Confederation are drafted. They link the thirteen states in a loose "League of Friendship," and are finally adopted in 1781.

1782 The War of Independence comes to an end. Peace negotiations begin in Paris, and the treaty is ratified the following year.

1786 Shays' Rebellion in Massachusetts, an attack by the debtors against their creditors.

1787 An assembly to draft a constitution convenes in Philadelphia.

1788 Sufficient number of states ratify new Constitution that it can be put into effect.

1789 George Washington is elected first President of the United States.

1791 Bill of Rights added to the Constitution.

Between the early 1770s and the early 1790s political events transformed the eastern seaboard from thirteen colonies ruled by Great Britain to thirteen states combined into one nation.

Establishing a Nation:
A Two-Stage Process

The American Declaration of Independence and the Revolutionary War shifted the center of political power from London to the newly independent states. Our early history thus anticipated the two-stage process through which many African and Asian nations are passing today as they liberate themselves from colonial rule. The first stage of this process involves capturing the centers of political power from the "false" rulers, the colonialists. Just as the American colonies gained their independence from Great Britain, so Kenya gained its independence from Great Britain, Indonesia from Holland, Congo from Belgium, and Algeria from France.

But it is not easy to establish a new nation, and so the first phase—gaining independence from a colonial power—is often followed by a second phase, *maintaining* the centers of power against centrifugal forces that are often set in motion by wars of liberation and that if unchecked can fragment and divide the new society. The successionist movement in the Congo (now called Zaire) is a clear example, as was the civil war between Nigeria and Biafra.

Our political history of the 1770s and 1780s followed a course similar to that of some of the new nations. The first phase, the Declaration of Independence and the ensuing War for Independence, severed the existing legal ties with the British colonial empire. The Articles of Confederation, creating a league of free and independent states, were adopted. But the Articles had a number of weaknesses, which we will discuss later in this chapter. So there followed the second phase; centrifugal forces, tending to disunity and differences, were set in motion. The drafting and subsequent adoption of the United States Constitution checked those divisive forces by shifting the center of political power from a loose league of states to a strong federal union. Without both of these acts—the writing of the Declaration of Independence and the making of the U.S. Constitution—there would be no United States as we know it today. A political order was founded and a constitutional contract accepted out of the events of the 1770s and 1780s.

The War for Independence

Acts of such magnitude as a revolution throw into sharp relief such abstract principles as authority and freedom. Men use these principles to justify the course of action decided on.

The Tories' Views: The Tory opposition to the "war of separation," as they called it, is illustrated in a series of weekly letters to the citizens of Massachusetts, written by Daniel Leonard, a brilliant Boston lawyer with strong loyalty to the Empire. The system of government designed by the

Anglo mind was, Leonard counseled, the "most perfect system that the wisdom of ages had produced." It is in the interest of the colonies to remain subject to the authority of parliament, he went on. And more than this, it is their moral duty, for "being part of the empire, subject to the supreme authority of the state, bound by its laws and entitled to its protection, were the very terms and conditions by which our ancestors held their lands, and settled the province."

The Patriots' Views: The Patriots were equally forthright. Thomas Paine, the remarkably effective agitator and pamphleteer, proclaimed in *Common Sense* that economic self-interest and natural right showed that it was absurd to suppose that a continent could be perpetually governed by an island. The argument for severing the contract with Britain was forcefully stated in the eloquent words of Thomas Jefferson as they appeared in the Declaration of Independence:

> We hold these truths to be self-evident, that all men are created equal, that they are endowed by their Creator with certain unalienable Rights, that among these are Life, Liberty, and the pursuit of Happiness. That to secure these rights, Governments are instituted among Men, deriving

The Declaration of Independence being read publicly.   (*New York Public Library Picture Collection*)

their just powers from the consent of the governed. That whenever any Form of Government becomes destructive of these ends, it is the Right of the People to alter or to abolish it, and to institute new Government, laying its foundations on such principles and organizing its powers in such form, as to them shall seem most likely to effect their Safety and Happiness. Prudence, indeed, will dictate that Governments long established should not be changed for light and transient causes; and accordingly all experience hath shown, that mankind are more disposed to suffer, while evils are sufferable, than to right themselves by abolishing the forms to which they are accustomed. But when a long train of abuses and usurpations, pursuing invariably the same Object evinces a design to reduce them under absolute Despotism, it is their right, it is their duty, to throw off such Government, and to produce new Guards for their future security. Such has been the patient sufferance of these Colonies and such is now the necessity which constrains them to alter their former Systems of Government. . . .

We should recognize that these elegant phrases convey economic as well as moralistic purposes. Major political events can seldom be understood unless one knows something of the economic interests involved. The immediate "abuses and usurpations" that Jefferson referred to were the arbitrary use by the British crown of the powers of taxation and regulation of trade. The thirteen colonies were part of a mercantilistic economic system in which trade, taxation, and other economic affairs were managed for the benefit of the small group of landlords and merchants who controlled the government in England, a government in which the colonies had no representation. Thus the call, "No taxation without representation."

Major Consequences of the War

But to view the War for Independence as a struggle between economic interests, one located on this side of the Atlantic and the other on the far side, would be to miss important issues. The successful War for Independence had consequences reaching beyond the settlement of economic squabbles. And these consequences are similar to those we now witness in those new African states which, like the United States two centuries ago, have successfully pursued the struggle for decolonization. There are certain regularities which follow successful political revolutions. A successful revolution intensifies commitment to the principles for which the war is fought. The people have been mobilized by a propaganda effort which stresses these very principles. In the American instance this meant that large numbers of citizens had now acquired a concrete view of freedom as separatism, individualism, absence of onerous taxation, and the right to rebel against central authority. Authority was illegitimate unless it rested on the consent of the governed, which in turn implied suffrage and political representation.

There was a second major consequence of the war. Among the small group of political leaders who served in the initial Continental Congresses, who framed the Declaration of Independence, and who financed and fought in the war were men who were beginning to think of themselves as a *national* political elite. Of course there was no "nation" either before or immediately after the war. Prior to 1776 there were thirteen colonies more or less self-governed with respect to internal matters but primarily under the authority of the British crown. For a few years immediately after the war there were thirteen autonomous states loosely linked together by the Articles of Confederation. Nevertheless, the men who came to prominence during the war years were conscious of their role in establishing a nation.

This national leadership recognized that, although revolutions are associated with the defiance of authority in the name of liberty, establishing regularized and effective procedures of government must be associated with obedience to authority in the name of stability. The history of "wars for independence" repeatedly illustrates the difficulties of reconstituting authority after a period of rebellion. The right of revolution so proudly proclaimed in the Declaration of Independence was soon viewed as having a disquieting effect on certain groups in the society. The obligations of contract must be reasserted over the excesses of freedom, the founding fathers agreed, and this is the story of the 1780s.

The Articles of Confederation: Their Weaknesses

The Articles of Confederation, framed in the spirit of the War for Independence, were put into effect in 1781, and lasted less than a decade. The Articles represented a compromise between complete state sovereignty and a strong central government. For the most part they reflected the belief that local self-rule could best preserve the liberties gained in the successful war. But to establish a confederation at all was to recognize that some centralized coordination among the thirteen states might work to the benefit of all. The inability of the Articles to provide such coordination, however, was quickly to discredit the Confederation.

There was provision for a Congress but not for an executive power; there was no one to administer legislation. The Congress itself consisted of delegates from each of the thirteen sovereign states. The delegates were similar to ambassadors in that they served entirely at the pleasure of the home government. Irrespective of size or resources each state had one vote, and it took the vote of only one state to veto any amendment to the Articles. It took nine votes, more than a two-thirds majority, to pass any legislation.

What the Congress was prevented from doing is even more interesting than what it was permitted to do.

Lack of Power over Individuals: Congress exercised no direct power over individuals. Men held citizenship only in their respective states. If Congress passed a law regulating the behavior of individuals, such as drafting them into the military, it would not be binding on an individual unless his state chose to enforce it, and many regulations were never enforced by state authority. An analogy with the United Nations is appropriate. If the UN Assembly passes a resolution advising trade sanctions against Rhodesia, no manufacturer or shipper can be punished for trading there unless his own nation passes similar legislation. Disregard for UN resolutions is as easy for us to understand as was disregard of congressional resolutions some 200 years ago. Both proceeded from the same conditions.

Lack of Power to Regulate Finances: The Congress could not tax. Although the Confederation was to be supported by state contributions levied in proportion to land values, the Congress could not enforce such contributions, just as today the UN cannot collect member dues from any nation that refuses to pay them. Early in 1781 Congress requested $8,000,000 from the states in order to pay war debts; three years later, less than a fifth of this money had been collected. The Confederation verged on bankruptcy.

In addition to levying states, the Confederation could raise money by selling the trans-Allegheny lands, which were held in common ownership by the Confederation, but the Confederation could not defend the frontier from Indians, and this discouraged settlement.

Lack of Power to Regulate Interstate Trade and Foreign Trade: The Congress could neither regulate commerce nor impose import duties. Thus another source of income was prohibited. Whereas individual states could, and did, impose tariffs on goods coming in from England, Spain, the West Indies, and other places, the Confederation itself was expressly prevented from doing so. Moreover, the inability of the Congress to regulate commerce among the states led to economic warfare. States issued their own money, and often would not accept that issued by another state. Any possibility of an emerging national economy was seriously threatened by absence of power to regulate commerce and money among the states.

Economic Groups Hurt by the Government's Lack of Powers

Creditor Class: Men who had loaned money for the war effort and who had been issued government bonds by the Continental Congress stood to lose everything if the government went bankrupt. Already they were fortunate to be paid ten cents on the dollar. The creditors included both foreign and American investors, and men such as Hamilton were aware that a government that defaulted on its public securities was a government with a ruined credit rating. Future financial support would not be forthcoming.

The creditor class had also been lending money to farmers, to enable them to purchase land, livestock, and basic supplies. States, often at the urging of farmers heavily in debt, began to issue paper money. Farmers were using this money to pay off debts in a currency far less in value than what they had initially borrowed, and the creditors were the losers.

Land Speculators: The inability of the central government to protect settlers from Indians, and indeed from British and Spanish soldiers who formed alliances with and armed the Indians, severely hurt land speculators. It was by no means certain that the rich and vast land from the Ohio River to the Mississippi River, called the Northwest Territory, could remain part of the United States. The British refused to be dislodged from their fur trading posts and from the garrisons they used to protect them. Control over the territory to the southwest was equally in doubt. The Spanish, through their control of the mouth of the Mississippi at New Orleans, were in a position to dictate the terms on which trade between the Westerners and the rest of the world would be carried out. Although pioneers were streaming across the Appalachians in the 1780s, these were people, often fleeing from debts and heavy taxation, who had no great love for the "Easterners" in control of the several states and the Confederation. Their loyalty very much depended on the ability of the government to remove the British from the fur posts, to open the Mississippi River for purposes of trade, and to protect them from Indians.

Merchant and Commercial Interests: In addition to creditors, land speculators, and settlers moving west, the merchant and commercial interests, small though they may have been, were suffering under the Articles of Confederation. State-imposed tariffs, often crippling small industries in a neighboring state, as well as general restrictions on interstate trade and the absence of common regulations on shipping, hindered the development of a national economy. Such an economy was necessary if commercial interests were to prosper.

In short, economic interests were severely hampered by the inability of the central government to maintain a standing army, to tax citizens and thereby pay off its debts, to regulate commerce among the states, to impose tariffs on foreign goods, and to protect economic investments.

The Conflict of Debtors vs. Creditors

But if some interests were hurt, others were promoted by the sovereignty of the states and the democratic spirit which prevailed within them. The population in the 1780s was overwhelmingly agrarian. Many of the farmers were heavily in debt, and did benefit from the cheap money being issued by state governments. Moreover, farmers were gaining control of state legislatures, and in the absence of strong state executives (itself a reflection of the prevailing hostile mood toward central authority), were able to pass laws delaying the collection of debts.

Debtors not only benefited from some of the economic conditions, they also stood to benefit from the lack of effective police power by the central government. Incidents of open rebellion against creditors were not unknown during the 1780s. There were refusals to pay debts and refusals to leave farms when authorities attempted to foreclose on mortgages. The most famous such rebellion, led by Daniel Shays, a veteran of Bunker Hill, even succeeded in capturing courthouses in several parts of Massachusetts. Although the rebellion was put down by a mercenary army paid by wealthy citizens, the lesson of Shays' Rebellion was not lost on citizens concerned about protecting property.

What if the "right of revolution" urged against the political tyranny of George the Third were to be reinterpreted as the "right of revolution" against the economic tyranny of local creditors? Increasingly at stake in the 1780s was the obligation of contract. Many citizens felt that the ties of authority had been too much weakened.

Recognition of the Need for a Strong Government: By the mid-1780s the Confederation entered the second phase that often follows a war of liberation: It was caught up in the action of centrifugal forces that cause tensions and disunity in the new society. Political leaders, recognizing the need to check these forces, moved to do so, and the result was the second great act—the writing of the Constitution—which established the United States of America. This time, however, national leadership advanced the cause of authority over the cause of liberty. In 1786 John Jay observed that "the mass of men are neither wise nor good" and that the people had too quickly confused "liberty and licentiousness." Hamilton insisted that there had been "an excess of liberty." In language similar to that heard in the law-and-order debates of the 1970s, he advised that durable liberty is possible only if the magistrate is given a "proper degree of authority to make and execute the laws with rigor." George Washington echoed a similar sentiment when he warned that "arbitrary power is most easily established on the ruins of Liberty abused to licentiousness."

There is no need to detail the steps by which it came to pass that 55 talented and powerful men gathered in Philadelphia in May 1787 to frame a new constitution. Congress had requested the thirteen states to send representatives to Philadelphia "for the sole purpose of revising the Articles of Confederation," but the men so assembled exceeded their mandate. They no sooner arrived than they agreed to two principles. First, the meetings were to be held in strict secrecy, and second, the articles were so inadequate that nothing would do but to create an entirely new Constitution. Knowing well that not all states would adopt the Constitution, they decided that the new Constitution would go into effect when only nine states had ratified. It is clear that the founding fathers violated the authority under which they were gathered, but the country was ready for something new, and these were the men who provided the leadership.

The Constitutional Convention

Writing a Constitution is difficult business. Men of influence are often strong willed, and if they differ in their views of the social order, in the personal interests they wish to protect, and in the constituencies they represent, to write a document agreeable to all is unlikely.

Yet over the span of a single summer fifty-five men did succeed in writing a Constitution that is hailed yet today as perhaps the most effective such document ever put to pen. Much is written about the statesmanship of Washington, the tactical brilliance of Hamilton, the profound insights of Madison, and the practical wisdom of Franklin. The founders and the wonder they wrought has now become political folklore and is passed on from generation to generation of American citizens.

The men gathered in Philadelphia were in fact a remarkable group. The document they fashioned reflected their wide political experiences as well as their close study of political philosophy and constitutional writings. As many as twenty of the delegates had had previous experience writing state constitutions, and in many respects the federal Constitution was an extension and elaboration of basic rules that had proved their worth in the different states. Thirty of the delegates were at the time of the convention serving in state legislatures. Thus they knew well the weaknesses of some of the existing charters, and were able to avoid certain mistakes. More than three-fourths had been members of the national Congress established by the Articles of Confederation. Their disappointment with this institution played a large part in the Philadelphia deliberations.

If the founders could draw on personal experience, they could also draw on political theory. John Locke's *Two Treatises on Government*, James Harrington's *Commonwealth of Oceana*, both seventeenth-century writings, and Montesquieu's *Spirit of the Laws*, written forty years before the Philadelphia convention, were familiar to all men of education. In these writings were many of the basic ideas which found their way into the Constitution. More than half of the delegates were trained in law, and thus had read some of the great commentaries on English common law, a system that remains today the basis of our own legal system.

The Constitution was not created out of a vacuum. It was a natural extension of ideas at least two centuries old, and an elaboration of practices common in many of the individual states.

It was nevertheless a difficult document to draft. Any constitution must balance freedom and authority—the freedom of citizens from arbitrary or unjust government, yet the authority of government to settle disputes and manage the society. There is no need to debunk the myth of the founding fathers as demigods, but it is important to recognize that the politics in the Convention Hall (and outside it) were as instrumental in the particular balance struck in the Constitution between freedom and authority as were the personal traits of the founders. Three political factors are relevant to understanding the considerable success of the Constitutional Convention: The framers were in agreement on certain basic issues, the convention skipped over the most difficult issue, and the delegates were willing to compromise when feelings ran high.

Agree on Basic Issues: Missing from the convention were two staunch conservatives, John Hancock and John Adams, who might have opposed the more liberal provisions of the Constitution. Also missing were several forceful democrats—Thomas Jefferson, Samuel Adams, and Patrick Henry —who might have refused to cede so much authority to a central government. Patrick Henry, for instance, on hearing of the convention refused to attend and commented, "I smelt a rat." He was subsequently to be a vigorous opponent of adoption.

The men who dominated the proceedings reflected the concerns of the solid, conservative financial interests of the country. Thus they had no difficulty in agreeing that the Articles of Confederation be dropped, and an entirely new document formulated. They shared a philosophy which included a mistrust of human nature, a belief in the sanctity of property, an anxiety about the excesses of democracy, and a self-assurance in their right to fashion a new government. But if they were in these respects conservative, they were also committed, though in varying degrees, to the experiment of self-government.

Through a process of self-selection and self-elimination the framing of the Constitution was left largely to men of influence with a basically similar political philosophy. Others either choose to ignore the proceedings or were not sent as delegates. For this reason, perhaps, the most difficult battles over the Constitution occurred not in Philadelphia but in the various state legislatures over ratification. For instance, the framers completely ignored the question of a Bill of Rights and were able to win ratification over the opposition of liberal critics in several states only when the first ten amendments were promised.

Skip the Hardest Issue: The strongest political feelings of the time centered on the locus of sovereignty. Should there continue to be state sovereignty such as existed under the Articles, or should there be a unitary government in which sovereignty rests with the central power? *Federalism*, in which sovereignty is shared between the states and the central government, was a brilliant compromise, and was probably the major reason that the Constitution was finally adopted. Yet the Constitution simply avoided the hardest

The founders simply passed the question of secession along to a later generation, and it finally took a bitter and destructive civil war to settle it.   *(Engraving: Culver)*

issue of all: whether member states had the right to secede. If the right to secede had been written into the Constitution, it is doubtful that the Union would have lasted more than a few decades. If the right to secede had been expressly prohibited, it is doubtful that there ever would have been a "united states." The founders simply passed this question along to a later generation, and it finally took a bitter and destructive civil war to settle it.

Compromise When There Is Strong Political Opposition: The Constitution was a compromise document on many counts. For instance, there is evidence that among the men gathered in Philadelphia were many who recognized that slavery was basically inconsistent with a government proclaiming the inalienable rights of men. But fearful that southern slave-owning states would never join the Union unless compromise with principle was made, the founders provided certain constitutional protections for the continuation of slavery. The most famous of the constitutional compromises was with respect to representation of the small and large states. At issue was whether states would hold membership in Congress based on their population size or on a "one state, one vote" rule. Small states such as Delaware and Maryland demanded equal voting rights, while large states such as

Pennsylvania and Massachusetts countered that representation should be based on population. The famous "Connecticut Compromise" allowed for equal representation in the Senate and representation proportionate to population in the House of Representatives.

For all the debate and concern over this compromise, there have been no significant political issues in our history that have led to small states aligned against large states. Many things divide different sectors of the nation: matters of economics, political style, personalities, and tradition. But never has there been a divisive issue just because some states have fewer people than other states. The most famous compromise of all was without much consequence.

Other compromises, however, have had more far-reaching consequences. Much in our political history is a working-out of the basic compromise contained in the Constitution between those who wished to extend popular participation in political life and those who feared "excessive" democracy, and wanted checks on popular participation.

Ratification: Despite the remarkable successes of the convention in drafting the Constitution, the hardest test was yet ahead: ratification. The individual states were jealous of their autonomy and would not willingly join a union that transferred many powers to a central government. Within several states were strong forces opposing the new Constitution. Knowing this, the framers—in violation of the Articles of Confederation—had decreed that the ratification by only nine of the thirteen states would be sufficient to establish the new national government. Still, ratification was difficult. Patrick Henry, a leader of the opposition, was to liken the "tyranny of Philadelphia" to the "tyranny of George III," and another opponent, from North Carolina, was to speak of a fortified Federal City from whence would come an army of perhaps 100,000 men who "will sally forth and enslave the people." These were strong words, and passions against the Constitution, especially the secret way in which it was framed and its lack of a Bill of Rights, were correspondingly strong. The debates that took place in Convention Hall in Philadelphia were to be repeated in the state conventions and in public meetings. The Constitution was not to be ratified by the necessary nine states until June 1788, nine months after it had been drafted by the framers. In several cases ratification was exceedingly close, especially in the critical states of Massachusetts (187 to 168), Virginia (89 to 79), and New York (30 to 27).

What Did the New Constitution Accomplish?

A complete review of constitutional principles is not possible in a single chapter. In later chapters, when we deal with federalism, the Supreme Court, Congress, and the Presidency, we will look more closely at aspects of the constitutional arrangements worked out in 1789. But it is important to review the fundamental principles embodied in the Constitution. What are these fundamentals?

A Federal System of Government

Much has been written about the alternative proposals at the Constitutional Convention regarding the struggle between large states and small states. But these differences ought not to obscure the fact that the delegates were in agreement on two principles. The first principle was that there indeed ought to be a central government with effective powers and effective institutions. Nothing else would guarantee social order, permit paying the public debt, provide a stable monetary system, and allow for the development of the economic resources of the country. The second principle was that the independence of the state governments ought also to be preserved. It would be clear that these principles are somewhat in contradiction with one another. The result was the federal system with its built-in tension and its constantly evolving structure.

The crucial decision for an effective central government came with the establishment of a Congress able to pass laws and rule directly over the people of America. In the old Articles of Confederation, the states were supreme. In the new Constitution, the laws of Congress passed under the Constitution and the treaties entered into by the federal government were to be the "supreme law of the land." In addition, there was provision for a federal executive and a federal court system—the latter with the all-important but as yet not fully recognized power to decide disputes about the allocation of powers established under the Constitution.

And the federal government received those specific powers that had been so noticeably lacking under the Articles. It received the power to tax directly, without which power it would have remained the subordinate creature of the states. The federal government also received the power to regulate interstate commerce, whereas the states were severely limited in their ability to control such commerce. It likewise received the power to effectively control foreign affairs. Without question, the Constitution gave us a truly national government.

But it also limited that government. Alongside the powers of the federal government were placed limitations on that power. One such limitation was built into the structure of the government in the requirement that all states, large or small, have equal representation in the Senate. Another restraint on the power of the federal government was contained in the first ten amendments (the promise of which was a crucial condition for ratification of the Constitution), which limited its legislative powers over citizens; moreover, the Tenth Amendment appeared to reserve to the states and the people all powers not delegated to the national government.

There are several bold and new steps reflected here. For one, citizenship was radically altered by the Constitution. No longer was the individual bound only to the state in which he lived. A nation was being created and the citizen owed his loyalty and his taxes to that nation. Failure to comply with national legislation was to risk punishment by the coercive power of the central government.

Another was the fact that the status of member states was radically altered by the Constitution. No longer was it possible to cooperate with other states only when interests and values so dictated. A nation was being created in which the various states entered a network of regulations and obligations that were enforced by a central government. States were now prevented from establishing their own tariff rates or from independently regulating shipping into and out of their harbors.

Not all authority shifted to the national government. Federalism was born of the need to share powers between a central government and its constituent parts. Federalism notwithstanding, the Constitution did nothing less than establish a new union out of previously separate peoples.

Popular, But Limited, Government

The constitution of a society will reflect in some measure the philosophical ideas acceptable to that society. And our Constitution does have a philosophical perspective, one acceptable to many citizens in the 1790s and one acceptable, we suspect, to many citizens today.

To get a glimpse of this perspective, let us listen to what John Adams had to say to his cousin, Samuel Adams:

> Human appetites, passions, prejudices and self-love will never be conquered by benevolence and knowledge alone. . . . 'The love of liberty,' you say, 'is interwoven in the soul of man.' So it is (also) in that of a wolf; and I doubt whether it be much more rational, generous, or social in one than in the other. . . . We must not, then, depend alone upon the love of liberty in the soul of man for its preservation. Some political institutions must be prepared, to assist this love against its enemies.

In other words, Adams was saying that men unencumbered by institutional restraints are not to be trusted. They would break their contracts with one another. Their passions and ambitions would dominate their reason and self-restraint. Minorities, if they controlled the means of coercion, would tyrannize majorities and plunder in order to expand their own privileges. Majorities, if unrestrained, would destroy the rights of minorities, forcing them to conform to majority wishes.

What was behind the writing of the Constitution, and was imbedded in the Constitution, was a pessimistic view of human nature but an optimistic view of social and civil institutions. A good political constitution, backed by the authority of the government, could protect liberties and could guard the social order.

But if there must be authority, it too must be curbed. No single group, be it a minority within government, the government itself, or the majority outside the governing circles, must be allowed final control of the coercive instruments of society. It is a tribute to the founders that they were consistent in applying these principles derived from a pessimistic view of human nature. They feared the unchecked ambitions of leaders just as they feared the excesses of the public. They were as careful to impose constraints on those who exercised authority as they were to guarantee the authority needed to govern the community.

The checks on authority are expressed through three constitutional fundamentals: popular control over elected representatives, a fragmentation and separation of governmental powers, and the idea of limited government.

A Representative Form of Government

Distrustful as the founders were of the excesses of democracy, they were also strongly opposed to arbitrary rule. They were sympathetic to republican government, and in this they were heirs of the seventeenth-century English political idealists who advanced the philosophy of political representation and popular rule. Did not the Declaration of Independence speak of the "consent of the governed"? And did not Madison report that "a dependence on the people is, no doubt, the primary control on the government"?

Titles of Nobility Abolished: One of the first accomplishments of the founders was to abolish hereditary titles of nobility and hereditary positions of power. This trend had started in the state legislatures, but to put it into the Constitution of the national government was to break sharply from practice common in Europe and England. Time and again the founders underscored their belief in the principle that no arbitrary criteria, especially those conferred by accident of birth, should give to some men the right to rule, and deny that right to other men. *The Federalist* (No. 57) asserts:

> Who are to be the objects of popular choice? Every citizen whose merit may recommend him to the esteem and confidence of his country. No qualification of wealth, of birth, of religious faith, or of civil profession is permitted to fetter the judgment or disappoint the inclination of the people.

Open Access to Office: To be sure, the founders did feel that the "right" persons should be chosen to rule. And they did retain a belief in the natural aristocracy of wealth, talent, and education. They themselves were far from a random sample of the total population. But the principle they asserted was that no man had a right to rule *just* because he was born of parents already in positions of rulership. Office was open to the talented and ambitious, whatever their social origins.

Periodic Elections: "Consent of the governed" found its most concrete expression in periodic elections. *The Federalist* explained the House of Representatives as follows:

> *As it is essential to liberty that the government in general should have a common interest with the people, so it is particularly essential that the branch of it under consideration should have an immediate dependence on, and an intimate sympathy with, the people. Frequent elections are unquestionably the only policy by which this dependence and sympathy can be effectually secured.*

The right of suffrage extended only so far, of course. Individual states were allowed to legislate their own voting regulations. Moreover, only members of the House of Representatives were directly elected by the citizenry. Senators, expected to be members of a more "aristocratic house," were indirectly elected, being nominated and chosen by the state legislatures. (Indirect election of senators was changed to popular election in 1913, with final ratification of the Seventeenth Amendment.) The President and Vice-President were even further removed from popular election, chosen by an electoral college, which in turn was appointed by the state legislature. And judicial posts, of course, were filled by appointment.

Though limited, the right of suffrage was firmly planted in the Constitution. And elections were to become a major prop supporting the evolution of representative government.

Limited Tenure in Office: Deriving from the two provisions just noted is the third, perhaps most significant, provision: limited tenure in office. Men served limited terms, at the end of which they returned to face the electorate or other agencies which had granted them power in the first place. The purpose was to create in political leadership a "habitual recollection of their dependence on the people," as *The Federalist* (No. 57) stated. In a manner which recalls that the framers shared with Lord Acton the belief that "power tends to corrupt," this passage continues:

> *Before the sentiments impressed on their minds by the mode of their elevation can be effaced by the exercise of power, they will be compelled to anticipate the moment when their power is to cease, when their exercise of it is to be reviewed, and when they must descend to the level from which they were raised; there forever to remain unless a faithful discharge of their trust shall have established their title to a renewal of it.*

This passage underscores much which is relevant to an understanding of representative government. Being elected to political office is to be "elevated" and being evicted from that office is to be "punished." Officeholders, therefore, exercise power in a manner "faithful" to the trust placed in them by the electorate.

Representative Government: The Constitution established a government that was to rest upon the consent of the governed. In reading back into history present-day conceptions about democracy, we very often misinterpret what happened in 1787, and either see the founders as more radical than they actually were or chastise them for being too cautious. Neither of these views fits the facts.

We today think of representative government as a compromise between the principles of "perfect" democracy, direct popular participation in making the laws that govern the people, and the realities of complex and huge nations. Because there is no way for the people to assemble, deliberate, debate, and decide, we compromise our commitment to these principles and institute representative government in which a select group of men meet and decide on the issues of the day, but are ever conscious of the wishes and the preferences of those who sent them. We can diagram the logic of this position, as shown in Figure 9.1.

What the framers had in mind was something far different. Because they feared arbitrary rule, they believed that men with political power must somehow be checked in their exercise of power. And because they felt some sympathy toward republican government, they envisioned a system of political representation as an appropriate check. Representative government was not a compromise with a deep commitment to democracy; it was a cautious move away from prevailing practices of hereditary rulership. Compare Figure 9.2 with Figure 9.1, and you will see that the initial conception of political representation was very different from how it is often thought of today.

The same point can be stressed from a second perspective. Whereas today we view representational processes as means by which the larger

Figure 9.1 Conception of Representative Government Today

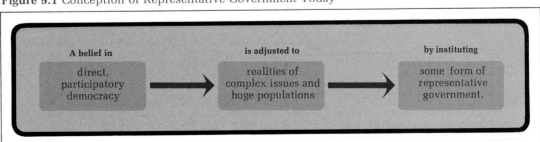

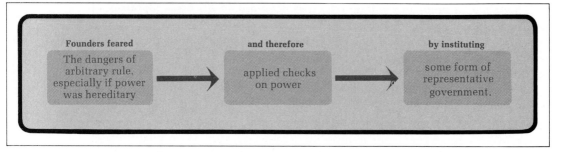

Figure 9.2 The Founding Fathers' Conception of Representative Government

population can express itself on political issues, the founders saw in representational arrangements the possibility of limiting the impact of public voices on specific politics. The representatives would be wiser and more cautious of the social order than were the masses at large. As Madison put it, instituting representative government would "refine and enlarge the public views by passing them through the medium of a chosen body of citizens."

In some respects, popular government has taken many turns never conceived of 200 years ago. But in other respects, the initial constitutional principles—open access to political office, periodic elections, probationary tenure of leaders—have had profoundly conservative consequences, rendering obsolete (whether unnecessary is a separate question) the "permanent revolution" once proposed by Jefferson. Much of what we record in this text can be viewed as describing a continuing struggle between those who would use representational processes to conserve a social or economic order and those who would use these same processes to challenge and to reform that order.

In addition to external checks whereby the citizens could restrain the use of authority, the founders considered internal checks whereby men in positions of authority checked one another.

Separation of Governmental Powers

The framers knew that there could be no nation unless a few had the authority to extract resources from the citizens, to regulate the actions of citizens, to establish binding contracts, and to punish offenders. Still, they were cautious about the implications of giving such powers to any single group of men, especially since it would necessarily be a small group. The memories of the arbitrary exercise of power by a central government, the British Parliament and the crown, were fresh in their minds. And certainly the citizenry was unlikely to tolerate a government that left central authority unchecked.

An elaborate system of divided powers was provided wherein those who administered one program would be given the constitutional means to resist encroachment by others, thus keeping any single interest from swallowing up the whole of governmental authority. In *The Federalist* (No. 51), it is remarked that public controls over government are always found inadequate. The defect must be remedied "by so contriving the interior structure of the government so that its several constituent parts may, by their mutual relations, be the means of keeping each other in their proper place." Here then was the principle of fragmenting authority. And in a passage which more clearly than any other expresses the assumptions behind this principle, *The Federalist* (No. 51) continues:

> *Ambition must be made to counteract ambition. It may be a reflection on human nature, that such devices should be necessary to control the abuses of government. But what is government itself, but the greatest of all reflections on human nature? If men were angels, no government would be necessary. If angels were to govern men, neither external nor internal controls on government would be necessary. In framing a government which is to be administered by men over men, the great difficulty lies in this: you must first enable the government to control the governed; and in the next place oblige it to control itself.*

Harking back to the principle of external control, this passage concludes that "a dependence on the people is, no doubt, the primary control on the government; but experience has taught mankind the necessity of auxiliary precautions."

The Separation of Powers System: These auxiliary precautions were achieved through the celebrated separation of powers system. *The Federalist* (No. 47) proclaims that "the accumulation of all powers, legislative, executive, and judiciary, in the same hands, whether of one, a few, or many, and whether hereditary, self-appointed, or elective, may justly be pronounced the very definition of tyranny." And we hear it as a passionate defense of a government of three separate branches: a branch that makes laws, a branch that executes the laws, and a branch that hears disputes arising out of conflicting interpretations of the laws. To separate the federal government into a legislative, executive, and judicial branch was to accomplish three goals.

First, the powers of government were to be fragmented. In this regard the federal form of government was complimented by separation of powers. The argument is stated clearly in *The Federalist* (No. 51):

> *In the compound Republic of America, the power surrendered by the people is first divided between two distinct governments (Federal government and the States), and then the portion alloted to each subdivided among distinct and separate departments. Hence, a double secur-*

ity rises to the rights of the people. The different governments will control each other, at the same time that each will be controlled by itself.

Second, through a checks and balances system each branch of government could intrude into the activities of the remaining branches. Congress legislates, but the President can veto. Then again the Congress can override the veto. The President appoints judges, though they are confirmed by the Senate. Then again the judges are appointed for life, unless impeachment proceedings initiated in Congress are successful. So it goes throughout the federal government, and every state government as well: a multitude of cross-checking restraints on authority. Table 9.1 shows how often some of these restraints have been used.

Third, the balances established in the Constitution required that various units of government cooperate with one another to reach common objectives. A wider range of interests would thereby be reflected in governmental policy. Moreover, each branch would bring its own institutional perspective. The blending of these differing perspectives should, in theory, result in superior government. The system of separated functions would also require a greater effort at communication among various constituencies. A merger of various strands of thought would be more likely to produce a true "national interest" than would a government under the control of a single branch.

It cannot be said that each of these goals has always been achieved in American political history. The separation of powers system has worked out differently than anticipated by the framers. Yet the basic fragmentation of authority and need for cooperation remain fundamental features of the government. And if one's time span is long enough, the goals of the framers have been remarkably well served.

Table 9.1 The Use of Checks and Balances from 1789 to 1970

Between 1789 and 1970

There were 2255 Presidential vetoes of congressional acts.

Congress subsequently overruled 75 of these vetoes.

The Supreme Court ruled 85 congressional acts or parts of acts unconstitutional.

Congress refused to confirm 27 nominees to the Supreme Court (out of a total of 138 nominees).

Source: First two items: Senate Library, *Presidential Vetoes* (New York: Greenwood Press, 1968). Data for Kennedy, Johnson, and Nixon taken from the *Congressional Quarterly*. Last two items: *Current American Government* (Washington, D.C., *Congressional Quarterly*, Spring 1973), p. 106.

Limited Government

A third basic principle of the Constitution is limited government. Here there are two things to keep in mind.

The Bill of Rights: First, there are certain things that government cannot and should not do. Specifically, it cannot restrict the protections for the individual citizen enumerated in the first ten amendments, the Bill of Rights. The government was explicitly prevented from denying citizens the right to religious practice of their choice, the right to say and write what they pleased, the right to assemble for political purposes, and the right to bear arms. Moreover the government could not take life, liberty, or property without due process of law, which included the right to a speedy, public, and fair trial and to a trial by a jury of peers in certain cases.

The complications and ambiguities of applying such principles in concrete cases will be discussed in Chapter 12. And scattered throughout the book are examples demonstrating that the protections promised by the Bill of Rights have had a checkered political history. At this point, however, we are interested in constitutional *principles* rather than political realities. The principle of limited government holds that the rights of man are derived from a higher law than government (natural law) and should be protected by placing limits on government, as in the Bill of Rights.

A "Government of Laws, Not of Men": The second idea behind the principle of limited government is constitutionalism itself. By this is simply meant the familiar phrase "government of laws, not of men." There is a basic law, against which all lesser laws should be measured. This basic law, the written Constitution in our case, rests on the consent of the governed. Any lesser laws passed in accordance with the Constitution, then, presumably also rest on the consent of the governed. Moreover, the basic law as well as the derivative laws regulate the operation of government, and thus the governors. No one is "a law unto himself" or should "stand above the law."

The Court System: The court system in the United States provides the vital forum for testing and thereby maintaining the constitutional character of the government. A citizen harmed by an act of government can challenge that action in the courts. If the courts accept jurisdiction, the government must show that its action was based on an authorizing law. Policemen cannot simply arrest citizens they dislike; they must first charge the citizen with violating a specified statute, and they must be prepared to specify the legal basis for their arrest. County welfare officials cannot simply issue checks to friends, or withhold payments from those whose hair styles they dislike; in each instance, they must be prepared to show in court that their decision was controlled by whether the applicant for welfare fell, or did not fall, into one of the welfare categories authorized by law. In principle, if not always in practice, courts offer the citizen the means for checking arbitrary governmental power.

But the courts play an even more distinctive role in American politics. Even if a government official can show that his specific act was in conformity with a local, state, or national law, his act can still be reversed if it can be shown in court that the *law itself* was contrary to the Constitution. The American system of government thus allows courts to limit what the popularly elected branches of government may authorize the government to do. Only a constitutional amendment—a cumbersome, time-consuming, politically awkward expedient—can reverse the United States Supreme Court's interpretation of the Constitution as barring some law of Congress or a state legislature.

As with the Bill of Rights, the idea of a "government of laws" has had a checkered history. Secrecy, duplicity, and lawlessness are not unknown in the highest government circles. The law can be, and often is, bent for those with power and money to do the bending. Some examples of this will appear in the chapter on the Supreme Court (Chapter 11), and indeed appear throughout the text. But however misshapen by political pressures, the principle of constitutionalism remains a constant check on arbitrary government.

Summary Thus Far

We have now covered two major topics: how the Constitution came to be written, and the fundamental principles on which it rests. The material provides a partial answer to the question at the beginning of the chapter, What is this Constitution which could so long endure and accommodate itself to a society so drastically transformed as ours has been over the past two centuries? One part of the answer is that the Constitution was and is a political document. And at least some of the political conflicts of the 1780s are still with us today, though in different guises. An example is the conflict between central power and local control. Thus a document sensitive to political realities remains workable insofar as these realities remain important.

Another partial answer derives from the constitutional fundamentals. Popular control over elected representatives, fragmentation and separation of governmental powers, and limited government were sufficiently attractive ideals in 1787 that a constitution built on them could be adopted. We can only surmise that they remain sufficiently attractive, despite substantial changes in society, that the Constitution continues to be supported. Political history reveals only one major challenge to the U.S. Constitution in two hundred years, the attempted secession of the Confederacy. The Civil War settled this constitutional impasse, a war fought to "defend and maintain the supremacy of the Constitution and to preserve the union," in the words of a congressional resolution of July 1861. Excepting the Civil War, no significant political movement has tried to call into question the Constitution.

But these are partial answers. A further explanation rests on the adaptability of the Constitution, and its constant reinterpretation to deal with new political realities and social conditions.

A Flexible Constitution

Four aspects of the Constitution contribute to its flexibility: (1) a formal amendment process through which specific changes are possible; (2) broad grants of authority, which allow considerable growing room for specific political institutions; (3) silences on certain key questions, which have permitted the growth of extraconstitutional political practices; (4) generalities of formulation, which have led to giving old words new meanings or giving old institutions new functions.

The Amendment Process

The formal amendment process has been used infrequently (leaving out the Bill of Rights, only sixteen times), and sometimes it has been used for minor changes in the mechanics of government. Most of the amendments, however, have been significant in adapting government to new social conditions. The famous "Civil War amendments" (Thirteenth, Fourteenth, Fifteenth) outlawed slavery, defined the privileges and immunities of national citizenship and set limits on state interference with equal protection and due process, and gave the right to vote without regard to race, color, or prior servitude. Other amendments have broadened the democratic meaning of the Constitution, providing for direct election of senators, women's suffrage, repeal of the poll tax, and a voting age lowered to 18. One of the most important amendments, the Sixteenth ratified in 1913, authorized the income tax.

Adding amendments is not easy. Proposed by a two-thirds majority of both houses, they must be ratified by three-fourths of the states before they go into effect. Thus, though permitting significant changes, the formal amendment process is less central to the flexibility of the Constitution than our other three factors.

Broad Grants of Authority

The Constitution seems in places to have been deliberately ambiguous. Perhaps ambiguity was the best way the founding fathers had of winning approval of the various factions disputing the document. In any case, this ambiguity has allowed later generations to interpret the Constitution as giving broad grants of authority to key institutions. We will see in Chapter

11 that the power of the Supreme Court to declare acts of Congress unconstitutional is not explicitly stated in the Constitution, nor is it denied. But
the Supreme Court ruled that it did have the power of judicial review, a
decision that greatly enlarges its political significance. The executive power
of the President is not clearly spelled out in the Constitution either. The
change from George Washington's staff of a half-dozen clerks to the huge
federal bureaucracy of the 1970s has been justified by the simple constitutional phrase, the President "shall take care that the laws be faithfully executed."

Constitutional Silences

One of the best examples of a constitutional silence permitting political
flexibility was noted earlier in our discussion of political parties. The political party system is entirely extraconstitutional, yet who could imagine
twentieth-century politics in the United States without some form of political parties? We have seen that every major elected official, and most appointed ones, take office under the banner of a political party. And political
parties largely organize and manage the elections, including primaries and
nominating conventions. All of this takes place outside the framework of
the Constitution, and indeed largely outside of any type of federal law at
all.

Thus it is that political institutions and the formal government adapt
themselves to the requirements of twentieth-century politics, and do so
very often because the Constitution has nothing to say on the matter.

Constitutional Generalities

Each of the three factors just reviewed contributes to constitutional flexibility, but none so much as the fourth factor, constitutional generalities.
These are the principles which were "to be accommodated to times and
events." No document could foresee future developments in detail, but it
could state general constitutional policy on the kinds of political choices
likely to face a nation.

New Meanings Given to Old Words: Thus the Constitution allows new
meanings to be put into old words. Consider the example of "unreasonable
searches." The framers disliked the manner in which the colonial officers
searched private homes at will, and so in the Fourth Amendment they
declared that "The right of the people to be secure in their persons, houses,
papers, and effects, against unreasonable searches and seizures, shall not be
violated. . . ." This language expresses a clear principle in sufficiently
general language that it can still be applied today, despite an entirely different technology of search and seizure. Today the right of government

agents to use electronic surveillance techniques—telescopic cameras, wiretaps, and hidden microphones—is challenged according to the principle and with the language of the Fourth Amendment as adopted in 1791. A new technology, yes, but an old argument which places individual rights above the government's right to know.

New Functions Replacing Old Functions—the Electoral College: As new meanings are put into old words, so also are new functions assigned to old institutions. One excellent example is the electoral college, which functions today in a manner never envisioned in 1787. The electoral college, as set down in the Constitution, was a method of choosing a President and Vice-President by a small group of respected citizens. Alexander Hamilton, in *The Federalist* (No. 68), states the case: The choice of a President "should be made by men most capable of analyzing the qualities adapted to the station. . . . A small number of persons, selected by their fellow citizens from the general mass, will be most likely to possess the information and discernment requisite to such complicated investigations." This small number of persons, the electoral college, was to be chosen by the state

Figure 9.3 Electoral Votes for Each State

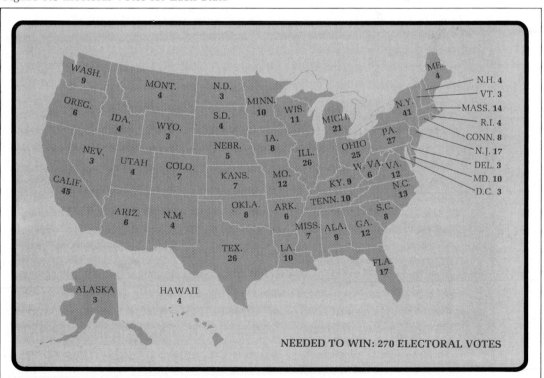

NEEDED TO WIN: 270 ELECTORAL VOTES

legislatures. Thus the election of a President was to be twice removed from popular vote: Voters elect state legislators, state legislators choose delegates to the electoral college, the electoral college selects a President and Vice-President. The provisions for an electoral college were slightly modified in 1804, through the Twelfth Amendment, but in essence remain as written into the original Constitution.

This ancient institution continues today to play a major role in Presidential selection, but it does so by performing a function not at all anticipated by the framers. It has been transformed into an institution of popular, democratic control. Each state has a number of electoral votes equivalent to the size of its congressional delegation. Figure 9.3 shows that at the present time electoral votes vary from 45 (California) to 3 (6 small states plus the District of Columbia have only 3 votes each). Electoral votes are bound by the unit-rule; that is, all of the electoral votes of a state go to the Presidential candidate who wins a plurality of the votes in that state. This unit rule enhances the political importance of the largest states, which is to say the urban, industrial states. For instance, the candidate who can win the two largest states (California and New York) has more than a third of the total electoral votes needed to win the Presidency (96 out of 270). Table 9.2 shows that 11 states can elect a President.

Winning the Presidency by winning electoral votes has had a substantial impact on twentieth-century politics. Because large states can be so much more important than small states (the electoral vote of California is worth the combined electoral vote of 13 small states), the large states tend to dominate the nomination process. This bias carries over into the campaign, as

Table 9.2   A Minimal Winning Coalition Needed to Secure 270 Electoral Votes and Thus Win the Presidency

California	45
New York	41
Pennsylvania	27
Illinois	26
Texas	26
Ohio	25
Michigan	21
Florida	17
New Jersey	17
Massachusetts	14
Wisconsin	11
	270

both political parties concentrate their energies on winning in the large pivotal states. One consequence of this has been to create a Presidential constituency which "overrepresents" urban, industrial interests. This in turn affects the relationship between the executive branch and the legislative branch of government, for the sum of all the congressional constituencies tends to "overrepresent" small-town and rural interests.

The electoral college, then, is an institution that has long ceased to perform as intended by the constitutional framers, but which now functions in support of different political goals altogether. The capacity of American politics to absorb and redefine the institutions and principles of the Constitution contributes further to the flexibility of the document, and to its staying power, despite the radical differences between our society today and that of the Eastern seaboard in the 1780s.

The Dynamics of Constitutional Change

To say that the Constitution is flexible is another way of saying that it does not provide ready-made answers for new political questions and social issues. We have now identified aspects of the Constitution that provide it with flexibility, but we have not yet accounted for specific instances of substantial constitutional change.

No general formula can account for each major change and reshaping of the Constitution, but it would help to hold in mind the following: The genius of the Constitution is also its vulnerability. A document that gives powers to different political institutions is sooner or later going to be caught in a squeeze when the interests of those institutions are in sharp conflict. Institutional clashes leading to constitutional crises have been of three general sorts: (1) clashes between the federal government and state governments, (2) clashes over the scope of authority of a particular branch of government, and (3) clashes over the separation of powers doctrine. Any such clash will occur in the context of immediate and volatile political issues. Let us briefly consider each type of institutional clash.

Federalism: In the next chapter we will learn how easy it is for clashes to occur over which level of government is responsible and authorized to do just what. The genius of the Constitution in splitting government powers between the national government and the independent states is also the vulnerability of the Constitution when conflict is sharp between different levels. The Civil War was fought to establish the supremacy of the national government, a supremacy ratified by the adoption of the Thirteenth, Fourteenth, and Fifteenth Amendments to the Constitution. The Civil War did not end jurisdictional disputes, and, as the next chapter will show, political issues continue to spill over various boundaries, thus testing the constitutional principle of federalism.

Scope of Authority: Many of the new social conditions with which government has had to deal over the past two centuries have been handled within the guidelines set by the original Constitution. But some conditions have presented such novel and complicated problems that traditional definitions of government authority have been found wanting. The interpretation of the Constitution has shifted in accordance with the emergence of these problems. As we shall see in Chapter 11, sometimes the courts have resisted the process of constitutional adaptation. Such was the case when the great economic depression of the 1930s seemed to require broad new grants of government authority and government programs. But the Supreme Court declared important new legislation unconstitutional, claiming that the Presidency was enlarging its scope of authority in an illegal matter. Intense political pressure from the Roosevelt administration led the Court to reverse itself. In other times it was the Court itself that stimulated constitutional adaptation. Thus the definition of citizenship rights and liberties was substantially enlarged by a series of decisions taken by the Warren Court (so called because the Chief Justice was Earl Warren) in the 1950s and 1960s.

Separation of Powers: We have noted that the constitutional framers feared a government in which all powers were concentrated in only one institution, and that they therefore devised a government in which different branches would have the means and the incentive to keep another branch in its proper place. The constitutional situation has led to innumerable disputes and conflicts between the Presidency and Congress, between Congress and the courts, or between the courts and the Presidency. For the most part these disputes have been resolved short of major constitutional revision, but we presently are in the midst of a separation of powers conflict that has broad constitutional implications.

The Watergate case reveals how the Constitution permits a branch of government to increase its role and its powers, while simultaneously showing the limits to such expansion imposed by the separation of powers system. In this instance it is the executive branch, especially the Presidency itself, which had steadily expanded its powers; and the Congress, the independent judiciary, and the press (sometimes, appropriately, called "the fourth branch of government"), which checked that expansion. Watergate illustrates dramatically how the constitutional system of checks and balances, competing power bases, conflicting political interests and ambitions, and a government of law can be triggered into action.

The fundamental premise of the Constitution—that ours is a government of laws and not a government *above* law—was initially upheld by the arrest, trial, and conviction of the burglars who broke into the Democratic Party National Headquarters at the Watergate Hotel. The principle of an independent judiciary, in the person of Judge John Sirica, who presided at the initial Watergate trial, was responsible for blocking an attempt by White

House staff persons to impede justice. Indeed, eventually there were no fewer than five grand juries convened around the country in an effort to unravel the complexities of the Watergate issue.

There could not have been full public disclosure of the Watergate scandal had it not been for the relentless digging of a few journalists from the *Washington Post* and *The New York Times*—a relentlessness protected by the First Amendment's guarantee of a free press. It is important to reflect that in only a handful of countries could the newspapers have played so full and aggressive a role. Even in democratic nations such as Britain, the press would have been legally inhibited from publically exposing the details of Watergate. But so strongly did the constitutional framers believe that openness is essential to the workings of a free government, that Jefferson once remarked that if faced with the choice between a government without newspapers and newspapers without a government, he would choose the latter.

Congress, too, moved in the face of Watergate to defend its constitutional position by launching major investigations in both the Senate and the House. The Senate as a body abandoned party lines and voted unanimously to create the Senate Select Committee on Presidential Campaign Activities for the purpose of investigating Watergate and the 1972 election as these matters related to the campaign practice laws as set down by Congress. Similarly, the House Armed Services Subcommittee on Intelligence Operations undertook an investigation as to whether the involvement of the CIA in Watergate had violated the authority of that agency as mandated by Congress. Such investigations served not only to fulfill the duty to recommend new legislation where revealed as necessary, but also to discharge the congressional role as "watchdog" over governmental operations.

And, not surprisingly, the executive branch acted to protect its perceived constitutional interests in the midst of the Watergate disclosures. Invoking the grounds of executive privilege, President Nixon refused to make available to the Congress or the courts certain requested documents and tapes pertinent to Watergate, claiming that if he were to relinquish such records he would violate his constitutional obligation to uphold the separation of powers.

It remains uncertain even today how important Watergate and its aftermath will prove in effecting any constitutional realignment between the branches of government. As shall be discussed in Chapter 14, there are some signs that one effect of Watergate may be to rejuvenate Congress in particular into becoming a more vigorous branch of government both in its own right and as a more active check upon the executive branch. If we can take some comfort and even pride in the resiliency of the Constitution as demonstrated in the Watergate crisis, we must at the same time take heed that—as Watergate demonstrates for better and for worse—the integrity of the Constitution is inseparable from that of those who endorse it.

Controversy

The American Constitution specified and (supposedly) limited the powers of the government as against the people. Authority was to be checked at every point, lest it become arbitrary and in this no different from the actions of a feudal lord or willful king. What has happened to the constitutional doctrine of limited government? Does not the enormous power today exercised by the U.S. government mock this doctrine?

One Side

For all practical purposes the doctrine of limited government is inoperable. There is really nothing that a popularly elected government cannot do. Our own history demonstrates this. Religious practices that offend the moral sensibilities of the majority have been prohibited, as in the case of the Mormon practice of multiple wives. Free speech has been curtailed in the interests of national security. It is easier to assemble politically if you wish to defend the prevailing political orthodoxy than if you wish to oppose it, as members of the Communist party or the Ku Klux Klan well know. A constitutional prohibition against cruel and excessive punishment did not outlaw the death penalty under all circumstances. Urban renewal programs had no difficulty condemning, then acquiring, the property of central city residents, usually poor and Black residents.

What does it mean to say that we have "limited government" if parents are told where to school their children; teenaged boys are told what wars to fight in; banks are told what interest rates to charge; farmers are told what crops to grow; home-builders are told what wiring to use; wage earners are told what programs they must support through their taxes? Take the example of cigarette advertising. Because some doctors (themselves in the employ of the government) find smoking to be harmful, legislation prohibits cigarette manufacturers from advertising on television. No doubt smoking is harmful. But are there no limits to what government can regulate? Why should private citizens not "harm" themselves if they freely choose to do so? Should TV ads for rich foods be outlawed because some citizens are tempted to gluttony?

There is a huge and growing body of law regulating individuals and institutions. Sum it all up and it hardly amounts to "limited government." The Constitution delegates broad grants of authority, and government agencies are delighted to interpret these grants in a manner that expands their functions and powers. They do not thereby act "unconstitutionally"; quite the opposite, by acting legally they can in effect act as they wish. We may have a government of law, but that principle itself tells us nothing about the content or the amount of law.

The Other Side

Limited government, it should be kept in mind, means two things: First, there are limits to what government can do; and second, there are limits to *how* it can do those things allowed. Consider the first meaning. To be sure, the powers of government have expanded enormously since 1787. But they stop short in many important areas. Only by being blatantly unconstitutional could the executive branch disband Congress, could a state religion be established, could private newspapers be banned, or could a national election be called off. Yet these are exactly the actions we have come to expect in nations where the doctrine of limited government is not adhered to.

The second meaning of limited government retains its significance as well. It is true that government now regulates what were once matters of individual conscience and private choice. And it is true that even such constitutional freedoms as free speech, religious practice, and assembly have been only partially protected. But *how* these regulations and curtailments have come about is important. Government has not acted in an arbitrary manner; that is, it has acted through popularly elected legislatures and executives. Maybe government actions sometimes reflect "manipulated consensus" rather than "true popular preferences," however one wishes to define these two notions. Even so, branches of government chosen by constitutional means are doing the acting.

Suggested Readings

The Federalist, originally written as newspaper essays urging the adoption of the new Constitution, under the authorship of Alexander Hamilton, James Madison, and John Jay, remains the most lucid interpretation of various constitutional principles. See also Max Farrand, *The Framing of the Constitution* (New Haven, Conn.: Yale University Press, 1926). Charles A. Beard, in his famous *Economic Interpretation of the Constitution of the United States* (New York: Macmillan, 1913), attempts to show that economic interests of influential delegates to the Constitutional Convention explain many of the Constitution's provisions. For refutations of Beard's thesis, see Forest McDonald, *We the People: The Economic Origins of the Constitution* (Chicago: University of Chicago Press, 1958); and Robert E. Brown, *Charles Beard and the Constitution* (Princeton, N. J.: Princeton University Press, 1956).

Two useful works on American political ideas are Louis Hartz, *The Liberal Tradition in America* (New York: Harcourt Brace Jovanovich, 1955); and Richard Hofstadter, *The American Political Tradition* (New York: Knopf, 1951). Robert A. Dahl, *A Preface to Democratic Theory* (Chicago: University of Chicago Press, 1956), deals in a more formalistic way with certain key ideas in democratic thought including the Madisonian formulations which so substantially influenced the Constitution.

A readable and informative account of the Constitutional Convention and of the battles over ratification is Catherine Drinker Bowen, *Miracle at Philadelphia* (New York: Bantam, 1968). This book would make excellent light reading as background to our discussion.

White House, State House, and City Hall: Federalism in America

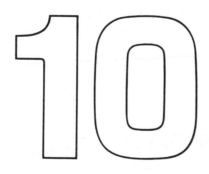

10

I f one wants to understand the full complexity of government in America it is important to keep one fact in mind: One cannot talk of American government, one must talk of American governments.

Number and Levels of Government

A major fact of political life is that there are many governments in America. The federal government in Washington is, of course, the biggest and the most powerful. But it is just one of a vast array of governments; there are also state governments, and a bewildering complexity, variety, and multitude of local governments.

State Governments

When we think of multiple governments, the first kind that comes to mind are the fifty state governments. The basic form of the American government is federal as set down and guaranteed in the Constitution. This means that there is a central government (in Washington) as well as separate governments for each of the states. And, even more important, neither level of government is completely subordinate to the other. Each is in some real way independent of the other. The federal government cannot abolish the states; the states cannot abolish the federal government. Each level can raise and spend money; each has power over certain aspects of our lives.

Two separate sets of governments ruling over the same territory and over the same citizens? Can such an arrangement be possible without constant clashes over who has jurisdiction over what? The designers of this system of government at the Constitutional Convention of 1787 thought that it was possible by differentiating the spheres in which the governments would be active: some powers to the state governments, some to the federal government. And indeed it has been possible; the states and the nation have lived side by side (or perhaps, better, the one inside the other). And they have generally been at peace with each other (at least since the Civil War settled some fundamental questions about their relationship). But the pattern of their relationship has never involved a simple division of labor with the states dealing with some problems, the federal government with others. Rather, the history of the relationship of the states and the nation is one of constant change, evolution, and complex interaction; more often a relationship involving shared and overlapping powers than separate and distinct ones.

Local Governments

The pattern of government in America would be relatively simple if one were dealing only with the national government and the states. Fifty-one governments is, after all, not that many. But there are many, many more governments in America—county governments, cities, towns, townships, as well as special districts for all sorts of purposes from education to sewage disposal to recreation to mosquito abatement. Indeed, as one can see from Table 10.1, there are over 80,000 governmental units in America today: almost 20,000 municipalities, almost 20,000 townships, and over 20,000 each of special districts and school districts.

Are these 80,000 units really governments? Some would say no. Only the federal government and the states are guaranteed existence and autonomy by the American Constitution. This means that in certain respects their authority is ultimate, deriving from no higher level of government. The Constitution, on the other hand, does not guarantee the existence of cities or counties—and certainly not mosquito abatement districts. Rather, these smaller local governments are the creatures of the states—set up by state governments and, at least as far as the United States Constitution is concerned, subordinate to the states.

Yet in fact, these 80,000 units have many of the features of governments. Some of them have guaranteed existence in state constitutions, though not in the federal Constitution. Many cities have powers clearly assigned to them by home rule laws. But above all, these political units are governments in that they have the power to raise revenue and to spend it. Sometimes (like city and county governments) they raise funds and spend them

Table 10.1 Number and Types of Local Governments, 1967

Counties	3,049
Municipalities	18,948
Townships	17,105
Special districts	21,264
School districts	21,482
All local governments	81,248

Source: Washington, D.C.: U.S. Bureau of the Census, *Census of Governments*, 1967, vol. 1, *Governmental Organization*, 1968, Table 1.

on a wide range of subjects; sometimes (like the special districts) they deal with quite specific and narrowly defined problems. But even in the latter case, these problems are seldom trivial, and these districts act as real governments.

Most important, we can consider these units as real governments because that is political reality: Cities, counties, and school districts are parts of American political life. The states neither could nor would want to abolish them. Nor are these local governments clearly lined up in a hierarchy with local governments dealing with the states and the states with the federal government. Local governments at times deal directly with the federal government, they deal with one another, and they deal with the states. And to complicate even further the crazy-quilt pattern of American governments, there are also numerous intergovernmental agencies—crisscrossing and combining various political units. The Port of New York Authority crisscrosses two states and seven counties in an attempt to organize some of the complex problems of transportation and commerce in the vast New York metropolitan area. As any observer of that powerful group can tell you, it is also a quite independent governmental unit. Problems of pollution or the control of water resources have led to many other such intergovernmental agencies in various parts of the nation.

That many local governments are single-purpose governments (set up to control pollution, get rid of mosquitoes, build sewers) does not make them any less real governments. Education is, in terms of spending, the largest domestic governmental activity. Over four-fifths of American public schools are under the jurisdiction of independent school districts—districts that are independent of other local governments even when they cover the same territory. These districts are run by independent school boards, often elected by the local residents or sometimes appointed by the local town council. These districts can levy taxes and float bonds to build schools, maintain schools, pay teachers salaries. They have much to say over curriculum, over special programs. It is true that they all must operate within guidelines set by the states (and federal guidelines if they have federal funds), and these may be more or less restrictive. But they usually have much discretion. On most any criterion, these school districts qualify as real governments.

Thus rather than there being two levels of government in America—the federal government and the states—there is a multiplicity of levels covering the same territory and overlapping one another. One estimate is that there are about 1500 governmental units in the New York metropolitan area. Or consider the number of units having jurisdiction in the Chicago suburb of Park Forest: "Cook County, Will County, Cook County Forest Preserve District, Village of Park Forest, Rich Township, Bloom Township, Monee Township, Suburban Tuberculosis Sanitarium District, Bloom Township Sanitary District, Non-High School District 216, Non-High School District

213, Rich Township High School District 227, Elementary School District 163, South Cook County Mosquito Abatement District.''[1]

These governments vary in size from small districts with budgets of a few thousand dollars affecting some small part of the lives of a few hundred citizens to governments like those of the cities of New York or Chicago—with budgets larger than those of all but a few of the members of the United Nations.

Why has this vast complexity evolved? Why so many governments? Why such a variety of types? And how can they possibly get along with one another?

To answer these questions, we shall have to do two things: First, we shall consider rather generally why it is that one might want a large government (like the federal government or the government of California) rather than a small government (like that of South Royalton, Vermont) and why one might want the opposite. And in the light of these general questions we shall consider how the particular pattern of American governments evolved. Having dealt with those two questions, we can then see how it is that these governments get along (and why it is they sometimes don't) as well as the consequences of having so many governments.

Centralization vs. Decentralization

We can understand this issue if we start with the example of a major governmental activity: education. It used to be said that the Minister of Education in France could look at his watch and say with confidence: "At this moment, every sixth-grade child in France is doing the following problem in math. . . ." And he could tell you the exact problem on which they were working. The story is a bit of an exaggeration, at least in its details, but it illustrates an important point about French education. It is a highly centralized educational system in which schedules, curriculum, standards and the like are all established by the Ministry of Education in Paris and then carried out in the local schools.

Compare this with the educational system in America. Suppose someone wanted to find out what pupils were doing in the sixth grade in the United States. He could go to the Office of Education in the Department of Health, Education, and Welfare in Washington. But he would get little enlightenment there. Matters of school schedule, curriculum, standards, and so forth are not decided in Washington. The American tradition in education is local control. Such matters generally are in the hands of the states or,

[1] Edward C. Banfield and Morton Grodzins, *Government and Housing in Metropolitan Areas* (New York: McGraw-Hill, 1958), p. 18; quoted in Advisory Commission on Inter-Governmental Relations, *Metropolitan America: Challenge to Federalism* (Washington, D.C., 1966).

The American tradition in education is local control.   (Photo: Irene Bayer, Monkmeyer)

indeed, in the hands of the school boards of counties, or cities, or towns, or school districts. If someone wanted to know about sixth-grade curriculum, he might have to visit each of the more than 20,000 separate school jurisdictions.

The Argument for Decentralization

The defender of the American way can make a strong argument for this diversity. After all, pupils differ in different parts of the country. They have different interests, needs, backgrounds. If some central government administrator were to try to establish a uniform curriculum for the ghetto school in Harlem, the suburban school in Grosse Pointe, Michigan, and the rural school in Towner County, North Dakota, he would create a curriculum that fits no place well. Only the local citizens and their local school authorities understand the educational needs of their own district and can create school programs to fit those needs. And this argument would be made not only by the farmers of North Dakota jealous of their freedom from domination by the big cities or by the affluent suburbanites of Grosse Pointe proud of their well-appointed schools, but also by many of the residents of Harlem eager to have a curriculum focusing on their own particular needs and their own particular heritage.

Furthermore, the defender of this system would argue that local control allows the community to decide how much it wishes to put into the school system; if the citizens in one community want to and can afford to have a luxurious school system, ought they not to be allowed to have such? Is that not better than a uniform standard applied across the country? Finally, the defender of the system would point to the huge and complex bureaucracy that would be needed to run a nationwide school system—a vast apparatus that would place the schools far beyond the control of the parents of the children who attend. The supporter of localism could cite several studies of the American public showing that the average citizen feels he understands local politics better than national, and feels he can have more influence on the local level. And, everything else being equal, citizens are more likely to be politically active where the political unit is small and relatively independent. In short, citizen control may be greater the more local the government.

The Argument for Centralization

But, the defender of the French centralized system might come back with the argument that a system of local control is chaotic and wasteful. For one thing there are no national standards to define an adequate education. And communities vary widely in their capabilities to provide such an education. The result, he might point out, is that some pupils get a much better education than do others who happen to be born in the wrong locality. Alabama, he might mention, citing well-known figures, spends about one-third as much on the education of a pupil as does New York. And these state-by-state variations mask greater variations within states. (See Figure 10.1.) Furthermore, local districts do not have the skills and specialists needed for a modern educational system; these could be provided by a centralized school system. Furthermore, he would say that our system is totally uncoordinated. A degree from a French lycée (high school) means something specific—you know what the student has studied and what he is capable of doing. In the United States, a high school diploma has no standard meaning. In some cases it means a student is prepared for the university, in some cases not. How can you run a complex society with such chaos? And he might point out that many of the most pressing urban problems derive from the disparity in school quality. If suburban schools were no different from those in the inner city, we would not be faced with as severe a crisis in many of our metropolitan areas—a crisis caused by the

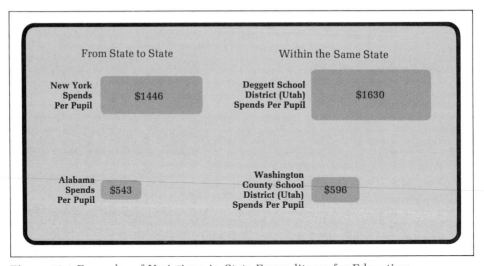

Figure 10.1 Examples of Variations in State Expenditures for Education

SOURCE: Based on data from *United States Statistical Abstract, 1972,* and *State Review of Government in Utah, 1972.*

fact that affluent citizens often move to the suburbs for the better schools, leaving the cities as the home of only the poor.

Finally, the defender of centralization might warn his opponents that they may be mistakenly identifying *decentralization* with *democracy.* That decisions are made within a local community does create a potential for greater control over such decisions by the average citizen, but this is only a potential. Local government may be democratic, with many opportunities for citizen participation and citizen control over the government. But it may also be just the opposite, run by a political "boss" or by a small group of wealthy local citizens. In such a case, more autonomy to the local community may imply less, not more, citizen control over governmental decisions.

Who Is Right?

It is hard to say who is right. Some may feel the weight of evidence lies on the side of local control; some may feel that the centralized system has more to recommend it. Few would argue that there is not something to be said for each side. And one can imagine a similar debate about central versus decentralized control over many other matters. On some matters — libraries or recreational facilities, say — the weight of the argument would favor decentralization. On others — transportation facilities that necessarily cross borders — more central control would seem desirable. But in all fields there are good arguments on both sides.

The Dilemma of
Centralization vs. Decentralization

The point is that there is a real dilemma when it comes to the issue of centralization versus decentralization—or to put the issue more concretely, when one argues over federal power versus states' rights, or over big government versus local government. Almost any solution stressing decentralization and local control can immediately be criticized: Coordination is lacking. Almost any solution emphasizing centralization and federal control can immediately be criticized: There is inadequate attention to local needs and desires. One can see this by exercising a little imagination. Many of us have had the daydream that we could ease many of the world's problems if we could just redesign the government. But suppose we could, and could create a government as big or as small as we wanted. It is clear that any proposal for a government bigger than, say, the small town or the neighborhood can be criticized as too big; there is inadequate chance for effective citizen participation. But it is also clear that any government smaller than that for the whole world could be criticized as too small; for is not the world one large interdependent system? And, it follows logically that any government of intermediate size, say the size of an American city, or an American state, or the size of the United States, could be criticized from both perspectives at once; it is both too big and too small.

Indeed, the dilemma is such that one can almost predict that a centralized system will come under pressure to decentralize and vice versa. In the United States, with its decentralized school system, there is pressure from many sources for more centralization and coordination. In France, with its centralized system, there is pressure for more local control.

The two principles generate an almost automatic tension. And that tension characterizes much of American political history and much of contemporary American politics. Indeed, the crazy-quilt pattern of American governments—the big governments in the state houses and large cities, the bigger government in Washington, the little governments overlapping and crisscrossing these, the intergovernmental agencies—can be viewed as one response to the dilemma of centralization versus decentralization. If neither solution is right, try both at the same time. In this sense one might find a logic in the multiplicity of governments in America: some small ones (like school districts) to deal with local problems, some big ones (like the federal government or the state governments) to coordinate things and deal with those problems that require larger government.

The Multiplicity of Governments:
A Result of the Constellation of Interests

The mixed pattern in America does not imply that the specific mixture always works. The pattern of central government mixed into local government that has evolved in the United States is not the result of a careful consideration of what powers and what functions ought to go to what levels. It is rather the result of a long historical process, a process dominated less by abstract considerations of what form of government best fits what problem than by the *constellation of interests* at the time.

This last point is important. The issue of centralization versus decentralization can be argued on the basis of general principles: the interdependence of society and the need for coordination on the one hand; the differences among areas and the desirability of local control on the other. But in any particular circumstance quite specific interests may lead one group to favor federal and another to favor local control, no matter what their general philosophy is about big and little government. If variations among the states in the regulation of commerce impede business activity, businessmen so affected may argue for uniform federal standards. If, on other matters, they believe they can more effectively influence state regulatory agencies than federal ones, they will argue for states' rights. Black leaders may want more centralization (federal involvement in local affairs) if they want to challenge the power of White-dominated governments or White-dominated school boards where they are a minority. In neighborhoods where they are a majority, they may call for local control.

And the history of federalism in America, and more generally of local government versus central government, is in large part the history of a clash of real interests. Since interests have pressed in both directions, toward centralization and decentralization, the final result has been the American hybrid. To see how this has worked out more concretely it is necessary to return to the constitutional arrangements worked out in 1787.

The Constitutional Evolution

We saw in the previous chapter how the authors of the Constitution attempted to change the balance of powers between the states and the federal government from the state-dominated system that had existed under the Articles of Confederation. They created a federal executive, gave Congress the power to pass laws that affected the lives of citizens directly, including the power to tax and to regulate interstate commerce, and they set up a federal court system able to adjudicate disputes between the states and the federal government. Thus the framers of the Constitution created a truly national government. Yet at the same time the framers balanced the scale by limiting that central government with such devices as the equal representation for all states in the Senate. In addition, the first ten amendments limited the powers of the federal government.

The balance seemed well struck, and few found fault with it at the time. In fact, the issue of the division of powers between the central government and the states was still to be worked out; worked out in numerous court decisions, worked out by the drift of governmental powers in one direction or another, worked out in the pressures of a changing America, and—on several crucial matters—worked out on the bloody battlefields of the Civil War.

But the framers of the Constitution could not be expected to anticipate these future changes; and even if they had foreseen future problems there is probably little they could have done about them at the time. The Constitution was a powerful document and has endured in part because things were not finally worked out. The ambiguities, the tensions built into the constitutional compromise between nation and states provided a framework within which future generations could work out the specifics of government and, in particular, the relative role of central versus decentralized government.

Why Did the Delegates to the Constitutional Convention Give Up the Power Held by Their States?

It will help us to understand the nature of the Union that was created and to understand its later evolution if we ask one question: Why were the delegates of the various states willing to give up the power that was held by their states to a central government? The reader ought to be aware of the importance of this question. Giving up power is a dangerous business—it may be hard to get it back; it may be used to damage your interests. For generations people have talked of a world federation, of a federation of Europe, of a federation of African states—new centralized governments that would replace the individual nation-states. Yet, except for such unions as are created by the force of arms (in which case the various parts do not *give up* their independence, but have it *taken away* from them) there are few examples of such successful voluntary federations.

Why were the states willing to give up their power in 1787? There are several answers:

Gains Were To Be Obtained from Union: The first answer has already been suggested above. There was something concrete to be gained from it. There had been commercial and administrative chaos under the Articles; trade among the states was inhibited; trade with other nations was difficult to regularize without a central treaty-making power; the rich new territories on which the states bordered could not be exploited without some central authority. The delegates to the Convention were men of affairs, and their affairs were not running very well. A central government would improve things.

The Union Was Based on a Relatively Homogeneous Society: As important as the issue of what gains were to be obtained from union was the issue of what losses might be suffered. A general principle is operative here, one that was explained when we considered problems of conflict and competition among groups in America: No group is likely to give up power to another group—to the opposition party, to a central government—if it feels that *its* vital interests will suffer. A *vital* interest is hard to define, because it boils down to what people think of as their vital interests. One thing that has impeded the union of nations throughout history is that they have different basic cultures—they speak different languages, follow different religions, lead different ways of life. One independent political unit is unlikely to give up its independence to a larger unit if it feels that the latter will not respect these vital aspects of its way of life. If an independent unit has such vital interests, it will join a larger union only if it can be guaranteed that its interests will be protected—usually by limitations on the power of the new central government to legislate on such matters. And, of course, the more extensive are such interests, the more limited will be the central government and the less meaningful the union.

The answer to why the states were willing to join a new central regime thus becomes obvious. There are few such vital interests that they felt they had to protect. They had a common language, they had a relatively common culture, they were not sharply divided on religion. In short, the Union was founded on the basis of a relatively homogeneous society.

The States' Vital Interests Were Protected: But there is a third reason why they were willing to join the new federation, a reason that serves as a qualification of the point just made. Where there was potential conflict over interests perceived by the states to be vital, they hedged the Constitution with protection for those interests.

For one thing, the Constitution did not destroy the states. Quite the contrary. Although the framers knew that power was being transferred from the state level to the national level, they also saw the Constitution as preserving the independence of the states in many important matters. The states had, after all, preexisted the Union, and the framers were not about to destroy them.

Small states, also, had some fears about their vital interests which they felt would be damaged in a union that could be dominated by a few of the larger, more powerful states. Thus they pushed to protect those interests through the provision for a Senate in which each state, no matter what its size, would have equal representation. The Convention spent a lot of time worrying about the large versus small state issue, though this has never evolved into a major conflict in America. But the next set of vital interests did and still does.

The South's Interests Were Protected: The most basic divergence of interest was between the economy and social system of the North and those of the South. The North had an expanding economy based on manufacturing. The South had an economy solidly based on the cultivation and export of cotton, and organized around the system of plantation slavery. The South (and by that one means the southern delegates representing the White population, for of course the slaves had no means of expressing their interests) had in this case a vital interest, and an interest that they feared might be damaged by a government dominated by northern states.

To protect these interests, certain clauses were entered into the Constitution. One such clause forbade the national government from levying taxes on exports, since the South depended on finding markets (often foreign) for its cotton. Another clause increased the representation of southern states in the House of Representatives by counting slaves when it came to apportioning seats in that House (though it counted them at only three-fifths of their actual number, while many southern delegates would obviously have preferred a full counting). And the Constitution forbade Congress from interfering with the slave trade until 1808. This latter point is a good illustration of what a group does or does not consider a vital interest. The southern delegates would not have compromised on the existence of slavery itself; this they considered vital. (In fact, there is little evidence that northern delegates were anxious to raise this question anyway.) But the compromise on the slave trade that allowed a future limitation on such trade was less vital, as the southern states were relatively able to breed enough slaves.

The issue of North versus South and the closely connected issue of slavery make it quite clear that the Constitution only temporarily settled matters as to the relations of the states and the nation. What the Constitution meant was not settled until the Civil War, and then only partially. Indeed, what the Constitution means and how the powers of the national and state governments are to be drawn—on racial matters and on other matters as well—remains open.

State and Nation: The Evolution

As with so many other issues in American political life, the Constitution did not settle the issue of federalism. Rather it provided a framework within which future changes would be worked out. The basic framework was the federal principle—a unified central government and a series of partially independent states. The Constitution established both contradictory principles—centralization and decentralization—without explicitly facing the fact that they were contradictory. And perhaps it is that fact that has allowed the evolution of the federal system within the framework of the

Constitution. The balance of power between the nation and the states has changed over time, but the framework of a central government and an independent set of states has survived.

The first era under the Constitution—from its writing to the Civil War—illustrates the tensions between the principles of centralization and decentralization. During this period a series of crucial Supreme Court decisions firmly established the fact of federal power over taxes, over interstate commerce, and in many other areas. These decisions made clear that the federal government was indeed a government and not simply the creation of the states. And at the same time, the Supreme Court established its own position as the supreme arbiter of what the Constitution meant.

The Principle of the Concurrent Majority

Concurrently, there was the counterpull of decentralization that was ultimately to lead to the Civil War. The issue revolved around the question of those vital issues that particular areas wanted to see protected. During this era, John Calhoun, a leading southern spokesman and senator, developed the idea of the "concurrent majority." According to this theory, no mere majority of the citizens of the United States nor a majority of the states themselves could tell the others what to do. Rather, policies had to be based on the agreements of majorities *within the regions involved*; that is, each section would have to give its consent when it came to policies that affected it. As one might expect, this general principle enunciated by Calhoun reflected the specific interests of his region, interests which the South wanted protected from the rest of the nation. The principle was, of course, quite contrary to the evolving strong federal government. Indeed the reader will recognize that the principle of the concurrent majority has a striking resemblance to the veto power exercised in the Security Council of the United Nations, whereby any of the major powers can block decisions with which it does not agree.

The Civil War partially resolved the tension of centralization versus decentralization. It settled the issue of the ultimate divisibility of the Union; decentralization could never go so far as to allow a state or a group of states to separate from the Union. But, as with the writing of the Constitution itself, the war did not finally settle the issue of the center versus the states. Nor did it do away with the issue of the concurrent majority whereby affected groups have a veto power over those laws that affect them. As we have seen when we considered the group process in America and as we shall discuss later, the notion of a concurrent majority still survives, though described in other terms. Specific groups still have a strong voice—often a deciding one—over policies that affect them. Often these groups are not specific states or regions, but rather economic interest groups. But the principle of decentralization that it implies remains.

Evolution of the Federal Principle

Since the Civil War, the evolution of the social and economic systems in the United States has been paralleled by an evolution of the federal principle. Most would agree that the general drift has been toward greater federal power. For a while this centralization was blocked by Supreme Court decisions limiting federal power. But a series of major Court decisions in the 1930s opened the way to federal intervention in almost all aspects of the economy; the New Deal era in the 1930s launched a period of great federal expansion. The major drift toward central government derives from the development of national problems that needed a national solution: the development of a national economy, of a national communications system, and, in more recent years, of such problems as pollution or the control of atomic energy that require central control.

It is difficult to imagine national air travel without a Federal Aviation Authority. *(Photo: John Sydlow, Photo Trends)*

Where Does Power Lie: State or Nation?

The drift toward the central government has led many commentators to declare that the federal principle is dead, that the states have lost so much power that they no longer can be considered independent entities, coequal to the federal government. There is much truth to this comment, as indeed the states have declined in influence vis-à-vis the federal government. But it is a great exaggeration. When one looks across the spectrum of governmental functions, one finds that all levels of government are active. One can, to be sure, find clear evidence for the growth of the federal sector. The budget of the federal government now greatly exceeds the combined budgets of state and local governments. Furthermore, state and local expenditures have come to depend more and more on federal grants-in-aid. (See Figure 10.2.) In 1973 it was estimated that federal assistance represented 22 percent of all state and local revenues, a percentage that had been growing steadily for several decades.

Yet one would not want to write off the state and local units as important actors. Counting only domestic programs (that is, excluding spending on defense or foreign affairs or space programs which form a large part of the federal budget), states and localities account for most—over 60 percent—of all government spending. Moreover, the states and localities con-

Figure 10.2 State and Local Expenditures Have Come to Depend More and More on Federal Grants-in-Aid

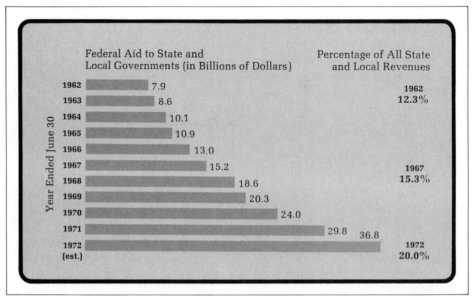

SOURCE: U.S. Office of Management and Budget (through 1971) and USN & WR Economic Unit (1972 estimate).

tinue to possess, and to exercise, substantial power over many of the most consequential sectors of public policy: the protection of life and property; the establishment of domestic or "family" laws covering such matters as divorce and abortion; the control of land-use through such means as the power of eminent domain, zoning restrictions, and so forth. Thus to the statement that federal power has grown, one would want to attach the qualifier that not only have the states and localities survived, but, indeed, they have retained major legal and financial responsibility over policy areas affecting all members of the political community.

The main conclusion, however, that would emerge from a close study of where governmental power lies is that such power is not as neatly compartmentalized as the framers of the Constitution envisioned. There are not some activities carried on by the federal government, some by the states, and some by localities. Rather, what one finds is a complex interaction among all these levels. Many governmental functions are shared.

Consider the area of public education. This has been traditionally an area of state and local control, not a federal matter. And so it remains, with the bulk of the funds for education being raised locally and spent locally. Yet, the federal government has been involved in one way or another from the very beginning. Indeed, before the writing of the Constitution a statute in 1785 provided for federal grants to local government for the construction of schools. Such federal aid continued in the nineteenth century when, under the Morrill Land Grant Act of 1862, federal grants of land were provided to the states to set up agricultural and mechanical colleges. In 1917 the Smith Hughes Act provided similar grants-in-aid for vocational education. And since then various federal programs have expanded federal aid to local education. During World War II legislation was passed to help "impacted" areas—that is, those places where governmental defense activity (a military base, for instance) put pressure on the local school system because of new population or because the use by the federal government of local land reduced the tax base. In such cases, federal funds were made available to build, operate, and maintain local schools. These programs were continued after World War II. In addition, when the first artificial satellite, Sputnik, was put into orbit, the federal government decided that a major effort had to be made to keep up with the Russians in technological education.

This led to the 1958 National Defense Education Act, an act that provided aid to local school districts to improve education in mathematics, science, and foreign languages, plus funds to improve school administration. In addition, it provided scholarship and fellowship funds in colleges and universities. And the massive Elementary and Secondary Education Act of 1965 involved fairly large grants of federal funds to school districts with large numbers of pupils below the poverty line.

It is likely that legislation in coming years will continue to increase the role of the federal government. But the history of the federal government's involvement in education illustrates a number of important general points about the way in which the states and the nation share functions.

How the State and the Nation Share Functions: Despite the expansion of the role of the federal government, it would be more than premature to talk of the eclipse of state and local powers over education. This largest of all government domestic programs is still heavily state and local. During the 1960s, the federal government's share of public education expenditures almost doubled. But this involved a growth from 6.1 percent in 1960 to 10.6 percent in 1971—indicating that the bulk of expenditure for public education still remains on the state and local level.

The increased federal involvement in education comes, at least in part, indirectly—that is, in response to other issues on which the federal government has always been involved. Thus, one main expansion of federal aid to local education derived from the federal concern with matters of defense: The defense system was putting too much burden on some areas of the country. The educational system was not adequate for providing the skills needed for defense. Similarly, the most recent expansion of aid to education has been tied to the federal government's involvement in problems such as poverty, a subject matter that has more traditionally (at least since the 1930s) been a federal concern.

However, one ought not to take the defense or poverty justifications too literally. In part, these bills were passed for the purpose of aiding education *per se*. But it is customary to justify the expansion of the government in one area in terms of more traditional federal activities.

The format of federal aid to education also illustrates the way in which the nation and the states share functions. The federal government itself does not take over schools. Rather the federal involvement is in terms of grants-in-aid to state educational commissions or to local school boards. The states and the localities continue to control the process of education. Federal aid, though, does usually have some strings attached, usually in the form of guidelines on educational practices or other issues, guidelines which must be complied with as a condition of receipt of the aid. How tight these strings are varies from issue to issue, but the guidelines do imply some federal involvement in the educational process. However—just to complicate things doubly and illustrate the tug in the federal-state relationship—the federal guidelines are often set up in close consultation with the states and with local school districts, so in part they involve standards the states and localities apply to themselves.

The evolving debate over the role of the federal government in the educational process illustrates the way in which the general principles of centralization versus decentralization interact with more specific interests. Opposition to the federal involvement in education is often framed in terms of general principles. On the one hand, it is argued that locally controlled education is better education than that dominated by a remote and cumbersome Washington bureaucracy. And the counter-argument comes back that national standards and equality of educational opportunity are more important values.

But, indeed, the alignment of forces for or against the federal involvement in education often depends not on these general principles of federalism, but where one stands on other issues. Thus federal aid programs to local schools have at times included desegregation requirements. One's position on school desegregation is more likely to affect one's attitude toward federal school aid than is the more general principle of central control versus local control.

The result, in relation to education, is a quite mixed system. The federal government is involved through its grants and through its guidelines, but the power over the educational system is certainly shared with the states. And this pattern can be found in many fields. The social security system set up in the 1930s involves a sharing of power and responsibility between the federal government and the states. Consider the program for unemployment insurance: Is it a federal or a state program? In most cases it is a state program, whereby the states levy a payroll tax used to provide unemployment insurance. But the states are induced to levy such a tax by a federal law, under which the federal government would impose such a tax if the states did not do so. Thus all fifty states levy the tax since it is to their advantage to comply. Furthermore, though they run their own programs, the states must act within the framework of federal standards. But the standards are flexible, giving the states much leeway.

If the previous paragraph leaves one uncertain as to whether the unemployment insurance program is a federal or a state one, the result is deliberate. As with many programs, the actual situation is a complex pattern of shared powers and overlapping jurisdictions.

Federal-State-Local Relations: What has been said about the sharing of functions between the federal government and the states applies as well to relations between those two levels of government and the more local governments—the cities, counties, towns, school districts. Local governments also share functions with the federal government. In some cases they receive federal aid indirectly through the state capitals. But in many cases they enter into direct relationships with the federal government—with aid going directly to cities or to school districts. In this sense, these local political units are full-fledged actors in the federal system in America.

Revenue Sharing Between the Federal Government and the States: The constantly evolving pattern of relations between the federal government and the states took on a new form in the early 1970s with the passage of President Nixon's proposals for revenue sharing between the federal government and the states. This multibillion-dollar program of federal aid to states and localities differs from previous grants by Washington. Most previous grants have been "categorical," that is, they are given to support specific programs. The funds from revenue sharing are allocated to states and localities for use more or less as they see fit. Such a program could represent a major change in the relations of federal and local governments. One major source of the growth of federal power has been the fact that the federal income tax is the most effective revenue-raising instrument, giving the federal government much greater financial resources than are available to the states and localities. Revenue sharing could give the states and localities access to these federal funds without restricting their freedom.

How revenue sharing affects the relations between Washington and the states will depend on the evolution of the program: how large the federal funds are that are allocated to the program, how many restrictions are placed on the use of the funds. Revenue sharing is the latest innovation in the long and complex development of federalism in America. And it illustrates the principle that federalism in America has not represented a clear conflict between federal powers and local powers, but rather an intertwining and sharing of powers across the various levels of government.

Why Has the Federal System Evolved as It Has?

No one reading the constitutional provisions that divide power between the federal government and the states—the provisions giving the federal government certain powers, the Tenth Amendment seeming to limit those powers—would be able on that basis alone to give an accurate description of what powers were where in our federal system. Its particular evolution depended on historical forces. Nor can we present a full analysis of the forces that led to the particular pattern of federal-state-local relations in every field. But two broad aspects of the federal system require explication.

Why has federal power grown so much beyond what the framers of the Constitution imagined? And why, despite the growth of the federal government, have state and local governments remained independent sources of power?

Sources of Expansion of Federal Power

The answer to the first question lies in the development of America as a nation. The framers of the Constitution wanted to create a unified nation, especially in relation to control over interstate commerce and foreign affairs. And these were two crucial powers, given the way in which the American nation evolved. The more it became a large continental economy and the more it became a world power, the more did the federal power grow.

Consider the federal government's power over interstate commerce. If the United States had remained an agrarian society, that power would have been important but not nearly as important as it became in a highly industrialized society, a society whose economic growth depended on the availability of vast internal markets. The more the nation needed a unified economy, the more the role of the federal government increased.

Development of a National Economy: The reason is that the development of a national economy makes it impossible for any one state to control it. If any one state tries to regulate business, and the businesses find such regulation onerous, they can move to another state. This inhibits state control over business and makes federal regulation more likely; indeed, the regulation of business activities (antitrust legislation, standards for goods, and so forth) has largely become a federal activity.

Or one can illustrate the pressure toward federal control in an area where the drift to centralization has not gone as far — welfare measures. If one state sets up a program with substantially higher welfare payments than other states, it may find its resources swamped by the movement of poor families from other, less generous states. Yet the state cannot, constitutionally, close its borders to citizens moving from other states. The one state that wants a more substantial welfare program is part of the same national economy as the others. What other states do affects its own programs. Under such circumstances of interdependence, pressures build for federal standards.

Growth Through Defense Power: Another source of expansion of federal power is the role of the United States in the world. Federal power has always grown in wartime, and the seemingly permanent high military budgets maintain that power. The example of the growth of the federal government through the defense power illustrates why the constitutional definition of the powers of the federal government is an inadequate guide to its real powers. Imagine that the power over national defense were the only one given to the federal government. It is easy to see how that single power could lead to all the other powers held by the federal government. The power to defend the nation is meaningless without the power to raise necessary funds; hence, the taxing power. One cannot defend the nation with inadequate technology; hence the federal government's involvement in education. Adequate defense requires good roads; hence the federal government's multibillion-dollar road-building program. And so forth, and so forth.

This imaginary circumstance is presented for two purposes. One, it is not completely imaginary. Federal power has grown over many fields as a concomitant of the defense power. We have seen the National Defense Education Act which involved massive aid to local school boards in the name of national defense. Federal involvement in transportation, in space research, in health programs has often had a defense-related basis. Second, the example of the defense power illustrates the more general principle that the specific powers given the federal government in the Constitution are infinitely stretchable. The courts have dealt with federal power through the doctrine of *implied powers*, a doctrine spelled out by Chief Justice John Marshall in 1819 in his decision on the case of *McCulloch* v. *Maryland*. Congress, he declared, was not limited in its powers to those *specifically* listed in the Constitution. Rather Congress had the full panoply of powers *necessary to carry out* the specific powers granted to it. And as we have seen, power over something such as defense could be interpreted to require almost every other power to carry out the former functions effectively. Though the Supreme Court, as we see in the next chapter, took a narrow view of implied powers in the 1930s, since then the Court has placed very few limitations on federal power.

Federal involvement in space research has often been defense related.　(Photo: NASA)

State courts, on the other hand, have been much more restrictive with local governments. They have tended to follow a rule opposite to that of implied powers, the so-called Dillon rule (named after a state judge who expounded it most fully). Authorizations of power to local governments have tended to be read quite narrowly. If a locality is given a specific power in a state law, it gets that power and nothing more. Thus federal court doctrine has allowed great expansion of federal power, but state courts tried to hold local powers more closely in check.

All this leads to our second question: What preserves the states and the localities?

What Preserves the States and the Localities?

The answer lies mainly in the structure of American politics, particularly in the organization of the American political parties. If the American political parties were—like the parties in some other countries—tightly organized and disciplined organizations, then the drift of power into federal hands would have proceeded more rapidly and more thoroughly. The legal potential for the "swamping" of the states by federal power exists. If the national administration controlled a party apparatus that stretched down into the grass roots, the legal potential would become a political reality.

In fact, as we have seen, the party system is quite the reverse in the United States. The political parties are essentially state and local organizations. They may develop a temporary national cohesion when it comes to Presidential elections, but this is only temporary (and not always that cohesive even then). Furthermore, the White House and the state houses (or the city halls) are not always controlled by the same party. And even when they are, this does not imply control over the local party by the party organization in Washington (which in fact hardly exists). In some countries the national party leadership decides who runs under the party label in local elections. If this were the case in the United States, governors and mayors would be under close control of the national party. In fact, who runs in state and local elections—indeed who runs for Senate and House of Representative seats—is a matter that is decided locally, not nationally. And this gives the local party independence from any national control. The result is that states and localities remain as independent governments because they have *political power,* not because of the legal requirements of the Constitution.

The Dispersal of Political Power

The power of the federal government may have grown, its budget (if one adds domestic and foreign programs) exceeds that of the states, and the states are increasingly dependent on grants-in-aid from Washington. But the dispersal of political power that derives from the party system means that the federal government is, at least in part, a creature of the states and of the localities—not in a legal sense but in a political sense. Congressmen are part of the federal government, but are deeply conscious of the fact that they represent particular areas. And even the two officials elected by the nation as a whole—the President and Vice-President—cannot but be aware of the importance of state forces and state parties in the nomination and election processes.

Two examples can illustrate this. When the social security legislation of the New Deal was prepared in the 1930s, the original plan was for a fully federal program. The program had been initiated in Washington, and many in the New Deal administration felt that it would be more effective if administered from there. In fact, the program that was submitted to and passed by Congress involved a vast amount of sharing with the states. A good deal of the program was administered by the states within the framework of federal guidelines—a pattern that has appeared in many other areas. The main reason was that the Roosevelt administration realized that the Congress would only accept a proposal with provision for the involvement of the states. If there had been tightly centralized party organizations in the United States, President Roosevelt as the head of the Democratic party would not have had to worry about the doubts of senators and congressmen; he could have controlled their votes on this measure. But these congressmen and senators—though technically part of the federal government—are the creatures of their locality, and often act to defend that locality.

Or take another example, involving an American city rather than a state. In 1965 the federal agency Office of Economic Opportunity (OEO) decided that the city of Chicago was not complying with federal guidelines on the desegregation of its schools. Federal aid to the school system of Chicago was massive and needed in order to keep that school system running. This, one would have guessed, would be a perfect example of the way in which federal involvement in local school matters could imply federal control of local school operations. The OEO did crack down and cut off school aid to Chicago. What was the result of this clash between the federal educational bureaucracy in Washington and the Chicago school district? Within a few weeks, the OEO had backed down and restored federal aid. And in the process, the OEO had been dealt a major blow to its prestige and authority within the government.

Why did this happen? The OEO was not exceeding its legal powers. It would probably have been backed up by the courts, which were themselves pushing in the same direction. And it did have the resources to back up its demand on Chicago; the school district could not have functioned without federal aid. It is indeed these two forces—the absence of court or constitutional restraints on the power of the federal government and the control over revenue sources by the federal government—that make the federal government as powerful as it is.

But the one factor that the educational bureaucracy in Washington did not reckon with was the *political power* of the Chicago Democratic organization and its leader, Mayor Richard J. Daley. The Chicago political machine—one of the most effective such organizations in the country at that time—controlled a number of vital political resources such as the crucial Democratic votes of a major state, numerous members of Congress, and an important bloc of delegates at Presidential nominating conventions. On the basis of such real political power, local government survives.

Of course, not all localities are as large as the city of Chicago; nor is it even a matter of size alone, for few other cities have local governments as powerful as that of Chicago. Yet the localities—even small ones—have some reciprocal power over the federal government because of their political independence and because of the fact that their representatives in Congress will act as defenders of that independence.

Washington, the States, and the Cities

The greatest single challenge to the American mixture of governments is found in the vast metropolitan areas. Can a constitution, written for a small agrarian society, deal with the contemporary city? Within the urban areas we see encapsulated all the problems of central versus local control, of multiple governments with overlapping jurisdictions, of federal-state relations, of federal-local relations. (See Figure 10.3.)

Metropolitan Areas

Consider the metropolitan areas. Two things become immediately clear: They are socially and economically interdependent, and they are politically divided.

The very definition of a metropolitan area, as used by the Census Bureau, stresses its interdependence: "the general concept of a metropolitan area is one of an integrated economic and social unit with a recognized large population nucleus." And the interdependence of the metropolitan areas takes many forms. People move easily from one part to another: They live in one area (perhaps a suburb) and work in another (perhaps the core city). The various communities in a metropolitan area share man-made facilities such as roads, public transportation, shopping areas. They are dependent on the same natural facilities such as clean water, pure air, space for recreation.

The term "spillovers" has come to be used to describe those activities of one community in a metropolitan area that affect its neighbors; and the

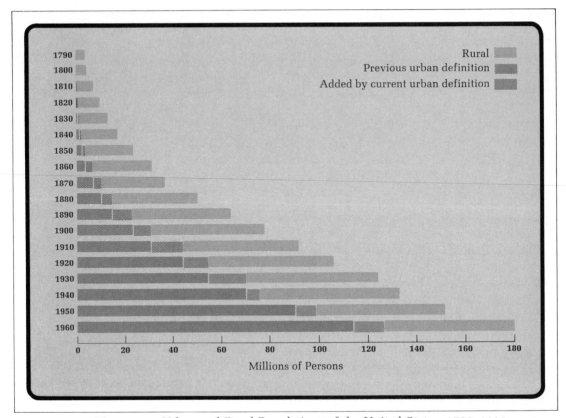

Figure 10.3 Urban and Rural Populations of the United States, 1790–1960

SOURCE: Irene B. Taeuber and Conrad Taeuber, *People of the United States in the Twentieth Century* (Washington, D.C.: U.S. Department of Commerce, Bureau of the Census, 1971).

spillovers are many. Smoke from a factory in one community pollutes the air of the community next door; if one community has an effective mosquito abatement program but the next does not, the former will suffer during the summer despite its efforts. If a suburb creates a zoning ordinance that limits housing to single-family homes on large plots of land, it will effectively keep out poor citizens, and in turn affect the population burdens of other communities.

Or there can be more beneficial spillovers. One community may provide parks and open them to all metropolitan residents. Or the central city may keep its streets clean, which are then used by commuters who live in the suburbs.

One could go on and on pointing to areas of interdependence. The major point should be clear: The metropolitan areas are social and economic units sharing problems. But overlaid upon this is the disorder of American local government—that curious mixture of local governments with overlapping boundaries, of state government, of federal government. As we have pointed out, one estimate is that there are about 1500 governmental units in the New York metropolitan area—and similar astronomical numbers would exist in most such areas. There is the government of the central city, separate governments for satellite cities, and for small and large suburbs. And these are overlapped and crisscrossed by county governments, by special districts, and by various state and federal jurisdictions.

The Advisory Commission on Intergovernmental Relations sums up the consequences well:

> *Fragmentation of this kind may appear to bring government closer to the people, but it compounds the difficulties of achieving coordination within metropolitan areas. Political responsibility for governmental performance is divided to the point of obscurity. Public control of government policies tends to breakdown when citizens have to deal with a network of independent governments, each responsible for highly specialized activities. Even when good channels are developed for registering public concern, each government is so circumscribed in its powers and in the area of its jurisdiction that important metropolitan action is virtually impossible for local governments to undertake.*
> *If a few governments are prepared to agree on joint or coordinated programs, their efforts can be blocked by others that are unwilling to cooperate.*[2]

What this circumstance means is that while problems cover a wide area, the solutions take place within individual parts of that area. This also often means a wide disparity between those who pay for services and those who receive them. The central cities provide clean streets and generally pay for these with taxes raised from their residents. The facilities are then used by suburbanites who pay their taxes to a suburban government. This disparity helps explain two common phenomena in America: the attempts by central cities to tax suburbanites who work in the city and (since the cities do not always succeed well in this) the fact that many cities have dirty streets and most have inadequate transportation facilities.

The Crisis in American Cities: More specifically, the contemporary crisis in American cities derives (at least in part) from the multiplicity of jurisdictions. The situation in the major American cities is by now quite clear. For a number of years the White middle classes have been moving out of the central cities of metropolitan areas into the suburbs. They have been replaced by poor minority groups—mostly Black. The 1970 census for instance shows that in the decade of the 1960s the White population of New York City decreased by 9 percent while the non-White population in-

---

[2] Advisory Commission on Inter-Governmental Relations, *Metropolitan America: Challenge to Federalism* (Washington, D.C., 1966).

creased by 62 percent. There are many reasons for the movement to the suburbs. In part it is a desire for fresh air, lawns, and the like. In part it is a desire to leave the problems of the cities—especially those of the urban poor—behind and to find school districts that are peaceful and homogeneously middle class.

The result is that the urban core of America is decaying, filled with the poor, the non-White. The suburbs are White and wealthier—and apprehensive about the cities. The situation was used in our chapter on group conflict to illustrate the kind of polarization of a population that can potentially tear a society apart.

And consider how the multiple jurisdictions of the metropolitan area help create this situation. What is crucial is that the White middle-class, when it flees the city, crosses a political boundary into another community. They no longer vote or otherwise take part in the government of the city; they no longer share its problems; and, above all, they no longer pay taxes to the city.

The result is great pressure on the central city to provide services for a growing population that needs such services badly—welfare services as well as the other necessities of urban life. But the cities come under these pressures just when the tax base required to provide the services is de-

It is difficult to integrate urban schools because there are not enough White pupils to go around.   (Photo: Don Sturkey, Black Star)

clining. Furthermore, the school-age population in the central cities comes to contain larger and larger percentages of non-Whites. And this phenomenon has two effects. It makes it difficult to integrate and obtain a racial mixture in the schools because there are not enough White pupils to go around. It also leads to an exacerbation of the problem as more and more Whites flee from what they see as ghetto schools.

Suppose the boundaries were different. Suppose the movement to the suburbs did not involve crossing the political boundary to another community. Surely that would not eliminate the problems but things would look somewhat different. The tax base of the cities would not change as drastically. The suburbs would still be part of the same district. Similarly, it would be easier to achieve racial balance in the schools if the entire population of the metropolitan district were considered at once, not the core cities and the suburbs separately. And the latter fact might eliminate much of the drive among the White middle classes to leave the city—since it would make less difference in the schooling of their children if they did. In short, the cities would have their problems still: The nature of the boundaries does not cause the urban problems. But the boundaries would not serve to make the problems worse.

Yet the situation does not lead to a clear solution, by which we mean one on which all participants would agree. Some solutions involve an increase in state responsibility for education; an issue before the courts is how much responsibility the states have to see that pupils in less affluent communities have as adequate an education as do those in more affluent places. But the boundaries of the urban problem are not coterminous with those of the states—many major metropolitan areas stretch across state borders as well.

The Federal Government and Housing: Another solution is greater involvement of the federal government in the metropolitan areas. The federal government has, in practice, had a long history of involvement through its programs in the urban areas of America, mostly in relation to housing. But the nature of that involvement is instructive. The first major federal program was the Housing Act of 1937, a program that set up the FHA mortgage insurance program. This program allowed many more people to build and own their own homes than would have otherwise been the case. But such a program was of greatest value to middle-class homeowners. And, indeed, the FHA program helped accelerate the growth of the suburbs at the expense of the inner city. The FHA program was balanced by federal support for low-rent housing, housing that almost always wound up in the central city. In short, the federal programs have helped create the current urban crisis.

The Federal Government and Urban Renewal: Or consider the involvement of the federal government in urban renewal, the major federal urban program of the past few decades. The purpose of the program was to renew central cities. Federal money was provided to allow local authorities to buy up blighted property (usually downtown slums, inhabited by non-Whites) and to clear the land. It was then sold to others for residential, commercial, or industrial development. The result was little that helped the poor population of the inner cities. What was supposed to be urban renewal turned out to be Black removal.

The Problem of Local vs. Federal Control: The story of urban renewal illustrates a major point often ignored in considering the problem of centralization versus decentralization. When you decentralize power, to whom do you decentralize it? The federal urban renewal program was run in a decentralized manner; federal funds were allocated to local authorities who planned the local renewal schemes. And what happens—in particular who benefits from such a program—depends on who is in power locally. Our previous discussions of who participates in politics (Chapter 5) and who is selected to occupy politically important positions (Chapter 6) suggest an answer. It is unlikely to be the urban poor themselves.

A distinguished observer of urban America comments on the effects of local control over federal funds:

> Local communities are allowed great latitude in deciding how federal funds will be spent on the bread-and-butter programs: urban renewal and public housing. If the Main Street merchants are in power, they can use renewal funds to tear down low-cost housing and put up luxury apartments near the department stores—in effect redistributing income from the poor to the well-to-do while reducing the stock of low-cost housing. If more generous souls are in power, the worst housing is torn down to make room for middle- or lower-middle-income housing; the income transfer from poor to not-so-poor is much less, but it is still in the wrong direction. And if the mayor simply is seeking funds with which to run his city in the face of a declining tax base, he discovers that he must join with those who want one of these urban renewal programs because that is about the only way he can get large-scale federal money into his city. He discovers, in short, that he has to hurt his poorest and weakest citizens in order to provide for the general welfare; his only option is to try to do it as humanely as possible. . . . The point is that for almost any legitimate community objective—improving the supply of housing, strengthening the tax base, etc.—urban renewal has in most cases proved to be an unwieldly and costly tool.[3]

The general point deserves emphasis: Local control means control by whoever it is that controls the local area. It is a misconception that local

[3] James Q. Wilson, "The War on the Cities," *The Public Interest*, No. 3 (Spring 1966), 30–31.

areas are homogeneous; they have leaders and followers in them. Citizens will often want local control when it means that they can control things. If they are not in control locally they may want outside control. Thus Blacks in the inner city sometimes call for local control over schools or the police, for they form a majority and could control these. But where they are a smaller group, they may prefer more federal control.

Where does this confusing situation leave us in terms of the "best" boundaries for the metropolitan areas? Should they all come under direct federal control; should there be massive metropolitan governments; should there be local jurisdictions as there now are; or should there be even more localism involving neighborhood governments?

It is, of course, not our mission in this book to suggest solutions to current problems—even if we knew them. Nor are these problems that would be solved solely by juggling boundaries. But the situation of the metropolitan areas illustrates aptly the paradox presented at the beginning of this chapter: All governmental units are too big, all are too small. Big units do not easily adjust to the problems of the local citizens nor do they give them adequate control. Small units need to be coordinated with the larger ones.

Let us see how this paradox applies to the cities. Suppose we have federal control or massive metropolitan governments. Many of the problems of lack of coordination would be gone and tax bases could be equalized. But could such a government adjust its policies to the specific needs of the citizens in various parts of the vast metropolitan areas? Does not each section of the area know best what it wants and have the right to run its own affairs? Such might sound like the question of an affluent White suburbanite who would prefer to ignore the problems of the inner city, but it might also be raised by a Black resident of the urban core. The latter also wants local control.

But will the opposite solution work: a small fragmented system of governments—perhaps like the one that already exists or one even more fragmented into neighborhoods? Certainly this has the advantage of giving the local residents more control over their own lives. Or does it? The problems with which they inevitably have to deal—transportation, housing, pollution, even education—transcend the boundaries of their neighborhood. Extreme localization of government would give the citizen more control over his local government, but it would be over a government totally incapable of dealing with the existent problems.

The best conclusion is that the dilemma of centralization versus decentralization is a real one, and the tension between the two principles will continue for many years to come. What particular solution is tried at a particular point in time will depend more upon the constellation of interests among the participants and their relative political power than upon abstract principles about the virtue of local government or the virtue of coordinated government.

Controversy

The tension between federal power and local control is an old and continuing problem in American politics. In recent years the tensions have increased because the pressures in both directions — toward greater federal power and toward greater local control — have grown. Nowhere is this seen more clearly than in American cities.

One Side

Government in the United States has grown so large that it is not in tune with the needs of the people. Planners and bureaucrats in Washington create programs without taking into account the differing needs of citizens in different parts of the country. And the same is true about city governments. Our cities have grown into vast impersonal institutions unable to respond to the real needs of citizens.

The main reason for this is size. Governmental units are too large. Planners in Washington cannot possibly pay attention to the specific needs of particular localities. They have to plan on a broad scale. And the same holds true for City Hall.

The only way to achieve government that can respond to citizens is to decentralize. In big cities, power should go to the neighborhoods. Here citizens know one another, they can meet and directly express their interests. Neighborhood government can control the schools, the police, the recreational facilities. In this way, citizens will lose the feeling that they are being manipulated by a distant government. Rather, they will come to feel that they are true participants in the governmental process.

The Other Side

Local control, neighborhood governments, government directly in the hands of the people — these are all romantic dreams of those who would return to the past. American cities in the 1970s cannot be run like New England towns. Whether one likes it or not, their problems can be dealt with only by a strong central government. The main problems of cities are not those of one neighborhood or another. Rather, they are problems that affect the entire metropolis. Mass transit is not a neighborhood problem; pollution is not a neighborhood problem. Why talk of neighborhood government when such governments could not possibly deal with the real urban problems.

In fact, even a strong metropolitan government cannot deal with the problems. What is probably needed is greater power for the federal government. In short, the advocates of neighborhood government have it backwards. We need stronger central government on the metropolitan level and, beyond that, a stronger federal government.

Suggested Readings

On federalism in America, see Morton Grodzins, *The American System* (Chicago: Rand McNally, 1966); Richard Leach, *American Federalism* (New York: Norton, 1970); and James L. Lundquist, *Making Federalism Work* (Washington, D.C.: Brookings Institution, 1969).

For a discussion of the urban problem, see James Q. Wilson and Edward C. Banfield, *City Politics* (Cambridge, Mass.: Harvard University Press, 1963); and Robert C. Wood, *1400 Governments: The Political Economy of the New York Metropolitan Region* (Garden City, N.Y.: Doubleday, 1964). For a general discussion of community government, see Alan A. Altshuler, *Community Control: The Black Demand for Participation in Large American Cities* (New York: Pegasus, 1970).

The Supreme Court in American Politics

11

Separation of powers is a central idea in our form of government. There is to be a legislature that makes laws, an executive that carries them out, and a court that passes judgment when controversies arise over the meaning and application of laws. We will have ample opportunity to see that such tidy distinctions rarely work out in practice. Separation of powers is actually a sharing of powers, and therefore a struggle for power.

Nevertheless, there is something called "legislation," and it primarily occurs in Congress; and there is something called "execution," and it primarily occurs through the Presidency; and there is something called "adjudication," and it primarily occurs in the court system. In this chapter adjudication, especially as practiced by the U.S. Supreme Court, will interest us. Because adjudication is not well understood, at least not nearly so well as legislation and execution, it is useful to start with a description of how courts operate.

What Do We Mean by Adjudication?

Courts differ from legislatures or executives in the way in which they establish new policies. Courts do not initiate action; rather, they wait until a case is brought before them. A case becomes the occasion for courts to proclaim a general rule.

To understand this distinctive characteristic of courts it is necessary to be clear about the role of the participants. American courts will hear only those cases in which a genuine controversy exists between two parties—a plaintiff and a defendant. Courts in the United States consistently refuse to accept jurisdiction over friendly, nonadversary proceedings whose object is to get a declaration of policy by the courts on a general social issue. The courts rule only if there is a genuine controversy—that is, if there is need to find a principle to resolve an issue in the case before them.

For the same reason, the courts generally decline to pronounce on cases in which the injury is merely a hypothetical future possibility. American courts are not a forum in which to discuss the probable benefits and costs, the apparent wisdom or demonstrable absurdity, of a public policy or private course of action. They exist to cope with the legal issues involving the suffering, or alleged suffering, of one party at the hands of another. Unless the courts can ascertain the actual injury one party has already experienced—or can be foreseen to experience in the absence of a court injunction—they cannot know what remedy will remove the injustice. This consideration underlies the extreme importance assigned by the courts to the seemingly technical question of whether an individual plaintiff has "standing to sue." To have "standing," one must demonstrate that one has suffered some wrong the courts can conceivably right by an exercise of their judicial power.

The court then presides over an adversary proceeding between two parties. If the case involves a challenge to an act of the government, one of the adversaries is the challenger: the convicted criminal who claims that he was not accorded the right to a fair trial guaranteed by the Constitution; the businessman who claims the government exceeded its authority under existing law in regulating his business; the schoolchild who claims he or she is not receiving equal protection of the law by being sent to a segregated school. The other adversary is the government: a state government if it is a state criminal proceeding that is challenged; the federal government if a federal regulatory act is being challenged; a local school board if it is the subject of the desegregation suit.

This same contest between adversaries applies to all court proceedings: the divorce contest where one adversary sues the other for divorce, the civil suit where one party accuses the other of injuring it, the criminal prosecution where the government prosecutor faces the lawyer of the accused. Because the outcome depends on this adversary proceeding we will look more closely at it.

The Role of the Lawyer

We begin with the lawyer. The role of the lawyer is subject to much misunderstanding. Lawyers do not necessarily sympathize with the aims of their clients. They may even strongly dislike the persons — or the objectives — they defend. But it is central to the lawyer's creed that his client receive the most forceful representation of his interests possible. Even accused criminals whom the lawyer himself believes guilty are entitled to have their rights adequately maintained.

The lawyer does not search dispassionately and disinterestedly on his own for "justice" or the "truth": These values will be secured, he believes, if lawyers on each side of the case present the strongest arguments they can muster. Lawyers are also "officers of the court." They state the claims of their clients in such a way that the issue can be resolved within the terms of the law: what specific interests are at stake, what legal remedies are sought, what facts and principles are to guide resolution of the dispute.

The Role of the Judge

The role of the judge, too, is often misunderstood. Unlike Continental European counterparts, the American judge is not expected to investigate on his own: to ascertain which allegations are true, which false, and which facts are being suppressed or overlooked by both parties to the controversy. On the contrary, he is expected to base his decision—or to instruct the jury to base theirs—solely on arguments and evidence presented to him in open contest. His responsibility is to assure that a proper adversary proceeding is observed: that legally correct claims and charges are entered; that each party is given ample opportunity to present his case; that irrelevant or prejudicial testimony is stricken from the record; that illegally obtained evidence is not admitted.

This description of adversary court proceedings is short and incomplete. And, in fact, many court proceedings depart somewhat from these norms. They are sometimes arranged to speed a divorce or to test the constitutionality of a law. Indigent clients sometimes receive less than full support from their lawyers. Some judges reach well beyond the necessities of the case at hand to make general pronouncements on controversial public policy. Yet the general norms of adversary proceedings help explain the moral force court judgments have in this country.

The Advantages of Adjudication

Why are such proceedings accepted as superior to rule making by a single disinterested body? For one thing, adversary proceedings are effective in revealing the specific interests actually affected by public policy. The most careful legislator cannot foresee all the future circumstances to which a general law will apply. Adjudication permits those actually affected by a law to bring forward the particulars of their case and to ask for a reasonable interpretation of the law in the light of problems revealed. Moreover, the adjudicatory process harnesses self-interest to the quest for the public interest by giving the participants a strong incentive to mobilize the full array of arguments on their behalf. Legislatures may casually vote through laws they half understand; they are apt to be swayed by superficial arguments, by time pressure, by abstract convictions unrelated to the actual costs their decision imposes. Adversaries in an adjudicatory proceeding cannot afford the indulgence of such abstraction.

Adjudication also invites attention to questions of fact and principle. It may seem curious to ascribe these characteristics to a process based on a highly partisan contest. But the motives of the participants should not be confused with the terms on which their arguments become effective. To win in court one does not have to show that public support is on one's side. Rather the participants must disprove charges or press claims based on rights to which they are entitled by virtue of the rules under which they have agreed to live. Arguments focus on the neutral principles of justice. To win it is necessary to show that the claim is *just,* or that an indictment is true.

This nonpolitical concern for fact and principle creates a third distinctive advantage of adjudication. It provides legal channels through which minorities can maintain their rights against majority preferences. The minorities that have thus benefited form a mixed lot — unpopular citizens accused of crimes, Blacks, the very wealthy, Jehovah's Witnesses, birdwatchers, corporations, and Communists. What these disparate groups have in common is that none would fare very well in an egalitarian democracy wholly controlled by majority rule. In acting on behalf of minorities, courts sometimes have blocked efforts at social reform by legislative majorities. They did so between the end of the Civil War and 1937 when they protected the giant corporations from government regulation. In these circumstances it is easy to see the courts as the defense of special privilege against the people's will. However, if at times the courts have protected privileges, they have also defended the rights of less privileged minorities. Blacks were long ignored by alternately indifferent and fearful legislatures; only a series of landmark judicial decisions has begun to right the wrongs of racial discrimination.

The Disadvantages of Adjudication

Against the advantages of adjudication must be placed its corresponding disadvantages. The case-by-case method of evolving a public policy may, while assuring attention to the impact of a general rule upon specific interests, also prove slow, cumbersome, and internally inconsistent as a means of regulating society. Judges in court constantly face a dilemma: If they confine their decisions strictly to the points requiring resolution in the case before them, they risk contributing a piecemeal solution to an interdependent problem demanding more uniform treatment; yet to the extent that they venture beyond these limits, they reduce the validity and moral force of their decision. The logic of the adversary process, moreover, encourages intense, unqualified statements of principle implying that only two possible points of view of the controversy exist, and that only one is right.

We have already noted that adjudication coexists uneasily with majority rule in this country. The strength of adjudication is that it helps minorities and the individual claimant. Now we must add that some of the "minorities" whose rights are upheld by the courts are often those who can pay for this protection. Adjudication is expensive, especially the cost of a lawyer. The procedures of the courtroom are complex and often cumbersome, and without a skilled lawyer one risks losing simply through failure to observe some highly technical procedural requirement. But there are many other expenses associated with a trial — courtroom fees, the cost of a delayed settlement, the expense of a transcript if one wishes to appeal the decision. Defendants in criminal cases who are too poor to hire a lawyer may have one assigned, but even the most conscientious assigned counsel is handicapped if he lacks funds to turn up the evidence he needs to win in court. Of course, one may lose the case, and thus lose not only the initial investment but also such additional damages and court costs as the judge may assess. It is scarcely surprising that many who feel certain their rights have been infringed nevertheless fear to go to court.

There are still subtler barriers confronting disadvantaged minorities. Because the courtroom is predominantly the preserve of those who can pay, it has acquired an aura peculiarly congenial to this class. Corporation lawyers, bankers, realtors, insurance agents, and automobile dealers are generally well informed of their rights under the law and are quick to institute legal action when it is to their financial advantage to do so. They mingle freely as social equals with judges and other lawyers, who share their interest in "practical" affairs and who—taken as a whole—have benefited from a longer and more expensive education than the general public. With good reason, the poor, the less-well-educated, and certain minorities feel out of place in court. They appear most often before the bar to meet charges of defaulting on contract or as defendants in criminal proceedings. Civil law is seldom written to yield benefits for them, and they are less likely to know how to turn the law to their advantage. They know that most judges and lawyers regard them as socially inferior, and that (at least until recently) the juries they confront will largely be drawn from the White middle classes.

The Effectiveness of Adjudication in Social Reform

A final question concerning adjudication relates to its effectiveness in social reform. It is sometimes argued that a single, decisive ruling by the courts may gain a reform far quicker than years of frustrating lobbying with an elected legislature. Lobbies to repeal antiabortion statutes, for example, now concentrate their efforts on bringing test cases to the courts. Environmental protection groups, discouraged by the slow progress of antipollution and land-use control bills through the state legislatures, have sought to short-circuit the process by obtaining favorable court rulings. Yet this increasingly popular strategy is open to question.

Democratic government rests heavily on persuasion, and on the formation of a community consensus. Judicial rulings offer a tempting short cut, particularly because they often enjoy an initial legitimacy not accorded to more overtly political prescriptions; but this legitimacy is easily strained by overuse. Courts lightly impose elitist solutions and frustrate the will of the popularly elected branches of government at their peril.

The Supreme Court: A Symbol
of the Restraints of the Constitution

This tension between courts and legislatures—more generally, between the legitimacy of adjudication and the legitimacy of mobilized popular sup-

For most Americans the Supreme Court symbolizes the principle that no government official may act above the law.   (Photo: Wide World)

port—is institutionalized in the central processes of American constitutional democracy. Its chief symbol is the United States Supreme Court. No other tribunal in the world has remained so dramatically in the public eye; none has so decisively checked so repeatedly the clearly expressed intent of the popularly elected branches of government and yet remained so firmly a part of a democratic political system. Although staffed by nine judges enjoying lifetime appointment, it has earned its place as a fully coequal branch—and, if public opinion polls are to be accepted, the most revered of the three branches—of the national government. For most Americans, the Supreme Court symbolizes the principle that no government official may act above the law. Because of the Supreme Court's special relation to constitutional government in the United States, we shall devote the remainder of this chapter to discussing its operations. The reader should, however, have in mind that the Supreme Court is part of a larger system of federal, state, and local courts. Figure 11.1 shows the major features of the U.S. court system.

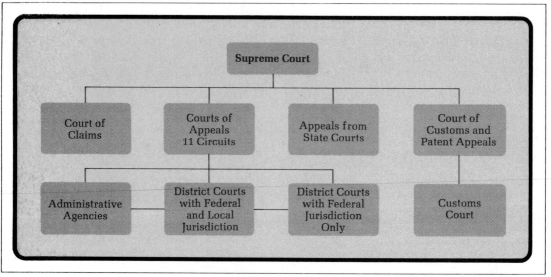

Figure 11.1 Major Units in the U.S. Court System

Executive Power and Constitutional Restraints: The Supreme Court and the President

The Case of the Cherokee Nation

At the beginning of the nineteenth century, the Cherokee Indian tribe was the largest and the most important single tribe in the southeastern United States. Its settled, advanced culture was based on agriculture; its members communicated through a written language of their own devising; its government was based on an elective chief and a two-chamber legislature. Although it had sided with Great Britain in the Revolutionary War and had continued the struggle with the ex-colonial "borderers" until 1794, it negotiated a peace treaty at that time that it scrupulously observed for the next three decades.

Then in 1828 two disasters befell the Cherokee nation simultaneously. Gold was discovered on Cherokee land by a prospecting White man. At about the same time, Andrew Jackson, himself a "borderer" and famous Indian fighter, was elected President of the United States. Immediately, a process now drearily familiar was set in motion. One of Jackson's first acts was to push through Congress "The Indian Removal Act," which granted the President authority to drive all Indian tribes west of the Mississippi. Following Jackson's lead, the Georgia legislature declared all treaties with the Cherokee Nation to be null and void. Former Cherokee lands were then distributed to interested Whites through a lottery system.

John Ross, the tribal chief, appealed in vain to President Jackson to halt the seizure. Appeals to other popularly elected public officials proved equally futile. But the Cherokee Nation still retained one last defense. The Georgia legislature's action was in flagrant violation of the treaty the Cherokee tribe had contracted with the federal government. It also ran afoul of the Fifth Amendment's prohibition against deprivation of property without due process of law. On these grounds, the Cherokee Nation carried its case to the United States Supreme Court. The Court first attempted to duck the controversy but was eventually prevailed upon to hear the case. In a statement affirming the "original natural rights [of the Cherokees] . . . and the settled doctrine of the law of nations," it pronounced the actions of the Georgia legislature as legally void.

President Jackson was furious. "John Marshall [the Chief Justice] has rendered his decision; now let him enforce it," he retorted. As Jackson knew very well, he proposed the impossible. A court of elderly jurists, lacking even the semblance of executive support, could never hope to reverse the actions of a popularly elected legislature. The Court and the Constitution had not stopped a determined legislature and a determined executive. In short order, a new federal treaty was signed with an unrepresentative small group of the Cherokee Nation, gold prospectors and other settlers poured in, and General Winfield Scott was sent to drive the Cherokees off their ancestral lands and burn their houses. Thus began the long march along the "trail of tears" to Oklahoma — a march during which 4,000 of the 14,000 tribesmen perished.

Harry Truman and the Steel Seizure Case

Somewhat more than a century later, President Harry S Truman found himself in an awkward, even alarming, position. American troops were at that time jointly engaged with South Korean troops in a desperate effort to hold the line at the 38th parallel against North Korean and Chinese Communist troops. In this effort they were dependent on the production of steel for helmets, shells, battleships, and warplanes. Yet federal arbitration boards had twice unsuccessfully attempted to mediate a wage dispute between the major steel companies and their employees, and the United Steelworkers of America had announced its intention of calling a strike to enforce its demands. The walkout was set for April 9, 1952.

In the hours before the threatened strike was to begin, the President reviewed his remaining options. Allowing the strike to proceed was politically and morally unthinkable in time of war. Further attempts at mediation were clearly futile. The Taft-Hartley Labor Disputes Act of 1947 had given him the authority to order striking workers back to work for an eight-day "cooling off" period if their strike would seriously endanger the public welfare. But Truman, who had centered his 1948 Presidential campaign as a Democrat on the "antilabor" features of the Taft-Hartley Act, could not bring himself to invoke its provisions. Relying instead on his general constitutional responsibility to maintain the security and welfare of the nation, he ordered his Secretary of Commerce to seize and operate the steel mills in the name of the federal government pending settlement of the dispute.

The mills complied with the seizure order but sought a federal court injunction restraining Secretary Sawyer from maintaining control of the mills. Because the dispute raised issues of urgent national importance, the Supreme Court accepted an appeal from the district court with unusual speed. On June 2 it ordered President Truman to return the mills to their former owners. The President promptly complied.

Public opinion was favorable to the outcome, and editorial comment echoed popular sentiment in portraying the Court's decision as a reaffirmation of the principle that even the President is firmly bound by the restraints of the Constitution.

Largely obscured by the excitement of the case was its most significant feature. Despite the national emergency the threatened strike created, despite the political embarrassment he sustained, President Truman unhesitatingly complied with the Supreme Court's directive. On all sides it was simply taken for granted that as the Court spoke, so would the President act.

This assumption is itself remarkable. As we have seen, President Jackson's violation of the Constitution a century before was far more flagrant, but he was strongly supported by public opinion. In the early nineteenth century the President could argue that his interpretation of the Constitution was as valid as the Court's. By the mid-twentieth century, this argument was unthinkable. Not only were Presidents to be bound by the Constitution; the Supreme Court alone could authoritatively declare what this document specified. This effective preemption of exclusive final constitutional interpretation by a tribunal of nine men—having neither Congress' power of the purse, nor the President's control over the military, nor the mandate of popular election that both Congress and the President possess—is ultimately the most dramatic element of the steel seizure case.

To understand how the Supreme Court has obtained this extraordinary ascendancy, it is necessary to go back to the cases in which the power of judicial review was first established.

A Broad, If Ambiguous, Grant of Authority: The Supreme Court and the Constitution

The Supreme Court's Right of Judicial Review: An Implicit Power

In what is known as the supremacy clause the Constitution declares that

This Constitution, and the Laws of the United States which shall be made in pursuance thereof . . . shall be the supreme Law of the Land;

*and the Judges in every State shall be bound thereby, any Thing in the
Constitution or Laws of any State to the Contrary notwithstanding.*

In this clause the framers were anticipating conflicts between state law and
laws of the federal government, and asserting that federal laws were to be
binding.

One might expect, therefore, that the framers would have said *who* was
to interpret the Constitution and to decide when various laws were in
conflict with it. But they did not. In particular they did not explain just
what role the Supreme Court was to play in judicial review.

The lack of explicit definition of the role of the Supreme Court perhaps
was deliberate. The framers knew that not all controversial questions could
be settled at a single convention. Had the delegates at Philadelphia proposed giving an elite body of life-tenure judges the authority to veto all statutes and acts of government contrary to their interpretation of the Constitution, the convention would almost certainly have broken up. States'
righters and populist democrats would have strongly objected. However, to
have failed to provide for a Federal Supreme Court of broad, if ambiguous,
responsibilities for guarding the Constitution would equally have alienated
the Federalists and Constitutionalists. All things considered, the wisest
course—and the one adopted at Philadelphia—was to establish a guardian
agency of great but uncertain potential and then leave it to define and test
the effective reach of its powers amid the unfolding political conflicts of
the future.

Hamilton's Support of Judicial Review

If the Constitutional Convention remained silent about judicial review,
not all of the delegates themselves were so constrained. Alexander Hamilton used *The Federalist Papers* to speak specifically to the role of the
Supreme Court within the scheme of the new government. His argument
was that the idea of judicial review by judges appointed for life was not inconsistent with majoritarian democracy. Two assumptions support his
position: First, all men are subject to the temptations of shortsighted ambition and self-interest; second, the Constitution reflects the fundamental
will of the American people, whereas acts of a legislature represent no
more than the preferences of temporary majorities.

Given these assumptions, Hamilton has little trouble showing that a constitutional government cannot depend on legislators' judgments of the constitutionality of their own acts. Legislators are men, and subject to the passions of men; self-interest will blind them to discrepancies between what
they desire and what the Constitution permits. A disinterested body external to the legislature—such as the Supreme Court—must perform the
function for which self-review by the legislature is insufficient. Only thus
can the American people be assured that their will, as embodied in the

Constitution, will remain supreme over the will of their temporary representatives in Congress.

Hamilton's first assumption might seem to undermine the claims of *any* group of men to sit in judgment on the constitutionality of an act of government. What makes the Supreme Court a more disinterested judge? Hamilton answers this question squarely. Supreme Court judges, he acknowledges, are no different from legislators and executives in their motives. They are, however, less to be feared. Lacking "influence over either the sword or the purse," the Court can exercise "no direction over either the strength or the wealth of the community." It can employ "neither FORCE nor WILL but merely JUDGMENT" in reaching a decision; it must judge "in accordance with rules that other agencies have prescribed," and must ultimately "depend upon the aid of the executive arm even for the efficacy of its judgments."

From these arguments Hamilton's chief conclusions all follow. The "least dangerous" branch of government offers no serious threat to the other two branches, or to the public generally. The dangers are quite different: that the judiciary will lose its independence, becoming absorbed into one of the other two branches; or that, in its isolation, it will prove ineffective in maintaining the rights of the citizens under the Constitution. Independent life tenure for the justices thus strengthens this "weakest of the three departments of power." The Constitution is intended to protect the enduring interests of the American people, but the Court will prove unable to uphold minority rights and basic freedoms if its members are subject to removal with every change in the mood of the electorate or its representatives in the government. Knowledge that a politically independent body of learned and honored men will refuse to enforce unconstitutional statutes will serve, Hamilton goes on, as a good influence in keeping the other branches of the government within constitutional bounds. Judicial review, he concludes, is therefore a necessary balancing mechanism for any popular government. *Elected* legislatures and executives are needed to assure a government responsive to the short-term preferences of the people; but so also an independent body is needed to guard the more enduring principles.

Hamilton's view was eventually to prevail, but not until two explosive political issues were settled. Lined up against Hamilton's position was, first, the argument that the Congress, as the constitutionally established legislature for the Republic, was the institution best suited to pass final judgment on the meaning of the Constitution. Alternatively, those committed to state "sovereignty" believed that the state supreme courts were fully empowered to interpret the Constitution in relation to the laws of the various states. It can be seen that two issues had to be resolved, one stemming from the ambiguities in "separation of powers" and the second stemming from ambiguities in "federalism." The first was resolved in favor of the Court over Congress; the second was resolved in favor of the federal government over the states. Let us look at the two landmark decisions.

Establishing the Right to Decide:
The Marbury and McCulloch Decisions

As early as the mid-1790s two factions were contesting for control of the Presidency. One faction, the Federalists, was led by John Adams (who became President in 1796), and the other was led by Thomas Jefferson. The Supreme Court was caught up in this bitter factional fight. During the election contest between Adams and Jefferson in 1800 several justices used their position as a forum for partisan speeches on behalf of Adams and the Federalist party.

The Marbury Case:
Cornerstone of Judicial Review

The massive popular endorsement of the Jeffersonian party at the polls in 1800 threatened the Supreme Court as an independent institution. The challenge was raised when outgoing President Adams, who had appointed as Chief Justice the outspoken Federalist John Marshall, rushed through a series of "midnight appointments" of new federal judges. With good reason, the supporters of Jefferson accused Adams of attempting to entrench in the judicial branch of government those Federalist views he had been unable to sustain in its elected branches.

It was clear that there would be a trial of strength between the President, controlled by the Jeffersonians, and the courts, controlled by the Federalists, and an issue was soon found: In its last-minute haste to pack the judiciary with Federalists, the Adams administration had neglected to deliver to William Marbury his commission to be justice of the peace for the District of Columbia. President Jefferson's secretary of state, James Madison, refused to deliver the commission, and Marbury sued for a writ of mandamus compelling him to do so. This suit placed the Marshall Court in an awkward position. The justices knew that Madison had not the slightest intention of delivering the commission to Marbury, and if the Court issued a writ of mandamus it would mean an open struggle with the executive branch responsible for enforcement of the writ. This tension between the executive branch and the judiciary would merely expose the Court's impotence and quicken the demand for the destruction of judicial independence. Yet simply to concede Madison's right to deny Marbury his commission would be a humiliating surrender.

Chief Justice Marshall was equal to the challenge. In an opinion that laid the cornerstone of judicial review, he granted to Jefferson his momentary objective while establishing a precedent of greater long-run importance. Jefferson and Madison's refusal to deliver the commission to Marbury, he wrote in his opinion, was patently illegal. The Supreme Court, however, lacked jurisdiction in this case. For although Congress, in the Judiciary Act of 1789, empowered the Court to issue writs of mandamus, that section of the law was contrary to the Constitution and thus was invalid.

As a masterpiece of judicial strategy, *Marbury* v. *Madison* (1803)[1] has never been equaled. Marshall managed to divert the attention of both parties from the petty quarrel to what was undoubtedly the most significant element in the decision—the bold assertion that the Supreme Court, on the basis of *its* interpretation of the Constitution, was empowered to set limits to what Congress could prescribe.

From the perspective of the twentieth century, *Marbury* v. *Madison* looms as the case that decisively established the Supreme Court's right to define the limits of governmental activity. This power of the Court has been used sparingly, however. Only 85 acts or parts of acts have been declared unconstitutional in the 170 years since *Marbury* v. *Madison*. Some of these acts have been very important ones, but most constitutional scholars believe that the significance of judicial review is not so much in the statutes declared unconstitutional as in the threat of a Supreme Court veto.

Marbury v. *Madison* served a second purpose nearly as significant as establishing judicial review. In 1800 localist impulses were still powerful in the new nation, and the Federalists saw in the Supreme Court an agency of great potential power for cementing national unity. By bringing a substantial measure of uniformity to judicial interpretations of federal law and the Constitution, and by giving an expansive construction to the constitutional powers of the federal government, they hoped to offset what they saw as dangerous tendencies toward secessionism. *Marbury* was an important step toward this end, for if the Court could hold the legislation of a coequal branch of government invalid, it could certainly do the same with regard to state legislation. But the contest between nationalist and localist forces was too explosive to be settled through a single judicial decision, and Marshall knew that the Court's own legitimacy was still too shaky for it to attempt any dramatic initiatives at this time.

By the end of President Madison's second term, however, Marshall felt sufficiently confident to lead the Court in his chosen direction. There followed a succession of landmark decisions in which the full weight of the Court was thrown behind the expansion and consolidation of the federal government's powers. We can here consider only one—*McCulloch* v. *Maryland* (1819)[2]—by common consent, John Marshall's greatest decision, and quite possibly the Supreme Court's single most consequential statement concerning the relation of the Constitution to the organization of the American government.

The McCulloch Case: The Principle of the Federal Government over the State

The *McCulloch* case arose from the efforts of the Maryland state legislature to protect the banks it had chartered against "outside" competition

[1] *Marbury* v. *Madison* 1 Cranch 137 (1803).
[2] *McCulloch* v. *Maryland* 4 Wheaton 316 (1819).

through the imposition of a tax on other banks. Of competing banks, the most feared and most unwanted was the Bank of the United States, which an act of Congress had established in 1816 to help finance the economic growth of the nation. McCulloch, cashier of the Baltimore branch of the Bank of the United States, refused to pay a $15,000 annual fee to the State of Maryland or to affix Maryland tax stamps to the bank notes he issued. Maryland obtained a judgment against McCulloch in one of its county courts, arguing that within its own borders it could tax as it pleased — even if it were taxing a bank founded by the United States Congress. The Bank's lawyers replied that Maryland's claim would hopelessly restrict the federal government's economic powers. The Maryland State Court of Appeals rejected their argument, so the Bank appealed to the United States Supreme Court. Here was a clear clash of federal versus state power.

Marshall, who fully agreed with the Bank's contention, rejected the argument that the powers of the federal government had been delegated to it by the sovereign states. Marshall wrote that the Constitution came into being as an act of a *sovereign people* and that all levels of government — state and federal — derived their authority from this sovereign instrument. No one level of government can therefore claim a natural preeminence over the others, he said; all must acknowledge their dependence on a single extraordinary expression of the collective national will. But precisely because this expression of national will happened rarely, it must not be narrowly interpreted in a manner befitting a routine legislative act: "We must never forget that it is a *constitution* we are expounding," he said.

We are in error, Marshall held, if we think that because a specific power is not listed in the Constitution, the national government lacks the constitutional authority to adopt necessary measures. A document "adapted to the various crises of human affairs," generous and flexible enough in scope to accommodate an uncertain future, will contain no such listing. The Constitution empowers the Congress "To make all Laws which shall be necessary and proper for carrying into Execution the . . . Powers vested by this Constitution in the Government of the United States." This clause of the Constitution, Marshall argues, gives the federal government broad powers:

> Let the end be legitimate, let it be within the scope of the constitution, and all means which are appropriate, which are plainly adapted to that end, which are not prohibited, but consistent with the letter and spirit of the constitution, are constitutional. . . .

The Maryland tax, which carries with it "the power to destroy," creates a clear impediment to the operation of an agency properly related to the goals of the federal government; therefore it must fall as constitutionally invalid.

The *McCulloch* opinion is an important landmark in the creation of the unique place of the Supreme Court as the interpreter of the fundamental law of the Union. The Supreme Court, in the *McCulloch* case, justifies both the expansion of federal power and the role of the Court in adjudicating disputes between the states and the federal government.

The Struggle for Judicial Supremacy: The Supreme Court as Regulator of the Economy

Throughout much of its history, the Supreme Court has remained a storm center of controversy. All adversary proceedings result in some losses to someone, and the natural impulse of the loser is to turn on the institution that gave the verdict. By all odds, however, the most sustained, serious, and widely supported challenge to the power of the Court occurred in 1937, at the beginning of President Franklin D. Roosevelt's second term of office. Not since the opening days of the Marshall Court had judicial independence been placed in such jeopardy.

The route to this near disaster for the Court is instructive to trace. Its starting point lies at the close of the Civil War. John Marshall's vision of one nation united under a federal constitution and a vigorous national government had become a firm reality by then through force of arms. The Supreme Court was now free to turn its attention to another concern: the relationship of the government to the economy. For the next seventy years, the Court saw as its dominant responsibility the maintenance of legal conditions favorable to the rapid growth of industrial capitalism. Both the federal and the state legislatures were checked if their actions threatened free enterprise. The effect of this self-appointed mission was to involve the Court ever more deeply with specific policies of the other branches of government.

In its usual manner, the Court embarked cautiously and tentatively on its mission. For some time, it was distracted by unsolved problems of the Civil War—most particularly, by cases involving the citizenship status of the newly emancipated Black. In 1883, however, the Court abandoned all efforts to protect Black people from legal oppression and popular prejudice. From then on its major work had to do with the economy, and by 1890 its decisions in economic controversies had formed a consistent pattern. This pattern, briefly described, was the preservation of unregulated, free enterprise.

The Due Process Clause Applied to the Economy

The Court held that the United States Constitution prohibited both the state and federal governments from interfering with competition in the marketplace. This legal case rested on several arguments. The foremost was the "due process" clause of the Fourteenth Amendment, which provided that "No State shall . . . deprive any person of life, liberty, or property, without due process of law," and which was intended to protect emancipated slaves from state action of a kind long prohibited at a federal level by the Fifth Amendment. This clause was almost immediately preempted by powerful corporate interests, whose lawyers urged the Court to interpret it as a constitutional barrier to limitations on profit. At first, some justices expressed astonishment at the proposal: At most, a strict reading of the due process clause would seem to require that state governments follow regular legal procedures of due notice and public hearings in regulating private property. But a dominant business opinion sustained by well-financed legal arguments reshaped this view. The due process clause of the Fourteenth Amendment emerged as a constitutional guarantee that owners of private property could enter a successful suit in court against virtually all forms of state regulation beyond those narrowly addressed to protecting the health and safety of the citizen.

The Court's Restriction of the Federal Government's Power over the Economy

Limitations imposed by the Supreme Court on the powers of the states to regulate business were extended to the federal government. The Constitution gave the Congress the power to regulate interstate commerce, but like all constitutional phrases, there was no clear and automatic definition of these terms. What was "commerce"? When did it become "interstate commerce"? What did the word "regulate" mean? For each of these questions the Court consistently gave answers that restricted the power of the federal government over the economy. In effect, the decisions provided a legal underpinning for the untrammeled and unregulated growth of American business. Had the industrialists of the period redrafted the Constitution, they could hardly have devised a concept more suited to their needs.

Hammer v. Dagenhart: Child Labor

The increasing subjectivity of the Court's interpretation of the Constitution was starkly illustrated in the notorious case of *Hammer v. Dagenhart* (1918).[3] For several years prior to World War I, congressional reformers had tried to prohibit mine and factory owners from employing young children. National legislation was required, because state governments that prohibited this source of cheap labor risked losing industrial firms to other states that allowed it. Lawyers noted that in a series of recent decisions the Court had upheld federal laws prohibiting the transportation of lottery tickets, prostitutes, and adulterated food and drugs across state lines. It would seem, then, that Congress could make child labor unprofitable by banning the interstate shipments of products produced with child labor. Acting on

---

[3] *Hammer v. Dagenhart* 247 U.S. 251 (1918).

In 1918 the Supreme Court declared that the attempt by Congress to ban child labor was unconstitutional.   (*Photo: National Child Labor Committee*)

this advice, Congress banned shipment of such products in the Child Labor Act of 1916.

A Mr. Dagenhart shortly afterwards brought suit in a local court to prevent enforcement of the act against a North Carolina cotton mill employing two of his now legally underage children. Lower courts upheld Mr. Dagenhart, and the case was appealed all the way through the North Carolina court system to the Supreme Court. Here Justice Day, speaking for a narrow 5–4 majority, upheld the lower courts by declaring that Congress had exceeded its constitutional powers in passing the law. Since Article I, Section 8 of the Constitution seemed to grant Congress unrestricted power to "regulate . . . Commerce among the several States," the Justice had some problem explaining how he had reached this conclusion. If this clause were read literally, he argued, and if "to regulate" were interpreted to encompass "to prohibit," then only congressional self-restraint could prevent the federal legislature from using this power to control all production dependent on an interstate market—a possibility too unthinkable to be held consistent with the intentions of the framers of the Constitution. It was true that on previous occasions the Supreme Court had recognized the power of Congress to bar certain "noxious" products from interstate commerce (liquor, dangerous explosives, adulterated eggs) or products that had harmful effects (lottery tickets, immoral women). But Justice Day distinguished these cases from one involving clothing, which—however it was produced—was neither intrinsically evil nor likely to produce evil results. The public welfare might well require "some limitations upon the right to employ children in mines and factories," and some uniformity among such laws might be desirable. But such limitations must be sought at the level of the several state governments, for "In interpreting the Constitution it must never be forgotten that the nation is made up of States to which . . . the powers not expressly delegated to the national government are reserved."

The decision reduced federal power substantially. The Court seemed to say that the federal government could exercise only those powers *expressly* listed in the Constitution, whereas previous interpretations of the Constitution made it a flexible document under which governmental power could expand as the times demanded. Justice Day's reading of the Constitution made it a much more restrictive document. The two interpretations represent polar opposite views of the nature of the Constitution and of the government it creates.

On purely technical grounds, *Hammer* v. *Dagenhart* marks a low point of judicial craftsmanship. In a dissenting opinion, Justice Oliver Wendell Holmes sharply criticized its logic. Justice Day could not explain why Congress was constitutionally entitled to use its powers under the commerce clause to strike at some kinds of evils, but not others. Congress could stop prostitution but not end the employment of ten-year-old children in the mines and mills. The weakness of the logic of the decision did much to weaken the respect of professional lawyers for the reasoning of the incumbent justices. And there were larger considerations. The revered Supreme Court had stood before the nation as an agency that could twist and bend the words of the Constitution to bring protection to the giant corporations that needed it least, while leaving small children subject to continuing economic exploitation. And Congress now found itself without any lawful means of remedying the evil.

FDR's Battles with the Supreme Court

In a period of normalcy, the Court would perhaps have gone unchallenged. But in October 1929 the Wall Street stock market collapsed, and with it the economic certainties of American capitalism. The idea of corporate immunity to government control was thrown on the defensive, as ruined speculators, bankrupt merchants, unemployed laborers, and farmers facing foreclosure joined in the demand for sweeping governmental action. From this point forward the Supreme Court became the defense against a massive coalition that was clamoring for a new economic order.

Thus as the economic crisis deepened, a governmental crisis grew. The reform administration of Franklin D. Roosevelt introduced legislation that attempted to deal with the crisis. But these new laws often ran into the roadblock of the Supreme Court. By 1935 the Court was rejecting as unconstitutional most of the major innovations of the New Deal. Between 1935 and 1937 the Court held constitutionally invalid a total of twelve congressional statutes—nearly one-seventh of all the federal laws so held in the nearly two centuries during which the Court had exercised judicial review. The Court overturned a succession of statutes designed to bring relief to the nation's farmers, to the oil industry, the coal industry, and the like.

The Court reasoned that it had no choice but to disallow these laws; they clearly went against constitutional provisions. And the Court appeared to believe that it could ignore the rising tide of public disapproval, congressional annoyance, and Presidential frustration. In other words, the Court believed that it was above politics and merely carrying out the "automatic" task of comparing laws to the Constitution and rejecting those that did not fit the provisions. In fact, as events showed, it was wrong on both counts. It could not ignore political currents, nor were its decisions inevitable ones based on the clear language of the Constitution. Other justices would see things differently.

Roosevelt's "Court-Packing" Scheme: For a time it appeared that the justices who opposed the New Deal legislation would succeed in halting all governmental efforts to deal with an economic crisis of unparalleled severity and duration. But this impression was always an illusion. The life-tenure appointments of the justices offered them seeming protection against popular sentiment; but in the end their power rested on the acceptance of their legitimacy, and this legitimacy was now fraying rapidly. President Roosevelt, fresh from an overwhelming electoral endorsement of his first term in office, tried to "pack" the Court through a law allowing him to add new justices of his own political persuasion. This was blocked, but it was a mere skirmish in the larger battle over judicial supremacy. And that battle was lost by the conservatives when the "swing men" on the Court, Justice Roberts and Chief Justice Hughes, decided to preserve that institution from a confrontation it could not win by making, in the newspaper language of the day, the "switch in time that saved nine."

In quick succession, measures hardly distinguishable from those found unconstitutional by 6–3 majorities were now upheld by a majority of five justices. On March 29, 1937, while the debate over the "court-packing" scheme was at its height in Congress, the Court found that the Fourteenth Amendment's due process clause no longer stood in the way—as it had in New York barely a year before—of a minimum-wage law in the State of Washington. Two weeks later, Chief Justice Hughes declared that Congress had the right to establish a National Labor Relations Board to deal with conflicts over union organization and collective bargaining rights. Four dissenting justices pointed out that in a long train of decisions, including several of the previous two years, the Court had ruled so sweeping a grant of power to be unconstitutional; but the Chief Justice brusquely responded that "These cases are not controlling here." And in 1941, in a case involving a Georgia lumber mill, the precedent created in *Hammer* v. *Dagenhart* was explicitly repudiated.

The change in the Supreme Court opened the way for wide government regulation of the economy. In a clash with the other branches of the government, the Supreme Court finally backed down. But, of course, this ought not to lead one to the conclusion that the Court is the weakest branch of the government, for it had dominated economic policy making for almost half a century despite the pressures from the elected branches of the government. It is a powerful institution but, as the events of the 1930s showed, not all-powerful.

Separate But Not Equal:
The Supreme Court and Racial Discrimination

In the years following the Civil War the Supreme Court's record shows that the Court did little to eradicate racial discrimination—in fact, some decisions reinforced it. In 1876 the Court drastically restricted a statute aimed at the Ku Klux Klan. In the same year it struck down two provisions of an act designed to secure Black voting rights under the Fifteenth Amendment.

The most famous case of the post-Civil War period was *Plessy* v. *Ferguson* (1896)[4]—involving a Louisiana law requiring segregated railroad facilities—in which the Court's decision replaced the principle of "equal protection of the laws" with the racist doctrine of "separate but equal." A nearly unanimous Court held that although the object of the Fourteenth Amendment was undoubtedly to enforce the absolute equality of the two races before the law,

> in the nature of things it could not have intended to abolish distinctions based on color, or to enforce social, as distinct from political equality, or a commingling of the races on terms unsatisfactory to either. . . . Legislation is powerless to eradicate racial instincts or to abolish distinctions based upon physical differences, and the attempt to do so can only result in accentuating the difficulties of the present situation. . . . If one race be inferior to the other socially, the Constitution of the United States cannot put them on the same plane.

And so, for the next half-century, the Supreme Court turned its back on America's Black minority. The one exception lay in the field of voting rights. Voting enjoyed a special status under the specific prohibitions of the Fifteenth Amendment, and the Court did deal with the more flagrant attempts to deny Blacks this most elemental of civic rights. As early as 1915,

[4] *Plessy* v. *Ferguson* 163 U.S. 537 (1896).

the Court invalidated Oklahoma's "grandfather clause," which required a literacy test of all voters but exempted all lineal descendants of those who had voted before January 1, 1866. Some ten years later it struck down efforts by Texas to bar Blacks from voting in the important primaries of the Democratic party. By the end of World War II, the unconstitutionality of any electoral device barring racial minorities from the polls was no longer at issue.

Civil Rights After World War II

World War II substantially transformed the status of Black Americans, though its effects were not immediately recognized. Blacks moved northward in large numbers from southern tenant farms to obtain relatively well-paying jobs in the defense industries, and most of them stayed on afterwards as semiskilled laborers to become critical "swing" constituencies in close elections in the northern cities.

These various developments evoked little immediate response within Congress; but President Harry S Truman, spurred both by personal conviction and by awareness of the strategic importance of Black voters in the northern industrial states, desegregated the armed services by executive order, created a new Fair Employment Practices Committee (FEPC) within the Civil Service Commission, and established a Civil Rights Commission to recommend and publicize further initiatives to reduce racial discrimination in public life.

The NAACP's Fight Against Racial Discrimination

The National Association for the Advancement of Colored People, convinced through experience that Congress could not be made responsive to its demands, decided to expand its long-standing fight in the courts by launching a series of carefully chosen suits with the judiciary to widen the range of constitutionally protected civil rights. Elaborate planning was needed, for experience had shown that litigation seldom brought basic social reforms. The plaintiff might run out of funds or lose interest in the case before it had been pressed to conclusion; he might compromise to accomplish his own purposes before the broad constitutional issues had been raised in appellate courts; or the courts, following their usual practice, might find nonconstitutional issues on which to settle the case. Even if the cases were won, the courts might define the constitutional issue so narrowly that the individual case would have little effect on the status of 15 million people. Some of the novel tactics — pro-NAACP articles in law review journals, for instance, tended to create a favorable climate among external groups (including particularly the United States Attorney General's office) who came to regard themselves as "friends of the court" in the matter—created uneasiness among conservative justices who felt that determinations of legal rights should not be influenced by pressure tactics and demonstrations of popular support. Nevertheless, the NAACP was strikingly successful in a number of cases involving state-supported discrimination in public transportation and housing.

The NAACP's Fight for Equal Education

But the biggest battle for the NAACP still lay ahead. Midway through the twentieth century, the schools of all the southern and border states were still segregated by law, and racially segregated housing patterns resulted in *de facto* segregation in a high percentage of northern schools as well. And education, as every Black parent well knew, decisively determined the life chances of his child. For this very reason the question of racial segregation in the public schools was the most explosive civil rights issue that could be placed on the Supreme Court agenda. Not until the constitutional foundations of racial desegregation had been firmly built up in other, less sensitive areas did the Court show a willingness to hear public school cases on appeal from the lower courts.

As first formulated, the crucial question before the Court appeared to be one of substantive equality. To meet the requirement that no person be denied the equal protection of the laws, the Court, in *Plessy* v. *Ferguson*, had assented that "separate" facilities for Blacks could be and were in fact "equal" to those provided Whites. That such facilities were inferior in almost all respects was common knowledge, but the Supreme Court for half a century had declined to look behind the factual determinations of the lower courts to assess the extent to which the facilities were in fact equal.

Sweatt v. Painter: It was a major victory for the opponents of racial discrimination, then, when the Supreme Court agreed to inquire closely into educational conditions for Black Americans in state-supported institutions. A key case was *Sweatt* v. *Painter* (1950).[5] Sweatt had been denied admission to the University of Texas Law School solely because he was Black. A trial court agreed that he had been unconstitutionally denied the equal protection of the laws, but continued the case for six months to give the state time to provide equal facilities for Blacks. In 1947 Texas opened the doors of a makeshift law school, with a faculty of five and a library of a few thousand volumes, to 23 Black students. Sweatt refused to accept this overnight institution as the equivalent of a law school with a student body of 850, a library of 65,000 volumes, and a distinguished faculty. He carried his case to the Supreme Court. The Court had little difficulty in finding it a matter of fact that the Whites-only University of Texas Law School was

[5] *Sweatt* v. *Painter* 339 U.S. 629 (1950).

substantially superior in its facilities. In a noteworthy passage, Chief Justice Vinson observed that a

> *law school, the proving ground for legal learning and practice, cannot be effective in isolation from the individuals and institutions with which the law interacts. . . . The law school to which Texas is willing to admit petitioner excludes from its student body members of the racial groups which number 85 percent of the population of the State and include most of the lawyers, witnesses, jurors, judges, and other officials with whom petitioner inevitably will be dealing when he becomes a member of the Texas bar.*

"With such a substantial and significant segment of society excluded," the Chief Justice asserted, no school, whatever its material facilities, could offer Sweatt an equal opportunity to acquire the experiences and social contacts required for successful participation in a nation dominated by Whites.

With *Sweatt* v. *Painter*, the long struggle to establish the fallacy of the "separate but equal" doctrine came to a close. It remained only to make clear to the general public how these principles bore on the continuing segregation of the vast public school system.

Brown v. Board of Education of Topeka: The NAACP believed it had at last found the ideal test case in *Brown v. Board of Education of Topeka* (1954)[6] for compelling the Supreme Court to address itself directly to the constitutional status of the "separate but equal" doctrine. The schools for Black children in Topeka, Kansas, were equal to White schools in all respects — physical plant and equipment, curricula, courses available, qualifications of and quality of teachers. Yet the crucial difference, and the one to be cited by the Court, was that Black children were deprived of the right to attend school with White children, and of course the opposite held as well. In 1954 a unanimous Court ruled that "In the field of public education the doctrine of 'separate but equal' has no place." The assertion of the Court was that "separate educational facilities are inherently unequal."

With this decision the Supreme Court reshaped the agenda of modern American politics. Racial discrimination could no longer be regarded as consistent with the constitutional principle of equality before the law. For another ten years, however, the judiciary was left to struggle on practically alone with the enormous task of implementing the government's newly defined legal and moral responsibility to Black citizens. The executive branch provided little aid in this task, and only in 1964 did the Congress begin to respond positively.

The conflict over desegregation of the schools is a highly sensitive, complicated problem that cannot be easily and readily solved. It is far from being settled, as our Controversy at the end of this chapter makes clear.

---

[6] *Brown v. Board of Education of Topeka, Kansas* 347 U.S. 483 (1954).

The Supreme Court
and American Politics: An Overview

To some observers the Supreme Court has always been an anomaly in America. What place, in a society based on principles of government accountability through elections, has a body of appointed officials enjoying life tenure? And in a government where one power is supposed to balance another, what place has a body with supposedly "supreme" power and ultimate decision over the constitutionality of laws? But as the description of some of the highlights of the Court's history should have made clear, the U.S. Supreme Court is by no means all-powerful.

Limitations on the Power of the Court

For one thing, the Supreme Court decides on the constitutionality of laws within the framework of the Constitution and the precedents of previous cases. This greatly limits the Court's discretion to write into a decision anything it sees fit. Some observers claim that the Supreme Court's activity is therefore essentially a mechanical one; justices apply no discretion of their own, but merely compare the clear words of the Constitution against the act of Congress or the state legislature that is in question. Justice Roberts of the Supreme Court stated this position:

> It is sometimes said that the court assumes a power to overrule or control the action of the people's representatives. . . . This is a misconception. . . . When an act of Congress is appropriately challenged in the courts as not conforming to the constitutional mandate, the judicial branch of the Government has only one duty — to lay the article of the Constitution which is invoked beside the statute which is challenged and to decide whether the latter squares with the former.

Most observers of the Supreme Court, however, would disagree with Justice Roberts. Indeed, this particular disclaimer of independent judgment was made in one of the most controversial decisions of the Supreme Court: the one that struck down the first Agricultural Adjustment Act on which the hope of millions of desperate farmers had rested. Comparing the statute being challenged with the Constitution to see if the former squared with the latter was hardly a mechanical act. In fact, within a few years, the Supreme Court had changed its mind on the issue.

The point is that the Constitution is rarely clear and unambiguous. Indeed it has survived throughout the years largely by being ambiguous — so that succeeding generations could interpret it to fit the needs and preferences of the times. When the Court rules on the constitutionality of a law it is guided by the Constitution and that limits its discretion; but it still must *interpret* and there it gets discretion. At times in its history it has been criticized for interpreting the Constitution too loosely, at other times for not interpreting it loosely enough. These controversies will continue, for the Court's actions are by no means mechanical.

Political Restraint: Another limitation on the powers of the Court is what may be called a political restraint. A widespread misconception about the Supreme Court is that the Court is a group of men isolated from the mainstream of American politics or the "real world" of America. In some small part this is true. The justices are not up for election; they do stay out of partisan politics; they are not directly visited by lobbyists or constituents. They are, as the founding fathers intended them to be, above politics in this sense.

Yet the justices are by no means cut off from the currents of American politics and from the preferences of the public. For one thing they are appointed by Presidents eager to see certain lines of policy pursued. Franklin D. Roosevelt, thwarted in his attempts at economic reform in the 1930s, appointed justices he believed would read the Constitution permissively when it came to the expansion of federal power. More recently President Nixon appointed justices he believed would reverse what he considered the overpermissiveness of the Court in matters of criminal prosecution. (Table 11.1 shows the current makeup of the court.)

Even after appointment, justices remain attuned to the "temper of the times." Judicial biographies as well as the swings in judicial opinions make it clear that the justices do not just read the Constitution—they read the newspapers as well. It would be an exaggeration to say that the justices "follow the election results"—that is, write their opinions on the basis of what the public seemed to want in the last election. But there is evidence that they have been sensitive to election results. This was seen in the 1930s when the Court turned from an institution acting as a staunch defender of free enterprise against government controls to an institution willing to allow the government to enact a wide range of controls over the economy.

Table 11.1 Members of Supreme Court, 1973

MEMBER	APPOINTED BY	YEAR
William O. Douglas	Roosevelt	1939
William J. Brennan, Jr.	Eisenhower	1957
Potter Stewart	Eisenhower	1959
Byron R. White	Kennedy	1962
Thurgood Marshall	Johnson	1967
Warren E. Burger	Nixon	1969
Harry A. Blackmun	Nixon	1970
Lewis F. Powell, Jr.	Nixon	1971
William H. Rehnquist	Nixon	1971

Self-Imposed Restraints: A further limitation on the power of the Justices is self-imposed. The Court ignores certain issues, even though they may be of major constitutional significance. For instance, it has rarely taken any position on the powers of the President in the area of foreign and military affairs. During the late 1960s and early 1970s, the question was constantly being raised as to the constitutionality of the war in Vietnam. The war was conducted without a declaration of war by the Congress; and yet the power to declare war was expressly given to the Congress in the Constitution. The Vietnam policies of Presidents Johnson and Nixon did clearly raise a constitutional issue. Yet the Court refused to review cases that attempted to challenge the actions of the government in Vietnam. Nor was this a position unique to the Vietnam war. In a number of earlier instances, the Supreme Court had steered clear of issues where the power of the President in the military and foreign policy field was involved.

Overruling by Amendment and by Avoiding Compliance: There is yet another way in which the power of the Supreme Court is limited. Even after it has declared an act unconstitutional the Court can be overruled. One way is through the process of constitutional amendment. This, as we have pointed out, is usually a slow and cumbersome process. But the Sixteenth Amendment directly overruled a Supreme Court decision barring the federal government from levying a federal income tax.

The amendment process is not the only way in which Supreme Court rulings can be negated. The Supreme Court has no direct enforcement arm. Although government officials will usually not openly disobey the decisions of the Court, there are many ways in which determined officials can avoid compliance. In cases where local officials disagree with a Court ruling, they can be very successful in limiting its effect. Two areas of concern where this has been the case involve the Court's decisions on school desegregation and the Court's decisions on barring prayers in the public schools. In each case the Court's decisions have as often been evaded as complied with.

Congressional Control over the Court's Powers: Finally, there are the limitations on the powers of the Supreme Court exercised through congressional powers to approve appointments and to impeach justices for misconduct in office.

Controversy

In the early 1970s the Supreme Court as well as the other federal courts became embroiled in an explosive controversy over the courts' attempts to have schoolchildren bussed in order to achieve desegregation of schools. *Brown* v. *Board of Education of Topeka* had ruled that legally *sanctioned* segregation of the public schools violated the Constitution. But as the years passed, it became clear that abolishing legally sanctioned segregation of the schools would not necessarily eliminate segregated schools. The reason was obvious. In many parts of the country housing patterns had come into existence whereby Black Americans and other minority groups lived in separate sections of metropolitan areas—usually in the center of the city—while Whites lived in other neighborhoods and in the suburbs. If children went to neighborhood schools, they would, in most cases, go to schools that were *de facto* segregated. The decision by some of the courts, therefore, was that only by bussing schoolchildren from one neighborhood to another, or even from one community to another, would racial imbalance be rectified.

One Side

Bussing schoolchildren is the only way to terminate segregated schools that are the result of *de facto* segregation. Under the *Brown* doctrine segregated schools are a violation of the Constitution whether they are the result of state laws or of the housing patterns. To put an end to *de facto* segregated schools, White pupils must be bussed into Black neighborhoods, or even from community to community, and Black students into White areas.

There is also the question of which branch of the government should assume responsibility for enforcing desegregation of the schools. It is the constitutional duty of the courts to do so. The President, the Congress, and state legislatures are powerless to act effectively to foster necessary social change because of political pressures brought to bear on them. To be sure, the courts may not be the best place in which substantive regulations for the desegregation of schools can be formulated, but in the absence of action by the other branches of the government, they are the only place where such necessary action can take place.

The Supreme Court is well aware of the complexity of the problem—it has taken upon itself an enormous task that it has had to carry on alone, with little aid from the executive and the legislative branches of government—and has acted in several instances in writing enforcement decisions on desegregation. Admittedly, the Supreme Court has not made a definitive decision on desegregation, but perhaps this is due to an exercise of judicial sensitivity to the complexity of the issue and the intense, explosive feelings surrounding it. And it may be that in view of the opposition to bussing that mounted with burning intensity, the Court is observing its own directions to the federal district courts in the *Brown* decision: Require the local state officials to move toward integration "with all deliberate speed."

The Other Side

The only way to terminate segregated schools that are the result of *de facto* segregation is to break down the barriers that force Blacks and other minority groups to live in restricted areas. Hence the solution is to get rid of the ghettos. Under the *Brown* doctrine *de facto* segregated schools do not violate the Constitution. Some courts have ruled to this effect: The *Brown* decision, they decided, applies only to those cases where segregation is the result of *discrimination by intent.*

It is the responsibility of the legislature and the executive to enforce desegregation — not that of the courts. If the courts rule that a local district has to bus children from one neighborhood to another to achieve racial balance — or even from one community to another, as some court decisions that demanded the merging of central city and suburban districts would have required — the courts are usurping the lawmaking role of the legislature, ignoring the opinions of the community, and reading the Constitution as they see fit, influenced perhaps by the personal preferences of the justices.

Further, correcting racial imbalance through drawing school boundaries and creating plans for bussing children from one area to another is too sensitive and complicated an issue to be handled by means of the awkward device of adversary proceedings in court.

Besides, court decisions can be circumvented. There is evidence that a host of means to circumvent them were being considered. First, various members of Congress considered introducing a constitutional amendment barring the bussing of children for the purposes of reducing segregation. Second, specific laws were passed — such as the Higher Education Act of 1972, which attempted to restrict the use of bussing for desegregation purposes. (The constitutionality of the laws still, of course, requires a court test.) Third, as might be expected in the light of his views on bussing, President Nixon made new appointments to change the direction of Court decisions on desegregation. And in fact some new appointments he made did turn the Supreme Court from one overwhelmingly in favor of desegregation to a Court more divided on the issue (though still leaning in the activist direction).

Then there is the role of the Supreme Court itself in enforcing desegregation. Granted, the Court took on a stupendous task when it handed down the *Brown* ruling. This is a sociological decision, and such decisions are difficult to enforce; it is not easy to change a person's attitudes, his beliefs, and his way of living. And if, as some think, the courts are the only place where movement toward desegregation can take place, why has not the Court made a definitive enforcement decision rather than, for the most part, leaving the responsibility to the lower courts to effect the desegregation ruling?

This conflict brings to mind another time when the Supreme Court raised a tornado of passionate anti-Court feelings. In the New Deal era of the 1930s the Court came under fire when it persisted in defending big business against the wishes of the people and their elected representatives for regulation of the economy. Then, sensitive to the climate of opinion, the Court eventually reversed its position. As in the 1930s, the bussing issue in the 1970s generated a series of vigorous and bitter attacks directed at the Court by many political forces: by the Congress, by the state legislatures, by the press, and in political campaigns. And, as in the 1930s, again the cry was "legislative usurpation."

Finally, there are the views of the majority of the citizens to be considered. Whether or not the courts are moving against the main current of public opinion is not yet clear. If this is the case, we must ask the question: Has the Court the right to enforce bussing to integrate the schools if such a policy goes against the deeply held convictions of the majority of the citizens?[7]

Suggested Readings

A standard work is Robert G. McClosky's *The American Supreme Court* (Chicago: University of Chicago Press, 1960), as is Alexander Bickel's *The Least Dangerous Branch* (Indianapolis: Bobbs-Merrill, 1962). There are numerous casebooks on constitutional law; a useful one is Alpheus T. Mason and William B. Beaney, eds., *American Constitutional Law* (Englewood Cliffs, N.J.: Prentice-Hall, 1965).

Herbert Jacob, Justice in America (Boston: Little, Brown, 1965), covers many relevant topics not reviewed in this chapter, especially material on the organization of American courts and appellate proceedings. For a broad and provocative view of the role of law in American society, see the collection of essays edited by Robert Paul Wolff, *The Rule of Law* (New York: Simon & Schuster, 1971).

---

[7] *Authors' Note:* As we write this book, the issue rages on the front pages of the newspapers. By the time the book is in the readers' hands, perhaps some new developments will have taken place—new laws of Congress or of the states will have been challenged in the courts; perhaps the Supreme Court will have made a definitive enforcement decision (as we write, the issue is still largely in the lower federal courts); perhaps even a constitutional amendment will have been passed. But because this issue invites strong resistance and heightened feelings of resentment, it appears that the issue will remain part of the American political scene for a long time.

Majority Rule, Minority Rights

12

If you were to ask the average citizen how political decisions are made in the United States, he very likely would answer "by majority vote." In some respects he would be right. A prime "decision rule" of a democracy is majoritarianism. This is a decision rule to which children are introduced very early, often by a "home room" teacher: "Today we must elect someone to represent our class on the student council. We have two nominees, Jennifer and Geoffrey. Write your choice on a piece of paper." When the ballots are counted, the teacher announces the results: "Jennifer gets 17 votes and Geoffrey gets 14. The majority decides, so Jennifer is our representative."

The Majority Decides, with Modifications

Although majoritarianism is a basic decision rule in our political life, it is subject to modifications. There are five of these modifications, as follows:

The Special Majority

There is the *special majority*. On some matters it is thought that the stakes are so significant that a "50 percent plus 1" majority is not large enough, that a larger majority should favor the decision before it is made. For example, a special majority would be required if Congress should pass a piece of legislation by a simple majority vote, 50 percent plus 1, and the President should then veto the legislation. Congress would then have the option of overriding the Presidential veto by a "special" two-thirds majority. The Constitution does not give the President ultimate power over legislation. But it does weigh the President's disapproval seriously, and thus it requires Congress to muster the so-called special majority if it is to pass the bill over his opposition.

The Voting Unit

A further modification of the majority rule concerns the choice of the *voting unit*. Federalism, as we saw in Chapter 10, assigns some responsibilities to units much smaller than the entire nation. Which voters should decide if the schools in Little Rock, Arkansas, are to be integrated—those of the Little Rock school district, those of Arkansas, those of the southern states, or those all over the United States? By shifting a choice to the larger unit, you risk an outcome that differs from what would occur in the smaller unit. The battle over states' rights is not a battle over majority versus minority rule so much as it is a battle over the geographic area within which majority rule is to prevail. When the decision is left to the local community or to the state, majority rule at the national level may be violated. When the decision is shifted to the national level, the majority preferences of the local community may be swept aside.

Plurality Counting

A third modification of the majority rule is *plurality counting,* which has the opposite effect of the special majority. Plurality counting allows the opinion of a group less than a majority to prevail, as long as that group is still larger than any other group. In 1968 Richard Nixon received only 43 percent of the popular vote, but this was more than Humphrey received (41 percent) and more than Wallace received (14 percent), so Nixon won the election. Because only 60 percent of the adult population voted that year, Nixon in effect was supported by approximately 27 percent of the eligible electorate. In fact Presidents are always elected by a minority of the voting-age population. (See Table 12.1.)

The Intense Minority

Another modification of the majoritarian decision rule results less from legal arrangements than it does from practical political considerations. This

Table 12.1   Presidents Are Elected by a Minority of Voting-Age Population

YEAR	PERCENTAGE OF VOTING-AGE CITIZENS VOTING	PERCENTAGE OF POPULAR VOTE RECEIVED BY VICTOR	PERCENTAGE OF VOTING AGE CITIZENS VOTING FOR VICTOR
1948	51.4	49.6	25.5
1952	62.6	55.1	34.5
1956	60.1	57.4	34.5
1960	64.0	49.7	31.8
1964	62.9	61.1	38.4
1968	61.8	43.4	26.8
1972	63.0	60.7	38.2

Source: Based on data from John H. Runyon, Jennifer Verdine, and Sally Runyon, *Source Book of American Presidential Campaign and Election Statistics, 1948–68* (New York: Ungar, 1971).

is the modification introduced by consideration for the *intense minority*. Sometimes a small group of citizens feel intensely about an issue, while the large majority are comparatively indifferent (see Chapter 4). Operating under the rule of thumb which says that the "squeaking wheel gets the grease," the response of authorities will often be to the vocal minority rather than the indifferent majority. In day-to-day politics this informal rule probably prevails more than the constitutional decision rule of strict majoritarianism.

The Constitutional Rights of Minorities

There is a final modification of majority rule: *the constitutional rights of minorities*. This modification is of such importance to American politics that we devote the remainder of the chapter to it. The principle of minority rights has, since the founding of the nation, been in tension with majoritarianism. If "50 percent plus 1" were the only rule for democratic decision making, the majority would be free to do whatever it wished to a minority group—it could take away their livelihoods, their homes, their freedoms, even their lives. And it would all be, by definition, democratic.

The "Tyranny of the Majority"

Many writers, indeed, have warned about the dangers of democratic tyranny—the so-called tyranny of the majority. Such a tyranny is possible. And in some respects it is more to be feared than the tyranny of a smaller group. The chances of successful resistance are, of course, less if a minority group has a majority united against it. Many foreign observers of life in America have commented on the power of public opinion, in particular the tyranny it can exercise over ideas and behavior that are deviant or unpopular. And when public opinion is coupled with the arm of government—that is, when one has a government exercising the will of the majority—it becomes a force that a deviant minority cannot easily resist.

Those who wrote the American Constitution were, as we have said, concerned with this problem. They built a government that operated in many respects to curb the power of the majority. The constitutional institutions of federalism, of checks and balances, of the Bill of Rights all help prevent the concentration of power in the hands of any one group—including the majority. In this, the role of the Supreme Court has been important. The nine justices symbolize in their mode of selection and their lifetime tenure the limitations on the majority built into the constitutional framework. In this chapter we look at the role of the Supreme Court and the Constitution in relation to majority rule and minority rights.

Reconciliation of Majority Rule
with Minority Rights: A Dilemma

The reconciliation of majority rule with minority rights represents one of the great dilemmas of democracy. If majority rule is not an easily acceptable absolute principle, neither is minority rights. Give all rights to all minorities—that is, give all minority groups in society the right to disregard the authority of the government—and one no longer has a society. Rather one has an anarchistic war of all against all. Each of us, after all, is a minority of one and could claim all such rights to ourselves.

But where then does one draw the line? What minorities are to be respected and in relation to what rights? Much of the debate on the nature of democracy—a debate found in the works of scholars but also in the debates on the Constitution and in the various decisions of the Supreme Court—revolves around this question. What rights are so important that they should be protected from the ordinary procedures of democracy whereby the wishes of the larger number become the rules for all? Historically several kinds of rights have been singled out for protection from the wishes of the majority:

1. The right to free speech, a free press, and freedom of assembly.
2. The right to freedom of religion.
3. The right to have one's property protected from the majority or from arbitrary acts of the government.
4. The right of "permanent minorities" to special protection from the majority.

Each of these rights has a somewhat different justification in democratic theory, and each set of rights has received, at one time or another, some special recognition.

The Right to Speak,
to Write, and to Assemble

These three rights—freedom of speech, press, and assembly—are thought by many to be the crucial rights that must be protected from the majority if democracy is to survive. They are provided in the First Amendment to the Constitution, which reads, "Congress shall make no law . . . abridging the freedom of speech, or of the press, or the right of the people peaceably to assemble. . . ." These three rights are what is meant by "civil liberties"; they are also sometimes called "First Amendment freedoms." The First Amendment protects these rights against acts of Congress. Over the years, the Supreme Court has extended the protection so that state governments are also barred from impinging on them.

First Amendment freedoms are central to the working of a democratic system because they are the key to effective majority rule. Effective majority rule depends on knowledge of alternatives, and depends on the ability of those with minority views to try to convince others. Only if there is freedom to present views on all sides of an issue can there be said to be a chance for real choice.

And these freedoms are particularly crucial to the minority, for a minority is politically disadvantaged by its size. It cannot expect to carry the day in governmental policy if it is but a small part of the decision-making unit. And if majority rule is the only accepted route to decision making, its situation would be hopeless as it lost out in one decision after another. But the guarantees of free speech, press, and assembly provide the minority opportunities to convince others to join with it, thereby forming a new majority. Today's minority can become the basis of tomorrow's majority. Put another way, First Amendment freedoms are supposed to prevent any given majority from becoming "frozen" and therefore excessively powerful. The role of the Supreme Court is important. If the majority attempts to repress political opposition or to outlaw picketing or to censor the press, then the Court is, presumably, the institution which blocks the majority.

> *When the channels of opinion and of peaceful persuasion are corrupted or clogged, political correctives can no longer be relied on, and the democratic system is threatened at its most vital point. In that event, the Court, by intervening, restores the processes of democratic government; it does not disrupt them.*[1]

Considerations such as these have given the First Amendment freedoms a special place in democratic thought. Some have claimed that they are "absolute" rights, never to be limited by the power of the majority or by the authority of the government supposedly speaking for the majority. According to this view, the correction for unpopular ideas or unpopular speech is found in the "free marketplace of ideas." No one—neither a minority nor a majority—can legislate truth. Therefore, a free society ought never to bar the expression of the views of any group no matter how unpopular.

Conflicts over the Limits of Free Speech

"Free speech without limitations" sounds like the only acceptable democratic position. But there are counter-arguments. For one thing, such an absolute position for free speech clearly violates the idea of majority rule. Suppose a majority of the American people want to bar some form of speech. What is the "democratic" thing to do under such circumstances— bar the speech and thereby violate the absolute freedom of speech, or allow

---

[1] Robert H. Jackson, *The Struggle for Judicial Supremacy* (New York: 1941), p. 285.

it and thereby violate the principle of majority rule? Such a situation is not merely hypothetical. As we saw in Chapter 3, majorities of the American people have at times favored the prohibition of speeches favoring communism or atheism. And public opinion polls on the issue of obscenity make it clear that if matters were put to a vote, a majority would oppose the distribution of many books and magazines found on newsracks or the screening of many movies currently in theaters.

The examples given above help us understand why conflicts over free speech arise. They arise when the speech endangers some other value that groups of citizens in society hold to be important. Consider some examples.

Libel and Obscenity: The right to say what one wants may be a value, but the right of the individual citizen to be protected against unjustified attacks is also a value. Thus limitations of free speech are found in libel laws that protect citizens from such attacks. Similarly, the right to publish what one wants may be a value, but others value the right to protect their children from exposure to writings that they think will hurt their morals or to protect themselves from speech they find offensive. Thus limitations of free speech are often found in laws controlling pornography.

But, as in most political issues, the general statement of the conflict of principles does not get one very far in practice. One may agree in principle that speech, the press, and movies ought to be free up to the point where they unfairly offend or damage some individual. At that point expression ought to be limited by the laws of libel. But applying the principle in practice is not so easy. For example, at what point does newspaper criticism of a public official become a libelous attack on the basis of which the official can sue the newspaper for damages? These are the issues that the courts—including the Supreme Court—are constantly in the process of working out in an attempt to balance the conflicting rights involved. On the issue of criticism of public officials, for instance, the courts have recently leaned in the direction of allowing a wide range of criticism even if it might be damaging to the government official. The right to criticize public officials is basic to a democracy. Thus one risks some weakening of the individual's right to be protected from unfair attack in order to make sure that the press is free to criticize government activities.[2]

Similarly with obscenity. On the one hand is the principle that free speech ought to be limited when it becomes pornographic—that is, all literature and movies ought to be allowed, except those that appeal solely to "base or prurient" interests and that have no "redeeming social value" or literary qualities. And on the other hand is the principle that all writings and movies should be allowed, regardless of their content. But even if the society accepts pornography laws, the task remains to define what books and movies fall beyond the line of acceptability. Many great literary works

[2] *New York Times v. Sullivan* 376 U.S. 254 (1964).

If the issue of pornography were put to a vote, most Americans would be more restrictive than the Supreme Court has been.   *(Photo: Geoffrey Gove, Rapho Guillumette)*

have been held by some to be so damaging to morals that they ought to be barred. In this difficult area, the burden falls on the courts to draw the lines.

Conflict Between Free Speech and National Security: Libel and obscenity represent two conflicts over the limits of free speech. But the major area of conflict—and the most important from the point of view of democratic politics—is the conflict between free speech and national security. Free speech is particularly crucial when it protects those with unpopular political opinions, especially opinions severely critical of government. But the right to express unpopular political opinions may conflict with another right: the right of the society to protect itself from those who would use violence against it.

As with libel and obscenity, it is easier to state principles than to apply them. For instance, the First Amendment guarantee of free speech does not give the citizen the right to commit sabotage or to use violence against government officials, and Congress can (and has) passed laws punishing those who commit or attempt to commit such acts. This principle should be easy to apply, but actually the boundary between speech and action is by no means clear. Speech, some have argued, can itself be violent. And there is no doubt that speech can be used to incite violent action.

Consider sabotage. The government is empowered to arrest and punish those who commit or attempt to commit sabotage. But:

1. What if I plan an act of sabotage with someone else? I tell him where to plant the bomb and when to do it. I only "speak." He does the actual bombing. Is my "speech" protected by the First Amendment?
2. What if I make a speech at a public meeting saying that people ought to sabotage government operations? After the meeting some of those who heard me speak go out and plant bombs at government installations. Is my "speech" protected?
3. What if I make a speech such as that described in Example 2, but no one acts? Is my "speech" protected?
4. What if I make a speech that merely says that there "are times when it would be justifiable to sabotage the government"? (That is, I do not directly advocate such sabotage.) Suppose someone hears the speech, decides that the current circumstances justify such sabotage, and attempts it. Is my "speech" protected?
5. Suppose I write a book on the history of sabotage and treat some famous saboteurs sympathetically? Is my "speech" protected?

It should be clear from these examples that the clash between the principle of free speech and the principle that the government can punish action directed against it can arise in many and varied circumstances. And at times it is unclear whether one is dealing with speech or action. For one thing it is hard to determine precisely when speech directly advocates action and when it does not. Under Example 1 above, it would seem clear that it does; perhaps under Example 2 as well. But what if one says, as in Example 4, "there are times when one must act"? Is that to be taken as advocating action?

And there is difficulty in determining whether the speech in fact leads to action. Again it would seem clear that it does in Example 1. But can we be sure, in Example 2, that the speech led to the action? (What, for instance, if the action comes a month or so later?)

Example 1 above represents a case where the "speech" involved would probably not be protected by the First Amendment. The "speech" is clearly part of a criminal action and punishable without a violation of the Constitution.

Example 5 represents a fairly clear case of "speech" that is protected under the First Amendment (even though it is possible that someone would read such a book and be motivated by a sympathetic portrait of a saboteur to imitate him).

Examples 2, 3, and 4 lie in between, and it is by no means clear whether the courts would consider the behavior to be *speech* protected by the Constitution or *activity* punishable as subversive. At times the courts have seemed to rely on a doctrine of "clear and present danger," first enunciated by Justice Oliver Wendell Holmes in 1919.[3] Under this doctrine, speech is punishable only when it is likely to lead immediately to illegal action and when the connection between the speech and the illegal action is unambiguous. But the "clear and present danger" doctrine is merely another way of expressing the problem involved in determining where speech ends and action begins. The issue remains as to when such a danger exists. The doctrine has, in fact, never represented a clear principle to be followed by the courts.

Governmental Actions Against Conspiracy and Subversion

Drawing the line between civil liberties and the right of the government to protect itself is made difficult by the fact that attempts to limit these liberties usually take place in times of national emergency—in particular, in time of war. At such times, the dangers of sabotage and subversion loom large in the eyes of the government and the public. At such times, civil liberties usually suffer. In the Civil War, for instance, President Lincoln suspended the writ of habeas corpus (a fundamental right guaranteed in the Constitution under which citizens cannot be held in jail without being brought into court or to trial). And in World War II, all Americans of Japanese ancestry, whether or not there was evidence of subversive activity, were forcibly moved from the West Coast to "relocation centers" in the Midwest where they were kept for the duration of the war.

In both of the above cases, the Supreme Court subsequently declared that the government had acted unconstitutionally, but in both cases the court decision came after the war was over and after the issue had ceased to be a real one.

The Smith Act of 1940: In the three decades since World War II, the issue of civil liberties versus national security has revolved around a series of laws aimed at blocking conspiracy and subversion. These laws, and the court cases relating to them, arose in periods when many felt that the nation was in danger—engaged in a cold war with the forces of communism. The Smith Act, passed in 1940, made it a crime to teach or advocate the overthrow of the United States government by force and violence. In 1951

---

[3] *Schenck v. United States* 249 U.S. 47 (1919).

During World War II all Americans of Japanese ancestry were forcibly removed from the West Coast to relocation centers.   *(Photo: Wide World)*

the Supreme Court upheld the conviction of Eugene Dennis, the head of the U.S. Communist party, under the Smith Act.[4] Critics of this decision (including the dissenting justices) argued that the defendants were convicted for speech, not action (for "teaching and advocating"), but the Supreme Court majority held that the government had the right to protect itself against the *actions* that the defendants taught and advocated. Therefore such teaching and advocacy was punishable.

In later cases the Supreme Court has generally upheld the provisions of the Smith Act. But the Court has put a heavy burden of proof on the government and has been narrow in its interpretation of the Act. In this way the Court has limited the extent to which the law can curtail speech, without ever concluding that provisions of the law violate the constitutional guarantees of free speech.

The McCarran Act of 1950:   The Court's ambivalence is also seen in its interpretation of another post-World War II law—the McCarran Act of 1950 requiring registration of Communist and Communist-front organiza-

---

[4] *Dennis et al. v. United States* 341 U.S. 494 (1951).

tions—which Congress passed at the outbreak of the Korean War. The Supreme Court held that although the registration requirements were constitutional, to compel the officials and other members of the party to register would mean that they could be required to testify against themselves, and this would be a violation of their freedom from self-incrimination guaranteed by the Fifth Amendment.[5] Thus the Supreme Court did not challenge the constitutionality of the registration requirements, but it did interpret them narrowly so as to limit the extent to which they inhibited freedom of association.

The Antiriot Bill: The most recent attempt by Congress to legislate against subversion came in response to the urban unrest and violence of the late 1960s. A 1968 antiriot bill contained a provision making it a crime to cross a state line for the purpose of inciting riots or conspiring to do so. The law was invoked in the trial of the "Chicago Seven" accused of conspiring to incite riots at the 1968 Democratic Convention in Chicago. No conspiracy was proved, but five of the defendants were convicted of crossing a state line to incite a riot. Those convictions were reversed in 1972 by a federal appeals court because of the way in which their trial had been conducted by the presiding government prosecutor and the judge. But the court upheld the antiriot law itself. As with the Smith and McCarran Acts, the courts provide narrow interpretations of antisubversive legislation that limit the impact of such laws on civil liberties but that do not challenge the laws directly (which makes it possible that the laws will indeed be *used* to limit free speech).

Freedom of Speech: Not an Absolute Right

In sum, the freedoms of expression guaranteed in the First Amendment remain real but by no means absolute. Attempts by the federal government to use antisubversive legislation to limit such freedom in the name of national security cannot obscure the fact that—unlike many countries—it is legal in the United States to express and publish strong criticism of the actions of the government. But the antisubversive laws passed by Congress, the enforcement of those laws by the Justice Department, and the interpretation of those laws by the courts make clear that the First Amendment freedoms are not given an absolute status. At times of crisis or political conflict the government is likely to attempt to prevent subversive acts and in so doing limit the voices of political dissent. The Supreme Court keeps a check on these limitations of free speech. But it often does so rather late (when the damage to free speech may be already done) and usually by restricting the government to narrow limits in its enforcement of these laws rather than by directly challenging the constitutionality of such legislation.

[5] *Communist Party v. Subversive Activities Control Board* 367 U.S. i (1961).

Freedom of Religion

The same constitutional amendment that guarantees free speech contains the equally basic guarantee of freedom of religion. The First Amendment prohibits the government from interfering with the religious practices of the American people—either by establishing a state-supported church or by favoring any one religion over another. This prohibition may be one of the cornerstones of civil peace in America. In a society with many religions there is potential for deep conflict if the government favors one over another. By keeping the government out of religion, the First Amendment minimizes the political divisiveness of religion.

Yet, as with freedom of speech, the wording of the First Amendment by no means settles the issue. The famous words of that amendment—"Congress shall make no law respecting an establishment of religion, or prohibiting the free exercise thereof . . . "—are ambiguous. The provision was meant to bar a state-supported religion, and to permanently separate church and state. But how wide that separation was supposed to be remains unclear, as does the issue of how to balance religious freedoms and other values.

The government cannot establish a church. But does this mean it cannot give aid to parochial schools? Does it mean it cannot provide buses for children going to such schools? What about providing policemen to direct traffic outside such schools?

The government cannot prohibit an individual from exercising his religion freely. But what if his religion tells him that he ought to practice polygamy or snake-handling? Or that he ought not to pay taxes? Or not serve in the armed forces? Or not salute the flag? Are all activities to be justified if they can be shown to represent "exercises of religion"? If not, has freedom of religion been limited?

Just as with free speech, it can be seen that the general rule laid down in the Constitution leaves unanswered questions. The result is a mixed, inconsistent system under which the government respects the separation of church and state in general, but not completely. It does not (under Supreme Court rulings) provide aid to parochial schools, but it is (also under Supreme Court rulings) allowed to provide buses for children going to such schools. Chapel attendance remained compulsory at the nation's military academies—West Point, Annapolis, the Air Force Academy—until 1972 when the Supreme Court ruled it unconstitutional. But the federal government still supports chaplains in the armed forces. And the sessions of Congress open with prayer. Those who object to such ceremonies for religious reasons can refuse to salute the flag. But citizens cannot refuse to pay taxes even if their religion so instructs them.

All these seeming inconsistencies stem from the same general problem spelled out when we discussed free speech—the need to balance one value (in this case freedom of religion) with other values. Consider the following aspects of church-state relations:

The Right to Worship as One Sees Fit

Freedom of religion is quite clearly specified in the First Amendment. The government can neither bar particular religions nor require adherence to any particular religion. Yet the boundaries of the free exercise of religion become controversial when that free exercise would violate some other principle. In the nineteenth century, the Supreme Court upheld the government's prohibition of polygamy even though this was a fundamental practice of the Mormon religion.[6] The court reasoned that polygamy so went against the American moral code that even though belief in polygamy was an article of religious faith in the Mormon church, it could not be allowed to continue. One wonders what decision the Court would reach today, when views about the nature of marriage have loosened somewhat. Perhaps the same. But even if the Court might decide that polygamy is no longer as shocking as it once was, there are certainly many other practices — such as public nudity — that the Court would continue to prohibit.

Freedom of Religion in the Field of Education

The field of education offers many examples of the delicate balance that the courts have drawn between freedom of religion and the requirements of the state. The Supreme Court has upheld compulsory education laws even for members of religious groups opposed to education — the Amish, for example. But it has allowed parents to choose religious schools for their children (as long as these schools meet state educational standards). This notwithstanding, religious schools are not eligible for government support. Apparently the Court believes on the one hand that there is a societal interest in having an educated citizenry that overrides the objections of some religious groups to compulsory education, but on the other that there is no overriding societal need for such education to take place in state-controlled schools.

The attempt to balance the rights of minority religious practices against obedience to general laws is found in the so-called flag-salute cases. The Jehovah's Witnesses — whose firm rejection of secular authority has led to many run-ins with the law and to numerous court cases — oppose the worship of images. They refused to allow their children to salute the flag. But laws existed that required a flag-salute ceremony at the beginning of the school day, the justification of such laws being that the state had the right to inculcate civic commitment in children and was empowered to require such ceremonies for that purpose.

In 1940 the Supreme Court upheld such a state law, saying that Jehovah's Witnesses could be compelled to salute the flag.[7] Three years later, the Court reversed itself — with four justices who had supported the right of

---

[6] *Reynolds v. United States* 98 U.S. 145 (1879).
[7] *Minersville School District v. Gobitis* 310 U.S. 586 (1940).

the state to compel a flag salute now supporting the right of the minority group to refuse to do so.[8] The new reasoning of the Court was that the state interest in such ceremonies as a flag salute was not important enough to override the right of the minority to follow its religious convictions.

Freedom of Religion for Nonbelievers

The provisions of the First Amendment were originally thought to prevent the government from favoring a particular religion over another. But might not the government favor those who were religious over those who were not? In many ways governmental policy seemed to do this. But in recent years the Court has moved to curb such practices. We have mentioned the abolition of compulsory chapel attendance at the military academies. As another example, the Supreme Court struck down as violating the First Amendment a long-standing provision of the Maryland constitution requiring that those holding public office declare a belief in God.

Conscientious-Objector Status: Similarly the Court has extended the right to conscientious-objector status with regard to military service to those who do not belong to an established religion or profess a belief in God. Earlier, those who claimed conscientious-objector status had to prove their right to it on religious grounds — usually a membership in some religious group that traditionally opposed military service. But in 1965 the Court found this to discriminate in favor of particular religions, and extended the right to conscientious-objector status to those who oppose war on ethical grounds.[9]

School Prayers: Perhaps the most controversial problem in relation to the protection of the rights of nonbelievers lies in the area of school prayers. Does it violate the freedom of nonbelievers if the government sponsors prayers in the public schools — even if the prayers are nonsectarian and are noncompulsory for those who do not want to join in?

Many school systems around the country traditionally opened the school day with the recitation of some prayer. In 1962 the Supreme Court barred such prayers.[10] It ruled that a school district in New York State violated the Constitution by requiring that classes be started with a nonsectarian prayer composed by the New York Board of Regents. The school board had specifically indicated that pupils could, at the request of their parents, be excused from the recitation. Yet the Court held that such prayers violated the separation of church and state since they were sanctioned by the government. And in a similar case, the Court barred a requirement in Pennsylvania that the Bible be read daily in the schools in that state.

---

[8] *West Virginia State Board of Education v. Barnette* 319 U.S. 624 (1943).
[9] *United States v. Seegar* 380 U.S. 163 (1965).
[10] *Engel v. Vitale* 370 U.S. 421 (1962) and *Abington School District v. Schempp* 374 U.S. 203 (1963).

There can be little doubt that the Court in so ruling was taking the side of a small minority. Public opinion polls have consistently shown large majorities of the public in favor of some religious observance in the schools. Those parents who objected to the religious observance (and brought the case to the courts) represented a small and generally unpopular group.

Here is a clear case where the issue of the proper extent of separation of church and state is far from settled. Critics of the Supreme Court's decisions contend that the minority who believe in no religion can expect tolerance for their views, but that such tolerance is adequately expressed in the fact that children do not have to take part in the prayers. Supporters of the Court's position argue that the Constitution requires a more positive neutrality than mere tolerance, and that school-sponsored prayers violate that neutrality.

Government Aid to Religious Schools

Another major controversy as to the proper extent of separation of church and state is over government aid to private religious schools. Does it violate the separation of church and state if the government provides support for such schools? The argument in favor of such support is that these schools contribute to society by educating children. And since parents who send their children to such schools are also taxed to pay for the general public school system, such parents who choose a religious school which they have to support as well are doubly burdened because of their beliefs. Opponents of such aid say that it would represent a discriminatory support for particular religions if all taxpayers were required to support Catholic or other denominational schools.

The Supreme Court has generally opposed support for religious schools. But, as in most of these issues, the position is by no means unequivocal. The Court has barred aid to religious elementary and secondary schools, but some aid to church-related schools on the college level is allowed. And various forms of indirect aid—such as government provision of school buses—is allowed.[11]

The Right to Property

Throughout American history a large share of the national wealth has been in the hands of a fairly small minority. This condition has persisted despite the principle of majoritarianism, which would seem to give to the poorer majority a means of using government to redistribute wealth on an equitable basis. As we saw in Chapter 2, this redistribution has not taken place.

[11] *Everson v. Board of Education of Ewing* 330 U.S. 1 (1947).

We reviewed some of the reasons in that chapter. Here we wish simply to emphasize that the Constitution helps protect the property rights of citizens.

In the 1780s, unlike today, there was no talk of property rights *versus* human rights. The rights for which the Revolutionary War was fought were the rights of political liberty and of property. "The true foundation of republican government," wrote Thomas Jefferson, "is the equal right of every citizen, in his person and in his property." This *did not* mean that every citizen would have equal amounts of property. The delegates to the Constitutional Convention in Philadelphia met not to redistribute property but to protect it.

The Protection of Property Rights

The protection of property rights was written into the Constitution and has since been elaborated extensively in legislation. There is, for example, a clause in the Constitution that prohibits any state from passing a law that would impair the obligations of contract. There is also a just compensation clause. The constitutional framers recognized that privately owned lands might sometime be needed for public projects, but they were concerned that the costs of such a project should be widely distributed. Thus the property owner would be fairly compensated out of the public treasury. Other clauses restrict both federal and state governments from depriving a citizen of his property without *due process of law*. Stemming from these comparatively simple constitutional provisions is an enormous range of laws and regulations which sustain the private property system in America. Standing behind this legal network is, of course, the police power of the government.

What is meant by "property rights"? We have in mind the basic right to own something, and by virtue of that ownership the right to prevent others from using it. So we put locks on doors. We mean also the right to sell or exchange the thing we own, be it a tangible property such as a car or house, or an intangible property such as stocks or bonds. And we mean the right to pass on property to chosen heirs. But the right to own, to sell, and to give are not unlimited rights. The courts and the legislatures in the United States have placed very many restrictions on private property. These restrictions raise complicated questions about "minority rights" in a majoritarian democracy.

The Property Owner vs. the Public Interest

Government restrictions on property often rest on the claim that the public interest supersedes the rights of property. The owner of a 300-horsepower automobile cannot drive it at its maximum speed because he would thereby endanger "the public safety." The homeowner with a diseased elm tree in his front yard is told he must cut it down to prevent the disease from spreading. The contractor building a downtown apartment building is instructed to include parking facilities so that the public nuisance of cars parked on the public streets will be minimized. In each of these cases the victim of the government regulation might well say, "Who are they to tell me what to do with my property?" The "they" is the government claiming to speak on behalf of the public interest.

The task of defining and then applying in specific cases something so vague as "the public interest" is exceedingly complex. The definition of this term varies from one area to another and from one time to another. Take, for instance, the question of billboard advertisements. The right of a property owner to lease some of his land to a billboard company was not challenged through much of our history. And thus our public highways are surrounded by private advertisements. But now, spurred by a different concept of "public interest," some local and state governments are beginning to restrict this practice. In this respect the United States is catching up with other nations of the world. You can drive from one end of Canada to the other and never once have your view of the scenery blocked by a billboard.

The Property Owner vs. Human Rights

On the 1964 ballot in California there was a proposed state constitutional amendment guaranteeing the right of any property holder in California to sell, lease, or rent his property to anyone he chose. This seems a reasonable enough proposal, and certainly is in line with property rights. The proposed amendment, however, was in fact in retaliation to an open-occupancy bill passed by the California legislature. The open-occupancy law prohibited racial discrimination in selling and renting property. Here is a clear case of "property rights" (the right of a citizen to do as he wants with his own home) versus "human rights" (the right of Black citizens not to be discriminated against). The voters of California passed the amendment overwhelmingly, but it was subsequently declared unconstitutional by the state supreme court, and this ruling was upheld by the United States Supreme Court.

The open-occupancy law in California is just one instance of how legislatures and courts restrict the uses of property when these uses violate other constitutional rights—in this case the right of equality before the law. When two constitutional rights are in conflict, it is the courts which must sit in final judgment. Sometimes this puts the courts on the side of the minority against the majority. Such was the case in California, when both the state and the federal courts overturned the clear majority preferences of the California citizens. The property rights of the majority were restricted on behalf of the human rights of the minority.

At other times it is the minority whose property rights are restricted in favor of the human rights of the majority. Progressive income taxes and

The right of the property owner to advertise as he sees fit is only now being challenged in the United States.　(Photo: American Airlines)

inheritance taxes can be interpreted in this light. A portion of the property wealth of the richer groups in society is taxed. This leads to some redistribution of wealth from a minority to the majority. We saw in Chapter 2 that this redistribution does not go very far; it nevertheless illustrates some attempt to restrict the property rights of a wealthy minority.

But despite limitations on property because of the public interest or because of competing constitutional rights, there remains firmly planted in our constitutional-legal heritage a strong respect for the rights of private ownership. What is remarkable are not the restrictions on property rights so much as the lack of restrictions. In this regard the principles of majoritarian democracy have been much less of a threat than many feared. John Dickinson, delegate to the Constitutional Convention in 1787, warned his colleagues that "the most dangerous influence" to public order was "those multitudes without property and without principle with which our country, like all others, will soon abound." But Dickinson was wrong on one very important fact: The multitudes have not been without property, and thus have not supported any sustained challenge to the rights of private ownership. Thomas Jefferson early realized the importance of widespread ownership of property when he remarked that "everyone, by his property, or by his satisfactory situation, is interested in the support of law and order." The support of law and order meant in Jefferson's time, as it does today, the use of the legal and police powers of the government to protect private property.

Permanent Minorities

Throughout this textbook, and especially in Chapter 11, we have reviewed the political and legal condition of Black citizens in America. Slavery was permitted by the Constitution. It has taken another century to begin to extend in full measure the rights of citizenship to Blacks.

Black citizens have been throughout American history what can be called a "permanent minority." Many factors have contributed to this. There is, first of all, the legacy of slavery, a legacy that separated the White and Black races by law and by social norms. Added to this legacy (and because of it) is the very real prejudice that many Whites continue to feel toward Blacks, and the resultant hostility toward Whites by Blacks. Social norms and prejudices have often been cemented in discriminatory legislation. Especially relevant to contemporary politics is the heritage of Jim Crow laws, which after the Civil War attempted to isolate completely the freed slaves, and "keep them in their place." These laws have now largely been declared unconstitutional, but the separation and second-class citizenship they imposed on Blacks have been less easy to eliminate.

Under the rules of majoritarian democracy a "permanent minority" is of course at a permanent disadvantage. At least this is so if the following conditions hold:

Majority interests and minority interests are opposed. For example, the White majority for various and complicated reasons does not want Blacks moving into their neighborhoods, but the Black minority wants to escape the inner-city ghettos with their poor housing, poor schooling, etc.

The majority votes according to its perceived interests. Thus the Whites vote for restrictive covenants and similar arrangements that prevent Blacks from moving into White neighborhoods.

Given the rules of majoritarian democracy, the majority interest would always prevail, and the minority interest would always lose. This example vividly illustrates the "tyranny of the majority," which many theorists have felt to be the most dangerous outcome of democracy.

Unless there are some constitutional restraints on the majority, the condition of the permanent minority cannot easily improve. What has happened in our political history is that the minority has invoked the constitutional principle "equality before the law." Blacks have claimed that their disadvantaged status is inconsistent with the principle of equality, and thus is unconstitutional.

To use this strategy the permanent minority needs allies. Without allies, the appeal of the minority remains just that, an appeal. But with an ally the appeal can become a potent political force. This we saw in Chapter 11, where we reviewed the role of the Supreme Court in the Blacks' struggle for equal status before the law. Especially with regard to voting rights and school integration the Supreme Court struck down discriminatory laws on the grounds that they were unconstitutional. The executive branch of the government has also at times been an ally, as when President Truman integrated the armed forces after the World War II and when President Johnson fashioned many economic opportunity programs which would specifically benefit Black citizens. The legislative branch has been the least consistent ally of all, but then it is the branch of government most continuously in touch with majority sentiment.

Indeed, the government, or any agency of it, is almost always a half-hearted ally of the permanent minority. This is what we might expect under the rules of democracy, for the government will remain somewhat responsive to the interests of the majority. The controversial issue raised at the end of the Supreme Court chapter asks whether the Court should enforce bussing to integrate schools if such a policy goes against the deeply held wishes of the majority of citizens. In discussing this complicated question you will undoubtedly have to balance the rights of the minority and the preferences of the majority.

Under the principle "majority wins" the rights of a permanent minority will depend on several things. It will depend on how seriously the majority accepts constitutional constraints on its own interests. And this in turn is likely to depend on how strongly the majority interests oppose those of the minority. Because of strong racial prejudices the Constitution very inadequately protected Black rights during the years from the end of the Civil War until the end of World War II. It will depend as well on how energetically the political authorities apply constitutional principles when those principles go against majority opinion. And of course it will depend on how strongly the permanent minority pushes to overcome its disadvantaged status. It was no accident that some of the most far-reaching legislation to extend civil rights to Black citizens occurred at the same time that Black protest movements were gaining in strength.

However, the disadvantages of the permanent minority would not be erased even if majority prejudices were lessened, if the authorities vigorously applied all constitutional principles, and if the minority itself was well organized and busy agitating for its rights. The reason is clear, and is illustrated in a current political debate about equality for Blacks.

Equality before the law is an elusive notion. Equal laws applied to groups unequal in resources and opportunities will not bring about equality. If two runners start a race at different points around the track, one from a point much farther along, the runner with a head start will win, even if they are equally fast and even if they run under the same rules. It is extremely difficult if not impossible *to equalize the starting point* at this late stage in the history of race relations in the United States.

This fact raises one of the most difficult questions facing the White American majority. Are Whites willing to apply reverse discrimination in order to compensate for the long-standing disadvantage of the Black minority? Or does reverse discrimination stretch too far the idea of minority rights? What happens to the idea of "majority rule" when government goes beyond the constitutional principle of equality before the law and starts to discriminate in favor of a particular group? We invite you to consider this issue in the Controversy section that follows.

Controversy

Systematic discrimination over a long period of time establishes social considerations nearly impossible to reverse by ordinary means. If, for example, the Black minority has been discriminated against by the White majority in schooling, in housing, in health care, and in employment, then turning to "equal status before the law" will not substantially improve the status of Blacks relative to that of Whites. The 1970 census was taken at the end of a decade unparalleled in its attention to racial justice—more books written, more meetings held, more marches organized, more legislation passed, more programs started, more commissions formed, more money spent on solving "the American dilemma" than in any other period of our history. At the end of that decade the median income of White families was $9,961 whereas for Black families it was $6,067. And this was not due simply to the fact that Whites have better jobs. Blacks are paid less than Whites for comparable jobs. The median income of White male "professional, managerial and kindred workers" in 1970 was $11,108. The median for the *same category* of Blacks was $7,659. Similar Black-White discrepancies appear in all job categories.

If these are the facts, what should be done?

One Side

It is the responsibility of government to put its enormous powers behind compensatory programs. An excellent place to begin would be educational and employment quotas. Universities and colleges should be required to hold approximately 10 percent of their places for Black applicants. Entering classes in medical schools should, starting now, admit 10 percent Blacks. If someday there is to be an equitable share of Black ownership of investment capital, then starting now all training programs and junior employees in banks, investment houses, insurance companies, and so forth, should include 10 percent Blacks. Similar quotas should be applied to construction unions, to army officers, college professors, to publishing firms, and on down the line.

There is a moral case to be made for reverse discrimination. After more than 200 years of slavery, another 100 years of Jim Crow laws, White prejudice, and institutional racism, American society does after all owe something to its Black citizens. But in addition to the moral case, and perhaps more important, is the very practical argument that equality between the races will result only if we go through a period of reverse discrimination and quota programs.

The Other Side

It is the responsibility of government to treat men and women simply as citizens, "regardless of race, creed, color, or sex." Insofar as public and private life in the United States discriminates on the basis of race (or any other arbitrary criteria), then government should step in and banish the practice.

But to replace one form of discrimination with another is violating the principle of government neutrality. No matter what moral or practical case can be made, it goes too far to say that government should deliberately favor one single group. This would be once again to make laws on the basis of race, exactly what the principle of equality before the law prohibits.

Quota programs, for instance, can be fair only if applied to every group equally. If there is to be a "Black quota" there should be an "Irish quota" or a "southern quota" or a "woman quota." If there is to be a Black studies program, there should be an Italian-American studies program and a Jewish studies program, and a women's studies program. To violate the principles of equality and fairness is no way to rid society of discrimination. It only changes its form.

Suggested Readings

On the general problems of "majority rule and minority rights," see the important analysis by Alexis de Tocqueville, *Democracy in America* (New York: Oxford University Press, 1947), and the illuminating treatment by Robert A. Dahl, *Preface to Democratic Theory* (Chicago: University of Chicago Press, 1965). John Stuart Mill's *On Liberty* (New York: Appleton, 1947), originally published in 1851, is the classic philosophical statement of the libertarian defense of freedom of speech. Bertrand Russell's *Authority and the Individual* (New York: Simon & Schuster, 1949) deals with the tension between political authority and individual freedom; and Henry David Thoreau's 1849 essay *On the Duty of Civil Disobedience* (New Haven, Conn.: Yale University Press, 1928) is a remarkable plea for the individual to resist unjust governmental authority. A widely read history on American civil liberties is Zechariah Chafee, Jr., *Free Speech in the United States* (Cambridge, Mass: Harvard University Press, 1941). On freedom of religion, see Leo Pfeffer, *Church, State, and Freedom* (Boston: Beacon, 1953).

The literature on civil rights and race relations is huge, and has been written from every imaginable perspective. Gunnar Myrdal's *An American Dilemma* (New York: Harper & Row, 1944) was a landmark study that helped launch the pressures that led to civil rights legislation in the 1950s and 1960s. A book by Louis Knowles and Kenneth Prewitt, *Institutional Racism in America* (Englewood Cliffs, N.J.: Prentice-Hall, 1971), collects contemporary materials documenting that discrimination against Blacks is part of the institutional arrangements of American society. The *Report of the National Advisory Commission on Civil Disorders* (Washington, D.C.: U.S. Government Printing Office, 1968) made famous the saying, "Our nation is moving toward two societies, one black, one white—separate and unequal." *The Autobiography of Malcolm X* (New York: Grove Press, 1964), by Malcolm X with the assistance of Alex Haley, is a powerful indictment of American racism as seen by a remarkable Black leader. See also Stokely Carmichael and Charles V. Hamilton, *Black Power* (New York: Random House, 1967), for the argument that popularized the slogan that gives this book its name.

A Note to the Student
Finding Out About Politics

In an earlier discussion of how we study politics attention focused on the opinions and behavior of the American public. There we reviewed the sample survey, which relies on interviews and questionnaires. Sometimes the technique of the sample survey is used for special "target populations." A target population might be state legislators or career officers in the State Department or lobbyists working in Washington, D.C., or party leaders. Much of the same guidelines discussed in our previous section are applicable when the sample survey methodology is used to investigate the opinions and behaviors of specialized groups of politically relevant persons.

For the most part, however, the sample survey is not the best strategy for studying political leaders. It is often difficult to get their attention and their time. And even if you can get them to answer a questionnaire on their opinions toward a range of political issues, their answers will not necessarily add up to a clear picture of what an actual public policy is and how it was made.

To study public policy, including the institutions in which policy is made and the persons who mostly make it, the political scientist concentrates primarily on what can be called "documentary research." This is a broad term that describes the many different ways in which politics is investigated through the records that government keeps about itself and the records that others outside of government publish about governmental activities and personnel.

Before discussing what documentary research involves we should get one important fact in mind. American government is enormous. It stands at the center of a complex technological society. Such a society cannot function well without a continuous flow of accurate data on very many aspects of human endeavor, including a great deal of data on the role of government in the society. A rational program of highway construction depends on detailed information about population movements, location of industries, where goods are produced and marketed, trends in home building, and so forth. International businesses need detailed information about markets abroad, tariff regulations, the shipping industry, the official policy of the government toward various nations, and so forth. These and many other examples suggest the importance of information to the making of policy in the public and the private sectors.

Thus in hundreds and hundreds of documents and reports the government describes its personnel, its activities, and its policies. It describes as well the personnel, the activities, and the policies of other sectors of American life. You can learn from government documents the number of scientists being trained in various universities, the number of private airplanes sold every year, the number of American businessmen living in Mexico, and the number of beds in private nursing homes. Very few activities in society, whether public or "private," escape the scrutiny of some government agency.

And because the government is so involved in such a wide range of activities, many nongovernmental agencies keep records about the government itself. The AFL–CIO, for instance, publishes the voting behavior of congressmen on all questions of importance to the labor unions. The budget and the policies of the National Science Foundation are reported in the journal of the American Association for the Advancement of Science, a private, nonprofit professional association.

The enormous "documentation deposit" describes in rich detail the agencies and the institutions that make public policy. Although this documentation is extensive in its coverage, it should nevertheless be approached with caution. Here are three things that the political scientist will keep in mind as he attempts to study politics through the use of public documents.

1. The Institutional Bias: Many government records are the product of self-reporting. The records of campaign contributions are filed by the political parties which collected the contributions. Crime statistics are made available by the FBI and by local enforcement agencies. An evaluation of the Head Start program is published by the Department of Health, Education, and Welfare under whose direction Head Start was initiated.

Self-reports often will be biased. They exaggerate facts that work to the credit of the reporting agency and underplay facts that would discredit it. For instance, an executive contributes $25,000 to a political party, but does so by sending 25 checks of $1,000 each to 25 different committees and candidates. If the political party wishes to stress that it depends on many small contributions instead of a few large ones, it reports this as 25 separate contributions. A city police department that feels itself short-handed and is looking for a budget increase might report crime statistics in such a way as to indicate an increase in crime. Perhaps it reports every loss of property as "suspected theft." Another police department that has just had a large budget increase and wishes now to justify it will produce statistics showing a decrease in crime. It reports only those cases where theft is clearly demonstrated.

This institutional bias by government agencies is easily understood. To stay in business an agency must demonstrate that it is doing what it is expected to do, and that it can do even better if only its budget were increased. But however understandable from a political point of view, the institutional bias imposes a difficulty on the researcher working with public documents. A careful researcher will attempt to locate possible sources of distortion, and will take this into account in his study.

2. The Durable Artifact: Have you ever wondered why archeologists can describe in detail the cultures of ancient Greece and yet provide such limited descriptions of the cultures of ancient Africa? Archeologists reconstruct how preliterate peoples lived by studying the things they left behind — monuments, temples, tools, weapons, ritual objects. These are the material artifacts of a culture. Some types of artifacts resist the erosive effects of time much more successfully than others, and this in part accounts for our uneven understanding of different cultures. The settled people of ancient Greece, who made their artifacts of metal or stone, left behind a much more complete record of their ways of life than did the nomadic people of Africa, who made their artifacts of animal skin or woven grass.

The idea of the "durable artifact" is today relevant to how we approach the records made available by governments. Some records are more durable than others. Those that have eroded with time present difficulties to the researcher who depends on documents for his data. For example, voter turnout in national elections is available since the earliest elections, but voter turnout in local elections can for some communities be retrieved only for the past ten or twenty years. This greatly hampers the researcher who wishes to compare turnout over time between the two levels of government. Another example comes from the study of comparative government. It is easy to get records on how England, for instance, administered its colonies in East Africa between 1920 and 1960. It is virtually impossible to get records on the many African movements that opposed the colonial government. The records that opposition movements kept of their own activities (their members, their resources, their plans) disappeared as the movements themselves were suppressed. And the records kept by the colonial government of how they suppressed these movements were destroyed by the colonial officials just prior to independence for the African nations.

3. Secrecy: In a democracy the business of government is presumably public. And in comparison to many nations of the world the amount of information about the U.S. government made public by the U.S. government is considerable. Yet very much government business even in the United States is conducted in secrecy or in semisecrecy. This is obviously true and for understandable reasons, as regards military and national security matters. Governmental secrecy, however, goes far beyond military and security agencies. Nearly everything that goes on inside the White House is made public only at the discretion of the President or his staff. Although floor debate in Congress is public, congressional subcommittees, and even full committees, often meet in private for the critical sessions that finish the drafting of legislation. (Forty percent of all congressional committee meetings were held in secret in 1972.) Supreme Court decisions are of course announced publicly, but the deliberations of the justices take place in private. Any of us can read the budget proposed by the Office of Management and Budget, but few of us can attend the meetings when the arguments for and against particular programs are being weighed.

In short, it is much easier to get information on the finished product of the legislative, executive, or judicial agency than it is to get information on the political process out of which that product emerged. And thus the study of public documents is always to some extent the study of what government chooses to let the outsider know about.

These three limitations plus others that could be listed serve to caution us about expecting too much from the study of the public record. But if we keep the cautions in mind we can learn a great deal about the institutions and the people of government and about the policies they make through careful study of government documents and similar materials. If you continue with your study of political science you will discover that many of the findings reported by political scientists depend on analysis of the public record. Examples have already appeared in this textbook; see, for instance, the discussion of inequality in Chapter 2 where we used income tax returns; or the discussion of political party differences in Chapter 8 where we used congressional voting records. We list here a few other examples just to show the kinds of studies that have been carried out using the public record.

1. Political Representation: Census data can be used to provide a profile of the citizens of a congressional district. Are the citizens generally poor or wealthy, generally Catholic or Protestant, generally rural or urban, and so forth. These profiles can then be compared to how the elected representatives vote on various public policies. We might be interested, for example, in seeing whether congressmen from rural districts favor farm subsidies, while congressmen from urban districts favor rapid transit subsidies. This research design can be elaborated by including data, again from the public record, on whether a given district has strong party competition or is generally safe for one or the other of the political parties. These three variables—social composition of the population, how the elected representatives vote on legislation, the strength of the political parties—can be combined to provide an overall picture of the political representation process.

2. The Legislative Process: No institution in government is so thoroughly documented as is Congress. And one of the most useful sources of information, though not the only one, is the Congressional Quarterly, published weekly. This publication reports the roll-call votes of all members of Congress, showing how the member votes on all key issues and whether his vote goes against his own party. It reports the record of action on major public bills: their subject matter and sponsors, the conclusions of committee hearings, the debate, amendments, and voting on the floor of Congress, and the results of any Senate-House conferences. It describes who has leadership in various committees, what lobbyists are active on which bills, and how any given legislation fits into the President's program.

Material such as this is invaluable for studying the legislative process. For example, you can see whether a committee headed by a southern Democrat handles a civil rights bill differently from a committee headed by a northern Democrat. You can learn which congressmen are likely to oppose the President's program, even if the President is of the same party. You can find out if cohesive subcommittees are much more successful in getting their bills enacted into legislation than divided subcommittees. You can trace the record of various pressure groups: how often the legislation they work on is favorable to their point of view and how often it is unfavorable.

Political scientists have used documentary data on Congress to study all of these issues. Out of these investigations has come a very detailed understanding of the legislative workings. Similar studies have been carried out in state legislatures and even in city councils, though the public record on legislative actions at the state and local levels is not as complete as it is for the national Congress.

3. The "Power Elite": There is a great deal of fascination with the actual persons who occupy the critical decision posts in American society. This fascination has resulted in a vast outpouring of descriptive material about the social backgrounds, the educations, and the careers of persons who reach the top offices. Sometimes this material appears in official or semiofficial publications, such as the Congressional Directory, the Biographical Dictionary of the American Congress, the latter going back to 1774, and the State Department Biographical Register. An even richer source of information is Who's Who in America as well as the dozens of more specialized biographical publications. There are, for instance, biographical reports on women, Blacks, Jews, corporation directors, educators, lawyers, and the rich. All of these publications choose persons in top positions and then provide basic social background and career information. This information is not always complete, and is more sketchy the further back into American history you go. But used judiciously it can provide the kind of evidence you need for testing various ideas about persons in powerful positions.

One question that has long interested political scientists is how much overlap there is between the various sectors of power in American society. That is, do the same people who serve on the board of trustees of large universities also come from the largest corporations? And are they the group that consults with government through such prestigious organizations as the Council on Foreign Relations? The extent of such overlap can be investigated from readily available biographical sources.

Another type of study is suggested by the social background information. You could learn, for example, whether leading career officers in the State Department and top diplomats come disproportionately from only a few states (as is sometimes charged) or whether they come from all regions of the country. You can study the social composition of Congress to see what changes have taken place: Did extending the vote to women result in women being elected to Congress? Has the percentage of Black congressmen increased much since the civil rights activity of the last decades? Are there proportionately fewer lawyers in Congress now than there were in the nineteenth century?

Yet another approach to the biographical data is suggested by books with such titles as the following: Who Rules America?, The Rich and the Super-Rich, American Political Dynasties, The Power Elite. Many authors have attempted to show that a distinct upper class in America supplies the persons who largely run the country. The analysis depends on social registers and other lists of wealthy and important people.

4. Priorities in Public Policy: Detailed and very suggestive data about public policy can be found in government budgets and reports of expenditures. Such information is published on a regular basis by every level of government. It can be very detailed—for instance, the exact amount of every contract the Department of Defense has with specific universities and research institutions; the salaries paid to every level of government employee; the cost of constructing a federal highway.

Budgetary data are an indicator of the priorities attached to different programs. We know, for instance, that for some time now military and security affairs have absorbed more than three out of every five dollars spent by the federal government, leaving all other federal programs to be funded out of the remaining 40 percent. Not only can you use budget data to compare priorities within a given budget, you can also compare across different units of government. To take an example at the local level, every city in California is required to have a planning commission, but there are no requirements concerning the funding of these commissions. Thus cities vary considerably in the proportion of the budget allocated to planning, some cities providing no funds and other cities providing sufficient funding to hire a full-time staff of experts.

5. Correlates of Government Expenditures: Perhaps more important than simply listing budget priorities are the studies that attempt to show what kinds of political or social factors seem to correlate with different priorities. Such studies usually obtain two different kinds of data from the public record: expenditure data and then a second kind that allows correlating expenditures against other considerations. For example, different planning expenditures in California cities can be correlated against the resources of the city (property taxes, for instance) and the pressures on the city (rate of population increase, for instance) to see if cities that might need the services of a planning commission manage to fund one no matter what their resources are. The measure of expenditures, of resources, and of need can all be taken from readily available statistics on California cities.

The correlation of public expenditures with specifically political factors is also illustrated in a series of comparative state studies. These studies have attempted to discover whether state expenditures on education, welfare, hospitals, and health, and so forth are correlated with voter turnout, party competition, or turnover of elected officials. For the most part it has been found that state expenditures correlate more strongly with social and economic factors than with political factors—that is, correlate more strongly with the per capita income in the state, say, than with the behavior of the electorate or the political parties.

A similar design is possible in the study of foreign relations. For *example, using public documents one could discover whether there is any pattern between how much military and foreign aid the United States gives to a particular country and how that country votes on issues in the United Nations. A comparison could be made between military expenditures abroad and American business investments abroad.*

Conclusions

These notes touch on only a few of the ways in which political scientists have used the "documentation deposit" to investigate politics and government in the United States. But they do illustrate the wealth of information available, and the importance of this information to systematic study. The sample survey is a powerful research tool, but is far too costly to use every time a researcher wants to learn something about government or public policy. Indeed, we use the sample survey primarily for studies of the entire population of the country because that is the only way to get data on public opinion or general political participation. But when we turn attention away from the population at large, and concentrate on specific groups or political institutions, the kind of data best suited to research is often found in documents, records, budgets, and the like.

Congress: Representation and Legislation

13

Article 1, Section 1, of the United States Constitution declares:

> All legislative Powers herein granted shall be vested in a Congress of
> the United States, which shall consist of a Senate and a House of Repre-
> sentatives.

Thus was created Congress, and in the remainder of Article I, the duties, powers, and responsibilities of that body are enumerated in detail.

The Roots of Congress

In creating a Congress the writers of the Constitution followed an ancient practice. In pre-Christian Greece and Rome specially selected assemblies were chosen to legislate on behalf of the entire community. And if we stretch the language a bit, the tribal elders gathered around the chief, a practice as old as mankind, resemble the legislative assembly. Americans, however, trace their legislative assembly to medieval British parliaments, the true precursors of modern-day legislatures. In these medieval parliaments, a selected few noblemen and clergymen met with the monarch to present the complaints and grievances of the estates on whose behalf they spoke. In its earliest days parliament was only a representative assembly; literally, it re-presented the viewpoint of the important sectors of society to the King. But it did not participate in lawmaking. The lawmaking powers remained exclusively with the King and his advisors. The evolution of parliament as a legislative assembly was to come later, and was not firmly established until the eighteenth century.

By the 1780s, however, the American colonies had extensive experience with their own legislative assemblies. And they liked what they had. The attempt of King George to whittle away at the authority of these legislatures provided impetus to the independence movement, for in the eyes of the colonized Americans, the royal governors (appointed by the King) in each colony were being given too much control over, especially, economic affairs. Thus was born the effective political slogan, "No taxation without representation." At first this was a rallying cry only for those who were demanding greater representation in the Parliament of England and greater autonomy of the colonial legislatures. When these demands were rebuffed, the rebel movement became an open claim for autonomy and eventually, of course, a demand for independence.

After the war was fought and won, the new nation had to fashion political institutions that would avoid the excesses and arbitrariness of executive authority, whether that authority was lodged in a Monarch or a Governor or a President. They devised the so-called separation of powers system in which Congress cooperates with the executive, but also stands against it. The power of political executives, thought the framers, is too often arbitrary and tyrannical and antidemocratic. A Congress would institutionalize a "counter-elite," an independent group of leaders who would owe their careers and authority to popular election. This counter-elite would check the excesses of executive power while at the same time remaining close in its thinking to the local constituencies it represents.

Representative Assemblies in the United States

Representative assemblies have proved enormously popular in the United States. In addition to Congress we have state legislatures, village, township, and city councils, school boards, special district commissions, and various county-level boards and commissions. All told, there are approximately 80,000 representative assemblies in the formal governmental structures in America. More than a half-million American citizens hold office as elected representatives. Representative institutions and principles have diffused well beyond formal government. We find them throughout our economic and social life. Stockholders elect a board of directors who presumably represent them and protect their interests against the managers of the firm. Union members elect their officials who presumably govern the union in a manner which reflects member preferences. Voluntary associations in the thousands are led by elected representatives. We are introduced to political representation at an early age, as for instance when we elect classmates to represent the home room on the student council or when we elect the officers of the school patrol or when we choose cheerleaders. No political ideal, with the exception of majority voting perhaps, is so deeply a part of our political culture as is the principle of representation itself.

Although there are many reasons why representative assemblies are so popular in America, we can single out three of particular relevance.

Political Representation—a Practical Consideration: "Representation is the grand discovery of modern times," wrote the Scottish philosopher James Mill, and his sentiment is widely shared. Political representation is viewed as a happy, workable compromise between the dangers of self-perpetuating leadership and the difficulties of participatory democracy. This compromise is based on a belief in popular sovereignty but recognizes that the people cannot actually govern themselves. Thus, as stated in The Fed-

eralist, political representation is an efficient "substitute for the meeting of the citizens in person."

Political Representation—a Normative Consideration: Not all citizens are equally enamored of politics. Some among us would just as soon not be bothered with the detailed, or even the broad, issues of public affairs. Such citizens demand the right to be apolitical, or to become political animals as infrequently and painlessly as possible (casting a ballot every two or four years). But if many citizens do not wish to pay the cost of heavy political involvement, neither do they wish to feel politically impotent. Political representation comes to their rescue. It allows a compromise between political indifference and preservation of the chance to intervene should matters take a turn for the worse. If you take a minute to become self-conscious about your own views, you might have strong positive feelings about the representative form of government for just this reason. You prefer to be about your own affairs, letting others worry about the trivia and intrigue of campus or national politics, but you reserve the right to complain, loudly, if things go wrong. The people working fulltime at politics are, after all, "your" representatives.

Political Representation—a Democratic Consideration: It has turned out to be exceedingly difficult to protect principles of popular sovereignty under the economic and social conditions of the twentieth century. Huge nation-states, swollen defense budgets, industrialization, the mass media, and complicated social and economic issues make nonsense out of the claim that people can govern themselves. Or, at least, it has happened that democratic principles have been undermined by the growth of gigantic bureaucracies and the steadily growing role of the state in organizing and regulating (and manipulating) social life. The fascist regimes of Europe shattered the naive belief that democracy was immune to tyrannical rule. Stalinism shattered the hope that communism as an economic system would somehow protect democracy where capitalism had failed. And the growth of the military-industrial complex has caused many in the United States to question whether our political arrangements can withstand tendencies for effective power to shift to a small number of men who manage the giant economic and political bureaucracies. Centralized organization and concentrated powers can too easily produce mass manipulation; democracy becomes the façade behind which the few direct the society. These are not groundless fears, and in some respects democracy is always a rearguard action against counter-tendencies. Political representation is nurtured as a major weapon of the resistance movement. If a democratic state can protect its representative assembly, then the trend toward concentrated, unaccountable power is checked. The legislature is rooted in popular choice and thus, presumably, constituency interests. If we cannot have government by the people, at least we can have government of and for the people.

Congress Under Attack

Congress has received more than its share of critical attention in recent years. Lethargic, labyrinthine, parochial, reactionary, inefficient, powerless, misguided, undemocratic—these are the adjectives used time and again in contemporary descriptions of Congress. As one of its own members has lamented, it is in the legislative branch of government that "political lag remains triumphant." That Congress is not yet part of the twentieth century is the implication, and Senator Joseph Clark is not alone in making this charge.

Congress Is a Local Institution
Dealing with National Issues

What appears to undergird widespread disenchantment with Congress is the complaint that the *institution* has not kept abreast of the *issues*. The issues with which the American government must deal are national in scope; Congress is essentially a local institution. This observation sums up the bewildering proliferation of criticisms of Congress.

American society has become a national society. The issues that count are those that affect the whole society. Transportation and housing and legal justice and national security and education are issues with ramifications in every corner of the society. The nationalization of issues has occurred hand in hand with the nationalization of social institutions. Consider the institutions that matter in our society: the *National* Council of Churches, the *National* Baseball League, the *National* Association of Manufacturers, the *National* Education Association, the *National* Federation of Independent Business, the *National* Broadcasting Company. The Main St. Methodist Church remains, as does the community baseball team, the local shoe factory, the Horace Mann PTA, the corner drugstore, and the town's radio station, but such local institutions as these have nowhere near the significance in American life of the gigantic national organization, product of the twentieth century.

The federal government has been part initiator and part victim of the trend toward nationalization. Federal agencies and activities have burgeoned in response to social problems that are national in scope. As transportation has become *trans-* and even *inter-*national, the government has had to organize itself through agencies such as the Federal Aviation Administration (FAA) to protect the safety and well-being of users. Medical research has implications for the entire nation, so the government has created institutions such as the National Institutes of Health or the National Science Foundation to fund and regulate this research. For every significant issue one can think of—fiscal policy, unemployment, civil rights, highway safety, consumer protection—federal agencies and programs exist in relation to them.

The charge is frequently made that Congress is ill equipped to play a serious role in the task of coordinating and formulating *national* programs. Yet Congress is supposed to be the institution that represents and legislates on behalf of the American public. When you are bothered about the quality of life in America—about traffic congestion, consumer prices, racial injustice, polluted rivers, street crime, mediocre schools, war expenditures—you in fact are bothered about issues which Congress has the constitutional authority to deal with.

Whether Congress is in fact failing the American public is a matter for inquiry, not unfounded assertion. Let us then look closely at the two responsibilities of Congress—representation and legislation.

Does Congress Represent the American Public?

Three arguments are voiced to prove that Congress is "unrepresentative." (1) Most congressmen are "parochial"; (2) Congress is dominated by a middle-class conservative coalition; and (3) our winner-take-all election system makes Congress a cautious, middle-of-the-road institution. After reviewing these arguments we will discuss the ways in which Congress does in fact carry out its representative functions.

Argument 1: Congressmen Are Parochial: Although serving in national office, congressmen are closely tied to one particular part of the country. The typical congressman lives his entire life in the district or state he represents. His education was in a local college or the state university. And if he went to law school, as more than half of the congressmen have, it was again to a local institution rather than a Yale or a Stanford. If his precongressional career was business, it was not as an executive of a national corporation who was frequently transferred around the country but, rather, of a business headquartered in his hometown.

The political career of the typical congressman often involves his working his way through local office and perhaps the state legislature. At the turn of the century three-fourths of congressmen had held state or local office before moving to the Congress; six decades later, despite the tremendous changes in American society over this period, this career pattern was still true of two-thirds of the congressmen. In contrast, while approximately one-half of the top administrative leaders had held state or local office in 1900, fewer than one-fifth of them had at the later period.

If the recruitment of the congressman stresses local ties, so does his continuing career. A member of the House of Representatives must stand for reelection every two years. He is hardly off to Washington before it is time to come home and campaign again. This ensures, as the writers of the Constitution intended, that the representative will not quickly forget his election promises. It has the further result of keeping him in close contact with local interests and his local campaign organizations. Actually, however, congressmen have rather long careers in Congress. Nine of every ten incumbent congressmen who stand for reelection are successful. Being a representative or a senator is a career in itself, with some men serving their entire adult lives. Thus Congress at any given time is composed mostly of veterans.

Lengthy tenure, it is claimed, contributes to the isolation of Congress from the changing issues of society. It leaves Congress under the control of persons who first put together their winning coalition two or more decades ago. As long as these veteran congressmen continue to satisfy the narrow interests of a few key groups in their home district or state, they can continue in their congressional career. The longer they stay, the easier it is to take care of constituency interests, for it is the old-timers who by virtue of seniority can control the allocation of defense contracts, federal loans, funds for road construction, and similar pork-barrel items. This leads to further entrenchment in the local area and increasing isolation from national problems.

As summarized by Senator Richard Neuberger: "If there is one maxim which seems to prevail among many members of our national legislature, it is that local matters must come first and global problems a poor second—that is, if the member of Congress is to survive politically." The senator is echoed by a colleague in the House: "My first duty is to get reelected. I'm here to represent my district. . . . This is part of my actual belief as to the function of congressmen. . . . What is good for the majority of districts is good for the country. What snarls up the system is these so-called statesmen-congressmen who vote for what they think is the country's interest. . . . We aren't . . . paid to be statesmen."[1]

Argument 2: Congress Is the Preserve of the Middle Class: Recently a Democratic congresswoman from New York, Rep. Bella S. Abzug, lamented the unrepresentative composition of Congress. In a speech to the National Women's Political Caucus she insisted that a representative Congress would have half women, 11 percent Blacks, more younger and more working-class people, and greater numbers of teachers, artists, and similarly unrepresented occupations. She correctly described Congress as dominated by men, mostly White, who are of a much higher education than the general population, and who are either from the professions (mostly law) or from the business and commercial sectors of society.

This has long bothered critics who speak in the populist tradition. Why should Congress have only 3 percent women members when women make up 51 percent of the population? Why should there be so few Black or

[1] The quotation from Senator Neuberger appears in Samuel P. Huntington, "Congressional Responses to the Twentieth Century," in David B. Truman, ed., *The Congress and America's Future* (Englewood Cliffs, N. J.: Prentice-Hall, 1965), p. 15. The following quotation appears in Lewis A. Dexter, "The Representative and His District," as reprinted in Theodore J. Lowi, ed., *Legislative Politics U.S.A.*, 2nd ed., (Boston: Little, Brown, 1965), p. 86.

Congresswoman Bella Abzug complains that Congress is dominated by men.
(*Photo: Bob Nadler, DPI*)

Chicano congressmen, despite the fact that minority groups make up 11 percent of the total population? (See Table 6.1 for Black and women members of Congress.) In short, why is Congress a preserve of White, middle-class America?

What the reformer counts on is the likelihood that changing the composition of Congress will change the social policies it pursues. When civil rights organizations campaign for Black candidates it is on the assumption that Blacks can best speak for the concerns of racial minorities; when the Women's Caucus demands more congresswomen it is on the assumption that the feminist viewpoint can be more forcefully presented by females than by males; when the United States Chamber of Commerce organizes political action groups it is on the assumption that businessmen in Congress will legislate policies favorable to commerce.

Although the populist assumption is a reasonable one, it should be taken cautiously. Just because a man works in a factory does not guarantee that he has the interests of the working class at heart; not all women believe with equal fervor in the feminist movement; and a Black skin covers the political views of an Uncle Tom just as it does those of a Black Panther. Conversely, being born of the middle class does not always imply antagonism toward the working class; not all men are indifferent to the cause of women's liberation; some Whites, including White congressmen, have been active in extending civil rights to Black citizens.

Political reformers are not unaware of this fact. The goal of proportionate representation is secondary to that of particular social policies. Thus the Women's Caucus aims "at the election of women *but also* men who declare themselves ready to fight for the needs and rights of women and all underrepresented groups." It is less the social composition *of* Congress than the social interests represented *in* Congress which bothers many critics.

What can be said about the social interests represented in Congress? We will return to this issue later, but some preliminary conclusions can be drawn at this point. Congress is not only the preserve of the middle class, it is the preserve of the more conservative viewpoints of that class. One reason is that congressional power goes to those who remain in Congress the longest, who gain seniority. By and large these are persons from "one-party" districts or states. Such noncompetitive areas of the country tend to be more conservative. Many of them are rural and many of them are in the South. Besides being generally conservative, these "safe districts" have overrepresented less populated areas and correspondingly underrepresented urban centers. This has happened because congressional districts can be very uneven in population size. The boundaries of districts are drawn by state legislatures, many of which are dominated by nonurban interests. One result has been fixing congressional districts in such a way as to reduce the number of congressmen elected from metropolitan centers. This practice, known as gerrymandering, has been made more difficult by the recent Supreme Court decision of "one man, one vote" which compels state legislative districts to be approximately equal in size. The long-term effect will be to shift some power, first in the state legislatures and eventually in the Congress, from the countryside to the cities.

Up to now, though, rural districts have for the most part sent conservative Republicans to Congress, and they have teamed up with conservative southern Democrats (often from safe districts) to block legislation in the area of civil rights, social welfare, programs for cities, and so forth. This "conservative coalition," as it has often been called, has defeated or delayed politics favored by a reform-minded, mostly urban-based coalition of liberal Democrats and Republicans.

It misses the point, however, to insist that this proves the unrepresentative character of Congress. To learn that a strategically placed group of conservative congressmen have obstructed certain social policies does not make them unrepresentative. It only makes them representatives of those social groups who oppose federal civil rights legislation or federal aid to education or a national medical service. To understand Congress accurately it is necessary to see it as a battleground between opposing interests and not to insist that if certain interests have consistently lost that therefore Congress is unrepresentative.

Argument 3: Congress Is a Centrist Institution: If some lament the parochial roots of Congress and others complain about its middle-class membership, yet other critics are disturbed about the way in which election procedures systematically penalize minority political viewpoints. According to these critics, Congress would be more representative if every shade of political viewpoint were represented in Congress in proportion to its electoral strength. If, for instance, there is a socialist viewpoint in the country, however few adhere to it, then it should have at least some congressional spokesmen. And the same logic holds for viewpoints more conservative than those currently represented in Congress. If the American Independent party is supported by 10 percent of the general electorate, it is only fair that Congress have that proportion of representatives so inclined. To exclude minority political views of either the political left or right is to make of Congress an "unrepresentative assembly." But this is often what does happen, for a very simple reason: Election to Congress is on a winner-take-all basis. Each district has only one representative, the person who gains a plurality of the votes.

Table 13.1 shows hypothetical results from a series of four congressional elections in a single district. As we can see from the table, the Republican party controls the congressional seat for four years, and then relinquishes control to the Democratic party. In such a congressional district, it makes sense for the two major parties to contest elections vigorously, for depending on conditions and the attractiveness of the candidate either party might win.

But the case is very different for the two minor parties. Although each represents a persistent viewpoint of a sizable group in the electorate,

Table 13.1   Results of Congressional Elections (Hypothetical)

	1968	1970	1972	1974
Republican Party	**47%**	**45%**	44%	43%
Democratic Party	40%	42%	**48%**	**46%**
American Independent Party	9%	10%	6%	8%
Socialist Party	4%	3%	2%	3%

neither can hope to win office. Thus if this district has 250,000 voters, about 20,000 supporters of the American Independent party are permanently unrepresented, as are about 8,000 voters with a socialist orientation. This is quite a few voters.

The winner-take-all feature of American congressional elections is not true of all national parliaments. Some nations have what are called multiple-member districts with proportionate representation. Italy is a notable example. The Italian Parliament is composed of representatives from perhaps a dozen political parties at any given time, representing every shade of political opinion from the far left to the far right. Each party wins seats in Parliament in proportion to its voter strength.

The United States Constitution, however, precludes proportionate representation. This penalizes minority viewpoints. Most students of American politics conclude that this is a good thing. If Congress duplicated the full range of political and social viewpoints in the society, it would greatly lessen its effectiveness as a legislating assembly. Too much diversity is said to create instability. No cohesive or persistent legislative program can emerge from a parliamentary situation in which authority is fragmented into many small groups. A Congress elected on a proportionate basis would decline in influence and effectiveness until nothing was left but a fractionated assembly unable to organize itself, let alone govern the country.

Other observers believe these to be exaggerated fears. They note that our election system produces a middle-of-the-road, essentially cautious Congress. Because neither of the two major parties can be effectively challenged by radical minorities on its left or right, the parties devise electoral strategies that attempt to control the middle of the political spectrum. In the hypothetical data presented above, the rational strategy for both the Republicans and Democrats is generally to move closer to each other in electoral appeal. Because the voters who are more liberal or more conservative than the major parties have nowhere to go, they will end up supporting one of the major parties. To achieve electoral success it is necessary for one party to attract voters from the other major party, and this often is accomplished by appealing to the political center. Those voters who have relatively unpopular, that is, minority, viewpoints are consequently unrepresented.

The three factors just reviewed—parochial origins of congressional careers, the middle-class conservative coalition that dominates Congress, and the centrist implications of the winner-take-all election system—and especially the first two, are often cited in support of the criticism that Congress is unrepresentative. This criticism emphasizes that the issues of American society are national in scope and urban in origin; a Congress still tied to parochial and sectional interests and still the preserve of an older political outlook is not equipped to deal with these issues. It is for this reason that the initiative in American politics has lately moved from the legislative to the executive branch, and even to the judicial branch in some cases. Although there is merit in the criticism, it overlooks several ways in which Congress does act as a representative assembly. It is to this issue that we now turn.

The Congressman as a Representative

Political representation is perhaps the most complex issue in democratic theory. Is the elected representative to carry out the wishes of his constituency, or is he to exercise his independent judgment on their behalf? One viewpoint holds that a representative who does not closely follow the instructions of his constituency is not a representative at all, for he is replacing his own views for those of the citizens of his state or district. The counter-position gives more emphasis to the idea of a deliberative legislature. If every representative is bound by the instructions of his home area, why bother to have a legislature? Why not simply decide public policy by plebiscite? But democracy by public opinion polling would be foolish, for it would ignore the benefits of an assembly in which debate and deliberation can evolve a policy that represents the general interest rather than being a hodgepodge of disconnected and parochial concerns.

The case for the legislator as an elected but nevertheless independent agent was forcefully presented by Edmund Burke two centuries ago:

> Certainly, gentlemen, it ought to be the happiness and glory of a representative, to live in the strictest union, the closest correspondence, and the most unreserved communication with his constituents. . . . It is his duty to sacrifice his repose, his pleasures, his satisfactions, to theirs; and, above all, ever, and in all cases, to prefer their interest to his own. But, his unbiased opinion, his mature judgement, his enlightened conscience, he ought not to sacrifice to you, to any man, or to any set of men living. These he does not derive from your pleasure; no, nor from the law and the constitution. They are a trust from Providence, for the abuse of which he is deeply answerable. . . . Parliament is not [where] local prejudices ought to guide, but the general good, resulting from the general reason of the whole. . . .[2]

In actual fact the large majority of congressmen steer a middle course between the two viewpoints. They either mix the two orientations depending on the issue at hand, or they lean toward the independence position except in cases which clearly affect the well-being of their home area. This can be seen by considering how the congressman represents individual citizens of his home area, how he represents the electorate, and how he represents organized interests.

[2] Edmund Burke, "Speech to the Electors of Bristol" (1774), *Works*, vol. II, p. 11.

Congress: Representing the Individual Citizen

In some descriptions of Congress, the picture conveyed is that of the interested citizen with a problem that he expects his elected representative to solve. This mythical citizen writes, calls, or visits his congressman, and the latter hastens to take care of the citizen's need, not only because the citizen represents a vote, but because such efforts are in the line of duty. Unrealistic as this picture at first appears, it conveys a great deal of truth.

The reason is simple. The federal bureaucracy touches the life of the individual citizen in dozens and dozens of ways: military draft, social security payments, income-tax laws, small business loans, Medicare, public employment, regulation of working conditions, consumer protection, and on and on. When the citizen is mistreated by an executive agency or needs some government service he turns to his congressman for help. And thus it is that the representational behavior of the congressman involves running errands for citizens or acting as an intermediary between constituent and bureaucracy. It is difficult to judge the amount of time a representative or a senator spends on errand running, though some estimates go as high as 50 percent. It is certainly true that the major amount of time given by a congressman's staff is to these individualized constituency problems.

Senator Vance Hartke, Democrat from Indiana, once inserted the following statement in the *Congressional Record* (no doubt so that he could subsequently have it copied and mailed, free, to Indiana voters):

> My office in Washington is a Hoosier headquarters. We receive an average of 275 phone calls a day, most of them from Indiana. We had nearly 6,000 visitors during the past year. . . . We received 45,938 letters and mailed out 50,678 letters. . . . We had 300 inquiries from people from Indiana who work for the Federal Government and wanted assistance with something pertaining to their jobs.
>
> The defense buildup has resulted in a great number of service and veteran problems. Since January 1, we have handled 709 of these problems, with the number growing daily. We assisted 261 Hoosiers with social security problems, 27 with draft board problems, 18 with railroad retirements, and 711 who sought patronage employment.
>
> I have helped also with 61 immigration cases who could be helped within the framework of the present law. Fifteen private immigration bills were introduced to assist those people who were worthy and who could not be helped through existing legislation. . . .
>
> It is my sincere conviction that I am in Washington to serve.

There is concern in some quarters that errand running absorbs so much congressional energy and time that Congress is in danger of being swamped with such requests and will eventually decline as a deliberative, legislative assembly. Rep. Reuss makes this point when he describes a congressman as a harried man and remarks that "the days are hardly long enough for him to think and act soundly on all the great issues of war and peace, national prosperity and civil rights," especially when the days are shortened by "the requests and demands from voters that require him to serve as their mediator with the Federal Government."

Few congressmen neglect these requests, however. Reelection can depend as much or more on your reputation as "available and helpful" than on your votes on bills before Congress. Errand running for constituents creates a bond between citizen and legislator, but a bond that has relatively little to do with substantive public policy. A request to protect a family's only son from the draft need have nothing to do with general policy on Vietnam; a request for help in dealing with the Internal Revenue Service need have nothing to do with tax reform or income distribution; a request for assistance in getting a small business loan need have nothing to do with government fiscal policy.

The gap between citizen request and policy issue can lead to a great deal of autonomy for the congressman. If he solves the citizen's problem, he can be reelected, whatever policies he supports on Vietnam, tax reform, or fiscal management. Thus in a somewhat paradoxical manner, while the congressman is paying very close attention to the citizen's *problems* he is paying less attention to the citizen's *viewpoints*. Of course, the congressman is not totally indifferent to the general policy orientations of his state or district, but as we will see in the next section there is little reason to think that the electorate delivers much of a mandate.

Congress: Representing the Electorate

It is often very difficult for a congressman to represent accurately the preferences of the voters who sent him to Washington. John F. Kennedy, when he was a senator from Massachusetts, wrote: "In Washington I frequently find myself believing that forty or fifty letters, six visits from professional politicians and lobbyists, and three editorials in Massachusetts newspapers constitute public opinion on a given issue. Yet in truth I rarely know how the great majority of the voters feel, or even how much they know of the issues that seem so burning in Washington."

Kennedy is here confessing to what has been called *mandate uncertainty*. Most congressmen are very uncertain about how to interpret election victory. Partly this is because voters do not have very well-informed viewpoints and do not participate in politics in great numbers (see Chapter 5). On the average, fewer than half the eligible electorate bother to vote in congressional elections. Turnout is especially low in "off-year" elections, the biennial election that does not correspond with a Presidential race. It takes the drama and press coverage of a Presidential campaign to attract attention even to contests for a senatorial seat. How can the successful congressional candidate consider his victory a mandate if less than one-quarter of the eligible voters in his district supported him? The difficulty is compounded by how little the average voter knows about his representative. Even in competitive congressional races, fewer than one-fourth of the voters know *anything* about either of the candidates and virtually none has any detailed information about the policy positions.

Mandate uncertainty is also caused by the multiplicity of issues in any campaign. A candidate simultaneously declares himself for and against a host of separate policies. He supports a negative income tax and revenue sharing with the state government, he opposes continued space exploration and federally funded cancer research, and he is largely silent on foreign policy issues. Did he win because of the issues he supported? Or did he win because he came out against certain policies? Or did he win because he veered away from foreign policy and concentrated only on domestic questions? And just as the winning candidate took pro and con stands on dozens of issues, so did his opponent. Maybe the winner did not gain votes by his stands so much as his opponent lost votes by *his* stands.

In addition to mandate uncertainty the sheer pressures of time and the complexity of congressional business render obsolete the view that the elected representative translates constituency preferences into public policy. The range of issues before Congress is immense: fiscal matters, civil rights, foreign treaties, appropriations for space exploration, wage and price policy, welfare programs, the military draft, revenue sharing, tax reform, and on and on. No senator or representative checks with his constituency before every roll-call vote, and of course none checks before a vote in committee or subcommittee, where most legislation is actually written. Only a tiny fraction of the voters will have the vaguest idea about the bills pending in Congress, let alone have any information about what their particular representative is doing.

These difficulties notwithstanding, it is wrong to conclude that the policy views of his electorate have *no* bearing on how a congressman votes. The typical citizens may not have detailed information about specific legislation, but they are not usually neutral about the major issues of war and peace, inflation and unemployment, civil rights, and so forth. The general tendencies within a district or state are known to the congressman and impose some limits on policies he supports. The civil rights voting record of Shirley Chisholm, liberal Black congresswoman from New York, bears little resemblance to the voting record of William Poage, ultraconservative Texas congressman, but a person with Chisholm's views would not be elected in Poage's district in Texas, nor would someone with Poage's views stand a chance of being elected in Chisholm's district.

Unfortunately we have very few systematic studies comparing the policy views of a congressman with those of the voters whom he represents. One such study, however, shows a high correspondence between the way in which congressmen vote and the preferences of their constituencies on bills having to do with civil rights and race relations.[3] The study found that

[3] The study cited here and in the next two paragraphs is from Warren E. Miller and Donald E. Stokes, "Constituency Influence in Congress," *American Political Science Review*, 57 (1963), 45–57.

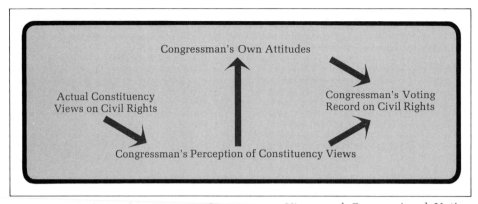

Figure 13.1 Relationship Between Constituency Views and Congressional Voting
SOURCE: Adapted from Warren E. Miller and Donald E. Stokes, "Constituency Influence in Congress," *American Political Science Review*, 57 (1963), Fig. 2.

congressional districts with a population generally liberal on civil rights issues are represented by congressmen who vote in favor of civil rights measures, and that districts with a more conservative population are represented by congressmen who oppose such measures.

This can be explained in two different ways. The congressman's own attitudes may be nearly identical to those of the constituency, in which case he need pay no attention to constituency preferences, for his vote will be in accord at any rate. Or perhaps the congressman may not always see eye to eye with the voters but fears to differ with them, at least on an issue as critical as civil rights and race relations. The evidence indicates that the latter explanation is more nearly the case: Congressmen appear to bring their own views about race questions into accord with what they perceive to be the views of their constituency. Furthermore, congressmen are remarkably accurate in judging what the voters do feel about civil rights. The relationship between constituency feelings and congressional voting can be diagrammed, as shown in Figure 13.1.

This study confirms that the broad stance of the constituency is translated into a vote pro or con in the Congress and indicates that the notion of mandate uncertainty may have been exaggerated. But before drawing this conclusion we should recall that the research found this pattern only in the area of civil rights. When voters and congressmen were asked about foreign policy and social welfare issues it was apparent that the attitude of the congressmen was not often in accord with that of their constituencies. On foreign policy in particular congressmen seem totally unfettered by the viewpoint of the constituency. Perhaps congressmen sense that voters feel less secure in their views about foreign policy and are willing to give Congress and the Presidency much more leeway. This study, however, was conducted prior to vocal opposition about Vietnam, and we today might find a closer fit between congressman and constituency in the area of foreign policy. The major conclusion to be drawn is that if the mandate *is* certain, the congressman generally votes in accord with constituency viewpoints.

Congress: Representing Interest Groups

Although a congressman may be uncertain about the views of the several thousands and even millions of individual voters in his district or state, he is not so uncertain about the views of the major groups back home, especially when legislation is pending that directly affects the interests of these groups. The contact that congressmen have with their constituents is most often contact with the active and organized sectors of the community: the interest groups.

Blocs of voters are more critical than the individual voter. The representative aiming at reelection must keep in mind the general policy preferences of groups which represent sizable voting power. And he does not have to work hard to learn these views. Organizations with a standing interest in legislative matters support a full-time staff in Washington whose job begins and ends with lobbying congressmen. Such organizations inform, cajole, and sometimes threaten in order to get favorable treatment from "their representative in Washington." The chief blandishment of course is electoral support, either in the form of campaign contributions or votes. It is generally accepted, though, that group leaders cannot easily control the voting choices of group members. But they do control campaign funds, and they distribute publicity to group members about the area's congressmen. Nearly all political pressuring in Washington comes through organizations. If the congressman receives a mass mailing on a labor issue it is because the union has organized that mailing; if the congressman is asked to speak to parents concerned about school bussing it is because a civic group has organized the meeting; if the congressman is asked to receive a delegation of farmers who will present a petition on wheat prices it is because a farmers' association has organized that delegation and collected the signatures. This type of pressure group activity is particularly important if there are only one or two major interests that dominate the district or state. Thus automobile manufacturers and the auto unions are listened to carefully by congressmen from Michigan; a citrus grower's association will be especially important to a Florida congressman.

One of the important differences between the Senate and the House of Representatives is suggested by this point. The constituency of a senator is nearly always more varied than that of the representative. Seldom will a single interest so dominate a state that its senators are in effect representatives only of that interest, though the influence of oil in Texas and of mining in Utah has at times approximated this situation. For the most part a senator will build a winning electoral constituency from a variety of groups and interests. It is for this reason that the Senate is said to have a constituency that is closer in kind to that of the President. The constituency of a senator, especially from a populous, urban state, is more a microcosm of the entire nation than is the constituency of a member of the House. Few senators will not have labor unions or civil rights groups among the organizations with which they deal, but numerous representatives are selected from districts totally lacking in unions or minority groups. Any given representative deals with a narrower range of constituency pressures than will nearly any senator (though a representative from New York City has a more varied constituency than a senator from Montana).

In one respect this discussion of group politics and representative behavior is somewhat misleading. Organizations are active in two respects. First, as we have suggested, they are active as local pressure groups attempting to persuade a congressman to support legislation beneficial to his area. This is the case of the businessmen of a community trying to control the routing of a federal highway, the case of a trade union trying to get a lucrative contract for a local industry, the case of a large university trying to obtain a federal research center, the case of a farmers' association trying to get more favorable soil bank terms. These are specific groups using what political influence they have to direct benefits to their specific area. They are not in competition with any other interest in the area, and they usually have no difficulty getting the help of their congressman. The struggle takes place *within* Congress, because more than one part of the country wants to affect the routing of the highway, wants the same defense contract, wants the same research center, or wants favorable treatment from the Department of Agriculture. Congressmen are evaluated in terms of how successfully they bargain and negotiate within the federal government on such matters. Listen to no less an authority than President Johnson:

> At the March 2, 1968, rollout ceremony for the giant C-5A cargo aircraft at the Lockheed Aircraft plant at Marietta, Ga., President Johnson warmly complimented the Georgia congressional delegation for helping to land the contract for their state. "I would have you good folks of Georgia know that there are a lot of Marietta, Georgias, scattered throughout our fifty states," the President said. ". . . All of them would like to have the pride [and cash inflow, we might add] that comes from this production. . . . But all of them don't have the Georgia delegation."

In contrast, groups can also operate in competition with different *groups,* both of them attempting to influence the course of broad legislative policy or of bills which may affect the well-being of an organization with a national membership. For example, congressmen often hear from such powerful national organizations as the political agencies of the AFL–CIO, the American Medical Association, the American Farm Bureau Federation, the American Legion, and the National Association of Manufacturers. With cause, these organizations claim to speak for a constituency scattered across the entire nation. With less cause, they claim to speak on behalf of the national interest.

When the national headquarters of mass member organizations join the legislative fray, the consequences are very different from those that occur when a local interest group contacts its congressmen, because the issues that involve the national organizations are nearly always divisive in one way or another. As the battle shapes up between business and labor or between farmers and consumers or between minority groups and states' rights organizations, Congress itself is the arena, and the individual congressmen are pressured from both sides.

Group Politics and Geographical Representation

The national organizations influence the congressional process in many ways, but here we are primarily interested in how they affect political representation. What seems clear is that national organizations substantially alter a representational system formally based on geography. The Constitution makes residence the basis for electing members of Congress, but geographic representation does produce anomalies. Does the doctor in St. Louis not have more in common with his fellow doctor in Dallas than he does with his next-door neighbor, a grocery store owner? You probably will answer that it depends on the issue. And of course you would be right. Politics is such a complex mixture of interests and issues that any election arrangement will sometimes make odd bedfellows.

Consider the alignment of three citizens on issues:

	CITIZEN A	CITIZEN B	CITIZEN C
Residence	Chicago suburb	Chicago suburb	Small town in Kansas
Occupation	Retired military	Public school teacher	Shop owner
Race	White	Black	White

On an issue directly related to residency, we would find Citizen A and B aligned against Citizen C, but on other types of issues, the alignment might well shift. For instance, it might look like this:

ISSUE	ALIGNMENT OF CITIZENS
Federal support for urban transit	A and B vs. C
Increased veteran benefits	B and C vs. A
Compensatory hiring of minority races	A and C vs. B

In this hypothetical case, residency aligns citizens in a meaningful way on the issue of federal support for urban transit but not the veteran-benefits or racial issues. By the same token, representation based on occupation does not make much sense on issues that directly benefit particular sections of the country or on issues having to do specifically with race. And race is inappropriate as a basis for representation on issues that involve residency or occupation.

Whatever anomalies it produces, the election of representatives on a geographical basis is a permanent part of our politics. No alternatives have ever received serious attention. Bearing this in mind, we can now appreciate the tremendous significance of national organizations in the legislative process. On many issues they crisscross arbitrary geographical boundaries and provide an umbrella under which citizens may gather on issues that affect them in their occupational roles or because of their sex or age or race or heritage or language or social outlook. The AMA collects the energies, the resources, and the viewpoints of doctors from Honolulu to Huzzah, from Mississippi to Maine. The National Council of Senior Citizens performs a similar service for older citizens, no matter where they live or what their sex or race. The constituencies of such organizations are in one respect narrow, primarily focused on a single set of issues, but they are broad in their national base. This combination adds potency to national organizations: Their focus adds strength to their claims when their interests are at stake and their broad base adds legitimacy to their demands.

Organizations with national constituencies introduce an element of functional representation that cuts across sectional boundaries and counteracts the parochialism that results from purely geographic representation. Insofar as Congress is responsive to national organizations on national issues, it is being much less localist than some critics have presumed.

Summary Thus Far

It is useful to give a brief review here. Congress, critics assert, is not fulfilling its representational responsibility. It is too much an institution of the nineteenth century, whereas the problems of the society very much belong to the twentieth century. Congress is parochial, middle class, conservative, and cautious—traits that ill equip it to play a creative role in formulating national programs. There is some truth to what the critics note. But the criticism does not take full account of the many ways in which congressmen do represent. As a direct result of expanding federal programs and activities, individual citizens make an enormous number of requests to their congressional representatives—and congressmen (with their staffs) respond enthusiastically. Second, in a general if vague manner congressmen do pay some attention to what they believe the electorate's position to be on major policy questions. Certainly there is no one-to-one correspondence between congressional voting and constituency viewpoints, but neither is there complete disjunction. Finally, congressmen are responsive to organized pressure. They attempt to satisfy important groups within the district or state, at least on matters directly affecting them. And in a broader sense legislative policy on national issues reflects in some measure the preferences of national organizations.

Before drawing our final conclusions we will examine the second major question—Congress as a legislative assembly.

Does Congress Legislate for the American Public?

Congress is simultaneously buffeted by two legislative struggles: One struggle pits the Congress against the Executive branch in a constant tug-of-war to control programs and resources of the federal government. The second legislative struggle takes place within the Congress, and it is exceedingly complex. In this struggle the House is sometimes pitted against the

Congress is where all the conflicting pressures, needs, and dreams of our society come together to focus on the specifics of public policy.   *(Photo: UPI)*

Senate, the Republicans against the Democrats, a regional group (Southerners) against another regional group (Northerners), an economic interest (the farm bloc) against another economic interest (urban programs), and sometimes it pits two different ideological groups against each other. To this legislative struggle within the Congress, influential lobbyists, the administration, and state delegations add their fuel. Congress is where all the conflicting pressures and needs and dreams of our society come together to focus on the specifics of public policy.

The Organization of Congress

How well Congress functions as a legislature under the conditions of legislative struggles is affected by how it organizes itself for action. In recent years Congress has been the object of criticism in a number of respects. One of the harshest criticisms is that Congress is poorly organized.

Criticisms of the Organization of Congress

The Ralph Nader Report charges that

Congress has shackled itself with inadequate political campaign laws, archaic rules, the seniority system, secrecy, understaffing, and grossly deficient ways to obtain crucial information. . . . It is a Congress which does not lead, but is led, and which continues to relinquish its constitutional authority and leadership role in government. Crushed by the burden of checking and balancing the executive branch, Congress operates nonetheless on a yearly budget equivalent to less than three days' expenditure of the Pentagon.[4]

We believe this criticism to be exaggerated. But we share with the Nader group the belief that internal organization and legislative outcomes are two sides of the same coin.

The Constitution separated Congress into two houses, the Senate and the House of Representatives, and then left the organization of those bodies up to the members themselves. How they select their leaders, how they divide responsibilities and duties, how they conduct debate, and how they vote on issues are all matters to be settled by the Congress.

Comparison of the Internal Organizations of the Senate and the House

In some respects the two houses of Congress have different internal organizations, reflecting their different characteristics. The Senate is the smaller

---

[4] Mark J. Green, James M. Fallows, and David R. Zwick, *Who Runs Congress? A Ralph Nader Congress Project Report* (New York: Bantam, 1972), p. 2.

and more prestigious group. Numbering only one hundred persons, two elected from each of the fifty states, it has a more informal or less ritualized manner of operation than does the House. "The Senate of the United States is a small and special world," writes one student of Congress. "The chamber is quiet. It must be, because there is no public address system and business is conducted in conversational tones. It is dignified: somber-suited men, a few quite old, move in the perpetual twilight of its high ceiling lights." This small and special world is "ingrown and not wholly immune from narcissism, yet its nerve ends are in the great world outside, and its reaction to events can be instantaneous."[5]

In contrast there are 435 members of the House of Representatives, apportioned among the states according to population size. The most populous state, California, has the largest delegation, 43; a half-dozen small states send only one representative each. Legislative business in the House is carefully regulated by an intricate set of procedures, and power is concentrated in the hands of a small proportion of its membership. As few as 10 to 15 percent of the House members control the flow of legislative business. Many members, especially those comparatively new to Washington, are without any effective power at all. One newcomer to Congress announced his retirement after serving only one term: "I could see I wasn't going to get any place. These old men have got everything so tied down you can't do anything. There are only about 40 out of the 435 members who call the shots. They're the committee chairmen and the ranking members and they're all around 70 or 80."[6]

The Senate is more nearly a club of equals. The senator's term of office is six years in contrast to only two years for the representative, and thus even a freshman senator will be around Washington long enough to be noticed. The House member needs to be reelected several times before he begins to count for much. Many senators are as well known as state governors, and a few are nearly as well known as the President himself. Indeed four of the last five Presidents were at one time senators: Truman, Johnson, Kennedy, and Nixon. Only in very unusual circumstances will a member of the House gain a national reputation, though it can happen as was evident in the long, powerful career of Speaker Sam Rayburn of Texas.

The Senate is generally more visible to the public. Senate debate, for example, receives more attention from the press and TV commentators than House debate. This is partly because Senate debate is unlimited except when closed off by the members themselves, and the practice of filibustering, where a tiny group can hold up Senate business for as long as it can talk, sometimes can extend debate on a single issue over days or even weeks. The legislative debate in the House is much less dramatic; the time given to any individual is sharply limited, usually five minutes, and only a certain number of pro and con speakers will debate a particular issue. The

[5] Ralph K. Huitt, "The Internal Distribution of Influence: The Senate," in Truman, p. 77.
[6] W. Burkhalter, as cited in the *Washington Post*, April 3, 1964.

daily workings of the House have much less flair and drama than do those of the Senate.

Although individual senators have on the average more power and prestige than individual representatives, this does not mean that the House as a collective body is less powerful than the Senate. Both parts of Congress share fully in the power to legislate, and bills must receive the stamp of approval in the Senate and the House before passing into law. There are certain powers assigned only to one of the houses. Most notable among these are the power of the Senate to confirm such Presidential appointees as Supreme Court justices (thus the involvement of the Senate in the defeat of two controversial Nixon appointees), and ambassadors and heads of major executive agencies, and the power of the Senate to ratify treaties. These special Senate powers are more than compensated for by the power of the House to originate all money bills, including those by which revenue is raised (tax bills and tariff legislation, for instance) and those by which money is appropriated to run the federal government. The "appropriation power" as it is sometimes called is only the power of initiation, for even revenue raising and appropriation bills must pass the Senate as well as the House. But the power to originate is the power to set the agenda, giving the House considerable influence in this, perhaps the most significant aspect of legislation.

Although the differences in size, in constituency, in tenure, in duties, and in internal organization between the Senate and the House are significant, the similarities between the two parts of Congress are striking. Each house starts from the same point: It is supposed to be a representative assembly that legislates in a manner reflecting the good of the nation. And in two very critical respects each house has organized itself similarly around (1) committee structure and (2) seniority rules.

Legislation by Committee

It is impossible for 535 persons to come together, deliberate the intricacies of dozens of complicated issues, and easily reach a collective decision. Even separating these persons into two groups, one of 435 and one of 100, does not solve the problem. Even if all their other commitments (running errands for constituents, ceremonial functions, meeting with organizational leaders, electioneering and political party work) allowed time enough for the legislators to meet and deliberate, no one of them could be even reasonably informed about the variety of things which require congressional action. How, for instance, is the single legislator to become sufficiently knowledgeable that he can deal in quick succession with a flood-control system for the Northwest, tariff policy on textile imports, wiretapping by the FBI, immigration quotas for Asian nationals, and a mutual defense treaty with Canada? To make matters more complex, each of these broad issues can be subdivided into dozens of minute but significant questions:

Should the flood control program be tied in with an irrigation scheme in the Southwest? Should there be matching funds from the various states, or should it be wholly federally financed? Is it the case, as the conservationists have claimed, that the proposal advanced by the Army Corps of Engineers will destroy a wildlife habitat?

Standing Committees of Congress

The more complicated the policy issue, the more complicated must be the legislation that deals with it, and the more necessary it is to delegate the drafting of the legislation to a small group of experts. Out of this necessity was born the *standing committees* of Congress. When a situation calls

Table 13.2   Standing Committees of Congress
(Ranked in Groups, by Order of Importance)

	SENATE (17)	HOUSE (21)
I	Appropriations	Rules
	Foreign Relations	Appropriations
	Finance	Ways and Means
II	Armed Services	Armed Services
	Judiciary	Judiciary
	Agriculture & Forestry	Agriculture
	Commerce	Interstate & Foreign Commerce
		Foreign Affairs
		Government Operations
III	Banking, Housing & Urban Affairs	Banking & Currency
	Interior & Insular Affairs	Education & Labor
	Labor & Public Welfare	Interior & Insular Affairs
	Public Works	Science & Astronautics
	Aeronautical & Space Science	Public Works
IV	Post Office & Civil Service	Post Office & Civil Service
	Government Operations	Merchant Marine & Fisheries
	Veterans Affairs	Veterans Affairs
		Internal Security
		Standards of Official Conduct
V	District of Columbia	District of Columbia
	Rules & Administration	House Administration

Source: Rankings based on data from several sources, including Donald H. Matthews, *U.S. Senators and Their World* (New York: Vintage, 1960); and H. Douglas Price, as cited in Stephen K. Bailey, *The New Congress* (New York: St. Martin, 1966).

for division of labor, the typical response is the committee. And this has been the response of Congress.

Standing committees in both houses have stated jurisdictions and defined responsibilities. These responsibilities include reviewing all bills referred to the committee, consulting relevant executive agencies about possible ramifications of the bills, writing and rewriting the actual legislation, holding public hearings if these seem necessary, and, finally, reporting the "finished" bill to the respective house of Congress *with the committee's recommendations.*

The preeminent characteristic of Congress is its committee structure. This is where legislation takes place, and where proposals for legislation are blocked. Insofar as Congress does govern the nation, or assists in that task, it does so through committees. Table 13.2 lists the standing committees of Congress, ranked according to their importance.

Subcommittees of Congress: Because the responsibilities of any single committee can encompass many issues and because the membership of even the committees themselves can be so large as to be unwieldly (the House Appropriations Committee has fifty members), there is need for a subcommittee structure. Indeed, subcommittees have flourished over the past several decades, and there now are nearly 250 subcommittees in Congress. Table 13.3 lists the subcommittees of the Senate Committee on Foreign Relations and those of the House Committee on Appropriations.

Table 13.3 Subcommittees of the Senate Committee
on Foreign Relations and of the House Committee on Appropriations

SENATE COMMITTEE ON FOREIGN RELATIONS	HOUSE COMMITTEE ON APPROPRIATIONS
African Affairs	Agriculture
American Republics Affairs	Defense
Canadian Affairs	District of Columbia
Disarmament	Foreign Operations
Economic & Social Policy Affairs	Independent Offices
European Affairs	Interior and Related Agencies
Far Eastern Affairs	Labor, Health, Education, and Welfare
International Organization Affairs	Legislative
Near Eastern and South Asian Affairs	Military Construction
State Department Organization & Public Affairs	Public Works
	State, Justice, Commerce, and the Judiciary
	Treasury, Post Office, and Executive Office

Committee Assignments

In the House of Representatives, each member normally is assigned to only one standing committee, although he may serve on several subcommittees. Senators, in contrast, will have at least two committee assignments and from seven to ten subcommittee assignments. This, by the way, increases the influence of the House, because, being so much larger, it can apportion legislative tasks more effectively than the smaller Senate. Consequently, House members can and often do develop great expertise in a legislative area—fiscal policy, say, or farm price supports. The harried senator is less likely to be a subject-matter expert, having to rely more on his staff than does the representative. The greater expertise of the House member is particularly valuable in conference committees, which are joint House-Senate committees to negotiate an agreed version of a bill that has passed both houses, though with different provisions.

Committee assignments are made by the party leaders of the Senate and the House, and committee seats are apportioned according to the relative strength of the two parties. Thus if two-thirds of the senators are Democrats and one-third are Republicans, each committee (and, less exactly, each subcommittee) will have approximately two-thirds Democrats and one-third Republicans.

Positions on the more powerful committees are highly coveted. This provides party leaders with one of their major sources of power. Appointing freshmen to committees and filling committee vacancies gives party leaders an opportunity to reward those they approve of and punish those who don't play by the rules. Newcomers to the House have difficulty getting appointed to the prestigious committees. "It would be too risky to put on a person whose views and nature the leadership has no opportunity to assess," said one veteran. A freshman representative fortunate enough to be appointed to the powerful House Appropriations Committee recalled how it happened: "The Chairman I guess did some checking around in my area. After all, I was new and he didn't know me. People told me that they were called to see if I was—well, unstable or apt to go off on tangents . . . to see whether or not I had any preconceived notions about things and would not be flexible—whether I would oppose things even though it was obvious."[7]

Being reelected to Congress can often depend on your committee assignment. Thus a congressman from a rural district tries to get a seat on the Agriculture Committee, the better to serve his constituents and to keep a watch on the Department of Agriculture. It is not uncommon for a congressional incumbent to claim that his seniority on a committee that directly benefits the home area is itself sufficient reason to return him to Washing-

---

[7] Cited in Richard F. Fenno, Jr., "The House Appropriations Committee as a Political System: The Problem of Integration," as reprinted in Leroy N. Riselbach, ed., *The Congressional System* (Belmont, Calif.: Wadsworth, 1970), p. 194.

ton. His opponent, he adds, would go to Washington as a powerless and inexperienced freshman. Such campaign claims reflect considerable truth.

Of course party leaders can try to hurt congressional careers by deliberately assigning "unwanteds" to committees that isolate them from the concerns of their constituents. Freshman Representative Herman Badillo, from the Bronx, was initially appointed to the Agriculture Committee, from which position he felt unable to do much for his urban supporters. As he told Speaker Carl Albert, "There isn't any crop in my district except marijuana." Outspoken liberal Shirley Chisholm, Black congresswoman from Brooklyn, also was initially assigned to Agriculture. She remarked that "apparently all they know here in Washington about Brooklyn is that a tree grew here." Both of these appointments, however, were changed following pressure from the New York delegation.

The request of a senator or a representative to serve on a committee related to the concerns of his constituents is reasonable, but it does contribute to the type of parochialism so bemoaned by critics of Congress. There is a price to pay for appointing lawyers to Judiciary, farmers to Agriculture, businessmen to Banking and Currency, urbanites to Education and Labor, or Westerners to Interior. Committees become the property of specialized interests, and public policy making the result of compromises among small groups more concerned with satisfying narrow constituencies than with evaluating national priorities.

One's influence within Congress is often directly related to his committee assignment. The more consequential his committee, the more bargaining power he has when trying to build support for his own proposals. In the House, for instance, a congressman could hardly do better than to become a senior member of the Rules Committee. This committee controls the legislative agenda; for the most part bills reach the floor for final action only after the Rules Committee clears them. This is not a mechanical administrative procedure. The fifteen members of the Rules Committee at times exact concessions as the price of putting the bill on the agenda; they can (and do) keep bills bottled up for weeks and months, sometimes never reporting them out. As Congressman Morris Udall wrote in a newsletter, "The Rules Committee has an almost complete power to determine on important issues *whether the rest of us can vote at all.*"

An example of turning committee position into bargaining power was illustrated in the career of the late Senator Robert S. Kerr, Democrat from Oklahoma. Although not a formal leader in the Senate, Kerr was certainly one of its three or four most powerful members.

The base of Kerr's power was never his major committees. Rather, it was his chairmanship of the Rivers and Harbors Subcommittee of the Public Works Committee, an obscure post that makes few national headlines, but much political hay. Kerr not only used it to consolidate his position in Oklahoma by festooning the state with public works but placed prac-

tically all Senators under obligation to him by promoting their pet home projects. He never hesitated to collect on these obligations later, when the votes were needed.[8]

Bases of Committee Powers

Committee powers derive from four factors: (1) their virtual monopoly over the flow of legislation, (2) the expertise developed by members and the mutual deference system among committees that results, (3) the clientele relationships committees have with executive agencies and interest groups, and (4) public hearings.

Control over the Flow of Legislation: The first of these is a direct result of congressional rules as well as ancient custom. It is the factor most often attacked by congressional reformers, but generally to little effect. What Woodrow Wilson observed 90 years ago needs only slight modification to be equally correct today: ". . . the practical effect of this Committee organization of the House is to consign to each of the Standing Committees the entire direction of legislation upon those subjects which properly comes to its consideration. As to those subjects it is entitled to the initiative, and all legislative action with regard to them is under its overruling guidance."[9] Today, the legislative agenda is largely set by the federal executive, but as regards the disposal of proposed policy within Congress, Wilson's description remains apt.

Expertise: The second base of committee power, expertise, is a natural outcome of the committee structure itself. Any organization which subdivides itself into working committees is simply recognizing the need for specialized counsel. Because all members cannot be equally knowledgeable about all issues, this is a practical arrangement. If, as in Congress, these working committees are permanent and if the same persons remain on them session after session, then it is hardly surprising that each committee develops considerable expertise in its area of jurisdiction. This is true as well of the subcommittee structure; thus the Foreign Relations Subcommittee on African Affairs will develop intimate knowledge of that continent, but have only superficial understanding of issues in Canadian-American affairs. On many matters of public policy, a system of mutual deference among committees and subcommittees emerges. Thus a congressman goes along with the recommendation of a committee with the comment, "They are the experts in this field, and usually know what they are doing." In the great majority of cases, the recommendation of the sub-

---

[8] Cited in Nelson W. Polsby, *Congress and the Presidency* (Englewood Cliffs, N.J.: Prentice-Hall, 1964), p. 38.

[9] From Woodrow Wilson, *Congressional Government*, first published in 1884.

committee is accepted by the full committee and the recommendation of the full committee is accepted by the House or Senate. It is inside the committee, or even subcommittee, that one must look for sharp debate, lobbying tactics, negotiations with the administrative agency, and the final shaping of legislation.

Relationships with Interest Groups and Executive Agencies: The third base of committee power is the relationships that a committee (or, again, even a subcommittee) forms with relevant interest groups and executive agencies. The fixed jurisdiction of the committees and the lengthy tenure of at least some of their members (the more powerful ones) facilitate close alliances with those sectors of society most affected by the legislative responsibilities of the committee. The two agricultural committees, for instance, will be led not only by congressmen from rural states but in all likelihood by congressmen who have long received campaign and electoral support from the American Farm Bureau Federation. The alliance is further cemented by the close relationship of farm interests and the committees with the Department of Agriculture. Each partner in this triple alliance is attentive and supportive toward the other two, protecting them from external "enemies" who might threaten the powers of either individually or the three collectively. Similar arrangements are common in the committees on labor, commerce, finance, welfare, education, space, defense, and nearly every other sector of American life.

In later chapters we will discuss some consequences of these arrangements. Here we merely note that the three-way partnership among congressional committee, federal bureau, and pressure group strengthens the control of committees over legislation. Programs concluded with relevant executive agencies and lobbies are not likely to be overridden on the floor of Congress.

Public Hearings: At their discretion, congressional committees and subcommittees can hold public hearings on legislation under consideration. These hearings perform several broad functions. Foremost, they assist congressmen in collecting information and opinion from interested parties. This helps Congress in drafting legislation, and it provides a means by which groups and individuals can try to influence policy. A public hearing on, say, price controls will be the occasion for a steady progression of "expert" witnesses. Of course testimony will clash, but congressmen, often being lawyers, use conflicting testimony much as a judge or jury uses it in a court case. (See Chapter 11 for a discussion of adversary proceedings.) Thus one expert may argue that price controls will damage the economy, while another will insist that controls will halt inflation and thus benefit the economy.

Witnesses before congressional committees will often be representing an executive agency, perhaps one of the President's senior economic advisers.

They may also be spokesmen for major interest groups affected by the proposed legislation. Sometimes a committee will wish testimony from an individual who is reluctant to appear. In such cases the committee can issue a subpoena requiring the presence of a witness.

One of the most complicated issues of the 1970s is whether the executive branch can claim "executive privilege" and thereby refuse to testify before Congress. This issue was brought sharply to public attention during the Watergate hearings. The special Senate committee on Watergate received wide press coverage, including live television. This had the purpose of educating the public about the need for reform of laws regulating political campaigning, but it also dramatized the issues that separate Congress and the Presidency. Such public hearings can contribute to the influence of a congressional committee and, as in the Watergate instance, contribute to the general resurgence of congressional power. We return to this issue in Chapter 14.

The Seniority Rule

Congress has its leaders, its near leaders, and its nonleaders. As we noted, this is especially the case in the House, where effective power is concentrated in a much smaller proportion of the total membership. In the Senate, power and influence are more equitably distributed, but even among these 100 national figures, some are more powerful than others. As with any group of men, power rests on many factors—friendship, expertise, persuasiveness, skill—but for the most part the relationships of power within Congress follow lines of formal authority.

Each house of Congress has two sets of authorities: those who achieve strong positions, mostly committee chairmanships, by virtue of seniority and those who are elected to positions of congressional leadership.

The Elected Leaders Within Congress

Elected leaders such as the Speaker of the House and the President *pro tempore* of the Senate are truly the elect of the elect. And just as each member of Congress earns his seat as a Democrat or a Republican, so do the elected leaders within Congress. In choosing leaders and elevating ranking members to committee chairmanships, party loyalty is unwavering. If the Democrats are the majority of the House, you can be sure that the Speaker is a Democrat; and the opposite is true when the Republicans are in control.

The Floor Leaders and the Whip: In addition to the presiding officers of the two houses, there are floor leaders and other party officers. The majority party and minority party floor leaders are responsible for guarding the party fortunes as these are affected by the bills in Congress. The party leaders keep in touch with fellow party members and, within limits, attempt to influence their votes in accord with the policy position of the party. This effort meets with only partial success. But the chief party leaders, assisted by party whips whose responsibility it is to secure attendance on critical votes and to act as a mediary between party leadership and membership, are not thereby powerless. They normally preside over the party caucuses which assign committee seats, and they give leadership to party steering committees which in a loose way act as the center of party strategy for each party in each house.

The Committee Chairmen: For the most part, however, power within each house of Congress devolves to the committee chairmen. Status, influence, and formal authority go primarily to the heads of the standing committees, who rule over their committees and ultimately over Congress itself by

Status, influence, and formal authority go primarily to the heads of the standing committees, who rule over their committees and ultimately over Congress itself by virtue of their many powers.   (Photo: Wide World)

virtue of their many powers. These formal and informal powers extend to such matters as appointment of subcommittee members, hiring and firing committee staff members, supervising the activity of the committee staff, calling committee meetings, determining the order of business and the agenda, deciding whether to hold public hearings, managing the floor debate, consulting with the executive branch and chairmen of other committees, and, when necessary, serving on the House-Senate conference committee, which irons out differences between the House and Senate versions of a bill. It is difficult to understate the power of a committee chairman. And though revolts against them can and occasionally do take place, for the most part the autonomy and influence of the chairman are jealously guarded.

How, then, do congressmen get to be chairmen of standing committees? The answer is simple: They get reelected, they continue to serve on the same committee, and they wait for their party to become the majority party, for committee chairmen are selected by the simple device of *seniority*. The ranking member on a committee of the majority party in Congress is the chairman. The ranking minority party member is the "shadow chairman," and in this role has some say over the committee's staff and over the appointment of his party's members to subcommittees. But his influence is always much less than that of the chairman himself, though he is in line for the chair should the fortunes of the next election return a majority of his party.

Criticisms of the Seniority Rule

Very many arguments are made against the seniority rule. There is, first, the complaint that the seniority system passes over ability or skill and puts a premium on mere length of committee service. This is recognized in a revealing comment by Senator Byrd of Virginia: "Seniority of service and committee rank have importance over and above the capabilities of the members." (A congressman gains seniority by virtue of committee service and not tenure in Congress, a fact that strengthens the tendency of congressmen to burrow deeper and deeper into a single legislative area rather than branch out by changing committees.) Seniority rewards chronological age as well as length of tenure, for the two cannot be separated. Congressional power passes into the hands of men in their sixties and seventies, many of whom built their winning coalitions around the issues of the 1930s. Sometimes these men grow with the times, adjusting to new groups and new issues. But sometimes they do not. Reelected from one-party, safe districts, they can easily remain insulated from a changing national political agenda. William Poage, a Texas congressman in his mid-seventies, is chairman of the House Agriculture Committee. In committee hearings on a food stamp program for the poor he asked a witness from the liberal Urban Coalition why he was "so concerned in maintaining a bunch of drones.

You know what happens in the beehive? They kill those drones. That is what happens in most primitive societies. Maybe we have just gotten too far away from the situation of primitive man."[10]

A further criticism of the seniority system is that it weakens the control of party leaders, and thus lessens the ability of the electorate to hold a political party accountable for the legislative record of Congress. Party leaders cannot withhold leadership positions from recalcitrant congressmen who ignore trends in public opinion; nor can party leaders reward congressman who show a sensitivity to public opinion and electoral mandates.

Defense of the Seniority Rule

Against the criticism of seniority as a method of selecting congressional leaders is the simple argument that nothing else will work as well. It is a system which, after all, is "natural" in that it recognizes that the less experienced legislators will normally defer to the more experienced members of Congress. Moreover, it is a system that eliminates conflict from leadership selection. Do away with seniority and, in the words of Senator Barkley, "The element of favoritism would come into play, and there would be logrolling and electioneering for the votes of the committee members by those who wanted to be committee chairman. . . . Jealousies, ambitions, and all the frailties of human nature would crop out in the electioneering methods of men who wanted to be chairmen of committees." In short, seniority is good because it resolves without a fight the most disruptive organizational problem of Congress, how to allocate power.

How Legislation Is Passed

Figure 13.2 pictures the typical process by which a proposed bill actually becomes a law. This process is dominated by the two organizational features of Congress we have been discussing: legislation through committee and influence through seniority. But analysis of the organization of Congress cannot fully explain what happens when individual congressmen must decide yea or nay on a particular proposal. Every year congressional decisions affect the spending of $250 billion of taxpayer's monies. The programs that are funded and those that are killed depend finally on a counting of heads. Legislation is passed when a simple majority of those in the House and the Senate so vote (unless they are voting to override a Presidential veto, which then takes a majority of two-thirds). We should, then, turn our attention to the factors that affect congressional voting.

[10] Cited in Green et al., p. 79.

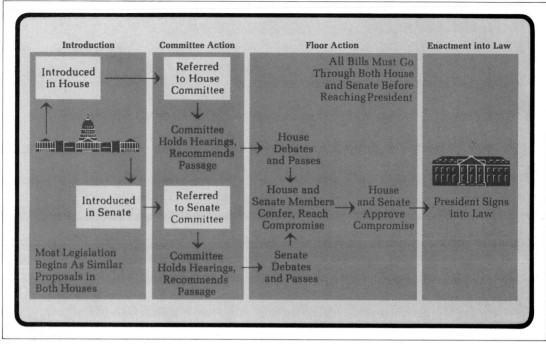

Figure 13.2 How a Bill Becomes a Law

Factors Affecting Congressional Voting

A congressional outcome reflects very many considerations: prior agreement with an executive agency, or fear of Presidential wrath; career aspirations, both inside and outside the Congress; conscience, conviction, and principles; instructions from party leaders; campaign promises; favors owed to lobbyists; thorough staff briefings; friendships, bargains struck and compromises negotiated; guesses as to probable constituency responses; and, of course, committee loyalties.

Sometimes the outside observer is dismayed at the seeming casualness of it all, of great issues of state being decided on what appear to be flimsiest of reasons. Here is one description:

> All but four of the one hundred senators' desks are unoccupied this afternoon. The debate on the pending amendment is sputtering along. In the visitors' galleries, groups of tourists, initially awed, then perplexed, have been filing in and out at the 15 minute intervals prescribed by the attendants. Now, after whispered consultations below, the debate ends and the voting bell sounds, reverberating through the vast Senate complex of Capitol Hill buildings. Scores of senators begin to converge upon the chamber.

Possessed of the prima donna's disdain for peers, compelled by their profession to fight one another on issues, they have often measured each other as enemies. But they are conscious, too, that they are brothers, that ambition makes them endure the same indignities, wage the same lonely struggle for career survival. And so they compensate for the mutual hostility inherent in their situation with the kind of exaggerated cordiality that is evident as they enter the doorways together.

But, as the senators approach their desks, the cordial glow is fleetingly interrupted by a look or perplexity — what the hell is the vote about this time? . . . To men so skilled, the minute remaining before the roll call should be adequate to identify the issue and divine the safe vote.

Covertly, they case the situation through the particular stratagem each has worked out over the years. Some have aides who now come forward to whisper a 30-second summary of the 3-hour debate. Some just follow their party leader, who has minions stationed about the floor to pass the word "aye" or "nay" to the faithful. Some, who are not faithful, follow the lead of their particular Senate guru. . . . Some, particularly those who are committee chairmen or near-chairmen, automatically support the position of the chairman who has jurisdiction over the measure — for they expect the same hierarchial support when they are piloting their own bills through the Senate.

And, too, there is a last-second vote hustling on the floor. "Give me a vote, Bill, if you can," the sponsor of the pending amendment will say to an undecided senator he has given a vote to in the past; and, if this is not one of those red-flagged issues of particular interest back home, the vote may well be given for "friendship's sake," with the donor carefully filing the incident away in his memory for future repayment.

Thus, by a variety of means most of them substitute for personal study and decision, the senators work their will, and the votes are counted.[11]

Although this is an apt account of much congressional voting, there are times when an issue is debated and investigated at length in the full chamber. One such occasion was the Senate vote in 1969 on President Nixon's plan to deploy the Safeguard anti-ballistic missile (ABM). A marathon debate, lasting nearly five months, involved scores of congressional witnesses, extensive media coverage, serious study by many senators, intense lobbying on both sides. The critical vote was a 50–50 tie, allowing Spiro Agnew (who as Vice-President officially presided over the Senate) to cast the deciding vote in favor of the administration's proposal. A few days

---

[11] James Boyd, "A Senator's Day," in Charles Peters and Timothy J. Adams, eds., *Inside the System* (New York: Praeger, 1970), pp. 101–103.

before the vote Senator Pearson, a Kansas Republican, thoughtfully observed, "You know, this issue will come as close as any to turning on the quiet conscience of the individual Senators. The Senate would be a powerful instrument if all the issues were debated in this manner."[12]

Harried men and women, having to consider dozens of major bills and hundreds of minor ones, seldom can afford the time necessary for the thorough debate that preceded the ABM vote. What are some of the factors that influence voting?

Bargaining: Often a vote reflects straightforward bargaining. "You help me this time, and I'll give you a vote when you need it." Here is an exchange that took place during a 1956 debate on acreage allotments for burley tobacco:

> Mr. LANGER (North Dakota): We do not raise any tobacco in North Dakota, but we are interested in the tobacco situation in Kentucky, and I hope the Senator will support us in securing assistance for the wheat growers in our state.
>
> Mr. CLEMENTS (Kentucky): I think the Senator will find that my support will be 100 per cent.
>
> Mr. BARKLEY (Kentucky): Mr. President, will my colleague from Kentucky yield?
>
> Mr. CLEMENTS: I yield.
>
> Mr. BARKLEY: The colloquy just had confirms and justifies the Woodrow Wilsonian doctrine of open covenants openly arrived at. (Laughter.)[13]

Friendship: Friendship also plays a role in building winning coalitions. In August 1971, the Senate prepared to vote on a bill to bail Lockheed Aircraft Corporation out of its financial difficulties by giving federal guarantees to a huge loan. One senator determined to vote against the bill was Lee Metcalf, Montana Democrat, who had assured his staff that he was no friend to "big-business slush funds." "But as he approached the floor he was cornered by his friend Alan Cranston of California, home of potentially unemployed Lockheed workers. Senator Cranston beseeched his Democratic colleague not to throw thirty thousand people out of work. Metcalf, weakened, finally chose employment over ideology and voted for the Lockheed loan, which slipped by the Senate 49–48."[14]

---

[12] Cited in Nathan Miller, "The Making of a Majority: Safeguard and the Senate," in Peters and Adams, p. 158.

[13] *Congressional Record*, February 16, 1956, pp. 2300–2301.

[14] Green et al., p. 211.

Economic Interests: Some Congressmen, of course, are interested parties to the legislation at hand. The Alabama Democrat James Eastland sits on the Agriculture Committee, from which commanding position he repeatedly votes against ceilings on farm subsidies. Perhaps it is not a coincidence that in 1971 his wife received $159,000 in agricultural subsidies for farmland held in her name in Alabama. Russell Long of Louisiana, chairman of the Senate Finance Committee, takes his stand against any changes in oil depletion allowances. Well he might. Between 1964 and 1969 his income from oil was $1,196,915, of which more than $300,000 was tax free. Reasons Long about the possible conflict of interest: "If you have financial interests completely parallel to [those of] your state, then you have no problem." The *Congressional Quarterly* in 1969 estimated that 183 congressmen held stock or other financial interests in companies doing business with the federal government, or subject to federal legislation.[15]

Committee Recommendations, Party Affiliations, Voting Constituencies:
Bargains, friendships, and economic interests undoubtedly influence some of the votes some of the time. But in the long run the factors that most determine legislative outcomes are committee recommendations, political party affiliations, and voting constituencies. Thus, as regards the first of these factors, a careful study of the 84th Congress found that if a sizable majority of the committee having jurisdiction over the bill support its provisions, then its chances of full Senate approval are nearly perfect. Indeed, 51 bills received at least 80 percent support in committee; every one of them passed. In 37 cases, committee support was between 60 and 80 percent; 32 passed. A recommendation from a divided committee passes only about half the time.[16]

It has often been observed that our congressional parties are "undisciplined," which means that individual party members are free to vote against the wishes of party leaders without fearing severe sanctions. In this respect our political parties are very different from, say, those of Great Britain, where disloyal voting by party members is a vote of no confidence in leadership and can bring the government down.

The lack of party discipline in the British sense does not mean lack of relationship between party affiliation and congressional voting. This we already saw in Chapter 8, where Democrats and Republicans in the House are compared on major legislative issues spanning a quarter-century. All things being equal, which they seldom are, congressmen prefer to vote with their party rather than against it. Usually this means that the congressmen of the same party as the President try to support administration programs, while the "opposition" party attempts to block those programs. Northern

[15] Evidence for this paragraph comes from Green et al., p. 140.
[16] Donald R. Matthews, *U.S. Senators and Their World* (New York: Vintage, 1960), p. 170.

Democrats in the House, for instance, gave President Kennedy an 84 percent support score on domestic legislation he favored. Southern Democrats were not quite so enthusiastic, giving him a support score of 57 percent. Republicans, however, lagged well behind with a score of 34 percent.[17] Various students of Congress have come to the conclusion that party pressure, whether direct or indirect, is the most pervasive and persistent pressure on congressional voting.

Insofar as Congressmen break party ranks on a regular basis the reason is usually to be found in our final factor influencing voting—*perceived constituency* preferences. We have stressed that citizens know little about their senator or representative, let alone how he might be voting on an intricate tariff amendment in a subcommittee meeting. Yet there are times when voters do know a great deal about the stands taken by their congressmen. A representative from Seattle, Washington, an area heavily dependent for employment on the Boeing Aircraft Company, would not have been likely to vote against federal funding for the supersonic-transport plane once being built there. No senator dependent on his state's labor unions for campaign funds and workers would support a bill that outlawed the right to strike. A congressman from a White, rural Alabama district need not ask what his constituents feel about compensatory hiring of Blacks; he knows what they feel and he knows how he will vote on any such bill.

Thus constituency opinion does matter—not always, not even usually. But it seems to matter most on those questions that matter most to the people back home.

Summary

Our review of Congress has covered much ground for good reason: Congress is at the center of our representative form of government. Some careful observers are in dismay that this is so, for they see in Congress the bankruptcy of our democracy. Other observers, equally thoughtful and equally insightful, believe the critics exaggerate the weaknesses and overlook the strengths of Congress. In this book we can give no final answers to our two major questions: How well does Congress represent? How well does it legislate? But we do invite the reader to ponder these questions in the light of materials reviewed in this chapter and elsewhere in the text. Indeed, more analysis is yet to come on the second question, when in the next chapter we include discussion about the role of the President as legislator. And on the first issue—How well does Congress represent?—we present a controversial question designed to help you think through your own answer.

[17] See Lewis A. Froman, Jr., *Congressmen and Their Constituencies* (Skokie, Ill.: Rand McNally, 1963), Table 7.1, p. 91.

Controversy

There has been much critical debate over *whether* Congress represents, but this debate misses the point. When congressmen try to get a pork-barrel federal program for their district, they are representing. Even when they favor policies that give tax advantages to wealthy constituents, they are representing. At issue is not whether Congress represents, but whether Congress should represent as best it can the interests of those who support and send them to Washington, or whether it should represent the broader public interest.

One Side

Congressmen should vote their constituency, at least insofar as they know what is in the interests of their constituency on a particular bill. Not only should they concern themselves with the voters back home, they should try to represent the groups and organizations that supply them with campaign funds. Someone who represents a wealthy community should try to whittle away at the progressive income tax, just as his colleague whose district is crowded with the poor should try to make taxes more progressive. If funds for the supersonic transport brings employment to your home state, your job is to fight for those funds. No one expects a Black congresswoman from a northern city to prefer farm subsidies for Montana wheat growers over an educational head-start program, and no one should expect her Montana colleague to favor the head-start program over wheat subsidies. A senator who consistently receives campaign funds from the AMA should oppose Medicare, just as a representative who accepts campaign help from the Senior Citizens should favor Medicare.

Take the case of Jamie Whitten, Democratic representative from the hill country of northern Mississippi. He is the powerful chairman of the House Appropriations Subcommittee on Agriculture. From this strategic position he forced the Department of Health, Education, and Welfare (HEW) to leave Mississippi out of the National Nutrition Survey, which was the first effort by the federal government to investigate malnutrition in the United States. He has delayed and blocked various programs that would provide surplus food to schoolchildren or other hungry citizens. He opposes any attempt to study how technological changes in farming might affect the livelihood of farm workers or sharecroppers. His record as an opponent of social reform measures is a consistent one. And it appears that this record impresses the constituents back home, for he has been reelected sixteen times.

Reelection—this is the true test of democracy. Congressmen are supposed to seek reelection, for this provides the major check which voters have over them. To seek reelection is to favor policies of direct benefit to local constituents or of particular concern to groups providing campaign funds. But this is what an elected representative assembly should do—represent those who send you to Washington. This quotation sums it up nicely:

> My first duty is to get reelected. I'm here to represent my district. . . .
> This is part of my actual belief as to the function of congressmen. . . .
> What is good for the majority of districts is good for the country. What
> snarls up the system is these so-called interests. . . . We aren't . . .
> paid to be statesmen.

The Other Side

Not all agree with the congressman who insists that he isn't paid to be a statesman. The argument against representing narrow constituency interests was effectively voiced two centuries ago, by Edmund Burke in a famous speech to the Electors of Bristol:

> Parliament is not a [collection] of ambassadors from different and hos-
> tile interests, which interests each must maintain, as an agent and ad-
> vocate, against other agents and advocates; Parliament is a deliberative
> assembly of one nation, with one interest—that of the whole—where not
> local purposes, not local prejudices, ought to guide, but the general
> good, resulting from the general reason of the whole. You choose a
> member, indeed; but when you have chosen him, he is not a member of
> Bristol, but he is a member of Parliament.[18]

Burke's observations merit careful reading. He believed that there is more to representative democracy then satisfying the immediate needs of your supporters. Someone must be thinking about the whole picture. Someone must be concerned about priorities, and trying to figure out which policies are best for the entire nation. The best place for this to happen is in an elected, deliberative assembly. In our government this would be the U.S. Congress.

Let us again consider Jamie Whitten. During World War II, some people in the federal government began to ask how the Black GI returning from the battlefields would adjust to conditions in the South. They thought it useful to plan a study that would help the government anticipate the range of social and economic difficulties likely to be faced by the returning war veterans. Jamie Whitten killed this proposal. As he saw it the task of the Department of Agriculture was to help the cotton planter and his crop, not

[18] Burke, *loc. cit.*

to engage in programs that might help the rural poor. His view no doubt reflected accurately the sentiment of his supporters.

But in killing the proposed study, and blocking many similar ideas, Whitten perhaps has contributed to the massive rural-urban migration which has drastically changed American society since the immediate post–World War II years. Northern cities, unprepared for the influx of rural poor and southern blacks, have faced the tremendous problems of urban decay, and have not had the resources to handle those problems.

It would be foolish and incorrect to say that Jamie Whitten somehow "caused" the urban crisis of the 1960s. It is not foolish and not incorrect to say that creative government programs started in the 1940s but anticipating the 1960s might well have eased the dislocations and sufferings brought about by the rural-urban migration. A Congress full of representatives concerned primarily with narrow and immediate constituency preferences is not likely to think up and fund such creative programs. But this is what a truly representative legislature would do.

Suggested Readings

A provocative book on Congress, very much in the muckraking tradition, is the Ralph Nader Congress Project report, *Who Runs Congress?* (New York: Bantam 1972). A more balanced though still critical review appears in the collection of essays edited by Senator Joseph S. Clark, *Congressional Reform: Problems and Prospects* (New York: T. Y. Crowell, 1965). This book ends with Clark's own recommendations for "Making Congress Work." Published in the same year are the very solid and informative essays in David B. Truman, ed., *The Congress and America's Future* (Englewood Cliffs, N.J.: Prentice-Hall, 1965).

The flavor of the House of Representatives is evoked in the late Clem Miller's *Member of the House* (New York: Scribner, 1962), a collection of newsletters written by this very gifted congressman. The book-length treatment of the Senate by Donald R. Matthews, *U.S. Senators and Their World* (New York: Vintage, 1960), includes readable discussion as well as useful data on a series of topics.

Much of the scholarly literature on Congress, of which there is a great deal, appears in journal articles. These are often collected in readers. For a representative selection of articles, see Robert L. Peabody and Nelson Polsby, eds., *New Perspectives on the House of Representatives* (Skokie, Ill.: Rand McNally, 1963); and Leroy N. Riselbach, ed., *The Congressional System* (Belmont, Calif.: Wadsworth, 1970).

The President and the National Executive

14

Shortly after winning the Presidency in the election of 1960, John Kennedy gave his view of the American President: "The history of this nation—its brightest and its bleakest pages—has been written largely in terms of the different views our Presidents have had of the Presidency itself." Perhaps this claim is exaggerated; a good deal more has gone into American history than how three dozen men have chosen to define their duty. But some truth remains to Kennedy's comment. More than other men, by a wide margin, the President of the United States can affect—though not control—history. What else did Kennedy think about the Presidency? Here are some excerpts from his speech:

> He must above all be the Chief Executive in every sense of that word. He must be prepared to exercise the fullest powers of his office—all that are specified and some that are not. He must master complex problems. . . . He must originate action. . . . It is the President alone who must make the major decisions of our foreign policy. That is what the Constitution wisely commands. And even domestically, the President must initiate policies and devise laws to meet the needs of the nation. And he must be prepared to use all the resources of his office to insure the enactment of that legislation. . . .
>
> No President, it seems to me, can escape politics. He has not only been chosen by the nation—he has been chosen by his party. And if he insists that he is "President of all the people" and should, therefore, offend none of them—if he blurs the issues and differences between the parties—if he neglects the party machinery and avoids his party's leadership—then he has not only weakened the political party as an instrument of the democratic process—he has dealt a blow to the democratic process itself.
>
> But the White House is not only the center of political leadership. It must be the center of moral leadership—a "bully pulpit," as Theodore Roosevelt described it. For only the President represents the national interest. And upon him alone converge all the needs and aspirations of all parts of the country, all departments of the Government, all nations of the world.

Whether Kennedy himself was aware of the inconsistencies and tensions inherent in this many-faceted view of the energetic President is not clear. But certainly we, as students of American politics, cannot but wonder that one man could assume so much.

Look at it this way. Suppose you were asked whether a government could be successful under the charge of a single man who was expected to do all of the following:

1. Symbolize the unity and common purpose of the nation. Give meaning to the idea that all citizens of the nation belong to one political community, a community with shared values and traditions. Articulate the national interest, and defend that national interest from enemies within or without.
2. Act as a strong partisan leader. Speak on behalf of one faction of the country in its battle with other factions. Recognize the deep divisions of opinion which split the citizens in many ways, and deliberately show favor toward particular groups.
3. Manage the day-to-day operation of the single biggest organization the world has even known, and carry out this executive task in an efficient and representative way.

What would you conclude? Probably that this government was in trouble, for how is it possible for the same person to act as Head of State and Head of Party and Head of Government? Nevertheless, for better or for worse, we have created just such a government. And the speech of President Kennedy makes it clear that he intended to carry out all three functions.

The President as Head of State

To understand what it means to be Head of State we must first be reminded of what a nation-state is. The State is in the first place the holder of legitimate physical force. Only the State can legitimately arrest, convict, and punish those who disobey its laws or who violate its borders. Only the State can instruct citizens to take up arms against another nation. If any other social institution uses physical force to achieve its goals, we cry out "that's not right, they just can't do that." Other social institutions can use persuasion or bribery or moral claims or inducements to get me to comply with their wishes, but they cannot force me to comply. The Catholic Church cannot make me worship according to its doctrines. Ford Motors cannot make me buy its cars. Duke University cannot make me enter its graduate school. If such institutions were to attempt physical coercion, we could and would resist and would call upon the government to protect us from illegitimate force. (Sometimes organized crime syndicates are called "private governments" because they do use physical force, but of course crime is illegitimate by definition.)

The State, then, is not like any other social institution. It has prisons. Not only does it have prisons, it has them with the support of the citizens, even including those citizens who might themselves end up serving time. As long as officials act constitutionally, they can arrest citizens, and can exact severe penalties for disobeying commands.

The President as Commander-in-Chief

Nothing indicates the President's role as Head of State so forcefully as his powers as Commander-in-Chief. If we define the State as the holder of legitimate physical force, then the person who has command over the instruments of force is indeed the Head of State. On matters of internal security and on matters of foreign involvements the President acts in his duties as Commander-in-Chief. An example of the former comes from the Presidency of Dwight D. Eisenhower, and an example of the latter comes from the Presidency of John Kennedy.

In 1957 a federal court order directed the Little Rock, Arkansas, school system to desegregate its public schools. The white citizens of Little Rock, the school officials, and even the governor of Arkansas were so outraged by this order that they refused to obey. When a federal court order is disobeyed, what is the President to do? In this case the President acted as Commander-in-Chief. Eisenhower sent federal troops to Little Rock. In a radio and television address to the nation he explained his action.

Good Evening, my Fellow Citizens:

For a few minutes this evening I want to speak to you about the serious situation that has arisen in Little Rock. . . . In that city, under the leadership of demagogic extremists, disorderly mobs have deliberately prevented the carrying out of proper orders from a Federal Court. Local authorities have not eliminated that violent opposition and, under the law, I yesterday issued a Proclamation calling upon the mob to disperse.

This morning the mob again gathered in front of the Central High School. . . . I have today issued an Executive Order directing the use of troops under Federal authority to aid in the execution of Federal law at Little Rock, Arkansas. This became necessary when my Proclamation of yesterday was not observed, and the obstruction of justice still continues.

The President, commenting on the necessity of his decision to send troops, reasoned that his responsibility to uphold the law was inescapable:

Unless the President did so, anarchy would result.
There would be no security for any except that which each one of us could provide for himself.
The interest of the nation in the proper fulfillment of the law's requirements cannot yield to opposition and demonstrations by some few persons.
Mob rule cannot be allowed to override the decisions of our courts.

Drawing on his powers as Commander-in-Chief, Eisenhower acted to uphold the laws of the land and to protect the security of citizens.

The same powers and responsibilities were cited five years later, this time by President Kennedy and this time in response to threat from outside the nation's boundaries. In October of 1962, as Kennedy breakfasted in his dressing gown, his chief of staff for national security affairs arrived with disturbing news. The Central Intelligence Agency had the night before provided irrefutable evidence that the Soviet Union was arming Cuba with intermediate-range ballistic missiles, sufficient to reach and destroy nearly any city in the United States. A week of intensive and very secret meetings between the President and his advisors resulted in the Cuban blockade, a military act that prevented Soviet ships from landing and installing the missiles. The President went on national television to dramatically announce his decision.

> *Whereas the peace of the world and the security of the United States and of all American states are endangered by reason of the establishment by the Sino-Soviet powers of an offensive military capability in Cuba, including bases for ballistic missiles with a potential range covering most of North and South America. . . .*
>
> *Now, therefore, I, John F. Kennedy, President of the United States of America, acting under and by virtue of the authority conferred upon me by the Constitution and statutes of the United States . . . do hereby proclaim that the forces under my command are ordered . . . to interdict, subject to the instructions herein contained, the delivery of offensive weapons and associated material to Cuba.*

Kennedy, as had his predecessor in office, committed the military force of the United States on behalf of a policy justified as being in the national interest. The wisdom of the policies may be debated, the authority of the Commander-in-Chief cannot.

The State is a social institution that uses force, if necessary, to realize its goals. The Head of State is the person who commands those forces. But the State is more than this. It is also the legitimate international actor.

The President as Chief Diplomat

Tradition and constitutional interpretation has established the federal government as the sovereign power in foreign affairs, and has established the President as the chief diplomat. Early in our history, however, these issues were matters of intense debate. Daniel Webster argued that the legislatures of the individual states were entitled to contract loans and otherwise form compacts with foreign nations: "Every state is an independent, sovereign political community," is how the senator stated his position. The contrary opinion was voiced by Chief Justice Taney who in 1841 argued that it was unconstitutional for the governor of Vermont to surrender an alleged fugitive to the government of Canada. "All the powers which relate to our foreign intercourse," wrote the Chief Justice, "are confined to the general government." The framers of the Constitution intended "to make us, so far as regarded our foreign relations, one people and one nation; and to cut off all communications between foreign governments and the several state authorities.''

Chief Justice Taney took certain liberties with the intentions of the framers. A close reading of the Constitution does not prove beyond a doubt that all powers in foreign matters were denied to the individual states. But the Taney doctrine has prevailed. And because it has, the relations this country has with another are all channeled through the federal government.

This sets the stage for the President to become the chief diplomat. But it is not a role that was automatically given to him. Whether foreign policy powers rest chiefly with the President or with Congress has long been debated; it was a debate fought anew in the 1960s and early 1970s in the struggle between legislature and executive as to who would control the direction of the Vietnam war.

Chief Justice John Marshall anticipated this debate as early as 1799. He asserted that "the President is the sole organ of the nation in its external relations, and its sole representative with foreign nations." The Constitution appears to confirm this judgment. Treaty-making powers are specifically assigned to the President, as is the responsibility to send and receive diplomatic messages and messengers. Yet the Constitution says that foreign treaties must receive the support of two-thirds of the Senate, and further that the appointment of diplomats is with the advice and consent of the Senate. Most important, the power to declare war is a legislative and not an executive responsibility. It is possible that the framers of the Constitution intended the President mainly to act as messenger between Congress and foreign countries. In this restrictive interpretation, the President would be explicitly instructed by Congress in his conduct of the nation's foreign affairs.

The President's Foreign Policy Powers

If it is difficult to decide just what the legal situation is, there is little doubt about what has happened in practice. Foreign policy initiative has been claimed by the Presidents, especially those of the last half-century. Only the President is in "continuous session" and for this reason, if for no other, many foreign policy powers are his to claim. It is said often that the world has shrunk in the twentieth century. Things happen quickly, and what happens in one part of the world affects what happens elsewhere. The business, military, and diplomatic empire of the United States is scattered around the world. Our military presence includes over 2,000 bases on foreign soil; U.S. government aid programs are in more than 80 different countries; and private economic investments abroad exceed $110 billion. A language riot in India, a border incident in Latin America, a monetary crisis in Europe, a new security pact in the Arab world—these and thousands of other happenings affect the interests of American programs and persons. They are viewed as requiring quick attention and action.

The President is in a position to act. He has authority over the network of ambassadors and consulates and technical aid offices spread throughout the world; he is responsible for the deployment of military forces; he has direct access to a huge international intelligence operation which provides the information on which foreign policy is based. In his actions as Commander-in-Chief and chief diplomat the President cannot avoid making policy. Nixon's dramatic visit to China in 1972 is a case in point. This visit was planned in strict secrecy. Congressional approval was not necessary. The American public was not informed until final arrangements were made. Yet the policy significance of this visit was perhaps greater than any other single action by Nixon in his first term in office. The visit had an immediate effect on China's admission into the United Nations, on U.S. military and technical aid policy toward the subcontinent of India, on security pacts with Japan, and on summit talks with the Soviet Union later in the year. The visit had longer-term consequences for our trade and tariff policies, our nuclear strategy, and our balance of payments.

But we do not react with surprise on learning that the President can alter our military stance and our foreign relations. After all, the Constitution prescribes such a role, and usage legitimates it. Most modern-day Presidents have been only too willing to engage in summit politics. Few Presidents seem able to resist the temptation to "remake" the world, or at least to take a direct hand in seeing that the enormous military, economic, and diplomatic resources of the United States are felt around the world.

Congressional Controls over Foreign Policy: The President vis-à-vis Congress

The President is not unfettered in his control over foreign policy. Congress periodically attempts to reassert its influence, primarily by threatening to shut off appropriations for foreign programs with which it disagrees. It can also refuse to agree to treaties, but the President has long since discovered a way to make this congressional power impotent. *Executive agreements* between the United States and another nation are routinely formulated by the State Department and put into effect by the President. Executive agreements need no congressional approval, and they can include such very significant arrangements as where to locate military bases and what types of technical and military aid programs to initiate.

The appropriations power is the other major control available to Congress, and its implications are more significant than treaty concurrence. For if there is no money to send bombers over Laos, they cannot fly; if there is no money for Voice of America, its broadcasts will stop.

There are times when the Congress does threaten to shut off funds, but the President is not defenseless. In the first place, Congress is often divided on such questions, and thus the President can play off one faction against another. In the second place, the President can take his case directly to the people, and can accuse Congress of obstructing programs that are in the national interest. If, as happens, a congressional committee requests the executive branch to prove that such-and-such a program is in the national interest, then "executive privilege" can be claimed. The chief national security advisor to Nixon, Henry Kissinger, was not atypical in refusing to testify before a congressional committee on grounds that what he knows should not be made public. As early as 1796 a President of the United States refused to make papers related to treaty negotiations (Jay's Treaty) available to Congress, on the judgment of the President that the papers were "of a nature that did not permit disclosure at this time." The contest between Congress and the executive has surfaced in modern times over the disclosure of the Pentagon Papers, the rights of congressional committees to review secret documents, and the obligations of military and State Department personnel, including most notably the Secretaries of Defense and of State, to testify and answer questions before Congress.

President Nixon also cited reasons of national security, along with the doctrine of separation of powers, in his refusal to provide documents and taped conversations to the Senate committee investigating Watergate. This refusal to cooperate with the Senate threw the issue of "executive privilege" into the courts.

The contest notwithstanding, and limitations and qualifications aside, the President is the center of the foreign policy powers. He may from time to time be hemmed in by congressional restraints, but as a matter of constitutional prerogative and political reality, it is the President who acts in the name of the United States in its dealings with the international community. Here, then, is the second major reason for seeing the President as Head of State. If the State is the legitimate actor in international politics, then the office which can act most regularly and decisively in those matters can rightly claim title to Head of State.

The President Speaks
and Acts on Behalf of the Nation

The President is Head of State in yet a third way. He is the central figure in the elaborate ceremonial life of the nation. A State is more than a collection of institutions, organizations, laws, and policies. It is also a political community. The community members share a "we-feeling." However much citizens may disagree with each other on many issues, they still see themselves as Americans. And this feeling separates them from citizens of other nations, just as citizens of other nations are separated from Americans by their own sense of political community. The political community is made concrete in symbols and ceremonies, in common heroes and a shared past, in public holidays and public monuments.

The President is the foremost symbol of the political community, and he is the central actor in its public ceremonies. It is the President who proclaims National Codfish Day, who dedicates a National Arts Center, who

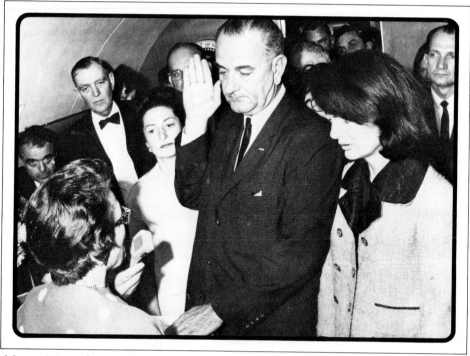

Many citizens best understand politics in terms of its most dramatic personalities, and the most dramatic of all personalities is the President.   *(Photo: UPI)*

annually pronounces on the State of the Union, and who toasts foreign dignitaries in the name of the United States. In these ceremonial tasks the President demonstrates that he is the single person who can speak for the entire political community. And he is looked upon in this way by the American public.

Try the following experiment. Ask a young child, say, five or six years old, what the United States is. The child will very likely respond by describing the President. The very abstract thing called a nation-state or a political community cannot be grasped by the child, but the very personal President can. Most of us first experience our nation in terms of its most dramatic personalities, and the most dramatic of all personalities is the President. Even as adults this tendency persists. The massive social and economic changes that took place in the 1930s are summarized as Franklin Roosevelt's New Deal. In the same way, we refer to Johnson's Great Society and to Nixon's New Economic Policy.

In the speech by President Kennedy quoted at the beginning of this chapter, the White House was likened to a pulpit, and by inference the President was likened to minister, priest, or rabbi. These are not far-fetched analogies. When Richard Nixon became President in 1969 he diagnosed our

national difficulties as a "crisis of the spirit" and he promised that his administration would meet that crisis with an "answer of the spirit." Somewhat later the widely read newspaper columnist James Reston commented
on the state of American society in similar terms. He presented a bleak picture:

> In the last few days the Administration has claimed that many of the
> income tax returns made out by tax advisers are fraudulent, that there
> is widespread price gouging and miscellaneous chiseling by producers
> at the expense of consumers and that organized labor is just as selfish
> in opposing the Pay Board as business is in evading the anti-inflation
> policies of the Price Commission. The picture of America that comes
> out of all this is a divided and selfish nation, dominated by powerful
> special interest groups that have no common concern for the national
> interest.

Reston mused about our difficulties, and despaired of the self-doubt that
seemed to afflict the society. He then wrote:

> In such a situation, the role of the Federal Government, and particu-
> larly of the President, is critical, for in a secular society that is full of
> doubt about the church, the university and the press, the White House
> is still the pinnacle of our civil life and the hope of some moral order
> and presiding national purpose. . . . More than anybody else, the Pres-
> ident has the power to establish the standard and set the model, to
> direct or manipulate the powerful forces of the nation, to encourage the
> best in us. . . .

The "Watergate scandal" brought the issue of moral leadership to public
attention in a dramatic way. Close associates and advisors of Richard Nixon
were implicated in a series of illegal and unethical campaign practices.
Prior to the reelection of President Nixon in 1972, Republican campaign
workers were arrested during an attempt to place electronic bugging devices in the headquarters of the Democratic National Committee. Investigation into this bungled affair revealed many other dubious campaign practices by the Committee for the Reelection of the President. At first Nixon
and his staff pleaded total innocence:

> June 22, 1972: "The White House has had no involvement whatever
> in this particular incident." —President Nixon

> August 29, 1972: "I can say categorically that his [John Dean's] in-
> vestigation indicates that no one in the White House staff, no one in
> this administration, presently employed, was involved in this bizarre
> incident." —President Nixon

> September 26, 1972: "I can say categorically than no one of responsi-
> bility in the White House or in the campaign committee had any knowl-
> edge [of the bugging]." —Attorney General Kleindienst

Several months later, however, investigations by a Senate committee, chaired by Sam Ervin (Democrat of North Carolina), as well as investigations by several Grand Juries, had indicated the involvement of top Presidential aides, and had cast suspicion on the President himself. Public opinion polls in the summer of 1973 revealed a lack of confidence in the President. Many thoughtful commentators felt that the President had let the nation down. In allowing the White House to become tainted with disreputable activities, he had failed to provide the moral and spiritual leadership that the Presidency, of all public offices, is best equipped to do.

The Watergate affair demonstrated that for better or for worse the President is the focal point of political hopes and political anxieties. The President is the one political figure with sufficient public personality to dramatize the nation to its members. When the drama is a noble one, national confidence increases. When the drama is a sordid one, a mood of cynicism sets in.

The President as Head of Party

As Head of State, the President presumes to speak and act on behalf of the entire nation. The same person, as Head of Party, speaks and acts on behalf of a *part* of the nation. No man since 1800 has reached the Presidency without first being a leader in one or another partisan faction in the nation. And for the last 100 years, no man has been President without being a Democrat or a Republican. This situation is not likely to change in the foreseeable future. Law does not prevent a third-party candidate from becoming President, but practical politics do. Voters, campaign workers, and campaign financers are, in the majority of cases, either Republicans or Democrats. From time to time a sufficient number of voters and party workers might be attracted to a third party, as in the case of George Wallace's American Independent party in 1968. But third parties are called "minor parties" for very good reasons. They cannot hope to capture the White House, or even more than a trace of congressional positions. (Even Wallace, the most successful third-party candidate in the last half-century, sought the Presidency in 1972 as a Democrat.)

As a partisan, the President favors one set of issues and policies over another set. He is followed by and in turn responds to a constituency that is less than the entire population. Indeed, the dictionary definition of partisanship suggests *bias*—favoring one point of view over another. The partisanship of the President sets up one of the most troublesome of all problems in American politics. As a partisan leader, the President leads one faction of the nation against another faction, but as the Head of State, the President must unify all factions. We return below to the complications of this dual role, but let us first review three ways in which the President's partisanship is revealed.

Presidential Patronage Powers

In creating the vast federal bureaucracy over the past century Congress has given, intentionally or not, extensive appointment-making powers to the Presidency. Of course these powers are legal rather than partisan ones, but they are exercised almost exclusively in a partisan manner.

Altogether there are approximately 6500 important federal appointments under the direct or indirect control of a new President. As many as one-fourth of these can be considered top policy-making positions: secretaries and undersecretaries, directors of executive agencies such as the CIA or the National Science Foundation, ambassadors and other appointments to foreign posts, members of important commissions such as the Atomic Energy Commission or the Federal Trade Commission, and of course the President's personal staff of advisors and consultants. From time to time a President will choose a member of the other party for a top position: Kennedy selected Republican McNamara to be his Secretary of Defense, and Richard Nixon appointed former Democratic Governor of Texas John Connally to be Secretary of the Treasury. But such cross-party choices are not usual, and often result in a change of loyalty by the appointed. (For instance, after serving in Nixon's cabinet, Connally in the 1972 Presidential campaign organized "Democrats for Nixon" in order to draw support and funds away from George McGovern, the Nixon challenger. In 1973 Connally joined the Republican party.)

Certain Presidential appointments, especially diplomatic posts, frequently are rewards for persons who contributed generously to the President-elect's campaign. Arthur K. Watson, an IBM executive, gave more than $50,000 to Nixon's 1968 campaign, and was named ambassador to France. An insurance company president, Guilford Dudley, Jr., also donated more than $50,000 to Nixon that year; he became ambassador to Denmark. All told, Nixon received nearly $300,000 in campaign donations in 1968 from backers subsequently named U.S. ambassadors.

Checks on the Appointment Powers of the President: The appointment powers of the President are not unchecked. Some of the most critical positions can be filled only with the "advice and consent" of the Senate. Supreme Court justices, for instance, must receive Senate approval; and the Senate refused two of Nixon's appointees on grounds that they were not fit for high office. Other "advice and consent" nominees include those for ambassadorships, for independent regulatory commissions such as the Federal Trade Commission, for higher office in the executive branch, including cabinet members, and for federal judgeships. Usually the Senate gives a new President a free hand in selecting his appointees. In turn, the President defers to the congressional leadership of a given state when making certain kinds of appointments, especially federal judges and post office positions, though the latter is now removed from direct executive control.

Constituencies with which a new appointee will work provide a further check on appointment powers. The Secretary of Commerce is almost certain to have been cleared by influential sectors of the business community. The airline industry will have something to say about who sits on the Civil Aeronautics Board. University presidents and deans along with officers of research institutes will be canvassed before a new head of the National Science Foundation is chosen. Such constituencies cannot dictate an appointment, but they can often determine the list from which the appointee will be chosen.

The President himself of course does not select each of the hundreds of important appointments made in the months immediately following his election. This is one of the busiest times of his tenure, and many issues compete for his time. What the President-elect does control is appointment to the highest positions—department heads, staff consultants, directors of commissions. These in turn influence appointments on down the line.

The entire hierarchy of appointments comes overwhelmingly from the party of the President. Patronage is used to reward those who have been loyal to the President, a loyalty often expressed as campaign contributions or other support which enabled him to win the nomination and then the Presidency itself. More than rewarding loyalty is at stake. The enormous range of government jobs that are filled by the President and his immediate advisors give a certain tone to any administration. The direction of economic policy can be shaped by the type of men chosen to head the Office of Management and Budget and the Council of Economic Advisers. Foreign policy will be shaped in the coming years by the men who direct the Departments of State and of Defense, those who head the CIA, and the Joint Chiefs of Staff, all of whom are invited to membership on the National Security Council.

Political patronage extends also to the judicial branch. Table 14.1 shows the percentage of judicial appointments that comes from the political party of the appointing President. As Philip B. Kurland, Professor of Law at the University of Chicago, says, "The judiciary has long been treated as the place to put political workhorses out to pasture. The great majority of America's judges have their posts because—and only because—of prior services rendered to the dominant political party."

The electorate not only chooses a President, it indirectly selects the several thousand persons who run the executive branch of government. That the councils, bureaus, departments, and commissions which comprise this branch of government are therefore filled on a partisan basis is to be expected. The President is elected as head of a party, and thus assumes that he has a "mandate" to put his party's program into effect. His central strategy for accomplishing this partisan goal is to fill government with "his men."

Implications of the President's Patronage Powers: The appointment powers of the President have implications for political representation. In the chapter on Congress we reviewed the failures and accomplishments of

Table 14.1 Judicial Appointments by President:
Roosevelt to Nixon (Federal, District, and Court of Appeals Judgeships)

	DEMOCRATS	REPUBLICANS	SAME PARTY AS PRESIDENT
Roosevelt (D)	188	6	96%
Truman (D)	116	9	93%
Eisenhower (R)	9	165	95%
Kennedy (D)	111	11	90%
Johnson (D)	159	9	95%
Nixon (R)[a]	12	165	93%

[a] Through 1972.
Source: Based on data from *Nixon: The Third Year of His Presidency* (Washington, D.C.: Congressional Quarterly, 1972), and Congressional Quarterly, Dec. 16, 1972.

Congress as an instrument of representation. It is equally important to consider the President in this connection. Some argue that the Presidency is a "more representative" branch of the government than the Congress. The case proceeds along two lines. The President, and only the President, is elected by a majority of the entire nation. Congress, in contrast, is elected by many different electorates that often have parochial and geographically specific interests to protect. It is the candidates for the White House who campaign before a *national* electorate and who must present themselves and their programs to the widest and most divergent audience. The winning coalition of a President will include a broader segment of the population than will the winning coalition of any congressman. No congressional candidate must simultaneously appeal to urban Blacks, southwestern oil men, Jews, prairie state isolationists, southern conservatives, and California dockworkers. But a Presidential candidate must appeal to these diverse groups, and many more besides. Thus is born the claim that the President speaks for the entire nation and represents its majority will.

This is an exaggerated claim of course. But the case for "representativeness" of the Presidency can be supported by another and more suggestive observation. We just noted that a chief executive influences the occupancy of several thousand major government positions. Thus when the White House changes party hands, as when the Democrats under Kennedy replaced the Republicans, and then the Republicans eight years later replaced the Democrats, a huge shift in government personnel occurs. This shift *far exceeds* any shift that follows a congressional election. No more than 10 to 15 percent of the congressmen will be new incumbents in any given session. But 100 percent of top executive positions can shift in the space of a few weeks. In choosing a new President the voters are in fact electing an entire administration. The Nixon administration represented a very different combination of men, issues, and outlooks from the Johnson administration it replaced.

The patronage powers of the Presidency have, thus, implications far beyond the rewards that go to the party supporters. Large numbers of people leave government office, presumably because programs of their party have ceased to satisfy majority preferences. And a new batch of people now take over the executive branch. From this vantage point they will reflect, or attempt to, the demands and goals of the majority electoral coalition that put their party leader into the White House. This is, after all, the purpose of elections in a democracy. And it is of some significance that this purpose seems better served by the election of one man, with immense appointment powers, than by the election of an entire legislature. The latter does not result in the same sense of changing vision and programs as happens when a new executive and his administration take over.

The President's Legislative Program

The constitutional doctrine of separation of powers draws a clear distinction between the branch that legislates, Congress, and the branch that puts the laws into effect, the Executive. This distinction is nowhere near as neat in practice. Historically, separation of powers has meant struggle for power. And in this struggle both the legislative and executive branches have devised numerous strategies not anticipated by the writers of the Constitution.

Chief among these strategies on the executive side is the President's legislative program. The Constitution provides that the President "shall from time to time give to the Congress information of the State of the Union, and recommend to their consideration such measures as he shall judge necessary and expedient." This is the opening wedge that all forceful Presidents have used to announce their own legislative program: Franklin Roosevelt's "New Deal" and John Kennedy's "New Frontier" and Lyndon Johnson's "Great Society" are examples. Legislative proposals are put forth in the State of the Union Address, the Budget Message, and the Economic Report. President Nixon added a State of the World Message in which he outlined his foreign policy goals. In addition to these formal addresses, the President can, and does, submit special messages to Congress at any time of his choosing.

The Partisan Role of the President: Of course a President in addressing Congress will verbally emphasize that he is above partisan politics. Republican President Nixon, in his State of the Union address in 1972, pleaded for nonpartisan treatment of his legislative program, a plea not without substance given that Democratic majorities firmly controlled both houses. Nixon recognized "honest differences of opinion, not only between the parties, but within each party." However, he immediately continued, "there are great national problems that are so vital that they transcend partisanship. And so let us have our debates, let us have our honest differences but let us join in keeping the national interest first." Later he urged that needed legislation "not become hostage to the political interest of any party." Yet these sentiments were immediately followed by a recital of *his* successes in contrast to the failures of the Democratic administration that had preceded him in office. Here are the words he used to describe the 1960s, when Democrats Kennedy and Johnson sat in the White House: "they were times of great agony—the agonies of war, of inflation, of rapidly rising crime, of deteriorating cities, of hopes raised and disappointed and of anger and frustration that led finally to violence and to the worst civil disorder in a century." As he presented the speciftcs of his legislative program for national defense, the environment, civil rights, farm support, health care, and crime, it is no surprise that Republican congressmen applauded enthusiastically and Democratic congressmen listened with polite attention. Democratic leaders went on television the following day to insist that though of course they would cooperate with the President in the national interest, the legislative program of the forthcoming Congress would have a Democratic and not a Republican imprint.

The legislative program of the President can hardly help being partisan. The President's campaign promises are many. If elected, he will do this and he will do that: start a program of public housing, oppose bussing to integrate schools, cut foreign aid, initiate tax reform, and so on. Campaign promises are phrased in such a way as to discredit the opposition candidate, and his party.

The legislative program of a newly elected or reelected President will, then, reflect partisan campaign promises. This is expected by his supporters. If not the President, who else can push for the announced policies of his party? Congress, we have seen, is divided into two houses, and then further split by the fact that each congressman is selected from a particular geographical area. It is the President who gives focus to party leadership; and it is the White House where power is sufficiently concentrated that a legislative program can be put together.

Together with his appointment powers, the legislative initiative taken by the President gives him great influence over the policy agenda that Congress must consider. If the President's party has a majority in Congress and if the President is an effective party leader—both big "ifs"—then the President can be enormously successful in having his policies enacted into law. The record of Lyndon Johnson is a good case in point. The civil rights legislation and the War on Poverty bills passed in the mid-1960s were fashioned by a Democratic administration and passed into law by a Democratic Congress.

Thus again we see the partisanship of the President. As party leader *and* chief legislator he is positioned to further the policy goals of his party, and block those of the opposition party. This is partisanship of the most significant kind. And it is remarkable that the same office from which it comes is that office which is also Head of State, and therefore the symbol of national unity. We will return to this ambiguity after considering still another way in which the President is a partisan figure.

The President as a Campaigner

In none of his activities is the President so unreservedly partisan as when he is campaigning. Actually the President is a campaigner in two major respects. First, on his own behalf when he must seek the Presidency, and second on behalf of congressmen and governors who campaign under his party's label. We first consider his own campaign.

Every four years the great American spectacle begins, first with the nominating process, including primaries and nominating conventions, and then to the general election itself. The six months prior to election day focus and intensify the partisan energies of American politics. These energies are most evident in the final month before election day, when both candidates (as well as minor party candidates) scurry about the country proclaiming their worth and denouncing that of their opponent. Depending on the personalities of the candidates, and the mood of the country, this intense partisan debate can get rather vicious. Sometimes the Presidential candidates themselves will refrain from mudslinging, but urge lesser figures, maybe a Vice-President, to let the opponent have it. Spiro Agnew, Vice-President under Nixon, was fond of casting doubts about the patriotism of those Democrats who objected to Nixon's policies in Vietnam. When McGovern was nominated by the Democratic party in the summer of 1972, Nixon observed a discreet silence, but Agnew accused McGovern of giving aid and comfort to the enemy, and other spokesmen for Nixon labeled McGovern a socialist.

Attacks on the personal virtue of one's opponent is a less significant aspect of the campaign than the legitimate debate that goes on between leaders of opposing parties. This debate is necessarily partisan. It is a debate that claims more leadership, wisdom, and talent for one side to the exclusion of the opponents. It is a debate that indirectly calls into question the judgment of every voter who would be so foolish or shortsighted as to support the other party. Actually, the Democratic party is normally more partisan in its appeals than the Republicans. The Democrats enjoy the status of majority party (more loyal followers than the Republicans) and thus need only attract traditional supporters. The Republican candidate heads the minority party; fewer citizens view themselves as Republicans than view themselves as Democrats. The Republicans therefore will more often make nonpartisan appeals, stressing that the voter should support the best man rather than a particular party. Nevertheless, the Presidential campaign intensifies partisan differences in the nation. Each candidate is viewed as

Table 14.2   Nixon's Campaign Efforts in the Congressional Election of 1970

Traveling to 24 states, President Nixon made an enormous personal effort to influence the 1970 election. The President made campaign appearances for 38 Republican candidates for governor and U.S. senator and also appeared on behalf of 236 candidates for the U.S. House of Representatives. The results:

	WON	LOST
For Governor	6	11
For Senator	8	13
For Representative	114	122

favoring programs and policies that benefit some groups in society, but not other groups.

Presidents differ in how actively they involve themselves in party affairs once they are elected. At one extreme is Eisenhower, who gave as little attention to the party as possible. At the other extreme is President Richard Nixon, who during his first term worked hard to strengthen the party. For instance, he helped raise large sums of money for Republican congressional candidates in 1970, and in the same year he campaigned vigorously to lend the prestige of his office to the candidacies of those he thought would support his legislative program. As Table 14.2 shows, the Republican party did not fare too well despite Nixon's efforts.

Even Presidents who downplay their party leadership once they have reached office are never totally free of party obligations. No President can completely shake the image of partisan leader, but he must adjust this image to that of Head of State, a figure ostensibly above factional fights.

He Can Win, But He Can't Govern

It is sometimes remarked about a President that he won the office, but could not govern the nation. This was observed about Lyndon Johnson before he stepped down from the Presidency in 1968. The remark reveals the ambiguity of the Presidential office. Getting it and effectively using it are very different matters. Getting it is primarily a partisan matter. It requires nomination by a political party and then campaign help, finances, and voter support from loyal partisans. Using the office to govern effectively involves much more than leading a party. It involves leading a nation. Here, then, is one of the standing tensions in the American form of government. It is a tension resolved in other nations by the separation of

Head of State from Head of Party. Great Britain is a well-known example. The Queen is the Head of State, and as such symbolizes the unity and common purpose of the people. The Prime Minister is Head of a Party, and as such is expected to show bias toward certain policies and programs. Prime Ministers can change from election to election, but the Queen remains. Our constitutional framers had such a bad taste in their mouth regarding the monarchy of King George III that no such solution was possible in our case. The framers hoped that political parties would not develop, but were naive in this regard. And they hoped that the President would somehow stand above factional battles, and again they were naive. What we have today is a single office on which is focused intense partisan differences and yet aspires to represent unity of purpose and the national interest. The ambiguity is well illustrated in the following news item:

> A U.S. conference of mayors voted today to back the [Republican] President's policy in Vietnam. An impassioned, shouting appeal for it by [Democratic] Mayor Richard Daley of Chicago had been greeted by cheering and footstomping.
>
> Mr. Daley, red in the face, gesturing in the air, called on the mayors, "In the name of God, stand behind the President."
>
> "No one would work harder against a Republican President than me," he said. "But maybe I'm old-fashioned or behind the times. The question is whether we are going to stand behind the President in foreign affairs."

The President as Head of Government

We have yet to account in full measure for the duties and powers of the President. Not only is he Head of State and Head of Party, he is Head of Government. "The executive power shall be vested in a President of the United States," is how the Constitution states it. The President is to "take care that the laws be faithfully executed." The Constitution also provides justification for a policy-initiating role: "He shall from time to time give to Congress information of the state of the Union and recommend to their consideration such measures as he shall judge necessary and expedient."

These phrases have become the license for the enormously important role the President plays as chief executive and for the significant powers he has claimed as policy maker. If a government is supposed to make and execute laws, then the President is in the thick of both of those activities.

Duties and Powers of the President

Initiating Legislative Programs: The requirement that the President keep Congress informed as to the state of the Union has given occasion for the President to announce his own legislative agenda. Modern-day Presidents do not just report on the state of the Union; they prescribe remedies. In domestic affairs alone President Nixon cited eighteen specific policy areas in his 1972 State of the Union address: technology, trade and monetary affairs, welfare reform, social services, environment, health care, hunger and nutrition, aging and the elderly, civil rights, women's rights, veteran benefits, youth, farmers, the cities, transportation, fighting crime, consumer protection, and school financing. In each area he referred to legislative proposals made in his first administration, or promised specific proposals over the course of the coming year. Here, for instance, is one paragraph from that speech:

> I shall soon send to the Congress a special message proposing a new program of federal partnership in technological research and development with federal incentives to increase private research, federally supported research and projects designed to improve our everyday lives in ways that will range from improving mass transit to developing new systems of emergency health care that could save thousands of lives annually.

Presidential proposals and special messages do become the legislative agenda for all practical purposes. In one year, for instance, President Johnson requested congressional action on 469 separate administration proposals. Approximately 80 percent of all major laws passed in the last two decades have started in the executive branch. Here is what one Republican congressman told an envoy from President Kennedy's Democratic administration: "We're not supposed to draw up these bills—that's your job, and then you bring them to us."

Staffing and Managing the Presidency: Where do administration proposals come from? Certainly not entirely, if much at all, from the head of one man. The ideas and efforts and responsibilities of the President are in fact the ideas and efforts and responsibilities of a network of Presidential advisors and assistants. This network is in effect the Presidency. It is the group that largely plans and carries out the Presidential program, and which attempts to organize a strategy for dealing with the several important constituencies—the Congress, the bureaucracy, the public—that will determine the program's success or failure.

The growth of the Presidency during recent administrations is one index of the increasing importance of the executive branch. As recently as the turn of the present century the President carried out his duties with the help of a secretary, someone to carry messages, and a few clerks, all paid from the President's personal funds. The modern Presidency actually dates only from the administrations of Franklin D. Roosevelt in the 1930s and 1940s. But even then the staff numbered only in the dozens, though during Roosevelt's administrations there was a separate budget to pay the salaries of the White House staff. The last 30 years have been a period of immense expansion. The total payroll for the executive office in fiscal year 1973 is more than $60 million, and Nixon's staff is estimated at more than 2000 persons.

The quality of leadership provided by the White House is largely determined by the persons staffing the Presidency. The collective energies and values of the Presidential network are what are meant by the phrases *Nixon's administration* or *Kennedy's team*. A critical task for any new President is finding the right talent to fill positions in the Presidency, and once the positions have been filled, the President must learn how to release rather than inhibit the talents and energies of the appointees.

Every President approaches the task of staffing and managing the Presidency somewhat differently. FDR fostered multiple lines of communication and overlapping jurisdiction, sometimes giving the same task to two separate agencies. He did this as a technique for keeping close control over the separate units of the Presidency. Eisenhower organized the Presidency in almost the opposite manner. Drawing on his military experience he established a firm hierarchy of responsibility; only the most critical issues were supposed to reach his desk. Kennedy had the habit of calling small, informal groups together to work on particular issues, and then disbanding them when the necessary decision was reached or program formulated. Nixon has relied heavily on a few key advisors, especially former Harvard professor Henry Kissinger in foreign affairs and former University of Chicago professor George Schultz in domestic and economic affairs.

Although there are differences of style from one President to the next, certain common problems endure in the relationship between President and staff. To get information and intelligent advice on dozens of matters, the President surrounds himself with experienced advisors. It is natural to expect that these advisors have firm ideas of their own. Yet the temptation to say what the "Chief" wants to hear is very great indeed. For at the same time that the President expects independent ideas from his staff, he expects loyalty to himself and the administration's program. From the President's point of view, his strong-minded subordinates must never sabotage, whether wittingly or unwittingly, the policy goals he has set. Early in his term Nixon fired a cabinet member, Walter Hickel (Secretary of the Interior), for writing a letter complaining that the Nixon administration was not being sensitive to the demands of college youth. As far as Nixon was concerned, the line between loyal dissent and disloyal opposition had been crossed by a member of the team, and off the team he went.

The Presidency: The Shaping and Enactment of Its Programs into Law

How Proposals Originate and Are Routed: The White House Staff does not have sole responsibility for the Presidential program. A specific proposal can originate from a variety of sources within the executive branch—and can be substantially modified or even blocked long before it reaches the President and his closest advisors. Although no single overview can describe how the executive program comes to be, here is one fairly common route:

A department or agency within the executive branch begins to formulate a new program, or to modify an existing one. The agency is likely to consult with a relevant congressional committee even at this very early stage, though the consultation is mostly informal. The agency might also check with any interest groups that normally have a position on such programs. If the Department of Health, Education, and Welfare has a group working on a program for federally financed university scholarships, for example, it is likely that they would be in touch with the staffs of congressional committees that normally handle bills on education. They would also be in touch with influential education organizations such as the American Association for the Advancement of Science. The program would begin to take shape, including some provisions (low-interest loans, perhaps), but dropping others (support for graduate teaching assistants) in response to actual or imagined opposition. As the proposal is taking shape, it would be sent to the Office of Management and Budget (OMB).

This is the chief clearinghouse. Here lies the responsibility for coordinating the hundreds of programs annually proposed by various executive agencies. Here also lies the considerable power of suggesting to the President, or his staff advisers, that a proposed program cannot be fitted into the budget this year. A proposal that does not pass through the clearance procedures of OMB has very little chance of reaching the President's desk, let alone being enacted into law. And of course OMB is also in constant contact with congressional leaders, keeping informed of what legislation might be incubating in a particular committee. Sometimes OMB will advise an executive agency to shelve its program because a group on Capitol Hill is working along the same lines, and already has the necessary congressional support for passage.

Even when an agency proposal gains clearance from the budget people, it will not necessarily become part of the President's own legislative initiatives. The executive agency may, however, be given the green light to try to get congressional sponsorship on its own. Franklin D. Roosevelt practiced this as early as 1935. To protect his own programs from various agencies in the federal bureaucracy, and to protect agencies from sniping at one another, for reasons of competing career ambitious and jealousies, he proposals into three categories:

> First, the kind of legislation that, administratively, I could not give approval to—[clearance] will eliminate that; secondly, the type of legislation which we are perfectly willing to have the department or agency press for, but at the same time we do not want it put into the [third] category of major Administration bills. Obviously I have to confine myself

to what the newspapers called last year "the comparatively small list of must legislation." If I make every bill that the Government is interested in must legislation, it is going to complicate things . . . very much; and where I clear legislation with a notation that says "no objection" that means you are at perfect liberty to try to get the thing through [Congress], but I am not going to send a special message for it. It is all your trouble, not mine.[1]

Of course from the Presidential viewpoint there is *must* legislation, and it is these proposals that receive his attention and effort. Yet we should not attribute too much of the President's legislative program to his own ideas. For the most part a President's personal policy views are only vaguely formulated in his mind. He does not have the time to think through the intricacies of legislative proposals. However, he is surrounded by advisors, staff, party leaders, and executive heads who do have "high-energy" interests, and who have career investments in specific policies. Most of the White House proposals to Congress came from these sources. And these "high-energy" policy advisors and policy formulators are themselves in touch with a larger elite network that includes influential congressmen, critical governors and other state officials, big-city mayors, powerful interest group leaders, and media people. Substantive proposals, then, reflect at least some shared perspectives.

This again illustrates the importance of the types of men and interests that a new administration ushers into Washington. A President understandably wishes to "leave his mark," another way of saying that he wants his place in history. To do so, he depends heavily on a staff that can shape a set of legislative proposals likely to receive support in Congress. Nixon entered the White House after eight years of Republican exile from power. He immediately organized interagency committees to deal with specific policies, such as committees—or "project teams" as they are called—on the delivery of health care, or the environment, or long-term strategic planning. Commenting on these project teams, *Science* magazine wrote:

The basic political drive behind all this planning activity is Nixon's need to fashion a distinctive and creative Administration. . . . The rhetoric of his State of the Union and State of the World speeches, as he enters his second year, suggests that his ambition is to mold the politics of the next 20 or 30 years, as Franklin D. Roosevelt set the context for domestic policies for the last 35 years, or as Harry S Truman defined the basic foreign policies of the last two decades.[2]

What a President sets out to get in specific policy areas, and what he actually gets are not the same thing. It is true that the chief executive and

---

[1] This statement was made at a meeting of the National Emergency Council, as recorded in the *Proceedings of the Twenty-second Meeting,* January 22, 1935, p. 2.

[2] *Science,* 167 (February 27, 1970), 1232.

his staff have many resources. Some of these we have named: executive agreements in foreign policy, party leadership and control over jobs, an enormous bureaucracy to supply him with information and proposals, the status of Commander-in-Chief, and ready access to the news media.

Presidential Tactics for Enactment of Their Programs into Law: In addition, the prestige of the office can be used in a highly personalized way to put pressure on critical congressmen. Johnson and Kennedy, both of whom had served in the House and Senate before reaching the Presidency, relied heavily on this tactic. Johnson was in close contact with congressmen when Presidential measures were at stake. Here is how one influential member of the House Committee on Rules commented on a telephone call from the President:

> What do you say to the President of the United States? I told him I'd sleep on it. Then the next day I said to myself, "I've always been a party man, and if he really wanted me of course I'd go along even if the bill wasn't set up exactly the way I wanted it." Probably I took half a dozen guys with me. We won in the crunch by six votes. Now, I wouldn't have voted for it except for this telephone call.[3]

In a second way Presidents use the prestige of the office to put pressure on Congress. They sometimes go on national radio or TV to speak directly to the public, and to urge the public to pressure Congress on behalf of Presidential programs. Franklin Roosevelt initiated this practice in his famous fireside chats. Here is Roosevelt in 1942 demanding congressional action on price controls:

> Today I sent a message to the Congress, pointing out the overwhelming urgency of the serious domestic economic crisis with which we are threatened. . . . I have asked the Congress to pass legislation under which the President would be specifically authorized to stabilize the cost of living, including the price of all farm commodities.

Roosevelt expected action within three weeks. If such action were not forthcoming he pledged to act anyway, citing the war as a cause. "In the event that the Congress should fail to act, and act adequately, I shall accept the responsibility, and I will act. The President has the powers, under the Constitution and under Congressional Acts, to take measures necessary to avert a disaster which would interfere with the winning of the war." Whether Roosevelt actually had those powers was never tested in the courts, for the Congress acted. Recent Presidents have followed Roosevelt's lead. Nixon was under congressional pressure to de-escalate the Vietnam war when he sent troops into Cambodia (1970) and later mined the harbor of Haiphong (1972). In both instances he went on national television to

[3] *Newsweek*, August 2, 1965, p. 22.

FDR initiated the practice of going directly to the public to gain support for his legislative proposals.   *(Photo: Wide World)*

plead for congressional restraint and for continued funding of the war. In both cases he asked the American public to support his decisions.

Constraints on Presidential Policy Making

It is true that the President's resources are many, but so are the constraints upon him. These constraints derive from the many constituencies that must be taken into account as the Presidental program is formulated. Chief among these are (1) the bureaucracy itself, and (2) the Congress. Each of these two constituencies has two different types of powers. Both have the power of preventing the White House from initiating a particular policy or program. And both have the power of noncompliance, of simply refusing to cooperate in the implementation of a policy initiated by the White House. On both counts the White House can fight back. There is then in American politics a constant tug-of-war between the Presidency and its various constituencies over both the initiation and the implementation of policy.

The Federal Bureaucracy

The federal bureaucracy is an immense, complicated organization. In layer after layer it descends from the White House to the lowest clerk on the government payroll. The multilayered executive branch is crisscrossed by thousands of separate agencies and programs, and by millions of employees. On any given day the executive branch of the United States government probably does more harm and more good than any organization in the history of mankind.

Bringing order to the federal executive is an impossible task. The 89th Congress alone (1964–1966) passed 21 new health programs, 17 new educational programs, 15 new economic development programs, 17 new resource development programs, 4 new manpower training programs, and 12 new programs designed to aid cities. This was Johnson's "Great Society" legislation, but how was it to be administered? In committee hearings Senator Edmund Muskie looked into federal support for individual states and cities; he reported that there were 170 different federal aid programs, financed by 400 separate appropriations, and administered through 21 departments and agencies, which included 150 Washington-based bureaus and over 400 regional offices empowered to handle applications and to distribute funds.

The President is constitutionally in charge of the executive branch, but in practice he is lucky to know what is taking place in even a tiny fraction of it. Consider the following news item, datelined Notasulga, Alabama, July 27, 1972:

> In 1932, Charlie Pollard, then a 26-year-old Macon County farmer, took advantage of a public health official's offer of a free blood test and was told a few days later that he had "bad blood."
>
> "They been doctoring on me off and on ever since then," Mr. Pollard, now 66, said yesterday. "And they give me a blood tonic."
>
> Mr. Pollard did not know until Tuesday that for the past 40 years he has been one of a constantly dwindling number of human guinea pigs in whose "bad blood" the effects of syphilis have been observed.
>
> U.S. Public Health Service officials revealed Tuesday that under a Public Health Service study, treatment for syphilis has been withheld from hundreds of afflicted Negroes for the 40-year period. For the past 25 years, penicillin has been generally available to treat it. The purpose of the study was observation of the course of the disease in untreated persons over a long period of time.

This study had been carried out by officials of the United States government and supported with funds from the public treasury. It spanned the Presidencies of Franklin D. Roosevelt, Harry S Truman, Dwight D. Eisenhower, John F. Kennedy, Lyndon B. Johnson, and Richard M. Nixon, all of whom headed the executive branch in which the Public Health Service is a small part. Any one of them would probably have stopped the program immediately had it come to their attention. But how can a single man know what is taking place in the name of the U.S. government in hundreds and hundreds of offices, laboratories, agencies, bureaus, departments, programs, and projects. Kennedy, it is said, was surprised to learn that the U.S. government as represented by the CIA was embarked on a plan to invade Cuba. Nixon was surprised to learn that contrary to orders, U.S. bomber pilots continued to fly over and bomb restricted parts of North Vietnam. Here is a snatch of conversation between Franklin Roosevelt and one of his top administrators:

> *"When I woke up this morning, the first thing I saw was a headline in the New York Times to the effect that our Navy was going to spend two billion dollars on a shipbuilding program. Here I am, the Commander in Chief of the Navy having to read about that for the first time in the press. Do you know what I said to that?"*
> *"No, Mr. President."*
> *"I said, Jesus Chr-rist!"* [4]

The sheer incapacity to deal with agencies legally subordinate to the White House is a significant check on Presidential powers. The organizational tools available to the President, his own staff and the cabinet, are not sufficient to the challenge of imposing Presidential control over the bureaucracy. Quite the opposite. They constitute part of the problem.

Competing career ambitions and disruptive jealousies natural to any fluid organization of powerful politicians and administrators cut into the organizational effectiveness of the executive office. Within the group surrounding the President there is a constant struggle to use the prestige of the President to advance particular policies, and this struggle creates animosities in the very organization that formulates and carries out the administration program. The success of any administration depends a good deal on who staffs the Presidency, and how cooperative the various parts are.

Many of the problems of President and Presidency are aptly illustrated in difficulties surrounding the role of Henry Kissinger, chief foreign policy advisor to Nixon. Kissinger was initially brought to the White House to give attention to long-term national security and foreign policy questions. To help him in this task he was given funds to support a highly professional group of personal advisors and researchers. His own group numbered about

---

[4] Cited by Sidney Hyman, ed., *Beckoning Frontiers* (New York: Knopf, 1951), p. 336.

The success of any administration depends a good deal on who advises the President.   *(Photo: Wide World)*

50 persons, chosen on the basis of impressive accomplishments in security, military, and diplomatic matters. Once assembled, the staff of Kissinger and Kissinger himself were soon involved in the immediate day-to-day decisions of foreign policy. Kissinger had responsibility for engineering the China and Russia summit meetings, and he took a personal hand in negotiating the end of the Vietnam war.

In short, Kissinger became his own "state department" and sometimes his own "defense department." In upstaging the units that traditionally supplied policy advice to the President on military and foreign matters, Kissinger and his staff attracted hostility. This hostility was expressed in a rather interesting way during the Pakistani-Indian clashes of late 1970. At a series of meetings of the Special Action Group, a unit of the National Security Council, Kissinger said things that could only be embarrassing if made public. The complete minutes of the meetings were leaked to a newspaper columnist. Informed comment on this breach of security concluded that a State Department official leaked top-secret materials as a deliberate strategy to undermine the credibility of Kissinger.

This type of tension between the White House staff and a cabinet official was not new with the Nixon administration. A very close advisor to

Lyndon Johnson explained to a questioner why Johnson had made his personal staff rather than the cabinet the logical extension of his power:

> Power, in the Presidential sense, is a very personal thing. It is invested in one man in the White House. Since power is his greatest resource, it is the instrument by which he works his will. It is not something he is likely to invest in people whose first allegiance is not to him. He is not likely to share what is his most precious resource with people whom he does not know well. Many Cabinet officers are men who are not well known to the President personally prior to his inauguration. They also become men with ties to their own departments, to the bureaucracy, to congressional committees, rather than exclusively to the President, as is the case with White House assistants.[5]

The President's Cabinet: The quotation above identifies one of the persistent difficulties a President has with his own cabinet. How should he use the cabinet? Each cabinet member normally has responsibility for a government department. Thus there is a Secretary of the Treasury, of Commerce, and so forth. The persons chosen to head the major government departments meet several criteria. They usually come from the President's party, they nearly always have had extensive executive experience, and that experience is normally in the area of expertise which the department is responsible for. The Secretary of Agriculture, for example, will have long been active in farm matters, and will be acceptable to the major clientele group with which his department works, including the large farmer organizations.

It is sometimes held that the cabinet should assemble at regular times, coordinate government strategy, and advise the President on pending policy matters. Few cabinets have performed in this manner. It is the rare head of a department who is not afflicted with what a general once termed localitis: "The conviction ardently held by every theater commander that the war was being won or lost in his own zone of responsibility, and that the withholding of whatever was necessary for local success was evidence of blindness, if not of imbecility, in the high command."[6] Localitis is an occupational disease of most cabinet members as they struggle to expand programs in their own departments. And though this preoccupation with departmental needs is expected of department heads, it hampers the cabinet from becoming a useful advisory group. Most Presidents use cabinet meetings to inform one department of government what other departments are doing. For actual consultation on policy matters Presidents use smaller, hand-chosen groups.

---

[5] Bill Moyers, taken from an interview conducted by Hugh Sidey, reprinted in Charles Peters and Timothy J. Adams, eds., *Inside the System* (New York: Praeger, 1970), p. 24.
[6] This remark is attributed to General George C. Marshall by Arthur M. Schlesinger, Jr., *The Age of Roosevelt: The Coming of the New Deal*, vol. II (Boston: Houghton Mifflin, 1958), p. 520.

But if the cabinet has relatively little influence as a collegial body, its individual members, in their roles as heads of departments, have a great deal of influence on policy making. Although the formal structure of the federal executive branch follows no set pattern, most of the government services and programs are provided in the cabinet-level departments: State, Defense, Treasury, Justice, Interior, Agriculture, Commerce, Labor, Transportation, Housing and Urban Development, and Health, Education, and Welfare.

Independent Agencies: Not all of the federal bureaucracy is organized under the major departments. Another organizational form of importance is the independent agency, which is usually more specialized and smaller than a department. Such agencies are often established in order to pioneer in a particular policy area, the National Aeronautics and Space Administration (NASA) being an obvious case in point. President Kennedy's promise to put a man on the moon before 1970 required an immense governmental effort and cooperation, and it was felt politically and economically useful to locate this effort in an independent agency. The Peace Corps was another independent agency established by Kennedy. Sometimes independent agencies (such as the Veterans Administration) are established to protect the interests of an important clientele group; efforts to locate this type of agency in an established department are strongly resisted.

We leave a false impression if the reader thinks that the federal bureaucracy is under the legal, let alone the practical, control of the President. The President's direct control leaves off at a very high level, that of the cabinet and the heads of the most important bureaus. And even his indirect control is substantially modified by the legalities and the politics of public administration.

The best way to understand the federal bureaucracy is to think of it as a fourth branch of government. It is at least partially independent of a President, the Congress, and the courts. For one thing, the federal bureaucracy is primarily directed by more than 5000 experienced career executives with permanent civil-service status. These men occupy the "supergrade" positions of the administration, and they remain in their positions despite changes in the White House or the Congress. Career executives are deliberately protected from partisan politics, and are expected to serve the "national interest" despite changes in the fortunes of the major parties.

Factors more significant than the status of government employees protect the federal bureaucracy from direct Presidental control. Over the years Congress as well as state legislatures have increasingly delegated to administrative agencies the authority and the funds to deal with citizens' needs as they arise. A water control agency, for example, will deal with a flood situation as it occurs, rather than having to wait for congressional approval. The Federal Bureau of Investigation operates under a broad authorization and with considerable resources in its mandate to control crime and internal subversion.

In its delegation of powers to administrative agencies, Congress has deliberately removed some of these agencies from Presidential control. This is one weapon that Congress has in the ongoing battle to protect its prerogatives from the executive. Federal programs not under the direct control of the President will be more dependent on the Congress.

Independent Regulatory Commissions: A particularly clear illustration of important federal agencies removed from Presidential control are the independent regulatory commissions. These commissions occupy a special place in the executive branch, for they are created to be *independent* of the President even though formally a part of the executive. Members of the commissions serve terms longer than the President, and have overlapping terms so that no single President can appoint the full membership. Unlike other executive appointees, commissioners can be removed only for gross misconduct or neglect of duty. That is, the President cannot remove a commissioner because he dislikes the commission's policies or because he feels a particular commissioner is not loyal to the Presidential program. The decision of a regulatory commission does not go to the White House for approval or veto.

Difficulty of Getting New Programs Started

Practical politics and legal limitations combine to limit what the President and his staff can accomplish. In addition the powers of the Presidency are limited by the sheer difficulty of getting new programs started. Attracting the talent, the resources, and the cooperation to initiate Nixon's wage and price guidelines, for example, proved nearly impossible in the time available for a successful program.

If things are hard to start, they are often even harder to dismantle. Government programs that have been in existence over the years have great momentum, for careers and vested interests are always linked to any ongoing program. Just because a new President comes to town, there is no guarantee that established programs can be easily changed. Most policy making is by accretion, adding a bit to or subtracting a bit from what has gone before. Every President wishes to leave his mark on history, but every President must adjust to the personalities, the quarrels, the values and commitments, and the inertia of the present day.

Eisenhower, the Republican, did not dismantle the New Deal programs that had been the product of Democratic administrations from 1932 to 1952. Nor did the eight years of Democratic control of the White House following Eisenhower's eight years in office represent a sharp break in public policy—though many new programs were added. Today President Nixon attempts to reduce expenditures for programs started in administrations prior to his, but he finds the task nearly impossible.

Here is his campaign pledge in 1972:

> We would like to operate the Federal Government at less cost, and we think we know how to do it. . . . We are for lower costs, for less function in the Federal Government. . . . My goal is not only no tax increase in 1973, but no tax increase in the next four years.

As one commentator observes:

> But where can the Administration cut enough to make its next budget consistent with this pledge? Roughly 40 per cent of the projected budgets are allocated to defense, space and related activities—and it is clear the Administration does not want to cut here.
>
> Of the domestic budget, well more than half goes directly to people, either in cash benefits (Social Security, unemployment insurance, veterans' pensions, welfare, civil-service retirement, etc.) or in kind (Medicare, Medicaid, public housing). These people have real needs, real votes and real representatives on Capitol Hill. It is inconceivable that the President would propose legislation to cut these benefits back or that the Congress would pass it.
>
> Contractual obligations of the Government, such as interest on the debt, cannot be tampered with, and no one really wants to cut out such services as national parks or fish and wildlife preservation.
>
> This leaves grants to state and local governments as the prime candidates for cuts. . . . In practice, however, it has so far proved . . . impossible to cut the total funds. . . . Each program brings identifiable benefits to a particular group which is aware that the program exists and resists its elimination. Moreover, and perhaps more important, most of these programs support the services of particular professional groups—librarians, vocational-education teachers, veterinarians, psychiatric social workers, sanitary engineers. Each of these groups believes it is doing something important and useful—and it doubtless is—and fights to preserve and expand the programs it knows will support its activities.
>
> Moreover, a Congressman likes easily identifiable programs and projects that he can point to with pride in an election year—a new hospital wing, a bridge, or a research center in his district.[7]

Nixon did reduce federal spending on certain social welfare programs; but as Figure 14.1 demonstrates, the trend toward increased spending was not reversed. The growth of the federal budget has persisted whether the President is a Democrat or a Republican. Once they are started, it is very difficult to bring programs to a halt.

[7] Alice M. Rivlin, "Dear Voter: Your Taxes Are Going Up," New York Times Magazine, November 5, 1972, pp. 113–114.

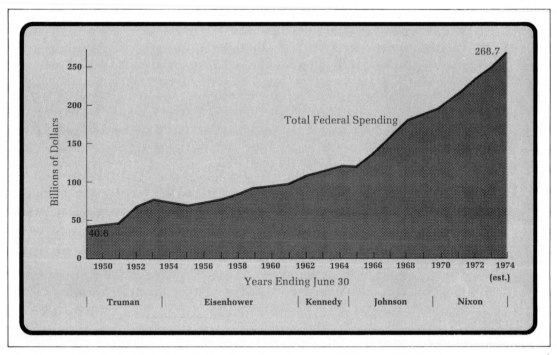

Figure 14.1 The Federal Budget Under Five Presidents (in Billions of Dollars)
SOURCE: U.S. Office of Management and Budget.

We have now reviewed several ways in which the President is limited even in the power he exercises over his own federal bureaucracy. These limits place important restraints on policy initiatives by the President. Even more significant restraints come from the fact that the executive branch is part of a "separation of powers" system of government. Despite the growth of executive power during the twentieth century, Congress continues to exert considerable authority over public policy.

The Battle for Legislative Powers Between Congress and the Presidency

The popular press frequently exaggerates the influence of the Presidency in making public policy. A distorted image is conveyed by the language used: Johnson's War on Poverty or Nixon's Revenue Sharing Plan. But seldom will a major legislative program be passed without some congressional imprint. An executive proposal sent to Congress is reworked by Congress and emerges as a bill reflecting compromise between congressional and Presidential wishes.

Influence of Strong Congressional Leaders: When Congress is not enthusiastic about a President's program, not much of it will be enacted into law. Running for the Presidency in 1960, John Kennedy proclaimed his New Frontier in campaign speech after campaign speech. Perhaps that slogan helped elect him, but it had little bearing on the electoral success of a half-dozen conservative southern senators who headed major Senate committees. James Eastland, the influential Democrat from Mississippi, won his Senate seat with 91 percent of the vote in Mississippi, while Kennedy was winning the Presidency by only one-tenth of 1 percent. Senators such as Eastland had strong positions in Congress and substantial constituency support back home. Once in office, Kennedy's limited success with his New Frontier program could be attributed to the lack of enthusiasm for them on the part of such powerful congressional leaders as Eastland. The President pushed for no civil rights legislation, for instance, leaving that issue to the law courts and the Attorney General's Office.

One source of congressional strength, as already noted, rests on its reputation of having roots back home. The Washington community, especially the executive branch, is more isolated from "public sentiment" than official rhetoric might suggest. As one long-time observer of Washington politics concludes:

> Congressional sentiment tends to be officialdom's pragmatic substitute
> for "public opinion" because it is on Congress, not the general public,
> that officials must depend, day after day, for legislation and for funds to
> keep programs and personnel alive. And bureaucrats are not the only
> ones who make that substitution. For comparable reasons it is made,
> much of the time, by diplomats of many countries, officers of every
> state, representatives of private interests, local party leaders, and even
> congressmen themselves.[8]

Congress' Legal Power of Control over the Executive Branch: Congress also has very specific legal powers of control over the executive branch. The four most significant powers held by Congress are: (1) organization—the departments and agencies of the executive branch are created by acts of Congress; (2) authorization—executive agencies operate within boundaries and on programs established by congressional legislation. The National Aeronautics and Space Administration (NASA) cannot design just any program of space exploration it wishes; its programs and its very existence depend on congressional authorization; (3) financing—Congress controls the purse strings, and programs that are not funded are programs that cannot be implemented. In a bitter battle between the President and Congress in 1970 Congress refused to provide funds necessary for the development of a supersonic transport (the SST), and Nixon had no choice but to let the project drop; (4) oversight—the executive agencies are subject

[8] Richard E. Neustadt, *Presidential Power* (New York: Wiley, 1962), p. 89.

to inquiry by Congress. Public hearings by a hostile congressional committee can embarrass an agency, and can do much to change administration policy.

There is, of course, a fifth power: impeachment. By a simple majority vote, the House of Representatives can vote to impeach the President (as well as other lesser officials). When this happens, the Senate convenes as a court, under the chairmanship of the Chief Justice of the Supreme Court, to weigh the evidence for and against the President. It takes a two-thirds majority of the Senate to convict. Only one impeachment trial of a President has ever taken place, and in this instance (President Andrew Johnson in 1868), the Senate failed by one vote to convict. The power of impeachment is very much a "last resort" measure and would not be used save in exceptional circumstances.

Congress has not, in recent decades, used its powers to the fullest. This has led some observers to conclude that Congress has ceased to check the executive. "No matter how hard the Congress may struggle on one issue, it is overwhelmed by the vastly greater forces of the presidency. Whether Congress wins or loses, the president ends up on top," is the conclusion reached by the Ralph Nader Congress Project.[9] A great deal of evidence lends substance to this conclusion.

For instance, even when Congress passes legislation viewed as undesirable by the President, the battle is not over. The President has the power to veto the legislation simply by refusing to sign into law the bill passed by Congress. Veto power was inserted into the Constitution, primarily as a Presidential check on unconstitutional or ill-conceived legislation. But usage has transformed the veto into an important policy power of the President; he can threaten to veto acts of Congress not in accord with the Presidential program. Here is Nixon in a special message to Congress as Congress prepared to vote on a major health bill and a major education bill:

> I will simply not let reckless spending of this kind destroy the tax-reduction we have secured and the hard-earned success we have earned in the battle against inflation. . . . With or without the cooperation of the Congress, I am going to do everything within my power to prevent such a fiscal crisis for millions of our people. . . . Let there be no misunderstanding, if bills come to my desk calling for excessive spending which threatens the federal budget, I will veto them.

Congress also has a veto power. It can override the Presidential veto with a two-thirds vote, but majorities of that size are not easily obtained. Franklin Roosevelt vetoed 631 separate congressional measures, and only 9 were subsequently overridden by Congress. Eisenhower vetoed 201 bills, only 3 of which were subsequently passed.

---

[9] Mark J. Green, James M. Fallows, and David R. Zwick, *Who Rules Congress?* (New York: Bantam, 1972), p. 94.

Executive power extends even beyond the veto. During Nixon's first term Congress authorized funds for waste treatment plants which Nixon considered excessive. Nixon vetoed the bill with a strong protest to Congress, but by an overwhelming bipartisan vote in both the House and the Senate the veto of the President was overridden. Normally the matter would have ended there, but it did not. Nixon ordered the relevant executive departments *not* to allocate the funds actually authorized by Congress to the various state projects. This order elevated executive will over congressional legislation, nullifying even the congressional overriding of a Presidential veto.

Such incidents as this give weight to the claim that the executive branch is taking over more and more of the legislative initiative traditionally (and constitutionally) belonging to the Congress. Yet it is easy to overestimate the significance of these incidents. Two things should be kept in mind. First, that which Congress gives, Congress can take away. Presidential initiative depends on a large and energetic White House staff as well as the establishment of executive agencies. Authorization and funds for these come finally from Congress. Should Congress decide to reassert its full control over legislation, there is nothing the Presidency can do. It is thought by students of the matter that the power balance between legislative and executive branches moves in cycles. It was just a decade ago that critics of the legislative branch were bemoaning how *effective* Congress was in obstructing the New Frontier legislation of President John F. Kennedy. The tug-of-war between the two branches goes on, and certainly it is premature to pronounce one branch dead.

There is a second observation to keep in mind. The complaint that the executive has supplanted Congress as the major force in American politics largely comes out of a period when foreign policy questions, and especially the Vietnam war, have dominated headlines. Now it is true that constitutionally the war-making power belongs to Congress. But tradition dictates otherwise. There is a long-standing, though tacit, agreement within our national government that matters of defense and national security should be delegated to the executive. In matters of warfare only the executive can act quickly and decisively; in matters of diplomacy and negotiations only the executive can act with the necessary secrecy. As Figure 14.2 shows, Congress backed away from this tacit agreement as the Vietnam war dragged on, but it never managed to substitute its own will for executive leadership in the arena of foreign affairs.

The other half of this agreement is that, finally, Congress controls the bread-and-butter domestic issues. No President, for instance, could expect to enact tax reform legislation. As columnist Russell Baker accurately noted, "no power is kept so zealously locked in the congressional safe as the power to decide who gets soaked and who gets the boons on April 15." It is to Congress and not the President that we look for final disposal of domestic welfare questions, such as revenue sharing or an education bill or a minimum-wage policy.

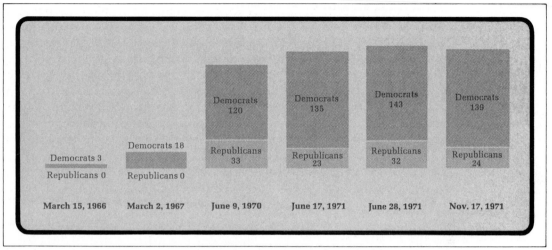

Figure 14.2 Antiwar Votes in House, 1966–1971

SOURCE: Based on data from *The Power of the Pentagon*
(Washington, D.C.: *Congressional Quarterly,* 1973), p. 112.

As the nation turns its mind from matters of war and diplomacy to matters of domestic policy, we are likely to witness a reassertion of congressional authority. This reassertion is being aided by the particular complications facing President Nixon due to the Watergate investigations. Watergate reveals how far the initiative in American politics had moved to the White House; it reveals also how sharply this initiative can be checked and perhaps reversed by a reawakened Congress. Yet the student of American politics should take care to separate immediate political happenings from longer-term trends. The weakening of a particular Presidential administration, because of an event such as Watergate, can be a temporary thing.

If a substantial amount of congressional control is to be exercised over public policy, it will be as much related to the shift of the political agenda from international to domestic issues as it will be to the specifics of the Nixon years. Whether you view the resurgence of congressional power as a good thing or a bad thing depends, of course, on your view of how Congress will dispose of domestic political and social problems. The controversial question posed at the end of this chapter provides an opportunity to debate the pros and cons of the "Congress vs. President" question.

The President's Position in American Politics

The President stands at the center of American politics. Presidential advisor and author Richard Neustadt tells why:

*Our Constitution, our traditions, and our politics provide no better
source for the initiatives a President can take. Executive officials need*

decisions, and political protection, and a referee for fights. Where are these to come from but the White House? Congressmen need an agenda from outside, something with high status to respond to or react against. What provides it better than the program of the President? Party politicians need a record to defend in the next national campaign. How can it be made except by "their" Administration? Private persons with a public axe to grind may need a helping hand or they may need a grinding stone. In either case who gives more satisfaction than a President? And outside the United States, in every country where our policies and postures influence home politics, there will be people needing just the "right" thing said and done or just the "wrong" thing stopped in Washington. What symbolizes Washington more nearly than the White House? [10]

Standing at the center of American politics, however, is very different from directing American society. Perhaps it is fair to say that the President is "the most powerful man" in the nation; if so, it should quickly be added that his powers are constrained and bound and limited from every side. At best he remains at the center of things for a limited number of years and it is remarkable how inconsequential ex-Presidents are. But even in office the President is as much a victim as the commander of his own bureaucracy, of the legislature and courts with which he shares his power, of public sentiments, and the victim of history itself.

Controversy

Is the Presidency or the Congress the appropriate branch of government for formulating national policy? Because the "Congress vs. President" debate is many sided, it is necessary to make certain simplifying assumptions in order to state a meaningful controversy. We ask the reader to make two such assumptions for the sake of the argument. (1) Rather than pursue the facts of the matter, we debate the "oughtness" of the issue. Relevant factual evidence is scattered throughout the preceding chapters, and it has been shown that how much power either branch has relative to the other depends on various conditions. (2) Let us assume that the agenda for public debate and governmental action is best formulated by only one branch of government. This assumption does not challenge the logic of separation of powers. It simply holds that sharpness of proposal and efficiency of action will be served if one branch of government has the clear responsibility to identify the national priorities and to formulate means for reaching them.

One Side

The Presidency is the appropriate branch of government for formulating national policy. The President is elected by a national constituency, rather than by hundreds of localized constituencies. The Presidential campaign focuses the attention of the nation on broad alternative strategies for dealing with social issues. Each of the major Presidential tickets presents a package of policies to which every region, every race, every social class, every occupational interest can respond favorably or negatively. Individual congressional contests present only partial programs, aimed at a particular constituency. An electoral victory or defeat at the Presidential level reflects the majority sentiment as it expresses itself across the entire society.

Only the executive branch is subject to large-scale turnover of personnel and priorities. When a new Presidential administration comes to power, "a thousand new officials descend on Washington, coming fresh from the people, representing the diverse forces behind the new President and bringing with them new demands, new ideas, and new power. Here truly is representative government along classic lines and of a sort which Congress has not known for decades."[11]

Not only does the Presidency represent national tides of public opinion, it can think and plan on a national level. By careful selection of White House staff, cabinet officers, and other high executive officials, the President brings together a group unparalleled in experience and talent. Although there will be honest differences within the executive office, there will also be common cause and shared vision. Out of this type of group can come a coordinated national program. Congress is much too much a potpourri of conflicting views to formulate any coherent perspective.

Finally the White House has the advantage because it can best bring together international and domestic considerations. Only the executive branch has the worldwide network and information flow so necessary to coordinating what goes on at home with what is going on abroad.

In short, the Presidential office is the truly national branch of government, and it has a global perspective. These are the conditions that will make for a meaningful articulation of social priorities and rational strategies.

The Other Side

The Congress is the appropriate branch for formulating national policy. Congress has one distinct advantage over the White House. It is the branch of government in continuous, direct contact with the citizens. Congressmen make frequent trips back home. They hear from constituents and from lob-

[11] Samuel P. Huntington, "Congressional Responses to the Twentieth Century," in David B. Truman, ed., *The Congress and America's Future* (Englewood Cliffs, N.J.: Prentice-Hall, 1965), p. 17.

byists on a daily basis. The White House, in contrast, is isolated for long periods of time. Many bureaucratic layers intervene between the President and his consultants and the public at large. The President deals with the public through the media or through intermediaries; the congressmen deal directly with the public. For this reason Congress is best equipped to outline a national program. Consider two points.

A program formulated by Congress will be more "democratic." It will reflect a compromised and negotiated version of what is on the mind of citizens spread across the nation. Perhaps Congress is tied to regional and parochial concerns, but these are exactly the concerns a government is supposed to service. Citizens want jobs, clean air and water, crime control, social services, and dozens of other specific things. But citizens are not of one mind regarding how much of which of these things they want from government, and at what cost. Only Congress reflects the bewildering and *necessarily* conflicting desires of more than 200 million individuals.

A program formulated by Congress will for this reason be more practical. Congress will come up with a national program that in truth is a jumbled compromise of dozens and dozens of regional claims and specialized requests. But such a program is realistic. The very contradictions and sharp disagreements within Congress reflect actual contradictions and disagreements within the nation at large. A program that fails to adjust and compromise such real differences is not likely to be accepted. And this is the danger to any highly coherent national program which comes from a star-studded staff of economists, planners, and strategists lodged in the White House.

Suggested Readings

A useful general book is Clinton Rossiter's *The American Presidency* (New York: Harcourt Brace Jovanovich, 1956). Two books written in the 1960s that make a case for stronger Presidential leadership are James M. Burns, *Deadlock of Democracy: Four-Party Politics in America* (Englewood Cliffs, N.J.: Prentice-Hall, 1963); and Richard E. Neustadt, *Presidential Power* (New York: Wiley, 1960). It is said that both of these works were closely read by John Kennedy, and may well have been the inspiration for his ambitions for the Presidency, as illustrated in the quotation that begins this chapter. A very telling critique of the Burns and Neustadt proposals can be found in Garry Wills, *Nixon Agonistes: The Crisis of the Self-Made Man* (Boston: Houghton Mifflin, 1969), which includes as well some fascinating interpretive discussions of what the election of Richard Nixon to the Presidency tells American society about itself.

Presidents and the Presidency have, of course, long fascinated observers. Many journalistic accounts have been written, and some of them contain rich descriptive material as well as sound analysis. Often, however, the reader will find that the preferences of the author color his perspective. The weaknesses as well as the strengths of such accounts appear in two highly readable books written about the

Kennedy years: Theodore C. Sorensen, *Decision-Making in the White House* (New York: Columbia University Press, 1963); and Arthur M. Schlesinger, Jr., *A Thousand Days* (Boston: Houghton Mifflin, 1965). On the Johnson Presidency, see Robert D. Novak and Rowland Evans, *Lyndon B. Johnson: The Exercise of Power* (New York: New American Library, 1966), which includes a useful account of his first years in office, when he managed to put through Congress much domestic legislation, but stops short of the years when Vietnam dominated his administration.

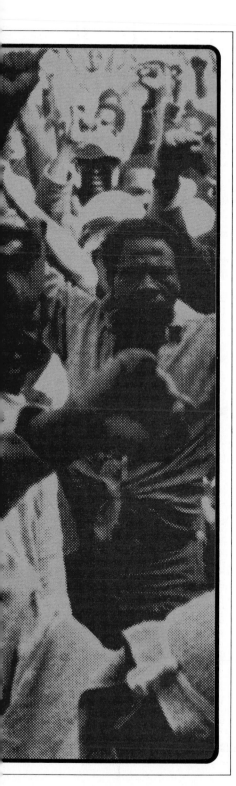

Who Gets
What and
How

15

Politics produces *policies*, and these policies affect the lives of all Americans. What the government does (or does not do) about pollution, the economy, mass transportation, or public safety makes the lives of Americans better or worse. Not that government policies have a uniform impact on all citizens. Quite the contrary. Some policies make the lives of some citizens better without affecting others. Some policies make the lives of some citizens better while making the lives of others worse. This fact of differential impact is what much of politics is all about. It makes it important who has access to the government, who has influence over its policies.

How is policy made in America? Who determines what the government does? Much of our book has been on this topic; we have looked at the various actors in American politics and the institutions within which they act from that point of view. What remains is to tie all this together by looking at the way in which policy is actually made.

What Is a Policy?

The activity of the government can be understood in terms of *policies* and in terms of *decisions*. Policies represent long-term commitments of the government to a *pattern of activity*. Decisions represent particular points where that pattern of activity changes. The United States had a *policy* toward China from 1949 to 1971, a rather hostile policy stressing nonrecognition, limitations on trade and contacts, and support for the government of Taiwan. In 1971 President Nixon made a *decision* to go to Peking, a decision that entailed a general change in the policy.

In some cases, policies continue for a long time while no decisions are made in relation to them. Sometimes policies are reinforced periodically by decisions. The decision year after year to oppose the entry of China into the United Nations reinforced the overall policy. And sometimes policies are constantly modified by decisions. Government policy on bussing to achieve school integration has constantly changed in recent years: Decisions by the courts, by the federal executive, and by the states kept changing the policy on this matter.

How to Understand Government Policy

To understand how government activities affect the lives of Americans, one has to understand the roots of long-term policies as well as the sources of the specific decisions that change those policies. Furthermore, one may have to look quite broadly to see what government policy actually is. We defined a policy as a long-term commitment to a pattern of *activity*. We are interested in what the government actually does in a particular area, not just what it says.

Study the Detailed Provisions: Many of the general statements about policy may be expressions of pious hope rather than descriptions of reality. If Congress passes a law declaring that all children have the right to an equal level of education, such a law has little meaning without a vast appropriation of funds to carry it out. Congress often passes laws expressing a high intent but backed up by a small budget. Furthermore, there is often a gap between the general preamble to a congressional measure and its actual provisions. The preamble gives the overall intent of the bill, but the detailed provisions often lead to results different from those expressed in the preamble. Tax policy is an example. A major tax bill has general purposes: to raise revenues, control inflation, perhaps redistribute wealth. These are expressed in the preamble of the bill. But the real policy is found in the many specific clauses of the bill, and these specific sections may lead to a result quite different from the general statement.

Observe Administration of a Policy: In addition, one has to follow a policy from its initial statement right through to its administration. The formal descriptions of American government tell us that Congress makes policies and administrative agencies carry them out. But this is not always the way it works, for how the general directives are administered may determine the effectiveness of policy. For example, Congress may pass a law to improve school conditions in the inner city; it may even appropriate funds for that purpose. But if the local school officials divert those funds to other purposes, the effective policy is not one of helping ghetto schoolchildren. Local school districts have sometimes used funds from the federal government to replace their own contributions to the inner-city school, thereby effectively leaving such schools in the same condition as they were before the policy went into effect, and making more funds available to schools in better neighborhoods. A similar pattern could be found in urban renewal — as we discussed in our chapter on federalism. The overall purpose of urban renewal as expressed in the preamble to the bill establishing the program was to preserve and improve conditions in the inner city by aiding in the removal of slums and replacing them by better buildings. But how that policy worked depended heavily on how the particular urban renewal plan developed locally. The specific plan determined who was moved out and where they were moved, what was built in place of the removed buildings, and who ultimately benefited from the program. For many cases it was the builders and the program directors rather than the people themselves who benefited.

Observe a Policy in Action: Congress in many cases passes laws whose meaning is quite vague—deliberately so because Congress wants administrative agencies to define the meaning more precisely. This increases the necessity of observing a policy in action rather than the policy as expressed.

The Supreme Court also makes important authoritative statements about policy, and like Congress, its policy statements are not always automatically put into effect once they are expressed. For example, in a variety of decisions, the Supreme Court has invoked the First Amendment on the separation of church and state to limit religious activities in the public schools. But individual school districts are sometimes slow to comply and quick to evolve alternative schemes to continue such practices. As one specialist on education and the law wrote: "School systems in virtually every state violate in some way the legal principles concerning religious instruction in the public schools."[1] And if no one in the community objects to these violations, little is done.

Or to take another example: In 1964, ten years after the Supreme Court's 1954 decision outlawing school segregation, only 2 percent of the Black children in the eleven southern states were attending integrated schools. Since then, more southern schools have been integrated, but only when rigorous enforcement by the Justice Department was begun.

In short, if you want to see what policy the government is pursuing in a particular area, you have to see what is actually happening and not what congressional law or Supreme Court edict tells you ought to be happening.

The Symbolic Response to a Demand for a New Policy: One perceptive scholar of American politics has noted a number of occasions where agitation for change—for a *decision* that would lead to a new *policy*—has been met by a *symbolic* response. A symbolic response is one in which the government—through a law of Congress or a major statement by the President—expounds a new policy: "No more rotten meat shall be sold"; "Railroads can no longer set fares to discriminate against some customers"; "Our rivers and lakes shall be clean." But beyond the broad symbolic statement, little is effectively done to carry out the policy. The real policy may look little different from that before the new "symbolic" policy. However, such symbols can have important consequences, particularly if those agitating for change are convinced that such change has in fact taken place. Nothing is different, but they are content and cease their agitation. For this reason, this scholar calls such policies "symbols of quiescence."[2] The example of such "symbols of quiescence" underlines our general point: To

---

[1] Frank J. Sorauf, "Zorach v. Clausen: The Impact of a Supreme Court Decision," *American Political Science Review*, 53 (September 1959).

[2] Murray Edelman, *The Symbolic Uses of Politics* (Urbana: University of Illinois Press, 1964).

understand a real pattern of policy, one has to look at how it is carried into effect.

The Unintended Consequences of a Policy: Not all policies work out as those who designed them or administered them intend them to. Often they have additional consequences, consequences that follow inevitably from the policy but that were by no means planned and intended. Policies pursued by school districts about uniform testing were not intended to discriminate against Blacks. But they have a discriminatory effect if the tests ask about aspects of life more familiar to middle-class Whites than to Blacks, or use a language structure more in tune with the language used in White homes than in Black homes.

Or take the example we cited in a previous chapter of the impact on urban America of federal policies on housing, urban development, and roads. These policies were not *intended* to create a situation in which inner-city ghettos are surrounded by more affluent White suburbs. The Federal Housing Administration (FHA) program was *intended* to allow citizens to buy their own homes. In practice, however, it led to White citizens' buying homes outside the city where land was available and where they believed they would find fresh air and green grass. The FHA policy was never overtly one against giving such loans equally to Blacks. But Blacks rarely could afford private homes. And even if they could, the FHA tended to guarantee loans only in neighborhoods that were not likely to become slums. That a Black family would want to buy a home in a particular neighborhood (or would be able to) made the agency dubious that such a neighborhood was a safe bet. The purpose of the governmental program: help citizens buy homes. The consequence: Black ghettos.

Government Action and Nonaction

To understand the full range of governmental policy one has to consider what the government *does not do* as well as what it *does*. If the government is inactive in some area, that is a policy as well, though not necessarily a planned policy. There may never have been a decision to do nothing. But the fact of inactivity has an impact nevertheless.

A visitor from another country, for instance, might ask about the policy of the American government in relation to the English language. "What do you mean by a language policy?" most Americans would reply. "There is no issue or problem here." Yet it is incorrect to say that we are a monolingual country. Most citizens speak English but substantial minorities speak Spanish. To have no explicit policy on the subject does not mean that there is not an *implicit* policy contained in the actuality of practice. To have no policy means that government business is conducted in English, civil service examinations are in English, literacy tests for voting are in that language, as well as school instruction. And all of these work to the disadvantage of those whose native tongue is not English. (Indeed, where previously only implicit policy existed in this area, today a conflict of interests has been recognized—leading to explicit policies in New York City and in California that recognize the multiplicity of languages.)

One could give many examples of where the absence of governmental activity is indeed a policy. What is government's policy on the length of vacations for workers? Surely we do not expect the government to have a policy on this subject, yet some countries do. In the United States, however, vacations are left to bargaining between employers and workers. We may consider that vacations are "in the natural order of things" not subject to governmental activity. But there was a time when we considered wages to be "naturally" a subject for private agreements among workers and management. Now of course we have numerous laws affecting wages. For many years the government was inactive in the area of medical care. This inactivity had the effect of a policy, for it meant that the individual citizen had to pay his own medical expenses.

How Issues Become Issues and How They Get on the Agenda

The discussion about action and nonaction points to a major consideration in understanding the pattern of governmental policies. The first issue may be: What are the issues? The impact that governmental policy has on the lives of citizens depends in part on how decisions are made about issues—whether the government appropriates funds for mass transport or for roads. But even more basic may be the question of how the issue of roads or mass transport gets *on the agenda* in the first place. How do roads become a topic for governmental decisions? Why is it governmental policy to be active in that area? In understanding governmental policy we shall have to consider the question of why issues becomes issues. Vehicle fumes were never until recently a public issue. Now they are. Vehicle noise was never a public issue. It still is not. What gets the first problem on the agenda, but not the second?

Setting the Agenda for Policy Making

The first political issue is the choice of issues; the first step in dealing with a problem is to recognize that it is a problem. Once a problem has been raised—"put on the agenda"—pressures can be brought to bear on the government by citizens and groups; debate can take place in the press, in the halls of Congress, in the executive branch; proposals can be made. Remember our stress on government inaction: When the government does nothing (about health care or pollution or automobile noise), that is in a real sense a policy. And nothing is done when an issue never makes it to the attention of the American people.

Lack of Procedural Rules for Setting the Agenda

Is there a "proper procedure" for putting problems on the political agenda? When we discussed Congress we dealt with the House Rules Committee, a powerful committee because it controls the agenda of the House of Representatives. It decides what bills come to the floor; it controls the debate. When it comes to American politics more generally, no such clear set of rules determines what problems get on the agenda. The relevant legal rules as to who can bring up an issue are found in the Bill of Rights—they are the right of free speech and the right to petition Congress for the redress of grievances. In this sense, anyone has the right to put a matter on the agenda—to write to his congressman saying that such and such should be done. But not everyone does so with equal effectiveness.

The process by which problems come to the attention of the American public and the American government has not been studied much. One reason is that it is difficult to locate and identify "nonissues"—that is, problems that have not yet been recognized. (If it were easy to do so, the problems would be recognized.) Social scientists as well as political leaders have been surprised by the sudden eruption of issues that were not expected. Women's liberation movements caught most off guard as, indeed, did many of the first Black protest activities in the 1950s. In retrospect one can say that these were "natural" issues certain to arise sooner or later. But that is hindsight.

Generalizations About How Problems Get on the Political Agenda

Though the study of how problems get on the political agenda is in its early stages, some generalizations are possible.

One view of how problems come to be on the political agenda is that they are forced on by objective reality. If the economy is going badly, economic problems automatically get on the agenda of politics; if it is going well, little attention is paid to them. In earlier days when our rivers and streams were pure, pollution was not on the agenda. Now they are filthy, and pollution is a major political issue. (See Figure 15.1.)

Such an explanation of the origin of political problems has some truth. One cannot imagine a pollution issue if all air and water were pure. In that sense an objective problem (dirty water) is a *necessary* condition, but it is not a *sufficient* condition. The "political agenda" is not merely a reflection of the "real" problems of a society. Our lakes and rivers were polluted long before the current concern with the problem—well back into the nineteenth century in some cases. Lake Erie became almost irreversibly polluted with little concern. Now that the same thing is happening to some of the other Great Lakes, it is an issue. Surely something other than the objective problem is responsible.

In the 1950s and 1960s the issue of race relations exploded on the Amer-

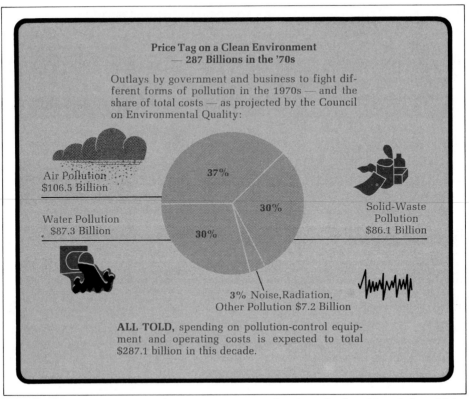

Price Tag on a Clean Environment — 287 Billions in the '70s

Outlays by government and business to fight different forms of pollution in the 1970s — and the share of total costs — as projected by the Council on Environmental Quality:

Air Pollution $106.5 Billion

Water Pollution $87.3 Billion

37%

30%

30%

Solid-Waste Pollution $86.1 Billion

3% Noise, Radiation, Other Pollution $7.2 Billion

ALL TOLD, spending on pollution-control equipment and operating costs is expected to total $287.1 billion in this decade.

Figure 15.1 Pollution Was Slow in Coming on the Agenda, but Now It Is a Major Government Concern

SOURCE: Reprinted from *U.S. News and World Report,* August 21, 1972. Copyright © 1972, U.S. News and World Report, Inc.

ican scene. Does that mean that there was less of an objective problem earlier? Quite the contrary. Data show a relative improvement of the life conditions of American Blacks at the same time as their struggle for equal rights heightened. What had to be added to the objective problems was the subjective awareness of them.

There is another reason why the agenda of politics is not a mere reflection of the objective problems of society. Each time a new problem arises it does not push the old ones off the agenda. It is often difficult for a new problem to get on the agenda. One political analyst found that the best predictor of what will be on this year's budget is what was on last year's budget. Just as most organization meetings have "old business" as the first agenda item, so does the American political structure. Once a problem has been recognized, that recognition tends to become institutionalized—that is, a government agency is set up to deal with it; it has an allocation on the government's budget; a congressional committee or subcommittee makes it the focus of attention. It is on the agenda, and year after year it stays there because the government agency and the congressional committee see to it. A new problem has no such institutionalized support, and may have to wait in the wings for a long time—sometimes years and decades—before it gets recognized.

A second view of agenda setting is that anyone can put a problem on the agenda. In some sense this is true but it is also somewhat misleading. As we pointed out, the Constitution guarantees the right to all Americans to petition Congress or to form a political group to press some issue. And such initiatives are taken in the United States, not by a majority of the people but by substantial numbers. But not all social groups are equally organized, and unorganized interests have less possibility of getting their problems placed on the political agenda than do organized ones.

That a serious problem exists does not make one active in trying to get the government to deal with that problem. This can be seen by a striking example. A study of political participation found that Black Americans were more likely to report that they had serious problems that could be solved by governmental activity than was the case among Whites. And the problems Blacks mention are serious: adequate jobs, income, housing. Blacks thus recognize their problems as political—that is, problems for which the government would be the institution most likely to solve them. But though Blacks are almost twice as likely as Whites to perceive problems that need governmental solution, they are less than half as likely to have contacted an official on such a problem. And when asked why they did not contact some official, the most frequent reasons given by Blacks was that they doubted their own effectiveness and the government's responsiveness.[3]

Of course, even if a group raises an issue for the political agenda, there is no certainty that it will have the issue accepted for serious consideration. The Constitution gives everyone the right to raise an issue; it does not ensure sympathetic reply. Thus, just as there is unequal likelihood that citizens will raise issues, there is even greater inequality in the degree to which the government is responsive.

A third point can be made about agenda setting. Just as there are certain people less likely to put their problems on the agenda, there are certain problems that are less likely to get on the political agenda. The "free enterprise" tradition in America makes it unlikely that an issue involving government ownership of industries will be raised or, if raised, will receive serious consideration.

There are a number of reasons why such issues might not be raised. Quite simply they may be considered "so far out of the question" that citizens would not think of raising them. Of course, what is "out of the ques-

---

[3] Sidney Verba and Norman H. Nie, *Participation in America: Political Democracy and Social Equality* (New York: Harper & Row, 1972), Chap. 10.

tion" may be difficult to tell until a question is raised. Many major changes were once considered unlikely or impossible. The notion that some issue is "out of the question" can be a self-fulfilling prophecy. People think something is out of the question and therefore do not raise the question. In this sense, the political agenda has a lot of inertia built into it. Some issues are just not thought of or not thought proper to raise.

Who Is Likely to Get Issues on the Agenda?

Those who are politically active are more likely to have the problems they face put on the political agenda. The reason is simple. Participation communicates to the government the views of the citizens. If the citizens do not participate, their views remain unknown. One study compared the views of citizens as to the major problems of their communities with the problems leaders felt were most pressing and upon which they were working. It found that leaders tended to have on their agendas those problems expressed by the *active* citizens. It was the activity of these citizens that communicated these preferences to the leaders. Thus the first generalization is that one has to be active to get one's problems on the political agenda.

Activity, however, may not be sufficient. This same study compared the effectiveness of political activity by upper- and lower-status citizens. Among the active citizens, it was found that those from upper social groups—the wealthy, the educated, those with high-status occupations—were very effective in getting their preferences on the political agenda. Those lower-status citizens who participated actively were less successful; the agendas of community leaders did not coincide very well with the preferences of lower-status citizens.

Why did these lower-status citizens who were active nevertheless not succeed in communicating their views as to the most pressing problems in the community to the community leaders? There are three possible answers, each of which tells us something of the dynamics of agenda building.

For one thing, the lower-status citizens who were active were socially very different from the community leaders. Community leaders tended to be wealthy and well educated; the lower-status activists tended to be poorer and less well educated. These differences may have made the leaders less attentive to them. Second, the particular problems that the lower-status citizens wanted to put on the agenda were different from those of interest to the upper-status citizens. The latter were interested in better community facilities, and perhaps also (inconsistently) in lowering taxes. The former wanted basic issues of welfare placed on the agenda. Third, though the lower-status activists were as active as the upper-status ones, there were fewer of them. Thus their views were drowned out by the views expressed by a larger group of upper-status activists.[4]

[4] *Ibid.*, chap. 20.

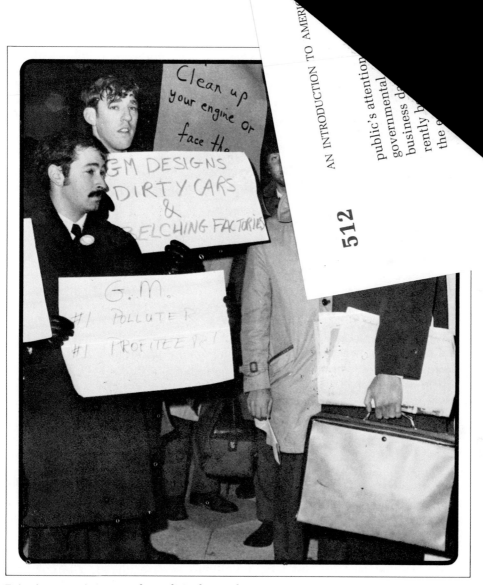

Bringing new issues to the political agenda is currently being carried on by leaders of the consumer movement.   (Photo: Wide World)

This discussion should help make clear why some groups turn to more direct, even violent, action to bring their problems to the attention of the government. Violent action, as we have suggested, is a *signaling* device, a way of capturing the attention of political leaders. Violent outbursts, whatever their other costs, are effective in calling the attention of leaders to problems they might otherwise ignore. It is a way of getting on the agenda.

There are also in America individuals and groups whose specialty is seeking and publicizing new problems. Such activity has a long tradition in America. Around the turn of the century, the muckrakers brought to the

numerous social problems and got these problems on the
agenda. Much of the legislation regulating the conduct of
tes from that era. The task of bringing forth new issues is cur-
ing carried on by the leaders of the consumer movement, those in
cology movement, and those in the women's rights movement.

Alternative Modes of Policy Making:
The Comprehensive vs. the Incremental Approach

Imagine a government official faced with a policy problem. Suppose he is
trying to write legislation to deal with automobile pollution. There are two
ways in which he can approach the problem: One we can call the *comprehensive* approach, the other the *incremental* approach.

Using the Comprehensive Approach

In using the comprehensive approach, the government official will consider all possible ways of handling the issue and all possible effects in relation to other problems. He will very clearly specify the goal he is trying to
achieve and relate it to other goals he considers important. He will then
choose the best possible means to achieve the goal.

Let us look at what a comprehensive approach to automobile pollution
might entail:

1. The past is no constraint: The planner dealing with the problem of automobile pollution in a comprehensive manner would not allow himself to
be constrained by what has come before. The past design of automobiles,
the number of older automobiles on the road, the historical evolution of the
automobile industry, and the pattern of use of the automobile as a means of
transportation would not interfere with his creation of a new comprehensive plan.

2. All possible policies and techniques will be considered: The comprehensive planner will not stop at considering schemes to modify current
cars; he will consider all possible technologies. Nor will he limit himself to
the existing means of transportation. He may very well consider the possibility of replacing the car with mass transit.

3. He will see the linkage of what he wants to accomplish to other policies,
and he will not hesitate to plan for changes in those policies if they are
related to automobile pollution. Does the private ownership of cars lead to
greater pollution? Then perhaps private ownership ought to be barred.
Perhaps government ownership of the automobile industry would increase
control over pollution. If so, that possibility ought to be considered as well.

4. The comprehensive planner, however, is not single-minded. He does not
consider only how to curb auto fumes. Rather, he is fully aware that we

have other values as well as a desire for less pollution. Pollution could be stopped by banning all cars, but that would hurt other values such as our desire to have a functioning economy and full employment, or our desire to get from place to place.

The comprehensive planner does not ignore these other values. Rather he takes them all into consideration. How much do we value curbing pollution? How much do we value curbing inflation? How much do we value full employment? How much do we value restricting government control over the economy? All of these values are related to pollution. A comprehensive planner will weigh them against the gain to be made by curbing car pollution.

5. The comprehensive planner considers all the ramifications of his scheme. What effect does it have on jobs, on housing, on other means of transport? Maybe a reduction in pollution will improve health. The planner might even go so far as to consider the need for new facilities for the aged, who will probably live longer in a pollution-free atmosphere.

Using the Incremental Approach

Consider, on the other hand, the incremental approach to policy making. It differs from the comprehensive approach in every respect. (See Figure 15.2.)

1. For the incremental planner, the past is a major constraint. He takes into account the current situation: how many cars are on the road, their eco-

Figure 15.2 The Incremental Model: Gradual Change Based on Past Policy Commitment

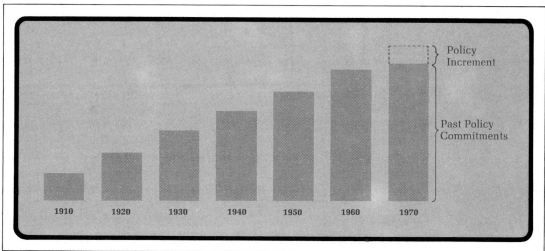

SOURCE: Thomas R. Dye, *Understanding Public Policy*, © 1972. Reprinted by permission of Prentice-Hall, Inc., Englewood Cliffs, N.J.

nomic significance, the current patterns of automobile use. Past policies, such as the policy not to support mass transit, will be considered as "givens" within the framework of which he must work.

2. Rather than considering all possible techniques for dealing with the problem, the incremental planner will take into account cars as currently designed and the modifications that could fit into currently workable technologies.

3. He will stick fairly closely to the technical problem of standards for automobile pollution and ignore changes that could come from a more comprehensive change in the economy. Such far-ranging schemes as the banning of the private automobile or the nationalization of the automobile industry would probably not even enter his mind.

4. The incremental planner would not spend too much time worrying about the ramifications of his plan in other areas. His area of concern is automobile pollution; let other governmental agencies worry about inflation or full employment. He will not comprehensively consider all other relevant values and weigh them against the value of cleaner air. Rather, he will ignore most other values, and think only of the narrower task at hand.

The results of the two modes of policy making would be quite different indeed. The comprehensive planner would almost redesign the world from scratch if he went at his task fully. The incrementalist will create a policy narrowly designed to deal with a specific problem, modifying but not scrapping current practices.

At first glance the comprehensive approach appears much more productive. Piecemeal solutions often accomplish little. And we have seen that failure to consider all the consequences of a policy can lead to unanticipated and unwanted results.

The Government Uses the Incremental Approach

Despite the seeming advantages of the comprehensive approach, most governmental policy takes the incremental approach. Policies tend to be based on previous policies and are worked out step by step, narrowly focusing on one aspect of the problem, for the following reasons:

First, comprehensive planning is, in fact, beyond the capability of planners. To consider all values explicitly and weigh one against the other is not possible. There is no precise way of saying (or knowing) how much one values clean air versus full employment. A plan that covered all relevant values and all possible ramifications of a decision could not be worked out, even with the most advanced computers.

Second, most governmental planners are not in an organizational position to consider all aspects of a problem at once. The official who was assigned to work on automobile pollution and came back with a scheme that

Mass transit has seldom been the result of comprehensive transportation policy.
(Photo: Sam Falk, Monkmeyer)

required vast funds for mass transit would be told to stick to his task. And that is what most public officials do. There are, of course, some institutions that are supposed to have a more comprehensive view of problems: the Presidency and the Congress. But even here, incrementalism may rule. Congress is empowered to make the broadest of legislation, but it itself is organized into specific committees that are geared to considering specific problems rather than planning comprehensively across all fields. And even the President, burdened with a press of particular problems that have to be dealt with at a particular time, may have trouble taking a more general view.

Many Presidents have complained about this lack of time to deal with a problem comprehensively. In the area of foreign policy, for instance, they have complained that the pressure of immediate decisions on emergency problems detracts from the opportunity to deal more generally with overall and long-term policy. They have often been more aware of the problem than capable of dealing with it.

Another reason why policy making tends to be incremental is the inescapable weight of history. Policy makers are faced with and cannot avoid the past decisions that have been made. Once a course is charted, one cannot easily change it without risking severe dislocations. If a governmental program of one sort has been set up, one cannot come along and start totally afresh without considering the status and consequences of the existing program. Furthermore, existing programs have built into them an organizational component; people become committed to those programs and exert pressures to keep them going. And the governmental planner must pay attention to this.

One major study of the expenditures of the government on various programs asked how one could predict for any state or city what it would spend on the various governmental functions — welfare, health, education, transportation, parks, and so forth. What was the best predictor, the study asked: the party that won the past election? the social composition of the locality? the changes in the problems the government faced? The answer was No. By far the best predictor of how a government will allocate its funds this year is how it allocated them last year. Changes there may be, but they will be marginal or *incremental* changes. Last year's budget tends to be the starting point for this year's.[5] And often the concluding point is not far away.

The weight of existing commitments falls on all governmental levels, high and low. After twenty years out of office, the Republicans elected a President in 1952. The previous two decades had seen the growth of vast governmental programs in the area of social welfare, programs that in their inception had been severely criticized by leaders of the Republican opposition. But none of these programs was removed. Some may have been changed somewhat in direction, some perhaps cut. But those were incremental changes, not comprehensive ones. The constraint of past commitments is also found in foreign policy. Each President inherits the policies of his predecessors. And though each President does move off in a different direction, it is almost always a less drastic difference than the public (or even the new President and his staff) expect. They may change course by 5, 10, 20 degrees — but rarely by 180.

The Argument in Favor
of Incremental Policy Making

Incremental policy making is a fact of American politics. That is how most policy is made. Its defenders argue that it is a most effective way of making policy. For one thing, they point out that such a narrow focus on one aspect of a problem is not a bad way to do things. It is not that other issues and other values are ignored. It is just that there are other governmental agencies worrying about the other problems. If the official concerned with air pollution does not face the issue of inflation, it does not

[5] Ira Sharkansky, *Spending in the American States* (Skokie, Ill.: Rand McNally, 1968).

matter. He would not have dealt with it adequately anyway. It is not his area of technical competence and he has other problems to worry about. Let some other part of the government worry about that. And if separate parts of the government worry about separate problems, all problems will be dealt with somewhere.

Furthermore, it is good to make policy without considering all ramifications. If one did, one would never act, for such consideration would require a lifetime of study.

The argument in favor of incrementalism is not without its flaws. It assumes that somehow each possible value has a governmental agency worrying about it. But of course that is not the case. Certain interests are preserved by certain parts of the government; others have no advocates. It is only in recent years that a governmental advocate of consumer interests has been appointed, and the organizational power of that branch of the government is much weaker than most other sectors. And while it is true that a comprehensive concern for all potential consequences might inhibit any policy making at all, one can find too many examples where unintended consequences have made the results of a policy almost the reverse of what was planned.

But whether one approves of it or not, one has to understand policy making in America as a process that goes on largely in an incremental way. And this is furthered by another basic tendency of American policy making: the tendency to *disaggregate* the policy-making process.

The Disaggregation of Policy Making

A major tendency in American politics is to divide the policy-making process into small units. In part this is reflected in the tendency to decentralize decision making into small governmental units — states, cities, towns, school districts. More generally it is a tendency to fragment policy making. Policy is made by a narrowly focused government agency for a particular constituency on a relatively narrow range of issues. Policy is not made for the economy as a whole. Rather, different parts of the government specialize in particular aspects of the economy. The regulation of one part of the economy is delegated to one specific branch of the government (a bureau in the Department of Agriculture, the Interstate Commerce Commission, the Bureau of Mines) that works closely with its particular constituency (the farmers growing a particular crop, the railroads, the mine interests). Disaggregated decision making means that those who are to be regulated are likely to take part in the regulation. President Nixon's Task Force for Business Taxation, appointed in 1969, was made up of four lawyers from corporate law firms, two New York investment bankers, three representatives of corporate accounting firms, two top officials of large industrial corporations, and three business-oriented economists. Policy is made in narrow confines. Each governmental agency is concerned with the problems of that particular part of the society in whose problems it specializes — with its constituency. It is not concerned with broader social issues. This disaggregation in the executive branch of the government is paralleled by disaggregation in Congress. The congressional structure of specialized committees and more specialized subcommittees makes for a similar narrow focus on the problems of a particular constituency.

Consequences of Disaggregated Policy Making

Policy making for narrow constituencies has important consequences. The top political institutions in the country — the parties, the President, Congress — have (or should have) broad rather than narrow constituencies. Their constituents come from all branches of the economy — workers and management, farms and industries. And they come from all kinds of farms and all kinds of industries, not just from wheat farms or from the aluminum industry. If policy is made by such multiconstituency institutions, it is likely to take into consideration many sides of a problem. If the constituency is broad, a suggestion for an increase in dairy prices would be considered not only from the point of view of the dairy farmers, but from the point of view of the consumers who must pay the prices. But if the constituency is narrow — if policy is made in a bureau of the Department of Agriculture that deals almost exclusively with dairy interests — policy will more likely be made with only that interest in mind.

How Does Disaggregation Come About?

Disaggregation is in part the inevitable result of the organizational structure of the government. It happens when major policy decisions are made within the confines of specialized agencies or committees. Disaggregation is furthered by the fact that American political parties do not provide broad programs among which citizens can choose. It also results from the tendency mentioned earlier for policies laid down in the laws of Congress to be extremely general and vague. This leaves a vacuum when it comes to the application of policy. Someone has to specify how the policy is to be applied, and that is left to administrative agencies with narrower constituencies.

Finally, the disaggregation of governmental policy derives from a general American belief that as much as possible of governmental activity should be freed from "politics." The slogan is heard in a number of fields: "Let's keep politics out of the schools!" "The Federal Communications Commission should not be placed under political pressure!" "Don't make Medicare a political football!"

What Does Keeping Politics Out of Policy Making Mean?

The slogans calling for keeping politics out of governmental activity are somewhat self-contradictory if one accepts our definition of politics—politics exists whenever binding decisions are made for the society. Whatever the Federal Communications Commission (FCC) does is, in our definition, political. Medicare, involving federal expenditures for medical care, is political. Education, the largest domestic governmental program, is political. The source of the confusion lies in the fact that our somewhat abstract "political science" definition of politics differs from the meaning implied in the slogans listed above. And to understand that difference is to understand something very important about policy making in America.

Removing Policy Making from Partisan Politics

When people talk of freeing some area of public concern—schools, communications policy, Medicare—from "politics" they generally mean freeing it from *partisan politics*. The particular policy, they believe, should not be the concern of the political parties, with each party trying to manipulate the policy as a means of getting votes. Similarly, the policy should be removed from the partisan control of the Congress. Certain policies, in short, should not be the subject of controversy and partisan struggle.

How then should communications, or education, or medical care policy be made? The answer will be that such policies should be impartial, objective, devised by technical experts. The regulation of the airwaves is a very technical problem. One needs specialists in communications policy. The allocation of a new TV license should not be the subject of partisan dispute, with the license going to the side that can muster the largest congressional backing. Education of children is a complicated business. It should not be subject to partisan pressures, but should be controlled by specialists in education.

This attempt to remove policy making from politics (in the narrow sense of *partisan politics*) characterizes much of American life. It is found in the federal administration with its specialized agencies, in Congress with its specialized congressional committees. It is found in the state governments, which develop a similar structure. It is found on the local level.

But—and here our broader definition of politics becomes important—to remove some governmental function from partisan politics is not to remove it from politics more generally. The decisions of technical experts remain political as long as they have behind them the force of the government, as long as they involve regulation of behavior or the allocation of tax money. What the removal of a subject from the partisan clash of politics means is that it is turned over to a narrow constituency. Communications policy is not made in a vacuum. Removing that policy area from partisan politics means that the vacuum is filled by the interest most specifically affected—the communications industry. It becomes the constituency of the government agency making that policy. The same is true of education policy. The role of organized educational interests—colleges of education, the educational bureaucracy, teachers' organizations—increases as the pressures of a broader constituency decline.

That many policies in America are made on a disaggregated basis—by particular parts of the government dealing with particular constituencies—ought not to be taken to imply that the President and Congress never act to make broad policy affecting groups across the nation. In the summer of 1971 President Nixon announced a major economic policy involving changes in the relation of the dollar to foreign currencies, controls over prices and wages, and a surtax on imports. Such a broad policy affects all Americans. It is quite the opposite of the disaggregated pattern of policy we have described. But two things ought to be noted: In the first place, such massive interventions are rare. Second, one has to look fairly closely at the way in which such a broad policy is carried out before one can be sure that it involves a comprehensive policy for all Americans. The actual administration of price and wage controls involves a number of specific decisions on the way in which these regulations should affect particular industries or particular firms. And these more specific applications can be a way of disaggregating the most general policy.

Those approving of disaggregated decision making argue that it gives significant control over policies to the specific groups that are most affected by the policy. The narrow constituencies that establish close relations with agencies of the government or committees of Congress are just those for whom the policy is most relevant. In this way power is dispersed in the society and policies can be adjusted to the needs of particular groups.

The counter-argument should by now be familiar: Not all potential constituencies are equally served. Many do not have powerful agencies with whom they can establish contact. Educational policy may be adjusted to the needs of colleges of education more than it is to the needs of teachers, and better adjusted to the needs of both of the former than to the needs of pupils. The education schools are better organized than the teachers, the teachers in turn better organized than the pupils. And last, broad concern with some more general public interest is missing when policy is disaggregated to these special policy areas.

Finally, it should be clear that the disaggregation of policy making inevitably leads to incremental policies. Those who make policy take no comprehensive view of social problems. Rather their attention is closely focused on the group nearest to themselves—their specific narrow constituency.

These tendencies in American policy making—toward incrementalism

and toward disaggregation—have a major effect on the kinds of policies that
are made. We will see how this is so in the next chapter when we take a
closer look at the making of particular policies.

The Actors in Policy Making

Who might be among the influential actors in relation to a particular policy? They can be individuals and groups in the government, or individuals
and groups out of the government. A list of potential actors in making federal policy follows:

1. *The Mass Public, Special Publics, Organized Groups.* One potential
actor is the *mass public* as a whole or that special part of it called the
"majority." Its opinion can be expressed in public opinion polls, in letters
to congressmen, perhaps at election time. If public involvement takes a
narrower form, *special publics* may be the actors. These so-called attentive
publics are likely to have some special interest in a policy: Union members,
for instance, are likely to be an attentive public for labor legislation, farmers for farm legislation, doctors for medical legislation. Or the actors may
be *organized groups.* And here we can make a useful distinction between
groups with a relatively broad constituency and those with a relatively
narrow one. A broad constituency would include a wide range of types of
citizens and interests; a narrow one would cover a much more precisely
defined group. A few examples will make the distinction clear: Groups
with broad constituencies include the so-called peak business associations that represent interests from many sectors of the business community:
organizations like the National Association of Manufacturers, or the U.S.
Chamber of Commerce representing all segments of industry, or the American Textile Manufacturers Institute representing many branches of a particular industry. In the labor field one would have the AFL–CIO representing
unions of all sorts. Other broad constituency groups might include the National Council of Churches (representing many specific church groups),
Common Cause (a lobbying group representing a loose coalition of liberals), or the Liberty Lobby (a parallel group from the other end of the
political spectrum).

More specific groups have narrower memberships. Particular labor
unions—the Auto Workers, the Teamsters, the Postal Workers—fall in this
category. So do groups representing specific industries or specific firms.
The United States Savings and Loan League and the National Association
of Retail Druggists speak for narrower interests than those mentioned above
as, of course, do the United States Steel Corporation and the International
Telephone and Telegraph Corporation. Groups representing particular
kinds of farmers—Wisconsin dairymen, cotton growers—fall into this

category as well. We distinguish between interest groups in this way because it makes a difference, in terms of the policy-making process, which kinds are involved. The more disaggregated the policy, the more will narrowly based groups be involved.

2. *The Party System.* Actors who come from the party system might include national party organs such as the National Committee or groups like the Young Democrats or the Ripon Society (a group of liberal Republicans). They might include also the state and local counterparts of these groups.

3. *State and Local Governments.* Other levels of government can be relevant actors on federal policy. The states, through their governors or other representatives, take part in federal policy making. And so do the cities and other local governments. At times it may be difficult to distinguish a state or local government as actor from a party group as actor. When Mayor Daley of Chicago used his political "clout" against the Office of Economic Opportunity—an event we described in Chapter 11—was he acting as Mayor of Chicago or as head of the powerful Cook County Democratic organization? The answer of course is that he was acting as both; and that is where the "clout" came from. (This example should serve as a warning that the distinctions among the groups mentioned are not always clear.)

4. *The Federal Government.* The most significant actors in the making of federal policy tend to come from within the federal government itself. The office of the President is crucial. This includes the President and his close advisers on the White House staff, as well as those governmental agencies closely attached to the White House. The more specific parts of the executive branch—the federal departments such as Agriculture, Commerce, State, and their various bureaus; the independent regulatory commissions such as the Interstate Commerce Commission, the Federal Communications Commission—all fall into this category.

The Congress acting as a whole, and acting through its many committees and subcommittees, is an important actor, as are the federal courts, especially the Supreme Court, but the lower courts are important too.

This compilation of actors is, we hope, familiar to the reader. It is merely a summary of those groups we have dealt with in our book thus far. Thus we already know a good deal about how they take part in the policy process. But we have dealt with each group separately. To see how they relate to one another, we shall have to see how they interact when making policy. We have introduced policy making in this chapter, but we have dealt with it only a rather general level. To get a better grasp of the policy-making process we turn to some specific areas of policy making in the next chapter.

Controversy

The American political agenda—those issues that are before the public and before the government—does change. From year to year new issues arise and old ones fade. One has only to follow the headlines for a few months to see this happen. But does this mean that the American political system is flexible and responsive to these new issues?

One Side

Yes, it does. Any important social issue can make it onto the political agenda. Just consider the past couple of decades. All sorts of issues have come before us: equal opportunities for Blacks and other minorities, as well as the rights of women. The consumer movement has grown from small beginnings to a major force. Or consider the increasing importance of pollution as an issue. One cannot really argue that issues have been "suppressed."

And the mass media help in getting issues before the public and the government. They are quick to pick up new trends. In fact, one can argue that they are more likely to exaggerate the importance of trivial issues than to suppress major ones.

Can those who claim that issues are kept from consideration name one such issue?

The Other Side

It may be true that all kinds of issues emerge onto the political scene. But that does not mean the political system is open and flexible. For one thing, when significant new issues have come to the attention of the public and the government, they have almost always done so very late in the game—after many years of being totally ignored. Furthermore, they are usually put on the agenda by groups who have to go outside the ordinary political channels to do so. Sometimes it takes violence or other direct action to catch the attention of political decision makers. And just because an issue gets into the newspapers does not mean that the government responds to it adequately.

Besides, not all issues make it to the front of the political stage. Some important ones never are raised. Just ask those people who are fundamentally critical of American society. A right-wing critic might mention the welfare state as something taken for granted. No one raises the issue of dismantling the many welfare programs in America. A left-wing critic might mention the capitalistic basis of our economy. No one raises the issue of fundamental economic change.

Suggested Readings

A good account of how policy is made in the all-important area of budgeting is Aaron Wildavsky, *The Politics of the Budgetary Process* (Boston: Little, Brown, 1964). An explication and defense of "incremental" policy making are found in Charles E. Lindblom, *The Policy-Making Process* (Englewood Cliffs, N.J.: Prentice-Hall, 1968), p. 68. A critique of this mode of policy making is in Theodore J. Lowi, *The End of Liberalism* (New York: Norton, 1969).

On the ways in which policies can have symbolic rather than substantive meaning, see Murray Edelman, *The Symbolic Uses of Politics* (Urbana: University of Illinois Press, 1964).

Patterns of Policy Making: Domestic and Foreign

16

In this chapter we present a few concrete case studies of how policy is made. The federal government is active in almost all aspects of our lives (and in the lives of people in other countries). To see how policy is made, we might have to look at thousands of issues, and at the activities of hundreds of bureaus, committees, and groups. We cannot, of course, do that. We must select some topics to study.

Yet the choice is difficult, for to study the policy process in one field may not tell us much about other fields. If we choose an unrepresentative policy area, we may learn little about other policy areas. How the government comes to policy decisions on nuclear weapons may tell us little about how agricultural policy is made.

In this chapter we will consider a range of policies that give some overview of the various ways by which policy is made, and the actors that get involved.

Government Regulation of Business

Government regulation of business activities illustrates a pattern of policy making common in many areas where the government acts to regulate citizens and organizations. Despite the talk of our "free enterprise" tradition, the government has been active for many years in regulating business activity. For certain kinds of businesses—public utilities, for instance, and the airlines industry, where a few firms have a monopoly over a vital public service—the government sets rates. In addition, the government controls certain businesses by allocating limited franchises to them, by giving a TV license to one firm rather than another, by allocating an air route to one carrier rather than another. For all kinds of businesses it sets standards that must be maintained: standards of cleanliness for foods, of purity for drugs, of safety for cars. The government is also empowered to maintain competition in business by enforcing the antitrust laws.

The regulation of business in the United States has had two major characteristics: It has tended to progress in a disaggregated manner, and it has tended to involve close cooperation between the government regulatory agency and the business being regulated.

Laws of Congress are, as we have pointed out, often remarkably vague. They receive meaning only when they are administered. Most of the major laws dealing with the regulation of industry have this characteristic. They direct the government agency administering the law to allocate radio and

The government is empowered to maintain competition in business by enforcing the antitrust laws.   (Cartoon: New York Public Library, Prints Division)

television licenses in accord with the "public interest and necessity" or to approve applications for air routes so as to maximize the "public convenience" or to see that public utility rates are "just and reasonable." Such general imperatives give almost no direct guidance to the administrators of these laws. What becomes vital, then, is who administers the laws and how?

Who Administers the Law and How?

Independent Regulatory Commissions: Many laws regulating business are administered by independent regulatory commissions. The first such commission was the Interstate Commerce Commission (ICC) created in 1887 to regulate the railroads and other interstate transportation industries. Over the years the Congress has created an "alphabet soup" of such agencies to regulate various aspects of the American business community: the Federal Trade Commission (FTC) to administer the antitrust laws; the Federal

The stock market is regulated by the Securities and Exchange Commission.
(*Photo: New York Stock Exchange*)

Power Commission (FPC); the Federal Communications Commission (FCC); the Securities and Exchange Commission (SEC) to regulate the stock market; the Civil Aeronautics Board (CAB); and so on.

Although they deal with different aspects of business, the commissions have a number of things in common. They are not directly under the control of the President or the Congress. The goal was to make them "nonpolitical" (in the narrow sense of that word as we discussed it in the previous chapter). These commissions were to be insulated from partisan politics. Their boards of directors must be bipartisan, and they are appointed for fixed terms to ensure their not being removed by a change in administration.

Regulation of business was to be handled as a technical problem for experts, not a political problem for the President and the Congress. But as we have argued, the decision to make something "nonpolitical" is in a broad sense itself a political decision. Decisions of regulatory agencies are inevitably political (in that the power of the government is involved). To detach them from the central decision-making institutions—the Presidency and the Congress—does not change that.

Furthermore, the result has hardly been decision making by technical experts serving some general public interest. Rather, the consequence is the creation of separate regulatory agencies isolated from the rest of the government. The regulatory agencies deal only with those industries they regulate—the FCC with the broadcast industry, the ICC with the railroads and truckers, the CAB with the airlines. Over time, these industries become the "constituency" of the agency; that is, the agency works closely with the industry it is regulating and gives first consideration to the welfare of that industry. In some sense the regulated and the regulator become one and the same working in close harmony.

Policy making becomes a totally disaggregated affair; policy for each industry is made by a separate agency responsible only for that industry. Congress and the Presidency—the branches of the government that have broad constituencies—are left out. The principal actors are the specific regulatory agency and the industry representatives working closely together. The final result often is that the regulatory agency starts being responsible *for* a particular industry and winds up being responsive *to* that industry. The result is usually regulatory policy that favors the industry regulated.

But it is important to note how this comes about. When we discussed the potential bases of group conflict in America, we distinguished between circumstances where the population is divided on a matter of principle from those where only narrow interests were at stake that did not appear to be in conflict with each other. If, as a general principle, the issue of the public good versus the good of the business community were to be raised, there is little doubt that the weight of influence would fall on the side of the public good. Who can oppose that? But by disaggregating policy making to specific agencies, each dealing with a specific type of business, the more general principle is never raised. Rather, the decision becomes one of making policy in relation to a particular industry. There are, in effect, no counter-participants; no one asking about the benefits to a larger public. In such circumstances, the important groups are not the broad organizations of the entire business community—the National Association of Manufacturers or the U.S. Chamber of Commerce, for example. Rather, the important groups are the organizations of the specific industries as well as the specific firms being regulated.

This pattern of regulation is found across much of the federal government. We have talked of the independent regulatory commissions whose particular legal status—formally independent of the Congress and the White House—reflects these tendencies. But the same pattern exists in the Department of the Interior in relation to the regulation of the petroleum industry, in the Treasury Department in relation to the regulation of banking, in the Department of Agriculture in relation to farm interests, in the Department of Commerce in relation to the vast variety of businesses with which it deals. Indeed, the same pattern applies to the Department of Labor in relation to the regulation of labor unions. In each case the distinction between public and private, between the governmental agency and the interest being regulated, becomes hopelessly blurred. Industry councils of various sorts, on which are represented the firms that are to be regulated, take a large part in the writing of the regulations. Such cooperation is, of course, useful for a federal agency. But such cooperation can lead to capture of the regulatory agency by that which was supposed to be regulated.

These agencies set up to regulate business go through an interesting "life cycle," a life cycle that illustrates the process of policy making in many areas of American life.[1]

The Birth of a New Agency: It all usually starts with massive public agitation about some abuse. There is a generally felt need in the public and in Congress for regulation. Such was the case when the ICC was created (to cope with major abuses by the railroads); it was the case when the SEC was founded (to cope with abuses of the stock market). At this stage of a regulatory agency's life, there are many actors involved: public and the press; specific groups of abused citizens (the farmers who did not like the railroads' rate policy, for instance); the political parties that make reform part of their platform; and the President and the Congress, who ultimately create the legislation. The business about to be regulated is also, of course, involved. And it may denounce the intended move as socialistic. In short, the vital elements are many actors, a major public issue, and moral fervor.

At this point, the new agency is born. Congress gives it its blessing, but little else in the form of guidance. As we have seen, the initial mandate is firm but vague.

The Young Agency: At first the new agency is vigorous in its regulations. The businesses to be regulated resist. The power of the agency is not completely clear, since it was not spelled out by Congress. And often one must wait years for the courts to decide on these powers. The businesses have good technical information and good legal advice. Often they are much better staffed than the agencies that are trying to carry out the regulation.

At this point something else of importance happens. The other actors who were there at the birth—the President, the Congress, the public—dispear into the background. For them the battle has been won. A law has been passed to correct the abuse, to regulate the industry. An agency has been set up. And indeed, from a *symbolic* point of view, all the right things have been done. In fact things may be working out differently. But by now the attention of the public and the Congress is elsewhere. The actors have become the agency and the business to be regulated.

The Mature Agency: In the end, the reforming zeal in the agency fades. New personnel come in. The agency becomes the protector of the industry, working closely with it. The regulation is no longer in the public interest

---

[1] The notion of a life cycle is developed by Marver Bernstein, *Regulating Business by Independent Commissions* (Princeton, N.J.: Princeton University Press, 1965).

but in that of the industry itself. The actors have narrowed to those most immediately concerned. At this "mature" stage, the two features of government regulatory policy are most apparent — disaggregation of the policy (a narrowly focused agency dealing with a narrow constituency) and cooperation between regulator and regulated.

The life cycle of a regulatory agency was forecast with amazing political insight in a letter written in 1894, on the occasion of the establishment of the ICC, which was to regulate railroads. The author of the letter, Attorney General Richard Olney, counseled the President of the Chicago, Burlington, and Quincy Railroad not to lobby against the ICC because:

> My impression would be that, looking at the matter from a railroad point of view exclusively, [abolition of the ICC] would not be a wise thing to undertake. . . . The Commission, as its functions have now been limited by the courts, is, or can be made, of great use to the railroads. It satisfies the popular clamor for a government supervision of railroads, at the same time that the supervision is almost entirely nominal. Furthermore, the older such a Commission gets to be, the more inclined it will be to take the business and railroad view of things. It becomes a sort of barrier between the business corporations and the people and a sort of protection against hasty and crude legislation hostile to railroad interests. . . . The part of wisdom is not to destroy the Commission but to utilize it.

One reason that a close relationship between the regulated and the regulator can occur is that there are no effective "counter-participants" defending the interests of other groups. The recent growth of consumer protection organizations is, in this sense, of considerable political interest. Public interest lobbies, such as Common Cause or the specialized groups associated with Ralph Nader, are potential counter-participants against the informal partnership between the regulating agency and the regulated industry. These relatively new public-interest lobbies have two resources not available to the general public: expertise and staying power. Drawing on these resources, consumer-protection organizations can help ensure that the process of regulation is sensitive to broader needs than just those of the regulated industry. As such, they are an important new actor in the policy area of government regulation of business. They perhaps will frustrate the political-economic arrangements so astutely predicted by Attorney General Olney in 1894.

Tax Policy

If someone wanted to choose that one area of governmental activity the understanding of which would lead to understanding of the government in general, he could do no better than to choose the area of tax policy. Taxes are, of course, the key to all other government programs. They provide the revenue for almost everything else the government does. Taxes touch the lives of all citizens. In terms of impact, everyone in America is a potential actor on tax policy.

The Purposes of Taxation

To Raise Revenue: In some sense, tax policy does derive from the pressures of "objective" reality. In general the government does not add on new taxes because it desires higher tax rates or because some influential group is pressing for them. Taxes are unpopular in the government and out of it. But the pressure for higher tax revenues comes largely from the increased costs of other government programs—the costs of defense and of domestic programs. As these programs become more and more costly, the government is forced to find new revenues. In this way all government programs are linked together by tax policy.

Of course, groups that agitate for new government programs or increased spending on old ones do not at the same time necessarily agitate for higher taxes to pay for them. Indeed, public opinion studies have found that just those citizens who want to see an increase in government spending on welfare programs want to see a decrease in taxes. This combination of desire for increased government spending and an unwillingness to pay the costs makes the allocation of tax burdens a tricky political business.

Although the main purpose of taxes is to raise revenue, one cannot understand tax policy fully without realizing that there are a variety of other purposes to which taxes can and have been put.

To Redistribute Income: Taxes can be used to transfer wealth from one segment of the society to another. The major way in which this is done is via the progressive income tax. The logic of a progressive income tax is that those with higher incomes can afford to pay a larger proportion of that income in taxes than can those with smaller incomes. Look at a federal income tax form and you will see that income tax varies from a few percent of the income of those in low income brackets up to 70 percent of income for those earning over $100,000 a year. If these funds are then used for government programs that benefit poorer people more than the wealthy (welfare payments, public housing, etc.) or even it they are used to pay for programs that benefit all citizens equally, it is clear that there has been a transfer of wealth from the more affluent to the less.

Such has been the goal of much of American tax policy—particularly that of the federal income tax. And the evidence is that tax policy does lead to some redistribution of income. Those in lower brackets get more out of the government than they put in; those in higher brackets get out less than they put in. But, as we noted in Chapter 2, the extent to which such transfer of income takes place is much less than a quick reading of basic income tax rates would lead one to believe. If indeed the poor paid only 2 or 3 percent of their income in taxes while the rich paid 70 percent, there would be quite a bit of income transfer. In fact, the rich rarely pay rates as high as 70 percent of income. The tax laws are riddled with loopholes — exclusions for income from certain kinds of investments, deductions for certain kinds of expenses and payments, lower rates for certain kinds of income. These loopholes tend to be taken advantage of by upper-income citizens, and this for two reasons. They tend to apply to kinds of income received by those with higher incomes. The average factory worker does not own many tax-free municipal bonds, nor is he likely to be able to take advantage of the lower "capital gains" tax rates applicable when one buys and sells real estate. The lower-income citizen is not likely to try to arrange his financial affairs in such a way as to minimize his tax liability. He probably has no way of doing this, even if he considered it. Anyway, most of his income comes from salaries and wages that are taxed at the highest rates. But upper-income citizens will adjust their financial affairs with the tax collector clearly in mind.

Second, the upper-income taxpayer is more likely to use professional help in preparing his tax return. The tax laws are infinitely complicated, and only a professional can take full advantage of the many — perfectly legal — deductions and exemptions that the law allows.

Indeed the relative burden of income taxes on rich or poor represents a perfect illustration of two of the principles of policy making we have set forth: (1) To understand a policy you have to look beyond the law as written to the details of the way the law is applied, and (2) policy making in the United States tends to bring the regulated into the picture as an active participant.

The first principle is illustrated by the fact that the actual tax burden that falls on a citizen is by no means clear from the basic tax bracket into which he falls. One has to look carefully at the specific income he has, its sources, and the tax loopholes of which he takes advantage. Thus, despite the very high peak rates for taxes, estimates are that almost no citizens pay an effective rate higher than 50 percent. Indeed, in 1970 it was discovered that there were Americans with incomes over $1,000,000 who paid no federal income tax.

The second principle — that those regulated are made partners in the application of that regulation — is illustrated by the procedure of self-reporting of taxes in the United States. In the United States, citizens calculate their own taxes, subject of course to audits by the Internal Revenue Service. What this means is that citizens may differ in the extent to which they take full advantage of the tax laws. No one has made careful calculations along these lines, but it is likely that many citizens — particularly those who do not use professional assistance — miss opportunities for deductions taken by those who have such assistance (in most cases those with higher incomes). The federal government has tried to equalize this situation by simplifying tax returns and by offering to calculate the tax for those who wish it. But it is likely that there are great differences among groups in the extent to which they *participate effectively* in the taxing process—that is, take full advantage of the laws as written.

Note that there is nothing illegal here. We are not talking about cheating on taxes. Rather we are talking of differential abilities to take advantage of perfectly legal tax arrangements.

There is another reason why taxes do not redistribute income as much as the basic federal income tax rates suggest they do. Income taxes are but one of the many forms of tax in the United States. They are the major way in which taxes are raised by the federal government, and they are an increasingly important way for states and some municipalities. But there are many other forms of tax, some of them less progressive and some of them regressive. Sales taxes are a major way in which revenue is raised for state and local governments. And such taxes tend to be regressive, which means that those with lower income pay a higher proportion of their income in sales taxes than do those of higher income—for the simple reason that poorer citizens spend more of their income on taxable goods. In addition, much local activity is supported by real estate taxes, which fall disproportionately on home owners. These additional taxes greatly modify the extent to which the total tax system in the United States involves a redistribution of income from rich to poor.

To Regulate the Economy: In addition to the raising of revenue and the redistribution of income, taxes can be used for other purposes. Tax policy is used as a means of regulating the economy. Higher tax rates may be used to curb spending in times of inflation or too rapid economic expansion. Tax rates may be lowered in order to increase spending and stimulate business in times of slowdown. Tax policy may be used as an indirect means of controlling certain activities. High taxes on alcoholic beverages and cigarettes reflect a governmental policy (not a very strong one) of limiting their use. Taxes can be used to stimulate particular segments of the economy—by so adjusting tax rates as to induce citizens to invest in those areas.

These alternative uses of the tax power are important to keep in mind, because they have an impact on how tax policy is made. They may bring different actors into the field.

How Is Tax Policy Made?

At first glance, tax policy in America would seem to be an uncongenial area for what we have called disaggregated policy making. Taxes affect all citizens; they touch all parts of the economy. Insofar as they have redistributive results they can become the subject of major clashes over the principles of free enterprise, over the proper role of the government in relation to the poor.

And, indeed, there are organized groups whose aim is to push general views of federal taxing policy—in particular, groups who want to limit that tax policy as much as possible. More important, the mass public is involved in taxes in a way in which it is not involved in the regulation of business. The public cares about taxes. In any election, national or local, tax rates are likely to be an issue. In public opinion polls, citizens consistently come out against tax increases. And government officials—particularly when they face an impending election—are very wary about raising taxes.

Even in this area, one finds a tendency to disaggregate policy to a series of narrow decisions.

One reason this happens is suggested by the complexity of the tax system in the United States. Federal income taxes are the largest single item on the citizen's tax bill, but he pays many other kinds of taxes as well. And these tax burdens are decided in the states, in localities, by special districts, by school districts. This dispersion of tax decisions into a large number of separate units has the usual consequences of disaggregated decision making: Decisions are made for one narrow constituency without considering their impact on other groups. The tax decisions of one school district in a metropolitan area affect all other parts of that area—in that they may stimulate population movement in or out of the particular district, affecting the policies of its neighbors. Indeed, as we have shown, one of the causes of the metropolitan crisis is exactly the disparities among the school systems within metropolitan areas. Yet each school district makes its own decisions as to how heavy a tax burden its citizens will bear. (This system is under challenge in the courts because of the inequalities it produces.)

Even federal income tax policy is subject to disaggregation into a series of more particular decisions in relation to small constituencies. We can see this by looking more closely at how federal income tax policy is made. The public is involved in tax policy—because of its concern about high taxes and because of government officials' reciprocal concern with how public attitudes will affect the next election. And the President is concerned as well—particularly insofar as higher taxes are needed to support foreign or domestic programs he favors, or insofar as he wants to use tax policy to slow down or speed up the economy. But in both cases, the pressure is a rather general one—for higher or lower tax revenues. It is less a pressure for a specific allocation of tax burdens among groups.

Congress' Role in Tax Policy Making: When it comes to specific allocations of tax burdens, the Congress plays a major role. The area of taxes is one where Congress has jealously maintained a strong role for itself. It supervises tax policy more than most other policies. In effect, though, it is not Congress as a whole that acts on tax matters but two specialized committees—the House Ways and Means Committee and the Senate Finance Committee.

And the procedure is not that different from the one used in relation to the regulation of business—although the formal structure is quite different. Congress does not turn policy on taxes over to a body formally independent of it as it does with much business regulation. The independent regulatory commissions are separate agencies; the House Ways and Means Committee and the Senate Finance Committee are parts of Congress. But a similar pattern takes place. The Congress starts with a vague general principle—a progressive income tax that is equitable. And the committee fills in the blanks. And it does so in a way that very much resembles the regulation of business, where decisions are made with a single constituency in mind (the business or industry to be regulated), but with little concern for the overall shape of public policy.

How Tax Laws Are Written: Numerous studies have been made of the process by which tax laws are written. And they agree that tax laws are agglomerations of specific decisions about specific types of income. Various industries, businesses, and other types of economic interests come forward with requests for tax relief: for special exemptions, lower rates, particular treatment for depreciation. In this, they are often represented by a congressman or senator with a particular interest in that economic sector—usually because it is heavily represented in his state or district. In these matters, most members of Congress tend to think of themselves as the defenders of the interests of their constituents—and since all other members of Congress are doing so, a congressman who does not play this role would be remiss and in danger of losing support.

The procedures for making tax law are particularly well set up to make the acquiescence to such requests easy. For one thing, the law is complicated and contains a great range of alternative tax schemes. Thus income can be taxed as regular income or as capital gains—the latter at a much lower level. It would be a major concession by Congress—and one that would lead to criticism in the press and by the public—if a certain kind of income were exempt from taxes completely or even given an arbitrarily lower rate. But to move one kind of income from regular salary to capital gains appears to be a much more technical decision, and one to which others are less likely to object. And, indeed, most special tax advantages come not from changing the basic tax rate, but by more subtle technical adjustments.

Second, the decisions are taken on an "interest-by-interest" basis; that is, they are disaggregated decisions. When the question of tax relief for a particular kind of farmer comes up, Congress tends to deal with it in terms of what is equitable in that case. It often seems easy, and of no harm to others, to offer a particular group relief from a tax burden it considers too high. There are more general principles involved: Who will have to pay higher taxes to compensate for the lower taxes paid by this group? What social programs will be hurt by the reduced revenues that result from the tax advantage just offered? Is the advantage given to this group commensurate with advantages received by others? But since each tax adjustment for each group is considered separately, one by one, these broader questions are not asked and not answered.

The system of specific adjustments to specific interests is also highly technical and does not come under much public scrutiny—despite the public's general concern with high taxes and despite the potentially hot political issue of unfair tax advantages. The public can be aroused by high taxes or clear unfairness. But when the tax adjustments for some groups are hidden in the intricacies of the tax law, little opposition can be aroused.

One result of all this is that special tax benefits go disproportionately to wealthier citizens. They are more likely to pressure Congress for relief from taxes and more likely to have the kind of earnings that benefit from special exemptions. As Table 16.1 shows, benefits from capital gains exemptions are more likely to help those with high incomes.

Nor does the Congress as a whole play much of a role. Indeed, the House Ways and Means Committee has over the years devised a procedure whereby it pushes through the House, without hearings and with little debate, "minor" tax bills that often cost the Treasury large sums.

These bills come up as "members' bills." They are brought up by specific congressmen to deal with specific cases of alleged tax inequity rather than to change general tax law. Each year, the Ways and Means Committee brings a long list of such bills before the House. They are called up under a rule that allows them to pass by unanimous consent without debate.

Only later is it discovered that some of these bills have given to a particular industry or firm a major tax break not available to others, and a benefit

Table 16.1 Capital Gains Benefits the Rich

IF YOUR ADJUSTED GROSS INCOME IS	YOU SAVE THE FOLLOWING AVERAGE AMOUNT THROUGH CAPITAL GAINS TAX EXEMPTION
Under $3,000	$ 1.66
$5,000–7,000	$ 7.44
$10,000–15,000	$ 16.31
$50,000–100,000	$ 2,616.10
Over $100,000	$38,126.29

Source: Based on data from *The Washington Monthly*, January 1973.

that costs the U.S. Treasury millions of dollars. There is no more explicit example of what we mean by a disaggregated decision.

The extent to which the final result is a tax policy hodgepodge of separate benefits guided by no overall structure can be seen by looking at the infamous oil-depletion allowance, the provision whereby the oil industry is allowed a 27.5 percent deduction against gross earnings because of the depletion of its resources. The logic of this provision was that it would stimulate the exploration of new petroleum sources, which are needed for national defense among other purposes.

Over time similar, though smaller, deductions have been allowed for other industries using natural resources that may disappear. Allowances

Table 16.2 One Estimate of Income That Escapes Federal Taxes

Tax Preference or Privilege	ESTIMATED INCOME REMOVED FROM TAX BASE IN 1972 (billions)	ESTIMATE LOSS IN TAX REVENUE
Tax exemption for transfer payments, including Social Security pensions	$55.1	$13.1
Special deductions, double exemptions for the aged and blind, and the retirement-income credit	$42.2	$14.2
Special benefits for home-owners, including deductions of mortgage interest	$28.7	$ 9.6
Special tax treatment of capital gains on sales of securities, other things	$26.0	$13.7
Exemption of interest earned on life insurance investments	$ 9.1	$ 2.7
Tax exemption of interest on state and local bonds	$ 1.9	$ 1.2
Tax exemption of up to $100 in annual dividends per person	$ 1.9	$ 0.7
Excess depletion and depreciation allowances	$ 1.1	$ 0.6
Total	$166.0	$55.8

Source: "Individual Income Tax Erosion by Income Classes," a study by Joseph A. Pechman and Benjamin A. Okner, Brookings Institution, published by the Joint Economic Committee of Congress on May 8. Reprinted from *U.S. News and World Report.* May 22, 1972. Copyright © 1972, U.S. News and World Report, Inc.

are made for the gravel and sand industry, though no one has argued that we have to locate more gravel and sand for national defense. Allowances are made for the coal industry. And there the logic is the opposite to that used to justify the depletion allowance for oil. It is not that we are running out, but that there is too much coal; it could not be sold because of competition from gas and oil. Indeed, the depletion allowance for oil (which leads to the production of more oil) creates the problem of the coal industry — by increasing the availability of the competing product!

In short, the various allowances to the mineral industry follow no overall logic or any general plan for the economy. Rather each represents an adjustment to that industry made in the light of its particular appeal, not in the light of general tax policy.

Tax policy, thus, works out in ways not so dissimilar to that of the regulation of business. The public is somewhere in the background pushing for lower taxes. But its voice is absent when it comes to the details of the tax law and how it is applied. The President is involved at certain crucial moments when there is a need for more tax revenues, or when the Treasury Department wants to use the tax power to regulate the economy. But this involvement is rather general as well, and does not determine how the tax burdens are distributed among groups. The Congress is involved, but only in a general sense. It sets an overall and loose framework within which tax law is made. The most effective actors — the ones who in some real sense make the tax law — are the specific businesses and other interests working closely with particular congressional committees and specific congressmen. What starts out to be a policy hard to disaggregate winds up being a policy disaggregated to the nth degree.

The result of these various specific tax exemptions is that many billions of dollars of income are exempt from federal taxes. In 1972 it was estimated that $166 billion of income was so exempt, and the federal government lost $55 billion in tax revenues by not taxing that income. The specific exemptions for specific interests add up. (See Table 16.2.)

Medical Care

The Medicare Program

In the early summer of 1965 President Johnson signed into law the Medicare program — a program of government support for the medical expenses of citizens over 65. The program represented a major step in a long battle over the role of the government in relation to medical expenses. The issue had been on the agenda for decades. Around the time of World War I, bills to set up state health insurance programs had been introduced in various state legislatures. In the early 1930s the New Deal administration had considered adding health insurance provisions to its social security legislation. In 1948 Harry Truman had made government-supported health insurance a major part of his campaign program.

In each instance the proposals came to nothing. A strong campaign was mounted by the American Medical Association, whose opposition to "socialized medicine"—as it labeled any program of government health insurance—had become a dominant feature of the public debate on the issue. The early state programs failed in the state legislatures; the New Deal program was never even submitted for fear that the addition of a controversial measure like health insurance would damage the chances of the rest of the social security program. And Truman's program died in committee in both houses of Congress. It never even came to a floor vote in 1949.

Policy on medical care is a perfect example of an instance where the absence of government action is, nevertheless, a policy. Medical costs for the American population had been rising precipitously with the improvement of medicine and the increase in specialization. Paradoxically the success of medical care was itself one of the sources of this increased burden of medical expenses: People live longer, and medical expenses are a particular burden to the aged. (See Table 16.3.) By the 1940s the United States had become the only industrialized nation of the world with no program of government health insurance, and many nations such as Germany had had such programs since the nineteenth century.

The program passed in 1965 was hailed as a great breakthrough for government health insurance. But indeed it did not nearly bring the United States into line with the other nations of the world. The Medicare program was limited to the medical expenses of the aged. In several major ways, the program represents an example of incremental policy making. Although more comprehensive medical care schemes had been prepared, the program that was able to pass Congress was one that involved incremental modifications of existing programs. For one thing, government assistance to the aged was a well-established program. This made a medical care program directed to the aged more palatable. Furthermore, the program was set up as an insurance scheme, whereby benefits become an "earned right" based on previous payments into the social security program. This too represented an extension of past practices. In this way Medicare became an extension of the social security laws. It was an important modification of those laws, but it was by no means a comprehensive program for medical care.

But one thing must be noted about incremental changes. Over time a number of small steps can add up to a comprehensive change. The supporters of federal medical assistance would have preferred a broader program. They supported the narrower one because its passage was possible by 1965, and because they felt it was the basis on which further small steps could be taken toward a comprehensive program. Each incremental step becomes a take-off point for the next. And indeed, the AMA shared this perspective,

Table 16.3 Health Care and People Over 65

With One Tenth of the Population, the Aged Account for One Quarter of Medical Spending

	SHARE OF POPULATION	SHARE OF HEALTH SPENDING
65 and over	9.9%	27.4%
Ages 19–64	54.4%	56.5%
Under 19	35.7%	16.1%

For Practically Every Type of Care, Bills Are Highest for the Aged

Health Spending Per Person in 1971

	65 AND OVER	AGES 19–64	UNDER 19
Hospital care	$410	$158	$ 41
Nursing home	$151	$ 2	—
Physicians' services	$144	$ 69	$ 45
Drugs	$ 87	$ 37	$ 20
Dentists' services	$ 19	$ 27	$ 16
Other health services	$ 50	$ 30	$ 18
Total	$861	$323	$140

Source: U.S. Department of Health, Education, and Welfare. Reprinted from *U.S. News and World Report*, January 22, 1973. Copyright © 1973, U.S. News and World Report, Inc.

though their evaluation of the situation was much more negative. For them the medical care program for the aged was a cause of concern because it was the "foot in the door" for comprehensive medical care.

How this will work out, only the future can tell. In any case the medical care for the aged program has become the basis upon which one can—by one step at a time—build a larger program.

The Actors in Medical Care Legislation

Who were the major actors in this long history of medical care legislation? In terms of impact, the issue of medical costs touches everybody. Of course, such expenses are a particular burden for poorer families. However, it was not just the very poor for whom medical care was a burden, for they could often obtain treatment in free clinics of one sort or another. The burden fell just as heavily on middle-income families, particularly when major debilitating illnesses hit them. And, above all, medical costs were a

---

major burden on the aged. Medical needs soar in later years just when income is declining.

The Public at Large: For a number of years, public opinion polls had found the American people in favor—usually by two to one—of government health insurance schemes; this despite a mass campaign by the AMA to label such schemes as "socialism" and therefore a threat to the American way of life. But this public support can be thought of as only a vague and general pressure on the government. Much more is needed to carry a new social program through Congress.

The Aged—A Noncohesive Group: Interestingly enough, even after the issue began to evolve into one of medical care for the aged, there was little direct involvement of the aged as a cohesive group. There were some organizations associated with the aged—senior citizens councils, golden age clubs—but these were small compared with the role of the major lobbying groups such as the AMA. This illustrates a generalization presented earlier—it is difficult to obtain organized pressure from "consumer" groups. Although the aged were major consumers of medical services and would be greatly helped by this legislation, they did not represent a self-conscious and organized group.

Interest Groups: The major public protagonists were organized interest groups. The proponents included the AFL–CIO, other labor unions, and charitable organizations. The opponents were led by the AMA and included the American Hospital Association, the Life Insurance Association of America, and other more general organizations like the National Association of Manufacturers (NAM) and the United States Chamber of Commerce. It was these organizations—because they were *organized*—who could carry on the battle, particularly in the halls of Congress.

But notice one major imbalance between the organizations who favored and those who opposed medical care programs. Those who favored it were well-organized and powerful groups such as the AFL–CIO. But these were organizations for whom medical care was only a side issue. Labor unions, after all, have many other purposes, and a more direct involvement in such matters as wages and labor conditions. When it comes to such matters as wages, the unions are in the category of the *producers* of services; when it comes to medical expenses, they are *consumers*. And—in accord with our generalization that citizens and groups become more active in relation to their interests as producers than as consumers—the unions are likely to be more effective and active on wage policy than on medical policy.

The contrast with the opponents of medical insurance is striking. The opponent groups were led by the organizations of the major producers of medical treatment—the AMA and the American Hospital Association. And such an organization as the Life Insurance Association of America also gets involved as a producer, since medical insurance programs would be in competition with private insurance. The involvement of these groups was much more intense and steady. And they were involved in many ways. For one thing, they claimed the special status of producer groups—the status of experts in the matter. But they were involved not merely on the technical side of things. Rather, the AMA maintained a long campaign to sway the public to the view that medical insurance was "un-American." In this way, the debate on the issue rose to the level of a more general ideological debate.

The AMA had several advantages. It was well financed. Medical problems were its main concern. And it could mobilize large portions of its membership. The nature of its membership is important. Doctors are members of a highly respected profession, they are spread throughout the country, and they are likely to be important citizens of their localities—just the kind of constituency to catch the attention of the members of Congress.

The Presidency and the Congress: If the battle were merely one between the interest groups, the stalemate in legislation might never have been broken. But there were other important actors—in the White House and in the Congress. Much of the pressure for medical care legislation came from the Presidency. Harry Truman made medical insurance one of his major legislative goals. In this he had the support of some influential members of Congress such as Senator Robert Wagner of New York, who introduced some of the major bills. Truman did not succeed. The program was blocked by a hostile congressional coalition of Republicans and conservative Democrats. But his support kept the prospects of medical insurance alive.

During the Eisenhower years, the program was dormant, for it had little White House support. But the prospects came alive again under President Kennedy and culminated with the Medicare bill under President Johnson. Without the strong push from the White House, no progress would have been made.

Government Specialists: In this process, a key role was played by those government specialists who shaped the legislation. Officials of the Federal Security Agency—men like Wilbur J. Cohen and I. S. Falk—had worked on medical care problems for years. And they played no small role in the passage of the legislation. Over the years such specialists had become the leading administrative spokesmen at congressional committee hearings. They played a major role in drafting the legislation and in adjusting the legislation in ways that would make it acceptable to Congress.

Congressional Committees: As with tax legislation, the crucial arena for Medicare legislation was the Congress, or rather the relevant congressional committees. The two powerful committees in this case, as in the tax case, were again the House Ways and Means Committee and the Senate Finance

Committee, with the House committee and its chairman, Wilbur Mills, playing a crucial role. The annual hearings before this committee represented the major public battleground in the war over medical insurance. It was here that the various interest groups testified. It was here that legislation would have to be initiated if it was to be successful in the House of Representatives.

The situation points up a key paradox of Congress' representative role. Congress is the institution most capable—in principle—of representing the views of the public: Its members are elected from all parts of the country; they consider themselves representatives of their constituents; and unlike such bureaus of the government as the independent regulatory commissions, they have broad constituencies. Each congressman represents many interests in his district, and all congressmen put together represent a wide range of types of citizens and of groups. Thus Congress should be able to make policy that represents the public's wishes.

But the organization of Congress is such that it rarely acts as a body. Rather, the key role is played by particular congressmen on particular committees. In 1961 President Kennedy—who favored a medical insurance program—had a Democratic majority in Congress. But this majority was, as was often the case, not adequate for carrying through a legislative program. It was made up of many conservative southern Democrats who often joined their Republican colleagues in opposition to the administration. As the leading student of the Medicare program describes the situation in 1961,

> Sixteen Ways and Means committee-men were known to oppose the [Medicare bill] including Wilbur Mills (Dem. Ark.) whose influence within the committee was formidable. Under these circumstances, the Gallup poll findings that "two out of three persons interviewed would be in favor of increasing the social security tax to pay for old-age medical insurance" provided little comfort to President Kennedy. Four votes—either of southern Democrats or northern Republicans—would have to change for the president to have a medicare majority within the committee, and the prospects were not good.[2]

The congressmen who play the key role in such matters are those with greatest seniority. They are thus likely to be those from safe districts. Mills and the other influential members of the Ways and Means Committee often ran unopposed for office and rarely had any serious opposition at all. Thus not only is the representative function of Congress diluted by the fact that particular congressmen play key roles, but the congressmen who play those roles are just the ones least likely to have to worry about reelection.

Such congressmen are not completely immune from pressure for change. Representative Mills' support was what ultimately got the measure passed.

[2] Theordore R. Marmor, "The Congress: Medicare Politics and Policy," in Allan P. Sindler, ed., *American Political Institutions and Public Policy* (Boston: Little, Brown, 1969), p. 33.

And in his change of mind the public did play a role—though indirectly. The landslide victory of Lyndon Johnson in 1964 brought with it both a larger Democratic majority as well as an apparent mandate from the people for some new legislation. "By changing from opponent to manager [of the Medicare bill], Mills assured himself control of the content . . . at a time when it might have been pushed through the Congress despite him."[3]

Assessment of the Outcome of the Medicare Issue

Of course, as we have seen from other legislative areas, what may really count is not the decision to have legislation, but the details of how that legislation is written and applied. And in working out these details, Representative Mills "called on committee members, HEW officials, and interest group representatives to lend their aid in drafting a combination bill."[4] In this way the interest groups, like the AMA—though they may have lost the overall battle against the legislation—did have some influence in the writing of the bill. For instance, one of the effects of the bill has been a substantial increase in the income of doctors, primarily because the bill neglected to define what it meant by "reasonable charges." The result has been of financial benefit to doctors, as they put their own definition on that term.

What can be said in conclusion about the actors in relation to the Medicare issue? For one thing, it shows that no one is all-powerful. The AMA did not have its way, in that it would have preferred no legislation. The President—even when he had a majority of the same party in Congress as did Truman and Kennedy—could not push through the legislation he wanted. The public, though it favored some program according to the polls, was not able to convert the preference into legislation.

If any institution appeared all-powerful, it was perhaps the House Ways and Means Committee and its chairman. But even he was movable when the forces changed. And he would not probably have held the position against a medical program for as long as he did were he not constantly supported in this by the AMA.

In the end, one may have to continue to pay tribute to the political efficacy of an organization like the AMA—especially when it has powerful allies at strategic points in the Congress. Such a combination can be a powerful force—especially when it is dedicated to holding the line against innovation. It is true that a bill was ultimately passed despite the objections of the Medical Association. But they held the line for a long time. Germany had a health insurance program in 1883!

Furthermore, by holding the line they also played a major role in setting the agenda of the debate on medical care. The bill that was passed was still

[3] *Ibid.*, p. 53.
[4] *Ibid.*, p. 52.

quite limited—at least in comparison to other more comprehensive schemes that had been proposed. And this limitation was largely due to the belief—probably correct—among the proponents of medical insurance that nothing more extensive could be passed. In this sense the antimedical insurance forces remained potent even when seeming to go down in defeat.

Desegregation of the Public Schools

The process of policy making in relation to desegregation of the public schools differs from that in relation to medical care in one important way: The major consumers of medical services who stood to benefit by new laws—the aged and their organizations—were not major actors in pushing for legislative action in that direction. The major "consumers" of education who stand to benefit by desegregated schools—Blacks and organizations representing them—were major actors. In particular, the National Association for the Advancement of Colored People (NAACP) played a major role in pushing through change. The difference is instructive and helps us understand the conditions under which groups can take a major role in the policy process. The aged do not form a cohesive and self-aware group. They are probably more divided by other social characteristics—by their religion, place of residence, race, income level—than they are united by their age. Blacks on the other hand, though they are by no means a fully cohesive and organized group, have a greater basis for such cohesion and organization. They have a common history, tend to live in racial neighborhoods, and throughout American history have been clearly singled out by informal norms and by laws for a special deprived status.

The Role of the Supreme Court in the Desegregation Issue

Segregation in public schools was formally adopted as policy by about twenty states in the 1890s. State law explicitly declared that White and non-White pupils had to attend separate schools. Such laws—as well as many other laws decreeing segregation in the use of public facilities—were coupled with legislation restricting Black participation in politics. And these undercut whatever improvement in the status of Black Americans one might have expected in the aftermath of the Civil War.

The laws requiring segregation in the schools were challenged in the Supreme Court as violating the equal protection clause of the Fourteenth Amendment. But in a famous 7 to 1 decision—*Plessy v. Ferguson*—the Supreme Court held in 1896 that the Constitution did not bar separate schools as long as they were equal. The "separate but equal" doctrine was to remain as the law of the land for decades.

But as we have seen, the mere statement of a doctrine such as separate but equal — even by a government body as respected and powerful as the Supreme Court — does not automatically put it into effect. To see the meaning of the doctrine, one has to observe how it works in practice. In connection with the separate-but-equal doctrine, the Court's views went into effect only in part. The schools were indeed separate, but they were rarely equal. The Court's doctrine was enforced in the first instance because that was the practice already, and local officials were in favor of keeping the schools segregated. The Court's doctrine was not enforced in the second instance, because equal schools were costly, because local officials were not particularly interested in that (Blacks, after all, had no political power, barred as they effectively were from the vote), and lastly because the Court established no mechanism to check on the equality of facilities.

The Role of the NAACP in Challenging School Segregation: The first challenge to school segregation was led by the NAACP, an organization founded by a small group of Black intellectuals led by W. E. B. Du Bois shortly after the turn of the century. After unsuccessful attempts to work through the legislative branch to obtain change in the conditions of American Blacks, the NAACP turned its attention to the courts. Unlike the Congress, where action could be stopped by a determined southern bloc representing the one-party and all-White politics of the southern states, the court was above such direct political pressures. Also the wording of the Fourteenth Amendment, declaring that no state could "deny to any person within its jurisdiction the equal protection of the laws," seemed inconsistent with the practices of the southern states — though the Court had not seen fit to rule that way.

The NAACP's appeals through the courts followed the by-now-familiar incremental approach: searching for step-by-step changes in the rules applying to segregation. At first they challenged the equality of the schools. In 1938 the Supreme Court ruled that the State of Missouri was not giving Black students equal education by providing scholarships for them to an out-of-state law school, there being only an all-White law school in Missouri. Equal education required that the state open a law school for Blacks within Missouri. Note that the Court allowed for a separate school, but was beginning to enforce equality.

In 1950 the Court went further to say that separate law schools — one for each of the races — were inadequate. Their very separateness made them unequal. As reviewed in Chapter 11, in 1954 the Supreme Court handed down its landmark *Brown* decision that segregation in the public schools led inevitably to unequal treatment of pupils and was unconstitutional.

The movement by the Court to the school desegregation decision was an incremental one. It dealt first with the issue of equality, only later with separation. It ruled first on graduate schools — not as hot an issue as the public schools — and only later on the public schools. And the school desegregation decision itself — with its call for "all deliberate speed" and allowances for delays in implementing specific plans—certainly fits the incremental mold.

The role played by the NAACP through the Supreme Court illustrates how a group can bypass the legislative branch of the government. The Court acted where the Congress was unable or unwilling to act. But a group that wishes to do this needs many resources. For one thing, it has to have a constitutional case it can make. Without the Fourteenth Amendment the NAACP would not have gotten far with this tactic. Another thing it needs is simply a lot of time and dedication. The constitutional road is a long one; cases have to be painstakingly prepared and argued up from the lower courts. The NAACP's success took many decades of steady work. Finally, it needs a great deal of skill; and the NAACP had this in a highly competent group of lawyers led by Thurgood Marshall, who later became the first non-White justice on the Supreme Court.

Our analysis of what happens to general statements of law—by Congress or by the courts—should warn the reader that the battle for equal schooling did not end with a declaration by the Supreme Court that segregated schools are unconstitutional. The decision of the Court was not self-administering. It turned the administration of the program over to local school districts and to the states—all under the supervision of the federal courts. But—as with the regulation of business we discussed above—this meant in effect turning the administration of the law over to those who were to be regulated. After all, it was the local school districts and the states who had been carrying out the segregation laws. These local districts dragged their feet, helped by the state legislatures in the South who used various devices to block implementation of court-ordered desegregation. The result was that a decade after the Court decision, less than 2 percent of Black children in the South attended integrated schools.

The slowness is in part a result of the dispersion of political power in America. Although the Supreme Court can interpret the Constitution and such interpretations are the "supreme law of the land," the effective power for enforcing that law lies in the states and the localities. They can effectively block federal action, especially if that action is embodied in a decision of the Supreme Court and not backed up by the other branches of the federal government.

President Eisenhower had used the U.S. Army to keep Governor Orville Faubus of Arkansas from blocking the court-ordered integration of Little Rock High School, and in that way had thrown the executive power behind the Supreme Court. But Eisenhower never spoke out directly on the issue of segregation, and never pressed for legislation to follow up the Supreme Court's ruling. And the Congress, as well, was inactive.

Progress in the elimination of legally supported segregation had to wait for a time when other parts of the federal government could take action. John F. Kennedy put his administration behind a bill enforcing school desegregation as did, with more force and success, Lyndon Johnson. The

Civil Rights Act, sponsored by the Johnson Administration, was passed in 1964. This act brought the enforcement power of the executive branch to bear on segregation. The Attorney General was empowered to initiate desegregation suits if asked to do so by local residents; the Office of Education had the power to survey the extent of segregation in a district. The federal government could thus become a powerful counterweight to local authorities.

The De Facto Desegregation Problem: A Major Issue

With the combination of federal forces, more progress was made in the elimination of de jure segregation in the South. But this of course did not eliminate school segregation. What was becoming clear in the 1960s was that school segregation was only in part a function of state law. At the end of the 1960s there was at least as much segregation in the North as in the South (perhaps more) because in the North segregated schools were a function of the segregated residential patterns that had evolved in northern cities over the decades. (See Table 16.4.)

De facto segregation may turn out to be a more difficult problem to handle than de jure segregation. For one thing, it is deeply rooted in the social structure and geographical layout of American cities. Its elimination requires either rearrangement of residential patterns—a long-term and difficult process—or large-scale bussing of children from school to school. On the bussing issue large segments of the public tend to be aroused, both Black groups and White groups.

Unlike most issues in American politics we have been discussing, the issue of school desegregation has not been turned into a disaggregated issue. As we pointed out above, many policies in America are disaggregated; a

Table 16.4 Percentage of Black Pupils Attending Schools More Than 95 Percent Black

Chicago:	85%
Baltimore:	76%
Washington, D.C.:	89%
Los Angeles:	78%
Mobile, Alabama:	85%
Nationwide:	61%

Source: U.S. Department of Health, Education, and Welfare.

policy is made to benefit a specific constituency—the railroads, say, or a particular type of farmer—without at the same time considering the impact of the benefit on other groups in society. Such policy making produces little conflict or opposition because the benefits accorded one group are not directly perceived by others as costly to them.

Matters of school desegregation—particularly those that involve bussing—often involve a direct conflict between those favoring integrated schools and those parents for whom bussing is seen as a direct cost to them. A policy seen as beneficial to Blacks is seen as costly to some Whites. Under such circumstances, the number of relevant political actors increases. Disaggregated issues tend to be decided quietly; issues that involve clashes among constituencies are more noisy. The press plays a major role, as overt conflict becomes news. The issue is likely to become a campaign issue, and indeed bussing was a major issue in the 1972 Presidential campaign.

In short, it is a policy area with many, many actors. The courts have remained active; Congress has become an important arena for debate on the issue of bussing; President Nixon was vocal on the matter and somewhat at variance with the other branches of government. The public—both Black and White—is aroused. Out of such clashes social change sometimes comes. but it is unlikely to come smoothly.

Policy Making in Foreign Affairs: Vietnam

If there was a crisis in American politics in the 1960s and early 1970s, the two issues around which this crisis centered were race and Vietnam. Race, as we have shown, has some "naturally" divisive characteristics—particularly if one race views benefits received by the other as directly damaging to it. Usually, a war has just the opposite effect. In most cases, wars have led to a rallying together of the nation, as in the two world wars. And even the Korean War, which was by no means as popular as World War I and World War II, did not lead to the kinds of stresses that grew out of Vietnam.

This is not a book about Vietnam. The histories of U.S. involvement will be written and rewritten, and we can only touch lightly on the complexities of that issue. But the history of policy making on Vietnam can tell us a lot about how governmental policy making is a useful case to study because it can illustrate how foreign policy is made in "ordinary" times and how foreign policy is made under the unusual circumstances when a foreign policy issue has aroused major public controversy.

Policy making on Vietnam under President Kennedy and during the first years under President Johnson resembled the way in which foreign policy is usually made—it was made with little public or congressional attention. Vietnam policy after 1964 or 1965 became a much more public issue. Yet, as we shall see, the control over such policy by the public or the Congress remained limited.

Vietnam Under President Kennedy

As Roger Hilsman, a leading student of foreign policy and Kennedy's Assistant Secretary of State for Far Eastern Affairs put it, "Any discussion of the making of United States foreign policy must begin with the President."[5] Despite the power over foreign affairs that would seem to lie in the Congress — based on its power to declare war, to appropriate funds, as well as on the power of the Senate to ratify treaties — foreign affairs has traditionally been the province of the President. He — or rather his administration — oversees the day-to-day conduct of foreign affairs; only the executive branch has the expertise and information needed for foreign policy making. Nor have the controls over appropriations or the power to declare war been major limitations on the President. President Truman committed American troops to Korea without congressional declaration of war or even a resolution supporting the move. And the growth of American involvement in Vietnam took place largely through a series of Presidential decisions.

It would be a mistake, though, to consider a President to be a fully free agent when it comes to foreign policy. To begin with, policies, as we have seen, have a history. At any moment a President must make decisions in the light of what has gone on in the past. Thus, when Kennedy took office in 1961 he inherited commitments made under Eisenhower to support the government of South Vietnam. As early as 1961 there were several hundred American military men in Vietnam working directly with the South Vietnamese government.

A President is not fully free in another way. He is very dependent on the foreign policy bureaucracy. They do not make decisions on foreign policy — at least not the major ones — but they can structure the decision for the President by the advice they give him, by the information they control. In "ordinary" foreign policy making — as was Kennedy's policy on Vietnam before it became a public issue under Johnson — the major institutions involved are the Presidency and those agencies that provide the Presidency with information — the State Department, the CIA, the military.

Thus, based on information from the CIA with regard to the needs of the South Vietnamese government, President Kennedy ordered in 1962 an increase of the American presence in Vietnam from a few hundred men to 12,000 men. The nature of the step is important. It was considered a limited response to a particular issue, not an open-ended commitment to preserve the South Vietnamese government at any cost. At least there is no evidence that the administration anticipated the massive bombings and the

[5] Roger Hilsman, *The Politics of Policy Making in Defense and Foreign Affairs* (New York: Harper & Row, 1971), p. 17.

half-million men who were to be there in a few years. In this way it was an example of an incremental policy, modifying somewhat an earlier policy.

But the policy cannot fully fit under the incremental rubric because it was also guided by an overall strategy, a strategy based on a desire to contain communism, and a strategy of which one major component was the "domino theory" that the loss of South Vietnam would topple the other Asian nations. It was the combination of small incremental steps upward, guided by an overriding concern not to "lose" South Vietnam that characterized Vietnam policy in the 1960s.

The Role of the Congress in the Vietnam Policy: The role of the Congress during this era is fairly easy to summarize: It was minimal. In 1961, 1962, and 1963 the Congress had little to do with Vietnam. Its attention was turned to other problems. The first major involvement of the Congress came in the summer of 1964, during President Johnson's first year in office. In response to a Presidential request on the heels of an alleged attack by North Vietnamese gunboats on two American destroyers, the Congress passed the so-called Tonkin Gulf resolution. It expressed support for the President in Vietnam and authorized him "to take all necessary measures to repel any armed attack against the armed forces of the United States and to prevent further aggression." The resolution, it later turned out, had been presented to Congress after the Tonkin Gulf incident but had in fact been prepared earlier for submission at the first opportune time.

The event is instructive for understanding the relative roles of the President and Congress in foreign affairs. That the President asked for such a resolution indicates that there is some sharing of power over foreign affairs. Otherwise such support would not have been sought. Yet the resolution indicates how little sharing there is. For one thing, it was the position of the President, and shared by many members of Congress, that the resolution was not necessary; the President already had the powers that it granted to him. In other words, congressional support was not a necessity, but rather a useful expression to strengthen the President's position.

Also indicative of the minimal role of Congress is the fact that the resolution passed almost unanimously—in the Senate it passed by 82 votes to 2 and in the House by 416 to 0. In the Senate the resolution was shepherded through by Senator William J. Fulbright, Chairman of the Senate Foreign Affairs Committee, who later was to emerge as a leading opponent of Vietnam policy.

Nor did Congress in this first era of Vietnam policy use its power over appropriations to limit Presidential action in Vietnam. For instance, in the spring of 1965 Congress passed a special 700 million-dollar appropriation for the military—occasioned largely by the needs of Vietnam. The vote was 88 to 3 in the Senate and 408 to 7 in the House.

The consultative role of the Senate was summed up by Senator Fulbright in describing the Presidential decision to bomb North Vietnam in February 1965:

The President called the congressional leadership to the White House and had the Director of the CIA, the Secretary of Defense, etc., all demonstrate to us the reasons why the only course of action open to us was to bomb. This was the "consultation" of the President with Congress on that important decision. Mike Mansfield and I were the only ones at that meeting to demur on the bombing . . . the President just did not give a damn.[6]

In short, then, the actors on Vietnam policy up till late 1964 or early 1965 are fairly clear and fairly limited. Policy was made in the White House; the major actors were the President and his close foreign policy advisors in the State Department, the Department of Defense, on the White House staff, and on the National Security Council, and all based their decisions on information from the CIA and the military. There is a controversy as to when the major decision toward a long-term commitment in Vietnam was made. But many commentators feel such a decision was made fairly early in 1964 before the Tonkin Gulf incident. If this is the case, it was made largely within the White House circle. If there was opposition—and there is some evidence that there was—it came from within the administration itself, not from outside.

Congress was quiescent; its only involvement was to give support when asked to in the summer of 1964. And the American public was not much concerned. In the 1964 election Vietnam figured relatively little. If it played any role it was because of some public concern over the position of President Johnson's Republican opponent, Barry Goldwater, whose more militant views made President Johnson the candidate of restraint in foreign military policy.

Vietnam Under President Johnson—The Issue Explodes

The "second era" of the Vietnam war dates from sometime in 1965; the first university "teach-ins" took place in the spring of that year. The second era was characterized by two changes from the earlier period. For one thing, the American involvement grew steadily and massively, culminating in 1968 with over a half-million American troops in Vietnam, large-scale bombings, and what is generally agreed to have been a domination of the effort in Vietnam by American troops. At the same time, Vietnam moved from the back of American consciousness to the forefront. In 1964, when the American people were asked in a survey to name the most important problem facing the nation, 8 percent mentioned Vietnam. By 1966 that figure had risen to 46 percent, and during the late 1960s the issue of Vietnam was consistently mentioned in public opinion polls as the most important problem facing the nation. Nor was public concern limited to results in

---

[6] Quoted in Eugene Eidenberg, "The Presidency: Americanizing the War in Vietnam," in Sindler, p. 122.

public opinion polls. Rather, the concern of at least some segments of the society was manifested in a growing number of protest marches and demonstrations linked to the war.

Protest against the war also moved to the floor of the Senate, where senators such as Fulbright, McGovern, Kennedy, and McCarthy came out in opposition to the policy. And in 1968 first Senator Eugene McCarthy and then Senator Robert Kennedy entered the Presidential primary races against President Johnson. The result was the President's withdrawal from the campaign.

Nor did the greater involvement cease after a new administration under President Nixon entered office after the 1968 election. Public opposition continued; student protest reached a new height after the President sent troops into Cambodia; and congressional critics were not silent.

But in some respects things changed relatively little. Vietnam exploded as an issue in America. The Congress was aroused, and many members were critical; the public was concerned, and large segments strongly opposed and became active in opposition. Yet the major way in which Vietnam policy was shaped—by the President on the basis of advice of his staff—did not change that much. They operated in a new environment where policy was under close scrutiny and constant attack, an environment quite different from that in the early 1960s. The President, however, remained what Hilsman has called the "ultimate decider."

Consider how the role of the various actors changed in the years after 1965. The Tonkin Gulf resolution represented the high point of the Senate backing of the President in Vietnam. From then on the Senate—or, rather, certain senators—became more critical. A series of public hearings on the Tonkin Gulf incident in 1968 brought out information indicating that the administration had been less than candid in the earlier event and had used it to take advantage of the Senate. Various resolutions were introduced in the Senate expressing disapproval of Presidential policy, calling for withdrawal of troops, and the like. But in all of these attempts the Senate acted as a critic of Presidential activity—a prestigious and often convincing critic at that. But what it did not do is intervene directly in the process of decision making on Vietnam. It could embarrass the administration—and indeed the pressure on the President may have weighed heavily in Johnson's decision not to seek reelection. But it did not shape policy.

The role of the Congress as critic is clearly seen in a resolution passed by that body in 1969, after hearings conducted by Senator Symington showed that there were American troops in Thailand and that the United States was supporting a clandestine army in Laos. The Congress this time remembered Tonkin Gulf and, in a move that was intended to counteract what many congressmen now felt had been a blunder and an unwarranted turning of power over to the President, passed a resolution expressing the wishes of the Congress that the President ought not to send troops to Laos or Thailand without the prior consent of the Congress.

Was this a major change in the structure of foreign policy making from the time when Congress gave the President *carte blanche* in Vietnam after the Tonkin Bay incident? Roger Hilsman's comment on two aspects of the resolution is instructive:

> *The first is that enough congressmen were sufficiently uneasy about tying the president's hand in some future crisis to defeat the resolution and would have done so if President Nixon had not let it be known that the resolution was in line with the Administration's policy. The second point is that a resolution does not have the binding effect of law, and if there were a crisis in the future sufficiently grave and sufficiently urgent to permit the President to justify sending American troops to Laos or Thailand on grounds of protecting the national security, there would in fact be no legal barrier. The resolution, in other words, is nothing more than the expression of a pious hope that the President will consult with Congress before making such a decision if it is possible and feasible to do so.*[7]

In the Tonkin Gulf resolution, the Congress had given the President a blank check, but ironically it was one that he did not need. According to both the President's interpretation as well as that of his senatorial critics, he had the power to act as the Tonkin Gulf resolution allowed him to do even without that resolution. When it came to Laos, congressional action was the opposite. It expressly called on the President not to act without first obtaining congressional approval. But ironically, this resolution had little more effect. The attitude of the Congress had moved from positive to negative, but its power had not changed that much. The Vietnam war remained in the hands of the White House.

There are many reasons for the relatively weak position of the Congress in relation to the President when it comes to foreign policy. For one thing, the constitutional balance of power lies in the direction of the President. The President's role as Commander-in-Chief of the armed forces was, to a large extent, the basis on which troops were committed in Korea and Vietnam. Once such commitments are made, Congress is reluctant to deny appropriations necessary to support the troops abroad.

More important than the constitutional grant of power is the importance of the administration's greater resources to coordinate policy, to gather information on foreign affairs, to present its position to the American people. The President controls the vast foreign policy bureaucratic apparatus in the State Department, in the Defense Department, in the Central Intelligence Agency, as well as a large White House staff. In comparison, the Congress is ill equipped.

For all senators and representatives, foreign affairs is only one of the many subjects they must deal with; and for all but a few it is not the most

[7] Hilsman, p. 81.

important. Senators and representatives are, as we pointed out, usually first and foremost representatives of their states and districts; they know local needs and problems. But such knowledge is not especially helpful in foreign affairs. They are specialists in satisfying local needs. And foreign affairs involvement takes away time from that. Foreign policy activities tend to gain a member of Congress few local votes. Senator Fulbright has been consistently criticized in his home state of Arkansas for ignoring the needs of his constituents while he pursues his job as chairman of the Senate Foreign Relations Committee. A foreign policy battle with the President can be damaging at home. It is perhaps no accident that both senators who voted against the Tonkin Gulf resolution (Gruening of Alaska and Morse of Oregon) were defeated in their next elections.

When it comes to foreign policy, the President remains most powerful. This is unambiguously the case when policy is noncontroversial and largely ignored by the Congress and the public, as was Vietnam policy in the early 1960s. But it does not change that much even when the issue becomes a massively public one, as in the late 1960s. This conclusion is underlined if we consider the role of the public in relation to Vietnam.

Vietnam and the Public

Vietnam during the earlier Kennedy years was a distant and unknown place for most Americans. In the Johnson years it became the major American problem as far as the public was concerned; the Vietnam battlefields dominated the evening news; the struggle over Vietnam at home also filled the news. And the steady increase in consciousness about the war was accompanied by a steady growth in disillusionment. In 1965 the Gallup poll found that about 22 percent of the American people thought that our entry into the war had been a mistake. The number rose steadily over the next five years, and from about 1969 on the polls consistently showed majorities of the public replying that our involvement in Vietnam was a mistake. And this was coupled with a growing unhappiness with the way in which the President was handling Vietnam.

The evidence is fairly clear that the public was deeply unhappy over Vietnam (see Figure 16.1), but the limitation of the public's voice in foreign affairs is emphasized by two additional facts. For one thing, the unhappiness of the public did not appear to be linked to the foreign aspects of the Vietnam war — that is, to the impact of the war on Vietnam or on American foreign relations more generally — but public concern seems to have derived from unhappiness over the domestic consequences of the war. In other words, a foreign policy problem — even one like Vietnam — breaks into the public consciousness only when it begins to have consequences nearer to home. Second, the public's unhappiness with the war was not coupled with any clear picture of what to do about it. Surveys showed, for instance,

Vietnam during the Kennedy years was a distant and unknown place for most Americans. During the Johnson years it dominated the news and the thinking of the American public.   (*Photo: Wide World*)

that among the growing group that believed the war had been a mistake, about as many favored escalation as favored withdrawal.[8]

In short, the public wanted something done about the war, but was by no means clear about what it wanted. This is reflected in the fact that the President's popularity during the Vietnam war usually went up whenever he did anything—increased the bombing or stopped the bombing, took a step upward in military pressure, or appeared to take a step downward. The new action, no matter whether it was escalation or de-escalation, brought the administration more support in the hope that it would mean an end to the war.

This characteristic of American opinion suggests the kind of constraint that the public can have over the conduct of foreign affairs. The President was not particularly pressured by the public to engage in one policy or another—to escalate or de-escalate the war. Rather, the public would support a variety of initiatives, as long as they tended to shorten the war. Thus

[8] See Milton J. Rosenberg, Sidney Verba, and Philip E. Converse, *Vietnam and the Silent Majority* (New York: Harper & Row, 1970), chap. 2.

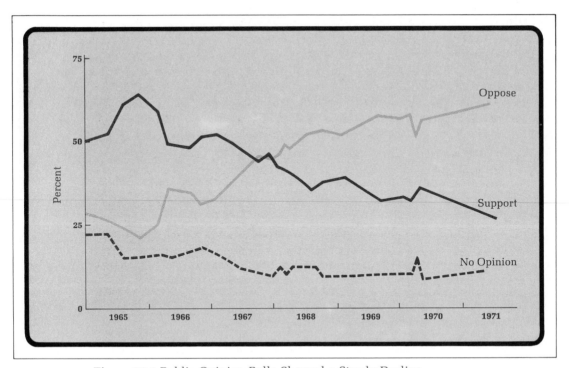

Figure 16.1 Public Opinion Polls Showed a Steady Decline
in Public Support of Administration Policy in Vietnam

SOURCE: John E. Mueller, *War, Presidents and Public Opinion* (New York: Wiley, 1973).
Reprinted by permission of John Wiley & Sons.

the public would judge the policy retrospectively in terms of how successful it was in that direction. Public opinion is a force to be reckoned with, not because it offers clear guidelines to the President for policy, but because it presents a threat to the President that it will react negatively to past failures.

Thus the White House cannot ignore these pressures; and it will be particularly sensitive to such pressures when elections approach. But the President maintains flexibility in terms of how he meets this pressure.

The role of the public in foreign policy thus appears to parallel in certain respects that of the Congress. Both the Congress and the public can apply pressure on the White House by withdrawing support, by threatening negative reactions in the future, by being critical. But neither the Congress nor the public initiates foreign policy.

Of course, as we have seen in relation to many issues, the balance of power among the various branches of the government is never rigidly fixed. During Nixon's second term in office, Congress attempted in a number of ways to limit U.S. military involvement in Cambodia (where U.S. bombings had continued after the American troop withdrawal from South Vietnam in the winter of 1973). And more general legislation was initiated to limit the power of the President to commit U.S. troops abroad without the explicit consent of Congress. This opposition from Congress was heightened by revelations in late 1973 that the executive branch had deliberately misled Congress and the public regarding bombing of Cambodia four years earlier. That deception had been carried out by listing as "killed in Vietnam" American troops actually killed in Cambodia. The hand of Congress was further strengthened by the defensive posture of the Nixon administration because of the Watergate scandals.

Such a challenge to the President's foreign policy powers may indicate the beginning of a more vigorous congressional role in foreign policy. But it is likely that when the particular problems faced by Nixon have passed into history, the overall balance in foreign policy making will still favor the Presidency over the Congress. The specialized features of foreign and military matters that have made the White House the central actor are not likely to change. And it is a safe guess that the executive branch will remain the initiator of foreign policy.

Controversy

It is the rare citizen who does not at one time or another feel strongly that some aspect of American policy needs changing: "It is obvious that the United States ought to get out of Vietnam." "We clearly need a more comprehensive medical care program." "Our economy will not survive if government regulations continue to stifle the initiative of businessmen." "The government has no business bussing children to achieve racial balance in schools." To paraphrase Lincoln, all citizens feel this way some of the time, some citizens feel this way all of the time—and over a wide range of issues.

But knowing one wants something done and getting it done are two different things. And thus most of us feel pretty much frustrated politically at times.

There are many strategies that citizens or groups of citizens can pursue in trying to develop some effective role in governmental policy. Two alternative strategies are what we can call the "grand coalition" and the "narrow thrust." Which strategy would you recommend to someone interested in radical social reform in America? (We realize that you may not, yourself, favor such change. But suspend your hostility for a moment and see which advice would be more useful for our hypothetical radical reformer.)

One Side

Change in America requires a broad coalition of the forces for change. Too often groups that could have much in common go off in different directions and do not give one another support. The peace movement goes one way, the ecologists another, and the Blacks and other minorities are always off by themselves. What is needed is a grand coalition of all forces for change. Only by creating such a broad coalition can one have sufficient numbers to make an impact on governmental policy. And only in that way can one achieve fundamental change rather than a piecemeal chipping away at this problem or that.

The Other Side

Any grand coalition must compromise its positions so much that it winds up standing for nothing. The Blacks don't get what they want, the ecologists no more so. What is the use of large size if there is no clear policy?

Furthermore, effective involvement in making policy requires close concentration on one issue or another. One can't reform everything. It is better for different groups to concentrate their efforts on one issue or another, rather than trying to deal with all issues at once.

Perspectives
on American
Democracy

17

Is America a democracy? This perhaps is the most controversial question to ask about American politics. It certainly is the most difficult. How you answer it will depend on what you think the word "democracy" stands for. It will depend also on how you emphasize different facts. We do not attempt an answer in this final chapter. We will, though, review two contrasting perspectives on the issue of democracy in America. The assumptions and facts stressed in one perspective lead to the conclusion that "Yes, on balance, America is a democracy," while the contrasting perspective emphasizes other facts and concludes that "No, America, is not really a democracy."

The first perspective is often summarized under the label *pluralistic democracy*, and gives emphasis to two major themes:

1. Power is widely shared across American society.
2. As voters and as members of interest groups the citizens exercise meaningful control over public policy.

The second perspective has been called the *power elite thesis*, and takes the opposite position on these themes:

1. Power is concentrated in the hands of a small group of persons.
2. The average citizen is isolated and ineffective when it comes to the making of public policy.

Pluralist Democracy

In the pluralist perspective, power is dispersed or fragmented. It is scattered among numerous competing interests. No single interest monopolizes control, and no single segment of the population is totally excluded. The competition among divergent interests — management versus labor, rural versus urban, Southerners versus Northerners, isolationists versus interventionists — expresses itself as the struggle between organized groups for relative advantage. Each group gets part of what it wants, but no group ever gets all of what it wants. Mutual adjustment and compromise prevail. The group struggle takes place in the public arena, with the government acting as umpire and mediator so that a workable balance is achieved, and the entire society benefits. In the pluralist conception, what begins as conflict between selfish and parochial interests ends up promoting the general welfare.

Three conditions in American society support a pluralistic politics.

There is, first, social pluralism or the heterogeneity of the population. Enormously varied types of people migrated to the United States during its first two centuries, resulting in a society that has correctly been called a "community of communities." Religious, ethnic, and racial diversity prevail. The life-styles of rural America continue side by side with the life-styles brought about by urbanization. It is the American creed to tolerate different life-styles, and though this tolerance has sometimes been strained (the attitude of many Americans toward the counterculture), the famous "melting pot society" has not in fact produced a homogeneous society.

There is, second, the often remarked-on tendency of Americans to form groups in order to satisfy a wide range of public and private needs. Evidence was reviewed in Chapter 7, where we saw that not all American citizens do belong to organizations. This qualification is important and we discuss it below. Still, there are an enormous number of formal and informal associations. The right to form groups is protected in the First Amendment freedom of association, and the habit of forming groups is as old as the Republic, at least if we accept the testimony of observers such as de Tocqueville:

> In no country in the world has the principle of association been more successfully used, or applied to a greater multitude of objects, than in America. In the United States, associations are established to promote the public safety, commerce, industry, morality, and religion. There is no end which the human will despairs of attaining through the combined power of individuals united in a society.[1]

Perhaps the folklore of voluntary associations in American society has exaggerated the numbers involved in group activity, but there is a complex network of private associations linking the individual citizen and his government.

A third significant condition of pluralistic politics is the structure of American government. We saw in Chapters 9 and 10 that the formal powers of government were deliberately fragmented, primarily through a separation-of-powers system, in which different duties are assigned to the judiciary, executive, and legislature, and through the federal principle, in which different duties are assigned to national, state, and local governments. This constitutional fragmentation of formal power provides multiple access points for citizens seeking favors from government. Numerous agencies and officials make decisions of concern to different interest clusters, a condition that promotes a multiplicity of groups. There are many pressure points and a corresponding proliferation of private organizations to take advantage of this condition.

What is striking about the pluralist theory is, of course, its perspective

---

[1] Alexis de Tocqueville, *Democracy in America*, vol. I, Phillips Bradley, trans. (New York: Knopf, 1944), p. 198.

on power. Power is viewed as fragmented or dispersed. Partly this is because different groups are active in different sectors of public life. Thus the groups that compete for advantage in the arena of public education are not the same as those that compete in the arena of veterans' benefits. If the National Federation of Teachers is influential when it comes to federal aid to education, it has little influence over health plans for returning servicemen. The opposite is true of the Veterans of Foreign Wars. The fact that different groups compete in different policy sectors goes far toward explaining why no single interest ever gets a monopoly of political power. Moreover, any given group varies in its political success. It wins one battle, but loses the next. The American Medical Association has certainly won its share of battles in the struggle to prevent establishment of public medicine and national health insurance programs; but it has not won all the battles, and the public health picture is not what it was a decade ago.

What emerges is a system not only of fragmented but also of balanced powers, according to the pluralists. The great economic interests of society—business, labor, agriculture, consumers—share power. The same can be said of interests lodged in geographic areas of the nation; some policies advantage the South, but others advantage the Midwest or the Northeast. No single region can monopolize public policy.

The portrait of American society painted by the pluralist has the various groups struggling for access and advantage: trade unions attempting to improve wages and working conditions while management organizations strive to protect corporate profits and investment capital; concerned parents agitating for a bond issue to raise teacher salaries but opposed by the homeowner association intent on keeping property taxes low; doves marching to end the war even as hawks are holding rallies to demand an increase in the military effort. These group conflicts magnified and repeated many times over are the stuff of American politics.

The conflict is never too disruptive, however, because the various interests are presumably agreed about the basic rules under which the political game is played. Despite sharp and divisive differences over substantive policy there is agreement about how differences are to be resolved—elections, due process, peaceful assembly and petitioning, legislative debate, court decisions, majority will, and so forth. This underlying consensus about how to adjust political differences reduces the social harm of group conflict. As the conflict proceeds within established channels, the antagonisms dissolve into compromises.

Consensus formation and conflict resolution are greatly aided by the government. In the pluralist view the state has no vested interest in the outcome of group conflict, and thus is a neutral arbiter. The government serves all interests—and thus all of society—by establishing the framework within which differences are peacefully resolved. The government also watches that no single interest monopolizes the power of society. If one interest cluster—say, business and commerce—appears to be growing too strong, then the government throws its weight behind the claims of the farmers or those of the workers. It is this process of countervailing powers that ensures that no segment of society is subordinated to another.

The public plays an active role at two critical points. First, it supplies the mass membership that makes interest groups the important actors they are in the policy process. Labor can stand up to business because 19 million American workers belong to trade unions. The antipollution policies of the last decade are at least partly in response to public pressure brought to bear by the many environmental protection groups in society.

In pluralistic democracy the public exercises effective control in another and even more significant way. The public is an electorate. As such, the public chooses its own representatives to umpire the struggle among competing groups. These elected representatives pay close attention to what they believe the public wants in the way of public policy. That is, their powers are not exercised free of public control. Because tenure in office depends on satisfying the voting public, representatives select policies thought to be in the public interest.

According to this perspective America is a pluralistic-representative democracy. Power is widely shared and public policy is largely under the

In pluralist democracy, one way citizens exercise control of public policy is by expressing their preferences through the ballot box.   (Photo: Joel Gordon)

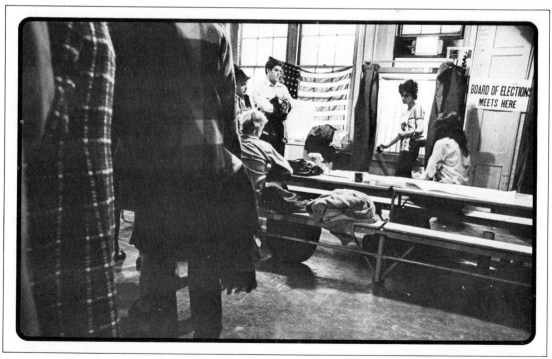

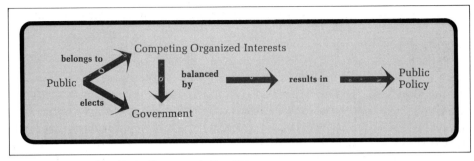

Figure 17.1 A Pluralistic-Representative Democracy

control of citizens as they express their preferences through their group memberships and through the ballot box. This perspective can be diagrammed as shown in Figure 17.1.

Some Doubts About Pluralist Democracy

The pluralist perspective has received sharp criticism. The critics say that it misrepresents the structure of power in the United States, and that insofar as elements of pluralism do operate, they have unfortunate consequences.

One glaring inadequacy of the pluralist conception is the assumption that no significant sectors in American society are excluded from the group process. The critics emphasize that many individuals remain unorganized and even that entire interests are never expressed through the group process. A good example of the latter is consumer interests. The unorganized consumer is buffeted by the inflationary policies shaped jointly by Big Labor and Big Business. Even federal agencies that attempt to regulate advertisements or that attempt to ensure fair competition find themselves largely captured by the industrial interests they are supposed to regulate. The individual consumer is a small voice in a world dominated by giant corporations, huge labor unions, and the mass media. The popularity of Ralph Nader suggests how eager the consumer is to have his interests protected. The difficulties Nader faces suggests how much the balance is weighed in favor of organized rather than unorganized interests.

The problem of the unorganized interest is compounded by the fact that the membership in groups is far from universal. Trade unions have enormous budgets and very effective lobbying staffs. It is understandable that in congressional committees or the Department of Labor, trade unions are viewed as the voice of the working class. But only one out of four American workers belongs to a union (19 million workers belong to unions, 60 million do not). Migrant workers, farm laborers, domestic help, small business employees, and many industrial workers, especially in the South and West, are not unionized. Some unions restrict membership, as when members of minority races are unable to join apprentice programs; thus the construction trades have been a White preserve for many years. Insofar as organized labor is the voice of the working class very many workers remain without a spokesman.

A similar bias can operate within the professions. The American Medical Association has long been viewed as the official spokesman for the medical profession, but fewer than one-half of practicing doctors today belong to the AMA. The doctor who refuses to join or who finds it difficult to get membership is typically in public health or in a university-based hospital. He often is unhappy with the conservative views of the AMA leadership, and even more unhappy with the influence of AMA in medical policy making. As long as health policy is dominated by the "organized viewpoint," the liberal perspective is disadvantaged. Liberal doctors attempting to formulate their own organization, just as the nonunionized workers do, find that the operating system of politics puts all the resources at the disposal of the already organized.

Many additional examples could be cited, but the point is clear. When social policies are promoted or blocked in the name of organized interests, many citizens are left out of consideration. It is a further point of the critics of pluralism that the bias in pluralistic politics favors the more conservative interests of society and it favors the more privileged groups.

The reason for the conservative bias is simple. Well-established, entrenched organizations are more powerful than organizations in the process of being born. The former have their budgets, their professional lobbying staff, their contacts in Washington and the state capitals, and a long record of public involvement. The upstarts lack all of these things. But it is usually the upstart organizations that are dissatisfied with the status quo and that enter politics with a reforming zeal. They are met, and more often than not beaten back, by the "conservatives" who shaped the status quo and, understandably, intend to protect it.

The pressure group system has also an upper-class bias. If one looks closely at the interests regularly and effectively represented in the group process it is evident that business and commercial organizations dominate. American politics regularly services their needs, as might be expected in a society committed to capitalism. From 60 to 75 percent of all organizations that have access to Congress and executive agencies represent the business community. In addition to the two giants—the National Association of Manufacturers and the U.S. Chamber of Commerce—there are hundreds of trade associations and independent corporations that maintain lobbyist activities. Business associations have a decided advantage in the group struggle because of the prior commitment of the society to capitalism, and because the commercial sector of society benefits from the high social status of their leaders and the deference given to their aims. Perhaps most significant, it is business groups and businessmen who provide the large share of the cash necessary for political campaigns and party activities.

The class bias of the pressure group systems is even evident when we look at organizations that purportedly represent the lower classes. The most active members of any group are its middle-class members, and its leaders are nearly always better educated than its average members. Thus such well-established minority group organizations as the NAACP or the Urban League are directed by Blacks whose social origins and educational attainments make them very atypical of the ghetto resident or southern share cropper. The same is true even of labor unions. In case after case the executives who shape the political program of the labor movement are not themselves workingmen, but instead are persons with college educations and often law degrees. Because large organizations — even those with a mass base — lack internal democracy, the critics conclude that power rests in the hands of an upper-class leadership.

Besides, say the critics, competition among organized interests has been grossly exaggerated in the pluralist interpretation. It is true that there is a plurality of groups. It is *not* true that they compete with one another for advantage. And even less does government moderate in a way that produces the best outcome for the entire society. A more accurate view of power sees that vested interests dominate the sector of public life that directly concerns them. In this criticism *capture* is a more appropriate term than *competition* to describe group politics.

Agricultural policy provides a clear example. Powerful interest organizations that represent the farmer, especially the large, commercial farmers, have literally captured the very government agencies that are supposed to regulate agriculture and balance the demands of farmers against the competing needs of consumers and other groups. Thus the Farm Bureau Federation controls the relevant congressional committees and subcommittees simply by electing friendly congressmen from the rural districts and then pressuring party leadership for their appointment to the relevant committees. A quid pro quo arrangement is reached with other dominant interests in society — similar treatment is accorded them with respect to committee assignments. It is no surprise that banking and currency committees are heavily staffed with congressmen representing financial interests or that interior and insular affairs committees in both the Senate and House have mostly congressmen from states with large public lands.

The same holds in the executive branch. Programs of the Department of Agriculture and related executive agencies are funded with public monies but controlled and administered by private farming interests. Thus the Soil Conservation Service or the Farm Credit Administration are practically self-administered by the farmer organizations most affected, and the taxpayer is the loser. Similar arrangements prevail elsewhere in the bureaucratic maze of Washington, D.C. The Department of Commerce is an adjunct to the business interests it presumably regulates. Indeed, the U.S. Chamber of Commerce was funded at the initiation of the Department of Commerce; the National Association of Manufacturers was organized out of a set of meetings arranged by and taking place in the offices of the Secretaries of Commerce and Labor.

In an extended criticism of pluralism it is argued that the all-important distinction between private power and public authority has nearly been eliminated in American society. "This has been accomplished not by public expropriation of private domain — as would be true of the nationalization that Americans fear — but by private expropriation of public authority."[2] In this criticism the much-vaunted pluralism is nothing but a façade behind which powerful private interests rule their own fiefdoms, but do so with the blessing of public authority and with the largess of the public treasury.

Dissatisfaction with pluralism as a description of power in American society has led to a view stressing a power elite. It is easy to see why. Because only the wealthiest interests in society are effectively organized and because they have appropriated the governing institutions to their own use, a reasonable view of power holds that a very small group of men are able to direct society according to their preferences.

Elitist Rule

Neither the mass public nor elected representatives nor interest groups have power. American society is ruled by a power elite. These are the men and women who "are in command of the major hierarchies and organizations of modern society. They rule the big corporations. They run the machinery of the state and claim its prerogatives. They direct the military establishment. They occupy the strategic command posts of the social structure, in which are now centered the effective means of the power and wealth and the celebrity which they enjoy."[3] In his enormously influential book entitled *The Power Elite*, C. Wright Mills swept aside previous interpretations of American politics and proposed instead a conception that was deeply pessimistic about the fate of democracy.

There are three sources of power in contemporary American society Mills suggested: the large corporations, the military establishment, and the political directorate. The economy is no longer a scatter of small productive units balanced by the workings of the marketplace, but "has become dominated by two or three hundred giant corporations, administratively and politically interrelated, which together holds the keys to economic decisions." The political order is no longer a decentralized arrangement with state and local autonomy, but "has become a centralized, executive establishment which has taken up into itself many powers previously scattered, and now enters into each and every cranny of the social structure."

---

[2] Theodore J. Lowi, *The End of Liberalism* (New York: Norton, 1969), p. 102.

[3] C. Wright Mills, *The Power Elite* (New York: Oxford University Press, 1956), p. 4.

The military order is no longer a weakling institution limited by the distrust Americans traditionally felt toward standing armies, but "has become the largest and most expensive feature of government, and, although well versed in smiling public relations, now has all the grim and clumsy efficiency of a sprawling bureaucratic domain."[4]

The powerful, Mills wrote, are persons able to realize their will, even if others resist it. In the contemporary United States it is clear to Mills that the powerful are those persons who head the corporate economy, the political directorate, and the military establishment. Men and women in charge of these dominant institutions are truly a power elite. They make the life-and-death decisions for the society. They not only do their duty, they define what their duty is. History is made by this elite, as is evidenced in such dramatic events as the Cuban missile crisis, the escalation of the war in Vietnam, the wage-price freeze, taking the dollar off the gold standard, and supporting China's entry into the United Nations.

These "history-making" events are not formulated by an actively involved public, by the huge number of elected representatives holding office in American politics, or by the leaders of interest groups. They are made by the persons who control one of the three dominant institutions. Other persons are relegated to the middle levels of power; here, in this category, belong most legislators, party bureaucrats, small-scale businessmen and entrepreneurs, interest group leaders, city mayors and even state governors. Below this middle level of power is a mass public, a powerless aggregate that has political anxieties but no political information, that is manipulated without being consulted, and that is acted upon rather than acts.

The hold the power elite has on society is aided by the interlocking nature of the three dominant institutions. According to Mills it is naïve to think that there are separate economic, military, and political elites, and it is wrong to view the economic, military, and political sectors as independent of one another. Power in American society results from the intermingling of the three sectors. Economic elites take into account and cooperate fully with political elites, and military elites are simultaneously involved in political and corporate decisions. Indeed, the different elites know one another; they attended the same private schools, the same prestigious universities and law schools, and they now vacation in the same resorts and appear at the same social gatherings. They often find themselves brought together by the intermarriage of their offspring. More important than the similar life experiences is the fact that the elites are often interchangeable. A retired general is invited to join the board of directors of a major defense industry; the president of Ford Motors leaves the corporate world to become Secretary of Defense; the defeated Presidential candidate joins a prestigious New York law firm that handles the affairs of giant cor-

[4] *Ibid.*, p. 7.

porations. These are not three separate elites in competition with one another, but a single elite that shares responsibility for three different sectors of society.

Private wealth is a significant advantage for recruitment into elite circles, as discussed in Chapter 6, though entry is not reserved only for the wealthy. Elite status can be attained by persons from various social backgrounds. But this does not mean that entry into the top positions is entirely open. On the contrary, it is prohibited or at least extremely difficult unless you share the general world-view of the dominant elite. The elite do not, of course, agree on many matters of specific policy, but they are agreed that private property is preferable to public ownership, that military force should be used to protect American investments and ideals abroad, that the public treasury must be used to bolster a faltering economy, and that the mass public requires and expects wise though strong leadership.

The last observation is particularly important to the power elite thesis. Even though America has the trappings of a democracy, effective democratic control is missing because citizens have become part of a mass either unable or unwilling to deal with the complexities of public policy.

In the first place the mass public would much prefer not to be bothered. The average citizen cares more for his family, his job, and how he spends his time than he does for the complicated and bewildering problems of society. Perhaps because he is largely indifferent to public issues, the average citizen is also very much ill informed about broad questions as well as specific issues. About all that he can be expected to know is the political party he prefers and for whom he should vote in order to put his party in office. You have learned that there is much empirical support for this characterization.

According to some elite theorists there is more than the apathy and ignorance of the mass public; there is also mass incompetence and perhaps irrationality. The public does not know what is in its best interests: If mothers could be trusted to boil milk, there would be no need to legislate about pasteurizing it. If workers were competent enough to save for their old age, there would be no need for compulsory social security. If people would wear seat belts, there would be no need for complicated engineering devices now being installed on cars. But the evidence is overwhelming that you cannot depend on the good judgment and competence of most citizens. Left to itself, the public would choose the immediate gratification and fail to plan for the future. Eventually it would bring ruin upon itself.

Thus the elite thesis does not find in the mass public a source of effective democratic control. And it dismisses as well most of the elected representatives, and even organized interest groups. It finds, instead, that power is concentrated in the hands of an elite that controls corporations, the military establishment, and the executive center of government. Competition may take place at the middle levels of power, but the higher reaches are in

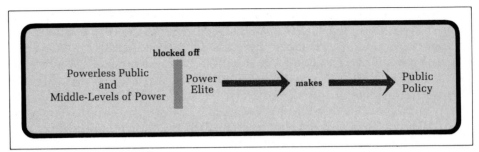

Figure 17.2 The Power Elite

general accord about the direction American society should take. This elite has the power to take American society in a direction of its own choosing. The viewpoint might be diagrammed as shown in Figure 17.2.

Some Doubts About the Power Elite Thesis

The elitist perspective has not escaped criticism. We cannot review all the criticisms, many of which are advanced by persons who hold to the pluralist viewpoint and who see competition among elites rather than a single dominant elite. We concentrate on one important observation.[5]

It may be true that a small group of men make many of the major decisions for society, and it is likely that these are the men directing the large corporations, controlling the machinery of the military, and in charge of the executive branch of government. It is not true that this small group is a *power* elite. In fact these men are powerless when confronted with active, popular opposition. A policy that loses widespread support will be pushed aside. And any policy that commands widespread and active support will eventually become the law of the land, no matter how much it might hurt the interests of the current elite. Examples might be pollution controls, consumer protection, and greater heed to environmental factors. Finally, it is not only the elites of the corporate, military, and political sectors who have veto power; so also does the public. There is evidence to suggest that the elites were willing and even eager to move much faster on civil rights during the 1950s and 1960s than was the general public. Social harmony and general stability work to the advantage of the elites, and integrating middle-class neighborhoods (where they do not live) or providing more blue-collar jobs (which they do not compete for) or improving ghetto schools (which their children do not attend) are not social policies that challenge either elite control or elite privileges. But the elite did not have the power to move the American public faster than it was willing to move. The elite, in short, are not a *power* elite.

[5] The point made below is developed more fully in Robert Paul Wolfe, *The Poverty of Liberalism* (Boston: Beacon, 1968), chap. 3.

Critics hold that the elite theorists overlook the significance of what might be called "constitutional opposition." Effective opposition to either the policies or the tenure of current rulers can be forestalled but not, in the final analysis, ignored. This opposition is not often mobilized. For the most part the elite do govern more or less as they see fit. But the threat of opposition is never absent. Especially potent is that opposition that can express itself through the ballot box. And consumer revolts, wildcat strikes, draft resistance, mass rallies, and similar instances of demonstration democracy can supplement and extend the voting process.

Of course the elite in the United States have used repressive tactics of questionable legality when they wish to suppress political opposition acting outside acceptable channels. And the elite are not reluctant to manipulate political symbols, keep secret what should be public information, and attempt to control or intimidate the mass media if they are threatened by an opposition movement; thus the practice during the 1960s of branding antiwar spokesmen as unpatriotic and the practice of suppressing negative reports from Vietnam while exaggerating the optimistic ones. Such tactics, however, are not the same as disbanding Congress, refusing to hold elections, banning newspapers, forcefully retaining office despite an electoral defeat, or calling out the troops to intimidate voters. These are common practices in nations where the elite is in fact a "power elite."

What remains is the idea that for the most part elites do rule. What is denied is that they rule despite widespread popular opposition to their decisions. If enough citizens are angry or dismayed by current policies, sooner or later this opposition will be mobilized by a counter-elite, and the ruling group will either change its tune or forego its positions. That this seldom happens only proves that the elite manage to mix propaganda, persuasion, manipulation, and acceptable policies in a manner that forestalls opposition. The American public is mostly ruled by default. And though the political indifference and quiescence of the public are in the interests of the elite, they cannot be brought about just because an elite wills them to be so.

The facts revealed in the investigation of Watergate indicate that members of the political elite are not completely restrained when it comes to such practices. Many who studied the political realities that nurtured the Watergate episode feel that the United States had drifted dangerously close to a subversion of the democratic process. This subversion would, in effect, transform a pluralistic democracy into an elite tyranny. On the first anniversary of the break-in of the Democratic National headquarters by staff of the Republican Committee to Reelect the President, the lead editorial of *The New York Times* asked, rhetorically, "What would constitute tyranny in the United States?"

It would involve reducing Congress to a peripheral role in making Government policy, discrediting the political opposition, suppressing the more aggressive forms of dissent, intimidating television, radio, and the press, staffing the courts with one's own supporters, and centralizing all of the executive power in the hands of the President and his anonymous, totally dependent aides.[6]

This newspaper reasoned that we had come close to such a situation. Indeed, members of the political elite, including even the ex-Attorney General of the United States, were testifying before a Senate committee that the "ends justify the means." This political philosophy does of course undermine the rule of law that presumably checks the power of the so-called power elite.

But if Watergate is evidence for those who insist that a power elite runs America, it is evidence for critics of this interpretation as well. We have repeatedly reviewed (especially in Chapter 9) the basic idea of separation of powers. This idea, which might also be called "institutional pluralism," is the constitutional doctrine that governs who gets how much power, and how they exercise it. Institutional pluralism continually places one set of leaders against another; or, more accurately, it leads to tension between the competing ambitions of different leaders. Watergate was viewed as a challenge to this institutional pluralism. The attempt by the political party in power to frustrate, illegally, the political ambitions of the opposition party, coupled with the attempts of the executive branch to frustrate the political role of the legislative branch, led to a large-scale counter-attack against those charged with responsibility for the Watergate affair.

This counter-attack was made possible by two political conditions. First, the counter-elite, which included leaders of the Democratic party, aggressive newspaper and television commentators, a Senate committee, and members of the judiciary, had power bases independent of the incumbent Republican President and his staff. Thus the counter-elite could not, finally, be silenced. Secondly, the mass public clearly favored a vigorous investigation of the Watergate affair. The public served as an aroused opposition against the excesses of a particular elite.

Political observers who doubt the accuracy of the power elite thesis for the United States will cite Watergate as evidence. They will point out that "institutional pluralism," "counter-elites" and "public opinion" do count in American politics.

Summary

These contrasting perspectives—pluralism vs. elitism—take from the political scene somewhat different facts, and give to these facts very different emphases. It is not likely that one perspective is entirely correct. More

---

[6] *The New York Times,* June 17, 1973.

likely, each perspective is partly accurate and partly inaccurate, as is nearly always the case when a single explanation is proposed for something so varied and complex as American politics. If you review materials presented throughout this textbook you will find evidence giving support to each perspective.

But to say that the truth is somewhere between the two perspectives is not to say that both are equally correct or equally incorrect. One perspective might on balance provide a better explanation for the facts of American politics. If despite its flaws you think the account advanced by pluralists is more persuasive, you probably will conclude that America at least approaches democracy: Power is widely shared across the society, and the institutions that allow for meaningful citizen influence over public policy are effectively operating. If, however, the power elite thesis seems to ring true, then you doubt that America is today really a democracy: Power is concentrated, and the powerful few are not really accountable for the kinds of policies they force on the society.

This, then, is the controversial question with which we end the book. And we invite you to draw on the material presented in previous chapters as well as on your independently developed insights and knowledge of political facts as you think through your own position.

Postscript:
Watergate and American Politics

This book goes to press exactly one year after Richard Nixon and Spiro Agnew won a sweeping electoral victory. In November of 1972 more than three out of every five American voters cast their ballot for these two Republican party leaders. The electoral mandate was interpreted as massive public support for the policies of the first Nixon administration and as an urging to continue these policies for another four years. It appeared that Agnew would be able to move from the Vice-Presidency to the Presidency in 1976.

Much changed in one year. Public opinion polls taken in November of 1973 showed that fewer than one-fourth of the population supported the President. A majority of Americans thought Nixon should resign from office. Agnew had already resigned. He had been charged by the Justice Department with involvement in a corrupt, illegal system of bribes and kickbacks. Rather than face trial, Agnew admitted guilt on one charge, payed a fine, and left office in disgrace.

The storm that raged around Nixon was much more intense. Public leaders around the country were openly questioning whether Nixon could govern the nation for the three remaining years of his term. The Judiciary Committee of the House of Representatives had begun inquiry into whether Nixon should be impeached. Editorials in several leading newspapers called for his resignation.

We add this Postscript in the middle of this political and constitutional crisis, and we cannot know for certain how it will end. Perhaps by the time you read these pages, Nixon will have resigned or will have been impeached; perhaps the controversy will be as intense, if unsettled, as it is today; perhaps it will have all blown over, and appear only to have been a difficult year for the President in an otherwise successful second term. In this Postscript we are not really interested in the specific fate of Richard Nixon; we are interested in what the Watergate crisis, as it has come to be known, can tell us about American politics.

During a crisis the basic governmental institutions of a nation are tested, and their workings are revealed more clearly than in normal times. We can take a look at the current crisis conditions as a way of further understanding many of the broad themes developed in the chapters of this text.

Watergate: What Is It?

Politics has a funny way with words. One of the most severe constitutional crises of our 200-year history as a nation is named after an apartment hotel and office complex in Washington, D.C. The summer of 1972 was an election summer, and it was in a suite of offices in the Watergate that the National Committee of the Democratic party had its headquarters. There, at 2:30 A.M. on June 17, 1972, five men, carrying electronic bugging equipment, were arrested. The initial public reaction to the bungled break-in was cynicism, disbelief, and even humor. The disbelief and the humor faded; the cynicism grew as one disclosure followed another. The Watergate incident has come to be recognized for what it was: one part of a large, complex political spying and sabotage operation, implicating the highest-level White House officials and financed with hundreds of thousands of dollars in secret campaign funds.

The investigations are far from over, but already two Cabinet members, a former Attorney General and a former Secretary of Commerce, have been indicted in connection with illegal campaign contributions and political favors; John D. Ehrlichman, formerly the President's chief domestic affairs adviser, along with two other White House aides have been indicted; a former legal counsel to the President has pleaded guilty to the obstruction of justice, as have a deputy campaign manager and another highly placed White House staff member; still others have publicly admitted that they lied under oath (committed perjury), destroyed evidence, and otherwise obstructed justice.

Some of the crimes, and the criminals, were uncovered as a result of the efforts of a special Watergate prosecutor, appointed by President Nixon after strong pressure from Congress and the press. The first prosecutor was, however, fired by the President over the issue of releasing White House tapes of conversations which some thought would implicate the President himself. Other activities were uncovered by a special Senate Committee, chaired by the Democratic Senator Sam Ervin, which conducted nationally televised hearings into the possible misconduct of Republican campaign activists and the cover-up by senior White House aides.

The Main Issues

Watergate and the events related to it have generated more congressional concern than any other issue in the last decades. Given that the 1960s was a decade of intense feelings over the Vietnam war, this is saying a lot. Why should Congress become so aroused over Watergate? Why is there active consideration of impeachment? Why has Congress pursued Watergate so tenaciously when at other times, as we have shown, Congress has tended not to question executive power? Watergate raised the issues of separation of powers and the constitutional authority of different branches of government in a way no other has since the Civil War, when the issue was federal versus state authority. To place the Congress versus Presidency conflict in perspective, we first take note of what Watergate meant for electoral politics.

Electoral Competition and American Democracy

The individuals who resorted to Watergate had, for the previous few years, viewed with increasing alarm and frustration the mass opposition to Presidential policies in Indo-China, as revealed by disorder on the campuses, acts of violence in the streets, and finally a pattern of leaks from within the executive branch in regard to foreign policy documents and the negotiations to end the Vietnam war. Well before the 1972 election campaign, these persons established a White House Special Intelligence Unit (later dubbed "The Plumbers"). This unit was under the direct control of the White House. It applied the methods and tactics of foreign spying to domestic political problems. This was justified in the name of national security.

It was a short step from these activities to the illegal actions associated with the election campaign of 1972. Men who see themselves beseiged can ill afford politics as usual. For high officials in the Nixon reelection effort, the national interest and the immediate political interest became one and the same thing. As John Mitchell, former Attorney General and campaign manager for Nixon, said when confronted by the illegalities of Watergate, "I still believe that the most important thing to this country was the reelection of Richard Nixon."

It was this attitude that aroused intense congressional anger. For the integrity of the American electoral process is viewed as absolutely central to democracy. The Senate investigations into Watergate revealed an attempt to subvert the electoral process that went well beyond the campaign corruption that has existed in previous elections. There were three characteristics of the illegal activities that caused particular concern:

1. Massive illegal contributions to the Republican campaign were discovered to have been made by American corporations and business interests under circumstances suggesting that they were in return for political favors. Campaign contributions in the hope of receiving favorable treatment are not new. But the scope and magnitude of the problem in 1972 exceeded previous experience.

2. There were hints that the vast police and intelligence powers controlled by the executive were used in the political campaign. Several of the Watergate burglars had worked at the CIA. And there was clear evidence that high administration officials had tried to involve the CIA and the FBI in the cover-up that followed the break-in. The concern this generated is easy to understand. As we have demonstrated in this book, the world role

of the United States has been accompanied by a growth in the executive power of the Presidency. Part of that growth in power comes from the President's control over intelligence networks. If that intelligence apparatus became involved in domestic party politics, it would be a dangerous force indeed. For that reason Congress had forbidden the CIA any domestic role. The fact that pressure for such involvement came from high administration persons revealed the potential for abuse in the vast executive apparatus.

3. Perhaps most important of all was the revelation that some of those involved — including the former Attorney General of the United States — believed that the election of the opposition candidate in 1972 (the Democrat, George McGovern) would be so bad for the country that any means were justified in seeing that he did not win. Such a belief is particularly devastating to a system of peaceful electoral competition in a democracy. Democracy rests, as we have shown, on the belief among the participants that it will work. And one fundamental component of these beliefs that support democracy is that those in power have sufficient trust in the political opposition that they are willing to yield that power when they lose an election. The principle is as obvious in the United States as it is rare around the world. In many nations, those in power would resist by any means a group that tried to replace them. That leading political figures in the United States believed the opposition was so dangerous that they could go beyond the law to prevent its victory indicated a movement far away from the basic trust that ordinarily undergirds American democracy.

Congressmen, as well as public leaders from the news media, universities, labor unions, business, and civic organizations, became deeply disturbed by the erosion of political trust so necessary to the workings of democracy. The sense of distress spread into the public. It was further aggravated by a major constitutional dispute over separation of powers.

The Controversy over Separation of Powers

The Constitution established an uneasy balance of powers across the key branches of government: legislative, judicial, executive. This uneasy balance has shifted often in response to social changes and political pressures and is likely to shift once again as a result of the Watergate crisis. The original separation of powers outlined in the Constitution was by no means a neat compartmentalization. Rather there was an intertwining of the powers of the three branches, each sharing in the overall power to govern. There have in our history been periods of congressional domination, periods during which the Supreme Court decisively shaped public policy, and periods of Presidential domination.

The years preceeding Watergate were clearly years of Presidential domination. We have already listed the reasons for this: the complex foreign and domestic problems facing the society, the clear need for nationally formulated policies, the weakness of Congress as a source of national policy making, the advantages of executive action in responding to international crises, the technical skills and information available to the President through the vast network of executive departments. Watergate, however, called into question whether Presidential domination had not come dangerously close to Presidential tyranny. This question was raised openly in the chambers of the Congress, and the following factors were cited.

Abuse of Executive Departments: There was, as we mentioned, concern about the possible involvement of the FBI and CIA in the 1972 election campaign, specifically the White House attempt to involve these agencies in the Watergate cover-up. Other revelations of the Watergate investigation suggested that the office of the President was using other executive agencies for specific partisan advantages. There was evidence that milk producers promised the Nixon administration $2 million in campaign support, while simultaneously seeking favorable rulings with regard to milk prices and import quotas on foreign milk products. These favorable rulings were forthcoming. Another large campaign contribution was connected with a favorable settlement of antitrust legislation against the giant corporation International Telegraph and Telephone. Some evidence appeared that the Internal Revenue Service was urged to use its powers to investigate tax returns in a manner that might embarrass enemies of the Nixon administration. And it was revealed that the President, during part of his first term, had paid almost no income tax because he claimed a huge and somewhat dubious tax deduction.

Executive Privilege: Concern about possible abuses in the executive branch was compounded by the difficulty of obtaining full information on these matters. One of the crucial issues was that of executive privilege — the right of the President to keep confidential the communications between his staff and himself. Few denied that there was such a right. Confidentiality was necessary for national security reasons and to allow the smooth functioning of the executive office. It could not, however, be used to conceal criminal activity.

But, as we have seen in most constitutional controversies, one can specify a general rule — executive privilege can only be challenged if it involves concealment of a crime — fairly easily. The application of the rule becomes more complex. *Who* decides whether the materials for which executive privilege is claimed contain information relevant to possible criminal activity? If the executive branch decides, then it is in the position of policing itself and there is no real external check on the abuse of executive privilege. But for the courts or Congress to decide, they will need access to material that might affect national security or the confidentiality of Presidential memoranda and conversations not related to any wrongdoing.

And, as with most such issues, the particular solution results from the constellation of political and legal forces operating at the time. The President's attempt to close off access to tapes of White House conversations and other memoranda led to such strong public and congressional protest that he reversed himself and released some of the material—though he never willingly gave full access to investigative bodies outside the executive.

Impoundment of Funds: Though this issue was not directly connected to the set of abuses associated with Watergate, it arose at the same time and revealed the same political battle over the relative powers of the Congress and the President. In a major attempt to expand Presidential powers, President Nixon impounded the funds voted by Congress for particular programs, thereby effectively refusing to execute laws passed by Congress. In this conflict between the Congress and the President over the power of the purse, the courts played a major role. In a number of cases, they declared one aspect or another of the impoundment policy illegal. And Congress in turn began to consider legislation that would explicitly remove the power to impound funds from the President.

The impoundment controversy illustrates how the three branches of the government intertwine in the law-making process. And the negative reaction to President Nixon's assertion of power in this respect may illustrate another facet of the growing opposition to executive power.

Changing the Constitution Within the Framework of the Constitution

Whatever the specific long-run effects of the Watergate controversies, it is most likely that one result will be a readjustment of the relative power of the executive, the legislative, and the judicial branches, with the latter two gaining power at the expense of the former. These changes illustrate the fact that basic constitutional questions as to the proper division of power among the branches of the government remain unanswered almost two centuries after the creation of the Constitution. The change in the balance illustrates the fact that the Constitution remains a flexible framework within which fundamental changes can be made.

But this flexibility ought not to obscure the extent to which the Constitution still provides the overall structure within which the conflict among the branches is worked out. Consider, for instance, the extent to which the power of the various actors in the Watergate controversy rests firmly on the Constitution.

1. *The President.* The great rise in Presidential power depended heavily on the grant to the President of the executive powers in the Constitution. In a complex society, the carrying out of that executive function meant a great increase in the size and scope of the executive branch. In particular, as we have shown, the powers of the President in military and foreign affairs

(also grounded in the Constitution) led to a major expansion of executive dominance over the other branches.

2. *Congress.* Though the relative power of Congress had been declining in the 1950s and 1960s, it still maintained its basic constitutional independence. The President could not dissolve or suspend the Congress or block their power to investigate him. And such congressional powers as that of the Senate to confirm appointments were used to place controls on the Presidency. Lastly, of course, the ultimate check by Congress on the power of the Presidency—the power to impeach the President—became of great importance during the controversy. This fundamental power had almost never been used in previous American history. Indeed, it took quite awhile before members of Congress would talk seriously about the possibility of impeachment. At first, consideration of such a move was considered too drastic. But the underlying importance of the constitutional structure is illustrated by the fact that this power, almost never used, could become so crucial in the early 1970s.

3. *The Courts.* At all stages of the controversy, the role of the independent court system was apparent. A major force behind the original revelations of Watergate wrongdoing was Judge John Sirica of the Federal District Court. And the controversy was punctuated by constant appeals to the courts from one side or the other. The controversy illustrates the crucial role played by the Federal Court system whenever there is conflict among the various coequal parts of the American government.

4. *The Press.* The actors in the Watergate affair were not limited to the branches of the government. The press and the public were also involved. Investigative reporting by the *Washington Post* and other papers first revealed many of the Watergate-related activities. And the point is obvious, but worth stressing, that the constitutional guarantees of a free press were the basis of what the press could accomplish.

5. *The Public.* The Watergate drama was enacted before the American people. Public response to the accusations, the defenses, the legal maneuverings, and the political developments was critical. For one thing, it is the public as electorate that would decide which political party and which public figures would ultimately benefit, or be punished, because of Watergate revelations. Public reaction could affect even very specific actions. Thus the flood of negative response when Nixon fired the first special prosecutor, Archibald Cox, led the President to reverse his position on the release of Presidential tapes.

In short, the Watergate controversy engaged all major actors in the political process. Each actor had its own basis of political influence that rested on a firm constitutional foundation: the independent power of the Congress to investigate, the responsibility of the courts to indict and convict, the authority of the executive to defend national security, the guaranteed freedom of the press resulting in public exposure of misdeeds in high office, and the ultimate power of the citizens to choose a new government in the next election.

Watergate and the Future of American Politics

The implications of Watergate extend well beyond the fate of Richard Nixon. Indeed, the implications extend beyond the many public careers that will be broken and the several others that will be made by the revelations now associated with the Watergate crisis.

One major repercussion has to do with the balance of powers in the federal government. It is likely that Congress will become a more vigorous partner in the governing process than had been the case during the 1950s and 1960s. At least some of this growth in congressional assertion will be at the expense of the Presidency. Still, however, the Presidency will remain a dominant force in American politics. The circumstances that led to the rise of Presidential power began decades before Watergate and progressed across the successive administrations of Roosevelt, Truman, Eisenhower, and Kennedy. Perhaps Nixon tried to push executive power to a new extreme, but the conditions that made this possible will not disappear with the disappearance of Nixon.

If anything, Watergate only makes clear one of the long-run problems facing American society: how to have an executive capable of coping with the nation's problems and yet accountable to the Congress, the courts, and eventually the public. Here is the dilemma as posed by one student of our political times:

> In a time of the acceleration of history and the decay of traditional
> institutions and values, a strong presidency is both a greater necessity
> than ever before and a greater risk—necessary to hold a spinning and
> distracted society together, necessary to make the separation of powers
> work, yet risky because of the awful temptation held out to override the
> separation of powers and burst the bonds of the Constitution. The na-
> tion requires both a strong presidency for leadership and the separation
> of powers for liberty.[1]

The second major repercussion of Watergate is being felt through the land. Support for a democratic political system depends, we have argued, on the trust and confidence citizens feel in their institutions. A trend spanning more than a decade was accelerated by the Watergate incidents. This trend shows a withdrawal of confidence in the major institutions of American society. Increasingly large numbers of citizens are doubting the leadership of major companies, of organized religion, of universities, of the press and TV, of organized labor, and of the military. These doubts derive partly from the seeming inability of society to deal with the problems of economic inflation, urban decay, environmental pollution, racial tension, and related domestic matters. Partly the doubts have roots in the long, inconclusive,

[1] Arthur M. Schlesinger, Jr., "The Runaway Presidency," *The Atlantic Monthly*, November 1973, 55.

and messy Vietnam war. Watergate did not "cause" the lack of public confidence in the institutions of society, but it did further this mood. And it dramatically turned attention to the weaknesses and, at times, corruptness of the institutions of government.

It is not easy to understand the public mood, let alone to forecast its turns and twists. Some commentators hope that Watergate will actually restore public confidence. They reason that the public discussions and the vigorous investigations going on in Congress and the courts demonstrate democracy at work. Wrongdoing was found out; wrongdoers were punished. This is as it should be in an open, healthy, democratic society.

But not all commentators are as optimistic. Certainly as we conclude this book it is not yet clear that all wrongdoers have been justly punished. Even if this were the case, it is not easy to have a "new beginning" however often our leadership may pronounce one. Those pessimistic about the nation point out that public cynicism is now so widespread that it will take years of exceptionally "clean politics" before the public will once again fully trust its leadership. In the meantime, social problems pile up and creative programs go untried. Trustful cooperative effort between citizen and government remains in short supply. It is not easy to solve a nation's problems without social trust; it is particularly difficult when that nation is attempting to make democracy work.

Thus it is that the consequences of Watergate will be felt long after the personalities and specific events will have been forgotten. It would be a valuable exercise for you, the reader, to think through for yourself what Watergate has meant for American democracy. The exercise will tell you something about yourself as a citizen; and it will tell you something about the vitality, or lack of vitality, of American democracy.

The Constitution of the United States

[Preamble]
We the people of the United States, in Order to form a more perfect Union, establish Justice, insure domestic Tranquility, provide for the common defence, promote the general Welfare, and secure the Blessings of Liberty to ourselves and our Posterity, do ordain and establish this Constitution for the United States of America.

ARTICLE 1

Section 1

[Legislative Powers]
All legislative Powers herein granted shall be vested in a Congress of the United States, which shall consist of a Senate and a House of Representatives.

Section 2

[House of Representatives, How Constituted, Power of Impeachment]
The House of Representatives shall be composed of Members chosen every second Year by the People of the several States, and the Electors in each State shall have [the] Qualifications requisite for Electors of the most numerous Branch of the State Legislature.

No Person shall be a Representative who shall not have attained to the Age of twenty five Years, and been seven Years a Citizen of the United States, and who shall not when elected, be an Inhabitant of that State in which he shall be chosen.

Representatives and direct Taxes shall be apportioned among the several States which may be included within this Union, according to their respective Numbers, which shall be determined by adding to the whole Number of free Persons, including those bound to Service for a Term of Years, and excluding Indians not taxed, three fifths of all other Persons. The actual Enumeration shall be made within three years after the first Meeting of the Congress of the United States, and within every subsequent Term of ten Years, in such Manner as they shall by Law direct. The Number of Representatives shall not exceed one for every thirty Thousand, but each State shall have at Least one Representative; and until such enumeration shall be made, the State of New Hampshire shall be entitled to chuse three, Massachusetts eight, Rhode-Island and Providence Plantations one, Connecticut five, New York six, New Jersey four, Pennsylvania eight, Delaware one, Maryland six, Virginia ten, North Carolina five, South Carolina five, and Georgia three.

When vacancies happen in the Representation from any State, the Executive Authority thereof shall issue Writs of Election to fill such Vacancies.

The House of Representatives shall chuse their Speaker and other Officers; and shall have the sole Power of Impeachment.

Section 3

[*The Senate, How Constituted, Impeachment Trials*]
The Senate of the United States shall be composed of Two Senators from each State, chosen by the Legislature thereof, for six Years; and each Senator shall have one Vote.

Immediately after they shall be assembled in Consequence of the first Election, they shall be divided as equally as may be into three Classes. The Seats of the Senators of the first Class shall be vacated at the Expiration of the second Year, of the second Class at the Expiration of the fourth Year, and of the third Class at the Expiration of the sixth Year, so that one third may be chosen every second Year; and if Vacancies happen by Resignation, or otherwise, during the Recess of the Legislature of any State, the Executive thereof may make temporary Appointments until the next Meeting of the Legislature, which shall then fill such Vacancies.

No Person shall be a Senator who shall not have attained to the Age of thirty Years, and been nine Years a Citizen of the United States, and who shall not, when elected, be an Inhabitant of that State for which he shall be chosen.

The Vice-President of the United States shall be President of the Senate, but shall have no Vote, unless they be equally divided.

The Senate shall chuse their other Officers, and also a President pro tempore, in the Absence of the Vice-President, or when he shall exercise the Office of President of the United States.

The Senate shall have the sole power to try all Impeachments. When sitting for that Purpose, they shall be on Oath or Affirmation. When the President of the United States [is tried] the Chief Justice shall preside: And no Person shall be convicted without the Concurrence of two thirds of the Members present.

Judgment in Cases of Impeachment shall not extend further than to removal from Office, and disqualification to hold and enjoy any Office of honor, Trust or Profit under the United States: but the Party convicted shall nevertheless be liable and subject to Indictment, Trial, Judgment and Punishment, according to Law.

Section 4

[*Election of Senators and Representatives*]
The Times, Places and Manner of holding Elections for Senators and Representatives, shall be prescribed in each State by the Legislature thereof; but the Congress may at any time by Law make or alter such Regulations, except as to the Places of chusing Senators.

The Congress shall assemble at least once in every Year, and such Meeting shall be on the first Monday in December, unless they shall by Law appoint a different Day.

Section 5

[*Quorum, Journals, Meetings, Adjournments*]
Each House shall be the Judge of the Elections, Returns and Qualifications of its own Members, and a Majority of each shall constitute a Quorum to do Business; but a smaller Number may adjourn from day to day, and may be authorized to compel the Attendance of absent Members, in such Manner, and under such Penalties as each House may provide.

Each House may determine the Rules of its Proceedings, punish its Members for disorderly Behaviour, and, with the Concurrence of two thirds, expel a Member.

Each House shall keep a Journal of its Proceedings, and from time to time publish the same, excepting such Parts as may in their Judgment require Secrecy; and the Yeas and Nays of the Members of either House on any question shall, at the Desire of one fifth of those Present, be entered on the Journal.

Neither House, during the Session of Congress, shall, without the Consent of the other, adjourn for more than three days, nor to any other Place than that in which the two Houses shall be sitting.

Section 6

[Compensation, Privileges, Disabilities]
The Senators and Representatives shall receive a Compensation for their Services, to be ascertained by Law, and paid out of the Treasury of the United States. They shall in all Cases, except Treason, Felony and Breach of the Peace, be privileged from Arrest during their Attendance at the Session of their respective Houses, and in going to and returning from the same; and for any Speech or Debate in either House, they shall not be questioned in any other Place.

No Senator or Representative shall, during the Time for which he was elected, be appointed to any civil Office under the Authority of the United States, which shall have been created, or the Emoluments whereof shall have been encreased during such time; and no Person holding any Office under the United States, shall be a Member of either House during his Continuance in Office.

Section 7

[Procedure in Passing Bills and Resolutions]
All Bills for raising Revenue shall originate in the House of Representatives; but the Senate may propose or concur with Amendments as on other Bills.

Every Bill which shall have passed the House of Representatives and the Senate, shall, before it becomes a Law, be presented to the President of the United States; if he approve he shall sign it, but if not he shall return it, with his Objections to that House in which it shall have originated, who shall enter the Objections at large on their Journal, and proceed to reconsider it. If after such Reconsideration two thirds of that House shall agree to pass the Bill, it shall be sent, together with the Objections, to the other House, by which it shall likewise be reconsidered, and if approved by two thirds of that House, it shall become a Law. But in all such Cases the Votes of both Houses shall be determined by yeas and Nays, and the Names of the Persons voting for and against the Bill shall be entered on the Journal of each House respectively. If any Bill shall not be returned by the President within ten Days (Sundays excepted) after it shall have been presented to him, the Same shall be a Law, in like Manner as if he had signed it, unless the Congress by their Adjournment prevent its Return, in which Case it shall not be a Law.

Every Order, Resolution, or Vote to which the Concurrence of the Senate and House of Representatives may be necessary (except on a question of Adjournment) shall be presented to the President of the United States; and before the Same shall take Effect, shall be approved by him, or being disapproved by him, shall be repassed by two thirds of the Senate and House of Representatives, according to the Rules and Limitations prescribed in the Case of a Bill.

Section 8

[Powers of Congress]
The Congress shall have the Power To lay and collect Taxes, Duties, Imposts and Excises, to pay the Debts and provide for the common Defence and general Welfare of the United States; but all Duties, Imposts and Excises shall be uniform throughout the United States.

To borrow Money on the credit of the United States;

To regulate Commerce with foreign Nations and among the several States, and with the Indian Tribes;

To establish an uniform Rule of Naturalization, and uniform Laws on the subject of Bankruptcies throughout the United States;

To Coin Money, regulate the Value thereof, and of foreign Coin, and fix the Standard of Weights and Measures;

To provide for the Punishment of counterfeiting the Securities and current Coin of the United States;

To establish Post Offices and post Roads;

To promote the Progress of Science and useful Arts, by securing for limited Times to Authors and Inventors the exclusive Right to their respective Writings and Discoveries;

To constitute Tribunals inferior to the supreme Court;

To define and punish Piracies and Felonies committed on the high Seas, and Offences against the Law of Nations;

To declare War, grant Letters of Marque and Reprisal, and make Rules concerning Captures on Land and Water;

To raise and support Armies, but no Appropriation of Money to that Use shall be for a longer Term than two Years;

To provide and maintain a Navy;

To make Rules for Government and Regulation of the land and naval Forces;

To provide for calling forth the Militia to execute the Laws of the Union, suppress Insurrections and repel Invasions;

To provide for organizing, arming, and disciplining, the Militia, and for governing such Part of them as may be employed in the Service of the United States, reserving to the States respectively, the Appointment of the Officers, and the Authority of training the Militia according to the discipline prescribed by Congress;

To exercise exclusive Legislation in all Cases whatsoever, over such District (not exceeding ten Miles square) as may, by Cession of particular States, and the Acceptance of Congress, become the Seat of the Government of the United States, and to exercise like Authority over all Places purchased by the Consent of the Legislature of the State in which the Same shall be, for the Erection of Forts, Magazines, Arsenals, dock-Yards, and other needful Buildings; — And

To make all Laws which shall be necessary and proper for carrying into Execution the foregoing Powers, and all other Powers vested by this Constitution in the Government of the United States, or in any Department or Officer thereof.

Section 9

[Limitation upon Powers of Congress]
The Migration or Importation of such Persons as any of the States now existing shall think proper to admit, shall not be prohibited by the Congress prior to the Year one

thousand eight hundred and eight, but a Tax or duty may be imposed on such Importation, not exceeding ten dollars for each Person.

The Privilege of the Writ of Habeas Corpus shall not be suspended, unless when in Cases of Rebellion or Invasion the public Safety may require it.

No Bill of Attainder or ex post facto Law shall be passed.

No Capitation, or other direct, Tax shall be laid, unless in Proportion to the Census or Enumeration herein before directed to be taken.

No Tax or Duty shall be laid on Articles, exported from any State.

No Preference shall be given by any Regulation of Commerce or Revenue to the Ports of State over those of another; nor shall Vessels bound to, or from, one State, be obliged to enter, clear, or pay Duties in another.

No Money shall be drawn from the Treasury, but in Consequence of Appropriations made by Law; and a regular Statement and Account of the Receipts and Expenditures of all public Money shall be published from time to time.

No title of Nobility shall be granted by the United States: And no Person holding any Office of Profit or Trust under them, shall, without the Consent of the Congress, accept of any present, Emolument, Office, or Title, of any kind whatever, from any King, Prince, or foreign State.

Section 10

[*Restrictions upon Powers of States*]
No State shall enter into any Treaty, Alliance, or Confederation; grant Letters of Marque and Reprisal; coin Money; emit Bills of Credit; make any Thing but gold and silver Coin a Tender in Payment of Debts; pass any Bill of Attainder, ex post facto Law, or Law impairing the Obligation of Contracts, or grant any Title of Nobility.

No State shall, without the Consent of the Congress, lay any Imposts or Duties on Imports or Exports, except what may be absolutely necessary for executing its inspection Laws: and the net Produce of all Duties and Imposts, laid by any State on Imports or Exports, shall be for the Use of the Treasury of the United States; and all such Laws shall be subject to the Revision and Controul of [the] Congress.

No State shall, without the Consent of Congress, lay any Duty of Tonnage, keep Troops, or Ships of War in time of Peace, enter into any Agreement or Compact with another State, or with a foreign Power, or engage in War, unless actually invaded, or in such imminent Danger as will not admit of delay.

ARTICLE 2

Section 1

[*Executive Power, Election, Qualifications of the President*]
The executive Power shall be vested in a President of the United States of America. He shall hold his Office during the Term of four Years, and, together with the Vice-President, chosen for the same Term, be elected as follows.

Each State shall appoint, in such Manner as the Legislature thereof may direct, a Number of Electors, equal to the whole Number of Senators and Representatives to which the State may be entitled in the Congress: but no Senator or Representative, or Person holding an Office of Trust or Profit under the United States, shall be appointed an Elector.

The Electors shall meet in their respective States, and vote by Ballot for two Persons of whom one at least shall not be an Inhabitant of the same State with themselves. And they shall make a List of all the Persons voted for, and of the Number of Votes for each; which List they shall sign and certify, and transmit sealed to the Seat of the Government of the United States, directed to the President of the Senate. The President of the Senate shall, in the Presence of the Senate and House of Representatives, open all the Certificates, and the Votes shall then be counted. The Person having the greatest Number of Votes shall be the President, if such Number be a Majority of the whole Number of Electors appointed; and if there be more than one who have such Majority, and have an equal Number of Votes, then the House of Representatives shall immediately chuse by Ballot one of them for President; and if no Person have a Majority, then from the five highest in the List the said House shall in like Manner chuse the President. But in chusing the President, the Votes shall be taken by States, the Representation from each State having one Vote; A quorum for this purpose shall consist of a Member or Members from two thirds of the States, and a Majority of all the States shall be necessary to a Choice. In every Case, after the choice of the President, the Person having the greatest Number of Votes of the Electors shall be the Vice-President. But if there should remain two or more who have equal Votes, the Senate shall chuse from them by Ballot the Vice-President.

The Congress may determine the Time of chusing the Electors, and the Day on which they shall give their Votes; which Day shall be the same throughout the United States.

No person except a natural born Citizen, or a Citizen of the United States, at the time of the Adoption of this Constitution, shall be eligible to the Office of President; neither shall any Person be eligible to that Office who shall not have attained to the Age of thirty five Years, and been fourteen Years a Resident within the United States.

In Case of the Removal of the President from Office, or of his Death, Resignation, or Inability to discharge the Powers and Duties of the said Office, the Same shall devolve on the Vice-President, and the Congress may by Law provide for the Case of Removal, Death, Resignation or Inability, both of the President and Vice-President, declaring what Officer shall then act as President, and such Officer shall act accordingly, until the Disability be removed, or a President shall be elected.

The President shall, at stated Times, receive for his Services, a Compensation, which shall neither be increased nor diminished during the Period for which he shall have been elected, and he shall not receive within that Period any other Emolument from the United States, or any of them.

Before he entered on the Execution of his Office, he shall take the following Oath or Affirmation: — "I do solemnly swear (or affirm) that I will faithfully execute the Office of the President of the United States, and will to the best of my Ability, preserve, protect and defend the Constitution of the United States."

Section 2

[*Powers of the President*]
The President shall be Commander in Chief of the Army and Navy of the United States, and the Militia of the several States, when called into the actual Service of the United States; he may require the Opinion, in writing, of the principal Officer in

each of the executive Departments, upon any subject relating to the Duties of their respective Offices, and he shall have Power to grant Reprieves and Pardons for Offences against the United States, except in Cases of Impeachment.

He shall have Power, by and with the Advice and Consent of the Senate, to make Treaties, provided two thirds of the Senators present concur; and he shall nominate, and by and with the Advice and Consent of the Senate, shall appoint Ambassadors, other public Ministers and Consuls, Judges of the supreme Court, and all other Officers of the United States, whose Appointments are not herein otherwise provided for, and which shall be established by Law: but the Congress may by Law vest the Appointment of such inferior Officers, as they think proper in the President alone, in the Courts of Law, or in the Heads of Departments.

The President shall have Power to fill up all Vacancies that may happen during the Recess of the Senate, by granting Commissions which shall expire at the End of their next Session.

Section 3

[Powers and Duties of the President]
He shall from time to time give to the Congress Information of the State of the Union, and recommend to their Consideration such Measures as he shall judge necessary and expedient; he may, on extraordinary Occassions, convene both Houses, or either of them, and in Case of Disagreement between them, with Respect to the Time of Adjournment, he may adjourn them to such Time as he shall think proper; he shall receive Ambassadors and other public Ministers; he shall take Care that the Laws be faithfully executed, and shall commission all the Officers of the United States.

Section 4

[Impeachment]
The President, Vice-President and all civil Officers of the United States, shall be removed from Office on Impeachment for, and Conviction of, Treason, Bribery, or other high Crimes and Misdemeanors.

ARTICLE 3

Section 1

[Judicial Power, Tenure of Office]
The judicial Power of the United States, shall be vested in one supreme Court, and in such inferior Courts as the Congress may from time to time ordain and establish. The judges, both of the supreme and inferior Courts, shall hold their Offices during good Behavior, and shall, at stated Times, receive for their Services, a Compensation, which shall not be diminished during their Continuance in Office.

Section 2

[Jurisdiction]
The judicial Power shall extend to all Cases, in Law and Equity, arising under this Constitution, the Laws of the United States, and Treaties made, or which shall be made, under their Authority;—to all Cases affecting Ambassadors, other public Ministers and Consuls;—to all Cases of admiralty and maritime Jurisdiction;—to Controversies to which the United States shall be a Party;—to Controversies

between two or more States;—between a State and Citizens of another State;—beween Citizens of different States;—between Citizens of the same State claiming Lands under Grants of different States, and between a State, or the Citizens thereof, and foreign States, Citizens or Subjects.

In all Cases affecting Ambassadors, other public Ministers and Consuls, and those in which a State shall be Party, the supreme Court shall have original Jurisdiction. In all the other Cases before mentioned, the supreme Court shall have appellate Jurisdiction, both as to Law and Fact, with such Exceptions, and under such Regulations as the Congress shall make.

The Trial of all Crimes, except in Cases of Impeachment, shall be by Jury; and such Trial shall be held in the State where the said Crimes shall have been committed; but when not committed within any State, the Trial shall be at such Place or Places as the Congress may by Law have directed.

Section 3

[*Treason, Proof and Punishment*]
Treason against the United States, shall consist only in levying War against them, or in adhering to their Enemies; giving them Aid and Comfort. No Person shall be convicted of Treason unless on the Testimony of two Witnesses to the same overt Act, or on Confession in open Court.

The Congress shall have Power to declare the Punishment of Treason, but no Attainder of Treason shall work Corruption of Blood, or Forfeiture except during the Life of the Person attainted.

ARTICLE 4

Section 1

[*Faith and Credit Among States*]
Full Faith and Credit shall be given in each State to the public Acts, Records, and judicial Proceedings of every other State. And the Congress may by general Laws prescribe the Manner in which such Acts, Records and Proceedings shall be proved, and the Effect thereof.

Section 2

[*Privileges and Immunities, Fugitives*]
The citizens of each State shall be entitled to all Privileges and Immunities of Citizens in the several States.

A Person charged in any State with Treason, Felony, or other Crime, who shall flee from Justice, and be found in another State, shall on Demand of the executive Authority of the State from which he fled, be delivered up, to be removed to the State having Jurisidiction of the Crime.

No person held to Service or Labour in one State, under the Laws thereof, escaping into another, shall, in Consequence of any Law or Regulation therein, be discharged from such Service or Labour, but shall be delivered up on Claim of the Party to whom such Service or Labour may be due.

Section 3

[*Admission of New States*]
New States may be admitted by the Congress into this Union; but no new State shall

be formed or erected within the Jurisdiction of any other State; nor any State be formed by the Junction of two or more States, or Parts of States, without the Consent of the Legislatures of the States concerned as well as of the Congress.

The Congress shall have Power to dispose of and make all needful Rules and Regulations respecting the Territory or other Property belonging to the United States; and nothing in this Constitution shall be so construed as to Prejudice any Claims of the United States, or of any particular State.

Section 4

[*Guarantee of Republican Government*]
The United States shall guarantee to every State in this Union a Republican Form of Government, and shall protect each of them against Invasion; and on Application of the Legislature, or of the Executive (when the Legislature cannot be convened) against domestic Violence.

ARTICLE 5

[*Amendment of the Constitution*]
The Congress, whenever two thirds of both Houses shall deem it necessary, shall propose Amendments to this Constitution, or, on the Application of the Legislatures of two thirds of the several States, shall call a Convention for proposing Amendments, which, in either Case, shall be valid to all Intents and Purposes, as Part of this Constitution, when ratified by the Legislatures of three fourths of the several States, or by Conventions in three fourths thereof, as the one or the other Mode of Ratification may be proposed by the Congress; Provided that no Amendment which may be made prior to the Year One thousand eight hundred and eight shall in any Manner affect the first and fourth Clauses in the Ninth Section of the first Article, and that no State, without its Consent, shall be deprived of its equal Suffrage in the Senate.

ARTICLE 6

[*Debts, Supremacy, Oath*]
All Debts contracted and Engagements entered into, before the Adoption of this Constitution, shall be as valid against the United States under this Constitution, as under the Confederation.

This Constitution, and the Laws of the United States which shall be made in Pursuance thereof; and all Treaties made, or which shall be made, under the Authority of the United States, shall be the supreme Law of the Land; and the Judges in every State be bound thereby, any Thing in the Constitution or Laws of any State to the Contrary notwithstanding.

The Senators and Representatives before mentioned, and the Members of the several State Legislatures, and all executive and judicial Officers, both of the United States and of the several States, shall be bound by Oath or Affirmation, to support this Constitution; but no religious Test shall ever be required as a Qualification to any Office or public Trust under the United States.

ARTICLE 7

[*Ratification and Establishment*]
The Ratification of the Conventions of nine States, shall be sufficient for the Establishment of this Constitution between the States so ratifying the Same.

done in Convention by the Unanimous Consent of the States present the Seventeenth Day of September in the Year of our Lord one thousand seven hundred and Eighty seven and of the Independence of the United States of America the Twelfth In witness whereof We have hereunto subscribed our Names.

Go. Washington
Presidt and deputy from Virginia

New Hampshire
John Langdon
Nicholas Gilman

Massachusetts
Nathaniel Gorham
Rufus King

Connecticut
Wm Saml Johnson
Roger Sherman

New York
Alexander Hamilton

New Jersey
Wil: Livingston
David Brearley
Wm Paterson
Jona: Dayton

Pennsylvania
B. Franklin
Thomas Mifflin
Robt. Morris
Geo. Clymer
Thos. FitzSimons
Jared Ingersoll
James Wilson
Gouv Morris

Delaware
Geo. Read
Gunning Bedford jun
John Dickinson
Richard Bassett
Jaco: Broom

Maryland
James McHenry
Dan of St Thos. Jenifer
Danl Carroll

Virginia
John Blair
James Madison Jr.

North Carolina
Wm Blount
Richd Dobbs Spaight.
Hu Williamson

South Carolina
J. Rutledge
Charles Cotesworth Pinckney
Charles Pinckney
Pierce Butler

Georgia	{ William Few Abr Baldwin

Amendments to the Constitution

[The first ten amendments, known as the Bill of Rights, were proposed by Congress on September 25, 1789; ratified and adoption certified on December 15, 1791.]

AMENDMENT I
[*Freedom of Religion, of Speech, of the Press, and Right of Petition*]
Congress shall make no law respecting an establishment of religion, or prohibiting the free exercise thereof; or abridging the freedom of speech, or of the press; or the right of the people peaceably to assemble, and to petition the Government for a redress of grievances.

AMENDMENT II
[*Right to Keep and Bear Arms*]
A well regulated Militia being necessary to the security of a free State, the right of the people to keep and bear Arms, shall not be infringed.

AMENDMENT III
[*Quartering of Soldiers*]
No Soldier shall, in time of peace be quartered in any house, without the consent of the Owner, nor in time of war, but in a manner to be prescribed by law.

AMENDMENT IV
[*Security from Unwarrantable Search and Seizure*]
The right of the people to be secure in their persons, houses, papers, and effects, against unreasonable searches and seizures, shall not be violated, and no Warrants shall issue, but upon probable cause, supported by Oath or affirmation, and particularly describing the place to be searched, and the persons or things to be seized.

AMENDMENT V
[*Rights of Accused in Criminal Proceedings*]
No person shall be held to answer for a capital, or otherwise infamous crime, unless on a presentment or indictment of a Grand Jury, except in cases arising in the land or naval forces, or in the Militia, when in actual service in time of War or public danger; nor shall any person be subjected for the same offense to be twice put in jeopardy of life or limb; nor shall be compelled in any criminal case to be a witness against himself, nor be deprived of life, liberty, or property, without due process of law; nor shall private property be taken for public use, without just compensation.

AMENDMENT VI
[*Right to Speedy Trial, Witnesses, etc.*]
In all criminal prosecutions, the accused shall enjoy the right to a speedy and public trial, by an impartial jury of the State and district wherein the crime shall have been committed, which district shall have been previously ascertained by law,

and to be informed of the nature and cause of the accusation; to be confronted with the witnesses against him; to have compulsory process for obtaining witnesses in his favor, and to have the Assistance of Counsel for his defence.

AMENDMENT VII
[Trial by Jury in Civil Cases]
In Suits at common law, where the value in controversy shall exceed twenty dollars, the right of trial by jury shall be preserved, and no fact tried by a jury, shall be otherwise reexamined in any Court of the United States, then according to the rules of the common law.

AMENDMENT VIII
[Bails, Fines, Punishments]
Excessive bail shall not be required, nor excessive fines imposed, nor cruel and unusual punishments inflicted.

AMENDMENT IX
[Reservation of Rights of the People]
The enumeration in the Constitution, of certain rights, shall not be construed to deny or disparage others retained by the people.

AMENDMENT X
[Powers Reserved to States or People]
The powers not delegated to the United States by the Constitution, nor prohibited by it to the States, are reserved to the States respectively, or to the people.

AMENDMENT XI
[Proposed by Congress on March 4, 1793; declared ratified on January 8, 1798.]
[Restriction of Judicial Power]
The Judicial power of the United States shall not be construed to extend to any suit in law or equity, commenced or prosecuted against one of the United States by Citizens of another State, or by Citizens or Subjects of any Foreign State.

AMENDMENT XII
[Proposed by Congress on December 9, 1803; declared ratified on September 25, 1804.]
[Election of President and Vice-President]
The Electors shall meet in their respective states, and vote by ballot for President and Vice-President, one of whom, at least, shall not be an inhabitant of the same state with themselves; they shall name in their ballots the person voted for as President, and in distinct ballots the person voted for as Vice-President and they shall make distinct lists of all persons voted for as President, and of all persons voted for as Vice-President, and of the number of votes for each, which lists they shall sign and certify, and transmit sealed to the seat of the government of the United States, directed to the President of the Senate; — The President of the Senate shall, in the presence of the Senate and House of Representatives, open all the certificates and the votes shall then be counted; — The person having the greatest number of votes for President, shall be the President, if such number be a majority of the whole number of Electors appointed; and if no person have such majority, then from the

persons having the highest numbers not exceeding three on the list of those voted for as President, the House of Representatives shall choose immediately, by ballot, the President. But in choosing the President, the votes shall be taken by states, the representation from each state having one vote; a quorum for this purpose shall consist of a member or members from two-thirds of the states, and a majority of all the states shall be necessary to a choice. And if the House of Representatives shall not choose a President whenever the right of choice shall devolve upon them, before the fourth day of March next following, then the Vice-President shall act as President, as in the case of the death or other constitutional disability of the President. — The person having the greatest number of votes as Vice-President, shall be the Vice-President, if such number be a majority of the whole number of Electors appointed, and if no person have a majority, then from the two highest numbers on the list, the Senate shall choose the Vice-President; a quorum for the purpose shall consist of two-thirds of the whole number of Senators, and a majority of the whole number shall be necessary to a choice. But no person constitutionally ineligible to the office of President shall be eligible to that of Vice-President of the United States.

AMENDMENT XIII
[Proposed by Congress on January 31, 1865, declared ratified on December 18, 1865.]

Section 1

[*Abolition of Slavery*]
Neither slavery nor involuntary servitude, except as a punishment for a crime whereof the party shall have been duly convicted, shall exist within the United States, or any place subject to their jurisdiction.

Section 2

[*Power to Enforce This Article*]
Congress shall have power to enforce this article by appropriate legislation.

AMENDMENT XIV
[Proposed by Congress on June 16, 1866; declared ratified on July 28, 1868.]

Section 1

[*Citizenship Rights Not to Be Abridged by States*]
All persons born or naturalized in the United States, and subject to the jurisdiction thereof, are citizens of the United States and of the State wherein they reside. No State shall make or enforce any law which shall abridge the privileges or immunities of citizens of the United States; nor shall any State deprive any person of life, liberty, or property, without due process of law; nor deny to any person within its jurisdiction the equal protection of the laws.

Section 2

[*Apportionment of Representatives in Congress*]
Representatives shall be apportioned among the several States according to their respective numbers, counting the whole number of persons in each State, excluding Indians not taxed. But when the right to vote at any election for the choice of electors for President and Vice-President of the United States, Representatives in

Congress, the Executive and Judicial officers of a State, or the members of the Legislature thereof, is denied to any of the male inhabitants of such State, being twenty-one years of age, and citizens of the United States, or in any way abridged, except for participation in rebellion, or other crime, the basis of representation therein shall be reduced in the proportion which the number of such male citizens shall bear to the whole number of male citizens twenty-one years of age in such State.

Section 3

[*Persons Disqualified from Holding Office*]
No person shall be a Senator or Representative in Congress, or elector of President and Vice-President, or hold any office, civil or military, under the United States, or under any State, who, having previously taken an oath, as a member of Congress, or as an officer of the United States, or as a member of any State legislature, or as an executive or judicial officer of any State, to support the Constitution of the United States, shall have engaged in insurrection or rebellion against the same, or given aid or comfort to the enemies thereof. But Congress may by a vote of two-thirds of each House, remove such disability.

Section 4

[*What Public Debts Are Valid*]
The validity of the public debt of the United States, authorized by law, including debts incurred for payment of pensions and bounties for services in suppressing insurrection or rebellion, shall not be questioned. But neither the United States nor any State shall assume or pay any debt or obligation incurred in aid of insurrection or rebellion against the United States, or any claim for the loss or emancipation of any slave; but all such debts, obligations and claims shall be held illegal and void.

Section 5

[*Power to Enforce This Article*]
The Congress shall have power to enforce, by appropriate legislation, the provisions of this article.

AMENDMENT XV
[Proposed by Congress on February 26, 1869; declared ratified on March 30, 1870.]

Section 1

[*Negro Suffrage*]
The right of citizens of the United States to vote shall not be denied or abridged by the United States or by any State on account of race, color, or previous condition of servitude.

Section 2

[*Power to Enforce This Article*]
The Congress shall have power to enforce this article by appropriate legislation.

AMENDMENT XVI
[Proposed by Congress on July 12, 1909; declared ratified on February 25, 1913.]
[*Authorizing Income Taxes*]

The Congress shall have power to lay and collect taxes on incomes, from whatever source derived, without apportionment among the several States, and without regard to any census or enumeration.

AMENDMENT XVII
[Proposed by Congress on May 13, 1912; declared ratified on May 31, 1913.]
[*Popular Election of Senators*]
The Senate of the United States shall be composed of two Senators from each State, elected by the people thereof, for six years; and each Senator shall have one vote. The electors in each State shall have the qualifications requisite for electors of the most numerous branch of the State legislatures.

When vacancies happen in the representation of any State in the Senate, the executive authority of such State shall issue writs of election to fill such vacancies: *Provided*, That the legislature of any State may empower the executive thereof to make temporary appointments until the people fill the vacancies by election as the legislature may direct.

This amendment shall not be so construed as to affect the election or term of any Senator chosen before it becomes valid as part of the Constitution.

AMENDMENT XVIII
[Proposed by Congress on December 18, 1917; declared ratified on January 16, 1919.]

Section 1

[*National Liquor Prohibition*]
After one year from the ratification of this article the manufacture, sale, or transportation of intoxicating liquors within, the importation thereof into, or the exportation thereof from the United States and all territory subject to the jurisdiction thereof for beverage purposes is hereby prohibited.

Section 2

[*Power to Enforce This Article*]
The Congress and the several States shall have concurrent power to enforce this article by appropriate legislation.

Section 3

[*Ratification Within Seven Years*]
This article shall be inoperative unless it shall have been ratified as an amendment to the Constitution by the legislatures of the several States, as provided in the Constitution, within seven years from the date of the submission hereof to the States by the Congress.

AMENDMENT XIX
[Proposed by Congress on June 4, 1919; declared ratified on August 26, 1920.]
[*Woman Suffrage*]
The right of citizens of the United States to vote shall not be denied or abridged by the United States or by any State on account of sex.

Congress shall have power to enforce this article by appropriate legislation.

AMENDMENT XX
[Proposed by Congress on March 2, 1932; declared ratified on February 6, 1933.]

Section 1

[*Terms of Office*]
The terms of the President and Vice-President shall end at noon on the 20th day of January, and the terms of Senators and Representatives at noon on the 3rd day of January, of the years in which such terms would have ended if this article had not been ratified; and the terms of their successors shall then begin.

Section 2

[*Time of Convening Congress*]
The Congress shall assemble at least once in every year, and such meeting shall begin at noon on the 3rd day of January, unless they shall by law appoint a different day.

Section 3

[*Death of President Elect*]
If, at the time fixed for the beginning of the term of the President, the President elect shall have died, the Vice-President elect shall become President. If a President shall not have been chosen before the time fixed for the beginning of his term, or if the President elect shall have failed to qualify, then the Vice-President elect shall act as President until a President shall have qualified; and the Congress may by law provide for the case wherein neither a President elect nor a Vice-President elect shall have qualified, declaring who shall then act as President, or the manner in which one who is to act shall be selected, and such person shall act accordingly until a President or Vice-President shall have qualified.

Section 4

[*Election of the President*]
The Congress may by law provide for the case of the death of any of the persons from whom the House of Representatives may choose a President whenever the right of choice shall have devolved upon them, and for the case of the death of any of the persons from whom the Senate may choose a Vice-President whenever the right of choice shall have devolved upon them.

Section 5

Sections 1 and 2 shall take effect on the 15th day of October following the ratification of this article.

Section 6

This article shall be inoperative unless it shall have been ratified as an amendment to the Constitution by the legislatures of three-fourths of the several States within seven years from the date of its submission.

AMENDMENT XXI
[Proposed by Congress on February 20, 1933; declared ratified on December 5, 1933.]

Section 1

[National Liquor Prohibition Repealed]
The eighteenth article of amendment to the Constitution of the United States is hereby repealed.

Section 2

[Transportation of Liquor into "Dry" States]
The transportation or importation into any States, Territory, or possession of the United States for delivery or use therein of intoxicating liquors, in violation of the laws thereof, is hereby prohibited.

Section 3

This article shall be inoperative unless it shall have been ratified as an amendment to the Constitution by conventions in the several States, as provided in the Constitution, within seven years from the date of the submission hereof to the States by the Congress.

AMENDMENT XXII

[Proposed by Congress on March 21, 1947; declared ratified on February 26, 1951.]

Section 1

[Tenure of President Limited]
No person shall be elected to the office of the President more than twice, and no person who has held the office of President, or acted as President, for more than two years of a term to which some other person was elected President shall be elected to the office of the President more than once. But this Article shall not apply to any person holding the office of President when this Article was proposed by the Congress, and shall not prevent any person who may be holding the office of President, or acting as President, during the term within which this Article becomes operative from holding the office of President, or acting as President during the remainder of such term.

Section 2

This Article shall be inoperative unless it shall have been ratified as an amendment to the Constitution by the legislatures of three-fourths of the several States within seven years from the date of its submission to the States by the Congress.

AMENDMENT XXIII

[Proposed by Congress on June 17, 1960; declared ratified on May 29, 1961.]

Section 1

[District of Columbia Suffrage in Presidential Elections]
The District constituting the seat of Government of the United States shall appoint in such manner as the Congress may direct:

A number of electors of President and Vice-President equal to the whole number of Senators and Representatives in Congress to which the District would be entitled if it were a State, but in no event more than the least populous State; they shall be in addition to those appointed by the States, but they shall be considered, for the purposes of the election of President and Vice-President, to be electors appointed by a State; and they shall meet in the District and perform such duties as provided by the twelfth article of amendment.

Section 2

The Congress shall have power to enforce this article by appropriate legislation.

AMENDMENT XXIV
[Proposed by Congress on August 27, 1962; declared ratified on January 23, 1964.]

Section 1

[*Bars Poll Tax in Federal Elections*]
The right of citizens of the United States to vote in any primary or other election for President or Vice-President, for electors for President or Vice-President, or for Senator or Representative in Congress, shall not be denied or abridged by the United States or any State by reason of failure to pay any poll tax or other tax.

Section 2

The Congress shall have power to enforce this article by appropriate legislation.

AMENDMENT XXV
[Proposed by Congress on July 6, 1965; declared ratified on February 10, 1967.]

Section 1

[*Succession of Vice-President to Presidency*]
In case of the removal of the President from office or of his death or resignation, the Vice-President shall become President.

Section 2

[*Vacancy in Office of Vice-President*]
Whenever there is a vacancy in the office of the Vice-President, the President shall nominate a Vice-President who shall take office upon confirmation by a majority vote of both Houses of Congress.

Section 3

[*Vice-President as Acting President*]
Whenever the President transmits to the President pro tempore of the Senate and the Speaker of the House of Representatives his written declaration that he is unable to discharge the powers and duties of his office, and until he transmits to them a written declaration to the contrary, such powers and duties shall be discharged by the Vice-President as Acting President.

Section 4

[*Vice-President as Acting President*]
Whenever the Vice-President and a majority of either the principal officers of the executive departments or of such other body as Congress may by law provide, transmit to the President pro tempore of the Senate and the Speaker of the House of Representatives their written declaration that the President is unable to discharge the

powers and duties of his office, the Vice-President shall immediately assume the powers and duties of the office as Acting President.

Thereafter, when the President transmits to the President pro tempore of the Senate and the Speaker of the House of Representatives his written declaration that no inability exists, he shall resume the powers and duties of his office unless the Vice-President and a majority of either the principal officers of the executive department or of such other body as Congress may by law provide, transmit within four days to the President pro tempore of the Senate and the Speaker of the House of Representatives their written declaration that the President is unable to discharge the powers and duties of his office. Thereupon Congress shall decide the issue, assembling within forty-eight hours for that purpose if not in session. If the Congress, within twenty-one days after receipt of the latter written declaration, or, if Congress is not in session, within twenty-one days after Congress is required to assemble, determines by two-thirds vote of both Houses that the President is unable to discharge the powers and duties of his office, the Vice-President shall continue to discharge the same as Acting President; otherwise, the President shall resume the powers and duties of his office.

AMENDMENT XXVI
[Proposed by Congress on March 23, 1971; declared ratified on July 5, 1971.]

Section 1

[*Lowers Voting Age to 18 Years*]
The right of citizens of the United States, who are eighteen years of age or older, to vote shall not be denied or abridged by the United States or by any State on account of age.

Section 2

The Congress shall have power to enforce this article by appropriate legislation.

Presidential Elections
1789-1972

YEAR	CANDIDATES	PARTY	POPULAR VOTE	ELECTORAL VOTE
1789	**George Washington**			69
	John Adams			34
	Others			35
1792	**George Washington**			132
	John Adams			77
	George Clinton			50
	Others			5
1796	**John Adams**	Federalist		71
	Thomas Jefferson	Democratic-Republican		68
	Thomas Pinckney	Federalist		59
	Aaron Burr	Democratic-Republican		30
	Others			48
1800	**Thomas Jefferson**	Democratic-Republican		73
	Aaron Burr	Democratic-Republican		73
	John Adams	Federalist		65
	Charles C. Pinckney	Federalist		64
1804	**Thomas Jefferson**	Democratic-Republican		162
	Charles C. Pinckney	Federalist		14
1808	**James Madison**	Democratic-Republican		122
	Charles C. Pinckney	Federalist		47
	George Clinton	Independent-Republican		6
1812	**James Madison**	Democratic-Republican		128
	DeWitt Clinton	Federalist		89

YEAR	CANDIDATES	PARTY	POPULAR VOTE	ELECTORAL VOTE
1816	**James Monroe**	Democratic-Republican		183
	Rufus King	Federalist		34
1820	**James Monroe**	Democratic-Republican		231
	John Quincy Adams	Independent-Republican		1
1824	**John Quincy Adams**	Democratic-Republican	108,740 (30.5%)	84
	Andrew Jackson	Democratic-Republican	153,544 (43.1%)	99
	Henry Clay	Democratic-Republican	47,136 (13.2%)	37
	William H. Crawford	Democratic-Republican	46,618 (13.1%)	41
1828	**Andrew Jackson**	Democratic	647,231 (56.0%)	178
	John Quincy Adams	National-Republican	509,097 (44.0%)	83
1832	**Andrew Jackson**	Democratic	687,502 (55.0%)	219
	Henry Clay	National Republican	530,189 (42.4%)	49
	William Wirt	Anti-Masonic	} 33,108 (2.6%)	7
	John Floyd	National Republican		11
1836	**Martin Van Buren**	Democratic	761,549 (50.9%)	170
	William H. Harrison	Whig	549,567 (36.7%)	73
	Hugh L. White	Whig	145,396 (9.7%)	26
	Daniel Webster	Whig	41,287 (2.7%)	14
1840	**William H. Harrison** (**John Tyler,** 1841)	Whig	1,275,017 (53.1%)	234
	Martin Van Buren	Democratic	1,128,702 (46.9%)	60
1844	**James K. Polk**	Democratic	1,337,243 (49.6%)	170
	Henry Clay	Whig	1,299,068 (48.1%)	105
	James G. Birney	Liberty	62,300 (2.3%)	
1848	**Zachary Taylor** (**Millard Fillmore,** 1850)	Whig	1,360,101 (47.4%)	163
	Lewis Cass	Democratic	1,220,544 (42.5%)	127
	Martin Van Buren	Free Soil	291,263 (10.1%)	
1852	**Franklin Pierce**	Democratic	1,601,474 (50.9%)	254
	Winfield Scott	Whig	1,386,578 (44.1%)	42
1856	**James Buchanan**	Democratic	1,838,169 (45.4%)	174
	John C. Frémont	Republican	1,335,264 (33.0%)	114
	Millard Fillmore	American	874,534 (21.6%)	8

YEAR	CANDIDATES	PARTY	POPULAR VOTE	ELECTORAL VOTE
1860	**Abraham Lincoln**	Republican	1,865,593 (39.8%)	180
	Stephen A. Douglas	Democratic	1,382,713 (29.5%)	12
	John C. Breckinridge	Democratic	848,356 (18.1%)	72
	John Bell	Constitutional Union	592,906 (12.6%)	39
1864	**Abraham Lincoln** **(Andrew Johnson**, 1865)	Republican	2,206,938 (55.0%)	212
	George B. McClellan	Democratic	1,803,787 (45.0%)	21
1868	**Ulysses S. Grant**	Republican	3,013,421 (52.7%)	214
	Horatio Seymour	Democratic	2,706,829 (47.3%)	80
1872	**Ulysses S. Grant**	Republican	3,596,745 (55.6%)	286
	Horace Greeley	Democratic	2,843,446 (43.9%)	66
1876	**Rutherford B. Hayes**	Republican	4,036,572 (48.0%)	185
	Samuel J. Tilden	Democratic	4,284,020 (51.0%)	184
1880	**James A. Garfield** **(Chester A. Arthur**, 1881)	Republican	4,449,053 (48.3%)	214
	Winfield S. Hancock	Democratic	4,442,035 (48.2%)	155
	James B. Weaver	Greenback-Labor	308,578 (3.4%)	
1884	**Grover Cleveland**	Democratic	4,874,986 (48.5%)	219
	James G. Blaine	Republican	4,851,981 (48.2%)	182
	Benjamin F. Butler	Greenback-Labor	175,370 (1.8%)	
1888	**Benjamin Harrison**	Republican	5,444,337, (47.8%)	233
	Grover Cleveland	Democratic	5,540,050 (48.6%)	168
1892	**Grover Cleveland**	Democratic	5,554,414 (46.0%)	277
	Benjamin Harrison	Republican	5,190,802 (43.0%)	145
	James B. Weaver	People's	1,027,329 (8.5%)	22
1896	**William McKinley**	Republican	7,035,638 (50.8%)	271
	William J. Bryan	Democratic; Populist	6,467,946 (46.7%)	176
1900	**William McKinley** **(Theodore Roosevelt**, 1901)	Republican	7,219,530 (51.7%)	292
	William J. Bryan	Democratic; Populist	6,356,734 (45.5%)	155
1904	**Theodore Roosevelt**	Republican	7,628,834 (56.4%)	336
	Alton B. Parker	Democratic	5,084,401 (37.6%)	140
	Eugene V. Debs	Socialist	402,460 (3.0%)	

YEAR	CANDIDATES	PARTY	POPULAR VOTE	ELECTORAL VOTE
1908	**William H. Taft**	Republican	7,679,006 (51.6%)	321
	William J. Bryan	Democratic	6,409,106 (43.1%)	162
	Eugene V. Debs	Socialist	420,820 (2.8%)	
1912	**Woodrow Wilson**	Democratic	6,286,820 (41.8%)	435
	Theodore Roosevelt	Progressive	4,126,020 (27.4%)	88
	William H. Taft	Republican	3,483,922 (23.2%)	8
	Eugene V. Debs	Socialist	897,011 (6.0%)	
1916	**Woodrow Wilson**	Democratic	9,129,606 (49.3%)	277
	Charles E. Hughes	Republican	8,538,221 (46.1%)	254
1920	**Warren G. Harding** (**Calvin Coolidge,** 1923)	Republican	16,152,200 (61.0%)	404
	James M. Cox	Democratic	9,147,353 (34.6%)	127
	Eugene V. Debs	Socialist	919,799 (3.5%)	
1924	**Calvin Coolidge**	Republican	15,725,016 (54.1%)	382
	John W. Davis	Democratic	8,385,586 (28.8%)	136
	Robert M. La Follette	Progressive	4,822,856 (16.6%)	13
1928	**Herbert C. Hoover**	Republican	21,392,190 (58.2%)	444
	Alfred E. Smith	Democratic	15,016,443 (40.8%)	87
1932	**Franklin D. Roosevelt**	Democratic	22,809,638 (57.3%)	472
	Herbert C. Hoover	Republican	15,758,901 (39.6%)	59
	Norman Thomas	Socialist	881,951 (2.2%)	
1936	**Franklin D. Roosevelt**	Democratic	27,751,612 (60.7%)	523
	Alfred M. Landon	Republican	16,681,913 (36.4%)	8
	William Lemke	Union	891,858 (1.9%)	
1940	**Franklin D. Roosevelt**	Democratic	27,243,466 (54.7%)	449
	Wendell L. Willkie	Republican	22,304,755 (44.8%)	82
1944	**Franklin D. Roosevelt** (**Harry S. Truman,** 1945)	Democratic	25,602,505 (52.8%)	432
	Thomas E. Dewey	Republican	22,006,278 (44.5%)	99
1948	**Harry S. Truman**	Democratic	24,105,812 (49.5%)	303
	Thomas E. Dewey	Republican	21,970,065 (45.1%)	189
	J. Strom Thurmond	States' Rights	1,169,063 (2.4%)	39
	Henry A. Wallace	Progressive	1,157,172 (2.4%)	

YEAR	CANDIDATES	PARTY	POPULAR VOTE	ELECTORAL VOTE
1952	**Dwight D. Eisenhower**	Republican	33,936,234 (55.2%)	442
	Adlai E. Stevenson	Democratic	27,314,992 (44.5%)	89
1956	**Dwight D. Eisenhower**	Republican	35,590,472 (57.4%)	457
	Adlai E. Stevenson	Democratic	26,022,752 (42.0%)	73
1960	**John F. Kennedy** **(Lyndon B. Johnson,** 1963)	Democratic	34,227,096 (49.9%)	303
	Richard M. Nixon	Republican	34,108,546 (49.6%)	219
1964	**Lyndon B. Johnson**	Democratic	43,126,233 (61.1%)	486
	Barry M. Goldwater	Republican	27,174,989 (38.5%)	52
1968	**Richard M. Nixon**	Republican	31,783,783 (43.4%)	301
	Hubert H. Humphrey	Democratic	31,271,839 (42.7%)	191
	George C. Wallace	American Independent	9,899,557 (13.5%)	46
1972	**Richard M. Nixon**	Republican	46,631,189(61.3%)	521
	George McGovern	Democratic	28,422.015(37.3%)	17

Because only the leading candidates are listed, popular vote percentages do not always total 100. The elections of 1800 and 1824, in which no candidate received an electoral vote majority, were decided in the House of Representatives.

Index

Decentralization
vs. centralization, 315–320
and Civil War, 324
Decision rule, majoritarian.
See Majority rule
Declaration of Independence,
44, 46, 277, 278, 281, 291
text of, 279–280
Declaration of the Rights of
Man and Citizens (1789),
57
Defense contractors, 33
Defense power, and federalism, 331–333
Democracy. *See also* Pluralist
democracy
belief in. *See* Political beliefs
and capitalism, 22–24
and Constitution, 25
and decentralization, 318
and equal status before law,
45–48
and equality, 44–45
and majoritarianism, 380–
381
and minority rights. *See*
Minority rights
model of, 79–82, 92–93
and political beliefs of
Americans, 78–79
and political capitalism, 37–
39
and political equality, 48–49
and political participation,
156, 181–182
and political recruitment,
187–192
and political representation,
415–416
and property rights, 395–398
and social-rights citizenship,
49–53
"Democratic class struggle,"
250–251
Democratic party. *See also*
Democratic party–Repub-
lican party comparisons;
Political parties
convention of 1968, 265
diversity within, 242
during election campaigns,
473
ethnic support for, 129
and religious groups, 136–
137
and White ethnics, 128, 129
Democratic party–Republican
party comparisons, 249–
253

and class antagonisms, 250–
251
and congressional voting,
258–260
by electorate, 252–253
and financial bases, 253–255
and political philosophies,
255–257
Democratic revolution, 187, 188
Demonstrations. *See* Protests
Dennis, Eugene, 389
Department of Agriculture,
228, 442, 453–454
and business regulation, 531–
532
Department of Commerce, 228,
572
and busines regulation, 531–
532
Department of Defense, 253
and Vietnam policy, 555
Department of Health, Education, and Welfare (HEW),
206, 207, 315, 404, 478, 547
Department of Labor, 228
Depression, federalism and, 304
Desegregation issue, 174, 369–
370, 373–376, 399, 504, 548
and *de facto* desegregation,
551–552
in Little Rock, Arkansas, 460
role of Supreme Court in,
548–551
Dickinson, John, 398
Dillon rule, 333
Direct action. *See* Protests
Disaggregated policy making,
552
and business regulation, 531–
532
consequences of, 518, 520–
521
methods of, 519–521
origins of, 518
and tax policy, 537, 538–539
Dixiecrats, 267
Documentation research
data sources for, 403–404
and durable artifact problem, 405
and institutional bias, 404–
405
and secrecy problem, 406
types of, 406–410
Domestic policy, and Congress
vs. executive, 493
Doves, 261
Downs, Anthony, 272
Drugs, public opinion on, 84,
85

Du Bois, W. E. B., 549
Dual citizenship, 46–48
Dudley, Guilford, Jr., 468
Due process clause, 46, 362–
363, 366
Dulles, John Foster, 34, 199
Durable artifact problem, 405

Eastland, James, 450, 490
*Economic Basis of Politics,
The* (Beard), 44
Economic inequality, 53–56
and capitalism, 21–22
and democracy, 22–24
persistance of, 56–59
political challenge to, 59–65
and political inequality, 8
and progressive income tax,
61–63
reduction of, 59–60
and social welfare programs,
63–65
and War on Poverty, 60–61
Economic-interest groups, conflict between public-interest groups and, 225–226,
228
Economic interests
under Articles of Confederation, 283
as basis for political groups,
123
and congressional voting,
450, 452, 453–454
Economic organizations, court
system and, 230
Economic policy, and Presidential appointments, 469
Economic reforms, of New
Deal, 32
Economic regulation. *See also*
Business regulation
and Supreme Court, 362–367
and taxation, 536
Economy, under Articles of
Confederation, 282–284
Edelman, Murray, 221n, 235,
504n, 524
Education
and centralization vs. decentralization, 315–319
and commitment to demo-
cratic values, 90
equality in, 369–370
federal aid to, 327, 328–329,
334–335
and freedom of religion,
392–393
and government aid to re-